THE ENCYCLOPEDIA OF
MAMMALS

THE ENCYCLOPEDIA OF
MAMMALS

VOLUME I

EDITED BY

PROFESSOR DAVID W. MACDONALD

Facts On File, Inc.

Published in North America by:
Facts On File, Inc.
132 West 31st Street
New York NY 10001

The Brown Reference Group plc
(incorporating Andromeda Oxford Limited)
8 Chapel Place
Rivington Street
London, EC2A 3DQ
www.brownreference.com

Editor Wendy Horobin
Archive Researcher Clare Newman
Indexer Kay Ollerenshaw
Art Director Sarah Williams
Managing Editor Bridget Giles
Production Director Alastair Gourlay
Editorial Director Lindsey Lowe

For Library of Congress Cataloging-in-Publication Data
please contact the Publisher.

ISBN: 0-8160-6494-6   (Set)
ISBN: 0-8160-6495-4   (Volume I)

Facts On File books are available at special discounts
when purchased in bulk quantities for businesses,
associations, institutions, or sales promotions. Please
call our Special Sales Department in New York at
(212) 967-8800 or (800) 322-8755.

You can find Facts On File on the World Wide Web at
http://www.factsonfile.com

Cover design by Dorothy M. Preston

Printed in China

10 9 8 7 6 5 4 3 2

Previous Edition
Editors Tony Allan, Peter Lewis, Mark Salad • Designers
Mark Regardsoe, Frankie Wood • Cartographer Tim
Williams • Picture Researcher Vickie Walters • Picture
Manager Claire Turner • Art Director Chris Munday
• Production Clive Sparling • Publishing Director
Graham Bateman

Photo page ii: *Gray squirrel* Photodisc

Advisory Editors

Dr. Richard Connor,
University of Massachusetts at
Dartmouth, North Dartmouth,
Massachusetts

Dr. Guy Cowlishaw,
Institute of Zoology,
London, UK

Dr. Christopher R. Dickman,
University of Sydney,
Australia

Professor Johan du Toit,
Department of Forest,
Range, & Wildlife Services,
Utah State University

Professor John Harwood,
Gatty Marine Laboratory,
University of St. Andrews,
Scotland, UK

Dr. Gareth Jones,
University of Bristol, UK

Professor Hans Kruuk,
Centre for Ecology and Hydrology,
Banchory, Scotland, UK

Dr. Erik R. Seiffert,
Department of Earth Sciences,
University of Oxford, UK

Professor Jerry O. Wolff,
University of Memphis,
Memphis, Tennessee

Assistant to the Editor
Kerry Kilshaw, WildCRU,
University of Oxford, UK

Artwork Panels
Priscilla Barrett
Denys Ovenden
Malcolm McGregor
Michael R. Long
Graham Allen

Southern Tamandua
see page 116

Contributors

INTRODUCTIONS pp. viii–xxxiii

KB   Kate Barlow, British Antarctic Survey, UK

RB   Robin Beck, School of Biological Sciences, University of New South Wales, Australia

OB-E   Olaf Bininda-Emonds, Technical University of Munich, Germany

MC   Marcel Cardillo, Imperial College, London, UK

RD   Richard Dawkins, University of Oxford, UK

JLG   John L. Gittleman, University of Virginia

RG   Richard Grenyer, University of Virginia

KJ   Kate Jones, Zoological Society of London, UK

DWM   David W. Macdonald, WildCRU, University of Oxford, UK

GM   Georgina Mace, Zoological Society of London

SP   Samantha Price, National Evolutionary Synthesis Center (NESCent), North Carolina

AP   Andy Purvis, Imperial College, London, UK

ERS   Erik R. Seiffert, Department of Earth Sciences, University of Oxford, UK

MONOTREMES, MARSUPIALS, AND INSECT EATERS pp. 2–83; 114–127

MLA   Mike L. Augee, University of New South Wales, Australia

GB   Gary Bronner, University of Cape Town, South Africa

LB   Linda S. Broome, New South Wales National Parks and Wildlife Service, Australia

AC   Andrew Cockburn, Australian National University, Canberra, Australia

CRD   Christopher R. Dickman, University of Sydney, Australia

GG   Greg Gordon, Queensland National Parks and Wildlife Service, Australia

TRG   Tom R. Grant, University of New South Wales, Australia

CEH   Clare E. Hawkins, Dept. Primary Industries, Water and Environment, Tasmania

PJ   Peter Jarman, Univ. of New England, Australia

CJ   Christopher Johnson, James Cook University, Australia

MJ   Menna Jones, Australian National University, Canberra, Australia

AKL   A. K. Lee, Monash University, Australia

DL   David Lindenmayer, Australian National University, Canberra, Australia

WJL   W. Jim Loughry, Valdosta State University, Valdosta, Georgia

CMM   Colleen M. McDonough, Valdosta State University, Valdosta, Georgia

VN   Virginia Naples, Northern Illinois University, De Kalb, Illinois

MEN   Martin E. Nicholl, Smithsonian Institution, Washington, D.C.

MAO'C   Margaret A. O'Connell, Eastern Washington University, Cheney, Washington

MP   Mike Perrin, University of Pretoria, S. Africa

SBP   Stephen B. Pyecroft, Dept. Primary Industries, Water and Environment, Tasmania

GBR   Galen B. Rathbun, California Academy of Sciences, San Francisco, California

EMR   Eleanor M. Russell, CSIRO Wildlife and Rangelands Research Division, Australia

JHS   John H. Seebeck, Department of Natural Resources and Environment, Victoria, Australia

ERS   Erik R. Seiffert, Department of Earth Sciences, University of Oxford, UK

RJvA   Rudi J. van Aarde, Univ. of Pretoria, S. Africa

JW   Jerry Wilkinson, University of Maryland, College Park, Maryland

RDW   Ron D. Wooller, Murdoch Univ., Perth, Australia

ELEPHANTS AND RELATIVES pp. 84–113

PKA   Paul K. Anderson, University of Calgary, Canada

RFWB   Richard Barnes, University of California, San Diego, USA, & Anglia Polytechnic University, Cambridge, UK

RB   Robin Best, Instituto Nacional de Pequisas de Amazonia, Brazil

DPD   Daryl P. Domning, Howard University, Washington, D.C.

ID-H   Iain Douglas-Hamilton, Save the Elephants, Kenya

HNH   Hendrik N. Hoeck, Kreuzlingen, Switzerland

CMJ   Christine M. Janis, Brown University, Providence, Rhode Island

AJTJ   A. J. T. Johnsingh, Wildlife Institute of India

WJL   W. Jim Loughry, Valdosta State Univ., Georgia

CMM   Colleen M. McDonough, Valdosta State University, Georgia

HM   Helene Marsh, James Cook Univ., Australia

JMP   Jane M. Packard, Texas A&M University

KP   Katy Payne, Cornell Univ., Ithaca, New York

GBR   Galen B. Rathbun, California Academy of Sciences, Cambria, California

HS   Hezy Shoshani, University of Asmara, Eritrea

ACW   A. Christy Williams, Wildlife Inst. of India

RODENTS pp. 128–247

GA   Greta Ågren, University of Stockholm, Sweden

KBA   Kenneth B. Armitage, University of Kansas, Lawrence, Kansas

CB   Claude Baudoin, University of Franche Comté, France

RB   Robin Boughton, University of Florida, Gainesville, Florida

PB   Peter Busher, Boston University

TMB   Thomas M. Butynski, Director, Eastern Africa Biodiversity Hotspots, Conservation International

MC   Marcelo Cassini, University of Lujan, Argentina

GBC   Gordon B. Corbet, Leven, Scotland, UK

MJD   Michael J. Delany, University of Bradford, UK

CRD   Christopher R. Dickman, University of Sydney, Australia

JFE   John F. Eisenberg, University of Florida, Gainesville, Florida

JE   James Evans, U.S. Fish and Wildlife Service, Olympia, Washington

JF   Julie Feaver, University of Cambridge, UK

THF   Theodore H. Fleming, Univ. of Miami, Florida

WG   Wilma George, University of Oxford, UK

DH   Donna Harris, WildCRU, University of Oxford, UK

GH   Göran Hartman, UC Davis, University of California, Davis, California

EH   Emilio Herrera, Simon Bolivar Univ., Venezuela

UWH   U. William Huck, Princeton University, Princeton, New Jersey

JH   Jane Hurst, University of Liverpool, UK

JUMJ   Jenny U. M. Jarvis, University of Cape Town, South Africa

PJ   Paula Jenkins, Natural History Museum, London, UK

CJK   Charles J. Krebs, University of British Columbia, Canada

TEL   Thomas E. Lacher, Texas A&M University, College Station, Texas

DWM   David W. Macdonald, WildCRU, University of Oxford, UK

KMacK   Kathy MacKinnon, World Bank, Washington, D.C.

JP   James Patton, University of California, Berkeley, California

DAS   Duane A. Schlitter, Texas A&M University, College Station, Texas

GIS   Georgy I. Shenbrot, Ramon Science Center, Mizpe Ramon, Israel

PWS   Paul W. Sherman, Cornell University, Ithaca, New York

GS   Grant Singleton, CSIRO Wildlife and Ecology, Australia

PS   Paula Stockley, University of Liverpool, UK

DMS   D. Michael Stoddart, Hobart University, Tasmania, Australia

RS   Robert Strachan, WildCRU, University of Oxford, UK

AT   Andrew Taber, Wildlife Conservation Society, New York, New York

RJvA   Rudi J. van Aarde, University of Pretoria, South Africa

JW   John O. Whitaker, Indiana State University, Terre Haute, Indiana

JOW   Jerry O. Wolff, University of Memphis, Memphis, Tennessee

CAW   Charles A. Woods, Florida State Museum, Gainesville, Florida

HY   Hannu Ylonen, University of Jyvaskyla, Finland

ZZ   Zhang Zhibin, Chinese Academy of Sciences, Beijing, China

LAGOMORPHS pp. 248–269

DB   Diana Bell, University of East Anglia, UK

DPC   David P. Cowan, Central Science Laboratory, York, UK

TH   Tony Holley, Brent Knoll, Somerset, UK

TK   Takeo Kawamichi, University of Osaka, Japan

CJK   Charles J. Krebs, University of British Columbia, Canada

ES   Eberhard Schneider, University of Göttingen, Germany

ATS   Andrew T. Smith, Arizona State University, Tempe, Arizona

CONTENTS

Red Kangaroo
see page 50

PREFACE

This book is dedicated to my wife,
Jenny, and Ewan, Fiona, and Isobel

Mammals are marvellous, and the aim of *The Encyclopedia of Mammals* is to relay this truth, in its myriad intriguing forms, to as wide a readership as possible. While zoologists continue to discover startling facts about the behavior and ecology of wild mammals and to develop new ideas to explain their discoveries, much of this information fails to reach even their professional colleagues, let alone percolate through to a general readership. My goal, then, has been to engage precisely these front-line researchers to produce a lucid, scholarly, and entertaining overview of all the world's mammalian species – some 5,096 in total. Happily, this venture has entailed no trade-off between scientific precision and user-friendly communication – the true stories of wild mammals are so fascinating as to require no embellishment: the reality of evolution renders our wildest fables dull by comparison.

A brief explanation of some organizing principles will help readers get their bearings. The Encyclopedia contains four distinct types of entries. First, for each order or group of orders, a general essay highlights the common features and main variations of the biology (particularly body plan), ecology, and behavior of the group in question and its evolution. Second, forming the bulk of each volume, are the accounts of individual species, groups of closely related species, or families of species. These entries cover details of physical characteristics, distribution, evolutionary history, diet and feeding behavior, social dynamics and spatial organization, classification, conservation, and relationships with people. Third, the special features – the fruit of authors' cutting-edge research – offer detailed insights into the social organization, foraging, breeding biology, and conservation of particular species. Photo stories showcase stunning sequences of wildlife photography.

To the nonscientist, the intricacies of classification (the ordering of animals into categories of increasing membership on the basis of common ancestry) can be difficult to comprehend – and the task is made harder by the common but mistaken belief that an omniscient authority knows the single correct answer! That is far from the truth. Not only are there many uncertainties and contradictory interpretations of the facts regarding the evolutionary relationships amongst contemporary mammals, but some distinctions are inherently imprecise and will always remain a matter of judgment or protocol. Nonetheless, to establish a firm footing on the shifting sands of taxonomy, I decided to adopt as the Encyclopedia's "baseline" Don Wilson and DeeAnn Reeder's *Mammal Species of the World*. Happily, while the current revision of *The Encyclopedia of Mammals* was being completed during 2005 and 2006 so, too, Don and DeeAnn were compiling a new edition of their mighty synthesis of the taxonomy and distribution of all mammal species. Kindly, they and their contributors gave us early sight of their proofs, enabling maximum concordance. Nonetheless, new techniques are constantly reshuffling old classifications, and authorities make different judgments, so

IUCN CATEGORIES

Ex Extinct, when there is no reasonable doubt that the last individual of a taxon has died.

EW Extinct in the Wild, when a taxon is known only to survive in captivity, or as a naturalized population well outside the past range.

Cr Critically Endangered, when a taxon is facing an extremely high risk of extinction in the wild in the immediate future.

En Endangered, when a taxon faces a very high risk of extinction in the wild in the near future.

Vu Vulnerable, when a taxon faces a high risk of extinction in the wild in the medium-term future.

LR Lower Risk, when a taxon has been evaluated and does not satisfy the criteria for CR, EN, or VU.

Note: The Lower Risk (LR) category is further divided into three subcategories: Conservation Dependent (cd) – taxa, which are the focus of a continuing taxon-specific or habitat-specific conservation program targeted toward the taxon, the cessation of which would result in the taxon qualifying for one of the threatened categories within a period of five years; Near Threatened (nt) – taxa that do not qualify for Conservation Dependent but which are close to qualifying for VU; and Least Concern (lc) – taxa that do not qualify for the two previous categories. The Conservation Dependent category, which is still currently used for some species until they are reassessed, is not included in the revised IUCN system.

while the newest Wilson & Reeder taxonomy is our baseline, I have opted to depart from it in the minority of cases where the first-hand experience of our own authors has led them to different conclusions. On the taxonomic panels (FACTFILES) that introduce each family or order, we draw attention in parentheses to any disparities between our species count and that of the 2005 Wilson & Reeder list; furthermore, in the species tables, as well as covering the species that are widely accepted, we also mention proposed new species or subspecies that some believe should be elevated to full species status.

Throughout the Encyclopedia we have added, wherever possible, the IUCN (World Conservation Union) Red List codes for each species, taking our data from the newly published 2005 lists, and the importance of these codes is explained in a new essay entitled Conservation (Vol. 1: xxvi–xxxiii). A new feature introduces the mammalian supertree (Vol. 1: xxiv–xxv), and presents the newest thinking on the ramifying branches of the mammalian lineage. In that context, the structure of this 2006 revision of the Encyclopedia differs radically from its predecessors – the hippos have been linked with the whales, the seals and sea lions with the carnivores, and the elephants with the aardvarks: all these changes reflect evolutionary revelations explained in What Is a Mammal? (Vol. 1: viii–xxiii). In making these revisions I am hugely grateful for the hard work of Kerry Kilshaw, as I was in the previous edition for that of Sasha Norris.

DAVID W. MACDONALD
UNIVERSITY OF OXFORD

What Is a Mammal?

MAMMALS COULD BE CATEGORIZED AS *a group of animals with backbones, and bodies insulated by hair, which nurse their infants with milk and share a unique jaw articulation. Yet this fails to convey their truly astonishing features – their intricate adaptations, thrilling behavior, and highly complex societies.*

A more satisfactory response might therefore be that the essence of mammals lies in their diversity of form and function, and above all their individual flexibility of behavior: the smallest mammal, the hog-nosed bat, weighs 1.5g (0.05oz), the blue whale weighs 100 million times as much; the wolf may journey through 1,000sq km (400sq mi), the naked mole rat never leaves one burrow; this latter species gives birth to litters of up to 28, the orangutan to only one; the elephant, like humans, may live three score years and ten, while the male brown antechinus never sees a second season and

dies before the birth of the first and only litter he has fathered. No facet of these varied lives is random; they are diverse but not in disarray. On the contrary, each individual mammal maximizes its "fitness," its ability, relative to others of its kind, to pass on genes, usually by leaving viable offspring.

There are some 5,096 species of mammals (modern molecular analysis has revealed a number of new ones), among which ancient relationships permit subdivisions into 1,188 genera, 153 families, 28 orders, and 2 subclasses. These subclasses acknowledge a 200-million-year separation between egg-laying Prototheria and live-bearing Theria. Moreover, a 150-million-year-old split within the Theria divides the marsupials from the living placental mammals. Some splits among the living placentals likely occurred over 100 million years ago.

⊙ *Below The mammal family tree showing the six main groups: Monotremata, Marsupialia, Afrotheria, Xenarthra, Euarchontoglires, and Laurasiatheria.*

Even within taxonomy's convenient compartments there is bewildering variation in the size, shape and life-histories of mammals. Indeed, it is especially characteristic of mammals that even individuals of the same species behave differently depending on their circumstances.

From Reptiles to Mammals
EVOLUTIONARY BIOLOGY

By the close of the Carboniferous period some 300 million years ago, the ancestors of today's mammals were no more than a twinkle in an ancient reptilian eye. The world was spanned by warm, shallow seas and the climate was hot, humid and constant. Among the reptiles of the late Carboniferous, one line heralded the mammal-like reptiles – the subclass Synapsida. The synapsids flourished, dominating the reptilian faunas of the Permian and early Triassic about 300–225 m.y.a. Over millions of years their skeletons altered from the cumbersome reptilian mold to a more racy design that presaged the early mammals. Yet, despite these auspicious beginnings, this was a false start for the mammals. The late Triassic saw the dazzling ascendancy of the dinosaurs, which in the Jurassic and Cretaceous era (200–65 m.y.a.) not only eclipsed the synapsids, but nearly annihilated them through competitive superiority. Inconspicuous synapsids evolved during the Triassic (250–200 m.y.a.) into true mammals, of which the first were 5cm (2in) long and nocturnal. Their unobtrusive scuttlings gave little evidence of what was to become the most exciting radiation in vertebrate history when, well over 100 million years later, in the late Cretaceous period, the nonavian dinosaurs lumbered into oblivion.

By the Triassic, among synapsids the therapsids prevailed and in the fossils of these mammal-like reptiles lie the roots of modern mammals. Over millennia, they developed an expanded temporal skull opening and a corresponding rearrangement of the jaw musculature; a secondary palate appeared, forming a horizontal partition in the roof of the mouth (formed by a backward extension of the maxillary and palatine bones); their teeth became diverse; six of the seven bones of the reptilian lower jaw were reduced in size while the fifth, the dentary, was hugely enlarged; ribs were no longer attached to the cervical and lumber vertebrae, but only to the thoracic ones; the pectoral and pelvic girdles were streamlined, and angles on the heads of femora and humeri altered so that the limbs were aligned beneath, rather than to the side of, the body. These and other changes promoted

EVOLUTION OF MAMMALS

Carnivores (Order Carnivora)
Pangolins (Order Pholidota)
Odd-toed Ungulates (Order Perissodactyla)
Whales, Dolphins, and Even-toed Ungulates (Order Cetartiodactyla)
Bats (Order Chiroptera)
Shrews, Moles, and Hedgehogs (Order Eulipotyphla)
Rodents (Order Rodentia)
Lagomorphs (Order Lagomorpha)
Primates (Order Primates)
Colugos (Order Dermoptera)
Tree Shrews (Order Scandentia)
Xenarthrans – Anteaters, Sloths, & Armadillos (Orders Pilosa and Cingulata)
Hyraxes (Order Hyracoidea)
Elephants (Order Proboscidea)
Dugong and Manatees (Order Sirenia)
Aardvark (Order Tubulidentata)
Sengis (Order Macroscelidea)
Tenrecs and Golden moles (Order Afrosoricida)
Marsupials (Supercohort)
Monotremes (Order Monotremata)

PLEISTOCENE
PLIOCENE
MIOCENE
OLIGOCENE
EOCENE
PALEOCENE
CRETACEOUS
JURASSIC
TRIASSIC

Laurasiatheria
Euarchontoglires
Afrotheria
SUBCLASS THERIA
INFRACLASS METATHERIA
SUBCLASS PROTOTHERIA

200   145   65   55   34   24   5   1.8
million years ago

more effective, agile, and swift working of the body. For example, the secondary palate forms a bypass for air from the nostrils to the back of the mouth, facilitating simultaneous eating and breathing, made more efficient by the evolution of the diaphragm – a muscular plate separating the chest cavity from the abdomen.

All modern mammals arose from a group known as cynodonts. These advanced synapsids, known primarily from the middle and late Triassic, were largely carnivorous, although herbivorous forms are known as well. A cynodont from the late Triassic beds of Argentina, *Probainognathus*, is thought to best represent the transition. It retains only the flimsiest articular–quadrate joint and illustrates the development toward the articulation between the dentary and squamosal bones. Moreover, the bones of the old reptilian jaw joint are juxtaposed so as to foreshadow their transformation into the ossicles of the mammalian middle ear apparatus (the angular, articular and prearticular, and quadrate become, respectively, the tympanic, malleus, incus). Remarkably, new evidence from the jaw of the early Cretaceous monotreme *Teinolophos* indicates that the final evolutionary transformation of postdentary bones into ear ossicles might have occurred independently in monotremes and therians.

Since soft parts rarely fossilize, the history of modern mammals must be traced from bones and

Note It is now generally acknowledged that the Cetacea are, with their cousins the Artiodactyla, part of a new order, the Cetartiodactyla. However, for the purposes of this edition they are treated as separate orders.

◁ *Left* The red fox (Vulpes vulpes) embodies several of the traits that characterize mammalian success – adaptability, opportunism, and intelligence, plus the capacity for intricate social relationships and subtle communication. It also epitomizes the grace and beauty that captivates people's enthusiasm for other members of our Class.

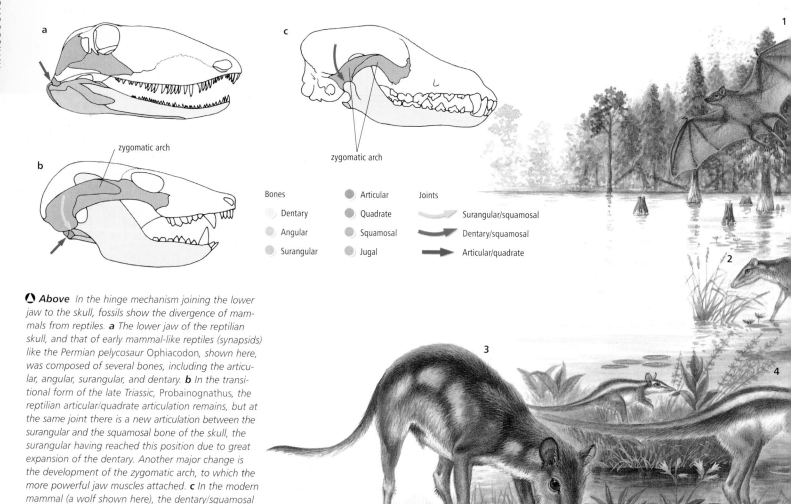

a

zygomatic arch

b

c

zygomatic arch

Bones			Joints
Dentary	Articular		Surangular/squamosal
Angular	Quadrate		Dentary/squamosal
Surangular	Squamosal		Articular/quadrate
	Jugal		

◐ **Above** *In the hinge mechanism joining the lower jaw to the skull, fossils show the divergence of mammals from reptiles.* **a** *The lower jaw of the reptilian skull, and that of early mammal-like reptiles (synapsids) like the Permian pelycosaur* Ophiacodon, *shown here, was composed of several bones, including the articular, angular, surangular, and dentary.* **b** *In the transitional form of the late Triassic,* Probainognathus, *the reptilian articular/quadrate articulation remains, but at the same joint there is a new articulation between the surangular and the squamosal bone of the skull, the surangular having reached this position due to great expansion of the dentary. Another major change is the development of the zygomatic arch, to which the more powerful jaw muscles attached.* **c** *In the modern mammal (a wolf shown here), the dentary/squamosal hinge remains, while the dentary is the principal bone of the lower jaw. Reptilian teeth are unspecialized (homodont), while those of modern mammals are specialized to fulfil different functions (heterodont).*

teeth. In addition to their jaw articulation and the features discussed earlier, modern mammalian skulls are distinguished by teeth that develop only from the premaxillary, maxillary, and dentary bones and that are generally diversified in function (heterodont, consisting of incisors, canines, premolars and molars). Typically, placental mammals have two sets of teeth, the milk, or deciduous, set often differing in form and function from the adult set; marsupials replace only the last premolar. All mammalian teeth consist of a core of bonelike dentine wrapped in a hard case of enamel (largely calcium phosphate). In most mammals the pulp cavity seals, and the tooth ceases to grow, once adult. But the incisors of rodents, the tusks of several species, and the grinding teeth of a few herbivores (such as wombats), all teeth experiencing rapid wear, remain open-rooted and ever-growing.

Experiments in Tandem
CONVERGENT EVOLUTION

From ancient starting points very distinct lineages have followed strikingly convergent routes to achieve a mammalian style of existence. Formerly, the marsupials were thought of as "primitive"

mammals, alongside the "advanced" placentals. Now, however, it is clear that they are the separate, intriguingly different yet amazingly similar results of an experiment begun more than 150 million years ago. The ancestral therian mammal lineage split along the two routes to form these lineages; in the later Cenozoic both faced the opportunities presented by the creation of continental climates and the emergence of grasslands and both arrived at the same solutions. For example, in tackling the challenges of herbivory, each array has produced both fore- and hindgut fermenters, using different microbial communities to achieve the same effects; both have solved problems of tooth wear on abrasive diets in parallel ways; and both evolved toe-reduction and sociality in response to predation risks while foraging in open habitats.

Since the turn of the 20th century, the field of molecular phylogenetics has radically altered our understanding of the interrelationships of placental mammalian orders, and has provided a fascinating new perspective on how mammals' remarkable anatomical and behavioral diversity came to be. Prior to the advent of large-scale sequencing of DNA, the evidence for deep splits

in mammalian phylogeny was a matter of persistent debate, with proposed supraordinal relationships generally being supported by only a few anatomical features. While genetic studies have confirmed a few phylogenetic hypotheses that were previously proposed on the basis of bones and teeth – for instance, a close relationship of rodents and lagomorphs in the superorder Glires, a grouping of hyraxes, sea cows, and elephants in the superorder Paenungulata, and some association of flying lemurs, tree shrews, and primates – this is where the similarities between the traditional morphological phylogeny and the new molecular phylogeny end.

Among the more surprising results is the discovery that Ungulata, the group that previously contained whales, even- and odd-toed ungulates, and paenungulates, is decidedly polyphyletic, that is, they do not share a unique common ancestor to the exclusion of other living placental orders. Indeed, perissodactyls, which were long considered by some anatomists to be the closest relatives of hyraxes, are in fact more closely related to placentals such as hedgehogs, shrews, and moles, while hyraxes and their paenungulate relatives are

◖ Above *An array of extinct mammals from the early middle Eocene (about 48 m.y.a.) were found near Lake Messel, Germany. This reconstruction shows a community at the dawn of the age of mammals: **1** Archaeo-nycteris, the first known bat; **2** Messelobunodon, an ancestral artiodactyl; **3** Propaleotherium, an ancestral horse; **4** Lepticidium, an insectivore; **5** Paroodectes, a miacid; **6** Eurotamandua, an anteater; and **7** Pholido-cercus, a hedgehog.*

more closely related to golden moles. The previously proposed relationship between Primates, Dermoptera, and Scandentia has been upheld, but the suggested inclusion of bats alongside the flying lemurs has been rejected. Chiropterans (the bats) are, in fact, more closely related to mammals such as perissodactyls, artiodactyls, and carnivorans, implying that the patagium that facilitates gliding in Dermoptera, and powered flight in Chiroptera, evolved convergently in the two orders. Perhaps least surprising is the realization the Insectivora or Lipotyphla – the long-acknowledged "taxonomic wastebasket" containing the various forms often considered to be among the most primitive placentals – is also polyphyletic. What is surprising is that these lipotyphlans do

not branch off near the base of the placental tree, as might have been predicted from their anatomical resemblances to Cretaceous placentals, but rather are deeply nested within Placentalia in two very distantly related groups: Eulipotyphla, which contains the shrews, moles, hedgehogs, and solenodons (some specialists continue to use the old name Lipotyphla for these taxa), and Afrosoricida, containing the tenrecs and golden moles (also sometimes referred to collectively as tenrecoids or tenrecomorphs).

As fascinating as these strange patterns are, they have also raised some troubling questions for morphologists and paleontologists. In particular, it must be asked whether these unexpected relationships imply that anatomy is so easily altered as to be uninformative for tracking deep divergences in the mammalian fossil record. The answer appears to be mixed. The new molecular phylogeny leaves it clear that morphology is, indeed, surprisingly malleable – strikingly similar adaptations have arisen convergently multiple times in distantly related lineages. But it is nevertheless quite likely that many of these convergences never would have appeared in the absence of certain other non-

biological forces, such as continental drift. Key to our understanding of early placental evolution and the origin of supraordinal diversity is the fact that the first divergences between the living placental orders first occurred in the late Cretaceous, probably between about 100 and 110 million years ago, when all of the major continental landmasses had been isolated from each other by plate tectonic activity. A greenhouse climate prevailed at that time, and elevated sea levels helped to further isolate these landmasses with shallow epicontinental seas. These conditions likely set the stage for a few chance events that would forever alter the course of placental evolution.

Available evidence indicates that placental mammals likely arose in Asia, which is also the probable source area for the earliest marsupials. At some point between about 105 and 80 million years ago, a primitive placental managed to disperse from Asia, or possibly Europe, across the Tethys Sea to Afro-Arabia, which was slowly moving north after its split from South America about 120 million years ago. This mammal would have been a distant relative of all other living placentals, and while we have no idea what it might have

◁ **Left** *The revolution in molecular techniques that has shed new light on mammal evolution has illuminated debates such as the classification of the red panda (now established in its own family, Ailuridae).*

looked like, we do know that around 80 million years ago its descendants gave rise to a spectacular radiation that produced forms as diverse as elephants, sea cows, hyraxes, aardvarks, sengis (elephant shrews), tenrecs, and golden moles. The earliest phases of this group's evolutionary history unfortunately are not known, because the late Cretaceous fossil record in Africa has not been well explored. However the earliest fossil records of the terrestrial members of these groups are all African; very primitive relatives of elephants, hyraxes, and sengis first appear in northwest Africa during the earliest part of the Eocene, between 55 and 50 million years ago. Given its presumed endemic African roots, this clade (or group that shares a single common ancestor to the exclusion of all other species) has been named Afrotheria, and its single origin is now supported by an impressive array of genomic information, including not only evidence from mitochondrial and nuclear DNA sequences, but also unique deletions within these sequences, chromosomal rearrangements, and a family of so-called jumping genes (or SINEs – shorthand for "short interspersed nuclear elements") whose unique insertion points throughout the genome should, theoretically, be almost completely immune to convergent evolution.

From the perspective of their body designs (morphology), the Afrotheria has been difficult to explain, because there are few features shared by all afrotherians that would clearly attest to the group's shared ancestry. Afrosoricids are particularly out of place – unlike other afrotherians, they exhibit many features, particularly in their dentition, that would not be unexpected in a very

primitive Cretaceous placental. An important clue to afrosoricid origins might be provided by their phylogenetic position within Afrotheria, however. The different forms of genomic data noted above appear to be converging on a phylogenetic arrangement in which aardvarks and sengis – which are, in many ways, morphologically similar to paenungulates – are consecutive sister groups of Afrosoricida. This phylogenetic pattern suggests that tenrecs and golden moles are not directly descended from the very earliest afrotherians, but may be members of a younger group whose members have undergone dramatic evolutionary reversals to conditions observable in much more ancient fossil placentals. If this is the case, then the ancestral afrotherian might have looked more like a proto- "ungulate" than an "insectivore."

At least two other ancient placental lineages dispersed south to Gondwana near the Cretaceous–Cenozoic boundary around 65 million years ago, presumably from North America into South America, and also underwent impressive adaptive radiations in isolation. The only surviving remnants of these dispersals are the peculiar xenarthrans, the Neotropical group that contains anteaters, sloths, and armadillos. Unlike Afrotheria, Xenarthra (now separated into the orders Pilosa and Cingulata) has long been easily distinguished by a number of morphological features, and as a group they are relatively well understood. South America's extinct "ungulate" radiation, which may or may not be a monophyletic group and may or may not have any real relationship to other "ungulates", went extinct only quite recently, and is much more mysterious. A shared origin with Xenarthra cannot be entirely ruled out, but

this hypothesis certainly finds no support from available fossil evidence. As marsupials also dispersed from North America into South America during the Paleocene, and anthropoid primates and rodents dispersed from Africa in the late Eocene or early Oligocene, the competitive landscape on that continent constrained any one of these invading lineages from diversifying to the extent that afrotherians managed in Africa.

What of all the other placentals? Afrotheria and Xenarthra are evidently distant relatives of the remaining 11 orders, which have now been placed in a group called Boreoeutheria. Within Boreoeutheria, there are two major subdivisions – Laurasiatheria, containing artiodactyls, perissodactyls, carnivorans, pangolins, bats, and eulipotyphlans, and Euarchontoglires, containing the remaining members of the old Archonta (now called "Euarchonta") and Glires. The evolutionary history of the nonvolant, nonaquatic boreoeutherian orders was primarily restricted to northern continents – Asia, Europe, and North America – until the early Miocene, when members of many of these orders migrated into Africa following the permanent reestablishment of land connections with Eurasia. Primates and rodents are some notable exceptions, with early members of those orders dispersing over the Tethys Sea to make it first into Africa, ultimately giving rise to living anthropoid and strepsirrhine primates and the living hystricognathous and anomaluroid rodents, and then heading west again over the Atlantic to produce the platyrrhine anthropoid and caviomorph rodent radiations in South America.

Some of the most interesting rearrangements within Laurasiatheria are found not at the supraordinal level (which is remarkable, given that all of the supraordinal relationships within the group are novel), but within certain orders. Certainly the most spectacular finding is that whales, which have long been phylogenetically enigmatic due to their extreme morphological adaptations for aquatic life, are not simply the sister group of artiodactyls (even-toed ungulates) as some had suspected, but are actually nested deeply within Artiodactyla as the closest living relative of the hippopotamus, thus forming a new order, the Cetartiodactyla. For many years this hypothesis was intensely disputed by paleontologists, who argued that cetaceans' evolutionary roots were clearly detectable among an extinct group of terrestrial carnivorous nonartiodactyl placentals called mesonychians. This debate was recently resolved by the timely discovery of a semiterrestrial early Eocene cetacean from Pakistan that preserves a number of artiodactyl-like features of the postcranium that are not present in mesonychians.

This discovery has revealed that it was actually the striking dental similarities of cetaceans and mesonychians that were phylogenetically misleading. Other relationships within Artiodactyla are also not quite what they seemed. The traditional grouping of pigs and peccaries with hippos as "suiforms" has been rejected in favor of a hippo–whale clade (named, rather light-heartedly, the Whippomorpha), but pigs and peccaries are evidently not even particularly close relatives of this new assemblage; instead hippos and whales appear to be more closely related to ruminants.

Other convenient taxonomic arrangements, such as the division between megabats and microbats within the order Chiroptera, have also been disrupted. The traditional view is that the relatively large nectar-, pollen-, and fruit-eating megabats and the smaller, more insectivorous, echolocating microbats shared a common ancestor that would have looked somewhat like a small megabat. However genetic data now indicate that the rhinolophoid microbats (rhinolophids, megadermatids, craseonycterids, and rhinopomatids) are in fact more closely related to megabats than to other microbats. This novel arrangement leaves it likely that echolocation evolved in the last common ancestor of all bats, and that megabats have subsequently abandoned the foraging strategies that required echolocation. This also implies that megabats are probably best seen as highly specialized microbats. As with whales, and possibly afrosoricids, megabats apparently provide another example in which dramatic morphological specialization has obscured the anatomical evidence for phylogenetic relationships.

The broad patterns emerging from the molecular phylogeny of Placentalia have some interesting implications for our understanding of the group's origin. For instance, while the ancestral placental may have had an insectivorous diet, there is now little reason to believe that this mammal would be identified as an "insectivoran" in the traditional taxonomic sense. With the former lipotyphlans now possibly best seen as highly specialized forms that are nested deep within Placentalia, it is no longer clear what type of morphology we should expect to find in the most basal placentals. It is certainly no longer inconceivable that early members of the afrotherian, xenarthran, and boreoeutherian lineages might have had relatively bunodont, low-crowned teeth, perhaps not unlike those of the late Cretaceous Asian zhelestids, which have traditionally been interpreted not as "insectivores" but as "archaic ungulates". More late Cretaceous fossils will be needed to test such hypotheses.

The new molecular phylogeny also has implications for the evolution of locomotor patterns. While the early Cretaceous stem placental *Eomaia* has been interpreted as a possible arboreal form, xenarthrans and all of the afrotherian orders are likely to have been ancestrally terrestrial, imply-

MESOZOIC MAMMALS

Popular accounts of vertebrate life during the Mesozoic almost unanimously state that mammals were outcompeted by dinosaurs, and that the former were only able to diversify following the extinction of the nonavian dinosaurs at the Cretaceous–Cenozoic boundary, about 65 million years ago. The fossil record remains reasonably consistent with this interpretation, but in the last few decades the number of newly described Mesozoic mammal genera has skyrocketed – while just over 100 were recognized only 25 years ago, that number is now rapidly approaching 300. This "burst" is, in large part, simply due to improved paleontological collecting techniques – because Mesozoic mammals are generally so small that they cannot easily be detected by scanning the surface of a fossil bed, their tiny teeth are most likely to be found by using sieves and microscopes. Thus while these diminutive mammals are certainly more difficult to find than dinosaurs, they were not necessarily exceedingly rare components of terrestrial vertebrate faunas as once thought.

Importantly, recent molecular dating of supraordinal divergences within the placental mammal radiation strongly suggests that placentals' early diversification must not have been unduly affected by the group's coexistence with dinosaurs during the latest Cretaceous, for even the most conservative studies indicate that stem members of almost every placental order had appeared before the nonavian dinosaurs went extinct. The smaller and more agile dinosaurs almost certainly consumed mammals, though, and such predation pressures could explain the fact that early diversification apparently occurred within a nocturnal radiation that rarely achieved body sizes larger than a shrew or mouse. Outside of Placentalia, however, there are exceptions to this pattern: the recent discovery of a "giant" (12–14 kg) triconodont mammal (*Repenomamus giganticus*), a primitive racoon- or opossum-like creature, in the early Cretaceous of China has not only demonstrated that some larger Mesozoic mammal lineages persisted despite their coexistence with agile carnivorous dinosaurs, but also deals an unexpected blow to another bit of received wisdom – the preserved stomach contents of *Repenomamus* include the remains of a young ceratopsian dinosaur. *R. giganticus* is one of the largest Mesozoic mammals known, and so its dietary habits are almost certainly anomalous within the broader Mesozoic radiation, but such discoveries leave it clear that we still have a great deal more to learn about the nature of mammalian evolution during the age of dinosaurs.

ing that the ancestral placental was as well. Full-fledged adaptations for habitual arboreal locomotion presumably first appeared within Euarchonta during the later Cretaceous, while various members of other placental orders experimented with arboreality at later points in time. With regard to morphological evidence for early placental phylogeny, it seems that features of the reproductive system, placentation, and early development might have more accurately tracked the molecular phylogeny than have other morphological traits. For instance, male afrotherians aside from the aardvark are relatively unusual in having completely intra-abdominal testes, while paenungulates, aardvarks, sengis, and potamogaline tenrecs are peculiar among placentals in having a quadrilobular allantoic sac. Afrotherians also tend to have relatively low core-body temperatures, and some forms are daily heterotherms. Whether these physiological features are adaptations or primitive retentions is, however, difficult to determine.

If these and other features are retentions from early placentals that have been improved upon within Boreoeutheria, they might help to explain some of the more recent patterns in placental evolutionary history. When land connections were reestablished between Africa and Eurasia in the early Miocene, afrotherians and boreoeutherians were finally placed in direct competition after at least 55 million years of relative isolation. For whatever reason, this was the beginning of the end for many afrotherian lineages, as these endemic groups were slowly out-competed by

○ Above *The complicated snout and enormous ears of Bate's slit-faced bat (*Nycteris arge*) are part of the remarkable apparatus of ultrasonic navigation that characterizes the microbats. They also belong to a family, Nycteridae, which is unique in that the tips of their tails are T-shaped.*

their northern competitors. Most notable was the loss of the diverse Paleogene hyracoid (modern hyraxes are survivors) radiation, which previously dominated the browsing and grazing niches in Africa and included tapirlike, bovidlike, and

piglike forms. The only remaining afrotherian "lipotyphlans" – the otter shrews and golden moles – became highly specialized and increasingly sensitive to habitat loss, while the invading boreoeutherian eulipotyphlans in Africa were quite successful and managed to range widely. Macroscelidine sengis diversified throughout the Miocene, and have the broadest geographic range of the nonpaenungulate afrotherians, but their living members bear little resemblance to their Eocene ancestors, possibly due to competition with boreoeutherian immigrants. When the Isthmus of Panama finally allowed for the Great American Interchange between North America and South America in the Pliocene, the story was similar. Various laurasiatherian carnivorans, perissodactyls, and artiodactyls, and even afrotherian (proboscidean) mastodons, moved south from North America, although some xenarthrans successfully moved north into North America. This influx was likely to have been largely responsible for the final extinction of the endemic South American "ungulates".

Interestingly, the other major group of endemic South American mammals – the marsupials – lived on despite the sudden influx of northern placentals. The ancestor of all living marsupials likely dispersed from North America to South America at some point in the early Paleocene, following at least 60 million years of evolution in Asia and North America. However it was yet another southern dispersal, from South America, into Antarctica, and then across to Australia (presumably early in the Eocene) that accounts for much of their current taxonomic and morphological diversity. Again, analysis of DNA has helped to resolve longstanding debates surrounding early marsupial biogeography by strongly suggesting that Australian marsupials – dasyuromorphians, diprotodontians, notoryctemorphians, and peramelemorphians – all derive from a common ancestor to the exclusion of the South American marsupials (didelphimorphians, paucituberculatans, and microbiotherians). Fossil marsupials from the Eocene of Antarctica support the hypothesis that landmass served as the likely dispersal route for the ancestor of the Australian taxa. Although it is clear that some of the South American "ungulates" also dispersed into Antarctica, alleged placentals from the early Cretaceous and Paleogene of Australia have not stood up to further scrutiny. For the time being it appears that marsupials were the only nonvolant mammals that managed to colonize Australia during the early Cenozoic. Like the various other mammalian clades that colonized Gondwanan landmasses devoid of therians, Australian "australidelphians" are a diverse radiation whose members evolved adaptations similar to those of other marsupials and placentals. Striking examples include the marsupial mole, whose external appearance is remarkably similar to that of the afrotherian golden mole, and the extinct Tasmanian wolf, which could, at first glance, easily be mistaken for a canid.

Mammal Central Heating
ENDOTHERMY AND ITS COSTS

Two fundamental traits of mammals lie not in their skeletons, but at the boundary of their bodies – the skin. These features are hair and the skin glands, including the mammary glands that secrete milk, and the sweat and sebaceous glands. They may not seem spectacular, and may even have evolved before mammal-like reptiles crossed the official divide. But these traits are associated with endothermy, a condition whose repercussions affect every aspect of mammalian life.

Endothermic animals are those whose internal body temperature is maintained from within (endo-) by the oxidation (essentially, burning) of food within the body. Some endotherms maintain a constant internal temperature (homeothermic), whereas that of others varies (heterothermic). The temperature is regulated by a "thermostat" in the brain, situated within the hypothalamus. In regulating their body temperature independent of the environment, mammals (and birds) are unshackled from the alternative, ectothermic, condition typical of all other animals and involving body temperatures rising and falling with the outside (ecto-) temperature. Endothermic and ectothermic animals are sometimes, misleadingly, called warm- and cold-blooded respectively. However, since the major heat source for, say, a lizard is outside its body, coming from the sun, it can have a body temperature higher than that of a so-called warm-blooded animal, but when the air temperature plummets the reptile's body temperature falls too, reducing the ectotherm to compulsory lethargy. In contrast, the internal processes of the endothermic mammal operate independently of the outside environment. This difference is overwhelmingly important because the myriad of linked processes that constitute life are fundamentally chemical reactions and they proceed at rates which are dependent upon temperature. Endothermy confers on mammals an internal constancy that not only allows them to function in a variety of environments from which reptiles are debarred, but also assures a biochemical stability for their bodies. The critical effect of temperature on mammalian functioning is illustrated by the violence of the ensuing delirium if the "thermostat" goes awry and allows the temperature to rise by even a few degrees.

Endothermy is costly. There are many adaptations involved in minimizing the running costs and the most ubiquitous is mammalian hair. The coat may be adapted in many ways, but there is often an outer layer of longer, more bristle-like, water-repellent guard hairs that provide a tough covering for densely packed, soft underfur. The volume of air trapped among the hairs depends on whether or not they are erected by muscles in the skin. Hair may protect the skin from the sun's rays or from freezing wind, slowing the escape of watery sweat in the desert or keeping aquatic mammals dry as they dive. Hairs are waterproofed by sebum, the oily secretions of sebaceous glands associated with their roots.

Mammals differ in their body temperatures – e.g., monotremes 30°C (86°F), armadillos 32°C (89.6°F), marsupials and hedgehogs 35°C (95°F), humans 37°C (98.6°F) and rabbits and cats 39°C (102.2°F). Some mammals minimize the costs of endothermy by temporarily sacrificing homeothermy: they do not maintain a constant internal temperature. The body temperature and hence metabolic costs of hibernating mammals drop while they are torpid, as do those of tenrecs and many bats during daily periods of inactivity. The body temperature of echidnas fluctuates between 25 and 37°C (77–99°F), falling much lower during winter torpor. Because of the huge area for heat loss in their hairless wings, some microbats cannot maintain homeothermy when at rest, but allow their temperature to fall. They get so cold that when they awaken they have to exercise vigorously to raise their temperature before takeoff.

The coiled sweat glands in the skin of mammals secrete a watery fluid. When expressed onto the skin's surface this evaporates, and in so doing draws heat from the skin and cools it. Mammals vary in the distribution and abundance of their sweat glands: primates have sweat glands all over the body, in cats and dogs they are confined to the pads of the feet, and whales, sea cows, and golden moles have none. Species with few sweat glands lose heat by evaporation of saliva, either by panting or by licking exposed skin.

Strange Senses and Perfumes
NAVIGATION AND COMMUNICATION

Many mammals have senses quite different to our own. Consider the electromagnetic sensory powers of platypus and echidna, or the ability of ele-

phants to detect low-frequency calls. An obvious example is the tremendous olfactory prowess of most mammals. Less obvious is the barometric sense of the Eastern pipistrelle bat, *Pipistrellus subflavus*. These bats have to conserve every possible calorie of energy and so must avoid fruitless foraging trips. Some nights are almost useless for catching insects, and on these occasions the bats would be better to rest, their metabolisms idling, deep in the shelter of their caves. Yet in these dark recesses there is neither light nor wind nor temperature fluctuation, so how are they to judge the weather outside? It happens that insect activity is greatest on warm nights, and the warmer the night the lower the barometric pressure. Remarkably, bats can read the barometer – the lower the pressure, the more active they are in the roost (at the lowest pressure their metabolic rate increases up to fourfold as they prepare to sortie forth). No-one knows how they sense barometric pressure, but it may be related to the paratympanic (Vitali) organ (which, alone among the mammals, bats possess).

Mammals are unique among animals with backbones in the potency and social importance of their smells. This quality also stems from their skin, wherein both sebaceous and sweat glands

become adapted to produce complicated odors with which mammals communicate. The sites of scent glands vary between species: they are aloft the snout in capybaras, on the lower leg in mule deer, behind the eyes in elephants, and in the middle of the back in hyraxes. It is very common for scent glands to be concentrated in the anogenital region (urine and feces are also socially important odors); the perfume glands of civets lie in a pocket between the anus and genitals – for centuries their greasy secretions have formed the base of expensive perfumes. (Glands around the genitals of musk deer serve a similar purpose.) Most carnivores have scent-secreting anal sacs, whose function is largely unknown, although in the case of the skunk it is clear enough. The evolution of scent glands has led to a multitude of scent-marking behaviors whereby mammals deploy odors in their environment. Scent marks, unlike other signals, have the advantage of transmitting long after the sender has moved on. They are often assumed to function as territorial markers, exerting an aversive effect on trespassers, but evidence of this is patchy. Probably most scents convey a plethora of information on the sex, status, age, reproductive condition, and diet of the

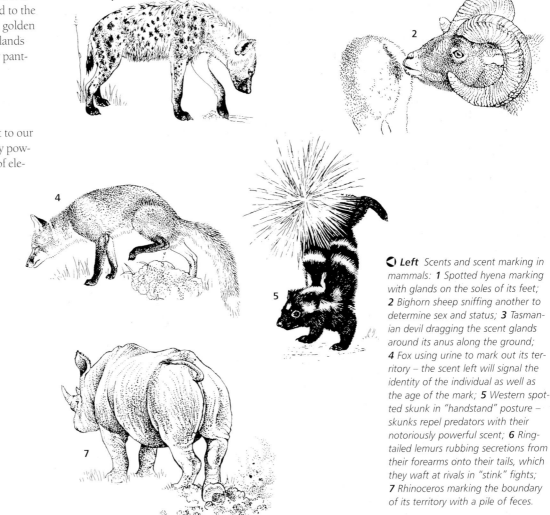

◖ **Left** *Scents and scent marking in mammals:* **1** *Spotted hyena marking with glands on the soles of its feet;* **2** *Bighorn sheep sniffing another to determine sex and status;* **3** *Tasmanian devil dragging the scent glands around its anus along the ground;* **4** *Fox using urine to mark out its territory – the scent left will signal the identity of the individual as well as the age of the mark;* **5** *Western spotted skunk in "handstand" posture – skunks repel predators with their notoriously powerful scent;* **6** *Ringtailed lemurs rubbing secretions from their forearms onto their tails, which they waft at rivals in "stink" fights;* **7** *Rhinoceros marking the boundary of its territory with a pile of feces.*

INFANTICIDE – A MAJOR FACTOR IN MAMMALIAN SOCIOLOGY

Among the subtleties of mammalian sociology is the importance of infanticide – the killing of young by conspecifics. Infanticide has been recorded in over 100 species from at least five orders and 18 families. Nor is this habit confined to one sex – infanticide by females is known for 25 species from three orders: lagomorphs, carnivores, and rodents. However, the potential motives may differ between the sexes – generally, males may be seeking to eat the babies or increase their mating opportunities, whereas females may be after foraging and nest sites.

Possible benefits of infanticide include: a) securing food (male and female chimpanzees eat their victims); b) eliminating competitors – including those of their future offspring (among common marmosets subordinate non-reproductive female helpers increase the weaning success of infants born to dominants; infanticide by the dominant provides her with a bereaved helper and removes rivals to her own offspring); c) stealing resources (infanticidal female rabbits and Belding's ground squirrels seldom eat their victims but do occupy their burrows); d) sexual selection – infanticide is adaptive for the infanticidal male that destroys a rival's offspring and causes the bereaved mother to stop lactating and come into estrus sooner (e.g. chimpanzees, lions, grizzly bears, and lemmings). Perpetrators reduce the risk of mistakenly killing their own offspring by being able to recognize their odor, or by sparing the offspring of females with which they have mated, or females in places where they have mated (in White-footed mice infanticide is generally by newly-arrived males, since resident males are inhibited from killing pups for the 35–40 days after mating, exactly the time needed for their progeny to mature and disperse); e) Parental manipulation, where parents regulate the sex ratio of a litter; and f) minimizing the risk of accidentally adopting non-kin and so wasting effort (perhaps applicable to the pinnipeds which commonly kill pups separated from their mothers).

Many aspects of mammalian behavior can be interpreted as counter-strategies against infanticide. For example, male deer mice defend territories around females at high (but not low) densities. Female counter strategies to male infanticide include mating with dominants, which are better defenders and would be a greater threat to the offspring had they not sired them. In Hanuman langurs, lions, and meerkats females at risk leave the troop to give birth and shelter their young. The infanticidal race brings costs: female prairie dogs fall victim to infanticide while they are out killing somebody else's pups.

Infanticide may have far-reaching consequences for mammalian society. In species in which males commit infanticide, the most obvious correlate is that females are promiscuous. Thus infanticide may be one of the underlying determinants of some mammalian mating systems. The risk of female infanticide may cause females to become aggressive and to space themselves out territorially, which may in turn may favour delayed emigration of their offspring if the habitat is saturated with territory holders, thus leading to kin-group formation and reproductive suppression and/or synchrony in female reproduction. This will influence a male's ability to monopolize females and thus the likelihood of the species having a monogamous, polygynous or promiscuous mating system.

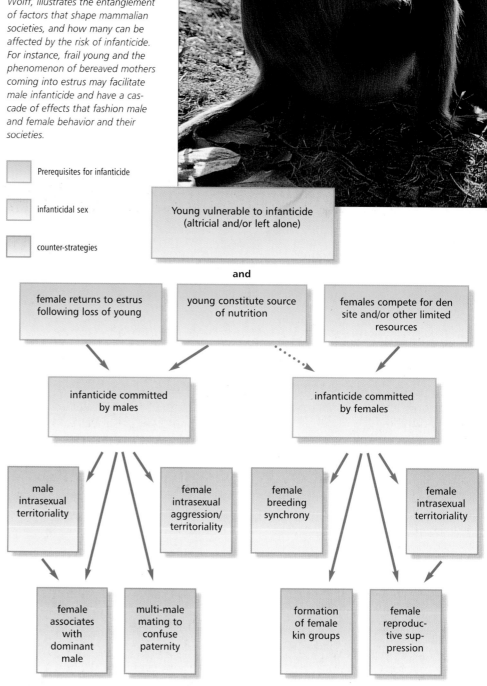

⬤ *Right* Infanticide is a key element of Hanuman langur societies. This brutality is balanced by equally intriguing acts of cooperation and care. Nonhuman primates demonstrate the complexity of cooperation, coalition, and conflict that may have been the driving force behind the evolution of the human's unique mental capacities.

⬤ *Below* Infanticide is the main form of infant mortality in certain species (e.g. lions, prairie dogs, and probably many primates). This scheme, devised by biologist Jerry Wolff, illustrates the entanglement of factors that shape mammalian societies, and how many can be affected by the risk of infanticide. For instance, frail young and the phenomenon of bereaved mothers coming into estrus may facilitate male infanticide and have a cascade of effects that fashion male and female behavior and their societies.

☐ Prerequisites for infanticide

☐ infanticidal sex

☐ counter-strategies

Young vulnerable to infanticide (altricial and/or left alone)

and

| female returns to estrus following loss of young | young constitute source of nutrition | females compete for den site and/or other limited resources |

infanticide committed by males

infanticide committed by females

male intrasexual territoriality

female intrasexual aggression/territoriality

female breeding synchrony

female intrasexual territoriality

female associates with dominant male

multi-male mating to confuse paternity

formation of female kin groups

female reproductive suppression

sender. Many mammals have several scent glands, each of which may send different messages, e.g., the cheek glands of the common dwarf mongoose communicate status, whereas their anal gland secretions communicate individual identity. In labs, almost identical mice have been bred, which differ by only one gene in their so-called Major Histocompatibility Complex (MHC) of genes (which is concerned with the immune system). These mice can nonetheless discriminate each other on the odor of their urine, showing that just one gene difference is sufficient to confer individuality on an odor.

Milk and Reproduction
PLACENTAL AND MARSUPIAL PREGNANCY
Mammary glands are unique to mammals and characterize all members of the class. The glands, which are similar to sweat glands, should not be confused with the mammillae or teats, which are merely a way of delivering the milk. Only females' glands produce milk (with the startling exception of the male Dayak fruit bat). Numbers of teats vary from two in, say, primates and the marsupial mole, to 19 in the pale-bellied mouse opossum. Generally, a female has twice as many mammaries as the average litter size.

Courtship among mammals varies from force (elephant seals) to elaborate enticement (Uganda kob). Pairings may be ephemeral (grizzly bears) or lifelong (silver-backed jackals), and matings mono-

gamous (sengis) or polygynous (red deer). In all cases fertilization involves intromission, which can last a few seconds (hyraxes) or several hours (rhinoceroses). Each of these variations correlates with the species' niche; for example, among cavy-like rodents duration of intromission is briefest in species that mate in the open, exposed to predators – the males of these species have elaborate penile adornments, perhaps to stimulate cervical contraction in the female.

The five monotreme species, sole survivors of the egg-laying subclass Prototheria, (like the marsupials, and some of the former Insectivora) have a cloaca (a common external opening of urinary and reproductive tracts); and their testes remain in the abdomen (as they do in elephants, rabbits, and some of the former Insectivora). As in birds, only the left ovary of the female platypus sheds eggs into the oviduct, where they are coated with albumen and a shell, and laid after 12–20 days. Echidnas incubate their eggs in a pouch, platypuses keep theirs in a nest where they are incubated for about three weeks. Meanwhile, the embryo is nourished from the yolk. On hatching, the young sucks milk that drains from mammary glands onto tufts of hair on the female abdomen. Monotremes lack nipples.

Among marsupials, eggs are shed by both ovaries into a double-horned (bicornuate) uterus. There the developing embryo spends 12–28 days, gaining nourishment from its yolk sac and "uter-

ine milk" secreted by glands in the uterine walls. The early embryo (blastocyst) rests in a shallow depression in the uterine wall, its vascular yolk sac (chorion) in contact with the slightly eroded wall of the mother's uterus. This point of contact allows limited diffusion between maternal and fetal blood and is called a chorio-vitelline placenta (the chorio-allantoic placenta in bandicoots is discussed below). At birth the marsupial infant is highly altricial (poorly developed), weighing only 0.8g (0.03oz) for the 20–32kg (44–70lb) female Eastern gray kangaroo. Nevertheless, its sense of smell and its forelimbs are disproportionately developed and enable it to work through the thicket of fur on its mother's belly to reach the teats, often in a pouch. The infant attaches to a single teat, which swells so as to plug into the baby's mouth. Marsupials detach from the nipple at about the same weight as that at which a placental mammal of comparable size is born.

Compared with this neat system, the prolonged pregnancies of placental mammals may seem ungainly. Placentals have evolved a chorio-allantoic placenta. This organ facilitates nutritional, respiratory, and excretory exchange between the circulatory system of mother and infants. The mother's enhanced ability to sustain infants in the uterus permits prolonged gestation periods and the birth of more developed (precocial) young. The placenta permits a remarkable liaison between mother and unborn infant. The blastocyst first adheres to the uterus and then, assisted by protein-dissolving enzymes secreted by its outer membrane, sinks into the maternal tissue, reaching an inner layer called the endometrium. The outer membrane of the embryo, the chorion, is equivalent to the one that lines the shell of reptile and bird eggs. Protuberances (villi) grow out from the chorion into the soup of degenerating maternal tissue known as the embryotroph. The villi absorb this nutritious broth. Blood vessels proliferate in the uterus at the site of implantation and the chorionic villi vastly increase the absorbtive surface – a human placenta grows 48km (30mi) of villi. The marsupial bandicoot's placenta lacks villi, and is thus inefficient compared with the placental mammal's version, but provides another stunning instance of parallel evolution. Mammalian orders differ in the extent to which the maternal and embryonic membranes of the placenta degenerate to allow mixing of parent and offspring fluids. Among pigs, lemurs, horses, and whales the chorionic villi simply plug into the maternal endometrium. This is a huge advance on the marsupial system, but nevertheless is 250 times less efficient at salt transfer from mother to fetus than the placentae of most sengis, rodents, rabbits, New World monkeys, and bats. In these cases the maternal and embryonic tissues are so eroded that the fetal blood vessels are bathed in the mother's blood. The great significance of the placenta is that without it the mother's body would reject the baby as a foreign body.

This tolerance of the embryo allows the placental mammals to have longer pregnancies and hence to bear precocial young, although not all do so. The placenta facilitates feeding the embryo during gestation, and milk nourishes it after birth. Yet both have an additional function, namely to transfer the mother's antibodies to her offspring, thus enhancing its immunity to disease. The afterbirth of placental mammals is the fetal part of the placenta.

Species differ in the duration of both gestation and lactation, and in their combined length. Gestation length is ultimately constrained by the size of skull that will fit through the mother's pelvis, but where agility, speed, or long travels put a premium on the mother's athleticism, then pregnancy will be short compared with the period of lactation, and birth weight of the litter relatively small.

Parental Care and Milk

LACTATION AND GESTATION

Mammals are not the only vertebrates to bear live young (viviparity), but they are unique in that the availability of milk buffers their infants from the demands of foraging for themselves while they are still small and undeveloped copies of their parents. To a large extent a young mammal prospers initially on the strength of its parents' competitive ability, as reflected in the supply of its mother's milk, until reaching an age and size when it can compete more or less on adult terms. In the tree shrew, parental care is entirely nutritional, the mother visiting her infants once every two days solely to suckle them for a few minutes. However, especially where food is elusive, additional parental care eases the transition to adulthood; indeed, since the female can store fat (and scarce minerals) in anticipation of nursing and then convert it to milk, she is free to spend more time with her offspring if necessary. Carnivora carry prey back to their offspring and may (e.g., wolves, African wild dogs) regurgitate for them. Koalas feed on toxic eucalyptus leaves and produce special feces of partially digested and detoxified material on which the weanling feeds, whereas the two-toed sloth overcomes a comparable problem by nursing for up to two years. Lactation not only prolongs infant dependence and accelerates growth, it detaches the infant mammal from the environment: short-term food shortages are ironed out as the mother continues to lactate, if necessary mobilizing her own tissue, minerals, and trace elements to provide abundant, digestible, and nutritious food for her young. For the young, suckling is hardly arduous, so it can devote more energy to growth than it could if hunting, doubtless inefficiently, for itself. Last but not least, parental care prolongs the young mammal's apprenticeship in complex adult skills.

The evolution of lactation has facilitated a marked increase in the sophistication of mammalian teeth. Once formed, mammalian teeth, encased in a dead shell of enamel, cannot grow in girth (some continue to grow outward). Lactation postpones the time when the teeth must erupt and this may have been a precondition for the evolution of the complex occlusion (fitting together) of cusps of teeth in upper and lower jaws (diphyodonty) that is characteristic of mammalian teeth and necessary for chewing. In a growing jaw such teeth would be thrown out of alignment. The importance of lactation is that it postpones the need for teeth until much of the jaw's growth is complete. As part of this process, mammalian jaws grow quickly; after birth, the growth of a mammal's head suddenly spurts relative to the rest of the body, giving infants their typically big-headed appearance. Furthermore, the growth of jaws and teeth is very resistant to variation, proceeding almost unabated whether the infant is starving or overfed. There are some interesting variations - it takes more than 30 years for an elephant jaw to reach full size, but nevertheless the upper and lower teeth are perfectly aligned throughout because their premolars and molars (in both milk and permanent teeth) erupt sequentially (as do kangaroos'), one at a time from the rear, a bigger tooth emerging and migrating forward along the jaw as the animal grows and as the previous one wears out.

Milk contains water, proteins, fats, and carbohydrates, but in proportions that vary widely between species. Mammals with high-protein milk grow fastest, but the diets of many species preclude their producing protein-rich milk. Pinnipeds have very fat-rich milk: that of California sea lions is 53 percent fat, perhaps because of the need for rapid weight gain prior to immersion in cold seas. Elephant seals born at 46kg (100lb) quadruple their weight in three weeks. Small

EVOLUTION, SOCIETY, AND SEXUAL DIMORPHISM

Thomas Malthus' 1798 *Essay on the Principle of Population* sowed a seed that germinated in Charles Darwin's mind as the theory of natural selection, in his *Origin of Species* (1859). Malthus observed that, although a breeding pair usually produce more than two offspring, many populations do not grow as fast as this would imply, if at all. Darwin was impressed by the subtlety of species' adaptations and saw that individuals differed in the perfection of their adaptations to prevailing conditions, or "fitness." The variation between individuals arose from the mixing of genetic material involved in sexual reproduction, and from mutation, although the link between these mechanisms and Darwin's theory was not realized until 1900, when Mendel's work was rediscovered.

Since populations do not necessarily grow, many of the young must die, and the variation among individuals facilitates selective death, allowing better adapted individuals to thrive. Traits that confer an adaptive advantage will thus spread, if they are heritable, since those that bear them will become an ever larger part of the breeding population. Natural selection fashions individuals of succeeding generations to be ever better adapted to their circumstances. The characteristics of a species represent the sum of the actions of natural selection on similar individuals.

It is wrong to say that animals behave "for the good of the species" – more accurately, individuals are adapted to maximize their own fitness, which is often equivalent to maximizing the number of their offspring that survive to breed. In fact, selection acts on the genetic material that underlies each individual's traits, and so individuals actually behave in ways that promote the survival of the genes for which they are temporary vehicles – hence biologist Richard Dawkins' now famous term, the "selfish gene." Sometimes an individual helps its relatives, behaving in a way that seems detrimental to its own interests but is on balance beneficial to its genes, and so improves its overall (or "inclusive") fitness.

Individual mammals behave so as to maximize their reproductive success and since the pattern of reproduction is the core of society, adaptations to this end are reflected in the huge variety of mammalian social systems. There is an asymmetry between males and females in this respect: sperm are cheaper to produce than ova, and only female mammals bear the costs of pregnancy and lactation. Thus males may more readily maximize their reproductive success by mating with many females. Females, in contrast, can mother only a relatively small number of young and so maximize their reproductive success by investing heavily in the quality of each and, in particular, securing the best (evolutionarily "fittest") father. Infanticide and helping are striking examples of the lengths to which individuals will go to spread their genes at the expense of their rivals'.

Females are a resource for which male mammals compete. The stringent natural selection that operates between competing males is called sexual selection. It explains why many mammals are polygynous (one male mates with several females) and why males are often bigger than females. A big male defeats more rivals, secures matings with more females and thus sires more offspring; if his size and prowess are passed to his sons they will in turn become successful, dominant males. So, females adapted to behave in a way that enables their sons to prosper will select only the most successful males as mates (but may still try to defray the infanticidal tendencies of other males my mating with them promiscuously). The situation is different if the species' niche is such that a male's reproductive success is affected by the quality of his parental care rather than simply by the quality of his sperm; for example, among canids the survival of young depends on their father providing them with prey, and the male would find it impossible to provide for more than one or perhaps two litters. In this case natural selection favors monogamy and sexual dimorphism is less pronounced. But it is less obvious why sexual dimorphism is especially prevalent among larger species. One possible answer is that energy demands are relatively less on larger species and so they can afford to invest more heavily in muscle and armaments. Of course, this is just one line of logic, linked to particular sets of selective pressures, which explains general trends, but there is variation in all these things: equids are not dimorphic but one male does monopolize a harem.

mammals also grow very fast; least shrews double in weight by the time they are four days old. The composition of milk may change during lactation: among kangaroos the early milk is almost fat free, but later it contains 20 percent fat; when the mother nurses two babies of different sizes each teat delivers milk with a fat content appropriate to the stage of development of the infant sucking it.

The timing of breeding in many mammals living in seasonal environments is critical, and often triggered by the effect of daylength on the pineal body of the brain. The costs of pregnancy and, even more, lactation are high and the weaned youngsters will place an additional burden on the food resources within their parent's range. Consequently, in seasonal environments, many species give birth at periods when food is most abundant. This can lead to extreme synchrony in mating time – in the marsupial brown antechinus all births occur within the same 7–10 days each year. The onset of heat (estrus) in some rodents is triggered by the appearance in their diet of chemicals contained in sprouting spring vegetation.

A difficulty may arise when other factors intervene to make it disadvantageous to mate one gestation period in advance of the optimal birth season. For example, Eurasian badgers give birth in February, but their gestation period of eight weeks would seem to necessitate them mating at a time when they are normally inactive, conserving energy while living on their winter fat reserves. Mammals have evolved some intricate adaptations to resolve this dilemma. In the case of the badger (and some other members of the weasel family, some pinnipeds, some bats, the roe deer, the nine-banded armadillo, and the Tammar wallaby) the adaptation is delayed implantation. This interrupts the normal progression of the fertilized egg down the oviduct to the uterus where it implants and develops: instead, the egg, at a stage of division called the blastocyst (where it consists of a hollow ball of cells), reaches the uterus where it floats in suspended animation, encased in a protective coat (zona pellucida) until the optimal time for its development. In the case of the Eurasian badger this means mating any time from February to September. The most protracted delay to implantation is in the fisher – a marten – whose total pregnancy lasts 11 months, the same as that of the blue whale. The fisher's "true" gestation is two months. Cetaceans (whales and dolphins) have very short pregnancies relative to their body weight. The longest mammalian pregnancy is 22 months in the African elephant. The shortest on record is 12.5 days in the short-nosed bandicoot.

Most kangaroos and wallabies exhibit nonseasonal embryonic diapause. A female conceives after giving birth (postpartum estrus) but so long as her current infant continues to suckle the new embryo does not implant in the uterine wall. The consequence is the ready availability of a replacement should one infant succumb, with the added

advantage of a rapid succession of offspring to be squeezed into good breeding seasons. Embryonic diapause or delayed implantation provide yet another example of an adaptation that has arisen separately in metatherians and eutherians.

A different method of ensuring that birth is at a convenient season is sperm storage. This is used by the noctule bat and other nontropical members of the families Rhinolophidae (horseshoe bats) and Vespertilionidae (vesper bats). All the males produce sperm in August (thereafter their testes regress). They continue to inseminate females, often while the latter hibernate throughout the winter. The sperm are stored for 10 weeks or more in the uterus, until ovulation in the spring.

Sons, Daughters, and Favoritism
INVESTMENT STRATEGIES
Some mammals treat their offspring differently depending on whether they are sons or daughters. In the two highly polygynous species of elephant seals, male pups are born heavier, grow faster, and are weaned later than their sisters. These differences arise partly because mother elephant seals allow their sons to suckle more than daughters. Similarly, male red deer calves are born heavier than females, after longer gestation. Thereafter, males suckle more frequently and grow faster and evidently cost their mothers more, since hinds that bear sons are inclined either to breed later in the succeeding season than hinds that rear daughters, or not at all. In these species mothers seem to invest more heavily in sons than in daughters.

The opposite pattern prevails amongst dominant female rhesus macaques, among which a mother that rears a son is more likely to breed the

⬥ **Above** *Because the thermal conductivity of water is greater than that of air, marine mammals face a special problem in conserving energy. They all need abundant insulation, a feature amply demonstrated by these hauled-out Atlantic walruses.*

following year than one that has reared a daughter. The implication is that a daughter costs her more, depleting her resources further than does a son. Amongst macaques it seems that part of the extra burden of bearing daughters is, remarkably, that females pregnant with female fetuses are more frequently threatened or attacked by other females than are those bearing male fetuses.

What underlies this favoritism? The answer lies in the limited time, effort, and resources that parents have at their disposal for investment in offspring. Natural selection will favor parents that invest more heavily in one sex of offspring if that investment is later repaid by the production of a larger crop of grandchildren. It is easy to see how just such a process has operated among elephant seals, red deer, and probably many polygynous mammals. In these species almost all females breed, but only a minority of very dominant males sire the great majority of the young.

Depending on status, males vary hugely in evolutionary fitness from indefatigable studs to reproductive flops. Attaining dominant status depends on a male's size and strength, and these attributes can be greatly influenced by early nourishment. A mother northern elephant seal that lavishes nourishment on her son is weighting the odds in his favor for the future day when he joins battle to win a harem. If he is victorious his brief but orgiastic reproductive career may secure for his mother up

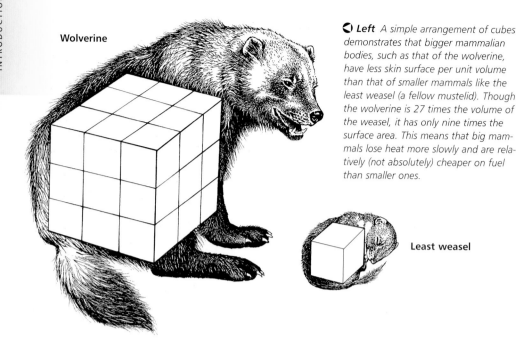

Wolverine

Least weasel

◁ **Left** *A simple arrangement of cubes demonstrates that bigger mammalian bodies, such as that of the wolverine, have less skin surface per unit volume than that of smaller mammals like the least weasel (a fellow mustelid). Though the wolverine is 27 times the volume of the weasel, it has only nine times the surface area. This means that big mammals lose heat more slowly and are relatively (not absolutely) cheaper on fuel than smaller ones.*

relative to weight (and volume) in smaller bodies is that energy consumption rises so steeply with diminishing body size that one of the smallest terrestrial mammals, the pygmy white-toothed shrew (2–3.5g/0.07–0.12oz), has to eat almost nonstop. The rate at which the body's chemical processes occur and at which it requires energy is called the metabolic rate, so fuel-hungry small mammals are said to have a high, or fast, metabolic rate.

Larger mammals score over smaller ones in conserving energy. On the other hand they are at a disadvantage when dissipating heat. Mechanisms for aiding heat loss include the elephants' ears and seals' flippers. The strictures of temperature are reflected in the wide geographical variation in the size of ears of North American hares: the arctic hare's ears are slightly shorter than its skull, while those of the antelope jack rabbit of Arizona are vast radiators, twice the length of its skull.

Body Size, the Cost of Living, and Diet
NUTRITION AND METABOLISM

The struggle to maintain body heat is especially acute for marine mammals. Many have evolved to gargantuan proportions to take advantage of a more favorable surface:volume ratio. Thus, the massive blue whale has a tenfold more advantageous ratio than a small porpoise. This, combined with its far greater depth of insulating blubber, puts the blue whale at a 100-fold thermal advantage in cold water. Because they lead an energy-expensive life generating adequate heat, smaller whales have even higher metabolic rates than would be predicted from their size. By contrast, fossorial (subterranean) rodents have a lower metabolic rate than to be expected for their size, because of the difficulty of dissipating heat in their humid, windless burrows where sweat cannot evaporate (perhaps relative freedom from predators also allows them to "tick over" more slowly.

If all else were equal, the energy-expensive metabolisms of smaller mammals would force them to eat relatively more than their larger cousins. However, all else is not equal, since foods differ in quantity and availability of energy. Animal tissues, fruits, nuts, and tubers are all rich in readily converted energy, in contrast to most vegetation, where each cell's nutrients are encased in tough cell walls of indigestible (without the aid of microbes) cellulose. The energy contained in a meal of meat is not only greater than that in a comparable weight of foliage, it is easier to digest. Thus, a carnivorous weasel is 26 times more efficient in extracting energy from its food than is its herbivorous prey, the vole. Smaller members of a mammal order tend to sustain their high energy demands

to 50 grandchildren each year for as many as 5 years – an ample return for that extra milk. Since in harem-living species all females breed, largely irrespective of strength, comparable extra investment in daughters' muscle-power would be wasted. Put another way, producing a feeble son that fails to breed is worse than useless, for the parental investment of time and energy is wasted on an evolutionary dead end. In short, if parents' investment influences the future reproductive success of their offspring, then natural selection will favor those parents that invest more in offspring of the sex that will benefit most from the contribution.

The same principle underlies the opposite result among dominant female macaques. These live in matrilinear groups whose members are linked by a female line of descent. Young males disperse, while mothers form coalitions with their adult daughters who thereby inherit their mother's social rank. The breeding success of a female macaque improves with the strength of the other females in her coalition. An attempt to promote this strength may explain why dominant females allocate extra investment to daughters. The attacks on females bearing female embryos (and later also upon female infants) may arise because mothers in rival coalitions react to these infants as potential competitors of their own daughters. How they perceive the sex of the unborn embryo is an unknown but fascinating twist to the story.

Not only do some species invest more in offspring of one sex than the other, some actually bear more of one sex. Among African wild dogs the sex ratio at birth is biased toward males (59 to 41 percent). This may have evolved because several males are required to rear the offspring of one female, so that parents producing a male-biased litter will thereby secure more grandchildren. In effect, a litter of African wild dogs requires the paternal investment of several "fathers" to

survive; thus to gain equal returns (i.e. future descendants) from their investments in sons and daughters, parents of this species may require more sons. Female coypu with ample fat reserves, and hence the opportunity of investing heavily in a litter, selectively abort small, mainly female litters. Later they produce larger litters, with the result that females in peak condition produce more sons. This is beneficial, since sons of females in good condition grow to be stronger and so, in a polygynous society, have a competitive advantage over the less robust sons of less healthy mothers.

Size and the Energy Crisis
ALLOMETRY

To survive, each animal must balance its income of energy with its expenditure. The particular problem for mammals is that their endothermy remorselessly imposes high expenditure. A mammal's body temperature is unlikely to be exactly that of its surroundings, so even when totally inactive the mammalian system must work to maintain its constant temperature and to avoid heat flowing out of or into its body: when at rest, 80–90 percent of the energy "burned" by endotherms is used solely to maintain constant temperature (homeothermy). As summer turns to winter, a mammalian body requires more energy, as it loses heat more quickly to the environment. The heat from the mammal's core is lost through its skin, and as a small mammal grows larger its volume increases faster than its surface area (the surface area of a body increases with the square of its length, whereas its volume increases with the cube). When inactive, the energy costs (and hence requirements) per unit weight of a horse are one-tenth of those of a mouse. This phenomenon, of bodily dimensions varying together but at different rates, is called allometry. A crucial upshot of this increase in surface area (and thus heat loss)

◁ **Right** *A polar bear mother nursing her cub. This species is a prime example of a K-selected mammal, whose reproductive strategy is to invest longer parental care in fewer offspring. Thus, polar bear cubs remain with their mother for well over two years.*

MAMMALS IN CONTEXT

The lives of mammals must be interpreted in the context of the creatures around them. Not only are they preyed upon by, and prey on, nonmammals, but they also compete with them. Take, for example, the two most abundant predators of South Georgia, the Antarctic fur seal, *Arctocephalus gazella*, and the macaroni penguin, *Eudyptes chrysolophus*. Both breed in the austral summer and the major component in the diet of both is antarctic krill, *Euphausia superba*. Scientists from the British Antarctic Survey have used satellite tracking to follow both species on forays from Bird Island, a tiny island on the northern tip of South Georgia. Most parents of both species travel north or northwest to feed, fur seals ranging to 150km/93mi (on trips of 3–5 days), penguins ranging to 50km/31mi on trips of 1–2 days when feeding chicks (and up to 400km/248mi over 15 days during incubation). Since exploitation of fur seals ceased 60 years ago, the population at South Georgia has grown from a few thousand to more than 3 million. Most of this increase has taken place since the 1970s. Over the same period the estimated population of macaroni penguins has halved to some two and a half million breeding pairs. Could these concurrent changes in numbers be related?

It is a fundamental ecological concept that two species cannot coexist stably when they are in direct competition for some limiting resource. In this case, in the summer, the seals and penguins take similar size-classes of krill from largely overlapping areas of ocean. To raise each pup to weaning, a female fur seal needs to catch over 900kg (1,984lb) of krill, whereas macaroni penguins need only to feed about 23kg (51lb) to fledge their chick. Nevertheless, energetic economics of larger size (female fur seals weigh 40kg/88lb, macaroni penguins 4kg/8.8lb), and the greater range of fur seals when both are rearing offspring, may mean that these seals outcompete the penguins within the latter's more restricted range. The penguins may increasingly be forced to work harder to find sufficient food, or switch to less profitable prey.   KB

by eating richer foods than do their large relatives. The 7kg (15lb) duiker selects buds and shoots whereas the 900kg (2,000lb) giant eland can survive on coarse grasses; a bush baby eats fruit but the gorilla eats leaves, and the bank vole eats seeds and roots while the capybara eats grasses. Among carnivores large size facilitates the capture of larger prey, which exempts them from the general rule that quality of diet declines with larger body size.

Diets differ in their availability. "High quality" foods are less abundant than "lower quality" ones. Overall, the abundance of food available to a species depends on which tier of the food chain it tries to exploit: since living things, like other machines, are imperfect, energy is wasted at each link in the chain and so less is available for creatures at the top. This is why the total weight (biomass) of predators is less than that of their prey and why that of herbivores is less than that of their food plants, which in turn are the primary converters of the sun's energy into edible form.

The general rule is that smaller species require more energy per unit weight than do larger ones, and so smaller species are pushed toward more nutritious diets and bigger species can tolerate less nutritious, but often more abundant food. So, for example, the 35g (1.2oz) bank vole has a higher metabolic rate than the 1.4kg (3lb) musk rat, even though they are close relatives (both are arvicoline rodents). Many of the species that defy this general rule do so in order to exploit a specialized diet: for example, ant and termite eaters, arboreal leaf eaters, and flying insectivores tend to have slower-than-expected metabolisms. Such mammals are united in their thrifty use of energy by the fact that their diets all preclude the possibility of a consistent and abundant supply of fuel necessary to run a fast metabolism; flying insects are only seasonally available, many tree leaves are loaded with toxins and deficient in nutrients, and quantities of indigestible detritus inevitably adhere together with termites to the anteater's sticky tongue and so diminish the rewards of its foraging. The difficulty of securing and/or processing fuel destines mammals in these niches to an economical "tick-over" metabolism that is sparing in its use of fuel, rather like a slow-running engine.

Other mammals have highly tuned, "souped-up" engines – their metabolisms burning energy even faster than expected for their body sizes. Among these are the seals and sea lions, whales and dolphins, and river and sea otters, which must generate heat to survive in freezing waters.

Quality versus Quantity
K- VERSUS R-SELECTION

Those, generally larger, mammals with a lower metabolic rate cannot grow so fast, and so their embryos have relatively longer gestations and their infants have slower postnatal growth. Litter-weight at birth is a smaller fraction of maternal body weight in larger species. Infants of larger

mammals thus require even longer postnatal care because they are born so small relative to adult size. The need for protracted parental care would be increased even further if the overall litter weight was divided into many smaller infants, rather than a few bigger ones, since the smaller infants would need even longer growing times. To minimize this problem larger mammals have smaller average litter sizes. These trends combine, so that mammals with lower metabolic rates have longer intervals between generations and a lower potential for population increase from one generation to the next.

Thus the rate of chemical reactions in the cells of a mammal species has repercussions throughout the species' life history and even determines the pattern of their population dynamics. Mammal species with fast, expensive metabolisms have a greater capacity for rapid production of young; they are preadapted to population explosions. Viewed against the variety of mammalian sizes from 1.5g (0.05oz) to 150 tonnes, this interaction between size, metabolic rate, and reproductive potential raises the intriguing possibility that while some species have evolved a particular size largely in order to overcome the mechanical problems of exploiting a particular niche, others may be a particular size largely due to selection for high reproductive potential of which their size is a secondary consequence. A giraffe has to be tall in order to exploit its treetop food and a harvest mouse must be small to clamber nimbly aloft grass stalks, and their sizes shackle them respectively to the reproductive consequences of slow and fast metabolisms – by the time a giraffe bears its first, single offspring, a harvest mouse born at the same time has already been dead four years, and potentially could have left behind more than 10,000 descendants.

On the other hand, mammals such as voles and lemmings, with high reproductive potential, are at a great advantage in unstable environments. Those that can breed prolifically and at short notice can take advantage of an unexpected period of bountiful food, and the capacity to breed fast requires the rapid growth permitted by the high metabolic rates typical of small body size. Mammals dependent upon unpredictable resources are therefore generally small.

The key feature of unstable environments is that supply of resources may exceed demand, for example when the few survivors of a harsh period find their food supply is replenished. In these circumstances, survival is no longer so dependent on population density or direct competitive prowess, and an individual will increase its reproductive success by investing more heavily in a larger number of offspring, and by breeding prolifically at the earliest opportunity, while the going is good. Though the term is now less current among scientists, species adapted to these conditions are called r-selected (selected for rate of increase, r).

⭘ **Above** *The gray squirrel has special enzymes that enable it to detoxify acorns. In its native North America this helps it flourish; in Britain, where it is introduced, it is helping it drive the native red squirrel to extinction.*

In a stable environment the situation is very different, because the population will be finely adjusted to the maximum that the environment can sustain, so competition for food and other resources will be intense. In these circumstances the pressure of natural selection increases in proportion to population density. Heightened competition in a saturated environment puts a premium on the competitive prowess of juveniles, and so parents must invest heavily in each offspring, preparing them for entry into the fray. Species adapted to these conditions have smaller litters, emphasizing the quality rather than quantity of infants born at a more advanced (precocial) stage of development, and infants are given more protracted parental care. Such species are said to be K-selected (selected to survive at carrying capacity, K). Clearly, the slower metabolism of larger mammals will push them toward K-selected life histories. It also makes them less able to recover from persecution, which is why many endangered mammals are large, slow-breeding species. All else being equal, K-selected mammals produce fewer young per lifetime than do r-selected ones, since not only do they have to invest more in each offspring, but they also have to invest heavily in their own competitive activities, such as territoriality, and in muscle power. The big decision in a mammal's life history is thus how to partition energy between reproduction and self-maintenance.

Spendthrifts and Population Explosions
RESPONSES TO UNSTABLE ENVIRONMENTS

The most dramatic illustration of this association between small size, rapid metabolism and great potential for population increase comes from mammals with an unexpectedly high metabolic rate for their size. Why do arvicoline rodents,

rabbits, and weasels spend extra energy on rapid metabolisms when comparably sized marsupials, anteaters, and pocket mice maintain homeothermy without recourse to such fuel-hungry "engines"? The answer is that these energy spendthrifts have apparently shouldered the additional burden of meeting extravagant fuel requirements so as to increase their reproductive potential as an adaptive response to unstable environments. The high "cost of living" of r-selected species such as the lemming, compared with the similarly sized (but K-selected) sengi, is thus a tolerable side effect of a reproductive rate that enables a female to have 12 offspring by the time she is 42 days old. A sengi would, at best, have two young in 100 days.

Considering mammals of similar size but different metabolic rate, those species whose populations tend to dramatic fluctuations and cycles (e.g., arvicoline rodents and lagomorphs) have more rapid metabolisms than species typified by stable populations (e.g. pocket mice and subterranean rodents). The arctic hare has an unexpectedly slow metabolism compared with other lagomorphs and its populations do not exhibit the dramatic population cycles typical of the otherwise similar snowshoe hare. Similarly, brown lemmings show population cycles with peaks of population density that exceed the troughs 125-fold; the collared lemming has a lower metabolic rate and shows a maximum of 38-fold variation in numbers (of course, there are added complications – the brown lemming feeds on abundant mosses and grasses, whereas the collared lemming feeds on less plentiful dicots and dwarf shrubs). The fluctuations in numbers of voles and lemmings result in huge variation in prey availability for weasels. The weasel's small body size and higher than expected metabolic rate enable it to breed twice a year (fast by carnivore standards), which may be an adaptation allowing them to respond as quickly as possible to such a sudden increase in prey numbers. This gives the weasel an advantage over one of its competitors, the stoat, which is broadly similar, but larger and can only breed once a year.

If small mammals can produce many more young, why are any mammals big? Competition drives mammals into countless niches on land, sea, and air and some of these can only be exploited by large species. Large size confers qualities that can be indispensable assets. Such advantages may include (depending on diet and other factors as well as size) the ability to survive on poorer food, to use longevity, efficient storage of metabolites, and memory to "iron out" environmental fluctuations, to travel farther and faster and hence to exploit widely separated resources, to repel larger predators and to survive colder temperatures. Thus, within an awesome diversity of size, shape and behavior, mammals and their characteristics can be categorized according to a series of trends that shimmer elusively through the cloud of adaptation and counteradaptation.   DWM/ERS

KIN SELECTION AND RECIPROCAL ALTRUISM

Optimizing conditions for gene survival

ADAPTATION SEEMS "AIMED" AT SURVIVAL, BUT survival of what? Not of the individual, for individual survival is only a means to reproduction, and even personal reproduction is not the whole story. Meerkats and wolves look after younger sisters and brothers, nephews and nieces. Naked mole rats go further, like worker ants even foregoing their own reproduction. Is the goal then survival of the colony, the species, or even the ecosystem? No, these are incidental consequences. We have to think harder, go back to Darwinian first principles.

A sharper consequence of successful individual survival and reproduction is survival of the individual's genes. This is significant, because genes have the unusual potential of immortality. Not the DNA molecules themselves, but the coded information in their nucleotide sequences can survive through unlimited generations. Not all of them do – that is natural selection – but successful sequences will still be here ten million generations hence. The world becomes full of successful genes.

So, having reached the level of the genes, we are finally talking about survival, pure and simple. If adaptations are "aimed at" anything, it is gene survival. But how do genes survive? By building individual organisms as receptacles or vehicles that take action to preserve them. That usually means take action to stay alive and reproduce. But if it is statistically likely that identical genes will be present in certain classes of other individuals, such as sisters or nephews, an individual may work to preserve them too, even at the expense of its own survival and reproduction. "Hamilton's Rule" states that a gene for altruism towards a particular class of relatives will spread if the cost C to the altruist is exceeded by the benefit B to the recipient devalued (multiplied) by the "coefficient of relationship" r (the proportion of genes shared, identical by descent, between them).

Some values of r, the Coefficient of Relationship:

Full sibling (also parent, offspring)	$1/2$
Half sibling (also grandchild, niece, nephew)	$1/4$
First cousin	$1/8$
First cousin once removed	$1/16$
Second cousin	$1/32$

When W. D. Hamilton first published the theory in 1964, he coined the term *inclusive fitness*, as a sympathetic gesture to biologists long comfortable with the notion that individuals work to maximize something: Darwinian fitness. Hamilton made the minimal adjustment necessary to accommodate fitness gained through other relatives such as brothers and nieces, as well as through offspring. Inclusive fitness has been informally defined as "That quantity which an individual will appear to maximize, when what is really being maximized is gene survival." Hamilton's own definition seems complicated, but the complications are strictly necessary if you want to focus on individual organisms as maximizing agents. If you are happy to talk, equivalently, about genes maximizing something, that something becomes simply gene survival, and the condition for an altruistic gene's survival is Hamilton's Rule, $rB > C$.

Hamilton's Verbal Definition of Inclusive Fitness:

"…the animal's production of adult offspring… stripped of all components…due to the individual's social environment…and augmented by certain fractions of the quantities of the harm and benefit the individual himself causes to the fitnesses of his neighbours. The fractions in question are simply the coefficients of relationship… ." (Hamilton 1964)

Kin selection is not an alternative to "individual selection," nor an unparsimonious complication to be "resorted to" only when individual selection fails. Animals are still maximizing inclusive fitness even when they stick ruthlessly to personal reproduction and never lift a finger for anybody else. Hamilton's Rule is still governing their behavior, but their ecology is such that $rB < C$.

Recipients of altruistic acts and cooperation are not always related to the donors. A supplementary theory is that of Reciprocal Altruism. The cooperation is mutual, and is based on what games theorists call a non-zero sum game. In human games of this kind there is a "banker" and the opportunity exists for the "players" to cooperate with one another at the expense of the banker. Each player brings something to the partnership which the other needs. The ratel or honey badger (*Mellivora capensis*) has the strength and immunity from stings to open bees' nests, but it cannot find them. A small flying bird, the honeyguide (*Indicator* spp.), can find bees' nests but cannot open them. The ratel eats honey but cannot digest wax. The honeyguide (uniquely among vertebrates) has a special enzyme which enables it to digest wax. These two "players," with complementary needs and skills, cooperate profitably at the expense of the 'banker' (the bees). Honeyguides have a special call with which they lead a ratel (or, opportunistically, a man) to a bees' nest. The ratel breaks open the nest and eats the honey, then the bird goes in and eats the wax and larvae.

The theory of reciprocation requires that for each player the cost of giving to the partner should be on average less than the benefit gained from the partner. In the honeyguide/ratel game, the condition is achieved by the complementarity of the needs and skills of the players. In other games, such as the vampire bat (q.v.) blood sharing scheme, the needs and skills of the players are on average the same, but they alternate on different occasions. Blood meals are hard to find but large when found. On a day when a bat is out of luck, it is saved from starvation by a gift of blood from a lucky, bloated colleague. The favor is repaid when the luck is reversed.

This raises the possibility of cheating. The second plank of reciprocation theory is that cheating must be reliably punished, otherwise natural selection will favor genetic tendencies to take when you need, but not give when your turn comes to pay back. This is modeled by the game of Prisoner's Dilemma (see box). Under the right conditions "Tit for Tat" (or "Reciprocal Altruist") is an evolutionarily stable strategy (ESS). As long as the frequency of reciprocal altruists in the population exceeds a critical number, a mutant cheat does not prosper.

In practice, reciprocal altruism is expected in species that live in stable groupings where repeated encounters with the same individuals are likely. As it happens, these same conditions favor kin-selected altruism, because stable groups are likely to be families. It is often difficult to decide whether cooperation evolves under the influence of one or the other selection pressure. It may often be a mixture of both.   RD

PAYOFF MATRIX	You cooperate	You do not cooperate
I cooperate	We both prosper at the banker's expense	I get the low sucker's payoff. You get the high cheat's payoff
I do not cooperate	I get the high cheat's payoff. You get the low sucker's payoff	Both get the low ("punishment") payoff for not cooperating

The Prisoner's Dilemma *Under the conditions given in the payoff matrix, the strategy Reciprocal Altruist (cooperate, but retaliate against cheats) is evolutionarily stable (ESS). So is the strategy Always Cheat. When two strategies are ESSs, whichever one chances to attain more than a critical frequency in the population will not be invaded by the other. The critical frequency will depend upon detailed circumstances. When the whole population is playing Always Cheat, a player wins and loses on different occasions. On average all score less than when playing Reciprocal Altruist. Here, no player wins, they draw prosperously, and the "banker" loses. It is to be expected that the Reciprocal Altruist ESS will be found in nature quite often.*

THE TREE OF LIFE

Deciphering the puzzle of relationships between mammals using supertrees

THE LONG-STANDING GOAL OF CLASSIFYING life – the science of systematics – is to uncover the Tree of Life, a detailed depiction of the evolutionary history of all life. Although the field of systematics is more than 200 years old, it is only recently that the "molecular revolution," and with it the ever-increasing ability to sequence the DNA of organisms quickly and cheaply, has brought the realization of the Tree of Life tantalizingly close. For instance, the complete nuclear genomes of several mammals are now known (human, chimpanzee, mouse, rat, and dog), with the genome projects of at least 26 other mammal species under way or nearing completion. Even better, the genome of the mitochondrion – small organelles inside the cell that each contain their own, smaller set of DNA (about 16,000 base pairs) separate from that in the nucleus – has been fully sequenced for more than 140 species spanning the breadth of mammals. However, molecular information remains limited outside these "model mammals." No single gene has been sequenced for every mammalian species: the best represented gene, cytochrome b, has been completely sequenced for less than one-third of all species. Similarly, as of March 2004, more than 99 percent of the nearly two million Carnivora sequences present in GenBank (an international database for genetic sequence data) were for the dog. With such incomplete information, how is it possible to reconstruct the evolutionary history of all mammals?

The key is to look beyond the DNA to take account of the entire body of information that has been amassed on the evolutionary relationships of a given species. Few species have been fully characterized on a molecular level, but some phylogenetic information exists for all mammals, if only relatively crude taxonomic information, such as the placement of a species in a genus, family, or order. A recent approach called supertree construction involves amalgamating all these fragments of information about a species' relationships into a single all-encompassing tree. Instead of analyzing characters of the organism directly (e.g., DNA sequences or morphological traits), a supertree is pieced together from the trees suggested by the separate lines of evidence. Roughly speaking, supertree construction is akin to building a single picture from multiple, incomplete jigsaw puzzles of that picture. But, because each puzzle overlaps with at least one other one, the supertree can be larger than any of the contributing puzzles, with the overlap showing how they fit together. Puzzles that do not overlap directly can be positioned relative to one another by a series of overlapping puzzles. Also, because the trees being combined need

not agree with each other absolutely, different analytical procedures are used to find the supertree that provides the best fit to the different puzzles.

The combining of trees in a supertree approach currently succeeds where direct analyses of character data fail because different data types often cannot be analyzed using a single analytical procedure. For instance, the evolution of DNA sequences is arguably best examined under a statistical, probabilistic framework that is generally not workable for morphological structures (e.g., dimensions of the skull or the presence or absence of a given feature). We can say how often we expect a specific change in a DNA sequence to occur (on average), but not how often we expect wings to arise within mammals. However, this problem of trying to analyze different types of information simultaneously does not apply when combining the trees that emerge from them. For example, two trees that conclude that mice and rats are more closely related to each other than either are to seals, can always be compared and combined, regardless of the data on which they are based.

The first attempt at a complete supertree of mammals shows the evolutionary relationships of more than 4,500 extant species, or >98 percent of all extant species (depending on the species list). As such, it represents by far the most complete Tree of Life for mammals yet produced and, because mammals are so well studied compared with other organisms, is one of the largest species-level trees ever assembled. Furthermore, divergence times throughout the tree were estimated by mapping DNA data from 66 genes onto the tree and calibrating them against 30 fossil time-points under a local variant of the molecular-clock hypothesis (which specifies that DNA or proteins evolve at a relatively constant rate). The supertree confirms the growing consensus (based largely on molecular studies) of relationships between the major lineages, but extends this information to the tips of the tree (species) for the first time. The egg-laying monotremes were the first group of mammals to branch from the tree and four major lineages (superorders) of placentals can be identified: the Afro-Arabian Afrotheria; the Euarchontoglires and Laurasiatheria, with roots in the ancient supercontinent of Laurasia; and the South American Xenarthra. The distinct biogeographic distribution of these superorders supports the hypothesis that the drifting of the continents caused by plate tectonics has helped drive evolution within placentals. Within these lineages, the whales (Cetacea) are shown to have evolved within the even-toed ungulates (Artiodactyla), with hippos being their closest living relatives. Insectivora – long the taxonomic

catch-all for any small, brown, furry nonrodent – actually comprises two distinct groups that have seemingly evolved in parallel, the African Afrosoricida (golden moles and tenrecs) and the largely New World, Asian, or northern hemisphere Eulipotyphla (remaining insectivores). However, this represents only one of many apparent instances of morphological convergence between the superorders. The divergence times reveal that most of the main placental lineages (roughly, the orders) originated up to eight million years before the Cretaceous–Tertiary boundary (65 million years ago), but that the diversification of the living members of these groups occurred only after this point (when the dinosaurs and many other forms of life went extinct). The supertree also reveals problematic areas that remain. The evolutionary history of the rodents is poorly resolved, partly because the group is so big (about 2,000 species) that it is hard to study, and has been comparatively little studied among mammals.

The impact of the mammal supertree goes far beyond its purely systematic aspects, where there is great optimism that it can be used to underpin a more complete understanding of mammals. Dating back to Darwin and Huxley, it has been appreciated that species do not represent independent data points for analysis because they are related through evolutionary history. As such, the biology of a species derives from both purely adaptive reasons and because it has been inherited from its ancestors (known as "phylogenetic inertia," although the individual traits usually remain adaptive). Disentangling these two factors naturally requires knowledge of evolutionary relationships and forms the basis of the so-called comparative method in biology. The more complete and well-resolved phylogenies currently offered by supertrees have the potential to increase both the scope of the biological questions that can be asked and the statistical power of the analyses, because comparisons across species are more successful when the data represent all or most of the species of interest. For instance, it is clear that wings have enormous adaptive benefits and affect the overall biology of those organisms possessing them greatly. If we were analyzing the evolution of flight but only had measures of one bat and one bird (and no nonflying vertebrates), then the conclusions would be severely limited. Further, without a phylogeny, it would be hard to know what to compare. Should comparisons be made among a few bats here and few birds there, or which species should be compared within bats? The most convincing results are those based on as many sam-

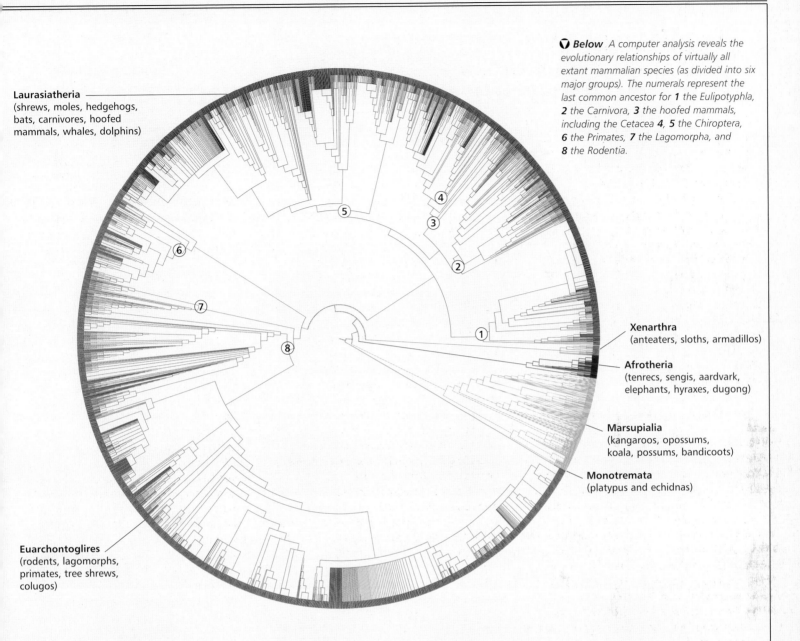

Laurasiatheria
(shrews, moles, hedgehogs, bats, carnivores, hoofed mammals, whales, dolphins)

Below A computer analysis reveals the evolutionary relationships of virtually all extant mammalian species (as divided into six major groups). The numerals represent the last common ancestor for **1** the Eulipotyphla, **2** the Carnivora, **3** the hoofed mammals, including the Cetacea **4**, **5** the Chiroptera, **6** the Primates, **7** the Lagomorpha, and **8** the Rodentia.

Xenarthra
(anteaters, sloths, armadillos)

Afrotheria
(tenrecs, sengis, aardvark, elephants, hyraxes, dugong)

Marsupialia
(kangaroos, opossums, koala, possums, bandicoots)

Monotremata
(platypus and echidnas)

Euarchontoglires
(rodents, lagomorphs, primates, tree shrews, colugos)

ples as possible, with the decision of what to compare with what having been set within a logical, phylogenetic structure.

For these reasons, complete supertrees open the door to tackling problems in biology that have previously been out of reach, and have provided new insights into the pattern and process of evolutionary change. As examples, a picture of the genealogical relatedness of all mammal species has shed light on questions about which species evolved when, about which characteristics are associated with rapid evolutionary change or no change, and about which characteristics are correlated with increases in species numbers. With continuing refinements in supertree analysis, some of the answers are now becoming apparent.

For example, species richness in mammals (that is, the number of species belonging to a cluster on the tree) is significantly correlated with life histories involving rapid reproduction – shorter gestation periods, quicker interbirth intervals, and larger litter sizes. Previously, with incomplete information

it was difficult to be confident whether such patterns were real or partly artifacts arising because parts of the tree were empty (that is, is a group species-poor because it is really species-poor or because it has been incompletely sampled?). Moreover, the same analyses revealed that the biological characteristics influencing species richness differ among groups: whereas population density is more important in Old World monkeys, body size is the key factor in carnivores.

Perhaps the most important task for a complete supertree is to help preserve mammal species and to understand the problems of their conservation. At present, about 25 percent of mammal species are threatened with extinction. Some groups are clearly more threatened than others: Afrosoricida, Artiodactyla, Dermoptera, Eulipotyphla, Hyracoidea, Monotremata, Perissodactyla, and Primates each contain a greater proportion of threatened species than the mammalian average. Understanding the biological and ecological processes that cause some species to be threatened while others

remain comparatively safe is a priority for conservation, and analyses based on supertrees have shed light in this area as well. For instance, it is now known that although geographic range is the most important of the many traits that increase the likelihood of extinction in mammals, group-specific biological characteristics become important additional determinants of extinction risk only for species greater than about 3kg in size.

These exciting examples reveal how having complete phylogenetic information has helped to solve problems that could benefit facets of society ranging from economics to agriculture to conservation to human health (see Beating Diseases in Primates) and that previously seemed lost to evolutionary history when branches of the tree were not represented in our phylogenies. Ultimately, our ability to better understand the complexity of the world's problems and to adapt to rapidly changing environmental issues will depend on our ability to build a more complete and accurate Tree of Life.

OB-E/RB/MC/JLG/RG/KJ/GM/SP/AP

Mammal Conservation: Planning for an Uncertain Future

the reader may marvel at the intricacies of adaptation, the process of natural selection, and the beauty of the creatures found in this encyclopedia, but there is great cause to be fearful for them.

Some losses have been dramatic: in the last 40 years, populations of the black rhino in Africa have plummeted from an estimated 100,000 in 1960 to 3,610 in 2003; since 1900 93 percent of Sumatra's orangutans (*Pongo pygmaeus abelii*) have gone (leaving only 7,300), while the inconspicuous water vole (*Arvicola terrestris*) has disappeared as fast or faster from the UK. Furthermore, things seem set to be getting worse; for example, about 40 percent of all the world's primate species are currently considered threatened with extinction. The oracle, in this context, is the IUCN Red List of Threatened Species, the most comprehensive source of information on the global (rather than national) conservation status of species, and which has served to highlight species at greatest risk of extinction (www.redlist.org). In 2004 the Red List recorded that at least 23 percent (1,101)

of all mammals, roughly one in four, face a high risk of extinction in the wild, either directly or indirectly as a result of human activities (including especially a preponderance of mammals inhabiting tropical montane forests and islands). Further, the conservation status of some 7 percent of mammalian species remains insufficiently known to classify their risk; the IUCN-led Global Mammal Assessment has been set up to remedy that by consolidating information on the systematics, distribution, habitat, ecology, and threats faced by all species of mammals, and to undertake complete reevaluations of the threat status of the world's mammals.

Nowadays the Red List assessments of extinction risk are based on rigorous quantitative criteria and draw on the knowledge of those – like a Delphic circle – who know most about each species. There are eight categories of threat: Data Deficient (DD), Least Concern (LC), Near Threatened (NT), Vulnerable (VU), Endangered (EN), Critically Endangered (CR), Extinct in the Wild (EW), and Extinct (EX). Categorizations of threat status are

made on the basis of five criteria that include factors such as range size, population size, fragmentation, and rates of population and range decline. VU, EN, and CR collectively qualify as threatened. Currently, the Red List includes 162 mammal species classed as critically endangered, 352 as endangered and 587 as vulnerable. In addition, 587 have so far been listed as near threatened and 380 as data deficient.

According to the Red List, 73 species of mammals have become extinct in the last 500 years, while at least another four are considered extinct

⊙ **Right** *The sea otter has made a remarkable recovery since a hunting ban imposed in 1911 reduced the numbers being killed for their fur. However, they are still vulnerable to the effects of human intervention, such as the Exxon Valdez oil spill, which killed an estimated 5,000 sea otters in Alaskan waters in 1989.*

⊙ **Below** *An African golden cat with her kitten in the evening sunlight. Encroachment by humans has already shifted the conservation status of this elusive cat from least concern in 1996 to vulnerable in 2002.*

in the wild. Without the dedicated conservationists of the last century, large charismatic species such as the tiger (*Panthera tigris*), rhinoceroses, elephants, cheetah (*Acinonyx jubatus*), and giant panda (*Ailuropoda melanoleuca*) and many more would certainly already be on this list. While some recently extinct mammals, such as the quagga, *Equus quagga quagga*, have become flagships for conservation efforts, others have simply been forgotten (as it happens, in the case of the quagga, the modern view is that it was "merely" a subspecies of the still-extant plains zebra, *Equus burchelli*). Of the 73 species listed as extinct by the IUCN, 12 are marsupials – the thylacine, *Thylacinus cynocephalus*, disappeared in the 1930s mainly as a result of human persecution. The first mammalian extinction of the 21st century took place only six days after millenium celebrations had ended, with the death of the last known Pyrenean ibex (*Capra pyrenaica pyrenaica*). This subspecies, formerly found in the Spanish Pyrenees, was widespread in the Middle Ages but by the 1990s had fallen to only 10 animals. The last one died in captivity in Ordesa National Park in Spain, on 6 January 2000, when a tree fell on it. This followed the first documented extinction in the 20th century of a primate: Miss Waldron's red colobus monkey, *Piliocolobus badius waldroni*, which, despite over two decades of warnings, was wiped out by indiscriminate hunting in West Africa (tantalizing reports that individuals may yet survive remain unconfirmed).

Unsafe Places

HABITAT AND DISTRIBUTION

Mammals, as with all biodiversity, are not evenly distributed across the globe; the greatest diversity of mammals is heavily concentrated in the tropics, particularly in tropical or subtropical moist broadleaf forests, and the East African woodlands and savannas. If we were to look at a map of the richness of mammal species worldwide, regions showing particular concentrations of threatened species would include the Andes, southern Brazil, West Africa, the montane regions of Africa, Madagascar, the Western Ghats of India, Sri Lanka, the eastern Himalayas, mainland Southeast Asia, Sumatra, Borneo, and the Philippines. Viewed at the level of political units, Indonesia has the largest number of threatened mammals in the world (146 species), followed by India (90), China (82), Brazil (74), and Mexico (73). Some countries have particularly high rates of threat among mammals; Madagascar, for example, a country that has lost more than 90 percent of

its original vegetation, is home to about one-quarter of all the world's threatened primates (20 species), represented by five endemic families of lemurs. Worryingly, preliminary results from the Global Mammal Assessment show that the true percentage of lemurs threatened is probably of the order of about two-thirds, largely because the effects of hunting have been so underestimated.

Conservation can be expensive, resources are inadequate and thus prioritization is essential. Where should effort be focused? Conservationists have identified 34 "biodiversity hotspots," regions characterized by both high threat and high endemism; about 72 percent of the world's critically endangered and endangered mammals occur in the hotspots, but more importantly nearly 60 percent occur only in the hotspots and nowhere else, so protecting these places is an obvious priority.

Protected areas, while not the only tool available, are probably the most effective means of conserving biodiversity. When the third World Congress on National Parks met in Bali in 1982 the protected area network covered 3.5 percent of planet's land surface. In 1992 the fourth World Congress met in Caracas and resolved that protected areas should cover 10 percent of each biome by the year 2000. In 2005 that target has been exceeded for 9 out of 14 major terrestrial biomes, and overall the protected percentage is 11.9 percent (although much of the increase is due to better reporting of reserves that already existed, and the figure is anyway closer to 5.1 percent if only protected areas designated specifically for biodiversity conservation are considered). The existence of more than 100,000 protected areas, spread between 227 countries or territories, prompts the question of where are the most important gaps? How much biodiversity is currently protected and where should new protected areas be established in order to move toward

complete coverage that takes account of vulnerability and irreplaceability?

The World Database on Protected Areas is a comprehensive global catalog of the world's protected areas and, if overlain by the distribution ranges of mammalian species, it can be subjected to gap analysis, which does as its name implies. So, if the world is divided into 105,086 half-degree grid cells, it is possible to calculate the percentage of each species' range that falls into unprotected cells, and for each of these cells to calculate its irreplaceability value (which is the extent to which the goal of achieving a given target of coverage depends on inclusion of that site). The first analysis of this type revealed that the geographic ranges of 258 species (4.8 percent of 5,416 described mammal species) overlapped no protected area. This figure paints far too rosy a picture. The mere fact that a species' geographic range happens to encompass a protected area will grossly overestimate the protection thus afforded. Many protected areas are perilously small, and not necessarily good quality (when the analysis was repeated considering only reserves larger than 10sq km (3.9sq mi) and affording the high levels of protection of an IUCN grading I–IV, then the percentage of mammalian "gap species" rose to 13.5 percent (26.0 percent [314 species] of the 1,063 threatened species of mammal). In many low-income countries some gazetted areas may be protected more in name than in practice. For example, the creation of Brazil's 38,000sq m (45,450sq yd) Tumumcumaque National Park, doubtless helped substantially achieve the target of 10 percent coverage, but involved no mechanisms for biodiversity protection (whereas elsewhere biodiversity was actively protected on some private lands, for example, the Pantanal).

What, then, is a sensible target level of coverage for a species to be considered "covered" by the global protected area network? Perhaps the network should encompass at least one viable population, but what constitutes a viable population? Viability necessitates not only a minimum number of individuals to forestall the genetic and demographic hazards of small populations, but also necessitates the ecological infrastructure that allows the population to persist in the long-term in the face of both natural and anthropogenic (for example, habitat fragmentation or climate change) variations in conditions. Pragmatically, the targets for coverage can be set, variously ambitiously, in terms of the percentage of a species' extent of occurrence that must overlap protected areas. The more restricted a species' range, the stronger the argument for setting the target coverage higher, insofar as smaller populations are subject to much greater risks. The most refined analysis of this sort to date therefore set a target of 100 percent coverage for species that occur in precariously small ranges (smaller than 1,000sq km/390sq mi) and 10 percent coverage for those with huge ranges of occurrence (of more than 250,000sq km/ 96,525sq mi, which includes about a third of mammalian species), with graduated targets in between. This analysis was completed for 276 mammals (of which 153 were threatened), of which 74 percent of species (and 89 percent of threatened species) did not achieve their coverage targets. Although in this analysis 6 percent of all mammals and 14 percent of all threatened mammals were "gap species" (their geographic ranges included no protected area), these average figures

differed between orders of mammal: not a single member of the Carnivora was deemed a "gap species," whereas 7 percent of all rodents (and 23 percent of threatened rodents) were. Perhaps this is because the carnivores generally have much larger ranges than do rodents and, because they are charismatic, many protected areas have been set up with carnivores specifically to include them – the same factors probably explain why mammals as a whole enjoy much better coverage by protected areas than do, for example, amphibians.

The next step is to identify the priority sites. For each candidate cell that might be recruited into the protected area network, its priority depends partly on its irreplaceability value and partly on the threat (based on IUCN risk categories) faced by the species living therein: the highest priority sites are both threatened and irreplaceable. Priority cells fall overwhelmingly on islands and, for those on continents, in the tropics, and especially on mountains. Asia emerges as extremely high priority for global mammal conservation (e.g., the Western Ghats, Sri Lanka, eastern Himalayas), with foci in southern and eastern China and especially Vietnam, northern Thailand, peninsular Malaysia, New Guinea and many Pacific islands, and the wet tropics of Australia's Queensland. In Africa priorities fall in mountains, such as the Cameroonian and Ethiopian highlands, and on islands such as the Seychelles, Mauritius, and the Comoros. In the western hemisphere priority sites for mammals are clustered in the Atlantic forests, the Andes, the Caribbean, and Central America.

Crucially, map-based gap analysis identifies much the same priority sites as did previous approaches such as biodiversity hotspots, Global 200 Ecoregions, and even Endemic Bird Areas. Indeed 97 percent of sites prioritized by gap analysis overlap with at least one of these three, and 59 percent overlap with all three. Most are in low-income countries in the tropics, which can least afford the costs of establishing and enforcing protected areas. Thus, if conservation is to succeed, the costs will have to be born by the global community. It should be remembered that, as the carnivores illustrate, the gap species are not necessarily the highest priority (either when creating reserves or on any other basis), nor indeed the ones that will benefit most from a new reserve.

The aforementioned analyses have identified the parts of the globe where new protected areas may have the highest pay-off, but in practice actually siting new reserves must take account of opportunity costs of income foregone (crucial in low income, tropical countries) and political feasibility. Exactly which populations of a threatened mammal should be protected? One answer lies in identifying Key Biodiversity Areas (KBA), a con-

Below *Sites known to hold the last remaining population of a critically endangered or endangered mammal species. Yellow sites are either fully or partially contained within declared protected areas, and red sites are completely unprotected or have unknown protection status (adapted from Ricketts et al. 2006; data vers. 2.1, courtesy of Alliance for Zero Extinction).*

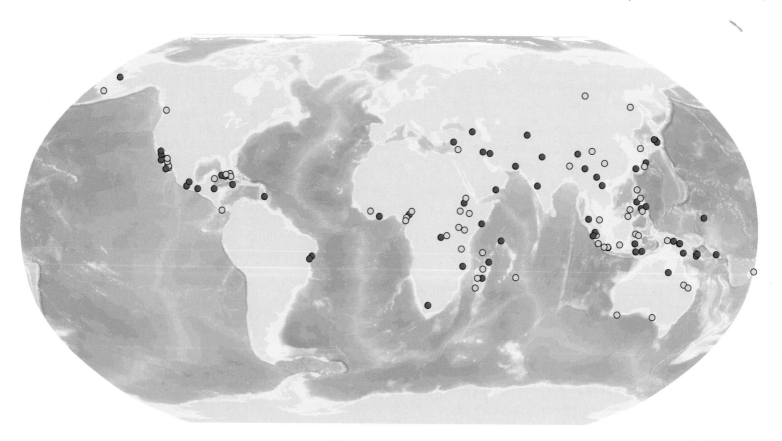

Above *Orphaned orangutans feed at the Sepilok sanctuary in northern Borneo. Most of these animals have been captured as babies and kept illegally as household pets. The aim of the sanctuary is to return the orphans to the wild after teaching them the skills they need to survive, such as finding food, building nests, and even how to climb properly.*

cept that conservationists have adapted from the idea of Important Bird Areas, conceived in the 1980s by BirdLife International. To qualify as a KBA the population of a species living there should be so significant that its conservation is likely to prevent a major deterioration of that species' global status. Sites at which a globally threatened species regularly occurs in significant numbers obviously rank highly. However, omitting an important site is a worse mistake than giving a questionable site the benefit of the doubt (that is, in conservation, errors of omission are generally more serious than errors of commission). Therefore, prudence dictates that for highly threatened species the presence of just one resident individual should trigger designation of a site (for species that are merely vulnerable the threshold might be lower, the presence of, say, 10 pairs or 30 individuals). Other criteria for identifying a KBA are that the site holds a significant proportion of the global population of one or more

restricted-range species, or that members of such a species congregates there, or which hold a significant proportion of a group of species whose distributions are restricted to a biome. What constitutes restricted range? The bird conservationists include species whose historical breeding extent of occurrence is 50,000sq km (19,300sq mi) or less, and adopting this definition would include about 25 percent of mammal species. Conveniently, the distribution of areas holding two or more restricted-range mammals is very similar to that for birds and amphibians (although a much higher percentage; close to two-thirds). Yet again, one pattern is evident: tropical islands and mountains predominate.

The KBA approach seeks to identify all the sites significant for the conservation of particular species or sets of species, but does not seek to minimize their collective area or apply any other system of prioritization – such economies are often tackled on the principle of complementarity – weeding out sites that duplicate each other so that the greatest benefit is achieved by the fewest sites. One recent study presents one means of prioritizing among such sites, by identifying those known to hold the last remaining population of a highly threatened species. Such sites, identified by a global partnership of like-minded conservation organizations, the Alliance for Zero Extinction,

represent immediate priorities for the conservation of the world's most threatened mammals. This study identified 131 species of mammals, 80 of which occur on islands, that require safeguarding at such sites.

Protected areas are very important, but they are not everything. For some species they have proven necessary but not sufficient – captive breeding and reintroduction programmes have been essential to the black-footed ferret (*Mustela nigripes*) and Arabian oryx (*Oryx leucoryx*). Some species range so widely that a single park is unlikely to contain them, and those, like the African wild dog, *Lycaon pictus*, that also occur, or disperse, at low densities need to be conserved at the scale of landscapes. For species that are colonial during the breeding season and then disperse widely, a protected area may be crucial during only part of the year. Worst of all, protected areas may do little to counter such pervasive, indirect manmade effects as introduced species (including diseases) and pollution. Mammal conservation, therefore, necessitates a multipronged approach to sites, species, and landscapes, and the diversity of local circumstances dictate that no aspect of conservation should be formulaic to the point of inflexibility. Furthermore, biology is a necessary but not sufficient foundation for conservation, which necessitates a web of other disciplines concerning the human dimension: economics, politics, law, development, health, and education among them.

Threats to Mammals
PREDATION AND HABITAT DESTRUCTION

There are three major threats to mammalian biodiversity: habitat loss, introduced species, and overexploitation. The global leader of this triumvirate is habitat loss and degradation – factors recently revealed to have provoked a devastating reduction in not only numbers, but also genetic diversity, of orangutans in just a few decades of deforestation. However, legions of species – including such mammalian notables as black (*Rattus rattus*) and brown (*R. norvegicus*) rats, red foxes (*Vulpes vulpes*), possums, American mink (*Neovison vison*), and gray squirrels (*Sciurus caroliniensis*) – have already been transported around the world, and globalization is increasing such movements (especially of diseases). Overexploitation may have shaped mammal faunas since the Pleistocene. Recent horror stories include the overhunting of saiga antelope (*Saiga tatarica*), which in the last 40 years has caused their numbers to plummet from 1,250,000 to 50,000. Appendix I of the Convention on International Trade in Endangered Species of Wild Fauna and Flora (CITES) lists 219 mammal species which are or may be affected by trade (another 364 and 56 species are on Appendices II and III, respectively). However, when it comes to conservation threats, be they direct or indirect, the really awesome figures are our own numbers (6 billion people, rising to 9 billion by 2050). Nowadays one human with a bulldozer can apply the power of 300 horses to modify the environment, and it would already require the resources of four planet Earths if everybody consumed at the level of the average US inhabitant. Humanity appropriates more than 30 percent of the net primary productivity (the green material) produced on Earth each year, consumes 35 percent of the productivity of the oceanic shelf, and uses 60 percent of freshwater runoff. No wonder, then, that in recognition of humanity's world-shaping impact, the current geological epoch has been named the "Anthropocene." One might therefore expect the size of the human "footprint" to be a major driver in the biodiversity crisis, and countless case studies confirm this. For example, 98 percent of the variation in extinction rates in national parks in Ghana over the last 30 years could be explained by the size of the park and the number of people living within 50km (31mi) of it – the higher the density and the smaller the park, the higher the extinction rate.

An individual's ecological footprint is a measure of the resources (the amount of land or sea) needed to support his or her consumption habits. In an attempt to add up all these ecological footprints into one giant global "human footprint" researchers mapped population density, measures of land transformation, accessibility (for example, within 15km/9mi of a road), and electrical power infrastructure (an indication of fossil fuel consumption), and thereby identified the places that might be conserved with minimum conflict with people. To ensure representation of all biomes in all realms involved identifying 568 of these "last of the wild" areas. However, identifying threats is only one side of the coin, because different species are differently susceptible to them.

Too Close for Comfort
ESTIMATING HUMAN IMPACT

One analysis of the extinction risk faced by carnivores explored how much of the variation in IUCN risk categories was explained (this is done using statistical techniques) by the human population density to which they are exposed, or by four biological traits, their geographic range size, population density, gestation length, and position in the food chain. Almost half the variation in extinction risk was explained by the biological factors (with a small geographical range being the most dangerous factor), whereas local human population density registered as unimportant. However, the universal everyday experience of practical conservationists is that the activities of people are the greatest threat to biodiversity, so it would be reckless to conclude from this finding that human impacts are unimportant. Rather, it may be that human population density is too coarse a barometer to reveal the threat people pose to carnivores (even where humans are few, a few of them can have enormous effects), and perhaps anyway the analysis may be too late, in that the species most vulnerable to human population density may already have been extinguished, or have contracted away from densely populated areas – an effect called the extinction filter.

The extinction filter reminds us that the current reality is already an impoverished shadow of biodiversity in the prehuman world. Conservation priorities are generally made on the basis of threat to the current (and thus both arbitrary and highly "unnatural") patterns of biodiversity. It is chilling to consider what has already been lost, and what plausibly might have been the case if people had not intervened. Taking the example of the species of lions that once spanned not only Africa and Asia, but much of Europe and North America, the contraction of their collective range, arguably due to the spread of humans, is equivalent to reducing their populations from many millions (one estimate makes it as many as 14 million) to the current 20,000 or so – a loss on a par with the recent anthropogenic devastation of the North Sea fish stock where it is estimated that about 97 percent of the "natural" biomass of large (4–16kg/9–35lb) fishes has been lost to fisheries exploitation (the difference is that the impact on lions has taken about ten millennia whereas that on fish has taken some ten decades). This "natural benchmark" provides a nonarbitrary perspective for taking stock, considering goals, and remaining alert to the corrosive effects of a shifting baseline.

If the Order Carnivora is split into species exposed to low (that is, 10 people per sq km in less than half their range) or high human densities, the proportion of variation in their IUCN risk status explained by biological factors jumped from 37.9 percent to 80.1 percent. For those living alongside few humans, the crucial risk factors were species population density and geographic range size (factors likely to be dangerous in the face of habitat loss), whereas for carnivore species living with populous humans a third factor – gestation length – became important (and this facet of reproductive output may be more likely to matter in the face of direct persecution). By plotting maps of predicted human population growth, the researchers could map which species currently exposed to low numbers of humans were likely to find themselves living alongside high numbers of people by 2030; the prediction is that human population increase is likely to cause eight species of carnivore to move from least concern to vulnerable by 2030, of which one, the African linsang, *Poiana richardsoni*, is catapulted to endangered status (the others included four more viverrids, the common genet, *Genetta genetta*, the giant forest genet, *G. victoriae*, the aquatic genet, *G. piscivora*, the Angolan genet, *G. angolensis*, together with two felids, the Chinese mountain cat, *Felis bieti*, and the African golden cat, *Caracal aurata* [so designated in 2002], and also the American hog-nosed skunk, *Conepatus leuconotus*).

Life Histories and Risk Factors
ASSESSMENT AND PREDICTION

For carnivores and primates low population density, slow life history, being high up the food pyramid (and thus being precariously dependent on those below) and, in particular, small geographic range size (invariably true of island life) are all independently associated with a high extinction risk in declining species, and together explain nearly 50 percent of the variation in their extinction risk. With these generalities in hand, biologists can use a species' biological characteristics to predict its likely extinction risk, and can then check how these match the risk assigned to that species through the Red List classification. Intriguingly, the predicted risks for some species, for example, gibbons and lemurs, are less threatening than the very high ranks accorded to them by the Red List – probably because the predictions failed to take account of threats posed by forestry that would doubtless have been at the forefront of the specialists' minds. The predictions similarly underestimated the risk to swift foxes (*Vulpes velox*), African wild dogs, and European mink (*Mustela lutreola*), and wolverine (*Gulo gulo*), all of which have faced particularly severe persecution. In contrast, the statistical predictions raise grave fears for some species that have

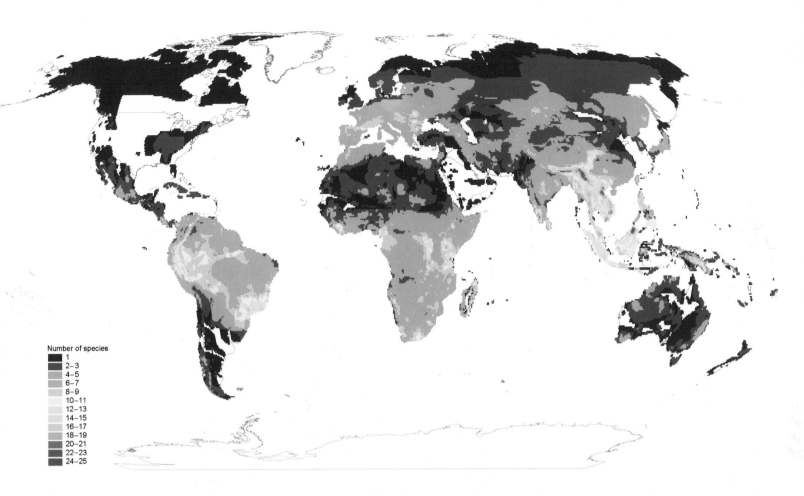

Number of species
- 1
- 2–3
- 4–5
- 6–7
- 8–9
- 10–11
- 12–13
- 14–15
- 16–17
- 18–19
- 20–21
- 22–23
- 24–25

less ominous Red List rankings, and these are mainly species living in very remote places such as the red-faced black spider monkey (*Ateles paniscus*) in Amazonia, the moupin golden snub-nosed monkey (*Rhinopithecus roxellana*) in montane reserves in central China, and hamadryas baboons (*Papio hamadryas*) in deserts; or species that do relatively well in disturbed, secondary jungle, such as the Guatemalan howler monkey (*Alouatta pigra*) or gorillas (*Gorilla gorilla*). Among carnivores the Red List had seemingly underestimated the threat to the sea otter, *Enhydra lutris* (a species with a very turbulent history with people) and to all felids (specialist predators, such as felids, do tend to have short longevity in the fossil record).

Although many of the mammal species with biological characteristics that make them susceptible to extinction risk are already threatened (or have gone), some survive in places where human impact is still low. Such species have a high "latent extinction risk" – disasters waiting to happen as human pressures penetrate their enclaves – and they are clustered around the world (for example in the boreal forests and tundra of North America, and islands from Indonesia to the South Pacific), in places that scarcely overlap with the priority hotspots identified on the basis of current risk and levels of endemism. Latent extinction risk identifies species likely to catapult through the risk categories when human influences reach them, as in

the unhappy case of the Guatemalan howler monkey, which has jumped from least concern in 2000 to endangered in 2005.

Too Big for Survival
INFLUENCING FACTORS

Being big is inherently dangerous for mammals. Of mammalian species in decline, those threatened with extinction have an average mass of 1.38kg (3.0lb) while their nonthreatened contemporaries average 139g (4.9oz). This sizist divide is conventionally explained because larger species tend to live at lower population densities, have lower intrinsic capacity to breed fast, and are disproportionately exploited by people. In smaller mammals (less than 3kg/6.6lb) risk is largely determined by geographic range and population density (that is, environmental factors), but in larger species a "slower" life history (for example, a longer pregnancy or later weaning age) becomes risky too. A practical conclusion might be that smaller mammals may generally be best conserved by the creation of protected areas, whereas larger ones may need bespoke plans.

Exceptions prove the rule, and regarding the risks of being big, it seemed as if Australian marsupials were such an exception. Nineteen of them (including the Lord Howe long-eared bat, *Nyctophilus howensis,* and the thylacine) have gone extinct, which is almost one-third the world

Above Global patterns of species richness for threatened mammals. The major risk areas for endangered mammals include southern Brazil, West Africa, the montane regions of Africa, Madagascar, and Southeast Asia. From Brooks et al. 2004; data compiled under the IUCN-led Global Mammal Assessment.

tally of recent mammalian extinctions. Most of these losses were not large- but medium-sized (35–5,500g/1.25–195oz). This gave rise to the idea that this "critical weight range" was prone to extinction. However, this turns out to be a fallacy. In fact, most Australian mammals (128 out of 210 species, excluding bats) fall in the critical weight range, so the loss of middleweights has not been disproportionate. Nonetheless, the cold shadow of extinction has not passed evenly over the marsupial orders. Some families have been largely spared. This particular analysis suggested that of 62 marsupial carnivores (Dasyuroidea) only 2 have gone extinct and 6 are threatened, whereas of 54 water rats and hopping mice (Hydromyinae) the figures were more than expected, 10 and 13, respectively. The 27 species of possums and gliders (Phalangeridae) escaped without an extinction, whereas the 11 Potoroidea (potoroos and bettongs) and 13 Perameloidea (bandicoots and bilbies) had more than expected, respectively, 3 and 4. Furthermore, extinctions have been more numerous in the arid zone of Australia (31 of 105 species) than the mesic zone (17 of 186 species). The arid zone has suffered relatively little habitat loss, but has been bombarded with introduced predators; there, extinction risk was much higher amongst larger species than smaller ones. In the mesic areas there are also introduced predators and habitat loss has been severe. In these regions body size was much less relevant to extinction risk and endangerment.

Glimmers of Hope
DISCOVERING NEW SPECIES

When, in April 2005, British biologist Rob Timmins came across a furry-tailed rat, unhappily deceased, in a bushmeat market in the Khammouan region of Laos, he did something that had, arguably, been achieved on only one other occasion since the end of the 18th century – he discovered a new mammalian family, the Laonastidae. The Loatian rock rat is known locally as the *kha nyou*, and to science as *Laonastes aenigmamus* (which translates as "enigmatic mouse inhabiting stones"). It is possibly the oldest surviving representative of the Hystricognath subfamily of rodents. The only other uncontroversial new mammalian family was found in 1974, the hog-nosed bat, *Craseonycteris thonglongyai* – the sole representative of the Craseonycteridae. Then, in

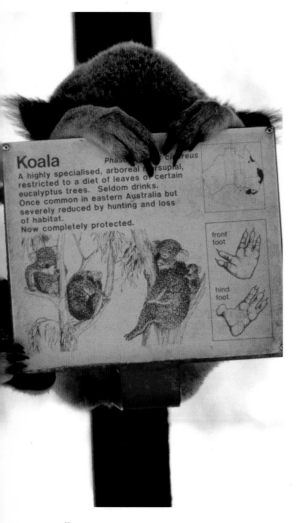

Koala
Pha...... ....reus
A highly specialised, arboreal marsupial, restricted to a diet of leaves of certain eucalyptus trees. Seldom drinks. Once common in eastern Australia but severely reduced by hunting and loss of habitat.
Now completely protected.

front foot

hind foot

December 2005 the world's press carried tantalizingly grainy photos of an unknown mammal recorded by a camera-trap in Borneo's Kayan Mentarang National Park – seemingly a new species widely said in the press to be a civet (although it looks to this author like a tree kangaroo – if so, it would have crossed Wallace's Line, which hitherto marked the northern extent of marsupials). Though nothing can offset the alarming rate of species loss, on the other side of the "balance sheet," new species of mice and bats are described every year. The black-faced lion tamarin, *Leontopithecus caissara*, was first described in 1990, in Atlantic forest just 200km (124mi) from Sao Paulo city. One man, Marc Van Roosmalen, has described 5 new species of Amazonian monkey, including two new species of *Callicebus* in 2002 (and claims to have discovered another 20 new species in the region). Between 1990 and 1995 two new species (and three new subspecies) of tree kangaroo were described from New Guinea – most recently the dingiso, or black-and-white tree kangaroo, *Dendrolagus mbaiso*, from the Sudirman Mountains of Papua, Indonesia.

One region in particular that has yielded many new mammal discoveries is the Annamite mountains between Laos and Vietnam. Indeed, five species of large mammals have been newly discovered or rediscovered in this region. The saola, *Pseudoryx nghetinhensis*, first became known to science in 1992 with the discovery of three horns in the Vu Quang Nature Reserve in Vietnam. This reserve also yielded the giant muntjac, *Muntiacus vuquangensis*, described in 1994. In fact, a number of new muntjac species have come to light since the early 1990s, including the Annamite muntjac *Muntiacus truongsonensis*, and the leaf deer, *Muntiacus putaoensis*.

Sometimes species thought extinct are rediscovered, as in the case of the Bornean bay cat, *Pardofelis badia*. This felid, endemic to the island of Borneo, was previously known only from six specimens, five of which were collected between 1855 and 1900. Then, in November 1992, an adult female was trapped in Sarawak. Another recent example concerns the Negros naked-backed fruit bat *Dobsonia chapmani*, presumed extinct since about 1970, and then recently rediscovered on the islands of Cebu and Negros in 2001 and 2002. The mountain pygmy possum, *Burramys parvus*, had been known only from fossils until 1966 when it was discovered alive in the mountains of southeastern Australia.

Protecting Imperilled Populations
CONSERVATION AND PROTECTION

The unhappy truth is that delight at the discovery or rediscovery of mammalian species is tempered by the fact that they invariably jump straight into a threatened category on the Red List. However, the news is not all doom and gloom. The efforts of conservationists are often rewarded, and there is a

small, but growing, body of evidence that targeted conservation action can have lasting positive benefits for species. Notable examples, described later in this book, are the cases of the Ethiopian wolf, (*Canis simensis*) whose tiny population has been protected from blights (ranging from rabies to hybridization) brought by domestic dogs, or the Andean vicuña (*Vicugna vicugna*), which has been brought back from calamitous decline, partly on the expectation of its beautiful wool generating wealth for local communities (sadly, no such rescue is on the horizon for the chiru – *Pantholops hodgsoni* – a Tibetan antelope with similarly exquisite shahtoosh wool). In both cases, success has rested heavily on highly focused, empirical fieldwork providing the evidence base on which an integrated conservation plan has been built, in collaboration with local and international stakeholders. A measure of success is the down-listing of the Ethiopian wolf from critically endangered to endangered – an endorsement for the evidence-based, integrated approach, but certainly no cause for complacency. Gray wolves (*Canis lupus*), sea otters, and southern white rhinos (*Ceratotherium simum simum*) provide other success stories.

The lessons of these examples of successful targeted, evidence-based conservation may be reflected in the recent findings of an overview of the Minimum Viable Population (MVP) estimated to secure, for example, a 99 percent probability of the continued existence of a population of a given species for at least forty generations. For 83 species of vertebrate for which there were detailed long-term population data, the calculations suggested that the MVPs varied between 633 and 2,724 individuals. But, within this great variation, what determined whether a lower or higher MVP was needed? The answer was not the life-history variables (such as geographic range, body size or reproductive biology) that so successfully predict a species' Red List category, and which indicate its susceptibility to the ultimate causes of decline and extinction. Rather, estimates of the MVP for a population (that has already declined precariously) depended heavily on local factors, such as the pattern of environmental fluctuations, interspecific competition and its contact with other populations. In short, while to "think globally" is indeed the way to understand wide-scale extinction risks, understanding, and thus being in a position to remedy, the plight of a particular population requires conservationists to "act locally," and on the basis of local evidence rather than on the basis of some wider generalization.

◁ **Left** *A koala sleeps behind its species description board at a wildlife sanctuary in Australia. The koala has suffered fragmentation of its habitat through forest clearance. Translocation programs have helped promote genetic diversity among southern populations, and relieved overcrowding among koalas in areas where habitat has been lost.*

Habitat loss is the most conspicuous threat to biodiversity, and it is the one that lends itself to systematic planning solutions (such as gap analysis). Other elements may be less amenable to formulaic or generalized solutions – as an example of overexploitation, the bushmeat problem might partly be tackled by providing substitute meat sources, and some invasive species (for example, red foxes, feral cats, and goats) can be tackled by eradication (a solution that, like all conservation issues, raises ethical issues). However, while the theory of conservation planning provides a useful framework and intellectual discipline – and perhaps also helps predict which currently safe species are likely to be in trouble next – the reality of conservation practice is that almost every case has to be tackled as a one-off, through understanding the particular, detailed local circumstances. DWM

Below Global distribution map showing a) irreplaceability, b) threat, and c) priority sites for the expansion of the global protected-area network, based on data for species of mammals, amphibians, turtles, and threatened birds. Regions of high priority are concentrated especially in the tropics, particularly the Andes, Caribbean, Central America, Brazil's Atlantic forest, montane Africa, Madagascar, the Western Ghats, and Southeast Asia. From Rodrigues et al. 2004).

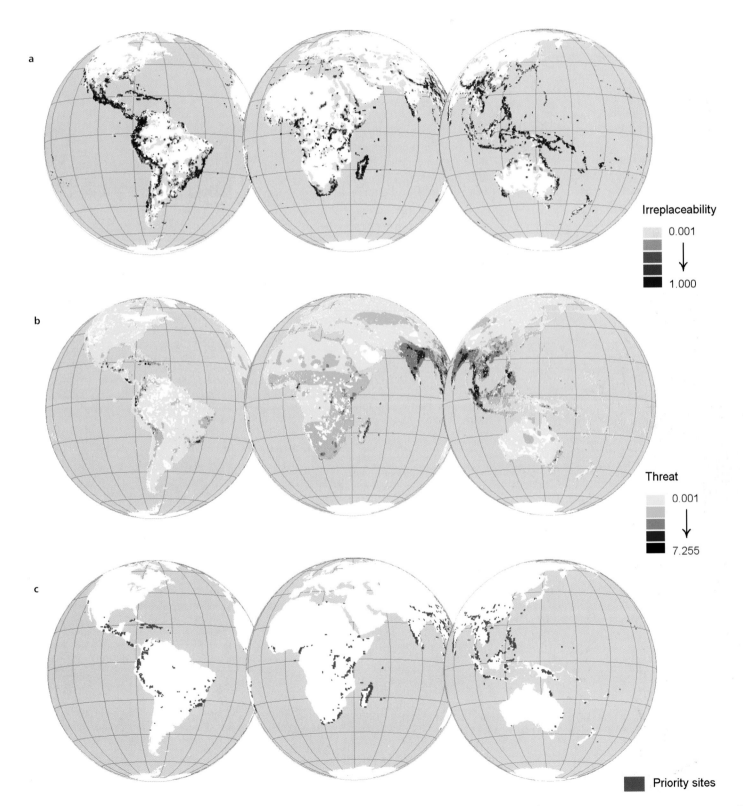

Irreplaceability

0.001

↓

1.000

Threat

0.001

↓

7.255

Priority sites

MONOTREMES

WHILE THE DESCRIPTION OF MONOTREMES *as "the egg-laying mammals" distinguishes them from other living animals, it exaggerates the significance of egg-laying in this group. The overall pattern of reproduction is mammalian, with only a brief, vestigial period of development of the young within the egg. The soft-shelled eggs hatch after about 10 days, whereupon the young remain (in a pouch in echidnas) dependent on the mother's milk for up to six months in echidnas.*

The platypus is confined to eastern Australia and Tasmania, the long-beaked echidna occurs only in New Guinea, while the short-beaked echidna is found in all of these regions, in almost all habitats. However, these distributions are relatively recent. There are Pleistocene fossils of long-beaked echidnas at numerous sites in mainland Australia and Tasmania. Fossil monotremes from the Pleistocene epoch (which began 1.8 million years ago) are much the same as the living types. A platypus fossil from the mid-Miocene (10 million years ago) has been found, which appears very similar to living platypuses except that it had fully developed, functional teeth as an adult. In 1991 paleontologists found isolated teeth in early Paleocene (60 million years ago) beds in Patagonia that are almost a perfect match for those of the mid-Miocene platypus. This, however, is not the oldest monotreme fossil; that distinction goes to a partially opalized jaw from the early Cretaceous (120 million years ago). These findings show that monotremes have undergone very conservative evolution, with little change over 100 million years. However, the fossils do not provide any evidence of the origins of monotremes and their ancestral relationships and how they relate to marsupial and placental mammals remains an enigma.

Strange Specialists
PHYSIOLOGY AND DISTRIBUTION

The term *egg-laying mammal* has long been synonymous with "reptilelike" or "primitive mammal," despite the fact that monotremes possess all the major mammalian features: a well-developed fur coat, mammary glands, a single bone in the lower jaw, and three bones (incus, stapes, and malleus) in the middle ear. Monotremes are also endothermic: their body temperature, although variable in echidnas, remains constant regardless of environmental temperatures.

Monotremes have separate uteri entering a common urinogenital passage joined to a cloaca, into which the gut and excretory systems also

enter. The one common opening to the outside of the body gave the name to the group that includes the platypus and echidnas – the order Monotremata ("one-holed creatures").

Monotremes are highly specialized feeders. The semiaquatic, carnivorous platypus feeds on invertebrates living on the bottom of freshwater streams. Echidnas are terrestrial carnivores, specializing in ants and termites (short-beaked or common echidna) or noncolonial insects and earthworms (long-beaked echidna). Such diets require grinding rather than cutting or tearing, and, as adults, monotremes lack teeth. In the platypus, teeth actually start to develop and may even serve as grinding surfaces in the very young, but the teeth never fully develop. Rather, they regress and are replaced by horny grinding plates at the back of the jaws. Reduction of teeth is common among ant-eating mammals, and echidnas never develop teeth, nor are their grinding surfaces part of the jaw. In the long-beaked echidna, a pad of horny spines is located in a groove on the back of the tongue, running from the tip about one-third of the way back. Earthworms are hooked by these spines when the long tongue is extended. The food is broken up as the tongue spines grind against similar spines on the palate. The long-beaked echidna takes worms into its

long snout by either the head or tail, and if necessary the forepaws are used to hold the worm while the beak is positioned. In the platypus, the elongation of the front of the skull and the lower jaw to form a bill-like structure is also a foraging specialization. The bill is covered with shiny black skin. Echidnas have a snout that is based on exactly the same modifications of the skull and jaws but is relatively smaller and cylindrical. The mouth is at the tip of this snout and can only be opened enough to allow passage of the cylindrical tongue.   MLA

THE POISONOUS SPUR

Monotremes are one of only two groups of venomous mammals (the other includes certain shrews). In the four species of echidnas, the structures that produce and deliver the venom are present but not functional. It is only the male platypus that actually secretes and can deliver the venom. The venom-producing gland is located behind the knee and is connected by a duct to a horny spur on the back of the ankle. This spur is completely lost in the female platypus, but in the male it is hollow and full of venom, which is injected with forceful jabs of the

hindlimbs. The poison causes agonizing pain in humans and can kill a dog. Because the venom gland enlarges at the beginning of the breeding season, it has been assumed to have a connection with mating behavior. The marked increase in aggressive use of the spurs observed between males in the breeding season may serve to decide spatial relationships in the limited river habitat. Yet this does not explain why, in echidnas, the system is present but nonfunctional. The spur in male echidnas makes it possible to distinguish them from females, which is otherwise difficult in monotremes since the testes never descend from the abdomen. However, the echidnas' venom duct and gland are degenerate, and the male cannot erect the spur. If it is pushed from under its protective sheath of skin, few echidnas can even retract the spur. It may be that the venom system in monotremes originated as a defense against a predator that has long since become extinct. Today adult monotremes have few, if any, predators. Dingos occasionally prey on echidnas, but dingos are themselves a relatively recent arrival in Australia.

◁ **Left** *The platypus's spur, which is curved and hollow, is connected by ducts to the venom glands.*

◖ Left A short-beaked echidna hatches from its soft-shelled egg. Following hatching the tiny newborn will increase in weight at an astonishing rate, perhaps 100–200 times in just a few weeks. The young stays in the pouch until its spines begin to emerge.

◓ Below The mouth of the echidna is positioned at the end of its snout, from which a long tongue is extended to catch termites and ants. The short-beaked echidna is widely dispersed throughout Australasia and New Guinea.

Platypus

eVER SINCE THE FIRST PLATYPUS SPECIMEN *(a dried skin) was sent to Britain from the Australian colonies in around 1798, this animal has been surrounded by controversy. At first it was thought to be a fake, stitched together by a taxidermist from the beak of a duck and body parts of a mammal.*

Even when the specimen was found to be real, the species was not accepted as a mammal. Although it had fur, it also had a reproductive tract similar to that of birds and reptiles. This led researchers to conclude (correctly) that the platypus laid eggs, and (incorrectly) that it could therefore not be a mammal; all mammals known at the time were viviparous (gave birth to live young). Ultimately, however, the platypus was recognized as a mammal when it was found to possess the essential characteristic from which the class Mammalia takes its name – mammary glands.

The Sleek Swimmer
FORM AND FUNCTION

At just under 1.7kg (3.7lb), the platypus is smaller than most people imagine. Females are smaller than males and the young are about 85 percent of adult size when they first become independent. The animal is streamlined, with a covering of dense, waterproof fur over its entire body except the feet and the bill. The bill looks superficially like that of a duck, with the nostrils on top, set immediately behind the tip, but it is soft and pliable. Its surface is covered with an array of sensory receptors, which have been found to respond to both electrical and tactile stimuli, and is used by the animal to locate food and find its way around underwater. The eyes, ears, and nostrils are closed when diving. Behind the bill are two internal cheek pouches opening from the mouth. These contain horny ridges that functionally replace the teeth lost by the young soon after they emerge from the burrows. The pouches are used to store food while it is being chewed and sorted.

The limbs are very short and held close to the body. The hindfeet are only partially webbed, being used in water only as rudders while the forefeet have large webs and are the main mode of propulsion. The webs of the front feet are turned back to expose large, broad nails when the animal is walking or burrowing. The rear ankles of the males bear a horny spur that is hollow and connected by a duct to a venom gland in the thigh. The venom causes extreme pain in humans; at least one component of the venom has recently been found to act directly on pain receptors, while other components produce inflammation and swelling. The tail is broad and flat and is employed as a fat-storage area.

⊘ **Below** *The prominent bill of the platypus is pliable and touch sensitive. Underwater, it is the animal's main sensory organ for navigation and locating food.*

Effective Care of the Young
SOCIAL BEHAVIOR

The platypus is mainly nocturnal in its foraging for prey items, which are almost entirely made up of bottom-dwelling invertebrates, particularly the young stages (larvae) of insects. Normal home ranges of platypuses vary with river systems, ranging from less than 1km (0.6 miles) to over 7km (4.3 miles), with many individuals foraging over 3–4km (1.8–2.5 miles) of stream within a 24-hour period. Two non-native species of trout feed on the same sort of food and are possible competitors of the platypus. Despite this dietary overlap, the platypus is common in many rivers into which these species have been introduced. A study in

one river system showed that the trout ate more of the swimming species of invertebrates, while the platypus fed almost exclusively on those inhabiting the bottom of the river. Waterfowl may also overlap in their diets with platypuses, but most also consume plant material that does not appear to be eaten by the platypus.

Certain areas occupied by platypuses experience water temperatures close to, and air temperatures well below, freezing in winter. When the platypus is exposed to such cold conditions it can increase its metabolic rate to produce sufficient heat to maintain its body temperature around its normal level of 32°C (89.6°F). Good fur and tissue insulation, including well-developed counter-current blood flow, help the animal to conserve body heat, and its burrows also provide a micro-climate that moderates the extremes of outside temperature in both winter and summer.

Although mating is reputed to occur earlier in northern Australia than in the south, it occurs sometime during late winter to spring (between July and October). Mating takes place in water and involves chasing and grasping of the tail of the female by the male. Two (occasionally one or three) eggs measuring 1.7 by 1.5cm (0.7 by 0.5in) are laid. When hatched the young are fed on milk, which they suck from the fur of the mother around the ventral openings of the mammary glands (there is no pouch) for 3–4 months while they are confined to a special breeding burrow. This burrow is normally longer and more complex than the burrows inhabited for resting. Such nesting burrows are reported to be up to 30m (100ft) long and be branched with one or more nesting chambers. The young emerge from these burrows in summer (late January–early March). It is not known how long they continue to take milk from their mothers after leaving the burrow, although they do feed on benthic organisms from the time they enter the water. Individual animals will use a number of resting burrows in an area but it is thought that there is attachment by breeding females to nesting burrows.

Although normally two eggs are laid, it is not known how many young are weaned successfully each year. Not all females breed annually, and new recruits to the population do not breed until they

◖ Above *The streamlined surface presented by the long guard hairs conceals the thick, dry underfur that insulates the platypus's body in cold water.*

are at least two years of age. In spite of this low reproductive rate, the platypus has returned from near extinction in certain areas since its protection and the cessation of hunting around 1900. This indicates that the reproductive strategy of having only a few young, but looking after them well, is effective in this long-lived species.

The platypus owes its success to its occupation of an ecological niche that has been perennial, even in the driest continent in the world. By the same token, because the platypus is such a highly specialized mammal it is extremely susceptible to the effects of changes in its habitat. Changes wrought by humans in Australia, particularly since European settlement began in the late 18th century, have brought about localized reductions and fragmentation of platypus populations. Care and consideration for the environment will have to be rigorously maintained if this unique species is to survive.   TRG

Echidnas

eCHIDNAS ARE READILY RECOGNIZED BY *their covering of long spines, which are shorter in the long-beaked species. There is fur present between the spines as well as on the head, legs, and ventral surfaces where there is an absence of spines. In both the long-beaked echidna and the Tasmanian form of the short-beaked echidna the fur may be longer than the spines.*

Both genera are further distinguished by their elongated, tubular snout, which in the case of the long-beaked echidna curves somewhat downward and accounts for two-thirds the length of the head. Echidnas are generally solitary creatures that are seen relatively infrequently, despite the fact that the short-beaked echidna is in fact quite common across its geographic range; the long-beaked echidna, however, is only found in the mountainous areas of New Guinea.

Spiny Anteaters
FORM AND FUNCTION

The echidna's coat of spines (it is sometimes called the spiny anteater) provides an excellent defense. If surprised on hard ground, an echidna curls up into a ball; on soft soil it may rapidly dig straight down, rather like a sinking ship, until all that can be seen of it are the spines of its well-protected back. By using its powerful limbs and erecting all its spines, an echidna can wedge itself securely in a rock crevice or hollow log.

Echidna spines are individual hairs that are anchored in a thick layer of muscle (*panniculus carnosus*) in the skin. The spines obscure the short, blunt tail and the rather large ear openings, which are vertical slits just behind the eyes. The snout is naked and the small mouth and relatively large nostrils are located at the tip. Echidnas walk with a distinctive rolling gait, although the body is held well above the ground.

Males can be distinguished from females by the presence of a horny spur on the ankle of the hind-limb. Males are larger than females within a given population. Yearling short-beaked echidnas usually weigh less than 1kg (2.2lb), but beyond that there is no way of determining age.

Echidnas have small, bulging eyes. Although they appear to be competent at telling objects apart in laboratory studies, in most natural habitats vision is probably not important in detecting food or danger; their hearing, however is very good. In locating prey, usually by rooting through the forest litter or undergrowth, they use their well-developed sense of smell. When food items are detected, they are rapidly taken in by the long, thin, highly flexible tongue, which short-beaked echidnas can extend up to 18cm (7in) from the tip of the snout. The tongue is lubricated by a sticky secretion produced by the very large salivary glands. Ants and termites form the bulk of

⊘ Below *Echidnas' sense of smell is particularly acute. They use their long snout to probe the undergrowth or leaf litter, and have even been seen to use it as a snorkel when crossing water.*

ECHIDNAS

Order: Monotremata

Family: Tachyglossidae

4 species in 2 genera

DISTRIBUTION
Mainland Australia, Tasmania, New Guinea (Short-beaked echidna); mountains of New Guinea (Long-beaked echidna).

SHORT-BEAKED ECHIDNA *Tachyglossus aculeatus*
Short-beaked or Common echidna (or spiny anteater) Australia, including Kangaroo Island (off S Australia), Tasmania, S and E New Guinea. In almost all types of habitat, from semiarid to alpine. HBL 30–45cm (12–18in); WT 2.5–8kg (5.5–17.6lb). Males 25 percent larger than females. Coat: black to light brown, with spines on back and sides; long narrow snout without hair. Breeding: gestation about 14 days. Longevity: not known in wild (extremely long-lived in captivity – up to 49 years). Conservation status: generally not threatened, though the Kangaroo Island subspecies (*T. a. multiaculeatus*) is classed as Lower Risk, Near Threatened.

SIR DAVID'S LONG-BEAKED ECHIDNA *Zaglossus attenboroughi*
Found only in the Province of Papua, New Guinea, Cyclops Mtns; 1600m. *Z. attenboroughi* is much smaller than the other species, possessing a shorter beak and shorter fur. Conservation status is currently unknown.

EASTERN LONG-BEAKED ECHIDNA *Zaglossus bartoni*
Interior New Guinea, east of Paniai Lakes, 600 to 3200m. The subspecies are all highly distinctive and may represent distinct species.

WESTERN LONG-BEAKED ECHIDNA *Zaglossus bruijni*
Long-beaked or Long-nosed echidna (or spiny anteater) New Guinea, in mountainous terrain. HBL 45–90cm (18–35in); WT 5–10kg (11–22lb). Coat: brown or black; spines present but usually hidden by fur except on sides; spines shorter and fewer than short-beaked echidna; very long snout, curved downward. Breeding: gestation period unknown. Longevity: not known in wild (up to 30 years in captivity). Conservation status: Endangered.

Abbreviations HBL = head–body length; WT = weight

---

the short-beaked echidna's diet. Around August and September short-beaked echidnas attack the mounds of the meat ant (*Iridomyrmex detectus*) to feed on the fat-laden females; this is done in the face of spirited defense by the stinging worker ants, although the mounds are prudently avoided for the rest of the year.

Males in Tow
SOCIAL BEHAVIOR

Short-beaked echidnas are essentially solitary animals, inhabiting a home range the size of which varies according to the environment. In wet areas with abundant food it covers some 50ha (124 acres). The home range appears to change little, and within it there is no fixed shelter site. When inactive, echidnas take shelter in hollow logs, under piles of rubble and brush, or in thick clumps of vegetation. Occasionally they dig shallow burrows up to 1.2m (4ft) in length, which may be reused. A female incubating an egg or suckling young has a fixed burrow. The home ranges of several individuals overlap.

During the mating season the female leaves a scent track by everting the cloaca, the wall of which contains numerous glands. This presumably attracts males in overlapping ranges. At this time echidnas break their normally solitary habits to form "trains," in which a female is followed by as many as six males in a line. In captivity, echidnas that are kept in spacious accommodation do not form any sort of groups but are mutually tolerant. By contrast, if they are kept in confined, overcrowded quarters they may form a size-related dominance order, but this does not seem to be a natural behavior.

The chief periods of activity are related to environmental temperature. Short-beaked echidnas

○ **Above** *The western long-beaked echidna feeds principally on earthworms. Echidnas can survive several weeks with no nourishment at all.*

are usually active at dusk and dawn, but in the hot summer are nocturnal. During cold spells they may be active in the middle of the day. They avoid rain and will remain inactive for days if it persists. In cold parts of their range, such as the Snowy Mountains of eastern Australia, echidnas hibernate during winter, with body temperatures as low as 5°C (41°F). Inactive echidnas may enter torpor, with body temperatures as low as 18°C (64.4°F), under less rigorous ambient temperatures.

The female pouch is barely detectable for most of the year. Before the start of the breeding season, folds of skin and muscle on each side of the abdomen enlarge to form an incomplete pouch with milk patches at the front end. There are no teats. The single egg is laid into the pouch by extension of the cloaca while the female lies on her back. After about 10 days the young hatches, using an egg tooth and a horny carbuncle at the tip of the snout. The young remains in the pouch until about the time spines begin to erupt. There are rare reports of females found moving about freely with an egg or young in the pouch. However, for most of the suckling period (up to six months), the offspring is left behind in the nursery burrow while the mother forages, often for days at a time. The young become independent and move out to occupy their own home ranges at about 1 year old.

The short-beaked echidna is widespread and common on mainland Australia and Tasmania. However, its status in New Guinea is uncertain. The long-beaked echidnas and several other similar genera were once distributed throughout Aus-

tralia but disappeared by the late Pleistocene. Today there are only three species, which are restricted to the New Guinea highlands. It is likely that the disappearance of long-beaked echidnas from Australia is related to climatic changes that have taken place there. Both the short-beaked and the long-beaked echidnas are hunted for food; most zoologists now consider the latter species to be under severe threat of extinction. MLA

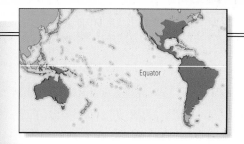

MARSUPIALS

aLTHOUGH MARSUPIALS HAD LONG BEEN *familiar to the indigenous peoples of the Americas and Australasia, they remained unknown to the rest of the world until the 16th century. The first marsupial seen in Europe was a Brazilian opossum that was brought back in 1500 as a gift to Queen Isabella and King Ferdinand of Spain by the explorer Vicente Yáñez Pinzón. Yet it was three centuries before zoologists ascertained that marsupials were not aberrant rodents but a distinctive natural group of mammals united by a unique mode of reproduction.*

From North to South
EARLY BEGINNINGS

The most ancient marsupial-like fossil, *Kokopellia juddi*, hails from early Cretaceous deposits in Utah aged at least 100 million years, but its position as a true marsupial is contentious. The earliest undisputed marsupial, from the now-extinct family Stagodontidae, has been dated at about 80 million years from other fossil deposits in Utah. At least

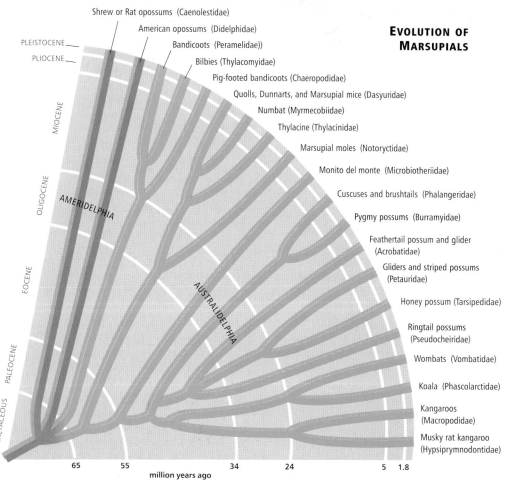

EVOLUTION OF MARSUPIALS

Shrew or Rat opossums (Caenolestidae)
American opossums (Didelphidae)
Bandicoots (Peramelidae))
Bilbies (Thylacomyidae)
Pig-footed bandicoots (Chaeropodidae)
Quolls, Dunnarts, and Marsupial mice (Dasyuridae)
Numbat (Myrmecobiidae)
Thylacine (Thylacinidae)
Marsupial moles (Notoryctidae)
Monito del monte (Microbiotheriidae)
Cuscuses and brushtails (Phalangeridae)
Pygmy possums (Burramyidae)
Feathertail possum and glider (Acrobatidae)
Gliders and striped possums (Petauridae)
Honey possum (Tarsipedidae)
Ringtail possums (Pseudocheiridae)
Wombats (Vombatidae)
Koala (Phascolarctidae)
Kangaroos (Macropodidae)
Musky rat kangaroo (Hypsiprymnodontidae)

PLEISTOCENE
PLIOCENE
MIOCENE
OLIGOCENE
EOCENE
PALEOCENE
CRETACEOUS

AMERIDELPHIA
AUSTRALIDELPHIA

65 55 34 24 5 1.8
million years ago

◑ Above *In spite of its distinctive appearance, the long-footed potoroo of Australia was identified as a separate species only as recently as 1980.*

◐ Right *At birth a koala weighs only one-fiftieth of an ounce. Weaning begins after five months when the mother provides partly digested leaves for the infant.*

20 other genera of slightly younger Cretaceous marsupials are known from other North American sites, suggesting that the group originated in that region. Despite their early ascendancy in the north, marsupials soon dwindled there as placental mammals increased in diversity, and they became extinct in North America by 20–15 million years ago. The one presently extant marsupial in North America, the Virginia opossum, recolonized less than 1 million years ago from the south.

Shortly after their appearance and radiation in North America, ancestral marsupials dispersed across land bridges to South America and also to Europe. Marsupial diversity in South America remained high from the middle Paleocene (60 million years ago) until the Pliocene (5–1.8 million years ago) during a period of "splendid isolation." In the Pliocene, a land bridge to North America reformed, allowing invasion of the southern continent by placental mammals including raccoons, bears, cats, and other carnivores. In the face of this onslaught, all South America's large (i.e. over 5kg/11lb) carnivorous marsupials disappeared. Its present marsupial fauna is dominated by omnivores

weighing less than 1kg (2.2lb), with a minority of species specializing on insects or small vertebrates. The marsupial emigrants to Europe arrived by the early Eocene (52 m.y.a.) and stayed for perhaps 35 million years. Although this radiation was not spectacular, comprising only six described fossil genera in the family Didelphidae, it extended to many parts of Europe, North Africa, and east to Thailand and eastern China.

The origin of Australasian marsupials is unclear, but the most likely scenario is an invasion of taxa with South American affinities sometime in the early Paleocene, some 65–60 million years ago. The earliest Australian marsupial fossils date to the early Eocene 55 million years ago and, intriguingly, two genera appear similar to marsupials of the same age from Argentina. During the Paleocene Australia, Antarctica, and South America were united as the last surviving remnants of the old supercontinent Gondwana. Australia severed its geological umbilical cord between 46 and 35 million years ago, while Antarctica and South America parted company 5 million years later. The climate of the early Eocene was warm and humid, with beech forest covering much of the Antarctic. That it was conducive to dispersal is suggested by the discovery of two genera of polydolopid marsupials from the middle Eocene of Antarctica.

Following its separation from Antarctica, the Australian ark drifted northward towards the equator, allowing its marsupial cargo to incubate in isolation. There is, frustratingly, a 30-million-year "dark age" lasting until the Miocene 24 million years ago that has yielded no fossils. However, by the early Miocene a spectacularly rich forest fauna had appeared, with many arboreal and browsing terrestrial marsupials represented. Climatic oscillations in the middle Miocene 15 million years ago were associated with losses of entire marsupial families, including the enigmatic miralinids, pilkipildrids, and wynyardiids. With the end of greenhouse conditions, forest contracted to coastal areas and savanna woodland and grassland dominated the interior. These shifts favored grazing marsupials, and set the scene for an explosive radiation of grazing kangaroos.

At the same time that the Miocene climate deteriorated, the Australian and Southeast Asian crustal plates collided, creating the highlands of New Guinea. These new mountainous areas, and parts of northeastern Queensland, allowed the continuation of lush conditions that had prevailed earlier in the Miocene, and provided opportunities for colonization for forest taxa. Many of the marsupials in New Guinea's rain forests now bear a striking resemblance to extinct taxa known only from fossils from the Miocene of central Australia. In contrast to the Australian marsupial fauna, in which only 30 of the 155 species are arboreal, at least 50 of New Guinea's 83 present marsupial species are restricted to the tree-top environment.

Modern Radiation
DISTRIBUTION PATTERNS

Although today's marsupials comprise only some 7 percent of the world's mammals, they occur widely in the Americas and predominate in Australasia. There is no evidence that marsupials ever dispersed naturally to New Zealand (the common brushtail possum was introduced to establish a fur trade in 1858, and a further six species of wallabies were introduced shortly after), but two species of cuscus occur on Sulawesi, one occurs throughout the Solomons, and others are scattered as island endemics in the Banda, Timor, Arafura, Coral, and Solomon seas. Australasian marsupials are ecologically more diverse than their American counterparts, and often occupy similar niches to placental mammals elsewhere. Thus, there are insectivores, carnivores, herbivores, and omnivores, and a honey possum that is unusual in specializing on nectar and pollen. All terrestrial habitats are exploited, from deserts to rain forests and high alpine areas. The smallest species, the long-tailed planigale, weighs no more than 4.5g, some 20,000 times less than male red kangaroos.

There is much that is still to be learned about the marsupials. Since the 1980s there has been a steady stream of discoveries of new species, for example, the distinctive long-footed potoroo in Australia in 1980, and two spectacular species of tree kangaroos in New Guinea in the early 1990s, the dingiso and the tenkile.

The Amazing Journey
REPRODUCTIVE STRATEGIES

Despite their ecological and morphological diversity, it is the mode of reproduction that unites marsupials and sets them apart from other mammals. In its form and early development in the

MARSUPIAL BODY PLAN

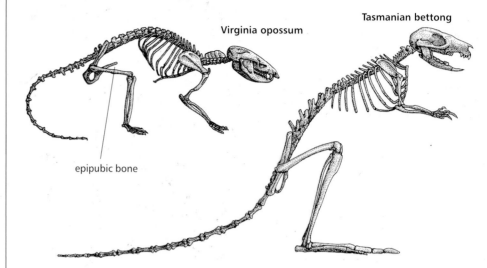

Virginia opossum

Tasmanian bettong

epipubic bone

⚪ **Above** Skeletons of the Virginia opossum and Tasmanian bettong. The Virginia opossum is medium sized, with unspecialized features shared with its marsupial ancestors. These include the presence of all digits in an unreduced state, all with claws. The skull and teeth are those of a generalist; the long tail is prehensile, acting as a fifth hand; and there are epipubic or "marsupial bones" that project forward from the pelvis and help support the pouch. The hindlimbs in this quadruped are only slightly longer than the forelimbs. The larger rat-kangaroo has small forelimbs, and larger hindlimbs for leaping. The hindfoot is narrowed and lengthened (hence macropodoid, "large footed"), and the digits are unequal. Stance is more, or completely, upright, and the tail is long, not prehensile but used as an extra prop or foot.

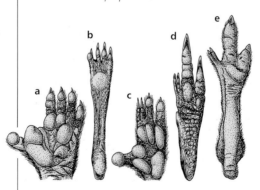

⚪ **Above** Feet of marsupials: **a** opposable first digit in foot of the tree-dwelling Virginia opossum; **b** long narrow foot, lacking a first digit, of the kultarr, a species of inland Australia with a bounding gait: both these species have the second and third digits separate (didactylous); in many marsupials (e.g., kangaroos and bandicoot) these digits are fused (syndactylous), forming a grooming "comb;" **c** opposable first digit and sharp claws for landing on trees in feathertail glider; **d** first digit much reduced In long foot of terrestrial short-nosed bandicoot – fourth digit forms axis of foot; **e** first digit entirely absent in foot of kangaroo.

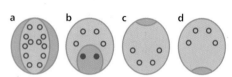

a b c d

⚪ **Above** Pouches (marsupia) occur in females of most marsupials. Some small terrestrial species have no pouch. Sometimes a rudimentary pouch **a** is formed by a fold of skin on either side of the nipple area that helps protect the attached young (e.g., mouse opossums, antechinuses, quolls). In **b** the arrangement is more of a pouch (e.g., Virginia and southern opossums, Tasmanian devil, dunnarts). Many of the deepest pouches, completely enclosing the teats, belong to the more active climbers, leapers, or diggers. Some, opening forward **c**, are typical of species with smaller litters of 1–4 (e.g., possums, kangaroos). Others **d** open backward and are typical of digging and burrowing species (e.g., bandicoots, wombats).

⚪ **Below** Anatomy of reproduction, and its physiology, set marsupials apart. In the female, eggs are shed into a separate (lateral) uterus, to be fertilized. The two lateral vaginae are often matched in the male by a two-lobed penis. Implantation of the egg may be delayed, and the true placenta of other mammals is absent. The young are typically born through a third, central, canal; this is formed before each birth in most marsupials, such as American opossums: in the honey possum and kangaroos the birth canal is permanent after the first birth.

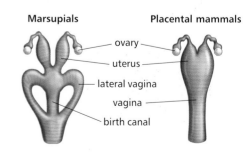

Marsupials   Placental mammals

ovary
uterus
lateral vagina
vagina
birth canal

Below *Marsupial skulls generally have a large face area and a small braincase. There is often a sagittal crest for the attachment of the temporal muscles that close the jaws, and the eye socket and opening for the temporal muscles run together, as in most primitive mammals. There are usually holes in the palate, between the upper molars. The rear part of the lower jaw is usually turned inward, unlike placental mammals.*

Many marsupials have more teeth than placental mammals. American opossums, for instance, have 50. There are usually three premolars and four molars on each side in both upper and lower jaws.

Marsupials with four or more lower incisors are termed polyprotodont. The eastern quoll (Dasyurus viverrinus) has six. Its chiefly insectivorous and partly carnivorous diet is reflected in the relatively small cheek teeth, each with two or more sharp cusps, and the large canines with a cutting edge. Its dental formula is I4/3, C1/1, P2/2, M4/4 = 42. The largely insectivorous bandicoot (Perameles) has small teeth of even size with sharp cusps for crushing the insects that it seeks out with its long pointed snout (I4–5/3, C1/1, P3/3, M4/4 = 46–48).

Diprotodont marsupials have only two lower incisors, which are usually large and forward-pointing. The broad, flattened skull of the leaf-eating brush-tailed possum contains reduced incisors, canines, and premolars, with simple low-crowned molars (I3/2, C1/0, P2/I, M4/4 = 34). The large wombat has 24 rodentlike teeth (I1/1, C0/0, P1/1, M4/4), all rootless and continuously growing to compensate for wear in chewing tough, fibrous grasses.

Eastern quoll
7 cm

Bandicoot
8 cm

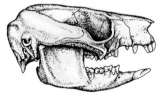

Brushtail possum
8 cm

Common wombat
18 cm

○ **Above** *A tiny, hairless, infant common brushtail possum attached to the mother's nipple in the pouch. It will be weaned at about six months.*

uterus, the marsupial egg is like that of reptiles and birds and quite unlike the egg of placental mammals (eutherians). Whereas placental young undergo most of their development and considerable growth inside the female, marsupial young are born very early in development. For example, a female eastern gray kangaroo of about 30kg (66lb) gives birth after 36 days' gestation to an offspring that weighs about 0.8g (under 0.03oz). This young is then carried in a pouch on the abdomen of its mother where it suckles her milk, develops and grows until, after about 300 days, it weighs 5kg (11lb) and is no longer carried in the pouch. After it leaves the pouch the young follows its mother closely and continues to suckle until it is about 18 months old.

Female young are ready to breed just after weaning, but males do not mature until aged two years or more. An extraordinary adaptation in kangaroos and all other marsupials studied is that the amount and quality of the milk changes during suckling, matching the needs of the growing young. Carbohydrates typically make up over half the solid fraction of milk for the first 6 months of lactation, and protein and fat the remainder. By 8–9 months carbohydrates have almost disappeared, and lipids constitute up to two-thirds of the solid bulk of the milk.

Immediately after birth, the newborn young makes an amazing journey from the opening of the birth canal to the area of the nipples. The forelimbs and head develop far in advance of the rest of the body, and the young is able to move with swimming movements of its forelimbs. Although

it is quite blind, it moves against gravity, locates (how is not yet known) a nipple and sucks it into its circular mouth. The end of the nipple enlarges to fit depressions and ridges in the mouth, and the young remains firmly attached to the nipple for 1–2 months until, with further development of its jaws, it is able to open its mouth and let go. In many marsupials the young are protected by a fold of skin that covers the nipple area, forming the pouch (see diagram).

As the main emphasis in the nourishment of the young in marsupials is on lactation, most development and growth occurs outside the uterus. For the short time that the embryo is in the uterus, it is nourished by transfer of nutrients from inside the uterus across the wall of the yolksac that makes only loose contact with the uterine wall. In eutherians, nourishment of the young during its prolonged internal gestation occurs by way of the placenta, in which the membranes surrounding the embryo make close contact with the uterine wall, become very vascular and act as the means of transport of material between maternal circulation and embryo. Although it is commonly believed that marsupials do not have a placentation system at all, the yolksac has a placental function; in bandicoots and the koala there is also development of a functional, albeit short-lived, placenta.

A further peculiarity of reproduction, similar to the delayed implantation found in some other mammals, occurs in all kangaroos (except the western gray) and a few species in other marsupial families. Pregnancy in these marsupials occupies more or less the full length of the estrous cycle but does not affect the cycle, so that at about the time a female gives birth, she also becomes receptive and mates. Embryos produced at this mating develop only as far as a hollow ball of cells (the blastocyst) and then become quiescent, entering a state of suspended animation or "embryonic diapause." The hormonal signal (prolactin) that blocks further development of the blastocyst is produced in response to the sucking stimulus from the young in the pouch. When sucking decreases as the young begins to eat other food and to leave the pouch, or if the young is lost from the pouch, the quiescent blastocyst resumes development, the embryo is born, and the cycle begins again. In some species that do not breed all year round, such as the Tammar wallaby, the period of quiescence of the blastocyst is extended by seasonal variables such as changes in day length. The origin of embryonic diapause may have been to prevent a second young being born while the pouch was already occupied, but it has other advantages, allowing rapid replacement of young which are lost, even in the absence of a male.

Four Strategies
SOCIAL ORGANIZATION

While large marsupials such as kangaroos and wombats usually produce single young, smaller species are not so constrained. Litter sizes in arboreal browsers, such as the common ringtail possum range from 1–3, while litters of 3–4 can be produced twice a year by the nectar-feeding honey possum, pygmy possums, and feathertail glider. Similar productivity occurs in omnivores, such as bandicoots and some didelphid species. Small insectivores such as antechinuses produce 8–12 young in a single bout of reproduction each year. Hensel's short-tailed opossum of southern Brazil has up to 25 nipples and probably rears the largest litters of any marsupial.

In species that produce litters of several young, individual young weigh less than 0.01g, by far the smallest of any mammalian species. At weaning, between 50 days in some didelphids to over 100 days in antechinuses, the combined weight of the young may be two to three times that of the mother. This represents an extraordinary investment of energy by females, and is often accompanied by high mortality of mothers. Not surprisingly, small marsupials tend to be shorter-lived than larger species and achieve reproductive maturity earlier

at 5–11 months. Larger litter sizes or more frequent bouts of reproduction compensate for their shorter life spans, with some species being capable of breeding year round. The shortest-lived marsupials are some male dasyurids that die after mating aged 12 months. In contrast, the mountain pygmy possum is the longest-lived of any small mammal; wild females may live for 11 years. Kangaroos live up to 25 years in the wild.

In some dasyurid marsupials, males disperse upon weaning up to several hundred meters from their mother's home range and then associate with unrelated females. Daughters remain at home, with one usually inheriting the maternal range after the death or dispersal of the mother. This pattern of dispersal reduces the chance of breeding among kin. Intriguingly, in species where females breed in two or more seasons, the sex ratio of the first litter is often skewed toward sons by a ratio of about 6:4, but returns to parity or less thereafter. The overproduction of sons by young mothers probably reduces the chance of future

⊙ **Below** *Red kangaroos watering. This species forms small social groups, known as mobs, which may contain between 2 and 10 members. These mobs are not temporary aggregations, but are quite organized.*

MARSUPIAL MOLES

The two species of marsupial moles are the only Australian mammals that have become specialized for a burrowing (fossorial) life. Others, including small native rodents, have failed to exploit this niche, except for a few species that nest in burrows.

Because of their extensive and distinct modifications, marsupial moles (*Notoryctes typhlops* and *N. caurinus*) are placed in their own order, the Notoryctemorphia. Both species are endangered. Their limbs are short stubs. The hands are modified for digging, with rudimentary digits and greatly enlarged flat claws on the third and fourth digits. Excavated soil is pushed back behind the animal with the hindlimbs, which also give forward thrust to the body and, like the hands, are flattened with reduced digits and three small flat claws on the second, third, and fourth digits. The naked skin (rhinarium) on the tip of the snout has been extended into a horny shield over the front of the head, apparently to help push through the soil. The coat is pale yellow and silky. The nostrils are small slits, there are no functional eyes or external ears, and the ear openings are concealed by fur. The neck vertebrae are fused together, presumably to provide rigidity for thrusting motions. Females have a rear-opening pouch with two teats. The tail, reduced to a stub, is said to be used sometimes as a prop when burrowing. Head–body length is approximately 13–14.5cm (5.1–5.7in), tail length 2–2.5cm (1in), and weight 40g (1.4oz). Dentition is I4/3, C1/1, P2/3, M4/4 = 44.

Little is known of these moles in the wild. They occur in the central deserts, using sandy soils in river-flat country and sandy spinifex grasslands. For food, they favor small reptiles and insects, particularly burrowing larvae of beetles of the family Scarabaeidae. In captivity, marsupial moles will seek out insect larvae buried in the soil and consume them underground. They also feed on the surface. They are not known to make permanent burrows, the soil caving in behind them as they move forward, and in this respect they are most unusual among fossorial mammals. Captive animals have been seen to sleep in a small cavity, which collapses after they leave.

Compared with other burrowing animals, marsupial moles show differences of detail in the adaptive route they have followed. The head shield is much more extensive than in many others, the eyes are more rudimentary than in most, and the rigid head/neck region with fused vertebrae appears to be specific to the marsupial moles.   GG

Olfactory communication occurs by passive deposition of urine and feces, but all species mark actively using secretions from glands in the skin. The secretions may be used to self-anoint, to mark other animals, or to lay claim to nests or other key sites. The sugar glider recognizes strangers on the basis of scent alone; it is likely that many other species share this ability. Most marsupials are nocturnal, so vision is relatively unimportant.

Four broad types of marsupial social organization can be identified. In the first, the social unit is an individual whose range overlaps with that of several others. Males have large ranges that take in those of several females, and mating is promiscuous. Marsupials with this social system often exploit dispersed food resources, and include small didelphids, dasyurids, and the honey possum. In a second type of social system, the unit is an individual with limited range overlap. Typically a male's home range overlaps that of one or two females who share exclusive mating rights. Arboreal folivores such as koalas and brushtail possums exemplify this type of system. A third type of social system is founded on cohesive family units that share a common, and often defended, home range. Groups may contain monogamous pairs and their offspring, or dominant males with several adult females and young. Group-living marsupials include sap- and exudate-feeding gliders and possums that may need force of numbers to defend focal food sources and shared dens. Finally, larger members of the kangaroo family exemplify the fourth type of social organization, in which the social unit is a flexible "mob" of gregarious individuals. Mobs have a promiscuous mating system, in which access to females is based on size and dominance.

Growing Human Encroachment
CONSERVATION ISSUES

Pressures on marsupial habitats have intensified in the last 200 years, with European colonization. Forests and woodland have been cleared for agriculture, while exotic herbivores and predators are widespread. Overhunting occurs in New Guinea. No marsupials have become extinct recently in the Americas or New Guinea, but 10 species and 6 subspecies have disappeared from Australia. A further 55 species in the Australasian region and 22 species from Central and South America are considered vulnerable or endangered.

Protection of habitat continues to be an important conservation measure. In New Guinea, where most of the land is owned by indigenous peoples, community support is crucial for conservation, but is sometimes subverted by the interests of rapacious multinationals. In southwestern Australia, a program of poisoning the red fox has aided the recovery of at least six marsupial species. Habitat protection and better ecological understanding will be the key to effective future conservation of marsupials.   CRD/EMR

conflict for resources with stay-at-home daughters. By contrast, in species where females usually breed just once, litter sex ratios are variable. Well-fed mothers produce more sons than daughters, perhaps providing the sons with an edge in growth that will allow them to compete successfully with other males and father more young themselves. Mothers in poor condition produce more daughters. Experimental provision of food allows female agile antechinuses, black-eared and American opossums to bias their litters in favor of sons, indicating the importance of body condition. The mechanism producing bias remains elusive, but appears to operate prior to fertilization.

Communication between marsupials is primarily through hearing and smell. Arboreal species in particular use sound to communicate over distances up to several hundred meters. Vocalizations range from chirps and squeaks in small possums to full-blooded bellows in the koala.

American Opossums

HEN MARSUPIALS WERE INTRODUCED TO *Europeans for the first time in 1500 AD, it was in the shape of a female southern opossum from Brazil, presented by the explorer Vicente Pinzón to Spain's rulers, Ferdinand and Isabella. The monarchs examined the female with young in her pouch and dubbed her an "incredible mother."*

Despite this royal introduction, the popular image of the opossum has never been a lofty one; the animals are often portrayed as foul smelling and rather slow witted. Although not as diverse as Australia's marsupials, the American opossums are in fact a successful group incorporating a variety of different species, ranging from the highly specialized tree-dwelling woolly opossums to generalists like the southern and Virginia opossums.

Generalists and Specialists
FORM AND FUNCTION

American opossums range from cat- to mouse-sized. The nose is long and pointed, and has long, tactile hairs (vibrissae). Eyesight is generally well developed; in many species, the eyes are round and somewhat protruding. When an opossum is aroused it will often threaten the intruder with mouth open and lips curled back, revealing its 50 sharp teeth. Hearing is acute, and the naked ears are often in constant motion as the animal tracks

Above *A dusky slender mouse opossum foraging on the forest floor in Venezuela. Animals of this species are mainly nocturnal and, in common with most other mouse opossums, feed primarily on insects and fruit.*

different sounds. Most opossums are proficient climbers, with hands and feet well adapted for grasping. Each foot has five digits, and the big toe on the hindfoot is opposable. The round tail is generally furred at the base, with the remainder either naked or sparsely haired. Most opossums have a prehensile tail used as a grasping organ when the animal climbs or feeds in trees. Not all female opossums have a well-developed pouch; in some species the pouch is absent altogether, while in others there are simply two lateral folds of skin on the abdomen. In males the penis is forked and the pendant scrotum often distinctly colored.

The Virginia opossum of North and Central America, the common opossum of Central and South America, and the white-eared opossum of higher elevations in South America are generalized species, occurring in a variety of habitats from grasslands to forests. They have cat-sized bodies, but are heavier than cats and have shorter legs. Although primarily terrestrial, these opossums are capable climbers. In tropical grasslands, the common opossum becomes highly arboreal during the rainy season when the ground is flooded. Opportunistic feeders, they eat fruit, insects, small vertebrates, carrion, and garbage, varying their diets with seasonal availability. In the tropical forests of southeastern Peru, the common opossum climbs to heights of 25m (80ft) to feed on flowers and nectar during the dry season.

FACTFILE

AMERICAN OPOSSUMS

Order: Didelphimorphia

Family: Didelphidae

92 species in 19 genera

HABITAT Wide ranging, including temperate deciduous forests, tropical forests, grasslands, mountains, and human settlements. Terrestrial, arboreal, and semiaquatic.

SIZE Head–body length ranges from 6.8cm (2.7in) in the Formosan mouse opossum to 33–55cm (13–19.7in) in the Virginia opossum; tail length from 4.2cm (1.7in) in the Pygmy short-tailed opossum to 25–54cm (9.8–21.3in) also in the Virginia opossum, whose weight is 2–5.5kg (4.4–12.1lb).

COAT Either short, dense, and fine, or woolly, or a combination of short underfur with longer guard hairs. Color varies from dark to light grays and browns or golden; some species have facial masks or stripes.

DISTRIBUTION Throughout most of S and C America, N through E North America to Ontario, Canada; Virginia opossum introduced to the Pacific coast.

DIET Insectivorous, carnivorous, or (most often) omnivorous.

BREEDING Gestation 12–14 days

LONGEVITY 1–3 years (to about 8 in captivity)

CONSERVATION STATUS 44 of the 92 Didelphidae species are currently listed by the IUCN. Of these, 3 are Critically Endangered, 3 are Endangered, and 16 are Vulnerable; most of the others are ranked as Lower Risk: Near Threatened.

See subfamilies box ▷

The four-eyed opossums from the forests of Central and northern South America are also mostly generalist species. They are smaller than the Virginia opossum, with more slender bodies and distinct white spots above each eye, from which their common name is derived. These opossums are adept climbers, but the degree to which they climb seems to vary between habitats. The four-eyed opossums are also opportunistic feeders; earthworms, fruit, insects, and small vertebrates are all eaten.

The yapok, or water opossum, is the only marsupial highly adapted to an aquatic lifestyle. The hindfeet of this striking species are webbed, making the big toe less opposable than in other didelphids. When swimming, the hindfeet alternate strokes, while the forefeet are extended in front, allowing the animals to either feel for prey or carry food items. Yapoks are primarily carnivorous, feeding on crustaceans, fish, and frogs as well as on insects. Although they can climb, they rarely do so, and the long, round tail is not very prehensile. Both male and female yapoks possess a pouch, which opens to the rear. During a dive, the female's pouch becomes a watertight chamber; fatty secretions and long hairs lining its lips form a seal, and strong sphincter muscles close it. In males, the scrotum can be pulled into the pouch when the animal is swimming or moving swiftly.

The little water, or lutrine, opossum is also a good swimmer, although it lacks the specializations of the yapok. Unlike the yapok, which is found primarily in forests, lutrine opossums often inhabit open grasslands. Known as the *comadreja* ("weasel") in South America, this opossum has a long, low body with short, stout legs. The tail is densely furred and very thick at the base. Lutrine opossums are able predators, being excellent swimmers and climbers and also agile on the ground. They feed on a variety of prey including small mammals, birds, reptiles, frogs, and insects.

The mouse, or murine, opossums are a diverse group, with individual species varying greatly in size, climbing ability, and habitat. All are rather opportunistic feeders. The largest species, the ashy mouse opossum, is one of the most arboreal, whereas others, such as the dusky slender mouse opossum, are more terrestrial. The tail in most species is long, slender, and very prehensile but in some species, including the elegant fat-tailed mouse opossum, it can become swollen at the base for fat storage. The large, thin ears may become crinkled when the animal is aroused. The females lack a pouch, and the number and arrangement of mammae vary between species. Mouse opossums inhabit most habitats from Mexico through South America; they are absent only from the high Andes, the Chilean desert, and Patagonia, where they are replaced by another small species, the Patagonian opossum, which has the most southerly distribution of any didelphid.

This opossum broadly resembles the mouse opossums, though the muzzle is shorter, allowing for greater biting power. In the light of this adaptation, and because insects and fruit are rare in their habitat, Patagonian opossums are believed to be more carnivorous than mouse opossums. The feet are stronger than in mouse opossums and possess longer claws, suggesting fossorial (burrowing) habits. As in some of the mouse opossums, the tail of the Patagonian opossum can become swollen with fat.

The short-tailed opossums are small didelphids inhabiting forests and grasslands from eastern Panama through most of northern South America east of the Andes. The tail of these shrewlike animals is short and naked; their eyes are smaller than

Right A large American opossum (Didelphis *sp.*) in Minnesota, near the northerly limit of its range. Since the 19th century these opossums have spread rapidly northward through the USA. However, they are poorly adapted to cold weather conditions. During severe spells they may remain inactive in their nests for days on end, although they do not hibernate.

THE MONITO DEL MONTE

The monito del monte or colocolo lives in the forests of south-central Chile. Once thought to belong to the same family as the American opossums, this small marsupial is now considered the only living member of an otherwise extinct order, the Microbiotheria.

Monitos ("little monkeys") have small bodies with short muzzles, round ears, and thick tails. Head–body length is 8–13cm (3–5in), and they weigh just 16–31g (0.6–1.1oz). They are found in cool, humid forests, especially in bamboo thickets. Conditions are often harsh in these environments, and monitos exhibit various adaptations to the cold. The dense body fur and small, well-furred ears both help prevent heat loss. During winter months when food (mostly insects and other small invertebrates) is scarce, they hibernate. Before hibernation, the base of the tail becomes swollen with fat deposits.

There are various local superstitions about these harmless animals. One is that their bite is venomous and produces convulsions. Another maintains that it is bad luck to see a monito; some people have even reportedly burned their houses to the ground after spotting one in their homes.

in most didelphids and not as protruding. As these anatomical features suggest, short-tailed opossums are primarily terrestrial, but they can climb. As in mouse opossums, the females lack a pouch, and the number of mammae varies between species. Short-tailed opossums are omnivorous, feeding on insects, earthworms, carrion, and fruit, among other foods. Often they will inhabit human dwellings, where they are a welcome predator on insects and small rodents.

The three species of woolly opossum, along with the black-shouldered and bushy-tailed opossums, are placed in a separate subfamily – the Caluromyinae – from other didelphids on the basis of differences in blood proteins, the anatomy of the females' urogenital system, and the males' spermatozoa. The woolly opossums and the black-shouldered opossum are among the most specialized of all didelphids. Highly arboreal, they have large, protruding eyes that are directed somewhat forward, making their faces reminiscent of those of primates. Inhabitants of humid tropical forests, these opossums climb through the upper tree canopy in search of fruit. During the dry season, they also feed on the nectar of flowering trees, and serve as pollinators for the trees they visit. While feeding, they can hang by their long prehensile tails to reach fruit or flowers.

Although the bushy-tailed opossum resembles mouse opossums in its general appearance and proportions, dental characteristics, such as the size and shape of the molars, indicate that it is actually more closely related to the woolly and black-shouldered opossums. This species is known only from a few museum specimens, all of them taken from humid tropical forests.

Back to North America
DISTRIBUTION PATTERNS

North American fossil deposits from 70–80 million years ago are rich in didelphid remains, and it was probably from North America that didelphids entered South America and Europe. Yet by 10–20 million years ago they had become extinct in both North America and Europe. When South America again became joined to Central America, about 2–5 million years ago, many South American marsupials became extinct in the face of competition from the northern placental mammals that took the opportunity to spread into their territory. Didelphids persisted, however, and even moved north into Central and North America.

During historical times, the early European settlers of North America found no marsupials north of the modern states of Virginia and Ohio. Since then, in the eastern USA, the Virginia opossum has steadily extended its range as far as the Great Lakes. Moreover, following introductions on the Pacific coast in 1890, this species has also spread from southern California to southern Canada. These expansions are most probably related to human impact on the environment.

Playing Possum
SOCIAL BEHAVIOR

Reproduction in didelphids is typical of marsupials: gestation is short and does not interrupt the estrous cycle. The young are poorly developed at birth, and most development takes place during lactation. In the past there was a popular misconception that opossums copulated through the nose and that the young were later blown out through the nostrils into the pouch. The male's bifurcated penis, the tendency for females to lick the pouch area before birth, and the small size of the young at birth (they are just 1cm/0.4in long, and weigh 0.13g/0.005oz) all probably contributed to this notion.

Most opossums appear to have seasonal reproduction. Breeding is timed so that the first young leave the pouch when resources are most abundant; for example, the Virginia opossum breeds during the winter in North America, and the young leave the pouch in the spring. Opossums in the seasonal tropics breed during the dry season, and the first young leave the pouch at the start of the rainy season. Up to three litters can be produced in one season, but the last litter often overlaps the beginning of the period of food scarcity, and these young frequently die in the pouch. Opossums in aseasonal tropical forests may reproduce throughout the year, as may the white-eared opossum in the arid region of northeast Brazil.

There are no elaborate courtship displays nor long-term pair-bonds. The male typically initiates contact, approaching the female while making a clicking vocalization. A nonreceptive female will avoid contact or be aggressive, but a female in estrus will allow the male to mount. In some species courtship behavior involves active pursuit of the female. Copulation can be very prolonged – for up to six hours in Robinson's mouse opossums (*Marmosa robinsoni*).

Many of the newborn young die, as many never attach to a teat. A female will often produce more

American Opossum Subfamilies

Subfamily Didelphinae

87 species in 16 genera. S and C America, E USA to Ontario. Virginia opossum introduced to Pacific coast.
Large American opossums (*Didelphis*, 6 species), including the Virginia opossum (*Didelphis virginiana*), Common opossum (*D. marsupialis*), and White-eared opossum (*D. albiventris*)
Mouse opossums (*Marmosa*, 9 species), including the Linnaeus's mouse opossum (*M. murina*) and Robinson's mouse opossum (*M. robinsoni*). 1 species is Critically Endangered, another Endangered.
Gracile mouse opossums (*Cryptonanus*, 5 species) including the Chacoan Gracile opossum (*C. chacoensis*); (*Gracilinanus*, 6 species), including the Wood sprite gracile mouse opossum (*G. dryas*). 1 species is Critically Endangered, 2 are Vulnerable.
Slender mouse opossums (*Marmosops*, 16 species), including the Dusky slender mouse opossum (*M. fuscatus*). 1 species is Critically Endangered, 1 Endangered, 2 Vulnerable.
Woolly mouse opossums (*Micoureus*, 6 species), including the White-bellied woolly mouse opossum (*M. constantiae*).
Short-tailed opossums (*Monodelphis*, 18 species), including the Gray short-tailed opossum (*M. domestica*)

and the Pygmy short-tailed opossum (*M. kunsi*). 1 species is Endangered, 8 are Vulnerable.
Gray and Black four-eyed opossums (*Philander*, 4 species), including the Gray four-eyed opossum (*P. opossum*).
Fat-tailed opossums (*Thylamys*, 10 species), including the Elegant fat-tailed opossum (*T. elegans*)
Brown four-eyed opossum (*Metachirus nudicaudatus*)
Water opossum (*Chironectes minimus*)
Lutrine opossum (*Lutreolina crassicaudata*)
Patagonian opossum (*Lestodelphys halli*). Vulnerable
Pygmy opossum (*Chacodelphys formosa*)
Kalinowski's mouse opossum (*Hyladelphys kalinowskii*)
Gray mouse opossum (*Tlacuatzin canescens*)

Subfamily Caluromyinae

5 species in 3 genera. S Mexico through C America and most of northern S America.
Woolly opossums (*Caluromys*, 3 species). 1 species Vulnerable.
Black-shouldered opossum (*Caluromysiops irrupta*). Vulnerable.
Bushy-tailed opossum (*Glironia venusta*). Vulnerable.

For full species list see Appendix ▷

young than she has mammae; for example, most female Virginia opossums have 13 mammae, some of which may not even be functional, but usually give birth to around 21 young (there is anecdotal evidence of 56 having once been produced). The number of young in an opossum litter that do attach ranges from one to 15, but varies both within and between species. Older females tend to have fewer young, and litters born late in the season are often smaller. Litter sizes in Virginia and common opossums seem to increase with increasing latitude. The number of mammae provides an indication of maximum possible litter size. In general, some species (e.g., Virginia and common opossums, short-tailed opossums, and the Robinson's mouse opossum) have comparatively large litters of about seven young, whereas others (for instance the gray four-eyed and woolly opossums) have 3–5 young. Females of some species, including the Virginia opossum, usually cannot raise a single offspring because there is insufficient stimulus to maintain lactation.

The rearing cycle in those species that have been studied ranges from about 70 to 125 days. For example, the gray four-eyed opossum and

◑ **Above** *Some representative American opossum species:* **1** *Derby's woolly opossum* (Caluromys derbianus) *resting in a tree;* **2** *Black-shouldered opossum* (Caluromysiops irrupta) *climbing down a branch using its prehensile tail;* **3** *Mexican mouse opossum* (Marmosa mexicana – *not shown to scale*) *foraging for fruit;* **4** *Gray four-eyed opossum* (Philander opossum) *eating an insect grub;* **5** *Water opossum* (Chironectes minimus)*; note the webbed hindfeet.*

woolly opossums are similar in size (usually about 400g/14oz), but the time from birth to weaning is 68–75 days in the former and 110–125 days in the latter. Initially the young remain attached to the mother's teats, but later they begin to crawl about her body. Toward the end of lactation, they begin to follow her when she leaves the nest to forage. Female Robinson's mouse opossums will retrieve detached young within a few days of birth; in contrast, Virginia opossum mothers do not respond to their distress calls until after they have left the pouch, at about 70 days.

Although individual vocalizations and odors allow for some mother–infant recognition, maternal care in opossums does not appear to be restricted solely to a female's own offspring. Female Robinson's mouse opossums will retrieve young other than their own, and Virginia and woolly opossums have been observed carrying other females' young in their pouches. Toward the end of lactation, females cease any maternal care, and dispersal is rapid. Sexual maturity is attained within 6–10 months. Age at sexual maturity is not related directly to body size.

SHREW OPOSSUMS OF THE HIGH ANDES

Six small, shrewlike marsupial species are found in the Andean region of western South America from southern Venezuela to southern Chile. Known as caenolestids or sometimes as shrew or rat opossums, they are unique among American marsupials in having a reduced number of incisors, the lower middle two of which are large and project forward. The South American group represents a distinct line of evolution that diverged from ancestral stock before the Australian forms did, and its members are now placed not just in their own family, the Caenolestidae, but are also assigned an order, the Paucituberculata, of which they are the only representatives.

Fossil evidence indicates that about 20 million years ago seven genera of shrew opossums occurred in South America. Today the family is represented by only three genera and six species. There are four species of *Caenolestes*: the gray-bellied (*C. caniventer*), northern (*C. convelatus*), Andean (*C. condorensis*), dusky (*C. fuliginosus*); the Incan (*Lestoros inca*) and long-nosed (*Rhyncholestes raphanurus*) caenolestids are placed in separate genera. Known head–body lengths of these small marsupials are in the range of 9–14cm (3.5–5.5in), tail lengths mostly 10–14cm (3.9–5.5in), and weights from 14–41g (0.5–1.4oz).

The animals have elongated snouts equipped with numerous tactile whiskers. The eyes are small and vision is poor. Well-developed ears project above the fur. The ratlike tails are about the same length as the body (rather less in the long-nosed shrew opossum) and are covered with stiff, short hairs. The fur on the body is soft and thick and is uniformly dark brown in most species. Females lack a pouch, and most species have four teats (five in the long-nosed caenolestid). Caenolestids are active during the early evening or night, when they forage for insects, earthworms, and other small invertebrates, and also small vertebrates. They are able predators, using their large incisors to kill prey.

Caenolestids travel about on well-marked ground trails or runways. More than one individual will use a particular trail or runway. When moving slowly, they have a typically symmetrical gait, but when moving faster Incan caenolestids, and possibly other species, will bound, allowing them to clear obstacles.

The northern and dusky caenolestids are distributed at high elevations in the Andes of western Venezuela, Colombia, and Ecuador. The gray-bellied caenolestids of southern Ecuador occur at lower elevations. The Incan caenolestid is found high in the Peruvian Andes, but in drier habitats than that of the other species; it has been trapped in areas with low trees, bushes, and grasses. The long-nosed caenolestid inhabits the forests of southern Chile, including Chiloé Island and adjacent Argentina. As winter approaches, the tail of this species becomes swollen with fat deposits. All these species are currently classified as lower risk, except the long-nosed caenolestid, which is vulnerable, and the Andean caenolestid, which has not yet been classified.

Very little is known about the biology of these elusive marsupials. They inhabit inaccessible and (for humans) rather inhospitable areas, which makes them difficult to study. They have always been considered rare, but recent collecting trips have suggested that some species may be more common than was previously thought.

In general, opossums are not long lived. Few Virginia opossums survive beyond 2 years in the wild, and the smaller mouse opossums may not live much beyond one reproductive season. Although animals kept in captivity may survive longer, females are generally not able to reproduce after 2 years. Thus, among many of these didelphids, there is a trend towards the production of a few large litters during a limited reproductive life; indeed, a female Robinson's mouse opossum may typically reproduce only once in a lifetime.

American opossums appear to be locally nomadic, and seemingly do not defend territories. Radio-tracking studies reveal that individual animals occupy home ranges, but do not exclude others of the same species (conspecifics). The length of time for which a home range is occupied varies both between and within species. In the forests of French Guiana, for example, some woolly opossums have been observed to remain for up to a year in the same home range, whereas others shifted home range repeatedly; gray four-eyed opossums were more likely to shift home range.

In contrast to some other mammals, didelphids do not appear to explore their entire home range on a regular basis. Movements primarily involve feeding and travel to and from a nest site, and are highly variable depending upon food resources or reproductive condition. Thus home range estimates for Virginia opossums in the central United States vary from 12.5–38.8ha (31–96 acres). An individual woolly opossum's home range may vary from 0.3–1ha (0.75–2.5 acres) from one day to the next. In general, the more carnivorous species have greater movements than similar-sized species that feed more on fruit. Male didelphids become more active during the breeding season, whereas reproductive females generally become more sedentary.

Most opossums use several to many nest sites within their range. Nests are often used alternately with conspecifics in the area. Virginia and common opossums use a variety of nest sites, both terrestrial and arboreal, but hollow trees are a common location. Four-eyed opossums also nest in holes and open limbs of trees, and additionally

◁ **Left** A bare-tailed woolly opossum perches on a branch in French Guiana. These opossums, which take their name from their long, thick fur, are agile climbers, using the five digits of all four limbs to help them clamber through the forests in which they live.

Above *Hanging from a branch, a short-tailed opossum mother in Brazil shows off her seven new-born young, each attached to a separate teat. Pouches are not developed in these species.*

Right *An infant Virginia opossum hitches a ride on its mother's back. For a month or two between leaving the pouch and achieving independence, this is the usual mode of transport for the young.*

on the ground, in rock crevices, or under tree roots or fallen palm fronds. Mouse opossums nest either on the ground under logs and tree roots or in trees, using holes or abandoned birds' nests. Occasionally mouse opossums make nests in banana stalks, and more than once animals have been shipped to grocery stores in the United States and Europe. In the open grasslands, the lutrine opossum constructs globular nests of leaves or uses abandoned armadillo burrows. In more forested areas, these opossums may use tree holes. Unlike other didelphids, yapoks construct more permanent nests; their underground nesting chambers are located near the waterline and are reached through holes dug into stream banks.

Opossums are solitary animals. Although many may congregate at common food sources during periods of food scarcity, there is no interaction unless individuals get too close. Typically, when two animals do meet, they threaten each other with open-mouth threats and hissing and then continue on their way. If aggression does persist (usually between males), the hissing changes into a growl and then to a screech. Communication by smell is very important; many species have well-developed scent glands on the chest. In addition, male Virginia opossums, gray four-eyed opossums, and gray short-tailed opossums have all been observed marking objects with saliva. Marking behavior is carried out primarily by males, and is thought to advertise their presence in an area.

In tropical forests up to seven species of didelphids may be found at the same locality. Competition between these species is avoided through differences in body size and varying tendencies to climb. For example, woolly opossums and the ashy mouse opossum will generally inhabit the tree canopy, the common mouse opossum mostly haunts the lower branches, common and gray four-eyed opossums are found either on the ground or in the lower branches, while short-tailed opossums live solely on the ground. Some species appear to vary their tendency to climb depending upon the presence of similar-sized opossums. For example, in a Brazilian forest where both gray and brown four-eyed opossums were found together, the former was more arboreal than the latter, yet in a forest in French Guiana where only the gray was present, it was primarily terrestrial, and elsewhere the brown four-eyed opossum is mostly arboreal.

Despite being hunted for food and pelts, the Virginia opossum thrives both on farms and in towns and even cities. Elsewhere in the Americas, man's impact on the environment has been detrimental to didelphids. Destruction of humid tropical forests results in loss of habitat for the more specialized species.   MAO'C

Large Marsupial Carnivores

*t*HE LARGE MARSUPIAL CARNIVORES CONSIST *of six species of the exquisitely spotted quolls, and the Tasmanian devil, a single species assigned to its own genus. Tasmanian devils are perhaps best known to the general public in the form of "Taz," the Warner Brothers cartoon character. But the comic image of a tail-spinning terror devouring everything in its path belies the true nature of the devil, as does its reputation in Tasmania itself as an odious scavenger. While belligerent towards other devils, these predators and specialized scavengers are responsive, intelligent, and full of character.*

Vertebrate prey is a major part of the diet of large marsupial carnivores. Current diversity is low, but fossil evidence suggests many more species existed in the past. At least 11 thylacinids and five thylacoleonids (marsupial lions) have roamed Australia; their heyday was during the Miocene era (24–5 million years ago), while during the Pleistocene (1.8 million–10,000 years ago), several species of giant dasyurids (quolls and devils) existed. The last thylacine, also known as the Tasmanian tiger or wolf because of its doglike appearance, became extinct only in the 1930s.

Marsupial carnivores are not exclusively Australasian. Three species of South American marsupials are highly carnivorous, and thylacine-like borhyaenids and sabretooth-catlike marsupial thylacosmilids roamed there in prehistoric times.

A Classic Case of Convergence
FORM AND FUNCTION

At least superficially, quolls look like mongooses, thylacines like dogs, while devils resemble small hyenas, even down to the sloping hindquarters and rolling gait. The remarkable similarities between marsupial and placental carnivores that have evolved on different continents can give the impression of parallel universes.

The observed similarities between the two groups are in fact related to these species leading similar lives. Devils, like hyenas, have highly carnivorous dentition and adaptations for bone consumption, including robust premolar or molar teeth used for cracking bones and a relatively short snout with massive jaw-closing muscles, giving the animals a strong, crushing bite. They are able to consume all parts of a carcass, including thick skin and all but the largest bones. With teeth that are adapted for crushing invertebrates as well as for slicing meat, quolls group with the mongoose and stoat families to fill the role of predator of small- to medium-sized mammals and invertebrates. The thylacine, on the other hand, was probably ecologically closer to smaller canids like the coyote than it ever was to the wolf. The animal's extremely long snout, very low rates of canine tooth wear and fracture, and limb ratios typical of slower runners, suggest that it hunted animals that were smaller than itself, such as wallabies, and did not use long, fast pursuits to obtain its prey.

Below *The Tasmanian devil is an effective hunter of medium-sized mammals, primarily wallabies. It is also a specialist scavenger and can eat all but the largest bones.*

FACTFILE

LARGE MARSUPIAL CARNIVORES

Order: Dasyuromorphia

Family: Dasyuridae

7 extant species in 2 genera; 1 species (*Thylacinus cynocephalus*) in the related Thylacinidae family recently extinct

DISTRIBUTION
Australia and New
Guinea

HABITAT Mostly
in rain forest or
woodland

SIZE Head–body length ranges from 12.3–31cm (5–12in) in the male Northern quoll to 50.5–62.5cm (20–25in) in the Tasmanian devil; **weight** ranges from 0.3–0.9kg (0.7–2lb) to 4.4–13kg (10–30lb) in the same two species.

COAT Short furred; upper parts mostly gray or brown, with white spots or blotches. The Tasmanian devil has thicker fur, and usually only one or two white patches.

DIET Smaller species eat mainly insects, but the Tiger quoll and the Tasmanian devil will take birds and mammals as large as wallabies.

BREEDING Mostly 4–8 young, carried in pouch for 8–10 weeks in smaller species but for 15–16 weeks in Tasmanian devil.

LONGEVITY Ranges from 12 months in the smaller species to 6 years in the Tasmanian devil.

CONSERVATION STATUS One of the 7 extant species is currently listed as Endangered, three as Vulnerable, two as Lower Risk, Near Threatened.

See species table ▷

Marsupial carnivore species exhibit variation in the strength of their canine teeth and temporal (jaw) muscles, which enables them to take prey of different sizes and consequently minimizes the competition for food. The shape of the canines is oval, being intermediate between the narrow canine teeth of the dog family and the more rounded canines of the cats. Marsupial carnivores kill their prey by use of a generalized crushing bite, which is applied to the skull or nape.

Two morphological features suggest that dasyuromorphs and carnivorans may simply have evolved different solutions to the same problems. Marsupials have a longer snout than the placental carnivores, suggesting that they may possess a weaker bite, but this comparative deficiency appears to be compensated for by extra space for larger jaw muscles, which is derived from their smaller brain cases. Limb–bone ratios suggest that devils, tiger quolls, and thylacines, but not the smaller quolls, are slow runners compared with their placental counterparts. The granular foot pads, which are limited to the digits in placental carnivores, extend to the ankle and wrist joints in the marsupial carnivores, which sometimes walk and rest on their heels, suggesting differences in their locomotory function.

⬤ *Above Four-month-old eastern quolls resting in a grass-lined den. Young are usually deposited in a den by the mother about ten weeks after birth, having spent their time up until then in their mother's pouch.*

There is a quoll adapted to every environment in Australia and New Guinea: tropical rain forest, monsoonal savanna, woodlands, deserts, grasslands, and temperate forests. The degree of carnivory increases with body size, from the quite insectivorous smaller quolls to the completely carnivorous tiger quoll, devil, and thylacine. The largest remaining guild, in Tasmania, had four species until the recent extinction of the thylacine: the eastern quoll, a small (1kg/2.2lb) ground-dwelling insectivore/carnivore; the tiger quoll, a middle-sized (2–4kg/4.5–9lb) tree-climbing predator; the devil, a larger (4.4–13 kg/ 10–30lb) ground-dwelling carnivore and specialist scavenger; and the predatory thylacine (15–35kg/33–77lb). Tiger quolls are naturally rare, perhaps because they are specialists on forest habitat and vertebrate food, and because they may compete for food with eastern quolls, devils, and introduced cats. Their tree-climbing abilities may allow them to exploit the tree-dwelling possum prey resource, however, which is less available

to other quolls and devils. Devils are the most common species; their larger size gives them an advantage in stealing carcasses from quolls and monopolizing them.

Solitary but Social
SOCIAL BEHAVIOR

Early settlers can be excused for giving the devil its alarming name. The sight of a jet-black animal with large white teeth and bright red ears (the ears of devils blush red when they are agitated) creating mayhem in a poultry coop, combined with spine-chilling screeches in the dark, must have been more than enough to convince them that they had indeed "raised the Devil." Devils make a wide range of sounds, including growls, whines, soft barks, snorts, sniffs, and whimpers. Devils are solitary creatures but highly social, feeding together at carcasses and developing affectionate relationships, especially while mating. Females and males, both devils and quolls, have very different agendas for mating, however. A female loves and leaves several males in succession over a period of a week, perhaps in an attempt to ensure that her young are sired by the best males available. Intent on protecting his paternity, the male devil indulges in "caveman" tactics, charging the escaping female and then using a neck bite to drag or lead her back to the den, where he will copulate with her for prolonged periods (up to 14 hours for tiger quolls). During the mating season female devils and quolls develop a swelling on the back of their neck that may serve to protect them from injury. Males fight for females, sustaining deep bites and gouges to the head and rump that may sometimes be life threatening.

Quolls, like devils, are solitary and rest underground or in hollow log dens during the day. Neither group is territorial, although female quolls of some species maintain an exclusive home range in part or whole, especially when they have young in a den. Male young are more likely than females to disperse away from the home range of their mother. Young devils disperse at 9 months of age, immediately after weaning, moving some 10–100 km (6–60mi) from their birth site. Scent is important in communication, with latrines possibly assuming the role of community noticeboards in some species. Devils frequently scent mark by dragging their cloacae on the ground. Quolls, unlike devils, call infrequently, making a variety of coughing and hissing sounds or else abrupt, piercing screams; or, in the case of the tiger quoll, screech like the sound of a circular saw.

The Threat from Placentals

CONSERVATION AND ENVIRONMENT

All Australian species have declined in range and abundance as a result of human presence. Concern has also been expressed for the quolls in New Guinea, although their conservation status is poorly known.

Devils and quolls, like many placental carnivores, are persecuted for attacking livestock. Both groups take insecurely penned poultry, and newborn lambs and sick sheep are also vulnerable. As a result, devils and quolls are trapped, shot, and poisoned in the tens and occasionally in the hundreds. Similar persecution, combined with loss of habitat and prey as a result of more sheep farming,

was a main cause of the thylacine's decline, leading ultimately to its extinction.

The greatest threats to marsupial carnivores, however, are loss of habitat and killings by introduced placental carnivores. These often go hand in hand. Like many carnivores, devils and quolls and require lots of space (home ranges of male devils average 20sq km/8sq mi) and often live at low density (one individual to 1–10sq km/0.4–4sq mi, depending on habitat, in tiger quolls). Extensive areas of habitat have been lost through degradation, in addition to direct losses to agriculture and intensive forestry, which in turn can limit the availability of prey, especially for the forest-dependent tiger quoll, which disappears if more

THE THYLACINE

Up to the time of its extinction, the thylacine was the largest of recent marsupial carnivores. Fossil thylacines are widely scattered in Australia and New Guinea, but the living animal was confined in historical times to Tasmania.

Superficially, the thylacine resembled a dog. It stood about 60cm (24in) high at the shoulders, head–body length averaged 80cm (31.5in), and weight 15–35kg (33–77lb). The head was doglike with a short neck, and the body sloped away from the shoulders. The legs were also short, as in large dasyurids. The features that clearly distinguished the thylacine from dogs were a long (50cm/20in), stiff tail, which was thick at the base, and a coat pattern of black or brown stripes on a sandy yellow ground across the back.

Most of the information available on the behavior of the thylacine is either anecdotal or has been obtained from old film. It ran with diagonally opposing limbs moving alternately, could sit upright on its hindlimbs and tail rather like a kangaroo, and could leap 2–3m (6.5–10ft) with great agility. Thylacines appear to have hunted alone, and before Europeans settled in Tasmania they probably fed upon wallabies, possums, bandicoots, rodents, and

birds. It is suggested that they caught prey by stealth rather than by chase.

At the time of European settlement, the thylacine appears to have been widespread in Tasmania, and was particularly common where settled areas adjoined dense forest. It was thought to rest during the day on hilly terrain in dense forest, emerging at night to feed in grassland and woodland.

From the early days of European settlement, the thylacine developed a reputation for killing sheep. As early as 1830, bounties were offered for killing thylacines, and the consequent destruction led to fears for the species' survival as early as 1850. Even so, the Tasmanian government introduced its own bounty scheme in 1888, and over the next 21 years, before the last bounty was paid, 2,268 animals were officially killed. The number of bounties paid had declined sharply by the end of this period, and it is thought that epidemic disease combined with hunting to bring about the thylacine's final disappearance.

The last thylacine to be captured was taken in western Tasmania in 1933; it died in Hobart zoo in 1936. Since then the island has been searched thoroughly on a number of occasions, and even though occasional sightings continue to be reported to this day, the most recent survey concluded that there has been no positive evidence of thylacines since that time. In 1999, the Australian Museum in Sydney decided to explore the possibility of cloning a thylacine, using DNA from a pup preserved in alcohol in 1866, although it admitted that to do so successfully would require substantial advances in biogenetic techniques. AKL

◐ **Left** *Rare or extinct over large parts of its range, the tiger quoll is vulnerable to habitat loss.*

◑ **Right** *The tiger quoll is an active hunter, killing its prey – which includes arboreal gliders, small wallabies, reptiles, and birds – with a bite to the back of the head.*

than 50 percent of the canopy is removed. The decline in the number of old hollow trees is a cause of particular concern; they support populations of hollow-nesting possums, which are major prey species for tiger quolls. The smaller quolls become increasingly vulnerable to predation by introduced predators if vegetative cover is removed by livestock grazing or frequent fires. northern, western, and eastern quolls have lost large tracts of habitat in this way.

Dingoes, cats, and foxes introduced to Australia by humans 3,500–4,000 years ago, in the 17th century, and in 1871, respectively, indulge in competitive killings of marsupial carnivores. The mainland Australian extinction of thylacines and devils coincided with the arrival of the dingo. The smaller species of quolls have been extirpated throughout the range of the fox. Physical refuges can mitigate predation risk; northern quolls experience increased mortality from predators after fire removes vegetative cover in savanna, but not in rocky habitats.

In the last 10 years, an apparently new disease, Devil Facial Tumor disease, has caused major population decline (locally up to 75 percent) across two-thirds of the range of the Tasmanian devil, and is still spreading. It is a neuroendocrine cancer and appears to be infectious, possibly spread by biting. It appears to kill most devils within a year of reaching adulthood, resulting in very young age-structured populations.

Populations of tiger and northern quolls are fragmented and declining. their survival and population ecovery will require a nationally coordinated approach, with habitat loss and predator control needing to be addressed. Fortunately, there is also some good news to report. The western quoll – once considered endangered – will shortly be removed from threatened-species lists, following the success of a recovery program that has translocated 200 captive-bred animals to four new sites since the early 1990s, although their continued survival will remain dependent on ongoing fox and cat control.   MJ

Northern quoll
Dasyurus hallucatus

Australia; N Northern Territory, N Queensland and N Western Australia. Formerly found in broad band across wet–dry tropics; now only in lowland savanna woodland and rocky terrain. HBL male: 12.3–31cm (5–12in), female: 12.5–30cm (5–12in); TL male: 12.7–30.8cm (5–12in), female: 20–30cm (8–12in); WT male: 0.4–0.9kg (0.8–2lb), female: 0.3–0.5kg (0.7–1.1lb). COAT: white spots on brown body, striated foot pads, clawless hallux (1st toe) on 5-toed hindfoot, long-haired tail. BREEDING: mates in June at 12 months old, usually up to 8 young (variation 5–10) carried in pouch for 8–10 weeks, weaned at 6 months. LONGEVITY: male 12–17 months, female 12–37 months. CONSERVATION STATUS: Lower Risk, Near Threatened; in extensive decline, with just six fragmented populations remaining.

Bronze quoll [Vu]
Dasyurus spartacus

SW New Guinea. Lowland savanna woodlands. Known from only a few specimens; recognized as a separate species from *D. geoffroii* in 1988. HBL male: 34.5–38cm (14–15in), female: 30.5cm (12in); TL male: 28.5cm (11in), female: 25cm (10in); WT male: 1.0kg (2.2lb), female: 0.7kg (1.5lb).

COAT: white spots on brown body, small hallux, long-haired tail. BREEDING: may be seasonal. CONSERVATION STATUS: Vulnerable.

New Guinean quoll [Vu]
Dasyurus albopunctatus

New Guinea. Widespread in rain forest habitats above 1,000m (3,300ft). HBL male: 22.8–35cm (9–14in), female: 24.1–27.5cm (9.5–10.5in); TL male: 21.2–29cm (8–11in), female: 22.1–28cm (9–11in); WT male: 0.6–0.7kg (1.5lb), female: 0.5kg (1.1lb). COAT: white spots on reddish brown body, well-developed hallux, short-haired tail. BREEDING: not seasonal, 4–6 young. CONSERVATION STATUS: Vulnerable.

Western quoll [Vu]
Dasyurus geoffroii
Western quoll or Chuditch

W Australia. Formerly over two-thirds of the county, from desert to forest, but now restricted to SW alone. HBL male: 31–40cm (12–16in), female: 26–36cm (10–14in); TL male: 25–35cm (10–14in), female: 21–31cm (8–12in); WT male: 0.7–2.2kg (1.5–4.9lb), female: 0.6–1.1kg (1.3–2.4lb). COAT: white spots on brown body, white belly, hallux, long-haired tail. BREEDING: mates in May–June at 12 months old, up to 6 young carried in pouch for 9 weeks, weaned at 6 months.

LONGEVITY: 3 years. CONSERVATION STATUS: Vulnerable; rare, currently occupies only 2 percent of its former range.

Eastern quoll
Dasyurus viverrinus

Tasmania; formerly also SE mainland. Grasslands and open forests. HBL male: 32–45cm (13–18in), female: 28–40cm(11–16in); TL male: 20–28cm (8–11in), female: 17–24cm (7–9.5in); WT male: 0.9–2.0kg (2–4.4lb), female: 0.7–1.1kg (1.5–2.4lb). COAT: white spots on brown body, white belly, no hallux on 4-toed hindfoot, long-haired tail. BREEDING: mates in May–June at 12 months old, as many as 30 young born in June, up to 6 carried in pouch for 8–9 weeks and weaned at 5.5 months. LONGEVITY: 3–4 years. CONSERVATION STATUS: Lower Risk, Near Threatened.

Tiger quoll [Vu]
Dasyurus maculatus

Tasmania (separate genetic unit); eastern states of Australia (smaller phenotypic subspecies). Formerly in South Australia. Forest-dependent in areas of high rainfall or predictably seasonal rainfall. HBL male: 45–51cm (18–20in), female: 40.5–43cm (16–17in); TL male: 39–49cm (15–19in), female: 34–44cm (13–17in); WT male: 3.0–7.0kg (6.6–

15.4lb), female: 1.6–4.0kg (3.5–8.8lb); all data are for southern subspecies. COAT: white spots on reddish brown body and on short-haired tail, cream belly, striated foot pads, well-developed hallux. BREEDING: mating April–July at 12 months old, up to 6 young carried in pouch for 8 weeks, weaned at 5 months. LONGEVITY: 3–5 years. CONSERVATION STATUS: Vulnerable, as is subspecies *D. m. maculatus*; Endangered as *D. m. gracilis*.

Tasmanian devil
Sarcophilus harrisii

Tasmania. Open forest and woodland. HBL male: 50.5–62.5cm (20–25in), female: 53.5–57cm (21–22.5in); TL male: 23.5–28.5cm (9–11in), female: 21.5–27cm (8.5–10.5in); WT male: 7.7–13.0kg (17–28.7lb), female: 4.5–9.0kg (9.9–19.9lb). COAT: black with variable white markings on chest, shoulder, and rump, fat store in tail base, no hallux on 4-toed hindfoot. BREEDING: mates in February–March at 12 months old, up to 4 young carried in pouch for 4–5 months, weaned at 9 months. LONGEVITY: 6 years. CONSERVATION STATUS: Lower Risk, Least Concern.

Abbreviations HBL = head–body length TL = tail length WT = weight

FACING DISASTER

A unique cancer strikes down Tasmania's icon

CAN A DISEASE BRING ABOUT EXTINCTION? Increasing awareness of the dramatic impacts of such diseases as rinderpest, avian malaria, and amphibian chytrid fungus has led conservation biologists to take wildlife diseases seriously. Although wildlife diseases might be perceived as a natural feature of the ecosystem, acting along with competition and predation to limit populations, human activities have, in many cases, heightened the threat posed by infectious disease to wildlife. Certainly, there are circumstances under which infectious disease might threaten

extinction – especially when a numerous host, such as humans or domestic animals, keeps an epidemic going that obliterates a rare species. Diseases that are infectious typically do not persist when population densities are low. The impact of infectious disease on a wild species will also depend on the probability of its killing individuals, the efficiency of transmission and the period between infection and death. Finally, the disease may occur in the presence of another threat to the population, and the combination of the two threats may be sufficient to bring about extinction.

In 1996, a wildlife photographer, Christo Baars, returned to a favourite spot for photographing wild Tasmanian devils (*Sarcophilus harrisii*): Mount William National Park, in northeast Tasmania. This area was well known for its extremely high numbers of devils. On this occasion, however, Baars had difficulties in finding devils. When, finally, he did, he found many of them had large, open tumors around their faces. His photographs were possibly the first reported observation of what has since become known as Devil Facial Tumor Disease (DFTD).

Above A young Tasmanian devil is released from a trap by a field biologist. The traps have been specially designed for the monitoring program set up by the Tasmanian state government. Each animal is carefully examined for any sign of disease, particularly around the mouth and head.

Below Blood samples are taken from a captured devil for analysis. So far, results have shown that the devils seem to respond very poorly to the infection, which allows it to take hold rapidly in an animal that has been exposed to the disease.

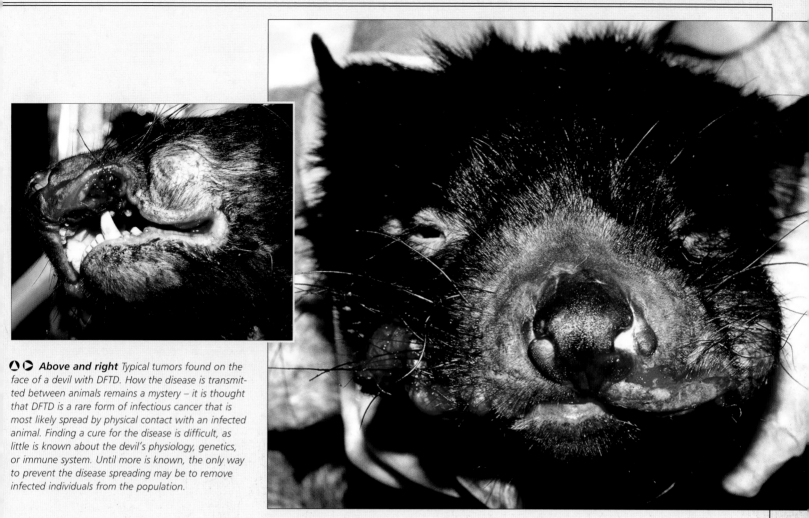

Above and right Typical tumors found on the face of a devil with DFTD. How the disease is transmitted between animals remains a mystery – it is thought that DFTD is a rare form of infectious cancer that is most likely spread by physical contact with an infected animal. Finding a cure for the disease is difficult, as little is known about the devil's physiology, genetics, or immune system. Until more is known, the only way to prevent the disease spreading may be to remove infected individuals from the population.

Since that time, it has become increasingly apparent that DFTD is widespread, and is having a serious impact on the devil population. By the end of 2004, it became clear that the disease was present in devils across more than half of Tasmania: specifically, the area in which devils were much more common, at densities of 1–3 individuals per sq km. At Mount William, where DFTD is thought to have been present longest, best estimates indicated that numbers had dropped by 80 percent since the first sighting of the disease, with lesser declines happening in all diseased areas. It is rare to find the tumors on a juvenile, but where the disease is established, all adults appear vulnerable to the disease. Most disappear from the population less than a year after first showing symptoms. No resistant or immune animals have been identified. A devil in a disease-free population typically lives 5–6 years, but at Mount William, it is rare to find an animal more than three years old.

Cancerous conditions have proved extremely difficult to understand and treat – even in humans, where vast health budgets are available and where there is already a profound knowledge of the species' physiology. The Tasmanian state government's Devil Disease Team has had the added challenge of needing first to establish an understanding of the physiology, immunity, and genetics of a healthy devil. They also lacked the luxury, often open to medical doctors, of studying millions of detailed case histories. Nonetheless, they have already discovered that the tumors observed on all devils in affected populations throughout Tasmania are all a single type of cancer. Such a widespread geographical distribution is not typical of cancer.

Microscopic study of the tumors reveals that their tissue structure and extremely complex chromosome rearrangement is almost identical in all individuals so far examined, suggesting that the tumors may have a single origin. Furthermore, no immune response to these tumors has yet been identified. In other words, the hypothesis is that one devil happened to develop a cancer composed of cells that were capable of being grafted onto other individuals. Instead of being rejected, these cells flourish, dividing to form further tumors on their new hosts. If this hypothesis is correct, DFTD is an infectious disease. Only one other cancer, canine transmissible venereal sarcoma, acts in this way.

To reduce the threat of the disease, both captive and wild options are being considered. Quarantined populations of devils from apparently disease-free areas have been established in captivity, to ensure that at least a minimum viable population of Tasmanian devils is kept safely in isolation from this disease. Very strict quarantine precautions are being followed until it is clear whether DFTD can be transmitted from a distance (for example via the proboscis of a biting insect) or only by direct contact. The Tasmanian government has also begun an adaptive management trial involving a wild population on a large peninsula. Here, the disease appears to have arrived relatively recently and its prevalence is still low. The devils can only enter or leave the peninsula across a broad canal or bridge, on which measures are being designed to restrict devil movement. Using this closed population, an experimental control program is under way – by trapping intensively in order to remove virtually all devils with DFTD symptoms, the authorities are seeking to find whether they can reduce or even bring about an end to the disease on the peninsula.

Since the demise of the thylacine, devils have been the top predator in Tasmania. The loss of a top predator from an ecosystem can have major effects on many other species. In Tasmania, the knock-on effects could be extreme, especially because red foxes are thought to have been introduced maliciously to the island at the turn of the 21st century. A plausible idea is that previous introductions of foxes have been thwarted because the Tasmanian devils killed the fox cubs. If the devil is not present in sufficient numbers to prevent the establishment of the fox, a large number of species extinctions are predicted on Tasmania. Fortunately, there is widespread support for efforts to save Tasmania's icon, and progress so far has been encouraging. CEH/SBP

Small Marsupial Carnivores

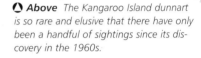

THE SMALL MARSUPIAL CARNIVORES INCLUDE some of the smallest mammals on Earth, yet the ferocity they display in hunting belies their size. All show a predilection for live food, preying mainly on insects and other invertebrates, but also taking lizards, fledgling birds, and other small mammals. However, their rapaciousness has sometimes brought them undeserved notoriety – for its attacks on poultry in the Sydney area, the diminutive brush-tailed phascogale, which weighs just 200g (7oz), was unfairly dubbed a "vampire marsupial" by early European settlers.

Although other marsupials such as American opossums, bandicoots, and the numbat eat animal flesh, most marsupial carnivores are dasyurids. The majority of species in this family weigh less than 250g (8.8oz) and representatives occur in all terrestrial habitats in Australia and New Guinea. Because of their conservative body form and appearance, dasyurids have long been considered as "primitive" marsupials structurally ancestral to the Australasian radiation. However, recent fossil discoveries show the family to be a recent and specialized addition to the region, with the ancestral dasyurid arising in the early to mid-Miocene, perhaps 16 million years ago.

Coping with Extremes
FORM AND FUNCTION

Despite showing three-thousand-fold variation in body mass, all dasyurids have distinctive pointed snouts with three pairs of similar-sized lower incisors, well-developed canines, and 6–7 sharp cheek teeth. This dentition allows prey to be grasped and quickly killed and then comminuted (chewed into small pieces) before swallowing. Dasyurids are united also in having five toes on the forefeet and 4–5 toes on the hindfeet, with all except the hallux (big toe) having sharp claws.

Unlike their larger relatives, the small marsupial carnivores mostly have uniform coat colors that range from shades of brown and gray to black. Three New Guinean dasyurids (the narrow-striped dasyure, broad-striped dasyure, and three-striped dasyure) are unusual in having dark dorsal stripes. All are partly diurnal, the coat pattern helping to camouflage them against the dark background of the rain forest floor. Two further diurnal species, the speckled dasyure of the New Guinea highlands and the dibbler of southwestern Australia, are also unusual in having grizzled, silvery gray coats that may again serve a camouflage function. In two species of phascogales, as well as in the mulgara and kowari, the terminal half of the tail is a spectacular black brush that contrasts greatly with the light body fur. The bushy tails are

○ **Above** *The Kangaroo Island dunnart is so rare and elusive that there have only been a handful of sightings since its discovery in the 1960s.*

thought to have a signaling function, but there are few observations of these species in the wild to confirm this.

The insectivorous diet of small marsupial carnivores has important implications for their physiology. Insects are rich in protein and fat, but have a free water content of more than 60 percent. Water turnover is relatively high in many dasyurids, with species weighing less than 25g (0.9oz) able to turn over their body weight in water each day. In arid areas, marsupial carnivores can obtain all their water from food for periods of months; juicy prey such as insect larvae and centipedes are preferred; water loss is reduced by the production of concentrated urine. If food is limited, several small marsupial carnivores can reduce their metabolic rates and drop their body temperatures by 10°C (18°F) or more to enter torpor. This can last at least 10 hours, reducing energy expenditure and allowing animals to ride out temporary food shortages. If food is not limited, dasyurids have an extraordinary ability to maintain their body temperatures, producing heat by elevating the metabolic rate 8–9 times its normal resting level. The desert-dwelling kowari maintains its body temperature for at least four hours by this method, even at –10°C (14°F). Alternative means of keeping warm include sun basking and sharing nests with individuals of the same or different species.

○ **Left** *The nocturnal fat-tailed false antechinus, which stores fat in the base of its tail, is found mainly on rocky hills.*

○ **Right** *Dubbed a "vampire marsupial" by early settlers for its attacks on poultry, the brush-tailed phascogale can erect the hairs at the end of its tail.*

SMALL MARSUPIAL CARNIVORES

Order: Dasyuromorphia

Families: Dasyuridae and Myrmecobiidae

62 species in 19 genera

DISTRIBUTION
Australia, Papua New Guinea, and Indonesia (Aru Islands).

HABITAT Diverse, from stony desert to forest and alpine heath.

SIZE Head–body length ranges from 4.6–5.7cm (1.8–2.2in) in the Pilbara ningaui to 24.5cm (9.7in) in the Numbat; tail length ranges from 5.9–7.9cm (2.3–3.1in) to 17.7cm (7in), and weight from 2–9.4g (0.07–0.33oz) to 0.5kg (1.1lb), both in the same two species. Males are slightly or much heavier than females.

COAT Varied in color, but mostly short and coarse furred.

DIET Mainly insects and other small invertebrates (e.g., beetles, cockroaches, arachnids). Also small mammals and birds, including house mice, lizards, and sparrows.

BREEDING Gestation period ranges from 12.5 days in the Fat-tailed dunnart to 55 days in the Fat-tailed false antechinus.

LONGEVITY In the Brown antechinus, males live for 11.5 months, females for 3 years.

CONSERVATION STATUS Seven species are classed as Endangered, eleven as Vulnerable, and seven as Lower Risk, Near Threatened.

See families box ▷

Lone Ranger of the Desert

DISTRIBUTION PATTERNS

Small marsupial carnivores occupy all terrestrial habitats in Australia and New Guinea. Up to nine species occur locally in some arid areas and in structurally complex forests, due to the diversity of foraging microhabitats that these environments provide. In contrast, only one or two species usually co-occur in woodland or savanna environments, due to the paucity of opportunities they provide for different species to segregate.

The spectacular success of small dasyurids in the deserts of Australia is perhaps the most remarkable feature of their modern radiation. Many denizens of the arid zone occupy drifting home ranges that appear to track changes in levels of food. The tiny lesser hairy-footed dunnart, for example, may move 2–3km (1.2–1.9mi) a night in search of food. Few small marsupial carnivores dig their own burrows, and those that inhabit the arid zone exploit soil cracks or abandoned burrows. Some dunnarts and ningauis will move several kilometers from drought-stricken areas toward rain. Lesser hairy-footed dunnarts have been recorded moving 12km (7.5mi) in two weeks, possibly following the scent of wet desert sand on the wind.

A Frenetic Search for Mates
SOCIAL BEHAVIOR

In the 12 species of forest-dwelling antechinuses and phascogales, as well as the little red kaluta, sexual maturity is reached when males and females are 11 months old. Matings occur over a short period (2–3 weeks), at the same time each year in any locality, with ovulation in females being stimulated by subtle increases in the rate of change of day length in spring. All males die at about 1 year of age within a month of mating, but females can survive and reproduce in a second or occasionally third season. All or almost all females breed annually, producing 6–12 young per litter. Male death in these dasyurids so soon after mating is due to increased levels of free corticosteroid (stress) hormones in the blood (see A Once-in-a-Lifetime Breeding Opportunity).

Other marsupial carnivores have more flexible life histories. In the sandstone antechinus, matings still occur synchronously in winter, but some 70 percent of males survive their first breeding season; about a quarter of individuals of both sexes breed at 2 years of age. Reproductive effort in this species is relatively small, as only 65–88 percent of females breed each year, and litter sizes seldom exceed 4–5 young.

In other species of marsupial carnivores, such as some dunnarts, sexual maturity is achieved at 6–8 months, and females are able to produce 2–3 litters over extended breeding seasons that can last

Small Marsupial Carnivore Families

Family Myrmecobiidae

One species, the **Numbat** (*Myrmecobius fasciatus*), SW Western Australia; formerly in NW South Australia and SW New South Wales. Vulnerable.

Family Dasyuridae

Divided into 2 subfamilies, Dasyurinae (with two tribes, Dasyurini and Phascogalini) and Sminthopsinae (with two tribes, Sminthopsinae and Planigale).

Subfamily Dasyurinae
Tribe Dasyurini

Genus *Dasycercus*: 1 species, the Mulgara (*D. cristicauda*), found in arid Australia from NW Western Australia to SW Queensland, N South Australia. Vulnerable as *D. cristicauda,* Endangered as *D. hillieri*. Rare or indeterminate.

Genus *Dasykaluta*: Formerly included in *Antechinus*. 1 species, Little Red Kaluta (*D. rosamondae*), NW Western Australia. Lower Risk, but rare.

Genus *Dasyuroides*: Formerly included in *Dasycercus*. 1 species, the Kowari (*D. byrnei*). Junction of Northern Territory, South Australia, and Queensland (C Australia). Vulnerable as *Dasycercus byrnei*. Rare.

Genus *Myoictis*: 2 species; Three-striped dasyure (*M. melas*) found in Prov. of Papua and NE Papua New Guinea; Salawati Isl. Also Waigeo, Yapen, possibly Batanta (Indonesia). Lower Risk (lc) and Wallace's dasyure (*M. wallacii*), Southern New Guinea and Aru Isls (Indonesia). Conservation status is unknown, but rare.

Genus *Neophascogale*: 1 species, Speckled dasyure (*N. lorentzi*). C New Guinea (highlands). Lower Risk. Uncommon.

Genus *Parantechinus*: Formerly included in *Antechinus*, a single species, Southern dibbler (*P. apicalis*), Inland periphery of SW Western Australia. Endangered.

Genus *Phascolosorex*: 2 species, Red-bellied marsupial shrew (*P. doriae*), W interior New Guinea, 100–2000m. Data Deficient. Narrow-striped marsupial shrew (*P. dorsalis*) W and E interior New Guinea (not known from central region). Lower Risk. Common.

Genus *Pseudantechinus*: Formerly included in *Antechinus*. 6 species, Sandstone dibbler (*P. bilarni*), Northern Territory (Australia), Lower Risk but rare; the Fat-tailed false antechinus (*P. macdonnellensis*), Uplands of Western Australia, and southern desert region of Northern Territory, from type locality north to about 19°S, Lower Risk; the Carpentarian false antechinus (*P. mimulus*), Northern Territory and North Isl, Sir Edward Pellew Group, Vulnerable; the Ningbing false antechinus (*P. ningbing*), Kimberley region, Western Australia, Lower Risk; Rory Cooper's false antechinus (*P. roryi*), Western Australia: Northern Pilbara, north of the Hamersley Range, into Great Sandy Desert as far east as Clutterbuck Hills; Cape Range Peninsula; probably Barrow Isl., and Woolley's false antechinus (*P. woolleyae*), Western Australia, Lower Risk.

Tribe Phascogalini

Genus *Antechinus*: Formerly included *habbema, melanura, naso,* and *wilhelmina,* which have been transferred to *Murexia* and a series of new genera (*Micromurexia, Murexechinus,* and *Phascomurexia*). 10 species including the Tropical antechinus (*A. adustus*), Australia: Dense tropical vine forests from Paluma to Mt. Spurgeon; Agile antechinus (*A. agilis*), Australia: Victoria (SW, and C, E and NE districts), and SE New South Wales north on the coast to Kioloa, and inland north to Mt. Canobolas; common. Cinnamon antechinus (*A. leo*), Cape York Peninsula from the Iron Range to the southern limit of the McIlwraith Range; Lower Risk, Near Threatened. The Brown antechinus (*A. stuartii*), SE Queensland, E New South Wales south to Kioloa. Bioclimatic modeling predicts an almost entirely coastal distribution, north to about 26°S, Lower Risk.

Genus *Murexichinus*: Separated from Murexia. Single species, Black-tailed dasyure (*M. melanurus*), New Guinea (Normanby Isl), sea level to 2800m. Lower Risk.

Genus *Murexia*: Formerly *Antechinus*; Short-furred dasyure (*M. longicaudata*), New Guinea, sea level to 1800m; Aru Isls; Yapen. Lower Risk.

Genus *Paramurexia*: formerly included in *Murexia*. Single species, the Broad-striped dasyure (*P. rothschildi*), SE New Guinea. Vulnerable.

Genus *Phascomurexia*: formerly included in *Murexia*. Single species, the Long-nosed dasyure (*P. naso*), Interior New Guinea. Data Deficient as *Antechinus naso.*

Genus *Phascogale*: 2 species, Red-tailed phascogale (*P. calura*), Inland SW Western Australia, formerly in Northern Territory, South Australia, NW Victoria, SW New South Wales, but probably extinct in all places except the Western Australian wheat belt; Endangered. Brush-tailed phascogale (*P. tapoatafa*), SW Western Australia, SE South Australia, S Victoria, E New South Wales, SE and N Queensland, Northern Territory. Lower Risk, Near Threatened.

Subfamily Sminthopsinae
Tribe Sminthopsini

Genus *Antechinomys*: A single species, Kultarr (*A. laniger*), Western Australia, S Northern Territory, N Victoria, W New South Wales, SW Queensland, N South Australia. Data Deficient.

Genus *Nigaui*: 3 species and an undescribed species of Ningaui which occurs in Northern Territory (Australia); Wongai ningaui (*N. ridei*), Northern Territory, South Australia, and Western Australia (deserts); Pilbara ningaui (*N. timealeyi*), NW Western Australia; Southern ningaui (*N. yvonnae*), Australia: Western Australia to New South Wales, Victoria. All three known species are Lower Risk. Common.

Genus *Sminthopsis*: 21 species, strongly distinct, and some of them may ultimately be given generic rank. Includes Kangaroo Island dunnart (*S. aitkeni*), Kangaroo Isl (South Australia), Endangered; Boullanger Island dunnart (*S. boullangerensis*), Boullanger Isl, and on the mainland at Lesueur, near Jurien; Near Threatened; Butler's dunnart (*S. butleri*), Western Australia, Kalumburu and Papua New Guinea, Vulnerable; Julia Creek dunnart (*S. douglasi*), Known in the "downs country" of NW Queensland; and possibly Mitchell Plateau, Western Australia, Endangered.

Tribe Planigalini

Genus *Planigale*: 5 species; Paucident planigale (*Planigale gilesi*), NE South Australia, NW New South Wales, and SW Queensland (Australia); Long-tailed planigale (*Planigale ingrami*), Australia: N and E Queensland, NE Northern Territory, NE Western Australia; Pygmy planigale (*Planigale maculate*), E Queensland, NE New South Wales, and N Northern Territory (Australia) and Narrow-nosed planigale (*Planigale tenuirostris*), NW New South Wales, and SC Queensland (Australia) are all Lower Risk. The New Guinean planigale (*Planigale novaeguineae*), Lowlands of S New Guinea is Vulnerable.

Classification of Sminthopsinae and Planigalini from Archer 1982. *Carnivorous Marsupials*, 2:439.

For full species list see Appendix ▷

for up to 8 months. Repeated reproduction is possible because the gestation period is short (10–13 days) and weaning occurs at 60–70 days. In antechinuses, false antechinuses, and phascogales, by contrast, gestation lasts 30–40 days and weaning occurs at least three months after birth. Four marsupial carnivores appear to have no seasonality in their breeding schedules. Northern Australian populations of the common planigale produce litters of 4–12 young in all months, while three species of antechinus in New Guinea produce smaller litters of 3–4 without any obvious seasonal break.

Differences in life histories of marsupial carnivores have probably arisen in response to variations in the duration and reliability of invertebrate food resources. In the antechinuses and phascogales, peaks in invertebrate abundance occur reliably in spring and summer, and mating is timed so that lactation and weaning coincide with these peaks. The chances of failing to breed at all due to food shortage is thus reduced. In dunnarts, ningauis, and other species where males survive or where females produce two or more litters in a season, food peaks may be smaller or less predictable. The chance of reproductive failure due to food shortage may be high, but the risk can be spread over more than a single litter.

Communication and social organization remain poorly known for most small dasyurids. Most or all species appear solitary except during the breeding season and when the young are dependent for food on the mother. In species that occur usually at low densities or occupy open habitats, such as ningauis, males continuously utter soft clicks or hisses to attract females, while females call in return during periods of receptivity. Loud hissing sounds are made by many species during aggressive encounters or during nest or food defense.

In the agile antechinus and some other forest-dwelling dasyurids, males disperse from the maternal nest at weaning and reside for periods of days or weeks with unrelated females. Toward the

THE NUMBAT – TERMITE EATER

The numbat (*Myrmecobius fasciatus*), the sole member of the family Myrmecobiidae, is a specialized termite eater and, perhaps because of the diet, is the only fully day-active Australian marsupial. It sports black-and-white bars across its rump, and a prominent white-bordered dark bar from the base of each ear through the eye to the snout. These distinctive coat markings and its delicate appearance make it one of the most instantly appealing marsupials.

The numbat spends most of its active hours searching for food. It walks, stopping and starting, sniffing at the ground and turning over small pieces of wood in its search for shallow underground termite galleries. On locating a gallery, the numbat squats on its hindfeet and digs rapidly with its strong clawed forefeet. Termites are extracted with the extremely long, narrow tongue which darts in and out of the gallery. Some ants are eaten, but it seems that the numbat usually takes these in accidentally while picking up the termites. It does not chew its food, and also swallows grit and soil acquired while feeding.

Numbats are solitary for most of the year, each individual occupying a territory of up to 150ha (370 acres). During the cooler months a male and female may share the same territory, but they are still rarely seen together. Hollow logs are used for shelter and refuge throughout the year, although numbats also dig burrows and often spend the nights in them during the cooler months. The burrows and some logs contain nests of leaves, grass, and sometimes bark. In summer numbats sunbathe on logs.

Four young are born between January and May, and attach themselves to the nipples of the female, which lacks a pouch. In July or August the mother deposits them in a burrow, suckling them at night. By October, the young are half grown and are feeding on termites while remaining in their parents' area. They disperse in early summer (December).

Numbats once occurred across the southern and central parts of Australia, from the west coast to the semiarid areas of western New South Wales. They are now found only in a few areas of eucalypt forest and woodland in the southwest of Western Australia. Habitat destruction for agriculture and predation by foxes have probably contributed most to this decline. While most of their habitat is now secure, remaining populations are so small that the species is classed as vulnerable. Efforts are being made to set up a breeding colony from which natural populations may be reestablished. **AKL**

breeding season, males appear to aggregate in tree-top leks where females come to "window shop." Both sexes mate with multiple partners. Females store viable sperm in the reproductive tract for up to two weeks, and produce litters sired by more than one father. For the female, mating with several males causes sperm competition, which may be beneficial in producing genetically diverse offspring. For the male, such competition reduces confidence in paternity and may drive the frenetic search for new mates.

Small Survivors
CONSERVATION AND ENVIRONMENT

In contrast to their larger relatives, the small marsupial carnivores have escaped the worst ravages of European settlement. No species has gone extinct, and only seven have suffered range reductions over 25 percent. Nonetheless, many species have small ranges or sparse populations: 15 Australian species are considered threatened, as is the New Guinean planigale. Clearing of vegetation for agriculture and predation by feral cats and foxes are serious threats. Populations of most of the threatened species occur at least partly on protected land. Control of introduced predators has stemmed population declines in the endangered red-tailed phascogale, and provides hope that it would protect other threatened species if implemented at a broad scale. **CRD**

◁ **Left** *The mulgara is not a common sight, however it is reported that observed numbers increase when plagues of house mice – a favored food – occur within its range. It eats a mouse from head to tail, inverting the skin of its victim as it goes.*

A ONCE-IN-A-LIFETIME BREEDING OPPORTUNITY

Sex and death in the antechinus

MANY MAMMALS GO TO GREAT LENGTHS FOR sex, but the prize for personal sacrifice has to go to those mammals that reproduce only once in a lifetime, exhausting their own bodies to fuel their reproductive urges. It is the sensible strategy of most mammals to start their reproductive lives with caution, rarely having their largest litter or fattest babies at the first attempt; at least initially, reproductive ability improves with age. In certain species, however, some individuals put all their eggs in one basket. An alpine vole that has survived the winter often produces only a single litter before it dies, and it will be the offspring of such voles that continue reproduction throughout the spring and summer. And in two groups of carnivorous marsupials, the Australian dasyurids and the American didelphids (opossums), all individuals of certain species commit themselves totally to reproduction at their first attempt. In these species, all the females come into estrus at the same time, once a year. After that all the males die, sometimes over a period of just three or four days. Indeed, all the males can be dead before the females have even ovulated. While the females live on to give birth and suckle their young, they also usually die after rearing only a single litter.

When organisms reproduce only once in their lifetime they are known as semelparous, in contrast

◑ **Above** *Some species of antechinuses – in this case a swamp antechinus (Antechinus minimus) – lack a pouch as such; instead they have a patch of bare skin from which the mammae or teats protrude.*

◐ **Below** *Raising litters of as many as ten young places a huge strain on the resources of a female antechinus. To ensure that she can produce enough milk to feed her offspring, the reproductive cycle is timed so that lactation coincides with the period of maximum prey availability, when she is well fed.*

with iteroparous organisms, which reproduce repeatedly. The former strategy is a strange and rarified phenomenon. True semelparity appears to have evolved at least twice in didelphids and five times among dasyurids, yet nowhere else among mammals or birds. The species involved range from the well-studied antechinuses, weighing a mere 20g (0.7oz), through the beautiful phascogales to the cat-sized northern quoll.

Semelparity only occurs in predictable, highly seasonable environments, and it has its "raison d'être" in the excruciatingly slow reproduction rate of small marsupials. The most famous of the semelparous marsupials, *Antechinus agilis*, has a four-week pregnancy, at the end of which it gives birth to young weighing only 16mg. The young are deposited in the shallow pouch, where their tiny bodies are unwound by a special swelling on their chest that allows them to attach to a teat, where they continue to develop. After a further 5 weeks of suckling, they have grown to a length of about 1cm (0.4in). They are not weaned until they are 14 weeks of age or more.

Because the mother may be suckling as many as ten young, her metabolic rate in late lactation can be ten to twelve times the basal rate – a mammalian record. Female reproduction is therefore timed to ensure that late lactation coincides with the period of maximum availability of the insect and spider prey on which the species feeds, which falls in late spring or early summer. Females must therefore get pregnant in the winter, when there is little food to eat. But males are put through a further test of endurance by having to congregate in special mating trees where the females come to mate. During the short rut, as many as twenty males may aggregate in the tree cavity, where they are visited by the females.

Males face a threefold dilemma. They have to mate in winter, and at a communal nest as much as 1km (0.6mi) from their own home range; and if they do try to feed at this time, they run the risk of missing the all-important visits by receptive females. It is now that the adaptive advantage of dying becomes apparent. Males resolve the challenge confronting them by exhibiting in an extreme form the stress response mounted by all mammals when presented with an external challenge, or stressor. This response involves the secretion of corticosteroids, of which cortisol is the most potent form in mammals. Cortisol suppresses appetite and promotes gluconeogenesis, the conversion of protein into sugars, which means that reserves other than rapidly consumed fat can be used to sustain the body during a crisis. Nonetheless, the stress response is a two-edged

◐ **Left** *A female antechinus returns to her litter of eight-week-old young in the hollow of a tree. Naked and helpless, they will be dependent on their mother's milk until they are weaned at 14 weeks or more.*

weapon. In addition to the benefits it brings, cortisol suppresses the immune and inflammatory responses, exposing stressed animals to a greater risk of disease. In most organisms this eventuality is prevented by corticosteroid-binding globulins that render some of the cortisol inactive, and by negative feedback in the brain that stops cortisol production. Semelparous marsupials, in a suicidal twist, radically reduce the level of binding globulins just as the breeding season starts, and the negative feedback cycle is turned off. As a consequence, males can digest and feed off their own bodies from within, but at the cost of condemning themselves to the most miserable of deaths. The commonest source of mortality is a massive hemorrhage of ulcers in the stomach and intestine, but parasites and other microorganisms that ordinarily have no effect can also often become pathogenic once the immune system fails. Females live on after the males have died, but they need to survive for another 16 months in order to successfully wean a second litter, and they often fail to do so.

This paradoxical solution to the stresses of mating has been arrived at evolutionarily by other organisms that also have to mate in a hostile environment, such as freshwater eels that migrate to the sea to breed or salmon that live in the ocean but spawn in fresh water. They use exactly the same hormonal system to sustain their migration, and they pay a similar price.

The curious life history of these small marsupials is fascinating in its own right, but the extremely simple population structure, producing individuals of identical ages, also provides a unique insight into other intriguing questions affecting mammalian society as a whole. In many mammals, juvenile males disperse, while females remain in the area where they were born. This behavior has been attributed to competition between fathers and sons for mating opportunities. But an alternative explanation, probably relating to incest avoidance, needs to be found for male-biased dispersal in the case of semelparous marsupials. They show extreme male bias in natal dispersal; females continue to live with their mothers after weaning, but all males leave, sometimes traveling many kilometers to a new home range – and this despite the fact that in these species fathers are dead long before their sons are born.　　　　　　　　　AC

Bandicoots

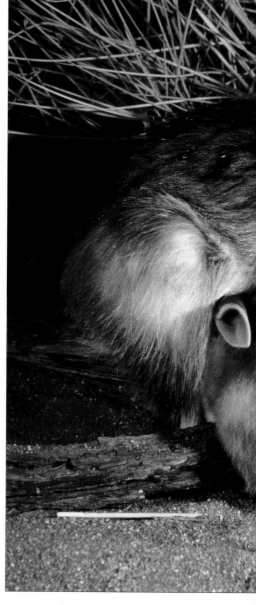

bANDICOOTS ARE RATLIKE MARSUPIALS, *agile, with long noses and tails. They share a common name and ancestry with the rabbit-eared bandicoots or bilbies, a smaller group adapted for arid environments, and distinguished not just by their long ears, longer limbs, and silkier hair but also by their burrowing habit. One of the two bilby species is now thought extinct, and the other is threatened.*

Bandicoots are notable for having one of the highest reproductive rates among marsupials, exceeded only by that of a single species of dunnart (family Dasyuridae). In this respect, they resemble the rodents in the placental world; like theirs, their life cycles centre on producing many young with little maternal care. Otherwise, these small insectivores and omnivores fit into an ecological niche similar to that of the shrews and hedgehogs.

Short Necks and Pointed Muzzles
FORM AND FUNCTION

Most bandicoots are rabbit-sized or smaller, have short limbs, a long, pointed muzzle, and a thick-set body with a short neck. The ears are normally short, the forefeet have three toes with strong, flattish claws, and the pouch opens backwards. The furthest from this pattern is the recently extinct pig-footed bandicoot, which had developed longer limbs and hooflike front feet as adaptations to a more cursorial life on open plains. The long-nosed bandicoots of the genus *Perameles* also have longer ears than the other species, but the longest of all are found on the bilby. Teeth are small and relatively even-sized, and have pointed cusps. Most bandicoots are omnivorous, characteristically obtaining their food from the ground by excavating small, conical pits.

Bandicoots are distinguished from all other marsupials by having fused (syndactylous) toes on the hindfeet, forming a comb for grooming, and

polyprodont dentition (with more than two well-developed lower incisors). The rear-opening pouch normally has eight teats. It extends forward along the abdomen as the young enlarge, eventually occupying most of the mother's underside, and then contracts again after they have departed. Litter size is normally 2–3.

Bandicoots' sense of smell is well developed. The animals are nocturnal and their eyes are adapted for night vision, although their binocular vision may be limited, perhaps because the elongated nose gets in the way. The long-nosed bandicoot produces a sharp, squeaky alarm call when disturbed at night, and bandicoots are also sometimes heard to sneeze loudly, probably to clear soil from their noses. They rarely if ever produce loud calls, but a very low, sibilant "huffing" with bared teeth is uttered as a threat by some species.

The dental formula is I5/3, C1/1, P3/3, M4/4 = 48, except in spiny bandicoots, which have four pairs of upper incisors (I4/3). Sexual dimorphism occurs in most species; in some, males may be up to 60 percent heavier and 15 percent longer than females. Males usually have larger canines.

The classification of bandicoots is not fully resolved, although all genera seem to be clearly defined. Currently three families are recognized, one of which (the Peramelidae) contains three distinct subfamilies (see box). Taxonomic relationships within the brown bandicoots and other groups and the taxonomy of most New Guinea forms warrants further study.

Brown bandicoots are stocky, short-eared, plain-colored animals. They inhabit areas of close ground cover, tall grass, or low shrubbery. The southern brown bandicoot favors heathland, whereas the northern brown bandicoot occurs in a wide range of habitats from wet forests to open woodland. All have inflated auditory bullae. Dwarfed forms occur, particularly on islands and in more open areas, perhaps as a result of scarcer

food resources. Variations in the angle of the ascending rear portion of the lower jaw, and the presence of an extra cusp on the last upper molar, have been used to differentiate between species, but the taxonomy is not satisfactorily understood. The distribution of southern brown bandicoots does not overlap that of the northern species, except for a single instance. There is, however, overlap between northern brown bandicoots and the golden bandicoot.

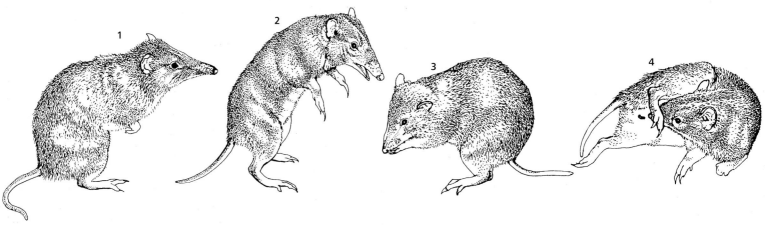

The long-nosed bandicoots are more lightly built, with a relatively longer skull, small auditory bullae, longer ears, and a preference for areas of open ground cover, although habitat use may be flexible; some species also exhibit barred body markings. The arid-zone species have a wide distribution, from Western Australia to western New South Wales; in contrast, the long-nosed bandicoot itself is restricted to the eastern coastal areas, and the eastern barred bandicoot to grasslands and grassy woodlands of the southeast mainland and Tasmania. Important variables between species are ear length and the size of the bullae, which both increase in arid areas, and the positioning of toes on the hindfeet. In addition, different species exhibit varying degrees of barring, which is absent in the forest species but conspicuous in grassland species.

Bilbies have lengthened ears, long, narrow rostra, and elongated limbs; other distinctive features include highly developed auditory bullae with twin chambers, long, silky fur, and a long, crested tail. The only burrowing bandicoots, they are an early offshoot from the main bandicoot stock that has become highly specialized for arid areas. Species and populations are differentiated principally by size, coat, and tail coloration, and also by the dimensions of the bullae, which were larger in the lesser bilby, now thought to be extinct.

The several New Guinea genera (the Peroryctidae) are poorly known. They tend to be little-modified, short-eared, forest bandicoots. The skulls are more cylindrical than in the peramelids, and in the spiny bandicoots and the Seram bandicoot the rostrum is long and narrow. The auditory bullae are small. Spiny bandicoots have short tails.

◐ **Above** *The greater bilby, seen here suckling its young, is a desert species. It now has a much-reduced distribution. Habitat loss and predation have severely reduced its numbers and it is listed as vulnerable.*

◗ **Below** *Behavioral postures of the northern brown bandicoot. It is nocturnal and frequently sniffs the air* **1** *to detect any danger. The usual gait is on all fours, but the larger hindlimbs are used in an aggressive hop* **2** *characteristic of males.* **3** *The northern brown bandicoot digs out food with its strong foreclaws. After the shortest gestation of perhaps any mammal, the newborn young crawl into their mother's rear-opening pouch* **4** *where they are carried for seven weeks, by which time* **5** *the pouch is bulging.*

FACTFILE

BANDICOOTS

Order: Peramelemorphia

Families: Peramelidae, Thylacomyidae, and Chaeropodidae

21 species in 8 genera

HABITAT All major habitats in Australia and New Guinea from desert to rain forest, including semiurban areas.

SIZE Head–body length ranges from 17–26.5cm (7–10in) in the mouse bandicoots to 50–60cm (20–23in) in the Giant bandicoot; tail length from 11–12cm (4.5in) to 15–20cm (6–8in), and weight from 140–185g (5–6.5oz) up to 4.8kg (10.5lb), both in the same species. Males of larger species may be up to 50 percent heavier than females.

COAT Mostly short and coarse in bandicoots (stiff and spiny in some New Guinean species); longer and silkier in the Greater bilby.

DIET Insects and other invertebrates, bulbs, roots, tubers.

BREEDING Gestation 12.5 days in the Long-nosed, Eastern barred, and Northern brown bandicoots, 14 days in the Greater bilby.

DISTRIBUTION
Australia, Papua New Guinea, West Irian

LONGEVITY About 2–3 years in the Eastern barred, and slightly more in the Northern brown bandicoot.

CONSERVATION STATUS Two bandicoot species – the Pig-footed (*Chaeropus ecaudatus*) and the Desert (*Perameles eremiana*) – have recently been declared Extinct, as has the Lesser bilby (*Macrotis leucura*). Several other species are also at risk; the Western barred bandicoot (*Perameles bougainville*) is listed as Endangered, and three other species are Vulnerable, including the Greater bilby (*Macrotis lagotis*). Little is known about the status of many New Guinea bandicoots; some species have only been collected on one or two occasions.

Habitat Specialists

DISTRIBUTION PATTERNS

In recent (Pleistocene) times, bandicoots have to a large extent evolved separately in Australia and New Guinea, as a result both of the intermittent separation of the two land masses and of the marked habitat differences. All but one of the New Guinea genera are endemic; only the long-nosed echymipera extends its range into northern Australia. Conversely, only one Australian species, the northern brown bandicoot, intrudes into the grassy woodlands of southern New Guinea. This suggests that the main influence of the two land masses on the different bandicoot fauna is habitat, not just the water barrier.

Within New Guinea, different species occur at different altitudes. The northern brown, giant, and most species of spiny bandicoots are lowland animals, but some range up to about 2,000m (6,500ft). The mouse, striped, and Raffray's bandicoots are all highland species, generally found above 1,000m (3,500ft). The Seram bandicoot is only known from high altitudes, at about 1,800m (6,000ft).

Within Australia, there are pronounced climatic influences on the distribution of species, which tend to fall into two groups. Species restricted to semiarid and arid areas have suffered large population declines since European settlement, and three (the desert and pig-footed bandicoots and the lesser bilby) are now probably extinct. The survivors include the western barred and golden bandicoots and the greater bilby.

This pattern is an effect, whether direct or indirect, of rainfall. The northern brown bandicoot, a coastal species of eastern and northern Australia, is widely distributed as far inland as the 72.5cm (28.5in) isohyet (rainfall line). Beyond this it tends to be largely confined to watercourses, which extend its range much farther inland,

Above *The southern brown bandicoot only overlaps with the northern form in an anomalous population in the Cape York peninsula of northern Australia.*

almost to the 60cm (23.6in) isohyet. Southern brown bandicoots are more confined to the coast (except in Tasmania), and the long-nosed bandicoot extends inland beyond the Great Dividing Range only in northeastern Victoria.

Opportunistic and Omnivorous

DIET

Although bandicoots are dentally specialized for feeding on invertebrates, feeding is opportunistic and omnivorous and includes insects, other invertebrates, fruits, seeds of nonwoody plants, subterranean fungi, and occasional plant fiber. Diet can also include a high proportion of surface food, and it is likely that bandicoots switch to other food when insects are unavailable. They locate food in the ground by scent and then dig it out with their strong foreclaws. The elongated muzzle is presumably used to probe into holes for food.

The northern brown bandicoot has a characteristic foraging pattern, moving slowly over its whole range. This is an adaptation for finding food that occurs as small, scattered items rather than being concentrated in a few areas. The eastern barred bandicoot concentrates on areas of increased soil moisture and vegetation diversity, where food species are both more abundant and more readily excavated.

Fast Breeders

SOCIAL BEHAVIOR

Most species are solitary, animals coming together only to mate, and there appears to be no lasting attachment between mother and young. Males are usually larger than females and socially dominant. Dominance between closely matched males may

Bandicoot Families

Family Peramelidae

Subfamily Peramelinae

Long-nosed bandicoots Genus *Perameles*
4 species: Western barred bandicoot (*P. bougainville*) and subspecies *P. b. bougainville* are Endangered, *P. b. fasciata* is Extinct; Eastern barred bandicoot (*P. gunnii*) and subspecies *P. g. gunnii* are Vulnerable, *P. g. nova* is Critically Endangered; Long-nosed bandicoot (*P. nasuta*). The Desert bandicoot (*P. eremiana*) is now listed as extinct by the IUCN.
Short-nosed or **Brown bandicoots** Genus *Isoodon*
3 species: Golden bandicoot (*I. auratus*) and subspecies *I. a. auratus*, and *I. a. barrowensis* are all Vulnerable; Northern brown bandicoot (*I. macrourus*); Southern brown bandicoot (*I. obesulus*).

Subfamily Echymiperinae

Spiny bandicoots Genus *Echymipera*
5 species: Clara's echymipera (*E. clara*) and Menzie's echymipera (*E. echinista*) are both Data Deficient and considered rare; Common echymipera (*E. kalubu*); David's echymipera (*E. davidi*), currently Data Deficient; Long-nosed echymipera (*E. rufescens*).
New Guinean mouse bandicoots Genus *Microperoryctes* 3 species: Mouse bandicoot (*M. murina*); Striped bandicoot (*M. longicauda*); Papuan bandicoot (*M. papuensis*). Two species are Data Deficient and considered rare.
Seram bandicoot *Rhynchomeles prattorum*

Subfamily Peroryctinae

New Guinea bandicoots Genus *Peroryctes*
2 species: Giant bandicoot (*P. broadbenti*) is Data Deficient, considered rare; Raffray's bandicoot (*P. raffrayana*).

Family Chaeropodidae

Pig-footed bandicoot (*Chaeropus ecaudatus*) is listed in Appendix 1 of CITES, but is now considered extinct by the IUCN.

Family Thylacomyinae

Rabbit-eared bandicoot or **Bilby** Genus *Macrotis*. Greater bilby (*M. lagotis*) is Vulnerable. The Lesser bilby (*M. leucura*) is listed in Appendix 1 of CITES, but is now considered extinct by the IUCN.

be established by chases or, rarely, by fights, in which the males approach each other standing on their hindlegs.

Male home ranges are larger than those of females; for the northern brown bandicoot 1.7–5.2ha (4.2–12.8 acres) in one study, compared to 0.9–2.1ha (2.2–5.2 acres) for females. Similar values were found for the eastern barred bandicoot, although these relate to core ranges not entire foraging area. The ranges of both sexes overlap extensively, although core areas may not. Females often dictate local distribution, selecting and perhaps defending high-quality nesting and foraging sites. Males patrol most of the home range each night, perhaps to detect other males or receptive females. In male-biased populations, many males may repeatedly mate with a single female.

Captive northern brown bandicoots showed intense interest in nests, which consist for them of heaps of raked-up groundlitter with an internal chamber, and dominant males commonly evicted others from them. Nests may therefore be a significant focus of social interactions in the wild in that species. Eastern barred bandicoots make several types of nest, the most complex being a lined, roofed excavation used when females have young. Many species have scent glands present behind the ears; the northern brown bandicoot uses this gland, which is present in both sexes, to mark the ground or vegetation during aggressive encounters between males. The high reproductive rate of bandicoots means that they are able to recolonize rapidly as habitat recovers from fire or drought.

The reproductive biology of Australian bandicoots has been studied in some detail and is well exemplified by the northern brown species. The young are gestated for only 12.5 days, less than half the length of time taken by most other marsupials and almost the shortest of any mammal. Development of the embryo is aided by a form of chorioallantoic placentation that is unique to bandicoots among marsupials, in that it resembles the placenta of eutherian mammals. Other marsupials form only a yolksac placenta, whereas bandicoots and eutherians have independently evolved both types of placentation.

At birth the young are about 1cm (0.4in) long and weigh about 0.2g (0.007oz), with well-developed forelimbs. The allantoic stalk anchors the

○ **Below** *The eastern barred bandicoot is virtually extinct on mainland Australia, being restricted to a tiny remnant population.*

young to the mother whilst the newborn crawls to the pouch, where it attaches to a nipple. The young leave the pouch after 49–50 days and are weaned about 10 days later. In good conditions, sexual maturity may occur at about 90 days, although it is normally attained much later. Females are polyestrous and breed throughout the year in suitable climates; in other conditions they breed seasonally. Mating can occur when the previous litter is near the end of its pouch life. Since the gestation is 12.5 days, the new litter is born at about the time of weaning of the earlier litter. Captive females may have 4–5 litters per year, and may therefore produce about 18 young in a lifetime; in the wild this figure is probably halved. In captivity only about 40 percent of young reach sexual maturity, while in wild populations the survival rate is as low as 11.5 percent, so, despite the high fecundity, recruitment is low.

The reproductive cycle is one of the most distinctive characteristics of bandicoots, setting them apart from all other marsupials. They have become uniquely specialized for a high reproductive rate and reduced parental care. In most bandicoots, this is achieved by accelerated gestation, rapid development of young in the pouch, early sexual maturity, and a rapid succession of litters in the polyestrous females. Female eastern barred bandicoots may become sexually mature at less than 4 months and, given normal climatic conditions, continue to breed throughout the year for up to 3 years. In one northern brown bandicoot population with breeding seasons stretching over 6–8 months, females produced an average of 6.4 surviving young in one season, and 9.6 in the next. Litter size, however, while higher than in many marsupial groups, is not exceptional, being smaller than in others, such as dasyurids.

○ **Above** *Young spiny bandicoots (Echymipera spp.) alone in a nest. Bandicoots expend little effort on parental care, relying instead on a high birth rate.*

Under Threat of Extinction
CONSERVATION AND ENVIRONMENT

Australian bandicoots have suffered one of the greatest declines of all marsupial groups. All species of the semiarid and arid zones have suffered massive declines or even become extinct; the survivors are reduced now to a few remnant populations that are still endangered. An important feature of most of the extinctions seems to be grazing by cattle, sheep, or rabbits, and the consequent changes in the nature of ground cover. Some authorities blame introduced predators. Removal of sheep and cattle is an important conservation measure in these areas.

Only a few species that occur in higher rainfall zones, including the long-nosed and the northern and southern brown bandicoots, can be considered secure, although all have been affected by European settlement. Even these "common" species are under threat of habitat alteration or alienation. For example, the long-nosed bandicoots have become all but extinct in Sydney, and the same is true of southern brown bandicoots in the Melbourne metropolitan area.

Conservation of the eastern barred bandicoot depends on an ongoing reintroduction program, in which captive-bred animals have been released to several protected sites in their former range. Success has been variable, with predation by the introduced red fox and habitat degradation by grazing herbivores, whether native (kangaroos) or introduced (rabbits), being constraining factors. Control management of these issues is required on a continuing basis, but after more than 10 years of effort some of the reintroduced populations have become successfully established. While the species is more common in Tasmania, the population there is also declining.   GG/JHS

Cuscuses and Brushtail Possums

1

2

dWELLING IN THE REMOTE OUTBACK AS well as in the suburbs of most Australian cities, the common brushtail possum is perhaps the most frequently encountered of all Australian mammals and is the most studied of the possums. But most of the remaining 26 phalangerid species are relatively unknown to science, either because of their cryptic behavior in dense rain forest or their restricted distributions; for example, the Telefomin cuscus, from the highlands of central New Guinea, is known from only five museum specimens.

The phalangerids are generally nocturnal, the outstanding exception being the bear cuscus of Sulawesi (*Ailurops ursinus*), which is the only one with circular pupils, a possible adaptation to diurnal living. The animals are usually arboreal; even the ground cuscus and scaly-tailed possum, which habitually rest by day in holes in the ground, spend the night in trees. Cuscuses and possums are careful and deliberate climbers, not given to spectacular leaps; among the adaptations that help them are curved and sharply pointed foreclaws, as well as clawless but opposable first hindtoes that aid in grasping branches, and prehensile tails with variable amounts of bare skin. Phalangers possess well-developed, forward-opening pouches.

Native Australians
EVOLUTION AND RADIATION

Phalangerids originated in the rain forests of what is now mainland Australia. The earliest fossils of modern genera – *Trichosurus*, *Wyulda*, and *Strigocuscus* – were found in the Miocene rocks of Riversleigh, northern Australia, and date from some 20 million years before the present. *Trichosurus* and *Strigocuscus* were also present in the early Pliocene of southern Australia about 5 million years ago. The genera *Ailurops*, *Phalanger*, and *Spilocuscus* have not appeared in the Australian fossil record and may have originated in New Guinea, possibly from the ancestral phalangerid stock closest to *Ailurops* at a time when New Guinea was connected to Australia during the Miocene or earlier.

Most phalangerid genera, even in the fossil record, are made up of between 1 and 4 species, the only exception being *Phalanger* itself, which numbers 13 species. The stimulus for *Phalanger*'s

proliferation was provided by the geographical isolation of its populations, either on islands or on remote mountain ranges in New Guinea, where it is the only genus occurring above 1,200m (4,000ft). *Strigocuscus* is now extinct in Australia, but it has been replaced by two other cuscus genera, the eastern common (*Phalanger intercastellanus*) and common spotted (*Spilocuscus maculatus*) cuscuses. Both are common lowland species in New Guinea that entered Australia less than 2 million years ago over the land bridge that linked the two landmasses during the Pleistocene.

Common and Uncommon
DISTRIBUTION PATTERNS

The common brushtail possum has the widest distribution of all phalangerids, covering most of Australia in a wide range of habitats from rain forests to semiarid areas; four subspecies are currently recognized. In temperate Tasmania individuals have thick coats and bushy tails and weigh up to 4.5kg (9.9lb), but there is a general decline in

size towards the tropics, with individuals across northern Australia attaining no more than 1.8kg (4lb), having thin coats and little bush to the tail. The predominant color is light gray, but in wetter habitats darker colors are common – black in Tasmania, dark red in northeastern Queensland. The common brushtail possum's congener, the mountain brushtail, is geographically much more restricted and not split into subspecies. These possums occupy dense, wet forests in southeastern Australia that are not usually inhabited by the common brushtail.

Cuscuses are rain forest dwellers, and species often have restricted geographical ranges, either confined to islands or to the highlands of mountain ranges. Most widespread is the common spotted cuscus, found in a range of rain forest habitats throughout New Guinea below an elevation of 1,200m (4,000ft), and also on many islands and on Australia's northeastern tip; this species seems able to persist near large centers of human population. Four geographically isolated subspecies are

FACTFILE

CUSCUSES AND BRUSHTAIL POSSUMS

Order: Diprotodontia

Family: Phalangeridae

27 species in 6 genera

DISTRIBUTION Australia, New Guinea, and adjacent islands W to Sulawesi and E to the Solomon Islands. Common brushtail possum introduced to New Zealand; Common and Spotted cuscuses introduced to many of the islands adjacent to New Guinea.

HABITAT All types of forest and woodland: rain forest, moss forest, mangrove, tropical, and temperate eucalypt forest and woodland, arid and alpine woodland.

SIZE Head–body length ranges from 34cm (13.4in) in the Small Sulawesi cuscus to 61cm (24in) in the Bear cuscus; **tail length** from 34cm (13.4in) to 58cm (22.8in), and **weight** from about 0.9kg (2lb) to 10kg (22lb), both in the same two species.

COAT Short, dense, gray (Scaly-tailed possum); long, woolly, gray to black (brushtail possums); long, dense, white to black or reddish brown, some species with spots or dorsal stripes (cuscuses).

DIET Leaves, flowers, fruits, seeds, shoots, insects, occasionally small vertebrates and birds' eggs.

BREEDING Gestation lasts 16–17 days in brushtail possums

LONGEVITY Up to 13 years (17 or more in captivity)

CONSERVATION STATUS The Telefomin and Black-spotted cuscuses are currently listed as Endangered, and the Rothschild's and Stein's cuscuses as Vulnerable. Three other cuscus and possum species are ranked Lower Risk, Near Threatened.

See species box ▷

currently recognized, and they exhibit considerable variation in color and size. The common spotted cuscus is remarkable in that there is a distinct color dimorphism between males and females: the males have large, irregular, chocolate brown spots on a creamy white background, whereas the females lack the spots – indeed, in one subspecies they are pure white. Two other members of the genus, the Admiralty Island and black-spotted cuscuses, are the only other phalangers with color dimorphism of the sexes.

The scaly-tailed possum inhabits very rugged, rocky country, with eucalypt forest and rain forest patches, in the remote Kimberley region of northwestern Australia. The last two-thirds of its tail is naked, prehensile, and rasplike, while the hands and feet have greatly enlarged apical pads as an adaptation to life among the rocks.

Of the nine mainland New Guinea cuscuses, the geographical ranges of some species overlap, whereas others fall within more or less exclusive (allopatric) altitudinal zones. These allopatric

⬤ *Above* *Brushtail possum and cuscus species: 1 the gray or northern common cuscus (Phalanger orientalis) lives in New Guinea; 2 Spotted cuscus (Spilocuscus maculatus); 3 the scaly-tailed possum (Wyulda squamicaudata) – only discovered in 1917; 4 Common brushtail possum (Trichosurus vulpecula).*

species all belong to the genus *Phalanger*, are very similar in body size (2.4–3.5kg/ 5.3–7.7lb) and habits, and are apparently unable to coexist. The restriction of Stein's cuscus, for example, to only a narrow altitudinal band of 1,200–1,500m (about 4,000–5,000ft), has been attributed to competition from the northern and southern common cuscuses, which occur abundantly below 1,200m (4,000ft), and the mountain and silky cuscuses, which occur at altitudes above 1,400m (4,600ft). In localities where the two highland species are absent, Stein's cuscus has been found up to 2,200m (7,200ft).

Where two species do overlap, they usually differ in size or habits. The ground cuscus, of the genus *Phalanger*, has the widest altitudinal range of all cuscuses, being found from sea level to 2,700m (8,900ft). It is heavier (at 4.8kg /7.0lb) than its congeners, is less arboreal, and has a more frugivorous diet.

Both species of *Spilocuscus* found on the mainland of New Guinea – the common spotted cuscus (6.0kg/8.2lb) and the black-spotted cuscus (6.6kg/8.8lb) – are heavier than the members of the genus *Phalanger*. They are confined to low altitudes below 1,200m (4,000ft), and cohabit

Cuscuses and Brushtail Possums

Cuscuses
4 genera, 21 species

Cuscuses Genus *Phalanger*, 13 species: Gebe cuscus (*P. alexandrae*), Mountain cuscus (*P. carmelitae*), Ground cuscus (*P. gymnotis*, formerly in *Strigocuscus*), Eastern common cuscus (*P. intercastellanus*, formerly in *P. orientalis*), Woodlark cuscus (*P. lullulae*), Blue-eyed cuscus (*P. matabiru*), Telefomin cuscus (*P. matanim*), Southern common cuscus (*P. mimicus*), Gray cuscus or Northern common cuscus (*P. orientalis*), Ornate cuscus (*P. ornatus*), Rothschild's cuscus (*P. rothschildi*), Silky cuscus (*P. sericeus*), Stein's cuscus (*P. vestitus*)

Spotted cuscuses Genus *Spilocuscus*, 4 species: Admiralty Island cuscus (*S. kraemeri*, formerly subspecies of *S. maculatus*), Common spotted cuscus (*S. maculatus*); Waigeou cuscus (*S. papuensis*, formerly subspecies of *S. maculatus*), Black-spotted cuscus (*S. rufoniger*)

Plain cuscuses Genus *Strigocuscus*, 2 species: Sulawesi dwarf cuscus (*S. celebensis*), Banggai cuscus (*S. pelengensis* formerly in *Phalanger*)

Bear cuscuses Genus *Ailurops* 2 species: Talaud bear cuscus (*A. melanotis*), Sulawesi bear cuscus (*Ailurops ursinus*)

Brushtail possums
2 genera, 6 species

Brushtail possums Genus *Trichosurus*, 5 species: Common brushtail (*T. vulpecula*), Short-eared possum (*T. caninus*), Mountain brushtail possum (*T. cunninghami*), Coppery brushtail (*T. johnstonii*), Northern brushtail (*T. arnhemensis*)

Scaly-tailed possum (*Wyulda squamicaudata*)

○ **Left** *A mountain brushtail possum feeding on eucalyptus leaves. This species is both nocturnal and arboreal and nests in tree hollows; the main elements of its diet are leaves, flowers, and young shoots.*

◑ **Right** *A white form of the spotted cuscus. Mainly inhabiting rain forest, it is active at night and tree-dwelling; the diet of the spotted cuscus comprises leaves, fruit, and flowers.*

with both the ground cuscus and one or other of the common cuscuses. The two *Spilocuscus* species may sometimes be found in the same districts; however, the black-spotted cuscus inhabits primary forest only, whereas the common spotted cuscus lives in a much broader range of habitats, including secondary forest.

Living Off Leaves
DIET

Most species are nonspecialist leaf eaters, but their relatively generalized dentition allows them to consume a wide range of foods – fruit or blossom, along with the occasional invertebrate, egg, or small vertebrate. The common brushtail possum's diet reflects its wide geographical distribution; in some areas up to 95 percent consists of eucalypt leaves, but usually a mix of tree species leaves is taken. In tropical woodland up to 53 percent of the diet may be made up of leaves of the Cooktown ironwood, which are extremely toxic to domestic stock such as cattle. In habitat modified for pasture up to 60 percent of its diet is pasture species, while in suburban gardens it has developed an unwelcome taste for rose buds. The brushtail relies on hindgut microbial activity to extract nutrients from its food, and the large cecum and proximal colon enable food to be retained for relatively long periods. Some cuscuses show evidence of particle sorting in

the cecum, which suggests that they have a more specialized leaf diet than the brushtail.

The ground cuscus is the most frugivorous phalangerid, with up to 90 percent fruit in the diet of captive animals. Its highly expandable stomach, well-developed pyloric sphincter, and long small intestine are all consistent with delaying the passage of food through the foregut to enable the digestion of lipids from the high fruit diet. Female ground cuscuses have even been reported to carry fruit back to the den in their pouches by local New Guineans.

A Scent-based Bush Telegraph
SOCIAL BEHAVIOR

Phalangerids are generally solitary, but with a well-organized spatial system based primarily on olfactory communication. The common brushtail possum actively uses four scent glands. Males, and to a lesser extent females, wipe secretions from mouth and chest glands on the branches and twigs of trees, especially den trees, and deposit sinuous urine trails, containing cells from a pair of paracloacal glands, on branches. These advertise both the presence and the status of the marker to other individuals. When a possum is distressed it produces a sticky, pungent secretion from a second pair of paracloacal glands; this is possibly used as an appeasement signal by low-status individuals. Estrous females produce a copious, gelatinous secretion from the cloaca that becomes smeared on branches and may advertise their readiness to mate.

Little is known about scent marking in cuscuses and the scaly-tailed possum, but the sternal and paracloacal glands are generally present, and males of the common spotted cuscus smear the sticky secretion from the paracloacal glands on branches. When distressed, the common spotted cuscus secretes a reddish brown substance on the bare skin of its face, particularly round the eyes.

Brushtail possums are one of the most vocal of marsupial genera, and many of their calls are audible to humans at up to 300m (1,000ft). They have about seven basic calls: buccal clicks, agonistic grunts, hisses, loud screeches, alarm chatters, very soft appeasement calls given by the male, and juvenile contact calls; a cartilaginous laryngeal resonance chamber, about the size of a pea and unique to the genus, presumably enhances the repertoire. Cuscuses and the scaly-tailed possum are not noted for their vocal repertoire, although

buccal clicks, hisses, grunts, and screeches are reported, and the female common spotted cuscus has a call, when in estrus, like the bray of a donkey.

Common brushtails are generally solitary, except when they are breeding and rearing young. By the end of their third or fourth year, individuals establish small exclusive areas centered on one or two den trees within their home ranges, which they defend against individuals of the same sex and social status. Individuals of the opposite sex or lower social status are tolerated within the exclusive areas. Even though the home ranges of males (3–8ha/7.5–20 acres) may completely overlap the ranges of females (1–5ha/2.5–12.4 acres), individuals almost always nest alone, and overt interactions are rare. Territoriality appears to break down in some tropical populations, because Aboriginal hunters may extract up to six individuals from the same hollow tree.

Females defend an individual distance of 1m (3.3ft) against the approach of a male. During courtship a consort male overcomes the female's aggression by repeatedly approaching her and giving soft appeasement calls, similar to those of juveniles. In the absence of a consort male, several males may converge on a female at the time of estrus, and mating is accompanied by considerable agonistic behavior. After mating, the male takes no further interest in the female and is not involved in the raising of the young.

Defence of den trees suggests that preferred nest sites are in short supply. Because few offspring (only 15 percent) die before weaning, relatively large numbers of independent young enter the population each year. These young use small, poor-quality dens, and up to 80 percent of males and 50 percent of females die or disperse within their first year.

Females begin to breed at 1 year and produce 1–2 young annually after a gestation period of 16–18 days. In temperate and subtropical Australian populations, 90 percent of females breed in the fall (March–May), but up to 50 percent may also breed in spring (September–November). In the less seasonal tropics, breeding appears to be continuous, with no seasonal peak of births. Only one young is born at a time, and the annual reproductive rate of females averages 1.4. Population density varies with habitat, from 0.4 animals per hectare (1 per acre) in open forest and woodland to 1.4 per ha (3.5/acre) in suburban gardens and 2.1 per ha (5.2/acre) in grazed open forest.

◗ **Right** The silky cuscus is found in the mountains of central and eastern New Guinea; they generally inhabit areas of tropical forest at altitudes above 1400m (4600ft). They are heavily built and possess a strong prehensile tail, which assists them in the trees. As is clearly evident here, the end portion of the tail lacks hair and is instead covered with scales. Insects, eggs, and small vertebrates are eaten, but the bulk of their diet is composed of leaves and fruits.

◖ **Left** A common brushtail possum carrying young on its back; the young leave the pouch after about five months, with weaning occurring within the next couple of months. Their prospects are not promising, with high numbers being lost during the dispersal period. Common brushtail possums have long been hunted for their fur in Australia and were introduced to New Zealand specifically for this purpose. However, dramatic falls in the price of pelts reduced numbers taken for the fur trade.

The mountain brushtail has a different strategy, associated to a more stable habitat. Far from being solitary, males and females appear to form long-term pair-bonds. In this species, mortality among the young is greatest before weaning (56 percent); about 80 percent survive each year after becoming independent. Females begin to breed at 2–3 years, produce at most only one young in the fall of each year, and reproduce at an annual rate as low as 0.73. The young are weaned at 8 months, as opposed to 6 for the common brushtail, and they disperse at 18–36 months (7–18 for the common brushtail). Population density is 0.4–1.8 per hectare (1–4.5/acre).

The scaly-tailed possum bears a single young, and its social strategy is closer to that of the common brushtail possum. Little is known about the pair relationship in cuscuses, but in the ground cuscus the male follows the female prior to mating and attempts to sniff her head, flanks, and cloaca; he may also utter soft, short clicks. The only

in Victoria and New South Wales, while in Queensland it frequently raids banana and pecan crops. The common brushtail also damages pines, and in Tasmania is believed to damage regenerating eucalypt forest.

A potentially much more serious problem is that the common brushtail may become infected with bovine tuberculosis. This discovery, made in New Zealand in 1970, led to fears that brushtails may reinfect cattle. Although a widespread and costly poisoning program was set up, infected brushtails remain firmly established.

More positively from the economic point of view, the common brushtail has long been valued for its fur. The rich, dense fur of the Tasmanian form has found special favor, and between 1923 and 1959 over 1 million pelts were exported. Exports from New Zealand have also grown rapidly (see box). In eastern Australia, however, the last open season on possums was in 1963, although in Tasmania the common brushtail is still subject to control measures in agricultural areas. Although the common brushtail is considered to be secure, there is a worrying trend of populations crashing in eucalypt woodlands over much of northern and inland Australia.

Cuscuses have long been valued by traditional hunters for their coats and meat, which are sold in local markets. Four cuscuses with restricted ranges or restricted habitats are now considered threatened by overhunting or habitat clearing. The black-spotted cuscus is particularly susceptible to hunting with firearms as it sleeps exposed on a branch; for the other three – the Telefomin, Stein's, and Rothschild's cuscuses – habitat clearing is the major threat. The conservation status of many other cuscuses is not known, but without protective measures the continued survival of the susceptible mainland species and the numerous island forms will be gravely threatened.   JW/CRD

phalangerid in which the female is known to take a proactive role in courtship is the common spotted cuscus; at 28-day intervals, assumed to coincide with estrus, she calls throughout the night, which excites males.

Most cuscuses also bear a single young, the exceptions being the two common cuscuses, for which twins are the norm. Long-term pair-bonding may only occur in the bear cuscus, the largest and most diurnal of the phalangerids. Male common spotted cuscuses may use sight in determining territoriality, since they are reputed to use daytime sleeping perches that provide clear views of neighboring rivals.

Pelts or Pests?
CONSERVATION AND ENVIRONMENT
The brushtail possums are of considerable commercial importance, in both a negative and a positive sense. On the downside, the mountain brushtail causes damage in exotic pine plantations

A MARSUPIAL INVADER: THE COMMON BRUSHTAIL IN NEW ZEALAND

When the first Australian common brushtail possums were imported to New Zealand around 1840, it was hoped that they would form the basis of a lucrative fur industry. The venture was manifestly successful. Aided by further importations until 1924 and by the freeing of captive-bred animals, populations increased prodigiously, so that sales of pelts became an important source of revenue.

However, the blessings of this marsupial invader are mixed. As well as carrying bovine tuberculosis (see above), the possum has been shown to have subtle but potentially damaging effects on the indigenous vegetation. New Zealand forest trees evolved in the absence of leaf-eating mammals, and, unlike the Australian eucalypts that produce poisonous oils and phenols, the leaves of most species are palatable and lack defenses against predators. When first introduced to particular New Zealand forests, the possums rapidly exploited the new food source, increasing in population density to up to 50 animals

per ha (120/acre) – some 25 times more than in Australia. By the time numbers had stabilized at 6–10 per ha (15–25/acre), trees such as ratas and konini had all but disappeared from many areas, and possums were turning their attention to less favored species.

Possums hasten tree death by congregating on individual trees and almost completely defoliating them. These normally solitary creatures evidently abandon their social inhibitions when food is abundant – and, in contrast to their Australian kin, the New Zealand possums occupy small (1–2ha/2.5–5 acre) and extensively overlapping home ranges.

The final verdict on possum damage is unclear. Young individual ratas and other exploited tree species are appearing in many localities, but they now seem to be distasteful to possums. Presumably possums are conferring a selective advantage on unpalatable trees, and so continue, subtly but surely, to alter the structure of the forest.   CRD

Ringtails, Pygmy Possums, and Gliders

tHE RINGTAIL POSSUMS, GLIDERS, AND PYGMY *possums of Australia and New Guinea inhabit a wide range of environments, including forest, shrubby woodland, and even (in the case of the mountain pygmy possum) alpine upland. Formerly included with the brushtail possums and cuscuses in the family Phalangeridae, they are now divided into four separate families. Although these families may appear superficially similar to one another, the differences between them in external form, internal anatomy, physiology, patterns of genetic variability, and the biochemistry of blood proteins are in fact as great as those between the kangaroos and the koala.*

When the Australian continent was invaded some 40–60 million years ago by primitive, possumlike marsupials, it was blanketed in a wet, misty, and humid rain forest. Opening of these forests in the mid-to-late Tertiary (32–35 million years ago) and their gradual replacement by the marginal eucalypt and acacia forests that now grow there forced this early fauna to seek refuge in the high-altitude regions of northern Queensland and Papua New Guinea, where the ringtail possums radiated to form a diverse family of leaf- and fruit-eating specialists. At the same time, the new nectar-, gum- and insect-rich Australian eucalypt and wattle (*Acacia*) forests provided many niches for the pygmy possums, feeding predominantly on nectar and insects, and the petaurid gliders, which fed on sap and gums. This diversification has led to remarkable convergences of form, function, and behavior with the arboreal lemurs, bush babies, monkeys, and squirrels of other continents.

The mountain pygmy possum adopted an alternative strategy to the arboreal habits of the other possums and gliders, retreating to a cool, alpine environment, where it became ground dwelling and inhabited rock deposits formed by periglacial activity. The mountain pygmy possum is the only Australasian small mammal to undergo deep, seasonal hibernation under snow cover for up to seven months of the austral winter.

Fitted for the Forests
FORM AND FUNCTION

The ringtail possums and gliders, and most pygmy possums, are predominantly arboreal, with handlike feet, an enlarged, opposable big toe on the hindfoot, and a range of adaptations suited to moving through wooded environments. In nongliding species, the tail is prehensile, and may be used for grasping branches and transporting nest material; a naked undersurface effectively increases friction. In gliders (but not the feathertail glider) the tail is heavily furred and either straight or tapering; it may be used for controlling the direction of flight. Gliding species are specialized for rapid movement in open forest and are thought to have evolved independently in three families during the mid-to-late Tertiary. In the eight species of gliders that survive today, gliding is achieved by use of a thin, furred membrane (patagium) that stretches from fore- to hindlimbs (wrist to ankle in the sugar glider, wrist to knee in the feathertail), increasing surface area in flight to form a large rectangle. It is retracted when not in use and may be seen as a wavy line along the side of the body. The effective surface area has also been increased by a lengthening of the arm and leg bones, and some species cover distances exceeding 100m (330ft) in a single glide, from the top of one tree to the butt or trunk of another. The heavier greater glider, with a reduced (elbow-to-ankle) gliding membrane, descends steeply with limited control, but the smaller gliders are accomplished acrobats that weave and maneuver gracefully between trees, landing with precision by swooping upwards. What appears to be a gentle landing to the human eye is in fact shown by slow-motion photography to be a high-speed collision. The animals bounce backward after impact and must fasten their long claws into the tree trunk to avoid tumbling to the ground. The fourth and fifth digits of the hand are elongated and have greatly enlarged claws that assist clinging after the landing impact.

Leaves, Insects, Sap, and Nectar
DIET

There are four major dietary groups of possums and gliders – folivores, sapivores and gumivores, insectivores, and nectarivores. All are nocturnal and have large, protruding eyes. Most are also quiet, secretive, and hence rarely seen. The only audible sign of their presence may be the "plop" of larger gliders landing on tree trunks, the yapping alarm call of the sugar glider, or the screeching or gurgling call of the yellow-bellied glider. Ringtail possums are generally quiet but occasionally emit soft twittering calls. The greater glider is totally silent, emitting only a quiet grumbling sound when being handled. Most possum species (except the greater glider) make loud screaming and screeching calls when attacked or handled.

Ringtail possums and the greater glider together form a highly specialized group (Family Pseudocheiridae) of arboreal leaf eaters (folivores), characterized by an enlargement of the cecum to form

▶ **Right** *A Herbert River ringtail displays the tightly-curled tip of the long, prehensile tail that gives these animals their common group name. Increased logging in Queensland is threatening this species' habitat.*

▶ **Inset** *Only 8cm (3in) long, a feathertail glider grooms itself on a branch. Also known as the pygmy glider, this species is the smallest marsupial capable of gliding, achieving flights of more than 50m (165ft).*

FACTFILE

RINGTAILS, PYGMY POSSUMS, & GLIDERS

Order: Diprotodontia

Families: Pseudocheiridae, Burramyidae, Petauridae, Acrobatidae

35 species in 13 genera

DISTRIBUTION SE, E, N, and SW Australia, Tasmania, New Guinea, offshore islands of New Guinea.

HABITAT Forests, woodland, shrublands, heathland, alpine heathlands

SIZE Head–body length ranges from 6.4cm (2.5in) in the Little pygmy possum to 33–38cm (13–15in) in the Rock ringtail possum; tail length from 7.1cm (2.8in) to 20–27cm (7.9–10.6in), and weight from 7g (0.2oz) to 1.3–2kg (2.9–4.4lb), both in the same two species.

FORM Coat gray or brown, with paler underside; often darker eye patches or forehead or back stripes (particularly in species feeding on plant gums); tail long, well-furred (in most gliders), prehensile, and part naked, or featherlike.

DIET Ringtails and gliders are primarily folivorous, although they also eat fruit; other species are more omnivorous, also including insects, larvae, spiders, scorpions, and small lizards in their diet.

BREEDING Gestation period 12–50 days; all young weigh less than 1g (0.035oz) at birth.

LONGEVITY 4–15 years (generally shorter in pygmy possums with large litters, and longer in ringtails and large gliders with single young).

CONSERVATION STATUS Four species are classified as Endangered, and five as Vulnerable.

See families box ▷

a region for microbial fermentation of the cellulose in their highly fibrous diet. Fine grinding of food particles in a battery of well-developed molars with crescent-shaped ridges on the crowns (selenodont molars) enhances digestion. Rates of food intake in these groups are slowed by the time required for cellulose fermentation, and nitrogen and energy is often conserved by slow movement, relatively small litter sizes (averaging 1–1.5 young), coprophagy (reingestion of feces), and adoption of medium to large body size (0.2–2kg/0.4–4.4lb). The preferred diet of the greater glider of eastern Australia is eucalypt leaves. The quantities of nutrients in these leaves vary substantially between different tree species, and this is a major factor underpinning the patchy patterns of distribution and abundance of the greater glider through the eastern Australian forests.

The five species of petaurid glider and Leadbeater's possum (all of the Family Petauridae) are specialist plant-exudate (sap and gum) feeders. Arthropods, pollen, and occasionally the green seeds of acacias are also eaten, providing an important source of protein. The petaurid possums and gliders are small-to-medium in size (70–650g/2.5–21oz). The most primitive member of the group, Leadbeater's possum, is virtually restricted to moist, high-altitude montane eucalypt forests, where it feeds on wattle or acacia gums, insects, and insect exudates. By incising notches in the bark of trees, the possum enhances gum production. Wattle gum is also a principal food of the sugar glider, and the species may travel hundreds of meters across open pasture to obtain it.

The sugar glider, which is distributed from Tasmania to northwest Australia and Papua-New Guinea and neighboring islands, also exploits the sap of eucalypts by incising the bark and licking up the sweet, carbohydrate-rich exudates. Such sap-feeding sites are highly prized and may be vigorously defended by chasing and biting intruders. Eucalypt sap also appears in the diet of the rare and highly endangered mahogany glider in the far northeast of Queensland. Like most other petaurid gliders, this species consumes gum exudates from acacia trees as well as insects. The diet of the

mahogany glider can also include gum tapped from the floral spears of grass trees. Eucalypt sap feeding has developed to an extreme in the yellow-bellied glider of eastern Australia, which cuts large notches into the bark of many tree species. The form of these notches varies from deep, V-shaped incisions to long strips of ruffled bark, depending on the eucalypt species that is tapped.

Although a minor component of their diet, pollen and insects are an important protein source for all members of the Petauridae. A high carbohydrate-to-nitrogen ratio in their diet provides additional energy for activity and territorial defense but has limited reproductive potential, and so births are restricted to seasons of insect abundance. The coats of the gum-feeding gliders and possums are characterized by a distinct black dorsal stripe. This is thought to camouflage them when they are feeding – the time when they are most vulnerable to predation by forest owls.

With Leadbeater's possum, the strikingly colored black-and-white striped possum and trioks are the nongliding members of the Petauridae. In a

Ringtail, Pygmy Possum, and Glider Families

Ringtail possums
Family Pseudocheiridae

17 species in 6 genera in 3 subfamilies.
Subfamily Pseudocheirinae: 10 species in 3 genera:
1 species of *Pseudocheirus,* Common ringtail (*P. peregrinus*), SE, E, N, SW Australia, Tasmania, New Guinea, and West Irian; 8 species of *Pseudochirulus*, including several poorly known New Guinea taxa such as the Weyland ringtail (*P. caroli*) and Pygmy ringtail (*P. mayeri*); 1 species of *Petropseudes,* the Rock-haunting ringtail (*P. dahli*) from N Australia.
Subfamily Heibelinidae: 2 species in 2 genera; the Greater glider (*Petauroides volans*) from E Australia, and the Lemuroid ringtail (*Hemibelideus lemuroides*) from NE Queensland, Australia.
Subfamily Pseudochiropsinae: 5 species in the genus *Pseudochirops*; including Green ringtail (*P. archeri*), D'Alberti's ringtail (*P. albertisii*), and the Plush-coated ringtail (*P. corinnae*) are both classed as Vulnerable.

Pygmy possums
Family Burramyidae

5 species in 2 genera: pygmy possums (4 species of *Cercartetus*), including the Eastern and Southwestern pygmy possums (*C. nanus* and *C. concinnus*), Tasmania, Kangaroo Island, SE, E, NE, SW Australia, New Guinea; Mountain pygmy possum (*Burramys parvus*), SE Australia. The Mountain pygmy possum is Endangered.

Gliders
Family Petauridae

11 species in 3 genera: 6 species of *Petaurus* (Tasmania, SE, E, N, NW Australia, New Guinea), including Yellow-bellied or Fluffy glider (*P. australis*), Squirrel glider (*P. norfolcensis*), Mahogany glider (*P. gracilis*), Sugar glider (*P. breviceps*), and two species confined to New Guinea – the Northern glider (*P. abidi*) and *P. biacensis*. The Petauridae also contain the monotypic genus *Gymnobelideus* (Leadbeater's possum, *G. leadbeateri*, Victoria) and four species of *Dactylopsila* (the Striped possum and the trioks). The Striped possum (*Dactylopsila trivirgata*) occurs in both NE coastal Queensland and New Guinea; the remaining three species (*D. megalura, D. palpator,* and *D. tatei*) are confined to New Guinea or adjacent offshore islands. The Mahogany glider, Leadbeater's possum, and Tate's triok are classed as Endangered; the Northern glider, and the Great-tailed triok (*P. megalura*) are Vulnerable.

Feathertail glider and Feathertail possum
Family Acrobatidae

2 species in 2 genera: Feathertail or Pygmy glider or Flying mouse (*Acrobates pygmaeus*), SE to NE Australia; Feathertail possum (*Distoechurus pennatus*), New Guinea.

For full species list see Appendix ▷

classic case of convergent evolution, the striped possum and the trioks, like skunks, emit a distinctive, musty odor that is particularly strong in the long-fingered triok from New Guinea. The four species are medium sized and are specialized for exploiting social insects, ants, bees, termites, and other wood-boring insects in the tropical lowland rain forests of northern Queensland and New Guinea. A suite of adaptations aids in the noisy extraction of insects from deep within wood crevices – feeding activity may produce a shower of woodchips. These adaptations include an extremely elongated fourth finger (like that of the aye-aye of Madagascar; see Primates: Strepsirrhines), an elongated tongue, and enlarged and forward-pointing upper and lower incisors.

Pygmy possums of the genus *Cercartetus* and the feathertail or pygmy glider form a fourth group that has diversified in the nectar-rich sclerophyllous Australian heathlands, shrublands, and eucalypt forests. Despite the small size of the feathertail glider, it is nevertheless highly mobile; the species can glide for distances exceeding 50m (165ft), often spiraling from high in the tree canopy toward the ground like a falling leaf before settling in a flowering shrub. The brush-tipped tongue of the feathertail glider is used for sipping nectar from flower capsules, and the small size

(under 35g/1.2oz) and extreme mobility of all five species increase nectar harvesting rates. In poor seasons, aggregations of many individuals may be found on isolated flowering trees and shrubs. Most species take insects and the abundant pollen available from flowers to provide protein. The eastern pygmy possum occasionally eats soft fruits and seeds. The combination of small size and abundant dietary nitrogen permit unusually large litter sizes (4–6), and rapid growth and development rates similar to those of the carnivorous marsupials. The other member of the pygmy possum group, the feathertail possum of Papua New Guinea, has a tail like that of the feathertail glider but is larger (50–55g/1.8–1.9oz) and has no gliding membrane. Its diet includes insects, fruit, and possibly plant exudates.

For its spring and summer diet, the mountain pygmy possum depends largely on bogong moths (*Agrotis infusa*) and other invertebrates. Huge numbers of these moths migrate to the mountains in spring. As bogong moths become scarce, fleshy fruits and seeds from heathland plants become increasingly important. The remarkable sectorial premolar tooth is adapted for husking and cracking seeds. Excess seeds may be cached for use during periods of winter or early spring shortage.

Smaller Size, Larger Nesting Groups
SOCIAL BEHAVIOR

Mountain pygmy possums have only one litter of four young per year, following snowmelt. This is an adaptation to the short, alpine summer and the need for both adults and young to gain sufficient fat reserves to enable them to survive the long period of winter hibernation.

Most Australian possums and gliders nest or den in cavities in large, old living or dead trees, although sometimes other types of nest sites are occupied, such as bark strips or fallen logs. The common ringtail possum can build a stick nest or drey, but in cold subalpine or seasonally hot woodland environments hollow trees are used in favor of dreys. Individuals of all hollow-using possums and gliders have den sites in many different trees and will often swap between them on a regular basis. The entrance to the hollow is typically just large enough to permit the entry of the occupant, but small enough to preclude predators and other species that may attempt to usurp the use of the cavity.

Patterns of social organization and mating behavior in possums and gliders are remarkably diverse, but to some extent predictable from species' body size and diet. The larger folivorous ringtail possums and the greater glider are often solitary; by day they sleep singly or occasionally in pairs in tree hollows or vegetation clumps, emerging to feed on foliage in home ranges of up to 3ha (7.4 acres) at night. Male home ranges of the greater glider are generally exclusive but may partially overlap those of one or two females. The occupation of exclusive home ranges by males and of overlapping home ranges by females is associated with a greater mortality of subadult males and a consequent female-biased sex ratio.

The tendency toward gregariousness increases with decreasing body size, the yellow-bellied glider forming nesting groups of up to five individuals, the common ringtail of eastern Australia up to six, the sugar glider up to 12, and the feathertail glider up to 25. Most nesting groups consist of mated pairs with offspring, but the feathertail glider and the petaurids may form truly mixed groups with up to four or more unrelated adults of both sexes (in the sugar glider), one male and one or several females (the yellow-bellied glider), or one female and up to three males (Leadbeater's possum). The chief reason for nesting in groups is thought to be improved energy conservation through huddling during winter. In one species, the sugar glider, large nesting groups disband into smaller units during summer. The aggregation of females during the winter enables dominant males to monopolize access to up to three females in the petaurid gliders, and a harem defense mating system prevails.

An entirely different mating system occurs in Leadbeater's possum. Individual females occupy large nests in hollow trees and actively defend a surrounding territory of 1–1.5ha (2.5–3.7 acres) from other females. Mating is usually monogamous, and male partners assist females in defense of territories. Additional adult males may be tolerated in family groups by the breeding pairs but adult females are not, and an associated higher female mortality results in a male-biased sex ratio. This pattern appears to be associated with the construction of well-insulated nests, avoiding the necessity for females to huddle together during winter, and with the occupation of dense, highly productive habitats in which food resources are readily defensible and surplus energy is available to meet the cost of territorial defense.

The mating patterns of some possum and glider species can be somewhat flexible, varying spatially and temporally depending on the availability and quality of food and other resources like den sites. For example, small, low-density populations of the greater glider that occupy eucalypt forests with low levels of foliage nutrients appear to be predominately monogamous. In contrast, higher-density populations in more nutrient-rich forest types maintain a polygamous mating system. The patterns of social organization, group size, and mating systems of Leadbeater's possum and the yellow-bellied glider may also change over time depending on, for example, year-by-year differences in the availability of food.

Selective pressures exerted during competition for mating partners have led to the prolific development of scent-marking glands in the petaurids, for use in marking other members of the social group. Leadbeater's possum, the most primitive member, shows the least development of special scent glands, and scent marking between partners involves the mutual transfer of saliva to the tail base with its adjacent anal glands. Sugar glider males, in contrast, possess forehead, chest, and anal glands. Males use their head glands to spread scent on the chest of females, and females in turn spread scent on their heads by rubbing the chest gland of dominant males. Male yellow-bellied gliders have similar glands, but scent transfer is achieved quite differently, by rubbing the head gland against the female's anal gland. Females in turn rub their heads on the anal gland of the dom-

⬥ Above *Dwarfed by their dinner, a pair of Tasmanian pygmy possums (Cercartetus lepidus) prepare to feed on nectar from a Banksia flower.*

inant male. Such behavior probably facilitates group cohesion by communicating an individual's social status, sex, group membership, and reproductive position.

In contrast to the small gliders, pygmy possums of the genus *Cercartetus* appear mainly solitary. Usually only lactating females share nests with their young, although several males may share a nest, sometimes with a nonlactating female. Mountain pygmy possums seem more social, with sedentary females forming kin clusters in high-quality habitats and sometimes sharing nests with nondependent, apparently related females. Nest sharing among males is common, and home ranges overlap. Although they are not sexually

dimorphic, female eastern and mountain pygmy possums may be behaviorally dominant. Mountain pygmy possum males leave the habitat of females after breeding and spend the winter in slightly warmer habitats, with more northerly and westerly aspects and lower elevations. It is still not clear whether the resulting sexual segregation during the nonbreeding season is a result of female aggression, or is simply a reproductive strategy.

The optimal temperature for hibernation in males is slightly higher than in females, and they arouse more frequently during winter and finish hibernation earlier in spring. This provides them with a reproductive advantage, because they can undergo spermatogenesis and be ready to breed. Because male survival is often lower than for females, sex ratios are frequently female-biased, especially in high-quality habitats. Pygmy possums generally have relatively short lifespans

world's tallest flowering plant and one of Australia's most valued timber-producing trees. Standing beneath such forest giants provides the most reliable method of catching a glimpse of a Leadbeater's possum, as the animals emerge at dusk from their family retreats in hollow tree trunks to feed. Less than 45 years after its rediscovery, however, the possum is once again threatened with extinction through a combination of inappropriate forest management and natural collapse of the large dead trees that provide nest sites in regrowth forests (in 1939 a fire devastated two-thirds of Victoria's mountain ash forests).

The mahogany glider was first described in 1883, but was misidentified at the time as a squirrel glider. Careful examination of specimens from the Queensland Museum subsequently revealed that gliders from a tiny coastal area in the far north of Queensland were, in fact, different in size, tail length, and a number of other particulars from the squirrel glider. The species has a highly restricted distribution and is confined to open woodlands and adjacent paperbark swamps. Most potentially suitable habitat has been destroyed, and the survival of the species continues to be threatened by land clearance, particularly for the establishment of sugar cane and banana crops.

The mountain pygmy possum was described from fossil remains in 1896 and was thought to be extinct until 1966, when one turned up in a ski lodge in the Victorian alps. Since it was believed that all pygmy possums were arboreal and nested in tree hollows, it was reasoned the animal must have been brought to the alps in a load of firewood. Searches were made in the forests at lower elevations, but to no avail. In 1970, however, another animal was trapped in rocky heath under snow gum woodland at the interface of the sub-alpine and alpine zones on the Kosciuszko plateau of New South Wales. This directed attention back to the ski lodge in Victoria, where trapping in the surrounding rocky heath quickly resulted in the capture of three animals. The following year, 11 animals were trapped well above the tree line on Mt Kosciuszko, the highest mountain on the Australian mainland (2,228m/7,300ft). Since then, intensive research has been conducted on the mountain pygmy possum. Not coincidentally, because of their requirements for high-elevation sites with good snow cover, the largest local populations all occur within ski-resort concession areas. Here, they are threatened by ski runs and general tourist development. An increasingly apparent and much less easily managed threat is that of increasing temperatures and receding snow cover resulting from global warming.

The survival of Leadbeater's possum, the mahogany glider, and the mountain pygmy possum – all of which are nationally endangered – is critically dependent upon effective government action, which is not yet forthcoming in the case of the latter two species.   DL/LB

(less than 3 years), but eastern pygmy possums have been known to live for more than 6 years. Mountain pygmy possums are remarkably long-lived, with females living for up to 12 years. This is probably a result of their relatively stable environment, single reproductive effort, larger size, and long periods of hibernation.

Back from the Dead
CONSERVATION AND ENVIRONMENT
The story of the discovery, apparent extinction, and subsequent rediscovery of three widely divergent species typifies the plight of the pygmy possums and gliders. In all cases, human pressure for land use is now once more placing their continued survival under threat.

Just after nightfall one evening in 1961, in the wet, misty mountains just 110km (70mi) from Melbourne, the attention of a fauna survey group from the National Museum of Victoria was caught by a small, bright-eyed, alert gray possum leaping nimbly through the forest undergrowth. Its size at first suggested a sugar glider, but the absence of a gliding membrane and the narrow, bushy, club-shaped tail led to the exciting conclusion that this was the long-lost Leadbeater's possum. This rare little possum is one of the State of Victoria's faunal emblems, and was first discovered in 1867 in the Bass River Valley. Only six specimens were collected, all prior to 1909, and in 1921 it was concluded that the destruction of the scrub and forest in the area had resulted in the complete extermination of the species. Surveys following the rediscovery, however, led to its detection at some 300 separate sites within a 3,600sq km (1,400sq mi) area. Its preferred habitat is Victoria's Central Highland forests, which are dominated by the majestic mountain ash (*Eucalyptus regnans*), the

Kangaroos and Wallabies

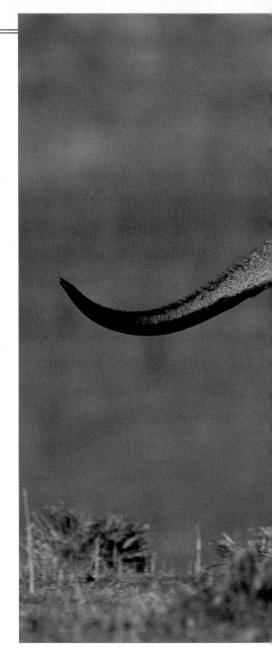

r ED KANGAROOS BOUNDING ACROSS THE *arid saltbush plains are one of the quintessential images of Australia. Yet the red is just one among a diverse array of about 69 recent species of kangaroos, wallabies, and rat kangaroos that make up the superfamily Macropodoidea. Desert-adapted, grass-eating kangaroos such as the red have in fact evolved only in the last 5–15 million years. Before then, Australasia was forested, and the ancestors of all macropods were forest-dwelling browsers.*

The suborder Macropodiformes takes its name from *Macropus*, the genus of the red kangaroo. The word means "big foot" in Latin, and long hindfeet do indeed characterize the animals. They are the largest mammals to hop on both feet, a very special gait for a large mammal. Even so, hopping is not the only way that kangaroos get about.

The Mechanics of Hopping
FORM AND FUNCTION

All macropods are furry-coated, long-tailed animals, with thin necks, prominent ears, and strongly developed hindquarters that make the forelimbs and upper body look small. A long, narrow pelvis supports long and muscular thighs; the even more elongate shin bones are not heavily muscled and end in an ankle that is adapted to prevent the foot from rotating sideways (so that the kangaroo cannot twist its ankle while

hopping). At rest and in slow motion, the long but narrow sole of the foot bears the animal's weight, making it in effect plantigrade. When hopping, however, macropods rise onto their toes and the balls of their hindfeet. Only two of the toes, the fourth and fifth, are in fact load bearing; the second and third are reduced to a single, tiny stump equipped with two claws that are used exclusively for grooming.

The first toe is entirely lost except in the musky rat kangaroo, the only surviving member of the primitive Hypsiprymnodontidae family. Short-faced kangaroos in the genus *Procoptodon* shed the fifth toe, too. *Procoptodon* went extinct 15–25,000 years ago at the peak of the last ice age, possibly as a result of human-lit fires and hunting, but rock paintings record its distinctive footprints. Limb-lengthening and toe reduction characterize many lineages of mammalian, terrestrial herbivores – they include horses among the perissodactyls and deer, antelopes, and pronghorns among the artiodactyls – that evolved speed to avoid running predators. In these and many other ways, macropods illustrate convergence for lifestyle between eutherian and metatherian mammals.

Macropods do not only hop; they also crawl on all fours when moving slowly, with the pairs of fore- and hindlimbs moving together rather than alternately. In medium and large macropodine species, the tail and the forelimbs take the animal's weight while the hindfeet are lifted and swung forward. This gait is called "pentapedal" (literally, five-footed). In the larger macropodines the tail is long, thick, and muscular, and the animal sits up by leaning back on it like a sportsman on a shooting stick; it can even briefly be the only means of support during fighting.

In smaller wallabies and rat kangaroos, the tail's major function is for balance and maneuvering, for instance as an aid in abrupt cornering. Most rat kangaroos also use the tail to carry nesting material; grasses or twigs are gathered into a bundle and pushed backward with the hindfeet against the underside of the tail, which curls over, holding the bundle against the rat kangaroo's rump as it hops away to the half-built nest.

In contrast to the hindlimbs, macropods' forelimbs are relatively small and unspecialized. The forepaws have five equal, strongly clawed digits set around a short, broad palm. Rat kangaroos dig for their food with elongate second to fourth digits with long claws. Macropods' forepaws can grasp and manipulate food plants; they also serve to grip the skin, hold open the pouch, or scratch the fur while grooming. The larger macropods also

Top left A swamp wallaby browses on foliage. *Despite the name, the species is found in open upland forests as well as in marshy regions and heathlands.*

use their forelimbs in thermoregulation, licking saliva onto the inner surface of the limb, where it evaporates, cooling blood in a network of vessels that lie just below the skin's surface.

At speeds slower than about 10km/h (6mph), hopping is at best an ungainly way of moving, but above 15–20km/h (9–12mph) it is extremely energy-efficient – more so than four-footed trotting or galloping. At the end of each bound, energy is stored in the tendons of the bent hindlegs, contributing to the next driving extension. Like the rider of a spring-loaded pogo stick, the kangaroo needs only to add a little extra energy in order to keep hopping. Yet hopping probably originated as a way of startling predators by making an explosive burst from cover, a strategy retained by the smaller kangaroos, which conceal themselves in vegetation, and the rat kangaroos, which hide in nests. That explosive burst requires long, strong,

FACTFILE

KANGAROOS AND WALLABIES

Order: Diprotodontia

Families: Macropodidae, Potoroidae, and Hypsiprymnodontidae

76 species in 16 genera

DISTRIBUTION
Australia, New Guinea; introduced into Britain, Germany, Hawaii, and New Zealand.

HABITAT Wide-ranging, from deserts to rain forests.

SIZE Head–body length ranges from 28.4cm (11.2in) in the Musky rat kangaroo to 165cm (65in) in the male Red kangaroo; **tail length** from 14.2cm(5.6in) to 107cm (42in), and **weight** from 0.5kg (1.2lb) to up to 95kg (200lb), both in the same two species.

COAT Macropod fur, mostly 2–3cm (0.8–1.2in) long, is fine, dense, and not sleek. Colors range from pale gray through various shades of sandy brown to dark brown or black.

DIET Mostly plant foods, including grasses, forbs, leaves, seeds, fruit, tubers, bulbs, and truffles; also some invertebrates, such as insects and beetle larvae.

BREEDING Gestation 30–39 days; newborn attach to a maternal teat within a pouch and remain there for a further 4–11 months.

LONGEVITY Variable according to species and conditions; larger species may attain 12–18 years (28 years in captivity), the smaller rat kangaroos 5–8 years.

CONSERVATION STATUS 2 hare wallabies and 2 wallabies are now listed as Extinct. Gilbert's potoroo is Critically Endangered. A further 9 species and subspecies of kangaroos and wallabies are Endangered, while 12 others are Vulnerable.

See families box ▷

Below Red kangaroos fighting. Before a fight two males may engage in a "stiff-legged" walk **1** in the face of the opponent, and in scratching and grooming **2**, **3**, standing upright on extended rear legs. The fight is initiated by locking forearms **4** and attempting to kick the opponent to the ground **5**.

Above With a baby, or joey, safely secured in her pouch, a female eastern gray kangaroo goes foraging in an Australian reserve. At full speed, large kangaroos can travel at over 55km/h (35mph).

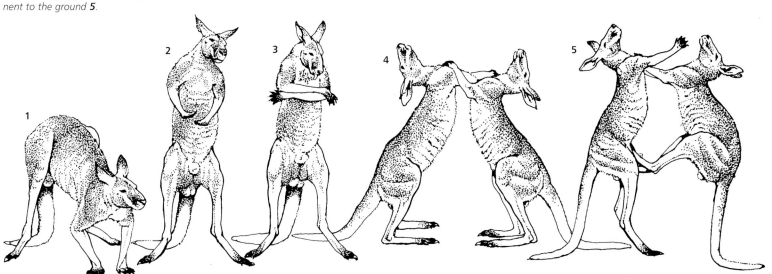

synchronized hindlimbs, and initiates a bounding gait. Large kangaroos can sustain hopping speeds faster than 55 km/h (35mph), and small species can manage bursts of over 30 km/h (20mph).

Some macropods are adapted to bounding up narrow ledges on near-vertical cliffs and even to climbing trees. Rock wallabies have rather broad hindfeet with nonslip soles, and long, bushy tails to help them keep their balance as they escape. Tree kangaroos find refuge high up in the rain forest. They climb by grasping the trunks with huge, heavily clawed forepaws on the ends of long, strong arms, and pushing upward on short, broad feet that grip the trunk or branches. Their tails are not prehensile. They descend awkwardly, tail first, but are able to jump short distances from tree to tree. When climbing or even moving along branches, their hindlimbs move synchronously – a remnant of their long-gone deerlike gait. Nevertheless, they can move them alternately (as all macropods do when forced to swim or while adjusting their stance).

Macropods' limbs, paws, and feet also function as weapons. Rat kangaroos and small wallabies fight by kicking out as they jump at each other, or else by grappling, rolling on the ground biting and scratching. They sometimes kill opponents with their hindfeet. The large kangaroos remain more

upright, wrestling with the forelimbs around the opponent's head, shoulders, and neck, and kicking with the powerful hindlimbs (the tail briefly taking the animal's weight), driving the large toes hard into the opponent's belly. The shoulders and forearms of males of larger kangaroo species are longer and more muscular than those of the females, and male forepaws are more heavily clawed. Males also grow a shield of thickened skin over the belly – more than twice as thick as on the flanks or shoulders – that helps absorb the impact of kicks to the gut.

Macropods have heads that superficially resemble those of deer or antelopes, with moderately long muzzles, wide-set eyes with some binocular vision, and upright ears that can be rotated to catch sounds from all directions. The upper lip is "split" like that of a hare or a squirrel.

The muzzles, teeth, and tongues of macropods are suited to taking small food items rather than large mouthfuls of food. Most macropods pluck single items, even blades of grass, one at a time. Behind the split upper lip lies an arc of incisor teeth surrounding a fleshy pad at the front of the palate. In macropodine kangaroos and wallabies, the two procumbent (horizontally set) lower incisors hold leaves against the fleshy pad while they are ripped off along the edge of the upper incisor arc. In potoroine rat kangaroos and the banded hare wallaby, the only living sthenurine, the lower incisors occlude with the second and

third upper incisors, while the central (first) upper incisors protrude and are used for gnawing.

Potoroine rat kangaroos' distinctive premolars form serrated blades to cut the tough and fleshy food that constitutes their diet (mainly plant storage organs or fungal fruiting bodies). Small macropodines have similarly sectorial, persistent premolars; but larger kangaroos shed their unspecialized premolars, opening the way for the molar teeth, which erupt sequentially at the back of the jaw, to migrate forward, being shed as they wear out. This adaptation to an abrasive diet (mainly of grasses) parallels that of elephants. Macropods with persistent premolars do not show molar progression, and all four erupted molars in each half jaw are in wear simultaneously.

Macropods can use their forepaws to handle or dig up food. This ability is most advanced in the potoroines, most of which depend to a large

⊙ Right *One of two remaining hare wallaby species, the rufous hare wallaby is itself listed as vulnerable, surviving on two islands off Western Australia.*

⊙ Below *Representative species of the larger kangaroos and wallabies:* **1** *Red kangaroo (Macropus rufus);* **2** *Wallaroo (Macropus robustus) with young in pouch;* **3** *Bridled nail-tailed wallaby (Onychogalea fraenata);* **4** *Red-legged pademelon (Thylogale stigmatica);* **5** *Whiptail or pretty-faced wallaby (Macropus parryi) in motion;* **6** *Goodfellow's tree kangaroo (Dendrolagus goodfellowi) resting on a branch.*

extent on digging up underground food items. However, even the largest kangaroos pull plants toward them with their paws, and use their "hands" to remove unwanted plant parts from their mouths.

Macropod digestion is aided by a forestomach enlarged to form a fermentation chamber. Longitudinal and transverse bands of muscles (haustrations) in the stomach wall contract to stir the stomach contents. A moderate-sized small intestine opens into an enlarged cecum and proximal colon, presumably a site for secondary fermentation, beyond which digested food flows through a long, water-resorbing distal colon.

The gut resembles that of some eutherian foregut fermenters, although the macropod stomach has not developed the compartmentalization of form and function to the same extent. The suite of bacteria, ciliate protozoa, and anaerobic fungi found in the stomachs of macropods performs the same functions as in ruminants, but the component species are quite different. Macropods may be less limited by poor-quality food than, for example, sheep. Some macropods recycle urea to help cope with low protein availability.

Macropod fur ranges in color from pale gray to dark brown or black. Many macropods have indistinct dark or pale stripes that visually break their outline: down the spine, across the upper thigh, behind the shoulders, or (most commonly) below or through the eye. The paws, feet, and tail are often darker than the body, and the belly is usually paler, making the animals appear "flat" in the dusk or by moonlight. In a few rock wallabies and tree kangaroos, the tail is longitudinally or transversely striped.

Males of some larger species are more boldly colored than the females; for example, the russet neck and shoulder coloring may be stronger in male red-necked wallabies. Male red kangaroos are mostly sandy red, while the females are blue gray or sandy gray. But the dimorphism is imperfect; some males may be blue gray and some females red. The sexes' colors are fixed from the time they first show hair, rather than being acquired under a hormonal surge at or after puberty as in many dimorphic ungulates.

Many macropod males spread scented secretions from the skin of the throat and chest onto trees (especially the tree kangaroos), rocks (rock wallabies), or bushes and tussocks of grass (large kangaroos). They may also rub the scent on females during courtship, indicating to other males their association. Other glands within the cloaca add their scent to the urine or feces.

All over Australia
DISTRIBUTION PATTERNS

The single extant Hypsiprymnodontidae species, the musky rat kangaroo, is confined to rain forests on the eastern side of Australia's Cape York peninsula. In contrast, the Macropodidae are represented by species of the Macropodinae subfamily all over Australia, in New Guinea, and on offshore islands; but the Potoroinae rat kangaroos (10 recent species) are confined to Australia (including Tasmania and other southern islands), and are rare in the tropical north. Two macropodine genera, *Dorcopsis* and *Dorcopsulus*, are confined to New Guinea; 8 of the 12 *Dendrolagus* tree kangaroos, and one of the seven *Thylogale* pademelon species, also occur only there. Just two species, the red-legged pademelon and the agile wallaby, occur in both Australia and New Guinea. Feral macropod populations occur in a few countries outside Australasia: brush-tailed rock wallabies in Hawaii; red-necked wallabies in England's Pennine hills and in Germany; and both those species plus Tammar and Parma wallabies in New Zealand.

Genera of macropodines that are restricted to the rain forest include *Dorcopsis* and *Dorcopsulus*, and the *Dendrolagus* tree kangaroos. Pademelons

are also associated with wet, dense forests, including eucalypt forests; they occur from New Guinea down the east of Australia to Tasmania. Except for the weakly social tree kangaroos, these forest-dwelling macropodines are solitary.

Hare and nail-tailed wallabies occur in arid and semiarid habitats including spinifex grassland, shrubland, savanna, and light woodland, and are confined to Australia. So are rock wallabies, which are found in habitats ranging from the arid zone of central, western, and southern Australia to rain forest habitats in the tropics. Yet their habitat always contains boulder piles, rocky hillsides, or clifflines to provide secure diurnal refuges.

The rich *Macropus* genus is almost confined to Australia. Its species occur in habitats ranging from desert to the edges of wet eucalypt forest, all characterized by grasses in the understory. The potoroines are confined to Australia. Potoroos occur in rain forest, wet sclerophyll forest, and scrub, always with dense understory. The bettongs are creatures of the open forest, woodland, and savanna, often with a grassy understory. The desert rat kangaroo used to occur in lightly-vegetated desert.

Macropod communities in Australia used to contain 5–6 sympatric species in the arid and semiarid regions, but as many as a dozen in broken woodland and forested country along the Dividing Range. Rain forest communities rarely exceed four species.

From Grass to Truffles

DIET

The musky rat kangaroo eats fleshy fruits and fungi and also regularly takes insects; in addition, it sometimes scatter-hoards seeds, although we do not know how efficient it is at finding them again. Macropodids depend on plants, although some of the smaller species (especially potoroines) will also eat invertebrates such as beetle larvae. Potoroos and bettongs feed largely on the underground storage organs of plants – swollen roots, rhizomes, tubers, and bulbs – and in addition eat the underground fruiting bodies (truffles) of some fungi, playing an important role in dispersing their spores (see A Mutually Beneficial Relationship).

Small macropodine wallabies that occupy dry habitats, including the hare and nail-tailed species, feed selectively on growing leaves of grasses and forbs, augmented with seeds and fruits. In mesic, forested habitats, macropodine diets include more fruits and dicot leaves, and these dominate the diets of tree kangaroos, swamp wallabies, and pademelons. Many macropodines feed opportunistically and seasonally from a large range of plant species and parts. *Macropus* species tend to have diets dominated by grass leaf, and also select seedheads of grasses and other monocots; and the largest kangaroos may rely entirely on grasses.

The smallest macropods tend to be highly selective in their feeding habits, seeking out scattered, high-quality food items, many of which have to be carefully sought and processed. In contrast, the largest species generally tolerate a lower-quality diet taken from a wide range of plant species, selecting mainly leaves but also some higher-value seeds and fruits.

Mobs and Loners

SOCIAL BEHAVIOR

At birth juvenile macropods are tiny, measuring just 5–15mm (0.2–0.6in); they look embryonic, with undeveloped eyes, hindlimbs, and tail. Using its strong forelimbs, the newborn infant will climb unaided up the mother's fur and into her forward-opening pouch. There it clamps its mouth onto one of four teats, remaining attached for many weeks of development – from 150–320 days, depending on species. The pouch provides a warm, humid environment for the juvenile, which cannot yet regulate its own temperature and can lose moisture rapidly through its hairless skin.

Once the juvenile has detached from the teat, the mother in many larger species will allow it out of the pouch for short walkabouts, retrieving it when she moves. She will prevent it from returning to the pouch just before the birth of her next young, but it will continue to follow her about as a dependent young-at-foot, and can put its head into the maternal pouch to suck the teat. The quality of milk provided changes as the joey matures, and a mother suckling a juvenile in the pouch at the same time as a young-at-foot will

---

Kangaroo and Wallaby Families

Family Macropodidae

Subfamily Macropodinae

Kangaroos, Wallaroos, and Wallabies Genus *Macropus*, 14 species: Red kangaroo (*M. rufus*); Eastern gray kangaroo (*M. giganteus*); Western gray kangaroo (*M. fuliginosus*); Wallaroo (*M. robustus*); Woodward's wallaroo (*M. bernardus*); Agile wallaby (*M. agilis*); Antilopine kangaroo (*M. antilopinus*); Red-necked wallaby (*M. rufogriseus*); Black-striped wallaby (*M. dorsalis*); Tammar wallaby (*M. eugenii*); Whiptail or Pretty-faced wallaby (*M. parryi*); Toolache wallaby (*M. greyi*); Western brush wallaby (*M. irma*); and Parma wallaby (*M. parma*). The Toolache wallaby is now listed as Extinct by the IUCN; the Black wallaroo and the Parma and Western brush wallabies are Lower Risk, Near Threatened.
Tree kangaroos Genus *Dendrolagus*, 12 species: Grizzled tree kangaroo (*D. inustus*); Bennett's tree kangaroo (*D. bennettianus*); Lumholtz's tree kangaroo (*D. lumholtzi*); Matschie's or Huon tree kangaroo (*D.matschiei*); Lowland tree kangaroo (*D. spadix*); Doria's tree kangaroo (*D. dorianus*); Dingiso (*D. mbaiso*); Tenkile (*D. scottae*); Ursine tree kangaroo (*D. ursinus*); Goodfellow's tree kangaroo

(*D. goodfellowi*); Golden-mantled tree kangaroo (*D. pulcherrimus*), Seri's tree kangaroo (*D. stellarum*). 11 *Dendrolagus* species are listed by the IUCN; Goodfellow's, Matschie's, and the Tenkile tree kangaroos are Endangered. Doria's and Dingiso tree kangaroos are Vulnerable.
Rock wallabies Genus *Petrogale*, 16 species including: Yellow-footed rock wallaby (*P. xanthopus*); Brush-tailed rock wallaby (*P. penicillata*); Proserpine rock wallaby (*P. persephone*); Black-flanked rock wallaby (*P. lateralis*); Cape York rock wallaby (*P. coenensis*); monjon (*P. burbidgei*); nabarlek (*P. concinna*); and Mount Claro rock wallaby (*P. sharmani*). Seven species are listed, including the Proserpine rock wallaby as Endangered, and the Brush-tailed rock wallaby, which is Vulnerable.
Hare wallabies Genus *Lagorchestes*, 4 species: Spectacled hare wallaby (*L. conspicillatus*); Lake Mackay hare wallaby (*L. asomatus*); Eastern hare wallaby (*L. leporides*); and Rufous hare wallaby or mala (*L. hirsutus*). The Eastern and Lake Mackay hare wallabies are now listed as Extinct by the IUCN; the Rufous hare wallaby is Vulnerable, while the Spectacled hare wallaby is

Lower Risk, Near Threatened.
Pademelons Genus *Thylogale*, 7 species: Red-necked pademelon (*T. thetis*); Red-legged pademelon (*T. stigmatica*); Tasmanian pademelon (*T. billardierii*); Brown's pademelon (*T. browni*); Calaby's pademelon (*T. calabyi*); Mountain pademelon (*T. lanatus*); and Dusky pademelon (*T. brunii*). The Dusky, Mountain, and Brown's pademelons are Vulnerable. Calaby's pademelon is Endangered.
Nail-tailed wallabies Genus *Onychogalea*, 3 species: Bridled nail-tailed wallaby (*O. fraenata*); Northern nail-tailed wallaby (*O. unguifera*); and Crescent nail-tailed wallaby (*O. lunata*). The Crescent nail-tailed wallaby is now listed as Extinct by the IUCN; the Bridled nail-tailed wallaby is Endangered.
Dorcopsises Genus *Dorcopsis*, 4 species: White-striped dorcopsis (*D. hageni*); Gray dorcopsis (*D. luctuosa*); Brown dorcopsis (*D. veterum*). Black dorcopsis (*D. atrata*) is Endangered.
Forest wallabies Genus *Dorcopsulus*, 2 species: Small dorcopsis (*D. vanheurni*); Macleay's dorcopsis (*D. macleayi*) is Vulnerable.
Quokka *Setonix brachyurus*. Vulnerable.
Swamp or **Black wallaby** *Wallabia bicolor*.

Subfamily Sthenurinae (Sthenurines)

Banded hare wallaby *Lagostrophus fasciatus*. Listed as Vulnerable by the IUCN.

Family Potoroidae

Bettongs Genus *Bettongia*, 4 species: Brush-tailed bettong or woylie (*B. penicillata*); Burrowing bettong or boodie *B. lesueur*; Northern bettong (*B. tropica*); and Eastern bettong (*B. gaimardi*). All 4 species are listed by the IUCN: the Northern bettong is Endangered, and the Burrowing bettong is Vulnerable.
Potoroos Genus *Potorous*, 4 species: Long-nosed potoroo (*P. tridactylus*); Long-footed potoroo (*P. longipes*); Broad-faced potoroo (*P. platyops*) and Gilbert's potoroo (*P. gilbertii*). Gilbert's potoroo is Critically Endangered, the Long-footed potoroo Endangered. Broad-faced potoroo is Extinct.
Desert rat kangaroo *Caloprymnus campestris* Listed as Extinct by the IUCN.
Rufous rat kangaroo *Aepyprymnus rufescens*.

Family Hypsiprymnodontidae

Musky rat kangaroo *Hypsiprymnodon moschatus*.

Below A red-necked wallaby and her young relax in the Tasmanian sun. Mothers bear a single young, but the short interval between births means that they often end up rearing an infant in the pouch while still continuing to feed an older offspring that has reached the "young-at-foot" phase.

produce different qualities of milk from the two teats – a feat achieved by having each mammary gland under separate hormonal control.

The musky rat kangaroo may give birth to litters of two or even three young, but all macropodids produce only one young at a birth. Few are strictly seasonal breeders; most can conceive and give birth at any time of year. In almost all species gestation lasts a few days short of the length of the estrus cycle – generally 4–5 weeks in macropodines and 3–4 weeks in potoroines.

Giving birth to such small babies is relatively effortless; the female sits with her tail forward between her legs and licks the fur between her cloaca and pouch, producing a path that will keep the climbing neonate moist until it enters the pouch. A few days after giving birth many macropods enter estrus once more. If they are mated and conceive, the new embryo's development halts at an unimplanted blastocyst stage. That embryonic diapause lasts until about a month before the current pouch young is sufficiently developed to quit the pouch. Then the blastocyst implants in the uterus and resumes development. A day or two before birth is due, the mother will exclude the previous young from the pouch, a rebuff that is difficult for it to accept as it has been taught to come when called and to climb back into the pouch. The mother then cleans and prepares the pouch for the next juvenile. Thus many macropod females can simultaneously support a suckling young-at-foot, a suckling pouch young, and a dormant or developing embryo.

The short interval between births allows females to quickly replace young-at-foot that are killed by predators. It also permits them to easily replace "aborted" pouch young. A female that is hard-pressed by a dingo may relax the sphincter muscles closing the pouch, dropping her young to get eaten while she escapes. Under the nutritional stress of drought a pouch young will also die, but will quickly be replaced by the dormant blastocyst, which is stimulated to implant and resume development as soon as the previous pouch young's suckling stops. At relatively low metabolic cost, a female in drought can maintain a succession of embryos ready to develop as soon as rains break and conditions turn favorable.

The young-at-foot phase comes to an end when the juvenile is weaned; it lasts many months in the large kangaroos, but may be almost absent in small rat kangaroos such as the rufous bettong. Similarly, large kangaroos grow through a prolonged subadult phase before breeding. Females of the large kangaroos begin breeding at 2–3 years, when they have reached half their full size, and may breed for 8–12 years. Some small rat kangaroos can conceive within a month of weaning, at 4–5 months, but may delay until 10–11 months.

Macropod males may mature physiologically soon after the females, but in larger kangaroos their participation in reproduction is socially inhibited. Female growth decelerates after they begin breeding, but male growth continues strongly, resulting in old males being very much bigger than younger males and females. Indeed, a female eastern gray or red kangaroo, in estrus for the first time and weighing as little as 15–20kg (33–44lb), may be courted and mated by a male five or six times her own weight. The large macropods exhibit some of the most exaggerated sexual size dimorphism known for terrestrial mammals, largely because the biggest male in the population gets the majority of the matings. In contrast, males and females of the smaller wallabies and rat kangaroos reach the same adult sizes.

With the exception of females accompanied by dependent young, most macropods are solitary or are found occasionally with one or two others.

Potoroines shelter alone during the day in a self-made nest, which a female may share with her unweaned young-at-foot. At night, when she emerges to forage, the female may be found and escorted by a male. In the nights before estrus, several males may attempt to associate with her.

Burrowing bettongs nest in self-dug burrows that form loose colonies, but they too are not truly social. The solitary macropodines that do not use permanent refuges (mostly smaller species living in dense habitat) behave much like potoroines, but association between a female and her most recent offspring may last many weeks beyond weaning. On the day of estrus, a female may be escorted by a chain of ardent males.

◑ **Left** *The musky rat kangaroo (Hypsiprymnodon moschatus) is a taxonomic oddity. Unlike all other kangaroos, which belong to the Macropodidae family, it is the sole representative of the Hypsiprymnodontidae. Its most distinctive anatomical feature is the presence of a first toe, lost in all other macropod species.*

◐ **Below** *Representative small- and medium-sized kangaroos and wallabies:* **1** *Proserpine rock wallaby (Petrogale persephone);* **2** *Yellow-footed rock wallaby (P. xanthopus);* **3** *Burrowing bettong or boodie (Bettongia lesueur);* **4** *Quokka (Setonix brachyurus);* **5** *Banded hare wallaby (Lagostrophus fasciatus);* **6** *Rufous rat kangaroo (Aepyprymnus rufescens). Several of these species are now listed by the IUCN as being at risk: the Proserpine rock wallaby is considered endangered; the quokka and burrowing bettong are vulnerable. The banded hare wallaby mainland subspecies is extinct and the island subspecies is vulnerable. Similarly, the boodie inland mainland subspecies is extinct and two island subspecies are vulnerable.*

Rock wallabies shelter during the day in caves and boulder piles, features that are clustered in the landscape, with the result that colonies of the animals inhabit clusters of daytime refuges. Individuals persistently use the same refuges, and males compete to keep other males away from the refuges of one or more females. In some rock wallaby species, males may consort closely with one or more females during the day, although they will not always forage together. A male tree kangaroo may similarly guard access to the trees used by one or a few females with which he associates.

Some of the largest *Macropus* species form groups (often called "mobs") of 50 or more animals. Membership of these groups is extremely flexible, however, with individuals joining and leaving several times a day. Some sex- and age-classes tend to associate with their peers or with specific other classes. Individual females may also associate with their female kin or with particular unrelated females; this association is frequent and persistent but not permanent. However, the stage of development of a female's young determines her association patterns; females with young about to be excluded from the pouch avoid others at the same stage by retreating to a part of their range generally not much used by other kangaroos, in order to stop the young from becoming confused during this period of rejection.

Males in these species move between groups more frequently than do females, and also move over larger ranges. No males are territorial, nor do any attempt to keep others out of a group of females. Males range widely, inspecting as many females as possible by sniffing the cloaca and urine tasting. If a male detects a female approaching estrus, he will attempt to consort with her, following her about and mating her when she enters estrus. However, he can be displaced by any larger and more dominant male.

In the medium and large macropods, hierarchical position, based largely on size and thus upon age in these persistently growing animals, is the principal factor in male reproductive success. In the eastern gray kangaroo, a locally dominant male may obtain up to a half of all matings within his home range. He will usually be able to hold top rank for one year only, however, and may have waited 8–10 years to reach that position. Most males never mate, and very few reach the top of the hierarchy. But those that do may father 20–30 offspring, or even more in dense populations.

In contrast, all females are likely to give birth to about one young a year throughout their adult lives. Among eastern gray kangaroos, the chances of the young surviving to adulthood are strongly

affected by the number of female relatives a mother has. Those with many female kin are much more likely to rear their own young, and especially their first, successfully through the young-at-foot period, the time of major mortality. In eastern gray kangaroos, the survival rate is 35 percent for the offspring of mothers whose own mother was still alive at the time of the birth, but only 8 percent if the mother had died. The chances of the first two joeys – baby kangaroos – surviving without a "grandmother" or "aunt" to assist in parenting is just 12 percent, rising to 25 percent when there is a grandmother but no aunts and to 42 percent when there are also one or more aunts.

Extraordinarily, these benefits seem to have translated into a maternal strategy of giving birth to females early in life, while sons are born correspondingly late in a female's breeding career. In eastern grays the ratio is about 1 daughter to 0.8 sons for the first two offspring, rising to 1 daughter to 1.3 sons in mid career and to 1 daughter to 2.9 sons in the final offspring.

The larger, social macropods all live in open country (grasslands, shrublands, or savanna), and were formerly preyed upon by cursorial and aerial predators such as dingoes, wedge-tailed eagles, and the now-extinct thylacine. Social grouping has conferred the same antipredator benefits on large kangaroos as on so many other animals, in that

dingoes are less able to get close to large groups, which can thus spend more time feeding. Group size of kangaroos relates to their density, the kind of habitat – especially its lateral cover – the time of day, and the weather.

Pests and Prey
CONSERVATION AND ENVIRONMENT

Between 2 and 6 million red, eastern, and western gray kangaroos and common wallaroos are shot every year in Australia because they are considered pests of pasture and crops. The cull is licensed, regulated, and for the most part humane. These large species were less numerous when Australia was first settled by Europeans, and from 1850–1900 several scientists feared that they might go extinct. Provision of pasture and of well-distributed water for sheep and cattle, together with (particularly) the reduction in numbers of dingoes, their main natural predators, as well as of hunting by Aboriginal peoples, all allowed the kangaroos to flourish.

Kangaroos used to be the main prey for Aboriginal hunters. Smaller wallabies were flushed by fire or driven into nets or else toward lines of hunters armed with spears and throwing-sticks. In New Guinea, they were once pursued with bows and arrows, but are now killed with firearms instead. In some areas commercial hunting is rapidly

○ Above *A kangaroo relaxes with her young in a refreshing pool of water. Large kangaroos mostly keep cool by resting in the heat of the day, coming out to feed at twilight or by night.*

depleting densities and endangering tree kangaroos and other restricted species.

In most of Australia outside the rain forest and wet sclerophyll forest, densities of macropod species with an adult weight of less than 5–6kg (11–13lb) have fallen during the last hundred years. On the mainland, several such species are now extinct or very severely limited in range outside the tropics, although some have survived on offshore islands. The extinctions have been caused by a combination of habitat clearing for (or modification by) introduced livestock and, most especially, the impact of foxes. Introduced for sport in Victoria from 1860–1880, foxes spread rapidly through sheep country, living primarily on rabbits, but taking as secondary prey bettongs and wallabies, which plummeted in numbers. On fox-free islands these species survived.

Where foxes have been suppressed, such species (if still present) have recovered their former densities. However, foxes, rabbits, and land-clearing are still widespread, and the battle to save small- and medium-sized macropods in Australia is not yet won. PJ

A MUTUALLY BENEFICIAL RELATIONSHIP

How rat kangaroos help cultivate the fungi they feed on

ON THE ROOTS OF MOST VASCULAR PLANTS LIVE fungi. The two symbiotically provide for each other; the plant supplies carbohydrate food, while the fungi enhance the uptake by the plant of nutrients (especially phosphorus) and of moisture from the soil. Associations of this sort between plants and fungi are known as mycorrhizal symbiosis, and they represent a very ancient liaison found in practically all terrestrial ecosystems.

Eucalyptuses typically have very high levels of mycorrhizal association, as Australian soils tend to be poor and deficient in phosphorus. So crucial is this relationship that foresters attempting to re-create natural forest must inoculate the trees with mycorrhizal fungi to ensure success. The fungi that associate with eucalypts are of two kinds. Some are mushrooms that produce fruiting bodies above ground and have spores dispersed by the wind; many others, however, fruit below ground. These hypogeous (subterranean) fungi are similar in many respects to European truffles; like them, they release delicious smells that attract mammals to dig them up and eat the fruiting bodies. The spores survive their passage through the mammals' digestive tracts, and germinate after being deposited on the ground in feces. They may, however, first be carried for quite long distances in the mammals' gut, so this is an effective means of dispersing spores throughout the forest.

For some species of fungus, passage through the digestive tract actually seems to stimulate the germination of spores. The "spore rain" produced by mammals is presumably important in maintaining the mycorrhizal association on mature root systems at a high level, as well as in rapidly establishing mycorrhizal fungi on the root systems of seedlings. Living on trees and dispersed by mammals, the fungi are a central link in the forest ecological web.

There are many willing takers for the proffered fungal delights. In Australia, the rat kangaroos (bettongs and potoroos) that live in eucalypt forests feed almost exclusively on these fungi. These animals will dig as deep as 20cm (8in) into the soil to find truffles, and in captivity they prefer freshly collected truffles over any other food. There are other species of mammals in eucalypt forests – bandicoots and many rodents – that feed on hypogeous fungi, but the fact that rat kangaroos eat fungi year-round and harvest fruiting bodies in large numbers must make them especially efficient spore dispersers.

In addition to promoting the reproduction of mycorrhizal fungi, rat kangaroos may also be responsible for protecting their diversity. It is common to find 20 or more different species of fungi living in stands of a single species of eucalypt, many of them on the root system of a single tree. Typically, a small number of these species are very abundant, while most are rare. Rat kangaroos are extremely adept at finding fungi of many different species; for example, a study of the long-footed potoroo showed that it was eating more than 40 species of hypogeous fungi over an area of only a few hectares, far more than even very experienced human mycologists were able to collect. In the absence of spore dispersal, the fungi would spread by growth of their hyphae – the fungal equivalent of root systems – through the soil, and those with the most vigorous growth would probably eventually displace others from the community. The fact that rat kangaroos are so effective at finding uncommon fungi and broadcasting their spores may be an important factor in keeping them healthy.

The rat kangaroos' role does not end there. Into the already complex but precisely choreographed web of life in an Australian forest comes the element of fire. Eucalypt forests are generally very fire-prone; many eucalypt species have features that encourage its spread as well as adaptations (such as stimulation of seed fall by heat and of seed germination by smoke) that link reproduction to the conflagrations. But if fires kill adult trees, this must lead to the death of their fungal associates soon after, so a mechanism is needed to ensure spore dispersal before the fungi die.

Rat kangaroos are very skilled at surviving fire. One study using radio tracking to follow brush-tailed bettongs during a hot fire showed that the animals managed to move around the flames while still remaining within their home ranges. After a fire, the rate of digging for hypogeous fungi by rat kangaroos increases dramatically, as animals in the area increase their feeding on the fungi and others move in from neighboring, unburned areas to feed over the burned ground. The result is that after a fire more fungi get dispersed, both within burned patches and from unburned to burned patches, ensuring that spores are introduced to new seedlings growing in the ashes. Thus the continuity of life is ensured.

There is a beautiful postscript to the story that brings an insect into the equation. Several dung beetle species have evolved specialized relationships with particular species of rat kangaroos. The beetles lay their eggs in dung, which their developing young subsequently eat. Unlike most such beetles, which search for fresh dung on the wing, these species cling to the fur at the base of a rat kangaroo's tail, waiting until feces are passed, when they drop off and bury them. This strategy gives the beetles first access to the feces, and the species that practice it tend to be poor competitors for dung. But the association also aids spore dispersal, providing a mechanism by which fungal spores are immediately transported close to the roots of trees, and so facilitating their germination and the reestablishment of the symbiosis.   CJ

◐ **Below** *Eastern bettongs are among the species that eat fungi and disperse their spores. Others include the northern and brush-tailed bettongs and all three species of potoroos.*

LIFE IN THE POUCH

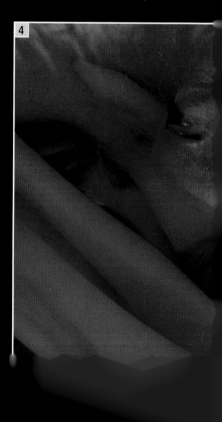

①② *What characterizes all macropods is their highly undeveloped state at birth. In comparison with the newborn of placental mammals, those of marsupials are in an almost embryonic state, with rudimentary hindlimbs and tail, ears and eyes closed, and no fur. Yet once the umbilical cord (seen left, below) breaks, the tiny infant is able to propel itself on its relatively strong forelimbs through its mother's fur to reach the safety of her pouch. The climb from birth canal to pouch will take about 2 minutes.*

③ *The teat (there are four in the pouch) fills the infant's mouth and holds it securely in place; this kangaroo is 4 weeks old. Kangaroos and wallabies suckle for 6–11 months.*

④ *By 12–14 weeks of age, a kangaroo has grown fast and acquired recognizable features. If a young kangaroo dies or is killed by predators, the mother does not need to mate again to conceive – a second, fertilized egg is immediately implanted in the uterus, and a new embryo begins development.*

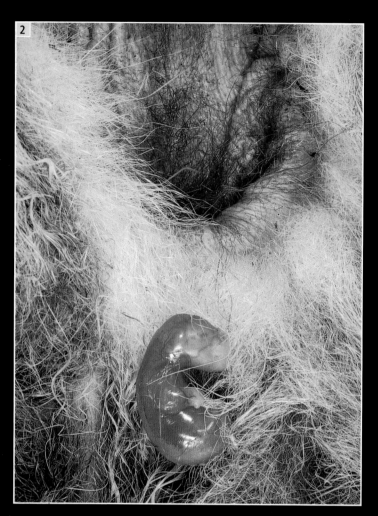

6 *An eastern gray kangaroo at the young-at-foot phase. Though it is now denied access to the pouch, it is still not weaned and will suckle for several months to come. To promote rapid growth, the walking young receives fatty milk, while the new infant inside the pouch is provided with fat-free milk. Nurturing two live young simultaneously, with an egg always ready for implantation, has proved an effective reproductive strategy for Australia's large marsupials.*

5 *Almost too large for its accommodation, a well-developed red kangaroo peers from its mother's pouch. This individual is at the stage of semi-independence, where it makes excursions outside but comes back to the pouch to sleep and suckle. It will soon be excluded for good, to make way for a newborn sibling.*

Koala

THE KOALA IS NOW AUSTRALIA'S ANIMAL ICON and one of the world's most charismatic mammals, but this has not always been the case. The first European settlers considered koalas stupid and killed millions for their pelts. Even more serious threats to the animals' survival came from the impact of forest clearance, large-scale forest fires, and the introduction of zoonotic disease, particularly domestic animal strains of chlamydia.

The threat to koalas reached a peak in 1924, when more than 2 million skins were exported. By that time, the species had been exterminated in South Australia, and had largely disappeared from Victoria and New South Wales. As a result of public outcry, bans on hunting were introduced, and intensive management, particularly in the southern populations from 1944 on, has subsequently reversed this decline. Koalas are now once more relatively common in their favored habitat.

⊙ **Below** A koala rides on its mother's back. At birth the single young is minuscule, weighing less than 0.5g (0.02oz). After 5 months it starts to feed on eucalypt leaves partly predigested by its mother. At 7 months the young leaves the pouch, but continues to travel with its mother for another 4 or 5 months.

Large Bellies, Small Brains
FORM AND FUNCTION

Trees from the genus *Eucalyptus* are widespread in Australia, and koalas are wedded to them. They spend almost their entire lives in eucalypts. Much of the day is taken up in sleeping (which occupies more than 80 percent of their time); less than 10 percent is required for feeding, and the rest is mainly spent just sitting.

Koalas display numerous adaptations for this relatively inactive, arboreal lifestyle. As they use neither dens nor shelters, their tailless, bearlike bodies are well insulated with a dense covering of fur. Their large paws are equipped with strongly recurved, needle-sharp claws on most digits, and these make the koala a most accomplished climber, able to ascend the largest smooth-barked eucalypts with ease. To climb, they grip onto the trunk with their claws and use their powerful forearms to heave upwards, while simultaneously bringing the hindlimbs up in a bounding motion. The forcipate structure of the forepaws (the first and second digits are opposable to the other three) enables them to grip smaller branches and climb into the outer canopy. They are less agile on the ground, but move frequently between trees, using a slow, quadrupedal walk.

The teeth of the koala are adapted to cope with eucalypt leaves, which are extremely fibrous. Using their cheek teeth, which are reduced to a single premolar and four broad, high-cusped molars on each jaw, they chew the leaves into a very fine paste. This digesta then undergoes microbial fermentation in the cecum, which, at 1.8–2.5m (5.9–8.2ft), is the largest of any mammal in proportion to body size, stretching three times the koala's body length or more.

The small brain of the koala may also be an adaptation for a low-energy diet. Energetically, brains are expensive organs to run as they consume a disproportionate amount of the body's total energy budget. Relative to its body size, the koala's brain is one of the smallest found in marsupials. The brain of a southern koala of average size (9.6kg/21lb)) weighs only about 17g/0.6oz (0.2 percent of body weight).

Male koalas are 50 percent heavier than females, and have a broader face, comparatively smaller ears, and a large, odoriferous sternal (chest) gland. The principal secondary sex characteristic of the females is the pouch, which contains two teats and opens to the rear.

Koalas have a broadly polygynous mating system in which some males do most of the mating, but precise details on the distribution of matings

KOALA

Phascolarctos cinereus

Order: Diprotodontia

Family: Phascolarctidae

Sole member of genus

DISTRIBUTION Disjunct in E Australia S of latitude 17°

Tropic of Capricorn

HABITAT Eucalypt forests and woodlands

SIZE Head–body length male 78cm (30.7in), female 72cm (28.3in); weight male 11.8kg (26lb), female 7.9kg (17.4lb). Animals from N of the range are significantly smaller, averaging only 6.5kg (14.3lb) for males and 5.1kg (11.2lb) for females.

COAT Gray to tawny; white on chin, chest, and inner side of forelimbs; ears fringed with long white hairs; rump dappled with white patches; coat shorter and lighter in N of range.

DIET Foliage, mainly from a limited range of eucalypt species, although leaves from some noneucalypts including *Acacia*, *Leptospermum*, and *Melaleuca* are also browsed.

BREEDING Females sexually mature at 21–24 months; single young born in summer months (Nov–March) after gestation of about 35 days. Young become independent after 12 months. Females are capable of breeding in successive years.

LONGEVITY Up to 18 years

CONSERVATION STATUS Lower Risk, Near Threatened. Common where habitat is intact, particularly in the south of its range, rarer in the north. Large-scale clearing of woodlands is threatening the northern populations.

between dominant and subdominant animals have not been comprehensively researched and await elucidation. Female koalas are sexually mature and commence breeding at 2 years of age. Males are fertile at the same age, but their mating success is usually poor until they are older, at about 4–5 years, when they are large enough to compete successfully for females.

Following the Forest

DISTRIBUTION PATTERNS

The koala is often thought of as a fragile and rare species, but in reality it tolerates a wide range of environmental conditions. The eucalypt forests on which koalas depend are widespread but fragmented, and the distribution of the animals now reflects the state of the forest.

Koala populations are often widely separated from each other, usually by extensive tracts of cleared land. Even so, they still occur across several

○ **Above** *Traveling between trees, a koala moves cautiously across the forest floor. The animals usually walk sedately, but can bound forward in emergencies.*

hundred thousands of square kilometers, stretching in a broad swathe across eastern Australia from the edge of the Atherton Tablelands in North Queensland to Cape Otway at the southernmost tip of Victoria.

Koalas occupy a surprisingly diverse range of habitats across this range. These encompass wet montane forests in the south, vine thickets in the tropical north, and woodlands in the semiarid west of their range. Their abundance varies markedly with the productivity of the habitat. In fertile, high-rainfall country in the south, abundances as high as 8 animals per hectare (more than 3 to an acre) are not uncommon, while in the semiarid zone 100 hectares (250 acres) may be required to support a single animal.

An Unpromising Food

DIET

As evergreen plants, eucalypts are a constantly available resource for leaf-eating animals. An adult koala eats about 500g (1.1lb) of fresh leaf daily, yet while there are more than 600 species of eucalypts to choose from, koalas feed from only 30 or so of these. Preferences differ between populations, with animals usually focusing on species growing in the wetter, more productive habitats. In the south *Eucalyptus viminalis* and *E. ovata* are preferred, while the northern populations feed predominantly on *E. camaldulensis*, *E. microcorys*, *E. propinqua*, *E. punctata*, and *E. tereticornis*.

Such a diet at first sight might seem unpromising. Eucalypt leaf is inedible, if not downright toxic, to most herbivores. It is low in essential nutrients, including nitrogen and phosphorus; it contains high concentrations of indigestible structural materials such as cellulose and lignin; and it is laced with poisonous phenolics and terpenes (essential oils). Recent research has shown that these last compounds may hold the key to koalas' preferences, as the acceptability of browse species has been found to correlate inversely with the concentration of certain highly toxic phenol–terpene hybrids.

The koala shows a number of adaptations that enable it to cope with such inauspicious food. Some leaves they obviously avoid altogether. Toxic components in others are detoxified in the liver and excreted. Coping with the low available energy provided by such a diet, however, requires behavioral adjustments, and koalas sleep a lot, for up to 20 hours a day. This has given rise to the popular myth that they are drugged by the eucalypt compounds they ingest. Koalas also exhibit very tight water economy and, except in the hottest weather, obtain all of their water requirements from the leaves.

Solitary and Sedentary
SOCIAL BEHAVIOR

Koalas are solitary animals. They are also sedentary, with adults occupying fixed home ranges. The size of these ranges is related to the productivity of the environment. In the more prolific forests of the south the ranges are comparatively small, with males occupying only 1.5–3ha (3.7–7.4 acres) and females 0.5–1ha (1.2–2.5 acres). In semiarid areas, however, they are much larger, and males occupy 100ha (250 acres) or more. The home range of socially dominant males overlap the ranges of up to nine females, as well as those of subadult and subordinate males.

Koalas are principally nocturnal, and in the breeding season adult males move around a great deal in the summer nights. Fights usually occur if they meet up with other adult males and matings if they encounter a receptive (estrous) female. Copulation is brief, usually lasting less than two minutes, and occurs in a tree. The male mounts the female from behind, usually holding her between himself and the branch while mating.

Females give birth to a single young, with the majority of births occurring in midsummer (December–February). The newborn animal weighs less than 0.5g (0.02oz) and climbs unaided from the urogenital opening to the pouch, where it firmly attaches to one of the two teats there. Over the next 6 months of pouch life, the young grows and develops while suckling this same teat. Weaning commences after 5 months, and is initiated by the young feeding on partially digested leaf material produced from the female's anus. The mother is able to clear the normally hard fecal pellets from the lower bowel before producing this soft material, and may be stimulated

into doing so by the young nuzzling the region. The high concentration of microorganisms in this pap is thought to inoculate the gut of the young with the microbes it needs to digest eucalypt leaf. Growth is rapid from this time onward. The young leaves the pouch after 7 months to travel around clinging to the mother's back. It becomes independent at around 11 months of age, but usually continues to live close to the mother for several months afterward.

Males bellow incessantly through the early months of the breeding season, and these calls, which consist of a series of harsh inhalations each followed by a resonant growling expiration, appear to serve both as an advertisement to potential mates as well as a warning threat to competing males. The call of one male usually elicits a response from all the adult males in the area. The only loud vocalization heard from females is a wailing distress call, usually given when they are being harassed by an adult male. At this time of the year males are often seen scent marking by rubbing their sternal gland against the trunk of trees, but the precise role of this behavior has yet to be elucidated.

When Clusters Become Crowds
CONSERVATION AND ENVIRONMENT

So far there has been no official attempt to enumerate the total population of wild koalas, but unofficial estimates range from 40,000 to more than 1 million. Genetic studies indicate strong differentiation between northern and southern populations, and suggest that there might be a

number of distinct subpopulations in the north. No such pattern has been detected among the southern populations, a fact that is thought to reflect the homogenizing effect of the extensive translocation program that has occurred there.

Habitat loss is threatening the viability of many koala populations, particularly in the northern part of their range. Urban and tourist developments are claiming important areas of habitat in coastal regions, but the situation is especially serious in the semiarid woodlands of central Queensland, where around 400,000 hectares (1 million acres) are being cleared annually for pastoral and other agricultural purposes. While environmentalists are attempting to stop this clearance, it is a politically difficult issue in the conservative farming areas of central Queensland.

Management problems in the south make koala conservation there an even more complex issue. Historically the koala has been a rare species on the mainland, but overpopulation has been a persistent problem in a few koala colonies established on offshore islands in the late 19th century. This issue has been addressed via translocations, and over the last 75 years more than 10,000 koalas have been relocated back to the mainland.

While the translocation program has reestablished the koala throughout most of its southern range, it has also transferred the problems of overpopulation and habitat degradation to many forest remnants on the mainland. Culling to control overpopulation is widely unpopular, and contraceptive methods are now being tried as a method of capping the growth of these populations. **RM**

Wombats

tHERE ARE ONLY THREE LIVING SPECIES OF *wombats, but they represent, together with the koala, one of the two great lineages of marsupial herbivores. The suborder Vombatiformes – which comprises the koala and wombats – diverged from the other marsupial herbivores at least 40 million years ago, and since then wombats have evolved a way of life that is unique among mammals.*

The wombats are large-bodied, burrowing herbivores. This combination of traits is extraordinary: the few other large mammals that burrow are either carnivores or specialized insectivores, while the numerous other burrowing herbivores are all small. Much of the interest in the biology of wombats comes from the fact that they defy the general rule which dictates that burrowing and large body size among herbivores are mutually exclusive. The time and effort required to dig a burrow are usually precluded by the need to feed constantly, in order to gain sufficient nutrition from low-energy grass or browse.

Equipment for Burrowing and Grazing
FORM AND FUNCTION
Wombats are stocky, with short tails and limbs. The pectoral girdle is heavy and strong, and the humerus is very broad relative to its length, making the shoulders and forelimbs exceptionally powerful. The forepaws are massive, and bear long, heavy claws. Wombats burrow by scratch-digging with the forepaws, throwing soil behind them with the hindfeet and using their ample rumps to bulldoze it clear of the burrow entrance. The wombat skeleton has many detailed features that increase the power of the limbs. For example, the posterior angle of the scapula (shoulder blade)

is extended to increase the lever arm for the *teres major* muscle. The male and female are similar in all species, but male northern hairy-nosed wombats have shorter bodies than females, along with thicker necks and heavier shoulders. The significance of this is unknown – perhaps their thick necks equip males for head-to-head confrontations down burrows.

Wombats feed primarily on grasses that are high in fiber and (especially on sandy soils) high in abrasive silica. The skull, teeth, and digestive tract are specially adapted to this diet. The skull is massive, broad, and flattened, allowing the jaws to exert great compressive force that is used to grind their coarse food. This compensates for the lack of a deeply furrowed rasping surface on the teeth, and enables wombats to grind their food to a very small particle size (about half that achieved by kangaroos). The teeth grow throughout life to compensate for tooth wear. The stomach and small intestine are small and simple and there is almost no cecum, but the colon is expanded and elongated, forming about 80 percent of total gut volume. Microbial fermentation takes place primarily in the colon, contributing about one-third of the total energy assimilated by the animal. Food passes slowly through the gut: particles remain there for an average of 70 hours and solutes for about 50 hours, far longer than in other similarly sized herbivores.

The Low-Maintenance Marsupial
SOCIAL BEHAVIOR
A common feature of all of the three species of wombats is their ability to maintain high population densities even in very unproductive habitats. Common wombats occur in alpine environments up to and above the snowline, as well as in sandy coastal environments where they may reach very high densities. Hairy-nosed wombats occur in dry habitats, where soil fertility may be too low to support grazing by domestic livestock.

Wombats thrive in such environments because they have extremely reduced energy requirements. The basal metabolic rates of wombats are very low – the southern hairy-nosed wombat has a rate only 44 percent of that predicted for eutherian mammals of similar mass – and their maintenance energy requirements are the lowest known for marsupials. The combination of low maintenance needs and efficient digestion of high-fiber diets means that the daily food intake of wombats is also very low – only about half that of similarly sized kangaroos. A wombat spends much less time foraging than might be expected for a

◑ Above *A common wombat mother and her offspring use a fallen tree trunk as a table for a meal of foliage. After leaving the pouch at the age of 6 months, the young may continue to follow their mothers about for as much as a year.*

◐ Above left *A southern hairy-nosed wombat displays the furry muzzle that distinguishes the two* Lasiorhinus *species from the common wombat.*

herbivore of its size. Total feeding times of as little as two hours per day have been recorded for northern hairy-nosed wombats in good seasons, and feeding ranges are only about 10 percent of those used by kangaroos in similar habitat. This extreme conservatism allows wombats to spend most of their time underground, and this behavior in turn contributes further to energy conservation by protecting them from unfavorable weather conditions. Although they do not enter torpor, wombats may spend several days at a stretch in their burrows, during which time their energy expenditure must be very low indeed.

Because wombats are nocturnal, secretive, and spend so much time underground, little is known of their behavior. Burrows may be 30m (98ft) or more long, and often have several entrances, side tunnels, and resting chambers. The southern

FACTFILE

WOMBATS

Order: Diprotodontia

Family: Vombatidae

3 species in 2 genera

DISTRIBUTION SE Australia

Tropic of Capricorn

COMMON WOMBAT *Vombatus ursinus*
Three subspecies: *Vombatus ursinus ursinus* (Flinders Island); *V. u. tasmaniensis* (Tasmania); *V. u. hirsutus* (mainland Australia). Temperate forests and woodlands, heaths, and alpine habitats throughout SE Australia, including Flinders Island and Tasmania. HBL 90–115cm (35–45in); TL c.2.5cm (1 in); HT c.36cm (14in); WT 22–39kg (48.5–86lb). Form: coat coarse, black or brown to gray; bare muzzle; short, rounded ears. Diet: primarily grasses, but also sedges, rushes, and the roots of shrubs and trees. Breeding: one offspring, may be born at any time of the year. Pouch life is about 6 months, and the young remains at heel for about another year; sexual maturity is at 2 years of age. Longevity: unknown in the wild, up to 26 years in captivity. Conservation status: Lower Risk.

SOUTHERN HAIRY-NOSED WOMBAT

Lasiorhinus latifrons
Central southern Australia; semiarid and arid woodlands, grasslands, and shrub steppes. HBL 77–94cm (30–37in); TL c.2.5cm (1 in); HT c.36cm (14in); WT 19–32kg (42–70lb). Form: coat fine, gray to brown, with lighter patches; hairy muzzle; long, pointed ears. Diet: grasses, including forbs and foliage of woody shrubs during drought. Breeding: single young, born in spring or early summer, remains in the pouch for 6–9 months; weaning occurs at approximately 1 year, and sexual maturity at 3 years. Longevity: unknown in the wild, more than 20 years in captivity. Conservation status: Lower Risk.

NORTHERN HAIRY-NOSED WOMBAT

Lasiorhinus krefftii
Sole population in Epping Forest National Park, near Clermont in central Queensland; semiarid woodland. HBL male 102cm (40in), female 107cm (42in); HT c.40cm (16in); WT male 30kg (66lb), female 32.5kg (72lb). Coat: silver gray, dark rings around the eyes. Diet: grasses, plus some sedges and forbs. Breeding: one young born in spring or summer; pouch life c.10 months; weaning age unknown; females breed on average twice every 3 years. Longevity: unknown in the wild; one captive animal lived at least 30 years. Conservation status: Critically Endangered.

Abbreviations HBL = head–body length TL = tail length HT = height WT = weight

---

hairy-nosed wombat inhabits large warrens that remain in constant use for decades. Groups of up to ten animals may live there, but interactions are rare and they feed solitarily. The family structure of these groups is unknown.

Among northern hairy-nosed wombats, burrows are arranged in loose clusters, with entrances about 10m (33ft) apart; different clusters are typically several hundred meters distant. Genetic relatedness is higher for animals in the same cluster than between neighboring clusters. There may be up to ten animals in a group, with equal numbers of males and females. This species displays an unusual pattern of dispersal, in which both young males and females remain in their home burrow cluster, but adult females may disperse to a different cluster after rearing an offspring. Dispersal distances of up to 3km (1.8mi) have been recorded. Common wombats appear to be more solitary than hairy-nosed wombats.

Cause for Concern

CONSERVATION AND ENVIRONMENT

Over the past 200 years both the common wombat and the southern hairy-nosed wombat have suffered range reductions of 10–50 percent as a result of habitat clearance and competition with rabbits, but they remain secure across much of

their original range. *Vombatus ursinus ursinus* has gone extinct from all the Bass Strait islands except Flinders Island. In parts of Victoria, common wombats are considered pests because of the damage they do to rabbit-proof fences, and some local control is carried out.

The northern hairy-nosed wombat is now one of the rarest mammals in the world. This species has only ever been confirmed in three localities, and it went extinct from two of these early last century as a result of competition with cattle and sheep, habitat change, and poisoning campaigns directed at rabbits. The last population was not finally protected until the 3,000-ha (7,400-acre) Epping Forest National Park was declared over its entire range in 1974 and cattle were excluded in 1980. At that time the population probably consisted of just 35 individuals. By 1995, capture–mark–recapture studies estimated a population of around 70 animals.

To date, the management of this population has focused on protection of its habitat, especially the control of fire and exclusion of cattle, while minimizing direct interference with the animals. This appears to have allowed the species to begin its recovery, but its fate remains precariously balanced, and plans are afoot to begin captive breeding and to establish other wild populations. CJ

Honey Possum

tHE HONEY POSSUM IS THE SOLE MEMBER *of a line of marsupials that diverged very early from possum–kangaroo stock. Although its entire fossil history is contained within the last 35,000 years, it probably evolved about 20 million years ago, when heathlands were widespread.*

Today, honey possums are most abundant in heathlands on coastal sandplains in southwestern Australia, one of 25 biodiversity hotspots worldwide, where about 2,000 species of plants ensure a yearlong supply of the flowers upon which the animals depend for their food.

Foragers among the Flowers
FORM AND FUNCTION

The honey possum's teeth are reduced in number and size, with a dental formula of I2/1, C1/0, P1/0, M3/3 = 22, but the molars are merely tiny cones. They use a long, protrusive tongue with a brush surface to lick nectar from flowers. Combs on the roof of the mouth remove pollen grains from the brush tongue. The contents of these pollen grains are digested during a rapid, six-hour transit through a simple intestine to provide the honey possum's sole source of nutrients; nectar (20 percent sugar solution) provides only energy and water. Unusual kidneys allow the animals to excrete up to their own weight in water daily. They feed mainly on banksias and dryandras, plants with large blossoms containing from 250 to 2,500 flowers. The food plants they favor have drab-colored flowers that are concealed either inside bushes or else close to the ground.

These tiny, shrewlike mammals use their long, pointed snouts to probe the flowers. The first digit of the hindfoot is opposable to the others for gripping branches, and all digits have rough pads on the tips, not claws. Honey possums run fast on the ground and clamber with great agility over dense heathland vegetation. A long, partially prehensile tail provides balance and support for climbing, and frees the grasping hands to grip branches and manipulate flowers while feeding.

Nonstop Motherhood
SOCIAL BEHAVIOR

Honey possums communicate through a small repertoire of visual postures and high-pitched squeaks, a reflection of their mainly nocturnal activity. Smell appears to be very important in their social behavior and also helps them locate the flowers of their food plants.

The short lifespan of honey possums is balanced by their continuous reproduction. A female carries young in her pouch for almost all of her adult life. Both sexes mature at around the age of 6 months. Many females breed for the first time while not yet fully grown, just 3 or 4 months after leaving the pouch in which they have spent the first 2 months of their lives. Births occur throughout the year, but reach very low levels when food is scarce. Population sizes are larger, body condition better, and births more common when nectar is most abundant. The timing of these cycles varies seasonally and between years in relation to rainfall, as well as geographically with differences in plant assemblages. Females appear to breed opportunistically whenever food is abundant, irrespective of the later consequences for their young.

A second litter is often born very soon after the first leaves the pouch or is weaned, since the honey possum exhibits embryonic diapause (the temporary cessation of development in an embryo). In good times, some females can give

FACTFILE

HONEY POSSUM

Tarsipes rostratus

Order: Diprotodontia

Sole member of the family Tarsipedidae

DISTRIBUTION
SW Australia

Tropic of Capricorn

HABITAT Heathland, shrubland, and low open woodland with heath understory.

SIZE Head–body length male 6.5–8.5cm (2.6–3.3in), female 7–9cm (2.8–3.5in); **tail length** male 7–10cm (2.8–3.9in), female 7.5–10.5cm (3–4.1in); **weight** male 7–11g (0.3oz), female 8–16g (0.3–0.6oz), averaging 12g (0.4oz). Females are one-third heavier than males, and are larger in the southern part of their distribution than in the northern.

COAT Grizzled grayish brown above, with orange tinge on flanks and shoulder, next to cream undersurface. Three back stripes: a distinct dark brown stripe from the back of the head to the base of the tail, with a less distinct, lighter brown stripe on each side.

DIET Nectar and pollen

BREEDING Gestation uncertain, but about 28 days

LONGEVITY Typically 1 year, never more than 2

CONSERVATION STATUS Lower Risk, but dependent on a continued supply of eucalyptus, banksia, and callistemon blossoms.

birth to four litters in a year. At birth, the young are the smallest mammals known, weighing only about 0.0005g (0.00002oz). Their subsequent development is typical of young marsupials. The deep pouch has four teats and, although litters of four occur, two or three are normal. No nest is constructed; instead, mothers carry their young in the pouch as they forage. The small litter size and slow growth of the young, which spend about 60 days in the pouch, indicate the difficulties mothers experience in harvesting enough pollen grains to supply the sucklings with milk.

The young leave the pouch weighing about 2.5g (0.09oz), covered in fur and with eyes open. They follow their mother around as she forages, suckling occasionally, and may even ride on her back. At this time a litter of four young weigh as much as their mother. They disperse to live independently within a week or two of leaving the pouch. Honey possums, especially juveniles, sometimes huddle together to save energy. Their unusually high body temperature and metabolic rate is offset by short-term periods of deep torpor in cold weather when food is short. At such times the body temperature may remain as low as 5°C (41°F) for 10 hours before reviving spontaneously.

Both sexes are solitary and sedentary, living in overlapping home ranges that average 700sq meters (0.17 acres) for females and 1,280sq meters (0.32 acres) for males. In captivity, females are dominant to males as well as to juveniles. In the wild, females that have large young appear to monopolize areas rich in food.

The larger home ranges of males reflect not just their wider search for food, but also their quest for females approaching estrus. Honey possum testes weigh 4.2 percent of the animal's total body weight, the largest proportion for any mammal. Their sperm is also the longest known among mammals (0.36mm). These features imply intense competition between males to father offspring. Courtship is brief; males follow a female nearing estrus, but are only able to mount her when the larger female allows this. DNA microsatellite profiling has shown that two or more males are responsible for fathering each litter.

The honey possum is still locally abundant in some areas, although its already restricted distribution continues to shrink. Clearance of habitat for agriculture has largely ceased, but within reserves plant diseases and introduced predators (cats and foxes) still pose threats. In addition, management burning can kill the food plants on which the honey possum depends.   RDW/EMR

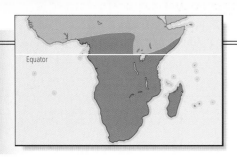

Equator

TENRECS AND GOLDEN MOLES

a *frosoricida is a recently named order of placental mammals that contains the enigmatic tenrecs (family Tenrecidae) and golden moles (family Chrysochloridae). The greatest morphological diversity within the Afrosoricida is found among Malagasy tenrecs, but afrosoricids are clearly of African origin – living and extinct golden moles, the extant potamogaline (otter shrew) tenrecs, and the most primitive fossil tenrecs are all African. Further-*

more, although morphologists had previously placed tenrecs and golden moles within the insectivorous order Lipotyphla alongside hedgehogs, shrews, "true" moles and solenodons, a wealth of diverse genomic data now strongly supports their placement in the superorder Afrotheria, which contains other historically African mammals such as sengis, aardvarks, and paenungulates (elephants, hyraxes, and dugongs and manatees).

Mysterious and Diverse
ORIGINS AND EVOLUTION

The phylogenetic position of afrosoricids within Afrotheria is now well resolved, but the nature of their placement within that clade has left the group's origin as enigmatic as ever. Golden moles' burrowing lifestyle has radically transformed almost every aspect of their anatomy, but tenrec morphology generally appears to be quite conservative, suggesting that afrosoricids derive from a

very primitive placental stock. For instance, both tenrecs and golden moles have cloacae and low body temperatures, and tenrecs' cranial and post-cranial bones are, in many ways, similar to those of the earliest fossil placentals. Most afrosoricids also have zalambdodont molars – a pattern in which the upper molars have only one major cusp (as opposed to three or more, as seen in most other placentals), and the crushing surface on the lower molars is either reduced or lost altogether. These specialized dental features likely evolved from a primitive molar pattern similar to that seen in Cretaceous placentals. Despite this, genetic evidence nests afrosoricids deep within the afrotherian radiation, as the sister group of either aardvarks or of sengis. This placement is peculiar, because the anatomy of sengis and aardvarks closely resembles that of early Cenozoic paenun-gulates, and bears little similarity to that of the afrosoricids. This pattern of relationships would seem to imply that afrosoricids' similarities to more primitive Cretaceous placentals are either entirely convergent – in which case the group may have actually evolved from a "protopaenun-gulate" ancestor – or that they are primitive within Afrotheria, and aardvarks' and sengis' paenungu-late-like features represent convergences.

Missing Ancestors

FORM AND FUNCTION

Recent molecular estimates suggest that afrosori-cids diverged from their afrotherian relatives a few million years before the end of the Cretaceous (possibly about 70 million years ago), and that tenrecs and golden moles went their separate ways at about the time of the K-T boundary, some 65 million years ago. Unfortunately, very little is known about afrosoricid evolution over the next 45 million years. Possible fossil afrosoricids are known from a handful of Eocene (55–34 million-year-old) deposits in north Africa, but none of the Eocene genera exhibit the zalambdodont tooth pattern seen in most extant afrosoricids. It is possible that that condition evolved independently in tenrecs and golden moles, because tenrecid otter shrews exhibit a non-zalambdodont molar pattern that provides more surface area for crushing (this could, however, also be a secondary adaptation related to otter shrews' tendency to feed on hard-bodied aquatic invertebrates). One thing that is clear from the meager afrosoricid fossil record is that the oldest undoubted golden mole, 20-million-year-old *Prochrysochloris*, differs very little from its extant relatives in aspects of craniodental morphology, and suggests that golden moles had probably entered into their highly specialized niche by the close of the Paleogene (24 million years ago), if not much earlier.

Almost all that is known about tenrec behavior and physiology is based on studies of the diverse Malagasy taxa, which include fossorial, semi-aquatic, spiny, and semiarboreal forms, among others. Genetic data indicate that the Malagasy tenrecs are monophyletic and probably the product of a single over-water dispersal from the African mainland. Available molecular evidence suggests that potamogalines had diverged from other extant tenrecs by 40 million years ago, but as yet no estimate has been calculated for the age of the last common ancestor of extant Malagasy forms. Unfortunately Madagascar has no pre-Pleistocene, post-Cretaceous mammalian fossil record, so little is known about the clade's evolutionary history on that island. ERS

◁ **Left** The fur of the Cape golden mole has a iridescent green sheen and is a character that led to the family name Chrysochloridae, from the Greek for "gold" and "green". Fur color can range from pale gold to almost black, depending on the species.

SKULLS AND DENTITION

The skull of the common tenrec has a long, tapered snout, and in the adult male, long canines, the tips of the bottom pair fitting into pits in front of the upper ones. The dental formula is I2/3, C1/1, P2/3, M3/3.

The skulls of chrysochlorids are well adapted to their burrowing lifestyle, with a pointed snout and wedge-shaped face. The cranial bones fuse early in life. Golden moles have a dental formula of I3/3, C1/1, p3/3, M2–3/2–3.

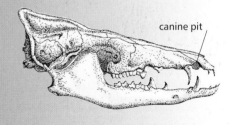

canine pit

Tenrec
11 cm

Tenrecs

t ENRECS AND OTTER SHREWS ARE REMARKABLE *in having a great diversity of shape and form. Yet this has been achieved in virtual isolation, since tenrecs themselves are confined to Madagascar, which they were one of the first mammals to colonize, and the otter shrews (Potamogalinae; sometimes regarded as a separate family) to west and central Africa.*

Tenrecs retain characters that were perhaps more widespread among early placental mammals. These conservative features include a low and variable body temperature, retention of a common opening for the urogenital and anal tracts (the cloaca), and undescended testes in the male. Some of the family comprise a conspicuous part of the native fauna, being either an important source of food, relatively large and bold, or conspicuously colored. Even though detailed studies of the family are few and restricted to a handful of species they provide an excellent basis for the elucidation of mammalian evolution. The earliest fossils date from Kenyan Miocene deposits (about 24 million years ago), but by then the Tenrecidae were well differentiated, and had probably long been part of the African fauna.

Diversity in Isolation
FORM AND FUNCTION

Among the largely nocturnal tenrecs and otter shrews, eyesight is generally poor, but the whiskers are sensitive, and smell and hearing are well developed. Vocalizations range from hissing and grunting to twittering and echolocation clicks. The brain is relatively small and the number of teeth ranges from 32–42.

The aquatic Tenrecidae are active creatures of streams, rivers, lakes, and swamps. The giant otter shrew and Mount Nimba least otter shrew are confined to forest, but the Ruwenzori least otter shrew and the aquatic tenrec are less restricted. All four species have a sleek,

△ **Above** *Species of tenrecs:* **1** *Aquatic tenrec (Limnogale mergulus);* **2** *Giant otter shrew (Potamogale velox);* **3** *Ruwenzori least otter shrew (Micropotamogale ruwenzorii);* **4** *Highland streaked tenrec (Hemicentetes nigriceps);* **5** *Common tenrec (Tenrec ecaudatus);* **6** *Lesser hedgehog tenrec (Echinops telfairi);* **7** *Long-tailed tenrec (Microgale melanorrachis);* **8** *Greater hedgehog tenrec (Setifer setosus);* **9** *Four-toed rice tenrec (Oryzorictes tetradactylus).*

7

8

9

elegant body form with a distinctive, flattened head that allows the ears, eyes, and nostrils to project above the surface while most of the body remains submerged. Stout whiskers radiate from around the muzzle, providing a means of locating prey. The fur is dense and soft; frequent grooming ensures that it is waterproof and traps insulating air during dives. Grooming is accomplished by means of the two fused toes on each hindfoot, which act as combs. All otter shrews and the aquatic tenrec have a chocolate brown back; the aquatic tenrec has a gray belly and otter shrews have white bellies. The Madagascan aquatic tenrec shows strong convergence with the least otter shrews, with a rat-size body and a tail approximately the same length. The Ruwenzori least otter shrew and the aquatic tenrec have webbed feet, which probably provide most of the propulsion in the water,

and their tails are slightly compressed laterally, providing each with an effective rudder and additional propulsion.

The Mount Nimba least otter shrew is probably the least aquatic, having no webbing and a rounded tail. However, all are probably agile both in water and on land. The giant otter shrew, which is among the most specialized of the aquatic Tenrecidae, often figures as part fish and part mammal in African folklore, giving rise to such names as "transformed fish." The unmistakable deep, laterally flattened tail that tapers to a point is the main source of such beliefs, even though it is covered by fine, short hair, but the animal's proficiency in water no doubt also plays a part. Sinuous thrusts of the powerful tail extending up the lower part of the body provide the propulsion for swimming, allowing a startling turn of speed and great agility. Although most of the active hours are spent in the water the agility also extends to foraging on dry land. The Boulou of southern Cameroon call the giant otter shrew the *jes*: a person is said to be like a *jes* if he flares up in anger but calms down again just as rapidly.

The long-tailed and large-eared tenrecs are shrewlike, and the former have the least modified body plan within the Tenrecidae. Evergreen forest and wetter areas of the central plateau of Madagascar are the primary habitats for long-tailed tenrecs, with only one species extending into the deciduous forests of the drier western region. These tenrecs have filled semiarboreal and terrestrial niches. The longest-tailed species, with relatively long hindlegs, can climb and probably spring among branches; jumpers and runners live on the ground, together with short-legged semiburrowing species. The large-eared tenrec is also semiburrowing in its western woodland habitat and is apparently closely related to one of the oldest fossil species.

The rice tenrecs, with their molelike velvet fur, reduced ears and eyes, and relatively large forefeet, fill a similar niche to the mole in Madagascar. In undisturbed areas of northern and western Madagascar, these tenrecs burrow through the humus layers in a manner similar to the North American shrew mole, but the extensive cultivation of rice provides new habitats for them.

The subfamily Tenrecinae contains some of the most fascinating and bizarre species. The tail has been lost or greatly reduced and varying degrees of spininess are linked with elaborate and striking defensive strategies. Both the greater hedgehog tenrec and its smaller semiarboreal counterpart, the lesser hedgehog tenrec, can form a nearly impregnable spiny ball when threatened, closely resembling the Old World hedgehogs. Continued provocation may also lead to them advancing, gaping, hissing, and head bucking, the latter being common to all Tenrecinae. The brown adult common tenrec, which is among the largest of the living Tenrecidae, is the least spiny species,

FACTFILE

TENRECS

Order: Afrosoricida

Family: Tenrecidae

31 species in 10 genera and 4 subfamilies

DISTRIBUTION Madagascar, with one species introduced to the Comoros, Réunion, and the Seychelles; W and C Africa.

HABITAT Wide ranging, from semiarid to rain forest, including mountains, rivers, and human settlements.

SIZE Head–body length ranges from 4.3cm (1.7in) in the Pygmy shrew tenrec to 25–39cm (10–15in) in the Common tenrec; tail length from 5–10mm (0.2–0.4in) to 4.5cm (1.8in), and weight from 5g (0.18oz) to 500–1,500g (18–53oz), both in the same two species.

COAT Soft-furred to spiny; coloration ranges from brown or gray to contrasted streaks.

DIET Tenrecs and otter shrews are opportunistic feeders, taking a wide variety of invertebrates as well as some vertebrates and vegetable matter. Rice tenrecs mostly live off invertebrate prey, but also consume vegetable matter. Fruit supplements the invertebrate diet of the more omnivorous species such as the Common and hedgehog tenrecs.

Equator

Common tenrecs are also large enough to take reptiles, amphibians, and even small mammals. The Streaked tenrec feeds on earthworms.

BREEDING Gestation relatively aseasonal within the Oryzorictinae, Geogalinae, and Tenrecinae where known (50–64 days); unknown in Potamogalinae.

LONGEVITY Up to 6 years.

CONSERVATION STATUS Seven species are considered Vulnerable or Endangered by the IUCN (4 Oryzorictinae, 3 Potamogalinae), while one – the Tree shrew tenrec (*Microgale dryas*) – is Critically Endangered.

See subfamilies table ▷

but it combines a lateral, open-mouthed slashing bite with head bucking that can drive spines concentrated on the neck into an assailant. A fully-grown male with a gape of 10cm (4in) has canines that can measure up to 1.5cm (0.6in), and the bite is powered by the massively developed masseter (jaw) muscles. A pad of thickened skin on the male's midback provides some additional protection. The black-and-white-striped offspring relies less on biting but uses numerous barbed, detachable spines to great effect in head bucking. Common tenrecs have better eyesight than most other species in the family but may also detect disturbances through long, sensitive hairs on the back. When disturbed, the young can communicate their alarm through stridulation, which involves rubbing together stiff quills on the midback to produce an audible signal. Streaked tenrecs are remarkably similar to juvenile common tenrecs in coloration, size, and possession of a stridulating organ. Like juvenile common tenrecs, they forage in groups, and their principal defense involves scattering and hiding under cover. If they are cornered, they advance, bucking violently, with their spines bristling.

Seeking Prey by Land and Water
DIET

Tenrecs and otter shrews are opportunistic feeders, taking a wide variety of invertebrates as well as some vertebrates and vegetable matter. Otter shrews scour the water, streambed, and banks with their sensitive whiskers, snapping up prey and carrying it up to the bank if caught in the water. Crustaceans are the main prey, including crabs of up to 5–7cm (2–3in) across the carapace. Rice tenrecs probably encounter most of their invertebrate prey in underground burrows or surface runs, but also consume vegetable matter. Fruit supplements the invertebrate diet of the more omnivorous species such as the common and hedgehog tenrecs. Common tenrecs are also large enough to take reptiles, amphibians, and even small mammals. Prey are detected by sweeping whiskers from side to side, and by smell and sound. Similarly, semiarboreal lesser hedgehog tenrecs and long-tailed tenrecs perhaps encounter and eat lizards and nestling birds. The streaked tenrec, which is active during daytime, has delicate teeth and an elongated, fine snout for feeding on earthworms.

Complex Multigenerational Groupings
SOCIAL BEHAVIOR

Tenrec reproduction is diverse and includes several features peculiar to the family. Where known, ovarian processes differ from those in other mammals in that no fluid-filled cavity, or antrum, develops in the maturing ovarian follicle. Spermatozoa also penetrate developing follicles and fertilize the egg before ovulation; this is known in only one other mammal, the short-tailed shrew.

Tenrec and Otter Shrew Subfamilies

Tenrecs
Subfamily Oryzorictinae

22 species in 3 Madagascan genera, including **Aquatic tenrec** (*Limnogale mergulus*); **rice tenrecs** (*Oryzorictes*, 2 species), **long-tailed tenrecs** (*Microgale*, 19 species, including the recently discovered *M. jenkinsae*). The Tree shrew tenrec (*Microgale dryas*) is Critically Endangered; the Pygmy shrew tenrec (*M. parvula*), Greater long-tailed shrew tenrec (*M. principula*), and Aquatic tenrec are Endangered; while the Gracile shrew tenrec (*M. gracilis*) is Vulnerable.

Subfamily Geogalinae

One species in one Madagascan genus: **Large-eared tenrec** (*Geogale aurita*).

Subfamily Tenrecinae

Five species in 4 Madagascan genera: **Greater hedgehog tenrec** (*Setifer setosus*); **Lesser hedgehog tenrec** (*Echinops telfairi*); **Common tenrec** (*Tenrec ecaudatus*), introduced to Réunion, Seychelles, and Mauritius; **Streaked tenrec** (*Hemicentetes semispinosus*); and the **Highland streaked tenrec** (*H. nigriceps*).

Otter shrews
Subfamily Potamogalinae

Three species in 2 African genera: **Giant otter shrew** (*Potamogale velox*), Nigeria to W Kenya and Angola; **Ruwenzori least otter shrew** (*Micropotamogale ruwenzorii*), Uganda, DRC; Mount Nimba; **Least otter shrew** (*M. lamottei*), Guinea, Liberia, and Côte d'Ivoire. All species are Endangered.

For full species list see Appendix ▷

TENREC BODY TEMPERATURE

Body temperature is relatively low among tenrecs, with a range of 30–35°C (86–95°F) during activity. The large-eared tenrec and members of the Tenrecinae enter seasonal hypothermia, or torpor, during dry or cool periods of the year, which ranges from irregular spells of a few days to continuous periods lasting six months; then it is integral to the animal's physiological and behavioral cycles. So finely arranged are the cycles of hypothermia, activity, and reproduction that the common tenrec must complete such physiological changes as activation of the testis or ovary while still torpid, since breeding begins within days of commencing activity.

The giant otter shrew, some Oryzorictinae, and the Tenrecinae save energy at any time of year because body temperature falls close to air temperature during daily rest. Interactions between these fluctuations in body temperature and reproduction in the Tenrecidae are unique. During comparable periods of activity in the common tenrec, body temperatures of breeding males are on average 0.6°C (1.1°F) lower than those of nonbreeding males. This is because sperm production or storage can only occur below normal body temperature. Other mammals either have a mechanism for cooling reproductive organs or, rarely, tolerate high temperatures. Normally, thermoregulation improves during pregnancy, but female common tenrecs continue with their regular fluctuations in temperature dependent on activity or rest, regardless of pregnancy. This probably accounts for variations in gestation lengths, as the fetuses could not develop at a constant rate if so cooled during maternal rest. Although torpor during pregnancy occurs among bats, it is well regulated, and the type found in tenrecs is not known elsewhere.

feeding throughout their brief spell of lactation. The striking similarity between juvenile common tenrecs and adult streaked tenrecs suggests that a striped coat associated with daylight foraging has been an important factor in the evolution toward modern streaked tenrecs.

Rain forest streaked tenrecs form multigenerational family groups comprising complex social groupings . Young mature rapidly and can breed at 35 days after birth, so that each group may produce several litters in a season. The group, of up to 18 animals, probably consists of three related generations. They forage together, in subgroups or alone, but when together they stridulate almost continuously. Stridulation seems to be primarily a device to keep mother and young together as they search for prey.

The primary means of communication among the Tenrecidae is through scent. Otter shrews regularly deposit feces either in or near their burrows and under sheltered banks. Marking by tenrecs includes cloacal dragging, rubbing secretions from eye glands, and manual depositing of neck-gland secretions. Common tenrecs cover 0.5ha (1.2–5 acres) per night, although receptive females reduce this to about 200sq m (2,150sq ft) in order to facilitate location by males. Giant otter shrews may range along 800m (0.5mi) of their streams in a night.

Mixed Fortunes
CONSERVATION AND ENVIRONMENT

Common tenrecs have been a source of food since ancient times, but are not endangered by this traditional hunting. Undoubtedly, some rain forest tenrecs are under threat as Madagascar is rapidly being deforested, but some species thrive around human settlements. Tourism may be a threat to other species. At the mid-altitude rain forest reserve of Analamazaotra, Madagascar, which is used for tourism, seven endemic tenrec species, and three endemic rodent species were recently found. Of the sites surveyed, most biological diversity was demonstrated at the most undisturbed site, though individual species abundance was reduced. Forest subjected to infrequent logging by local people exhibited an intermediate level of species richness, and it seems apt to conclude that core areas of the reserve should be left undisturbed in order to preserve small mammal species diversity. Forest destruction is also reducing the range of the giant otter shrew and perhaps also of the Mount Nimba least otter shrew and the Ruwenzori least otter shrew.   MEN

Most births occur in the wet season, coinciding with maximum invertebrate numbers, and the offspring are born in a relatively undeveloped state. Litter size varies from two in the giant otter shrew and some Oryzorictinae to an extraordinary maximum of 32 in the common tenrec. This seems to be related to survival rates, which in turn are conditioned by the stability of the environment. For example, oryzorictines in the comparatively stable high rain forest regions seem to be long lived and bear small litters. Average litter size of common tenrecs in relatively seasonal woodland or savanna regions with fluctuating climatic conditions is 20, compared with 15 in rain forest regions, and 10 in Seychelles rain forests within 5° of the equator. Weight variation within the litter can reach 200–275 percent in common and hedgehog tenrecs.

A recent study of large-eared tenrecs revealed that four out of ten breeding females exhibited postpartum estrus, the first time this phenomenon has been recorded within the Tenrecidae. Gestation length is around 57 days, confirming that all tenrecs have a uniformly slow fetal development rate. Pregnant females may enter torpor, which contributes to variety in length of gestation. Litter size ranged from 2–5 neonates.

The common tenrec feeds her offspring from up to 29 nipples, the most recorded among mammals. Nutritional demands of lactation are so great in this species that the mother and offspring must extend foraging beyond their normal nocturnal regime into the relatively dangerous daylight hours. This accounts for the striped camouflage coloration of juveniles, which only become more strictly nocturnal at the approach of the molt to the adult coat. Moreover, adult females have a darker brown coat than adult males, presumably because it affords better protection for daylight

Golden Moles

gOLDEN MOLES ARE SO CALLED FROM THEIR *family name, Chrysochloridae, deriving from the Greek terms for "gold" and "pale green." The appellation refers to the iridescent sheen of coppery green, blue, purple, or bronze on the animals' fur rather than to the color of the fur itself, which varies from pale yellow to black, depending on the species.*

Golden moles are known from as far back as the late Eocene, about 40 million years ago. Climatic modifications may be responsible for their present discontinuous distribution, but they have special adaptations for a burrowing mode of life in a wide geographic range of subterrestrial habitats.

Equipped for Extremes
FORM AND FUNCTION

Golden moles are solitary, burrowing insectivores with compact, streamlined bodies, short limbs, and no visible tail. The backward-set fur is moisture repellent, remaining sleek and dry in muddy situations; a dense, woolly undercoat provides insulation. The skin is thick and tough, particularly on the head. The eyes are vestigial and covered with hairy skin, and the optic nerve is degenerate. The ear openings are covered by fur, and the nostrils are protected by a leathery pad that assists in soil excavations; in some species such as the yellow golden mole, the nostrils also have foliaceous projections that prevent sand from entering the nose during burrowing. The wedge-shaped head and extremely muscular shoulders push and pack the soil, whereas the strong forelimbs are equipped with curved, picklike digging claws.Of the four claws, the third is extremely powerful, while the first and fourth are usually rudimentary. The hindfeet are webbed with five digits, each bearing a small claw, and are used to shovel loose soil backward along tunnels.

The key to the evolutionary success of golden moles lies in their unique physiology. They have a low basal metabolic rate and do not thermoregulate when at rest, thereby considerably reducing their energy requirements. All species studied so far enter torpor, either daily or in response to cold. Body temperature in the thermal neutral zone is lower than in other similarly sized mammals. A lowered metabolism and efficient renal function reduce water requirements to the extent that most species do not need drinking water. Far from being primitive characters, such physiological specializations allow the moles to survive in habitats where temperatures are extreme and food is scarce.

The chief senses in golden moles are hearing, touch, and smell. The ear ossicles of some species are disproportionately large, giving great sensitivity to vibrations, which trigger rapid locomotion either toward prey or toward an open burrow entrance (on the surface) or to greater depths (when underground). Those species without enlarged ear ossicles have a well-developed hyoid apparatus that may transmit low-frequency sounds to the inner ear. Golden moles also have an extraordinary ability to orientate themselves underground; when parts of burrow systems are damaged, the new tunnels that repair them always link up precisely with the existing tunnels.

Golden moles forage in subsurface tunnels, visible from above as soil ridges. Desert-dwelling species "swim" through the sand just below the surface, leaving U-shaped ridges. Most species also excavate deeper burrows connecting grass-lined nests, defecation chambers, and spiraling boltholes, depositing excess soil on the surface.

Sustained burrowing in the Hottentot golden mole lasts for about 44 minutes, separated by inactive periods of about 2.6 hours. Nonrandom surface locomotion minimizes foraging costs.

The Underground Larder
DIET

Golden moles are opportunistic foragers, preying predominantly on earthworms and insect larvae. Grant's golden moles feed mainly on soft-bodied termites, a sedentary prey occurring in patches of high concentration. De Winton's golden moles also prey on legless lizards, using their long, slender claws to hold these reptiles. Giant golden moles feed mainly on oniscomorph millipedes, which abound in leaf litter, and giant earthworms (*Microchaetus* spp.); they probably also consume small vertebrates they may stumble across. Captive moles take a wide spectrum of terrestrial invertebrates except for mollusks, and can be trained to eat sliced lamb kidney.

FACTFILE

GOLDEN MOLES

Order: Afrosoricida

Family: Chrysochloridae

21 species in 9 genera

Habitat Almost exclusively burrowing.

Size Head–body length ranges from 7–8.5cm (2.7–3.3in) in Grant's golden mole to 19.8–23.5cm (7.8–9in) in the Giant golden mole.

LARGE GOLDEN MOLES Genus *Chrysospalax*
The two largest species: **Giant golden mole** (*C. trevelyani*), forests in E Cape Province, Endangered; and **Rough-haired golden mole** (*C. villosus*), grasslands and swamp in E South Africa, Vulnerable.

SECRETIVE GOLDEN MOLES Genus *Cryptochloris*
2 species, both found in arid regions of Little Namaqualand, W Cape: **De Winton's golden mole** (*C. wintoni*), Vulnerable; and **Van Zyl's golden mole** (*C. zyli*), Critically Endangered.

CAPE GOLDEN MOLES Genus *Chrysochloris*
3 species: **Stuhlmann's golden mole** (*C. stuhlmanni*), mountains in C and E Africa; **Cape golden mole** (*C. asiatica*), W Cape to Little Namaqualand; and **Visagie's golden mole** (*C. visagiei*), succulent karoo of W Cape, Critically Endangered.

AFRICAN GOLDEN MOLES Genus *Chlorotalpa*
2 species: **Sclater's golden mole** (*C. sclateri*), high-altitude grasslands and scrub in W Cape, Lesotho, E Free State, and Mpumalanga, Vulnerable; and **Duthie's golden mole** (*C. duthieae*), coastal forests in W and E Cape, Vulnerable.

SOUTH AFRICAN GOLDEN MOLES Genus *Amblysomus*
5 species, including the **Hottentot golden mole** (*A. hotten-*

DISTRIBUTION
Sub-Saharan Africa, including Somalia.

Equator

totus), all found in grasslands and forests in W and E Cape, KwaZulu-Natal, NE Free State, Mpumalanga, Swaziland.

GENUS *NEAMBLYSOMUS*
2 species: **Gunning's golden mole** (*N. gunningi*), forests in Limpopo Province, Vulnerable; and **Juliana's golden mole** (*N. julianae*), sandy soils in savannas of Gauteng and Mpumalanga, Critically Endangered.

GENUS *CALCOCHLORIS*
3 species: **Yellow golden mole** (*C. obtusirostris*), Zululand to Mozambique and SE Zimbabwe; **Congo golden mole** (*C. leucorhinus*), forests of W and C Africa; **Somali golden mole** (*C. tytonis*), NE Somalia, Critically Endangered.

GRANT'S GOLDEN MOLE *Eremitalpa granti*
Sandy desert and semidesert of W Cape, Little Namaqualand, Namib Desert. Vulnerable.

AREND'S GOLDEN MOLE *Carpitalpa arendsi*
Forests and adjacent grasslands in E Zimbabwe and NE Mozambique.

For full species list see Appendix ▷

Contacts between the Burrows

SOCIAL BEHAVIOR

Territorial behavior is influenced by the availability of food. Hottentot golden mole burrow systems are more numerous in the summer when food is more abundant, and a certain amount of home range overlap is tolerated. The systems are larger and more aggressively defended in less fertile areas; a neighboring burrow may be taken over by an individual as an extension of its home range. Occupancy is detected by scrutiny of tunnel walls by smell. Fighting occurs between individuals of the same sex, and sometimes between male and female. Hottentot golden moles tolerate herbivorous mole rats in the same burrow systems, and in the Drakensberg range golden mole burrows open into those of Sloggett's vlei rats (*Otomys sloggetti*).

Courtship in Hottentot golden moles involves much chirruping vocalization, head bobbing, and foot stamping in the male, and grasshopper-like rasping and prolonged squeals with the mouth wide open in the female. Both sexes have a single external urogenital opening. Females display aseasonal polyestry. Litters comprise 1–3 (usually 2) naked young with a head–body length of 4.7cm (1.9in) and a weight of 4.5g (0.16oz). Birth and lactation take place in grass-lined nests, and eviction from the maternal burrow system occurs once the young weigh 35–45g (1.2–1.6oz).

Sadly, eleven species of golden moles are now threatened with extinction owing to habitat degradation induced by human activities. These threats include urbanization, the mining of alluvial sands for diamonds and building materials, poor agricultural practices, and predation by domestic dogs and cats.   GB/MP

▷ **Right** A telltale ridge of earth indicates the location of a golden mole foraging tunnel. Most species dig deeper nesting burrows.

▽ **Below** In the Namib Desert in southern Africa, a Grant's golden mole feeds on a locust – a change from its usual diet of soft-bodied termites.

SENGIS

a PPEARING MUCH LIKE GIANT VERSIONS OF
true shrews, elephant shrews, now known as
sengis, were not described in the scientific literature until the mid-19th century, partly because they
are cryptic, difficult to trap, and confined to Africa.
Almost another century passed before a few short
notes on their natural history appeared in print.
Knowledge of them has expanded greatly over the
last 50 years, revealing for the first time just how
unique these animals really are.

In the past, sengis were sometimes referred to
as "jumping shrews," but this is something of
a misnomer because none jump or hop bipedally
like a kangaroo; the normal method of locomotion
is to walk or run on all fours. The name "elephant
shrew," bestowed by field naturalists in Africa,
alludes to their long snouts. With large eyes, a
trunklike nose, high-crowned cheek teeth, and
a large cecum similar to that found in herbivores,
long legs like those of small antelopes, and a long,
ratlike tail, sengis sometimes seem like walking
anthologies of other animals.

Anteaters on Stilts
FORM AND FUNCTION

The sengis of today give little insight into the
family's long and diverse evolutionary history
in Africa. Fossil sengis first appeared in the early
Eocene 50 million years ago, but they reached
their maximum diversity by the Miocene (24
million years ago), when they comprised six subfamilies. One included a small, herbivorous form
(Mylomygale) weighing about 50g (1.8oz) that
resembled a grass-eating rodent; another a large
plant eater (Myohyrax) ten times that weight was
so like an ungulate it was initially thought to be a
hyrax. Today, all that remains from these ancient
forms are representatives of two well-defined,
insectivorous subfamilies, the giant sengis
(Rhynchocyoninae) and the soft-furred sengis
(Macroscelidinae). The other four subfamilies
mysteriously died out by the Pleistocene, 1.5
million years ago.

Taxonomically, sengis have long been a source
of controversy. At first, biologists included them
with other insect eaters in the Insectivora. Then
they were briefly thought to be distantly related
to ungulates. Next there was a scheme to include
them with the tree shrews in a new grouping, the
Menotyphla. More recently, they have been associated with rabbits and hares. Most biologists now

agree that sengis belong in their own order, the
Macroscelidea. To avoid the old association with
true shrews (family Soricidae), many biologists are
replacing the common name "elephant shrew"
with sengi, a name derived from several African
Bantu languages.

So what is their exact phylogenetic relationship
with other mammals? With the advent of molecular techniques to unravel evolutionary relationships, there is a growing consensus that the
Macroscelidea belong to an ancient radiation of
African mammals that today share few obvious
morphological similarities. The latest proposal
includes the sengis in the superorder Afrotheria,
which also includes elephants, hyraxes, sea cows
(the Paenungulata), aardvarks, golden moles,
and tenrecs.

Widespread, but Not Common
DISTRIBUTION PATTERNS

Sengis are widespread in Africa, occupying very
diverse habitats. For example, the distribution of
the round-eared sengi (Macroscelides proboscideus)
includes the Namib Desert in southwestern Africa
as well as gravelly thornbush plains in South
Africa's Cape Province, while the three rock-
dwelling species in southern Africa (Elephantulus
myurus, E. rupestris, and E. edwardii) are largely
restricted to rocky outcrops and boulder fields.
Most other species of Elephantulus live in the vast
steppes and savannas of southern and eastern
Africa. The three giant sengis of the Rhynchocyon
genus and the four-toed sengi (Petrodromus tetradactylus) are restricted to lowland and mountain
forests and associated thickets in central and
eastern Africa. Elephantulus rozeti is found in arid
rocky habitats in extreme northwestern Africa,
isolated from all other species by the Sahara. The
absence of sengis from western Africa has never
been adequately explained. Nowhere are sengis

particularly common, and despite being highly
terrestrial and mostly active above ground during
the day and in the evening, they often escape
detection because of their swift locomotion and
secretive habits.

Golden-rumped sengis spend up to 80 percent
of their active hours searching for invertebrates,
which they track down in the leaf litter on the
forest floor by using their long, flexible noses as
probes, in the manner of coatis or pigs. Rhynchocyon species also use their forefeet, which have
three long claws, to excavate small, conical holes
in the soil. Important prey include beetles, centipedes, termites, spiders, and earthworms. The
soft-furred species spend only half as much time
foraging. They normally glean small invertebrates,
especially termites and ants, from leaves, twigs,
and the soil's surface, but they also eat plant matter, especially small, fleshy fruits and seeds. All
sengis have long tongues that extend well beyond
the tips of their noses and are used to flick small
food items into their mouths.

Monogamy and Trail-Clearing
SOCIAL BEHAVIOR

While sengi species look diverse and live in vastly
differing habitats, they all have similar sex lives.
Individuals of the golden-rumped, four-toed,
round-eared, rufous, and western rock species
live as monogamous pairs, but there appears to
be little affection between partners.

Rufous sengis that inhabit Kenya's densely
wooded savannas are distributed as
male–female pairs on territories that
vary in size from 1,600 to 4,500sq m
(0.4–1.1 acres). The same pattern is
found in golden-rumped sengis in
coastal forests of Kenya, although the
territory sizes are larger, averaging 1.7ha
(4.2 acres). Although monogamous,

Right *Representative species of sengis:* **1** *Checkered sengi (Rhynchocyon cirnei) scent marking with its anal glands;* **2** *Rufous sengi (Elephantulus rufescens) foraging for insects;* **3** *Round-eared sengi (Macroscelides proboscideus) clearing a trail;* **4** *North African sengi (Elephantulus rozeti) washing its face;* **5** *Four-toed sengi (Petrodromus tetradactylus) extruding its tongue after insects;* **6** *Black-and-rufous sengi (Rhynchocyon petersi) tearing at prey with its teeth and claws;* **7** *Golden-rumped sengi (R. chrysopygus) stalking before a chase.*

ORDER: MACROSCELIDEA

Sengis or Elephant shrews
Family: Macroscelididae
2 subfamilies; 4 genera; 15 species

Distribution N Africa, E, C and S Africa, absent from W Africa and Sahara

Habitat Varied, including montane and lowland forest, savanna, steppe, desert.

Size Ranges from Round-eared sengi, with head-body length 10.4–11.5cm (4.1–4.5in), tail length 11.5–13cm (4.5–5in), weight about 45g (1.6oz), to the Golden-rumped sengi with a head-body length of 27–29.4cm (11–12in), tail length 23–25.5cm (9.5–10.5in), weight about 540g (19 oz).

Coat Soft, in various shades of gray and brown in the soft-furred species, giant sengis have silky, colorful fur.

Diet Beetles, spiders, centipedes, earthworms, ants, termites and other small invertebrates; also fruits and seeds.

Breeding Gestation 57–65 days in the Rufous sengi, about 42 days in the Golden-rumped sengi.

Longevity 2½ years in the Rufous sengi (5½ in captivity), 4 years in the Golden-rumped sengi.

Conservation status *R. chrysopygus, R. petersi,* and *E. revoili* are classed as Endangered; *R. cirnei, M. proboscideus, E. edwardii,* and *E. rupestris* as Vulnerable.

GENUS *RHYNCHOCYON*

Golden-rumped sengi (*Rhynchocyon chrysopygus*), Black-and-rufous sengi (*R. petersi*), Checkered sengi (*R. cirnei*).

GENUS *PETRODROMUS*

Four-toed sengi (*Petrodromus tetradactylus*)

GENUS *MACROSCELIDES*

Round-eared sengi (*Macroscelides proboscideus*)

GENUS *ELEPHANTULUS*

Short-nosed sengi (*Elephantulus brachyrhynchus*), Cape sengi (*E. edwardii*), Dusky-footed sengi (*E. fuscipes*), Dusky sengi (*E. fuscus*), Bushveld sengi (*E. intufi*), Eastern rock sengi (*E. myurus*), Somali sengi (*E. revoili*), North African sengi (*E. rozeti*), Rufous sengi (*E. rufescens*), Western rock sengi (*E. rupestris*).

Note: Sengis have recently been reassigned, with other endemic African placentals (e.g. golden moles, tenrecs, and elephants), to a new grouping, the Afrotheria.

Right *Sengi tails – the one shown is from the four-toed sengi – are lined with knobbed bristles. Their exact function is controversial, but it has been noted that, during aggressive and sexual encounters, individuals lash their tails across the ground, dragging the bristles across the substrate. It may be that the animals are scent marking through this behavior, with the knobs acting as swabs to spread scent-bearing sebum from large glands on the undersurface of the tail.*

Right *Rufous sengis visibly mark their territories by creating small piles of dung in areas where the paths of two adjoining pairs meet. Occasionally aggressive encounters occur in these territorial arenas. In these situations, two animals of the same sex face one another and, while slowly walking in opposite directions, stand high on their long legs and accentuate their white feet, much like small mechanical toys. If neither of the animals then retreats, a fight usually develops and the loser is routed from the area.*

Below *A perfect ball of fur but for the protruding nose, a round-eared sengi basks in the sun. The species – the only representative of the Macroscelides genus – is limited to a region of about 20,000sq km (7,700sq mi) of southern African plain and desert, and is listed as vulnerable by the IUCN.*

individuals of both species spend little time together. The male and female share precisely the same territory, but defend this area individually, with females seeing off other females and males evicting intruding males. This system of monogamy, characterized by limited cooperation between the sexes, is also found in several small antelopes, such as the dik-dik and klipspringer. As in most monogamous mammals, the sexes are similar in size and appearance, but male giant sengis have larger canine teeth.

In territorial encounters, visual signals are important, but sengis also bring to bear their scent glands to mark out their land. These are located on the bottom of the tail in several *Elephantulus* species, on the soles of the feet in the rufous sengi, on the chest of the dusky-footed, rufous, and Somali sengis, and just behind the anus in the giant sengis of the *Rhynchocyon* genus. Vocal communication is unimportant, although the four-toed sengi and most species of *Elephantulus* create sounds by drumming their rear feet on the ground, while *Rhynchocyon* species slap their tails on the leaf litter. When captured, several

sengi species emit sharp, high-pitched screams, although all are surprisingly gentle when handled and rarely attempt to bite humans despite their well-developed teeth.

In several respects sengis are similar to small ungulates, especially in their avoidance of predators. Initially they rely on camouflage to elude detection, but if this fails they use their long legs to swiftly outdistance pursuing snakes and carnivores. This is no mean feat for a creature standing only 6cm (2.4in) high at the shoulder and weighing 58g (2oz); the trick is achieved by using a system of trails to rival the road network of a city like London.

Even so, this explanation begs a question about the purpose of monogamy in the case of the golden-rumped sengi, which does not clear trails, apparently leaving the male of the pair jobless. A possible answer lies in the forest habitat it inhabits. The tropical climate allows these particular sengis to breed continuously throughout the year, and their food resources are relatively evenly and widely distributed. Under these circumstances, the most productive strategy for a male may be to remain with one female, ensuring that he fathers her young, rather than to wander over huge expanses of forest trying to keep track of the reproductive condition of more than one female, and thereby running the very real risk of missing opportunities to mate. This mate-guarding explanation for monogamy is also thought to explain the paired sex lives of several small antelopes, such as the dik-dik and some duikers.

In contrast to the path-using four-toed and rufous sengis, several other sengis, including the round-eared, western rock, and bushveld species, dig short, shallow burrows in sandy substrates for shelter. Where the ground is too hard, these species will use abandoned rodent burrows. But even the burrow-using sengis do not incorporate nesting material in their shelters, as do most rodents. The giant sengis are more typical of small mammals, in that they spend each night in a leaf nest on the forest floor. To deny predators the reward of a meal in each nest that they find and tear open, the sengis build several nests and then sleep alone in a different nest every few nights.

ON THE TRAIL OF THE RUFOUS SENGI

Near Tsavo National Park in Kenya, the rufous sengi lives in dense thickets in which each pair builds, maintains, and defends a complex network of crisscrossing trails. To enable the sengis to run at full speed along these paths, the trails must be kept immaculately clean. Just a single twig could break an sengi's flight from a fast-moving predator with disastrous consequences, so the sengis regularly go road sweeping. Every day, individuals of a pair spend 20–40 percent of the daylight hours separately traversing much of their trail network, removing accumulated leaves and twigs with swift sidestrokes of their forefeet. Little-used paths consist merely of a series of small, bare, oval patches on the sandy soil on which the sengi lands as it bounds along the trail; those that are heavily used form continuous bare channels through the litter.

The trails of rufous sengis, and also those of *Petrodromus*, are exceptionally important because neither species nests or lives in burrows or shelters. They spend their entire lives relatively exposed, as would small antelopes. Their distinct black-and-

white facial pattern probably serves to disrupt the contour of their large black eyes, thus camouflaging them from predators while they are exposed on the trails.

The rufous sengi produces only 1 or 2 highly precocial and independent young per litter. Since the female alone can nurse her young, the male of the pair can do little to assist. This begs the question of why the animals should be monogamous in the first place.

In the rufous sengi, part of the answer may relate to the system of paths. Males spend nearly twice as much time trail cleaning than females – a rather similar arrangement to that of mara couples, which are also monogamous and in which the males put their effort into vigilance, freeing the female to graze. Although this sort of indirect help is not as obvious as the direct cooperation of wolf and marmoset pairs in raising their altricial young, it is just as vital to the sengi's reproductive success, for without paths, its ungulate-like habits would be completely ineffective.

Sengis in the tropics produce several litters throughout the year, but at higher latitudes reproduction becomes seasonal, usually in association with the wet season. Litters normally contain one or two young, but the North African sengi and checkered sengi may produce three young per litter. Although all sengis are born in a well-developed state with a coat pattern similar to that of adults, the young of giant sengis are not as precocial as those of the soft-furred species, and thus they are confined to the nest for about three weeks before they accompany their mother.

Giant sengis are exceedingly difficult to keep in captivity, and only recently have black-and-rufous sengis been bred in captivity. In contrast, rufous and round-eared sengis have been successfully exhibited and bred in several zoos, which has resulted in numerous laboratory studies of their

△ Above *Looking somewhat like a miniature anteater, a melanistic variant of the checkered sengi (Rhynchocyon cirnei) combs the forest floor for insects with its long, sensitive nose, which it uses as a probe to search for food items among the leaf litter.*

biology. For example, physiological studies of round-eared sengis have shown that they can go into torpor, with body temperatures dropping from about 37°C (98.6°F) to as low as 9.5°C (49°F) for short periods when food resources are limited. This is thought to be an adaptation to conserve energy. Research on captive rufous sengis has shown that they can recognize the identities of family members and neighbors from scent marks alone, so individuals can presumably closely monitor the use of their large territories by smell as well as by sight.

Disappearing Forests
CONSERVATION AND ENVIRONMENT

Generally, sengis are of little economic importance to man, although golden-rumped and four-toed sengis are snared and eaten along the Kenya coast. This subsistence trapping is illegal, but so far is thought to be sustainable. A bigger problem for these forest dwellers is severe habitat depletion, especially for those species occupying small, isolated patches of woodland in eastern Africa that are being degraded by tree cutting for the wood-carving trade, or else being destroyed outright to make way for subsistence farming, exotic tree plantations, or urban developments. It would be a dreadful loss if these unique, colorful mammals were to disappear after more than 50 million years just because their dwindling patches of forest could not be protected adequately.　　　GBR

ESCAPE AND PROTECTION

The tactics and adaptations of the golden-rumped sengi

THE AFRICAN SUN WAS JUST STARTING TO SET when a golden-rumped sengi made its way up to an indistinct pile of leaves about 1m (3ft) wide on the forest floor. The animal paused at the edge of the low mound for 15 seconds, sniffing, listening, and watching for the least irregularity. Sensing nothing unusual, it quietly slipped under the leaves. The leaf nest shuddered for a few seconds as the sengi arranged itself for the night, then everything was still.

At about the same time the animal's mate was retreating for the night into a similar nest located on the other side of the pair's home range. As this sengi prepared to enter its nest, a twig snapped somewhere. The animal froze, and then quietly left the area for a third nest, which it eventually entered, but not before dusk had fallen.

Every evening, within a few minutes of sunset, pairs of sengis separately approach and cautiously enter any one of a dozen or more nests they have constructed throughout their home range. They use a different nest each evening to discourage forest predators such as leopards and eagle owls from ascertaining exactly where they will be spending the night.

Changing nests is just one of several stratagems golden-rumped sengis regularly use to avoid predators. The problem they face is considerable. During the day they spend over 75 percent of their time exposed while foraging in leaf litter on the forest floor, where they fall prey to black mambas, forest cobras, and snake eagles. To prevent capture by such enemies the animals have developed tactics that involve not only the ability to run fast but also a distinctive coat pattern that is notable for its flashy coloration.

Extraordinarily, golden-rumped sengis can bound across open forest floor at speeds above 25km/h (16mph)—about as fast as an average person can run. Because they are relatively small, they can also pass easily through patches of undergrowth, leaving larger terrestrial and aerial predators behind as they do so. Despite their speed and agility, however, they still remain vulnerable to ambush by sit-and-wait predators, such as the southern banded snake eagle. Most small terrestrial mammals have cryptic coloration on their coats or skins to serve as camouflage. However, the forest floor along the coast of Kenya where the golden-rumped sengi lives is relatively open, so any defense against predation that relied on camouflage would be ineffective.

Instead, the sengi's tactic is to actively invite predators to take notice of it. It has a rump patch that is so visible that a waiting predator will discover a foraging sengi while it is too far away to make a successful ambush. The predator's initial reaction to the sight, such as rapidly turning its head or shifting its weight from one leg to another, may be enough to reveal its presence. By inducing the predator to disclose prematurely its intent to attack, a surprise ambush can be averted.

A sengi that discovers a predator while still outside its flight distance does not bound away; instead it pauses and then repeatedly slaps the leaf litter with its tail at intervals of a few seconds. The sharp sound produced probably conveys a message to the predator: "I know you are there, but you are outside my flight distance, and I can probably outrun you if you attack." Through experience, the predator learns that when it hears this signal it is generally futile to attempt a pursuit,

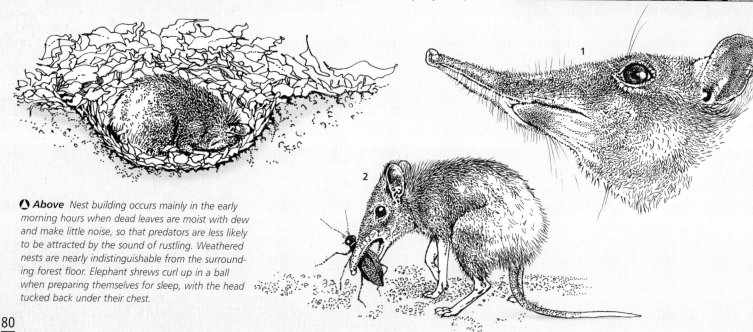

⬥ **Above** *Nest building occurs mainly in the early morning hours when dead leaves are moist with dew and make little noise, so that predators are less likely to be attracted by the sound of rustling. Weathered nests are nearly indistinguishable from the surrounding forest floor. Elephant shrews curl up in a ball when preparing themselves for sleep, with the head tucked back under their chest.*

nearest cover as the bird swoops to make its kill, noisily pounding the leaf litter with its rear legs as it bounds away. Only speed and agility can save it in such a situation.

The golden-rumped sengi is monogamous, but pairs spend only about 20 percent of their time in visual contact with each other; the remainder is spent resting or foraging alone. So for most of the time they must communicate via scent or sound. The distinct sound of a sengi tail-slapping or bounding across the forest floor can be heard over a large part of a pair's 1.5ha (3.7 acre) territory. These sounds not only signal to the predator that it has been discovered, but also communicate to the sengi's mate and young that an intruder has been detected.

Each pair of sengis defends its territorial boundaries against neighbors and wandering subadults in search of their own territories. During an aggressive encounter a resident will pursue an intruder on a high-speed chase through the forest. If the intruder is not fast enough, it will be gashed by the long canines of the resident.

These conflicts between sengis can be thought of as a special type of predator–prey interaction, revealing yet another way in which the animal's coloration may serve to avoid successful predation. The skin under the animal's rump patch is up to three times thicker than that on the middle of its back. The golden color of the rump probably serves as a target, diverting attacks on such vital parts of the body as the head and flanks to an area of the body that is better suited to take assaults.

Deflective marks are common in invertebrates, and have been shown to be effective in foiling predators; for example, the distinctive eye spots on the wings of some butterflies attract the predatory attacks of birds, allowing the insects to escape relatively unscathed. The yellow rump and the white tip on the black tail of the sengi may serve a similar function by attracting the talons of an eagle or the fangs of a striking snake, thus improving the animal's chances of making a successful escape. GBR

◁ ◖ **Above and Left** *Foraging in the leaf litter on the forest floor. The golden-rumped sengi has a small mouth located far behind the top of its snout* **1**, *which makes it difficult to ingest large prey items. Small invertebrates are eaten by flicking them into the mouth with a long, extensible tongue.* **2** *In the Arabuko-Sokoke forest of coastal Kenya, sengis feed mainly on beetles, centipedes, termites, cockroaches, ants, spiders, and earthworms, in decreasing order of importance.*

◖ **Right** *Sengis chase intruders from their territory using a half-bounding gait.*

because the animal is on guard and can easily make its escape back to a place of refuge.

The situation is very different when a sengi becomes aware of a predator – say, for example, an eagle – so close that a safe escape cannot be guaranteed. In those circumstances, the animal will take flight across the forest floor towards the

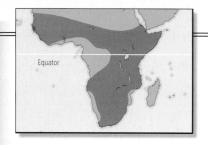

AARDVARK

FEW PEOPLE HAVE HAD THE FORTUNE OF A *close encounter with the aardvark, one of Africa's most bizarre and specialized mammals. Nocturnal and secretive, this ant and termite eater is the only living member of the order Tubulidentata. Because of its elusiveness, it is also one of the least known of living mammals.*

Aardvark means, literally, "earthpig" in Afrikaans, but the resemblance to a pig is purely superficial. The animal has large ears, a coarse-haired body, and a tubular snout – but one much longer than any pig's, and shaped to the requirements of a diet specialized on ants and termites.

Fossil evidence suggests that members of the Tubulidentata are descended from primitive ungulates and spread from Africa to Europe and Asia during the late Miocene (about 8 million years ago). As a result, aardvarks were previously included within the Paenungulates, however, recent molecular data suggest that the aardvark is more closely related to the endemic African insectivores (sengis, golden moles, and tenrecs). Three of the four genera are now extinct.

Adaptations for Ant-eating
FORM AND FUNCTION

Many adaptations in the aardvark's anatomy equip it for eating ants and termites. With its tubular snout close to the ground, it can make sweeping motions 30cm (12in) wide, following a zigzag course sniffing for food. The same route may be used on consecutive nights. Pushing the end of its soft nose firmly into a suitable patch of ground, the aardvark inevitably sucks up some soil, which is prevented from entering the lungs by a filter of dense hairs in its nostrils. A wall between the nasal slits is equipped with a series of thick, fleshy processes, probably used for sensing the jittery prey.

When an aardvark finds the prey that it is seeking, it will rapidly dig a V-shaped furrow with its forefeet. Its short, powerful limbs have four digits on the front feet and five on the back, all equipped with long, sharp-edged, spoon-shaped claws that make light work of digging. A sticky, round, long, thin tongue and well-developed salivary glands act like flypaper to ensure aardvarks get the most out of every termite mound. Their stomachs have a muscular pyloric area, which functions like a gizzard, grinding up the food. Aardvarks therefore do not need to chew their food and so have no need for incisors or canine teeth; instead, their continuously growing, open-rooted cheek teeth consist of two upper and two

lower premolars and three upper and three lower molars in each half-jaw. The cheek teeth differ from those of other mammals in that the dentine is not surrounded by enamel but by the thin, bonelike tissue known as cementum.

Both male and female aardvarks have anal scent glands that emit a pungent, yellowish secretion, probably to advertise social status. Large ears signal the animal's acute hearing, but their typical posture during foraging is vertically upward, not earthward. This suggests that aardvarks do not strain to hear the sounds of termites, but rather listen out for predators.

In order to get enough nourishment, aardvarks readily eat more than 50,000 insects in a night. In one study, they were found to consume 21 different species of ants, plus 2 species of termite (the latter mostly in the winter). Aardvarks share their habitat with a variety of other termite- and ant-eating animals, including hyenas, jackals, vultures, storks, geese, pangolins, bat-eared foxes, and aardwolves, but all of these also take other prey, so reducing competition.

Nighttime Foragers
SOCIAL BEHAVIOR

Aardvarks are almost exclusively nocturnal and solitary. They normally emerge from their burrows shortly after nightfall, though they may come out late in the afternoon in winter. Individuals tracked by radio in South Africa's arid Karoo plateau were found to be most active in the early evening, from 8pm to midnight, though the moon was apparently not a factor in their decision to venture forth. Their home ranges are well organized, with a system of burrows that provide very efficacious refuges for animals seeking shelter from storms or hungry predators. The animals in the Karoo

Above Once a termite mound is located, the aardvark assumes a sitting position and inserts its mouth and nose. Feeding bouts, lasting from 20 seconds to 7 minutes, are interrupted by periods of digging.

study foraged over distances varying from 2–5km (1.2–3mi) each night, covering an average distance of 550m (1,800ft) an hour without stopping to rest. Their nightly route was circular, but did not encompass their entire home range. Other studies suggest that aardvarks may range as far as 15km (9mi) during a 10-hour foraging period, covering up to 30km (19mi) in a night.

In the Karoo survey, home ranges for both males and females varied from 133–384ha (328–949 acres), and overlapped considerably with those of adjacent animals. Individuals spent half their time in a core area that took up 25–33 percent of the range. The proportion of time spent above ground feeding was higher in summer than in winter. In winter, aardvarks may remain active above ground for an average of 5 hours, regularly returning to their burrows before midnight, but in summer their nightly sorties may last 8–9 hours.

Aardvarks make burrows of three main types: those dug when looking for food; larger, temporary sites, scattered through the home range, that may be used for refuge; and permanent refuges in which the young are born. The latter are deep and labyrinthine, up to 13m (43ft) long, and usually have more than one entrance. Aardvarks like to change the layout of their homes regularly, and can, if necessary, dig new burrows with considerable speed, disappearing below ground within 5–20 minutes. In the Karoo study, burrowing was estimated to affect 0.05 percent of the total land area per year, and burrows were used for between 4 and 38 consecutive nights, after which they were abandoned. Only mothers and their young share burrows. Droppings are deposited in shallow digs throughout their range and covered with soil.

Little information is available on reproduction, but a single offspring is born weighing around 2kg

ORDER: TUBULIDENTATA

Family: Orycteropodidae
One species. 18 subspecies have been listed, but most may be invalid; there is insufficient knowledge of the animal for firm conclusions to be drawn.

AARDVARK *Orycteropus afer*

DISTRIBUTION Africa S of the Sahara, excluding deserts.

HABITAT Mainly open woodland, scrub, and grassland; rarer in rain forest; avoids rocky hills.

SIZE Head–body length 105–130cm (41–51in); tail length 45–63cm (18–25in); weight 40–65kg (88–143lb). Both sexes same size.

COAT Pale, yellowish gray, with head and tail off-white (the gray to reddish brown color often seen results from staining by soil, which occurs when the animal is burrowing). Females tend to be lighter in color.

DIET Mainly ants and termites.

BREEDING Gestation 7 months.

LONGEVITY Up to 10 years in captivity.

CONSERVATION STATUS Not threatened.

(4lb), probably just before or during the rainy season, when termites are readily available. The infant first ventures out of the burrow to accompany its mother when only 2 weeks old. It will start digging its own burrows at about 6 months, but may stay with the mother until the onset of the next mating season.

Specialists Ill-fitted for Change
CONSERVATION AND ENVIRONMENT

Due to their specialized food preferences, aardvarks are extremely vulnerable to habitat changes. Intensive crop farming may reduce their density, but increased cattle herding benefits them, as trampling creates the right conditions for termites. However, little progress can be made in formulating management policies until more is known about the behavior and ecology of the animals.

⬖ **Above** The aardvark's long, tubular ears give it vital early warning of predators. Once it has dug far down into the soil, it can fold its ears flat, so preventing them from filling with earth and impairing its hearing. Aardvarks are fast diggers and can excavate a new burrow in as little as five minutes.

Aardvarks are killed not just for their flesh, which is said to taste like pork, but also for their teeth, worn on necklaces by members of the Margbetu, Ayanda, and Logo tribes of the Democratic Republic of the Congo to prevent illness and as good-luck charms. The animal's bristly hair is sometimes reduced to a powder that is regarded as a potent poison when added to the local beer. It is also believed that the harvest will be increased when aardvark claws are put into baskets used to collect flying termites for food.   RJvA

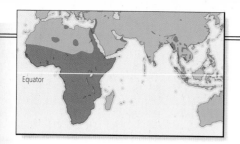

ELEPHANTS AND RELATIVES

t HE HUGE ELEPHANT, THE RELATIVELY SMALL *hyrax, and the aquatic dugongs and manatees all look markedly different from one another. And yet, zoologists believe that these three orders of animals are more closely related to each other than they are to other mammals, and so have grouped them together in the superorder Paenungulata (sometimes called subungulates).*

This surprising relationship between such diverse mammals has been corroborated by research into the animals' molecular biology and anatomy. It has also recently been shown that these animals are not closely related to the other ungulate orders (Artiodactyla and Perissodactyla) but instead belong to the basal placental African endemic group, the Afrotheria. All of these mammals (with the exception of the sea cows) have an initial appearance and early diversification in Africa, and this may reflect the early isolation of a common ancestor on this continent.

The three orders of paenungulates proper – the Hyracoidea (hyraxes), Sirenia (sea cows), and Proboscidea (trunked mammals, today represented only by the elephants) – share certain derived anatomical characters, including details of the structure of the skull, wrist, and placenta. Indeed, it has even emerged that the sea cows, which belong to the order Sirenia (see Dugong and Manatees) may be more closely related to the elephants than are the hyraxes. The grouping of sea cows and elephants is called the Tethytheria, which also includes an extinct group of amphibious mammals, the desmostylians, as well as the more terrestrial embrithopods. They have short,

nail-like hooves (secondarily lost in sirenians), and share the peculiar feature of a styloglossus muscle, running between the base of the skull and the tongue, that is forked at its insertion into the tongue. The females have two teats between the forelegs (hyraxes have an additional two or four on the belly); the testes remain in the body cavity close to the kidneys (this latter feature being true of all Afrotheria aside from the aardvark).

Out of Africa
PAENUNGULATE ORIGINS

The Paeungulata (also called the Subungulata) evolved in Africa, during this continent's isolation, from an ancestral immigrant mammal that also gave rise to the rest of the Afrotheria. By the early Eocene (about 54 million years ago), the Paenungulata had already separated into the three distinct orders. The Tubulidentata (represented only by the aardvark) diverged early on, possibly during the late Cretaceous and specialized in feeding on termites and ants.

The Hyracoidea proliferated about 40 million years ago, but spread no further than Africa and southern Eurasia (including China). Today, their only Eurasian stronghold is around the eastern Mediterranean (hyraxes are the "conies" mentioned in the Bible). Some of them became as large as tapirs, but now only the smaller forms remain. The decline of the Hyracoidea during

the Miocene, 25 million years ago, coincided with the radiation of the Artiodactyla, against whom it is likely that they were unable to compete.

The Proboscidea were a very successful order that went through a period of rapid radiation in Africa and then spread across the globe except for Australia and Antarctica. The most obvious feature of the Proboscidea is, of course, their large size. Associated with this are their flattened soles, elongated limb bones, and the modifications to the head and associated structures. Modern elephants are only a remnant of a previously vast diversity of proboscideans, many of which survived into the Pleistocene. Elephants are distinguished by having upper tusks only and a dentition adapted for eating grass. The deinotheres, known from Africa and Asia, had lower tusks only, and appear to have been specialized browsers with tapirlike molars. The mastodons, which spread to North America, were also browsers and, like elephants, eventually lost their lower tusks. Gomphotheres had piglike molars, indicating an omnivorous diet. Most forms kept their lower tusks, and they spread not only to North America but also into South America.

◐ **Right** *Evolution of the elephant. Beginning with the small, tapirlike* Moeritherium **1***, in the early Oligocene (34 million years ago), proboscideans became a large widespread group by the mid-Miocene (around 15 million years ago).* Trilophodon **2** *was one of a family of long-jawed gomphotheres found in Eurasia, Africa, and North America from the Miocene to the Pleistocene (24–1.8 million years ago).* Platybelodon **3** *was a shovel-tusked gomphothere found in the late Miocene (about 12–5 million years ago) of Asia and North America. The imperial mammoth (*Mammuthus imperator*) **4***, the largest ever proboscidean, flourished in the Pleistocene of Eurasia, Africa, and North America. Unlike the earlier forms, it had high-crowned teeth, like those of the modern savanna elephant (*Loxodonta africana*) **5***.

Highly Specialized Teeth
DENTITION

All paenungulates show specializations of the molars (grinding teeth) and incisors, and all have independently lost their canines. The elephant's upper incisors have become its characteristic tusks, and the same teeth have been enlarged in both the hyraxes and the dugong (while manatees have no front teeth at all). Elephants and hyraxes have transverse ridges on their molars, while those of the sirenians are secondarily simplified. Hyraxes have molars very much like those of the primitive horses, which is why the earliest known horse was originally called *Hyracotherium* (having been mistaken for a hyrax). However, the other paenungulates are more specialized. The molars of the dugong are continuously replaced from the back and shed from the front. Elephants have very high-crowned molars, and both elephants and manatees have taken advantage of the fact that mammalian molars erupt in sequence from the back of the jaw in a way so as to prolong the effective life of their dentition. Elephants delay the timing of molar eruption so that only one tooth is in use in the jaw at any one time. Each tooth has been greatly enlarged to the size of the entire back of the jaw; when one tooth wears down, the erupting tooth behind moves in to take its place. Elephants have six teeth in each jaw half (upper and lower, left and right), which represent the normal mammalian complement of three milk molars and three true molars, but when the last tooth has been worn down the elephant is all out of dentition. In contrast, manatees do not enlarge the individual teeth, but have added to the normal mammalian complement, and have a virtually never-ending supply of erupting teeth throughout their life (at least 20 in each jaw half), erupting from the back of the jaw and falling out of the front when worn down. CMJ/RFWB

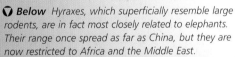

◗ **Below** *Hyraxes, which superficially resemble large rodents, are in fact most closely related to elephants. Their range once spread as far as China, but they are now restricted to Africa and the Middle East.*

85

Hyraxes

NTRIGUINGLY, THE ANCIENT HEBREW AND *Phoenician word for the hyrax, shaphan, (meaning, literally, "the hidden one") was responsible for a geographical misnomer. Some 3,000 years ago, Phoenician seamen sailing west through the Mediterranean sighted a coastline teeming with animals they thought were hyraxes, familiar to them from their homeland in the Levant. Accordingly, they called it* Ishaphan *("Island of the Hyrax"). The Romans later modified this to* Hispania, *root of the Spanish* España. *But the animals the sailors saw were in fact rabbits, and so Spain is actually misnamed.*

During the Pliocene – approximately 7–2 million years ago – hyraxes were both widespread and diverse: they radiated from the southern parts of Europe to China in the east, and one fossil form, *Pliohyrax graecus*, was probably aquatic. However, in the present day they are confined to Africa and the Middle East.

The rock hyraxes have the widest geographical and altitudinal distribution, while the bush hyraxes are largely confined to the eastern parts of Africa. Both are dependent on the presence of suitable refuges in "kopjes" – rocky outcrops – and cliffs. As their name suggests, the tree hyraxes are found in arboreal habitats of Africa, but in the alpine areas of the Ruwenzori Mountains they are also rock dwellers. The eastern tree hyrax might be the earliest type of forest-living tree hyrax, being a member of the primitive fauna and flora of the islands of Zanzibar and Pemba.

Small but Solidly Built

FORM AND FUNCTION

The odd appearance of the hyrax has caused even further confusion. Their superficial similarity to rodents led Storr, in 1780, mistakenly to link them with guinea pigs of the genus *Cavia*, and he thus gave them the family name of Procaviidae or "before the guinea pigs." Later, the mistake was discovered, but the group was given the equally misleading name of hyrax, which comes from the Greek and means "shrew mouse."

Hyraxes are small and solidly built, with a short, rudimentary stump for a tail. Males and females are approximately the same size, reaching a maximum length of about 60cm (24in) and rarely weighing more than a little over 4kg (9lb). The feet are ill-equipped for digging, but have rubbery pads containing numerous glands that exude sweat when the animal is running, which greatly enhances their climbing ability; additionally, part of the underside of the foot can be retracted, which creates something akin to a suction pad to afford the animals extra grip. Species that live in arid and warm zones have short fur, while tree hyraxes and the species that is found in alpine areas have thick, soft fur. Hyraxes have long, tactile hairs at intervals all over their bodies, probably to aid in orientation when they are in dark fissures and holes. They also have a dorsal gland, which is surrounded by a light-colored circle of hairs that stiffen whenever the animal is excited. The function of this gland is unknown; however, it is thought that it might be important for intraspecific odor communication.

Fossil beds in the Fayum, Egypt, show that 40 million years ago hyraxes were the most important medium-sized grazing and browsing ungulates. At the time there were at least six genera (though there could have been many more), which ranged in dimensions from their present size to those that were the size of tapirs. With the first radiation of the bovids (a more advanced mammal) in the course of the Miocene – about 25 million years ago – hyrax populations were considerably reduced and, correspondingly, hyraxes became much less diverse; the animals survived only among the rock and tree habitats into which the bovids did not go.

Modern-day hyraxes retain some primitive features, notably an inefficient feeding mechanism that involves cropping food with the cheek teeth or molars instead of with the incisors, as is the case with modern hoofed mammals. Additionally, hyraxes also possess short feet and have poor body-temperature regulation.

◁ **Left** *Found from southeastern Egypt to northeastern South Africa, Bruce's yellow-spotted hyrax obtains most of its food from browsing. Dominant males will stand guard on high rocks and keep watch while the rest of the group feeds below, though they have also been observed keeping watch while the rest of the group bask on the rocks. If danger approaches, they give a shrill alarm call.*

Coping with a High Fiber Diet

DIET

Hyraxes consume a wide variety of plants. Rock hyraxes feed mainly on grass, which is a relatively coarse material, and therefore have hypsodont dentition – high crowns with relatively short roots, whereas both the browsing bush hyraxes and the tree hyraxes have a diet that is based on softer food and therefore have a brachydont dentition, which comprises short crowns with relatively long roots.

Hyraxes do not ruminate. The morphology of the digestive tract differs from most other animals. The gut is complex, with three separate areas designed for the digestion of fibrous diets by means of microbial fermentation. Their kidneys are efficient enough to allow them to exist on only a minimal moisture intake. In addition, they have a high capacity for concentrating urea and electrolytes, and excrete large amounts of undissolved calcium carbonate. As hyraxes have the habit of consistently urinating in the same place, the crystallized calcium carbonate forms deposits, which whiten the cliffs. These crystals were used as medicine both by several South African tribes as well as by Europeans. The crystals were used for the treatment of such ailments as epilepsy, hysteria, St. Vitus's dance, injuries, and as an abortivum.

KOPJE COHABITANTS

The dense vegetation of the Serengeti and Matobo National Parks, in Tanzania and Zimbabwe respectively, supports two species of hyraxes – the gray-brown bush hyrax and the larger dark brown rock hyrax – living together in harmony. Whenever two or more closely related species live together permanently in a confined habitat, at least some of their basic needs must differ, otherwise one species will eventually exclude the other. In the case of these two species, the division of food resources is the key factor that allows them to cohabit successfully – thus while the bush hyrax browses on leaves, the rock hyrax feeds mainly on grass. Both species consume plants that are poisonous to most other animals.

When bush and rock hyraxes occur together, they live in close contact. In the early mornings they huddle together after spending the night in the same holes. They use the same urinating and defecating places. Births tend to be synchronous, and they show cooperative behavior. Newborns are greeted and sniffed intensively by members of both species.

The juveniles associate and form a nursery group; they play together with no apparent hindrance, as play elements in both species are alike. Most of their vocalizations are also similar, including sounds used in threat, fear, alertness, and contact situations. Such a close association has never been recorded between any other two mammal species except among primates and whales.

Even so, bush and rock hyraxes do differ in key behavior patterns. Firstly, they do not interbreed, because their mating behavior is different and they also have different sex organ anatomy: the penis of the bush hyrax is long and complex, with a thin appendage at the end, arising within a cuplike glans, while that of the rock hyrax is short and simple. The male territorial call, possibly intended as a "keep out" signal, is also different.

⊙ **Below** *A mixed group, comprising Johnston's hyrax and Bruce's yellow-spotted hyrax bask on rocks together in the Serengeti National Park.*

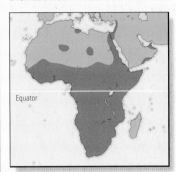

Gregarious Group-Dwellers

SOCIAL BEHAVIOR

Hyraxes have a poor ability to regulate body temperature, and a low metabolic rate. The extent to meet energetic requirements depends on the interaction of ambient temperature, food availability, food quality and foraging efficiency in the presence of predators. Each of these factors influence the behavior on a daily and seasonal basis. To control body temperature, hyraxes huddle together and bask in the sun. They are also relatively inactive, which enables them to exist in very dry areas that provide food of poor quality. A crucial requirement, however, is shelter that provides them with relatively constant temperature and humidity, as well as protection from predators.

Hyrax social organization varies in relation to living space. On kopjes smaller than 4,000sq m (43,000sq ft), both rock and bush hyraxes live in cohesive family groups consisting of 3–7 related adult females, 1 adult territorial male, dispersing males, and the juveniles of both sexes. Larger kopjes may support several family groups, each occupying a traditional range. The territorial male repels all intruding males from an area encompassing the females' core area (the average for bush hyraxes is 27 animals in 2,100sq m/22,600sq ft, and for rock hyraxes 4 animals to 4,250sq m/45,750sq ft).

The females' home ranges are not defended and may overlap. Rarely, an adult female will join a group and will eventually be incorporated. Females become receptive about once a year, and a peak in births seems to coincide with rainfall. Within a family group, the pregnant females all give birth within a period of about three weeks. The number of young per female bush hyrax varies between 1 and 3 (mean 1.6), and in rock hyraxes between 1 and 4 (mean 2.4). The young are fully developed at birth, and suckling young of both species assume a strict teat order. Weaning occurs at 1–5 months and both sexes reach sexual maturity at about 16–17 months. Upon sexual maturity females usually join the adult female group, while males disperse before they reach 30 months. Adult females live significantly longer than adult males.

There are four classes of mature male: territorial and peripheral, plus early and late dispersers. Territorial males are the most dominant. Their aggressive behavior toward other adult males escalates in the mating season, when the weight of their testes increases a record twentyfold. These males monopolize receptive females, and show a preference for copulating with females over 28 months of age. A territorial male monopolizes "his" female group year-round, and repels other males from

> **Right** A Cape hyrax with its offspring. The young are usually born in a crevice, in a litter that may vary in size between a single young and perhaps half a dozen, though most commonly will comprise 2–3. The young are born with hair and become mobile quite soon after birth, usually within 24 hours or so.

> **Left** A southern tree hyrax eating Acacia leaves. Although one genus is commonly referred to as the "tree hyraxes," all hyraxes are adept at climbing and those from other genera will sometimes bask in trees. However, the tree hyraxes' arboreal dependence puts it most seriously at risk from deforestation.

> **Right** Mating in hyraxes is both brief and vigorous. The anatomy of the penis varies quite significantly between the three genera. In rock hyraxes it is short, simply built, and elliptical in cross section; in tree hyraxes it is similarly built and slightly curved; in bush hyraxes, illustrated here, it is long and complex: on the end of the penis, and arising within a cuplike glans penis, is a short, thin appendage, which has the penis opening. **1** The male presses the penis against the vagina; **2** violent copulation takes place, in which the male leaves the ground; **3** the female moves forward, causing the male to withdraw.

sleeping holes, basking places, and feeding areas. Males can fight to the death, although this is probably quite rare. While his group members feed, a territorial male will often stand guard on a high rock and be the first to call in case of danger. The males utter the territorial call all year round.

On small kopjes, peripheral males are unable to settle, but on large kopjes they can occupy areas on the edge of the territorial males' areas. They live solitarily, and the highest-ranking takes over a female group when a territorial male disappears. These males show no seasonality in aggression but call only in the mating season. Most of their mating attempts and copulations are with females under 28 months – older males probably do not bother mating with females this

young as first pregnancies tend to have a higher mortality rate.

The early dispersers include the majority of the juvenile males. These leave their birth sites at between 16–24 months old, soon after reaching sexual maturity. The late dispersers leave a year later, but still leave before they are 30 months old. Before leaving their birth sites, both early and late dispersers have ranges that overlap with their mothers' home ranges. They disperse in the mating season to become peripheral males. Almost no threatening, submissive, or fleeing behavior has been observed taking place between territorial males and late dispersers.

Individual rock and bush hyraxes have been observed to disperse over a distance of at least 2km (1.2mi). However, the greater the distance a dispersing animal has to travel across the open grass plains, where there is little cover and few hiding places, the more the animal is at risk, either of predation or as a result of its inability to cope with temperature stress.

Long-term observations in Serengeti, Matobo (Zimbabwe), and Israel show that hyrax colonies fluctuate, and that small colonies are prone to extinction. Preliminary DNA analysis of rock and bush hyraxes in the Serengeti suggests that there is little genetic variation among kopjes. Dispersing occurs among closely located kopjes (around 10 km/6mi distance). Migrating bush hyrax females prevent inbreeding and are mainly responsible for the long-distance gene transfer between kopjes.

Enemies Within and Without
CONSERVATION AND ENVIRONMENT

The most important predator of hyraxes is the Verreaux eagle, which feeds almost exclusively on them. Other predators are the martial and tawny eagles, leopards, lions, jackals, spotted hyenas, and several snake species. External parasites such as ticks, lice, mites, and fleas, and internal parasites such as nematodes, cestodes, and anthrax, also probably play an important role in hyrax mortality. In Kenya and Ethiopia it was found that rock and tree hyraxes might be an important reservoir for the human parasitic disease leishmaniasis.

The eastern tree hyrax is extensively hunted for its fur in the forest belt surrounding Mt. Kilimanjaro; it takes 48 pelts to yield one rug. Because African forests are disappearing at an alarming rate, the tree hyraxes are probably the most endangered of all the hyrax species, especially in small areas of woodland such as those on the islands of Zanzibar and Pemba and in the Usambara Mountains of Tanzania. No recent information is available on the status of the two bush hyraxes *Heterohyrax antineae* in Algeria or *H. chapini* in Congo, but their status is deemed to be vulnerable.   HNH

Elephants

MODERN ELEPHANTS ARE THE LARGEST *extant land mammals; they have the biggest brains in the animal kingdom, live as long as humans, are able to learn and remember, and are adaptable as working animals. The antecedents of today's elephants are* Phosphatherium, *the earliest proboscidean, which lived around 55 million years ago, and* Moeritherium *(named for Egypt's Lake Moeris, near which its remains were discovered), from around 35 m.y.a.*

For millennia, elephants' great strength has been exploited in agriculture and warfare, and even today, notably in the Indian subcontinent, they are still important economically and as cultural symbols. But over the past 150 years growing human populations causing habitat loss and the demand for elephant tusks, the main source of commercial ivory, has brought about a drastic decline in elephant populations across most of their range.

Big Bodies, Big Brains
FORM AND FUNCTION

Though African and Asian elephants are ecologically very similar, there are physical and physiological differences between the two. In addition to visible distinctions, the African species have one more pair of ribs than their Asian counterpart (21 versus 20).

Of the African elephants, the savanna species is better understood than the forest elephant, since it is far easier to study behavior in the open grasslands of East Africa than in dense forest habitats.

Savanna bulls are also the biggest and heaviest elephants of all. The largest known specimen, killed in Angola in 1955 and now on display in the Smithsonian Institute in Washington DC, weighed 10 tonnes and measured 4m (13.1ft) at the shoulder. Body size continues to increase throughout life, so that the biggest elephant in a group is also likely to be the oldest.

The characteristic form of the cranium, jaws, teeth, tusks, ears, and digestive system of elephants are all part of the adaptive complex associated with the evolution of large body size (see box). The cranium, jaws, and teeth form a specialized system for crushing coarse plant material. The skull is disproportionately large compared with the size of the brain and has evolved to support the trunk and heavy dentition. It is, however, relatively light, due to the presence in the cranium of interlinked air cells and cavities.

The tusks are elongated upper incisors. They first appear at 2 years of age and grow throughout life, so that by the age of 60, a bull's tusks may each weigh 60kg (132lb). Such massive "tuskers" have always been prime targets for ivory and big-game hunters, with the result that few remain in the wild today. Elephant ivory is a unique mixture of dentine and calcium salts, and a transverse section through a tusk shows a regular diamond pattern not seen in the tusks of any other mammal. The tusks are used in feeding for such purposes as prizing the bark off trees or digging for roots, in social encounters as instruments of display, and also as weapons.

The upper lip and the nose of elephants have become elongated and muscularized to form a

trunk. Unlike other herbivores, an elephant cannot reach the ground with its mouth. The fact that early proboscideans did not evolve an elongated neck may have been due to the weight of their heavy cranial and jaw structures. Besides enabling elephants to feed from the ground, the trunk is also used for feeding from trees and shrubs, breaking off branches, and picking leaves, shoots, and fruits. Further uses include drinking, greeting, caressing and threatening, squirting water and throwing dust, and the forming and amplifying of vocalizations. Elephants drink by sucking water into their trunks, then pouring it into their mouths; they also throw water over their backs to cool themselves. At times of water shortage they sometimes spray themselves with water that they have stored in a pouch in the pharynx. The trunk can also serve as a snorkel, enabling an individual to breathe if submerged, for instance during a river crossing. Elephants use their trunks to rub an itchy eye or to scratch an ear. Trunks are also employed to gesture at enemies, to throw objects, or to use tools such as sticks to scratch the skin.

The most common elephant vocalization is a growl emanating from the larynx (what hunters used to call the "tummy rumble"). This sound can carry for up to 1km (0.6mi), and may be used as a warning, or to maintain contact with other elephants. When feeding in dense bush, members of a group monitor each other's positions by low growls with a strong infrasonic component (see box). They vocalize less frequently when the bush is more open and the group members can see one another. The trunk is used as a resonating chamber to amplify bellows or screams so as to convey a variety of emotions. New evidence suggests that another organ, high in the trunk and known as the alinasal cartilage, may also modify sounds. This cartilage divides the bony opening where the trunk begins (the external nares) and can be used to direct the flow of air. The loud trumpeting of elephants is used mainly when they are excited, surprised, about to attack, or interacting in play.

Visual messages are conveyed by changes in posture and the position of the tail, head, ears, and trunk, which besides the other uses described earlier has a secondary value in communication. Though powerful enough to lift whole trees, the trunk is also an acutely sensitive organ of smell and touch. Smell plays an important part in social contacts within a herd and in the detection of external threats. As to touch, the trunk's prehensile two fingerlike lips, endowed with fine sensory hairs, can pick up very small objects. In addition, elephants often touch each other using the trunk;

African elephant

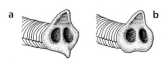

Asian elephant

◐ **Above** *African and Asian elephants compared. The African elephant is bigger, with a concave back and larger ears. Its trunk has two processes ("lips")* **a** *rather than the Asian's one* **b***. Whereas both sexes of both African species generally have tusks, these are mainly confined to male Asian elephants.*

⊲ **Left** An African elephant cow and calf. The huge ears, which give the elephant such a distinctive frontal appearance, function as radiators for cooling its bulky body by creating a vast surface area over which heat is lost.

ELEPHANTS

Order: Proboscidea

Family: Elephantidae

3 species in 2 genera

DISTRIBUTION Africa S of the Sahara; S Asia.

Equator

SAVANNA ELEPHANT *Loxodonta africana*
Sub-Saharan Africa. Savanna grassland, bushland, and woodland. SH male 3.3m (10.8ft), female 2.7m (8.9ft); WT male up to 6 tonnes, female 3 tonnes. In its densest places, the skin is 2–4cm (0.8–1.6in) thick and sparsely endowed with hair. The Savanna elephant typically has only four toes on the forefoot and three on the hindfoot. Breeding: gestation averages 656 days. Longevity: 60 years (more than 80 in captivity). Conservation status: Vulnerable.

FOREST ELEPHANT *Loxodonta cyclotis*
C and W Africa; dense lowland jungle. SH male 2.2m (7.2ft), female 1.8m (5.9ft); WT up to 2.5 tonnes. Tusks straighter and ears more rounded than Savanna elephant. In common with Asian elephants, five toes on the forefoot and four toes on the hindfoot. Conservation status: Vulnerable.

ASIAN ELEPHANT *Elephas maximus*
Indian subcontinent and Sri Lanka, Indochina, parts of peninsular Malaysia, Thailand, and SE Asian islands. Evergreen and dry deciduous forests, thorn scrub jungle, swamp and grassland; from sea level up to 3,000m (10,000ft). Three subspecies: *E. m. maximus* on Sri Lanka, *E. m. sumatranus* on Sumatra, and *E. m. indicus* on mainland Asia. HBL 5.5–6.4m (18–21ft); SH 2.5–3m (8–10ft); WT male 5.4 tonnes, female 2.7 tonnes. Skin: dark gray to brown, sometimes marked with flesh-colored blotches on the forehead, ears, and chest. Breeding: gestation 615–668 days; normally a single calf is born, weighing about 100kg (224lb). Longevity: 75–80 years in captivity. Conservation status: Endangered.

Abbreviations HBL = head–body length SH = shoulder height WT = weight

a mother will continually use hers to guide her infant. When elephants meet, they often greet each other by touching the other's mouth with the tip of their trunk.

The brain of an elephant weighs 4.67kg (10.3lb) in females and 5.0kg (11lb) in males. It has a temporal lobe that is highly convoluted – even more so than in humans – thus increasing the active surface area. Its size may be associated with the need for storage space for information, for elephants need to differentiate identities, to record memories of other elephants' behavior, and to store experiences of droughts, dangerous places and situations, and promising feeding sites. Some

of their social behavior suggests that they possess the mind tools to imagine what other elephants are feeling. Given their long lives, there is a survival premium for families led by matriarchs that make the right decisions on movements in times of peril or drought. All these factors favor the development of intelligence.

Besides their role in communication, the elephant's large ears act as radiators to prevent overheating, always a danger for animals with large, compact bodies. They are well supplied with blood, and can be fanned to increase the cooling flow of air over them; on hot, windy days, elephants sometimes spread their ears to let the breeze blow over them. Observation of blood vessels on the medial side of the ear show that when the ambient temperature is cool the vessels are normal and do not protrude beyond the skin, but when temperatures are high, the blood vessels dilate and rise above the skin. Elephants also have a keen sense of hearing and communicate mainly through vocalizations, especially the forest species.

The massive body is supported by pillarlike legs with thick, heavy bones – this is called graviportal stance. The bone structure of the forefeet is semidigitigrade (a horse has a digitigrade stance, with the heel raised high off the ground), whereas the hindfeet are semiplantigrade (a man has a plantigrade posture, with the heel on the ground). Elephants usually meander, but at other times walk quickly at about 1–2km/h (0.6–1.2mph). A charging elephant is said to reach 32km/h (20mph); at this speed over short distances it would easily outstrip a human sprinter, but it is doubtful whether it has ever been measured accurately.

Elephants have a nonruminant digestive system similar to that of horses. Microbial fermentation takes place in the cecum, which is an enlarged sac at the junction of the small and large intestines.

Elephants spend at least three-quarters of their time searching for and consuming food. In the wet season, savanna elephants eat mainly grasses, plus small amounts of leaves from a wide range of trees and shrubs. After the rains have ended and the grasses have withered, they turn to the woody parts of trees and shrubs. They will also eat large quantities of flowers and fruits when these are available, and they will dig for roots, especially after the first rains of the season.

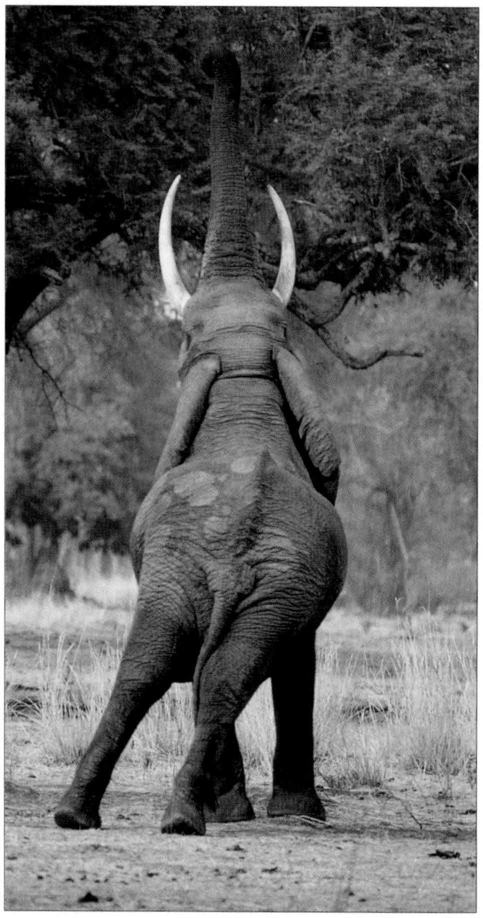

Above The elephant's dextrous trunk serves many purposes, including plucking succulent leaves and shoots from high branches. Browse is the staple diet of elephants, supplemented by fruit and grass at certain times of the year.

Asian elephants eat a varied diet that includes up to 100 species of plant; however, more than 85 percent of it derives from between 10 and 25 favorite foodstuffs. Crops also play a part, as the elephants live in landscapes dominated by agriculture. As cultigens like cereal and millet are essentially grasses that have been selected by humans for their high protein and other nutrient content, it is hardly surprising that elephants generally find them more attractive than wild grasses.

Because of their large body size and rapid rate of throughput, all elephants need large amounts of food: an adult requires 75–150kg (165–330lb) of food a day, or over 50 tonnes per year. Less than half of this is thoroughly digested. Elephants rely on the gut microflora to help them with digestion; babies, having no microflora of their own, ingest them by eating the dung of older family members.

In addition, elephants require 80–160 liters (20–40 US gallons) of fluid every day, an amount they can imbibe in less than 5 minutes. In the dry season they may dig holes in dry riverbeds with their trunks and tusks to find water.

Matriarchs and Musth Bulls

SOCIAL BEHAVIOR

Most of the information on elephants' ranges now comes from radio tracking, which has been used in Africa since 1969. In addition, improved radio collars using global positioning technology were deployed at the end of the 20th century, allowing very accurate positions to be collected every hour.

Cumulative average daily movements vary greatly from one elephant to another. In a study in Kenya, an elephant living in a well-watered

WHY ELEPHANTS GREW BIG

At their evolutionary peak, elephants living and extinct spread to all parts of the globe except Australia, New Zealand, and Antarctica, and until the Pleistocene (about 2 million years ago), elephants occupied a range of habitats from desert to montane forest throughout their range. This wide radiation was related to their most outstanding feature: the evolution of large body size.

In order to understand their evolutionary success, one must first consider the early large-herbivore community. The first sizable mammalian herbivores in Africa were perissodactyls – ancestors of the horse – which arose in the late Paleocene, about 58 million years ago. They remained dominant until the coming of the ruminant artiodactyls – predecessors of the antelopes – in the middle Eocene, some 46 million years ago. It is likely that while each perissodactyl species ate a wide range of plants, taking the coarser parts, the ruminants ate a narrower range, taking the softer parts.

The earliest proboscideans appeared in the late Paleocene; the elephantids arose in the late Miocene, at a time when the highly successful ruminants were continuing to evolve and to colonize new ecological niches. As nonruminants, members of the Elephantidae were able to feed on plant foods that were too coarse for the ruminants, but this brought them into competition with the perissodactyls.

For a given digestive system, differences in metabolic rate enable a large animal to feed on less nutritious plant parts than a smaller one can. There was, therefore, a strong selective pressure for the elephantids to increase their body size and so reduce the competition with perissodactyls. The most nutritious plant parts, such as leaf shoots and fruits, are produced only at certain seasons, and even then may be sparse and widely scattered; but coarse plants are more abundantly distributed both in space and time. By permitting the digestion of the latter, the elephants' evolutionary strategy thus enabled them to feed on plant parts that were not only abundant but also available all the year round. In particular, it enabled them to feed on the woody parts of trees and shrubs, and so to tap a resource which other mammalian herbivores could neither reach nor digest. At the same time, they remained able to eat rich plant parts such as fruits whenever these were available. This catholicity enabled elephants to thrive in a wide range of habitats. RB

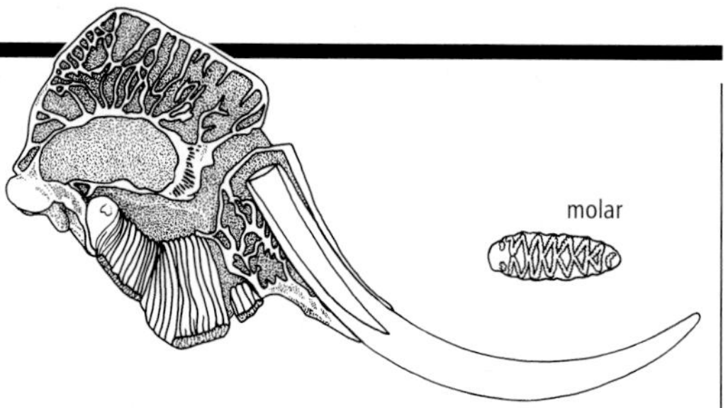

Above The elephant's skull is massive, comprising 12–25 percent of its body weight. It would be even heavier if it were not for an extensive network of air-cells (diploe). The dental formula is I1/0, C0/0, P3/3, M3/3. The single upper incisor grows into the tusk and the molars fall out at the front when worn, being replaced from behind. Only one tooth on each side, above and below, is in use at any one time.

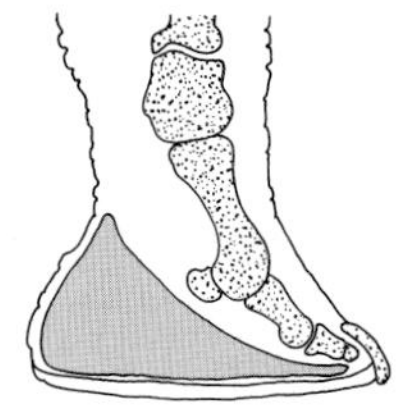

Left The elephant's foot is broad and the phalanges (fingers and toes) are embedded in a fatty matrix (green) that cushions the animal's weight and enables it to move silently through the bush..

forest averaged a mere 3km (1.9mi) a day, while others living in an arid northern area covered 12km (7.5mi) a day. Typically, an elephant will meander over a cumulative daily distance of 7–10km (4–7mi).

A striking feature of elephant movements is the behavior known as "streaking." This involves a spell of relatively rapid motion – typically at 3–4 km/h (2–2.5mph) – with a strong directional component, usually down corridors connecting distinct segments of the animals' range. Streaking, which is fairly rare and often takes place at night, may serve to get elephants rapidly across dangerous areas from one safe haven to another.

Elephants also respond speedily to sudden rainfall, and may travel more than 40km (25mi) to reach a spot where an isolated shower has fallen, so as to exploit the lush growth of grass that soon follows. Likewise in the forest they may make long journeys to find rare trees in fruit. When elephants venture into dangerous feeding zones such as farmlands, they tend to do so only at night. Elephants appear to be able to learn which areas are safe and will venture right up to the edge of a protected area before turning back at the border. Repeated movements often carve broad "elephant roads" cutting through even the densest jungles, which may subsequently be used by many other species including humans.

Some elephant ranges have surprisingly complex structures. By enclosing the outside points of a range, the rough area can be calculated for

⬣ **Above** *Herds of elephants often lift their trunks high into the prevailing breeze and use their acute sense of smell to gain advance warning of any approaching threat.*

⬣ **Below** *Despite its thickness – in places, up to 4cm – the elephant's skin is highly sensitive and requires frequent bathing, massaging, and powdering with dust to keep it free from parasites and diseases.*

comparative purposes. Within this area there may be discrete segments, linked by elongated corridors and empty zones where the elephants never venture. Ranges as small as 10sq km (4sq mi) have been described in one forest in Tanzania, while others of up to 21,000sq km (7,000sq mi) were observed in a desert area in Mali. In a study in Kenya, the home ranges of savanna elephants in a woodland and bushland habitat were found to average 750sq km (290sq mi) in an area of abundant food and water, and 1,600sq km (617sq mi) in a more arid area. Detailed studies of the ranging behavior of the forest species were initiated at the beginning of the 21st century, and first results indicate that the ranges can be as much as 60km (37mi) across, far larger than previously thought. Radiotelemetry studies of Asian elephants have revealed that female groups in India range over 180–600sq km (70–230sq mi) or more, while males typically use an area of 160–400sq km (60–150sq mi).

Elephants live in groups and display complex social behavior. The advantages of living in society lie in group defense, the teaching of the young,

COMMUNICATING OVER LONG DISTANCES

Elephants make calls that are rich in infrasound – sound below the range of human hearing. Forest elephants make calls as low as 5Hz, two octaves below the lowest sounds that humans ordinarily hear (c. 20–20,000Hz). Many of the calls of Asian and of African savanna elephants have fundamental frequencies of 14–20Hz. A person standing close to a calling elephant may hear a soft rumble, but at even a short distance some calls that are perfectly audible to elephants are not perceived by humans.

Elephants use their calls in long-distance signaling, since very low-frequency sound loses exceptionally little energy in traveling. Playback experiments show that calls at 119dB (SPL) are powerful enough to elicit responses from other elephants as far away as 4km (2.5mi) in the middle of the day. In the evening, distances increase as a result of atmospheric conditions. On a clear savanna night (as 80 percent are in the southern African dry season), a temperature inversion forms. A layer of hot air is trapped under cold air, forming a ceiling at 300m (1,000ft) or below that reflects Earth-generated sounds back down to the surface, enhancing sound propagation at or near ground level, especially at low frequencies. One model projects that at such times the calling area for loud elephant calls expands tenfold, from 30 to 300sq km (11.5 to 115sq mi).

Long-distance communication appears to be crucial to reproduction in free-ranging elephants. Adult males and females move about independently most of the time. When a female comes into estrus, she will emit a series of powerful, low-pitched calls to announce her condition. Reproductive males then gather rapidly from varying distances and all directions. It is essential for them to detect her condition quickly, because the estrus periods are extraordinarily short and rare – on average, according to data from Amboseli Park, Kenya, encompassing only 2–4 days every 5 years.

Elephants' powerful infrasonic calls also have long-distance functions in other circumstances. In times of excitement, distress, or separation, family members listen for one another's calls and aggregate. Noisy events that result in aggregation include aggression or calf rescue as well as courtship and mating. Listening males and females are selectively attracted to the site, to help in or to take advantage of the situation. Related families sometimes coordinate their movements for weeks at a time over distances of several kilometers without actually meeting. This appears to be how they avoid exhausting the resources on which they depend while remaining available to one another for purposes of mutual support.   KP

🔅 **Below** *As well as long-distance calling, close-quarters interaction – here, a bull tests a cow's receptivity – is a key part of the reproductive cycle.*

and enhanced mating opportunities. Female elephants live in family units, which typically consist of closely related adult cows and their immature offspring. The adults are either sisters or else mothers and daughters. A typical family unit may contain two or three sisters and their offspring, or one elderly cow in company with one or two adult daughters and their offspring. Strangers may also sometimes join a group permanently. When the female calves reach maturity, they may stay with the family unit, where they usually then breed. As the family grows in size, a subgroup of young adult cows will gradually separate to form their own unit. As a result, related family units are sometimes separated, but usually move together in a coordinated fashion. Groups of 2–4 related families that travel around together are known as kinship groups or bond groups.

The oldest female, the matriarch, leads the family unit. The social bonds between the members of the family are very strong. In times of danger, the family forms a defensive circle with calves in the middle and adults facing outward. The matriarch or other adult females will check the bearing of

the threat, generally a human being. Usually she will retreat, but sometimes she may advance to confront the danger, spreading her ears and giving vent to trumpeting and thunderous growling. A threat charge, with ears outstretched, is often enough to deter an aggressor. But occasionally, the charge is followed through. Unfortunately, this defensive behavior exposes the matriarch to danger, so she often is first to fall victim to poachers, leaving the rest of the family leaderless.

If a family member is shot, wounded, or tranquilized, the rest of the group, or strangers, may well come to its aid. With much noise and excitement, they will try to lift the animal to its feet and carry it away, with elephants supporting it on either side.

In Asian elephants too, the basic social structure is a family group of 2–10 females and their offspring, with an average size of 6.7 animals. Intensive studies conducted in Rajaji National Park in northern India have shown that groups of three or less adult females and their associated offspring are highly stable, spending up to 90 percent of the time together. Such groups will meet

up from time to time with other groups (maybe related) when grazing in open grasslands or near waterholes, though the intense greetings described in African elephants have not been documented, and the bigger groupings seem to be merely transitory.

In contrast to their sisters, young male elephants leave or are forced out of the family on reaching puberty. Adult bulls tend to associate with one another in small groups that constantly change in number and composition; they also spend short periods alone. The traditional picture has been one of weak associations and little cooperative behavior between bulls, but recent research in Kenya shows that short-term intensive associations may be repeated time and again, with intervening periods of separation. In northern Botswana, small bull populations of several hundred individuals maintain close associations by focusing their activities on waterholes, often provided by the local Department of Wildlife.

Male Asian elephants start to move away from the family group at around 6–7 years of age. Fully-grown adult males are solitary and are rarely

seen with female groups unless a cow is in estrus. When they reach the age of 20, mature males start coming into a phase called "musth," in preparation for the rigors of competing for females and mating. Musth (a Hindi or Urdu word meaning "intoxicated") aptly describes this extreme physiological condition, in which the levels of testosterone in the blood may increase by a factor of twenty or more. The animals typically display agonistic or aggressive behavior. In the Rajaji National Park study, the biggest adult males came into musth during the period when most of the females would have been in estrus. Fully grown adult males (up to 35 years) remain in musth for about 60 days, during which time they wander widely in search of females in estrus.

African elephants also experience musth, though in a less pronounced form. In Kenya's Amboseli Park, where social behavior has been more intensively studied than elsewhere on the continent, the bulls normally do not come into musth until nearly fully grown at 29 years old. Musth usually lasts for 2–3 months and tends to coincide with periods of high rainfall.

Musth bulls are more likely to be involved in fights than others, and occasionally this can result in the death of one of the contenders. During musth, elephant bulls dramatically decrease their food intake, burning up accumulated fat reserves. Musth bulls emit signals that notify other elephants of their state. The temporal glands between the eye and the ear swell up and discharge a viscous aromatic secretion. They discharge a continuous dribble of urine containing soluble pheromones. The posture of musth bulls is also quite distinct; they carry their heads much higher than normal, and their ears are held high and spread out. There is also a characteristic vocalization, the "musth rumble," which consists of low, pulsating growls somewhat like a low-revving diesel engine.

The purpose of musth seems to be to increase temporarily the status of a bull and to help it win fights; even a small bull in musth will normally prevail over a larger, non-musth bull. Cows are in estrus only 2–4 days during the estrous cycle that lasts about 4 months if females are not pregnant, or every 4–5 years if she conceived, had a successful delivery, and raised the young. During estrus, bulls must be able to locate the females rapidly. Musth bulls travel longer daily distances than other bulls. Females in estrus attract musth bulls with a very loud infrasonic call. It appears that females prefer large bulls to small ones and musth bulls to non-musth. They exercise choice as to which bull to mate with; if a female does not want a particular individual, she will run away, and even if he catches up with her she will refuse to stand still long enough for him to mate successfully.

Female estrus usually comes on during the rains, and bulls of the highest rank come into musth at this time. The presence or absence of larger musth bulls apparently affects the age at which a bull comes into musth and the length of time it stays in the condition, apparently through an intimidation effect. In one population in South Africa, the introduction of older bulls subdued the highly aggressive behavior of young bulls that had been killing the resident rhinos.

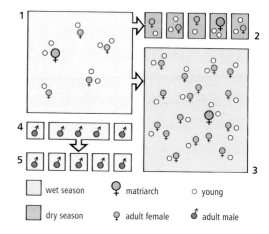

wet season   matriarch   young

dry season   adult female   adult male

Above A typical elephant family unit is made up of closely related cows (with one dominant cow, the matriarch) and their offspring **1**. When food is scarce **2**, the family groups tend to split up to forage. In the wet season **3** family units may merge to form groups of 50 or more. Bulls leave at puberty to join small, loose herds **4** or live alone **5**.

Below A large group of elephants of varying ages and comprising a number of family groups assembles at the onset of the wet season.

Cows reach sexual maturity at about 10 years of age, but this may be delayed for several years during drought or periods of high population density. Once a cow starts to breed, she may produce an infant every three or four years, although this period too can be extended when times are bad. Females are most fecund from the age of 16 to 40.

Most elephant populations show an annual reproductive cycle that corresponds to the seasonal availability of food and water. During the dry season when food is scarce, cows may cease to ovulate. When the rains break and the food supply improves, a period of 1–2 months of good feeding is needed to raise the female's body fat above the level necessary for ovulation. Thus females are in heat during the second half of the rainy season and in the first months of the dry season.

Elephants have an exceptionally long gestation period, averaging 630 days or sometimes not far short of 2 years, which means that the calves are born early in the wet season, when conditions are optimal for their survival. In particular, abundant green food helps ensure that the mother will lactate successfully during the early months. First-year survival of calves varies from 48 percent in drought years to 95 percent in times of plenty. The calves of older mothers have a greater chance of surviving their first year.

At birth, the African elephant weighs about 120kg (265lb). The lengthy gestation is followed by a long period of juvenile dependency. The infant suckles (with its mouth, not its trunk) from the paired breasts between the mother's forelegs, which are roughly the size and shape of large human breasts. (Both elephants and humans have nipples, not teats, an error often found in the literature.) The young elephant grows rapidly, reaching a weight of 1 tonne by the time it is 6 years old. The rate of growth decreases after about 15 years, but growth continues throughout life; males grow faster than females.

During a birth, other cows may collect around the new calf, and so-called midwives may assist by removing the fetal membrane. Others may help the infant to its feet. Young female elephants called "allomothers" play a key role in bringing up young elephants. They increase the calves' chances of survival by their efforts, and at the same time gain experience for the time when they too will become mothers.

The supposed existence of elephant graveyards is a myth, although it is possible that old elephants whose days are numbered may congregate on riverbanks to feed on the lush vegetation. Some countries have also seen elephant killing-fields, where poachers have left dead elephants strewn across the landscape. This happened, for example, in the Murchison Falls National Park in Uganda, which used to be home to 8,000 elephants; they were killed for their ivory by poachers, many of them soldiers of Idi Amin's army, who reduced the population's numbers to less than 100 in the early 1980s.

A real mystery of elephant life lies in the way the living treat the dead. They exhibit an extraordinary interest in elephant carcasses and bones, and will spend hours sniffing the remains and investigating them with their trunks, picking up some bones and putting them in their mouths or carrying them on their heads. So far there is no satisfactory scientific explanation for this behavior, although it seems that elephants are able to identify particular individuals from the smell of the remains, suggesting a level of understanding that remains a challenge to science.

Stemming the Ivory Trade
AFRICAN ELEPHANT CONSERVATION

Man's relationship with elephants is beset by contradictions. On the one hand, they are regarded with awe and fascination; while on the other, whole populations are eradicated in pursuit of land or ivory. Even though elephants do have natural predators – the young are often killed by lions, hyenas, or crocodiles – by far their most dangerous enemy is humankind.

As far back as classical antiquity, North African elephant populations were dwindling rapidly. They finally disappeared during the Dark or Middle Ages. The Arab ivory trade, which started in the 17th century, precipitated a further rapid decline among elephant populations in both West and East Africa. The colonial era accelerated the process by opening up previously inaccessible areas and introducing modern technology, notably high-powered rifles; in Africa, the destruction of elephants peaked between 1830 and 1910 and again between 1970 and 1989. Today, continuing deforestation and the encroachment of roads, farms, and towns into former elephant habitats threaten both African and Asian elephants by restricting their range, cutting off seasonal migration routes, and bringing them into more frequent conflict with people.

Perceptions of the main conservation issues involved have changed radically since the 1960s, when the debate centered on local overpopulation of elephants in protected areas. In the 1970s and 1980s the concern was that elephants were being decimated by poaching for ivory. It used to be thought that the worldwide economic recession of the early 1970s encouraged investors to switch to ivory as a wealth store, but studies by the Ivory Trade Review Group have since demonstrated that it was rather the increase in the buying power of ordinary Japanese citizens, coupled with a desire to possess ivory seals as status symbols, that trig-

Above In inaccessible parts of the Indian subcontinent, such as Nepal and the Andaman Islands, Asian elephants still play a key role in forestry, carrying logs or clearing vegetation. Here, a mahout – an elephant owner and driver – guides his animal through dense undergrowth in Chitwan National Park, Nepal.

Left In the dry season, when food is at a premium, elephants become extremely destructive, stripping and eating bark and even felling trees to get at leaves and twigs. Elephants also devastate planted crops, leading to conflict with rural communities in Africa and Asia.

Above *Ivory poaching was the scourge of elephant populations at the end of the 20th century, and is still rife. Here, tusks seized from poachers are destroyed.*

Right *Asian elephants still feature prominently in religious and cultural festivals, such as this night procession through Kandy, on the island of Sri Lanka.*

gered the upsurge in killing by stimulating a much higher price for ivory in the 1970s and 1980s than in previous decades. The result was a dramatic decline in elephant numbers; for instance, the Kenyan population fell from 167,000 in 1970 to 60,000 by 1980 and to about 22,000 by 1989. In 1979 a wide-ranging survey estimated that 1.3 million elephants survived in Africa, but by 1989 the number had fallen to 609,000, suggesting that more than half of Africa's elephants had been lost to ivory poaching in a single decade. In response, the movement to ban the trade reached a climax in 1989, when a meeting of the Convention on International Trade in Endangered Species of Wild Flora and Fauna (CITES) voted in favor of a moratorium on all trade in elephant products.

There has since been much controversy over whether or not the ivory ban has been effective in lowering elephant killing. In places where monitoring is possible, elephant mortality dropped in the 1990s compared with the previous decade, although some attribute this effect to better policing. What is certain, however, is that ivory prices fell after 1989, reducing the incentive for poaching.

On the other hand, some southern African countries, claimed they depended upon ivory sales to finance their conservation programs. Their elephant populations have been steadily increasing, and they contend that they are unnecessarily penalized by the ban. Throughout the early

1990s, they sought to reopen a limited ivory trade with Japan, and in 1997 succeeded in having restricted exports reestablished. However, policymakers in East, Central, and West Africa feared that even this small-scale revival might revive poaching in their own countries. To forestall this possibility, all parties at the 2000 CITES conference resolved to suspend ivory trading until an adequate system of monitoring illegal killing had been put in place.

Since the original ivory trade ban of 1989, conflict between elephants and rising human populations has played an increasing role in conservation thinking, for while the elephant population outside of the southern countries more than halved in the preceding two decades, the human population more than doubled. Attitudes toward elephants remain contradictory, varying from the sheer animosity felt by many agriculturalists within elephant ranges, through the indifference shown by most local people, to the tolerance generally exhibited by certain pastoralist peoples such as the Masai and the Samburu – and finally, of course, to the adoration of safari tourists. The key to the animals' survival would seem to lie in extending tolerant attitudes and in educating people to recognize elephants as a valuable natural resource, at best as cultural assets or at least as a potential means of livelihood.

Even though protecting elephants is costly, many conservationists regard the elephant as a so-called keystone species – namely, one that pays dividends by benefiting other animals within its ecosystem. Thus, elephants play a pivotal role, dispersing seeds, transforming savannas into grasslands, distributing nutrients in their dung, providing water for other species by digging waterholes, supplying food for birds by disturbing insects and small animals while walking in tall grass, and even alerting small animals to approaching predators. Moreover, since larger species require greater quantities of food and water and larger home ranges than smaller species, an area large enough to support an elephant will automatically support several other species.

In 2002, the African Elephant Specialist Group analyzed all available data to reach the following estimates. Some 402,000 individuals definitely survived, while a further 59,000 probably and 100,000 possibly did so; the existence of an additional 99,000 animals on top of these figures was considered speculative. A comparison of aerial surveys showed that in the late 1990s elephant numbers had increased in southern Africa, while the apparent increase in Eastern Africa was not statistically significant. The data were inadequate to determine quantitative trends for West and Central Africa where many estimates were out-of-date or were only guesses. However, the CITES program for monitoring the illegal killing of elephants reported a high rate of carcass finds and suggested that poaching was at crisis levels in much of Cen-

tral Africa. In 2002 elephants were found in 37 countries in Africa, of which seven probably had less than 200: Eritrea, Guinea-Bissau, Rwanda, Senegal, Sierra Leone, Somalia, and Togo. Elephants were found in 13 Asian countries (estimated between 36,000 and 50,000), of which Nepal and Vietnam probably had less than 200.

Working Elephants
ASIAN ELEPHANT CONSERVATION

Like their African relatives, Asian elephants also now occupy a much-reduced range. The total estimated population of Asian elephants in the wild is 37,000–57,000, occurring across an area of some 500,000sq km (193,000sq mi). In addition, there are about 15,000 elephants in captivity. It was captive elephants that allowed the British to open up forests in the region for logging in colonial times. Subsequently, the decline of the timber industry across south Asia, Indochina, and Southeast Asia has led to a decline in numbers, though some countries such as Myanmar still have a sizable population of 5,000 or so timber elephants.

Habitat loss and poaching are still the main threats to Asian elephants. The tusked males alone are targeted by the poachers, which radically affects breeding patterns. In Periyar Tiger Reserve in south India, for example, where poaching has left only 1 male for every 100 females, fewer than one-third of adult females are accompanied by calves less than 5 years old; in Rajaji National Park, in contrast, the sex ratio is 1 male for every 2 females, and more than 90 percent of the adult cows are accompanied by a calf. Elephant–human conflict mostly arises on the borders between elephant habitats and inhabited lands; in India about 300 people and 200 elephants per year die through poaching, crop protection incidents, or accidents.   ID-H/RFWB/HS/ACW/AJTJ

AN ELEPHANT'S EARLY YEARS

❶ *Only an hour old, an elephant calf pulls itself to its feet and takes its first tentative steps. An African elephant weighs about 120kg (265lb) at birth, the Asian elephant about 100kg (220lb). The calf remains closely dependent on its mother for its first 10 years of life, and continues learning social and survival skills until it is about 17. Elephant society is close-knit and matriarchal, and in addition to its mother, a calf has the support and attention of an extended family of aunts, cousins, and subadult males.*

❷ *The newborn calf will be immediately encouraged to suckle from its mother's nipples, which are located between her front legs. Milk is the most important food for the first two years of a calf's life, and the mother does not have another calf during this time. Milk continues to be part of the calf's diet until it is 3 or 4 years of age. If the calf's mother dies, the calf usually starves; other females will not suckle it at the expense of their own offspring.*

5 The sense of touch plays a crucial role in elephant society, but especially between mothers and calves, which are rarely more than a trunk's reach apart. In adult life, elephants touch one another frequently throughout the day, and greet each other by standing close and twining their trunks.

3 **4** Play is an essential part of the physical and social development of elephant calves. Spreading its ears wide, a four-month-old calf threatens an imagined enemy. Early morning is a favorite time for playing. Chasing and head-to-head sparring are the preferred games for males, while running through tall grass, chasing birds, throwing sticks, and attacking imaginary enemies are those of female calves. Both sexes, especially juveniles, seem to enjoy rough and tumble games where one elephant clambers over another.

6 Baby elephants learn to eat by putting their trunks inside their mothers' mouths to take food. From the age of 6 months a calf will supplement its milk diet with vegetation and will sample food it sees other herd members eating. Elephants know instinctively which foods are good and which are poisonous, although they can sometimes ingest a toxic meal by accident – a poisonous mushroom growing in the grass, for instance.

Dugong and Manatees

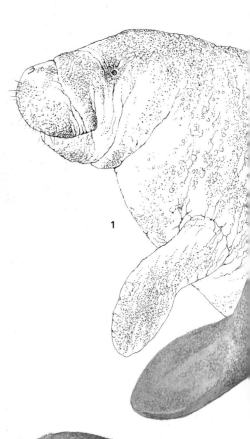

1

LTHOUGH SIRENIANS HAVE STREAMLINED *body forms like those of other marine mammals that never leave the water, they are the only ones that feed primarily on plants. This unique feeding niche is the key to understanding the evolution of the order's form and life history, and possibly explains why it contains so few species.*

Sirenians are descended from terrestrial mammals that once browsed the shallow, grassy swamps of the Paleocene, some 60 million years ago. These herbivores gradually became more aquatic, yet their closest modern relative remains a land mammal, the elephant.

Current theories suggest that, during the relatively warm Eocene period (55–34 million years ago), a sea cow (*Protosiren*) that was the ancestor of the modern dugong and manatees fed on the vast seagrass meadows found in shallow tropical waters of the west Atlantic and Caribbean. After the global climate cooled during the Oligocene (34–24 million years ago), the sea grass beds retreated. The manatees (family Trichechidae) appeared during the Miocene (24–5 million years ago), a geological period that favored the growth of freshwater plants in nutrient-rich rivers along the coast of South America. Unlike the sea grasses, these floating mats of river grass contained silica, an abrasive defense against herbivores, which causes rapid wearing of the teeth. To counter this deterrent, manatees have an unusual adaptation that minimizes the impact of wear: throughout their lives, worn teeth are shed at the front and are replaced at the back (see box opposite).

Today, there are only four sirenian species: one dugong and three manatees. A fifth, Steller's sea cow, was exterminated by humans in the mid-1700s. Adapted to the cold temperatures of the northern Pacific, Steller's sea cow was a specialist, feeding on kelp, the dense marine algae that became abundant after the retreat of the sea grass beds (see An Extinct Giant box).

Large, Slow, and Docile
FORM AND FUNCTION

Sirenians are nonruminant herbivores, like the horse and elephant but unlike sheep and cows, and they do not have a chambered or compartmentalized stomach. The intestines are extremely long – over 45m (150ft) in manatees – and between the large and small intestines there is a large midgut cecum, with paired, blind-ending branches. Bacterial digestion of cellulose occurs in this hindpart of the digestive tract and enables

the four species to process the large volume of relatively low-quality forage they require to obtain adequate energy and nutrients; this amounts to 8–15 percent of their body weight daily.

Sirenians expend little energy: for manatees, about one-third that of a typical mammal of the same weight. Their slow, languid movements are said to have reminded early mariners of mermaids – sirens of the sea. Although capable of rapid movement when pursued, they have little need for speed in an environment without humans, having few other predators. Living in tropical waters, sirenians can afford to have a low metabolic rate, because they expend little energy on regulating body temperature. Sirenians also conserve energy by virtue of their relatively large body size.

Manatees have the typical sirenian body form and are distinguished from the dugong mainly by their large, horizontal, paddle-shaped tails, which move up and down when they swim. They have only six neck vertebrae; all other mammals have seven. The lips are covered with stiff bristles, and there are two muscular projections that grasp and pass the grasses and aquatic plants that they feed on into the mouth.

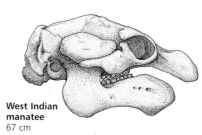

4

SKULLS AND DENTITION OF SIRENIANS

Adult dugongs of both sexes have only a few, peglike molar teeth, located at the back of the jaws. Juveniles also have premolars, but these are lost in the first years of life. Adult males also have a pair of "tusks": incisor teeth that project through the upper lip a short distance in front of the mouth and behind the disk. The uses to which these stubby tusks are put are not clear, but it is thought that the males may use them to guide their slippery mates during courtship.

A unique feature of manatees is a constant horizontal replacement of the molar teeth. When a manatee is born, it has both premolars and molars. As the calf is weaned and begins to eat vegetable matter, the mechanical stimulation involved in chewing starts a forward movement of the whole tooth row. New teeth entering at the back of the jaw push each row forward through the jawbone until the roots are eaten away and the tooth falls out. This type of replacement is unique to manatees.

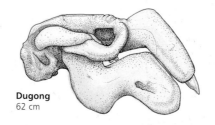

Dugong
62 cm

West Indian manatee
67 cm

2

3

WEST INDIAN MANATEE *Trichechus manatus*

West Indian or Caribbean manatee
SE North America (Florida), Caribbean, and N South America on Atlantic coast to C Brazil. Shallow coastal waters, estuaries, and rivers. 2 subspecies – *T. m. manatus* and *T. m. latirostris* – have been proposed for the North and South American coastal population and the Caribbean populations respectively, but such a division is probably not justified because detailed comparative studies of the two groups have not yet been made. Head–tail length 3.7–4.6m (12.1–15.1ft); weight 1,600kg (3,500lb). Skin: gray brownish and hairless; rudimentary nails on foreflippers. Breeding: gestation approximately 12 months. Longevity: 28 years in captivity, probably longer in the wild. Conservation status: Vulnerable.

WEST AFRICAN MANATEE *Trichechus senegalensis*

West African or Senegal manatee
W Africa (Senegal to Angola). Other details, where known, are similar to those of the West Indian manatee. Conservation status: Vulnerable.

AMAZONIAN MANATEE *Trichechus inunguis*

Amazonian or South American manatee
Amazon river drainage basin in floodplain lakes, rivers, and channels. Head–tail length 2.5–3m (8–10ft); weight 350–500kg (770–1,100lb). Skin: lead gray with variable pink belly patch (white when dead); no nails on foreflippers. Breeding: gestation not known, but probably similar to that of the West Indian manatee. Longevity: greater than 30 years. Conservation status: Vulnerable.

DUGONG *Dugong dugon*

Dugong or Sea cow or Sea Pig
SW Pacific Ocean from New Caledonia, W Micronesia, and the Philippines to Taiwan, Vietnam, Indonesia, New Guinea, and the N coasts of Australia; Indian Ocean from Australia and Indonesia to Sri Lanka and India, the Red Sea, and S along the African coast to Mozambique. Coastal shallows. Head–tail length 1–4m (3.3–13ft); weight 230–900kg (500–2,000lb). Skin: smooth, brown to gray, with short sensory bristles at intervals of 2–3cm (0.8–1.2in). Breeding: gestation 13 months (estimated). Longevity: to around 60 years. Conservation status: Vulnerable.

◖ **Left** *Sirenians have only foreflippers, the hindlimbs having been lost, leaving a vestigial pelvic girdle; the head is large, with small eyes and tiny ear openings. The biggest species was Steller's sea cow (*Hydrodamalis gigas*)* **1***, extinct since 1768, which had a tough, barklike skin.* **2** *Amazonian manatee (*Trichechus inunguis*), feeding on floating vegetation and showing the rounded tail typical of all manatees.* **3** *West African manatee (*Trichechus senegalensis*) displaying the strong bristles on very mobile lips typical of sirenians.* **4** *West Indian manatee (*Trichechus manatus*) carrying vegetation with its flippers. This manatee has vestigial nails.* **5** *Dugong (*Dugong dugon*) showing the tail with a concave trailing edge. The dugong has no nails, and its nostrils are placed further back than those of manatees.*

5

The eyes of manatees are not particularly well-adapted to the aquatic environment, but their hearing is good, despite the tiny external ear openings. They seem particularly sensitive to high-frequency noises, which may be an adaptation to shallow water, where the propagation of low-frequency sound is limited. The hearing abilities of manatees and other marine mammals may have also been shaped by ambient and thermal noise curves in the sea.

Being unable to hear low-frequency noises may be a contributing factor to the manatees' inability to effectively detect boat noise and therefore avoid collisions. They do not use echolocation or sonar, and may bump into objects in murky waters. Nor do they possess vocal cords. Even so, they do communicate by vocalizations, which may be high-pitched chirps or squeaks; how these sounds are produced is a mystery.

Taste buds are present on the tongue, and are apparently used in the selection of food plants; manatees can also recognize other individuals by "tasting" the scent marks left on prominent objects. Unlike toothed whales, they still possess the brain organs involved in smell, but since they spend most of their time underwater with the nose valves closed, this sense may not be used.

Manatees explore their environment by touch, using their highly developed muzzle and muscular lips. The tactile resolving power of their bristlelike hairs is lower than that of pinnipeds, but compares well with that of the trunk of Asian elephants. This increases grazing and browsing efficiency and maximizes the potential of the manatee as a generalist feeder.

Manatees can store large amounts of fat as blubber beneath the skin and around the intestines, which affords some degree of thermal protection from the environment. Despite this, manatees in the Atlantic Ocean generally avoid areas where temperatures drop below 20°C (68°F). The blubber also helps them to endure long periods of fasting – up to six months in the Amazonian manatee during the dry season, when aquatic plants are unavailable.

The dugong grows to a length of 3m (10ft) and a weight of 400kg (880lb). In contrast to the three manatee species, all of which spend time in fresh

to the warmer waters of the western bay, they feed during the winter months by browsing the terminal leaves of *Amphibolis antarctica*, a tough-stemmed, bushlike sea grass.

In both feeding modes, the dugong's foraging apparatus is the highly mobile, horseshoe-shaped disk at the end of its snout. In the disk, laterally-moving waves of muscular contraction sweep away overlying sediments, while stiffer bristles scoop up exposed rhizomes and any leaves that may remain attached. A meandering, flat-bottomed furrow is left behind on the seabed as evidence of a dugong's passage. Foraging dugongs rise to the surface to breathe every 40–400 seconds; the deeper the water, the longer the intervals become.

Isolated Survivors
DISTRIBUTION PATTERNS

The four sirenian species are geographically isolated. The dugong's range spans 40 countries from east Africa to Vanuatu, including tropical and subtropical coastal and island waters between about 26° and 27° north and south of the equator. Their historical distribution broadly coincides with the tropical Indo-Pacific distribution of sea grasses. Outside Australia, the dugong probably survives through most of its range only in relict populations separated by large areas where it is close to extinction or even extinct. The degree to which dugong numbers have dwindled and their range has fragmented is unknown.

The West African and West Indian manatees have been isolated for long enough to become distinct since their supposed common ancestor migrated to Africa across the Atlantic Ocean. Each can occupy both saltwater and freshwater habitats. The Amazonian manatee apparently became isolated when the Andes mountain range was

⬆ Above *An Amazonian manatee displaying its rubbery, almost seal-like skin. The Amazonian is the smallest of the three manatee species and is the only one that occurs exclusively in freshwater environments. Other distinctive features are flippers that usually lack nails and an elongated snout.*

◀ Left *Fearlessly approaching the photographer, a West Indian manatee demonstrates the curiosity that is a feature of all sirenian species. One reason why they may wish to explore unfamiliar newcomers from close up is that their eyesight is poor; touch and hearing are more important weapons in their sensory arsenal.*

⬇ Below *A dugong cruises the Pacific shallows in search of sea grass to graze on. Dugongs are less bulky than manatees, and can most easily be distinguished from them by the shape of the tail; this is rounded or fan-shaped in the manatee, but in the dugong is indented to form a shallow V.*

water to varying degrees, it is the only extant plant-eating mammal that spends all its life at sea. Unlike those of manatees, its tail has a straight or slightly concave trailing edge. A short, broad, trunklike snout ends in a downward-facing flexible disk and a slitlike mouth.

Dugongs appear to "chew" vegetation, mainly with rough, horny pads located in the roof and floor of the mouth. While their preferred feeding mode is piglike, rooting out carbohydrate-rich rhizomes (underground storage roots) from the seabed, the name "sea cow" is not always a misnomer. At Shark Bay, Western Australia, low winter temperatures drive the herds from their summer feeding grounds and their choicest food plants. After a migration of over 160km (100mi)

Below The mother–child bond, exhibited here by a West Indian manatee and her calf, is easily the strongest social tie in the sirenian world. Cows give birth to a single offspring once every other year, and the young stay with them for 12–18 months, learning about choice feeding areas and annual migration routes.

uplifted in the Pliocene 5–1.8 million years ago, changing the river drainage out of the Amazon basin from the Pacific to the Atlantic Ocean. Amazonian manatees are not tolerant of salt water and occupy only the Amazon River and its tributaries.

Despite the manatee's ability to move thousands of kilometers along continental margins, genetic studies have revealed strong population separations between most locations. These findings are consistent with tagging studies, which indicate that stretches of open water and unsuitable coastal habitats constitute substantial barriers to gene flow and colonization. Conversely, within Florida and Brazil, manatees are genetically more similar than might be expected, which may be explained by recent colonization into high latitudes or bottleneck effects. Adult survival probabilities in these areas appear high enough to maintain growing populations if other traits such as reproductive rates and juvenile survival are also sufficiently high. Lower and variable survival rates on the Atlantic coast are a cause for concern.

Grazing the Shallows
DIET

Sirenians have few competitors for food. In terrestrial grasslands there are many grazers and browsers, requiring a complex division of resources; but the only large herbivores in sea grass meadows are sirenians and sea turtles. Marine plant communities are low in diversity compared with terrestrial communities and lack species with high-energy seeds, which facilitate niche subdivision among herbivores in terrestrial systems. It is not surprising that dugongs and manatees dig into the sediments when they feed on rooted aquatics; over half of the mass of sea grasses is found in the rhizomes, which concentrate carbohydrates. In contrast, the cold-blooded sea turtles subsist by grazing on the blades of sea grasses without disturbing the rhizomes, and appear to feed in deeper water. Thus even the herbivorous sea turtles probably do not compete significantly for food taken by the sirenians.

As aquatic herbivores, manatees are restricted to feeding on plants in, or very near, the water. Occasionally, they feed with their head and shoulders out of water, but normally they consume floating or submerged grasses and other vascular plants. They may eat algae, but this does not form an important part of the diet. The coastal West Indian and West African manatees feed on sea grasses growing in relatively shallow, clear marine waters, and also enter inland waterways to feed on freshwater plants. Amazonian manatees are surface feeders, browsing floating grasses (the murky Amazon waters inhibit the growth of submerged aquatic plants). The habit of surface feeding may explain why the downward deflection in the snout of Amazonian manatees is much less pronounced than in bottom-feeding West Indian and African species. Some 44 species of plants and 10 species

○ **Above** *The sensitive vibrissae (whiskers) on a manatee's protruding upper lip play an essential part in feeding. With their aid, an animal can feel its way through clumps of floating vegetation or root for nutrients on the seabed, much as pigs do on land.*

◐ **Left** *A West Indian manatee feeds on aquatic plants off Florida. As the downward-pointing snout might suggest, this species spends some of its time grazing on the seabed, in contrast to the Amazonian manatee, which is almost entirely a surface feeder.*

of algae have been recorded as foods of West Indian manatees, but only 24 for Amazonian manatees.

Many food plants on which the manatees graze have evolved antiherbivore protective mechanisms – spicules of silica in the grasses, and tannins, nitrates, and oxalates in other aquatics – that reduce their digestibility and lower their food value. Microbes in the manatees' digestive tract may be able to detoxify some of these chemical defenses.

Dugongs feed on sea grasses – marine flowering plants that sometimes resemble terrestrial grasses and are distinct from seaweeds. Sea grasses grow on the bottom in coastal shallows, and dugongs generally feed at depths of 2–6m (6–20ft), though characteristic rooting scars have been observed in sea grass beds at a depth of 23m (75ft). The food they most prefer is the carbohydrate-rich rhizomes of the smaller sea grass species.

The Cow–Calf Bond
SOCIAL BEHAVIOR
The large sirenian body size, dictated by the requirements of nutrition and temperature regula-

tion, is associated with traits seen in other large mammalian herbivores as well as large marine mammals. The life span is long – ages of 30 or more have been recorded in captivity – and the reproductive rate is low. Females give birth to a single calf after about a year's gestation, calves stay with the mother for 1–2 years, and sexual maturity is delayed for 4–8 years. Consequently, the potential rate of population increase is low. It is possible that rapid reproduction brings no advantage where the renewability of food resources is slow and there are few predators.

Manatees are extremely slow breeders: at most they produce only a single calf every two years, and calves may be weaned from 12–18 months. Although young calves may feed on plants within weeks of being born, the long nursing period probably allows them to learn the necessary migration routes, foods, and preferred feeding areas from their mother.

In highly seasonal environments such as the Amazon, and probably also at the northern and southern limits of their distribution, the availabi-

lity of food dictates when the majority of manatee females are ready to mate, and this, in turn, results in a seasonal peak in calving. The reproductive biology of male manatees is poorly known, but it is not uncommon for a receptive female to be accompanied by 6–8 males and to mate with several of these within a short time. Direct observation and radio-tracking studies have shown that manatees are essentially solitary, but occasionally form groups of a dozen or more.

Little is known about the behavior and ecology of dugongs, for they are not easily studied. The waters where they are found are generally turbid, and their shyness frustrates close observation. When disturbed, their flight is rapid and furtive; only the top of the head and nostrils are exposed as they rise to breathe. When underwater visibility is adequate and they are approached cautiously, they will come from 100m (330ft) or more to investigate a diver or a small boat, probably alerted by their extremely keen underwater hearing. Normal behavior stops until their curiosity is satisfied; then they swim off, frequently on a zigzag course that keeps the intruder in view with alternate eyes.

The dugongs' curiosity suggests that, as adults at least, they have few predators, although attacks by killer whales and sharks have been recorded. Dugongs have smaller and less complexly structured brains than whales and dolphins, and their greater tendency to approach and investigate objects visually is consistent with a lack of echolocation apparatus. Known dugong calls include chirps, trills, and whistles, which may signal danger and maintain mother–young contact. Large size, tough skin, dense bone structure, and blood

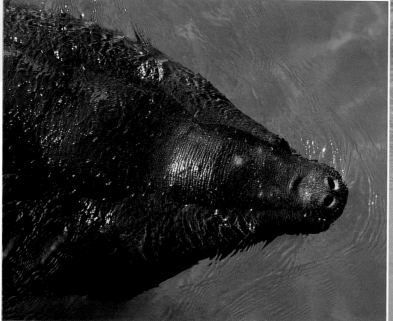

 **Left** *A manatee raises its nostrils to the water's surface to take in air. Manatees normally breathe at intervals of less than a minute, though dives of more than 15 minutes have been recorded.*

that clots very rapidly to close wounds seem to be an adult dugong's main means of defense.

Dugongs sometimes form large herds, but are more often found in groups of less than a dozen; many individuals may be solitary. Sexing is difficult in the wild, but the groups generally appear to include one or more females with calves. In some habitats, herds 60–100 strong may gather to exploit rich seagrass resources; "cultivating" the beds cooperatively with their grazing.

Radio tagging has shown that dugongs are mostly quite sedentary, inhabiting home ranges of a few dozen square kilometers. Sometimes, however, for reasons unknown, they make excursions of hundreds of kilometers.

Tropical environments make long mating seasons possible, and dugongs may mate over a period of 4–5 months. In at least one area males gather at a traditional lek site where they patrol and vocalize. Territorial males perform "situps" that appear to serve a display function. The dugong is the only marine mammal that displays this classic lekking pattern. Females become sexually mature at 10–17 years, and give birth to a single calf after a gestation of about 13 months. Few births have been observed, but it seems that the females seek out shallows at the water's edge. The calf keeps close contact with its mother for up to 2 years, suckling from a single teat in the axilla of each flipper while lying beside her and taking refuge behind her back in the presence of danger. Although females can become pregnant while lactating, interbirth intervals average from 3–7 years. Females may live to more than 60 years old.

⬤ **Right** *In Florida, a pair of manatees share a snack at a favorite feeding spot. Although the big animals are not highly social, they tolerate one another's company without showing aggression, and enjoy apparent play activities that include nuzzling and "kissing."*

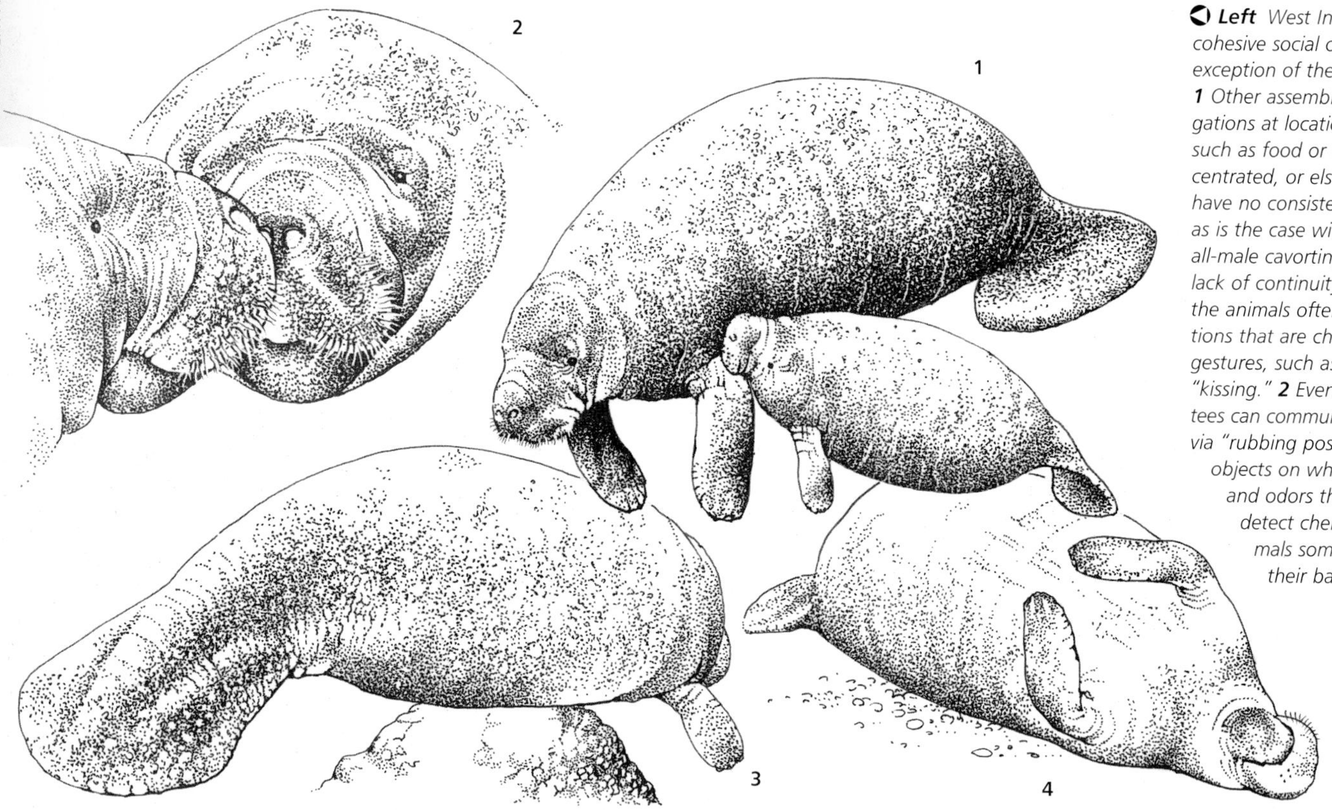

Left *West Indian manatees lack any cohesive social organization, with the exception of the mother–calf bond.* ***1*** *Other assemblages are either aggregations at locations where resources such as food or warm water are concentrated, or else are ephemeral and have no consistency in composition, as is the case with mating herds and all-male cavorting groups. Despite the lack of continuity in social groupings, the animals often exhibit social interactions that are characterized by simple gestures, such as physical contact and "kissing."* ***2*** *Even when alone, manatees can communicate with one another via "rubbing posts"* ***3****, prominent objects on which they deposit tastes and odors that other manatees can detect chemically. The big mammals sometimes relax by lying on their backs on the seabed* ***4****.*

Lambs to the Slaughter

CONSERVATION AND ENVIRONMENT

Docility, delicious flesh, and a low reproductive capacity are not auspicious characteristics for animals in the modern world. The dugong and manatees have all three, and are consequently among the most threatened of aquatic mammals.

All three species of manatees are considered by the IUCN to be vulnerable as a result of both historic and modern overhunting for their meat and skins; they are also at risk from more recent threats such as pollution and high-speed pleasure craft. One study estimated that a 10 percent increase in adult mortality or reproduction would drive the Florida population to extinction over a 1,000-year timescale, whereas a 10 percent decrease in adult mortality would allow slow population growth. They are protected under the Convention on International Trade in Endangered Species of Fauna and Flora (CITES), and legally in most countries where they exist.

In Costa Rica, local residents blame an apparent decline in their numbers on illegal hunting, high levels of toxicants in coastal waters, ingestion of plastic banana bags, and increased motorboat traffic. Badly managed "ecotourism," and environmental degradation have also played a part. A study of manatee carcasses in Florida revealed that most deaths there were due to human interaction, especially captures and watercraft collisions. When a manatee does die of natural causes, it is usually a dependent calf.

Amazonian manatees have been commercially exploited for their meat and hide since 1542, and

AN EXTINCT GIANT

The only close relative of the dugong to survive into historic times was Steller's sea cow. This giant marine grazer was the largest sirenian of all, with a body length of up to 7.5m (25ft) and a weight of 4.5–5.9 tonnes. The sea cow was unique among mammals in having no phalanges. The pectoral flipper had a stumpy, densely bristled termination described by the biologist Steller as "hooflike." Sea cows were apparently unable to submerge, and instead used these appendages to support themselves against rocks while they fed on kelp. Fossil evidence suggests that 100,000 years ago their range extended along northern Pacific coasts from Baja California up through the Aleutian Islands as far as Japan.

Its inshore feeding habits made Steller's sea cow vulnerable to hunters in small boats. Native peoples almost certainly hunted it, so, even before the arrival of Western explorers, the population had probably already been severely reduced to as few as 1,000–2,000 animals. When shipwrecked Russian sailors first sighted it in 1741, it was restricted to two subarctic Pacific islands, each 50–100km (30–60mi) long. The survivors killed and ate the sea cows out of dire necessity, and thereafter fur-hunting parties overwintered on the islands to exploit this ready food supply. Moreover, by slaughtering sea otters the hunters caused a boom in the urchin population, which stripped the kelp beds, the sea cows' main food. By 1768 the sea cows were extinct.

In later times, several isolated dugong populations seem to have suffered similar fates. Even though there are still a few surviving herds as numerous as those of Steller's sea cow were at the time of its discovery, the story of the extinction of the species' huge relative nevertheless has an obvious moral for the present day. PKA

Below *A fanciful 18th-century illustration of Steller's sea cows.*

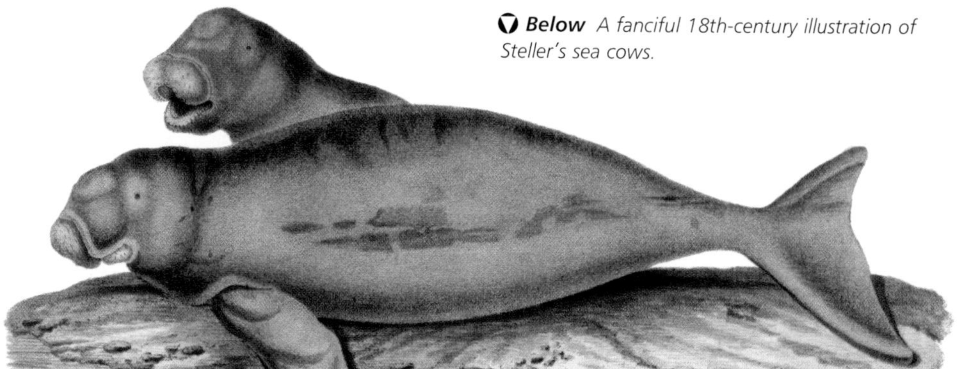

they are now considered an endangered species. Although they have been legally protected since 1973, exploitation for meat has in fact continued without any practical restrictions. Manatees are also hunted in Peru, and are sometimes taken incidentally in fishing gear.

Another important factor in manatee deaths are blooms of toxic algae that may be exacerbated by pollution. During a period of several weeks in the spring of 1996, over 200 manatees were found dead or dying in Florida's coastal waters or on the beaches of the west coast. At the same time, high densities of a dinoflagellate that produces a potent neurotoxin that binds to manatee brain cells were observed in the same coastal areas. Yet another threat is morbillivirus, which may cause fatal infections and possibly also more insidious effects on the immune system or reproduction.

Improving the manatee's lot will require proactive management. Scientific research, rescue, and rehabilitation also have their place. Boat-free zones provide sanctuaries for manatees in Florida, and are an effective management tool. If speed and boating regulations are effectively enforced in 13 key coastal counties, Florida's manatees should be able to coexist indefinitely with human recreational requirements, whereas if regulation is unsuccessful, the population is likely to decline slowly toward extinction. Control of hunting and management of tourism may also make the manatee's future more certain elsewhere.

In recent times, people have found a nonlethal employment for manatees that they seem only too happy to fulfill: that of clearing weeds from irrigation canals and the dams of hydroelectric power stations. It is thus possible that the animals' gentle, herbivorous lifestyle might yet help them to survive in an aggressive world.

As a marine creature, the dugong has had less direct contact with people than the riverine manatees, but even so the relationship has not been a happy one. Dugongs have traditionally been hunted by coastal peoples in most of their range. In recent times, the increase in human populations and the growing availability of nylon gill nets and boats with outboard motors have led to the decimation of dugong populations outside of Australia and the Persian Gulf. PKA/JMP/GBR/DPD/RB

○ **Above** Caught in a fish-trap off Sulawesi (Indonesia), a young dugong uses its sensitive snout to investigate its prison. Over the centuries hunting has driven the dugong from much of its former range.

GRAZING THE SEA GRASS MEADOWS

Feeding strategy of the dugong

A PERSON WANDERING THE INTERTIDAL SEA GRASS meadows of northern Australia will likely notice long, serpentine furrows devoid of all vegetation. These are the feeding trails of the dugong, a large marine mammal that uproots whole sea grass plants, including their roots and rhizomes. Dugongs prefer small, delicate, "weedy" sea grasses that are low in fiber, yet high in available nutrients and easily digested – mainly species from the genera *Halophila* and *Halodule*. Experiments simulating dugong grazing indicate that their feeding alters both the species composition and nutrient qualities of sea grass communities, causing them to become lower in fiber and higher in nitrogen. In effect, dugongs are like farmers cultivating their crops. If these animals were to become locally extinct, the sea grass meadows would, in turn, deteriorate as dugong habitat.

Over most of its range, the dugong is known only from incidental sightings, accidental drownings, and the anecdotal reports of fishermen. However, within Australia, intensive aerial surveys have produced a more comprehensive picture of dugong distribution, which is now known to extend from Moreton Bay in Queensland, on the east coast, around to Shark Bay in Western Australia. These same surveys show dugongs to be the most abundant marine mammal in the inshore waters of northern Australia, numbering some 85,000 individuals. What is more, this figure is probably an underestimate, since some areas of suitable habitat have not been surveyed and the mathematical correction for animals that cannot be seen in turbid water is conservative. In other words, Australia is the dugong's last stronghold.

More than 60 individual dugongs have been tracked using satellite transmitters. Most of their movements have been localized to the vicinity of sea grass beds and are dictated by the tide. At localities where the tidal range is large, dugongs can gain access to their inshore feeding areas only when the water depth is at least one meter (3.3ft). In areas with low tidal amplitude or where sea grass grows subtidally, dugongs can generally feed without making significant local movements. However, at the high-latitude limits of their range, dugongs make seasonal movements to warmer waters. While overwintering in Moreton Bay, many dugongs frequently make round trips of 15–40km (9–25mi) between their foraging grounds inside the bay and oceanic waters, which are, on average, up to 5°C warmer. Dugongs also apparently relocate within Shark Bay itself, moving from east to west, where the water is warmer. Some travel for long distances; for example, in the Great Barrier Reef region and the Gulf of Carpentaria, several

◐ ◑ Above and Right *Sea grasses grow abundantly in the shallow waters that surround northern Australia. This plentiful supply of vegetation attracts great numbers of dugongs. Stirring up the substrate as they browse, these sedate marine grazers appear when seen from the air almost like combine harvesters moving slowly across a field of crops.*

dugongs have been recorded making trips of 100–600km (62–372mi) over just a few days. Many of these movements were return trips. One plausible explanation for such long journeys is that dugongs are checking the status of the sea grass beds in their region. Many sea grass meadows arise and promptly disappear again, for no apparent reason. Sometimes hundreds of kilometers of sea grass may be lost after storms or flooding.

Dugongs are long lived, with a low reproductive rate, long generation time, and a high investment in each offspring. On the basis of annual growth rings in its tusks, the oldest dugong was estimated to be 73 years old when she died. Females give birth aged 10–17, and the period between successive births varies from three to seven years. The gestation period is around 13 months, and the (almost always single) calf suckles for at least 18 months. Dugongs start eating sea grasses soon after they are born and grow rapidly during the suckling period. Population simulations indicate that a dugong population is unlikely to be able to increase by more than 5 percent annually. This makes the dugong highly susceptible to overexploitation by indigenous hunters or to incidental drowning in fishing nets. Consequently, they are classified as vulnerable to global extinction.   HM

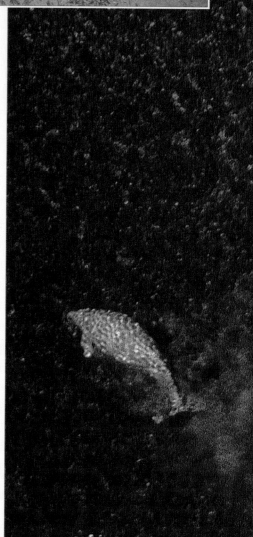

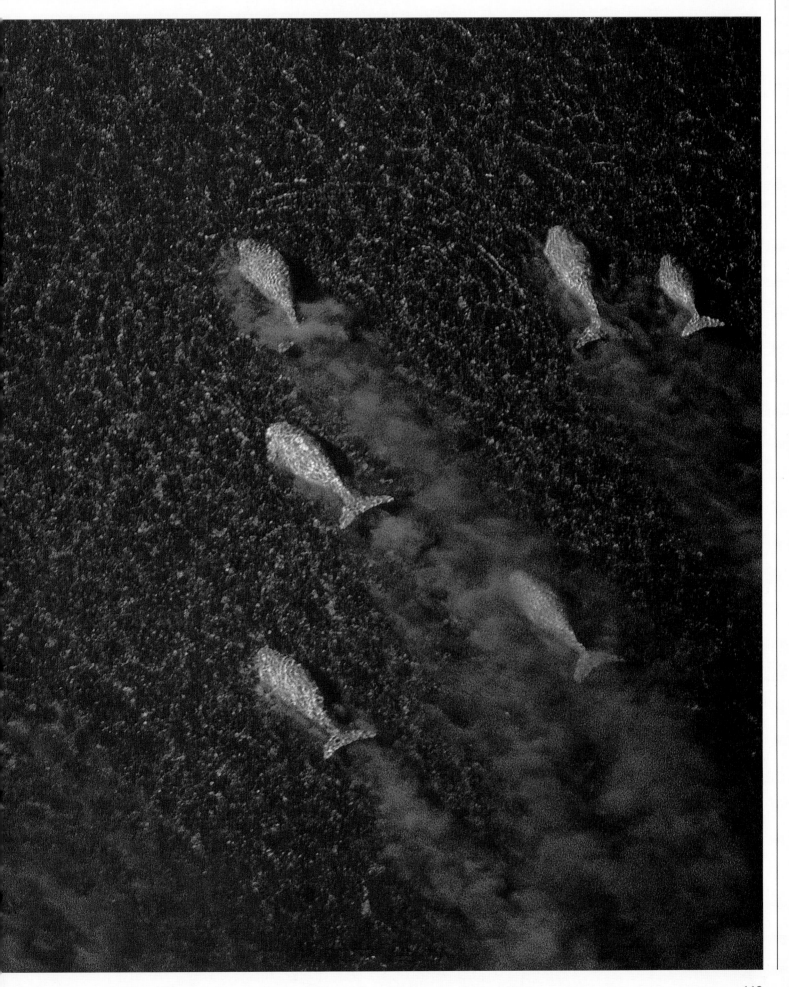

ANTEATERS AND RELATIVES

tHE TERM EDENTATES, *OFTEN USED TO describe a group of niche food specialists is a misnomer. Firstly, it contradicts the fact that most species in the group are not toothless, but have at least vestigial teeth. Secondly, it has no taxonomic validity; the order Edentata, which once embraced anteaters, sloths, armadillos, pangolins (and even the aardvark), is now defunct. The perceived similarities that occasioned such a grouping are now thought to be the result of convergent evolution, and not of any phylogenetic connection. Edentata was replaced with the order Xenarthra, which grouped the clearly related anteaters, sloths, and armadillos, and the pangolins were placed in a separate order, the Pholidota.*

By the early Tertiary 60 million years ago (the beginning of the "Age of Mammals"), the ancestral "edentates" had already diverged into two quite distinct lines: the Palaeanodonta, (ancestor of the pangolins, Pholidota), and the Xenarthra. The xenarthrans were on the brink of a spectacular radiation that was later to produce some of the most distinctive and bizarre of all the New World mammals. More recently, the species previously belonging to the xenarthrans have been divided into two separate orders; Pilosa (anteaters and sloths) and Cingulata (armadillos).

▌ Sluggish Specialists
ANATOMY AND EVOLUTION

The living and recently extinct members of the Pilosa and Cingulata are distinguished from all other mammals by additional articulations between the lumbar vertebrae, which are called xenarthrales (or xenarthrous vertebrae). These bony elements provide lumbar reinforcement for digging, and are especially important for the armadillos. The living pilosans and cingulatans also differ from most mammals in having a double posterior vena cava vein (single in other mammals), which returns blood to the heart from the hindquarters of the body. Females have a primi-

◐ **Right** *Prehistoric edentates. The edentates produced three major groups: "shelled" forms (Loricata), including the extinct glyptodonts and living armadillos; "hairy" forms (Pilosa), including the extinct giant ground sloth and living tree sloths; and the anteaters (Vermilingua).* **1** *The giant ground sloth (Megatherium), from the Pleistocene of South America, was up to 6m (20ft) long.* **2** *Glyptodon panochthus, a giant shelled form from the Pleistocene of South America.* **3** *Giant anteater (Scelidotherium), from the Pleistocene of South America.* **4** *Eomanis waldi, a small armored pangolin from the Eocene of Germany.*

tive, divided womb only a step removed from the double womb of marsupials, and a common urinary and genital duct, while males have internal testes, and a small penis with no glans.

Despite these unifying characteristics, the extinct xenarthrans differed greatly in size and appearance from their modern relatives and, in terms of numbers of genera, were more than ten times as diverse. The rise and fall of these early forms is closely linked to the fact that throughout the Tertiary South America was a huge, isolated island. At the beginning of this epoch, ancestral xenarthrans shared the continent only with early marsupials and other primitive mammals, and flourished in the virtual absence of competition. By the late Eocene (38 million years ago), three families of giant ground sloths had emerged, with some species growing to the size of modern elephants. In their heyday during the late Miocene, 30 million years later, ground sloths appeared in the West Indies and southern North America, appar-

ently having rafted across the sea barriers as waif immigrants. Four families of armored, armadillo-like xenarthrans were contemporary with the ground sloths for much of the Oligocene. The largest species, *Glyptodon*, achieved a length of 5m (16.5ft) and carried a rigid 3m (10ft) shell on its back, while the related *Doedicurus* had a

1

4

massive tail with the tip armored like a medieval mace. Although *Glyptodon* and the giant ground sloths survived until historical times – and are spoken of in the legends of the Tehuelche and Araucan Indians of Patagonia – only the smaller tree sloths, anteaters, and armadillos persisted to the present day.

The extinct xenarthrans are believed to have been ponderous, unspecialized herbivores that inhabited scrubby savannas. They were probably out-competed and preyed upon by the new and sophisticated northern invaders. In contrast, the success of the living pilosans and cingulatans was due to their occupation of relatively narrow niches, which allowed little space for the less specialized newcomers. The anteaters and leaf-eating sloths, for example, have very specialized diets. To cope with the low energy contents of their foods, both groups evolved metabolic rates that are only 33–60 percent of those expected for their body-weights, and variable but low (32.7–35°C/91–95°F) body temperatures that burn fewer kilojoules. Armadillos eat a wide range of foods, but are specialized for a partly subterranean way of life; they also have low metabolic rates and body temperatures (33–35.5°C/91.5–96°F) to avoid overheating in their closed burrows. Lacking similarly sluggish metabolisms, the invading mammals were not able fully to exploit these habitats, so competition was probably minimal.

Living in Niches

SOCIAL BEHAVIOR

As consequences of specializing and slowing their metabolisms, the sloths and anteaters use energy frugally, and generally move slowly over small home ranges. Females attain sexual maturity at 2–3 years of age and breed only once a year thereafter. They produce small, precocious litters (usually one young), and invest much time and energy in weaning and post-weaning care. Defense against predators is passive and primarily dependent on cryptic camouflage. While anteaters, and occasionally sloths, may try to flee from an assailant, they more often stand their ground and strike out with their claws. Sloths are reputedly able to survive the most severe injuries; bite wounds and deep scars rarely become infected, and heal completely within weeks. Armadillos show similar trends toward economizing their use of energy, but these are not as marked as in their ant- and plant-eating relatives. The armadillos are less constrained because of their more varied and energy-rich diets, and the ability (at least of some species) to store fat and enter torpor.

The social lives of pilosans and cingulatans are probably dominated by the sense of smell. All species produce odoriferous secretions from anal glands, which are used to mark paths, trees, or conspicuous objects; these probably advertise the presence, status, and possibly the sexual condition of the marking individual. Scent marks may also serve as territorial markers, and allow individuals priority of access to scarce resources, such as food. CRD

SKULLS AND DENTITION

Pilosans and cingulatans have the least complex skulls of all mammals. Although once described as edentates ("without teeth"), it is in fact only the anteaters (such as the southern tamandua) that are completely toothless. Both sloths and armadillos are equipped with a series of uniform, peg-shaped cheek or grinding teeth (premolars and molars). These lack an enamel covering and have a single so-called open root that allows continuous growth of the teeth throughout life. True incisor and canine teeth are absent in all species of these orders, but sloths have enlarged, caninelike premolars.

The diet of pilosans and cingulatans ranges from an almost total reliance on ants and termites in the anteaters, through a wide range of insects, tubers, and carrion in the armadillos, to plants in the sloths.

2

3

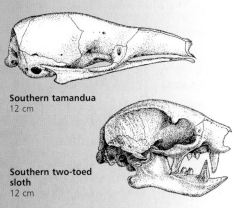

Southern tamandua
12 cm

Southern two-toed sloth
12 cm

115

Anteaters

aNTEATERS FEED EXCLUSIVELY ON SOCIAL insects, primarily ants and termites. Their adaptations to this diet affect not only masticatory and digestive structures but behavior, metabolic rate, and locomotion. Anteaters are solitary, except that a mother may carry her young on her back for up to a year, until it is nearly adult in size.

While the different anteater species do not overlap greatly in distribution, they nonetheless operate at different times and in different strata: the giant anteater feeds mostly by day (although it becomes nocturnal when it is disturbed by people), whereas tamanduas are variably active both by day and by night and the silky anteater is strictly nocturnal. Similarly, giant anteaters are terrestrial, tamanduas partially arboreal, and silky anteaters almost exclusively arboreal. All anteaters can both dig and climb, as well as walk on the ground. However, the giant anteater rarely climbs and the silky anteater descends to the ground only infrequently. There is further niche separation in diet, with giant anteaters eating the largest-bodied ants and termites, tamanduas the medium-sized insects, and silky anteaters the smallest.

Toothless Insect-eaters
FORM AND FUNCTION

Anteaters were previously grouped in the Xenarthra with the sloths, armadillos and the extinct glyptodonts. The anteaters now belong in the order Pilosa with the sloths, but are the only toothless (edentulous) members of the order. Mouths in all species are small and only open to a small oval. Anteater snouts are disproportionately long, the giant anteater's head appearing to be almost tubular and over 30cm (12in) in length. Their narrow, rounded tongues are even longer than their heads; the tongues of tamanduas protrude some 40cm (16in), while that of the giant anteater can extend up to 61cm (24in). In all anteaters, the tongues are covered in minute, posteriorly directed spines and coated with a thick, sticky saliva secreted from salivary glands relatively larger than those of any other animals. Anteater stomachs are unusual in not secreting hydrochloric acid, but depend instead on the formic acid content of the ants they eat to assist with digestion.

The only natural predators of giant anteaters are pumas and jaguars – if threatened they rear up on their hindlegs, slashing with claws that can be up to 10cm (4in) in length. They have even been known to embrace and crush an attacker. The

◗ Right The southern tamandua has strong claws and a powerful tail, which is used to gain additional purchase when climbing in trees. The tail can also act as a prop, enabling the animal to rear up on its back legs.

largest claws are on fingers two and three in giant and silky anteaters, but digits two, three, and four in tamanduas. All have five fingers and four or five toes, although some fingers are reduced in size and enclosed within the skin of the hand. The fifth finger of the giant anteater and the first, fourth and fifth fingers of the silky anteater are the reduced digits. Anteaters move with the fingers of the forefeet flexed and turned inward to keep the sharp claw tips from contacting the ground. Sometimes they walk on the sides of their hindfeet, turning the claws inward, much as did some of the extinct ground sloths to which they are related. Climbing in trees the tamanduas and silky anteaters use their prehensile tails, and claws that may be up to 400mm (16in) in length to grip branches. When threatened, a tamandua on the ground balances on hindfeet and tail, swiping ferociously with the foreclaws. The defensive posture of silky anteaters also uses the prehensile tail and hindfeet to grasp a supporting branch, but initially the forefeet are raised to the level of the shoulders with the claws aimed forward and inward. Amazingly, silky anteaters can stretch out horizontally from the supporting branch, an unusual feat (shared with tree sloths) made possible by additional (xenarthrous) articulations

between vertebrae. Furthermore, an additional (and unique) joint in the sole of the foot allows the claws to be turned back under the foot to enhance the grasp. The most common predators of arboreal anteaters include harpy eagles, hawk eagles, and the spectacled owl. These hunters fly above the canopy and search visually for prey; thus, the coat of the silky anteater, which closely resembles the massive balls of silvery fluff that make up the seed pods of the silk-cotton ceiba tree, may serve as protective coloration. Silky anteaters are frequently found in these trees. None of the anteaters is particularly vocal, but giant anteaters bellow when threatened. If separated from the mother, young animals produce short, high-pitched whistles.

Digging for Dinner
DIET

Anteaters detect prey mainly by smell, but their vision is probably poor. Giant anteaters feed on large-bodied colonial ants and termites. Anteaters feed rapidly. Typically they dig a small hole in the nest, and lick up worker ants as they emerge, and with tongue movements as rapid as 150 times a minute take larvae and cocoons as well. Insects trapped on the sticky saliva-coated tongue are

FACTFILE

ANTEATERS

Order: Pilosa

Families: Myrmecophagidae and Cyclopedidae

4 species in 3 genera

DISTRIBUTION
S Mexico, C & S America S to Paraguay and N Argentina; Trinidad.

FAMILY MYRMECOPHAGIDAE

GIANT ANTEATER *Myrmecophaga tridactyla*
C America; S America E of the Andes to Uruguay and NW Argentina. Grassland, swamp, lowland tropical forest. HBL 1–1.3m (3.3– 4.2ft); TL 65–90cm (25.5–35.5in); WT 22–39kg (48–86lb); male anteaters are 10–20 percent heavier than females. Coat: coarse, stiff, dense; coloration gray with black-and-white shoulder stripe. Breeding: 1 young born in spring after a gestation of 190 days. Longevity: unknown in the wild, but up to 26 years in captivity. Conservation status: Vulnerable.

NORTHERN TAMANDUA *Tamandua mexicana*
Northern tamandua, Northern collared or lesser anteater S Mexico to NW Venezuela and NW Peru. Savanna, thorn scrub, wet and dry forest. HBL 52.5–57cm (21–22in); TL 52.5–55cm (21–21.5in); WT 3.2–5.4kg (7–12lb). Coat: light fawn to dark brown with variable patches of black or reddish brown from shoulders to rump. Breeding: Gestation 130–150 days. Longevity: unknown in the wild but to at least 9 years in captivity.

SOUTHERN TAMANDUA *Tamandua tetradactyla*
Southern tamandua, Southern collared or lesser anteater S America E of the Andes from Venezuela to N Argentina; Trinidad. HBL 58–61cm (23–24in); TL 50–52.5cm (19.5–21.5in); WT 3.4–7kg (7.5–15.5lb). Coat: as for Northern tamandua, but black "vest" is only present in specimens from SE portion of range.

FAMILY CYCLOPEDIDAE

SILKY ANTEATER *Cyclopes didactylus*
C and S America, from S Mexico to the Amazon basin and N Peru. Tropical forest. HBL 18–20cm (7–8in); TL 18–26cm (7–10in); WT 375–410g (13.2–14.4oz). Coat: soft, silky gray to yellowish orange, with darker mid-dorsal stripe.

Abbreviations HBL = head–body length TL = tail length WT = weight

◐ **Left** A giant anteater with offspring in Brazil. The young anteater may continue to ride around on its mother's back for up to a year, well past the weaning stage, which occurs at about six months.

crushed against the hard palate prior to swallowing. Anteaters avoid large-jawed ant and termite soldiers. Even though the skin on their muzzles is thick it is evidently not impervious to the bites of insect soldiers. Because they use each nest for only a short period, and take as few as 140 insects (only about 0.5 percent of their daily food requirement) per feeding bout, anteaters cause little permanent damage to nests. Their density appears to depend on the number of nests that are available in a given area; many must be visited daily to get sufficient nutrition (which may amount to 35,000 ants a day). Beetle larvae are also taken. Water requirements are generally met by their food.

The way anteaters eat is unique among mammals. They contract their chewing (temporal and masseter) muscles to roll the two halves of the lower jaw towards the middle, thereby separating the anterior tips to open the mouth. The mouth is closed by the pterygoid muscles that pull the lower rear (posteroventral) edges of the two lower jaw bones inward (medially), raising the anterior tips to close the mouth. The result is simplified and minimal jaw movement which, when coupled

with movements in and out of the tongue and nearly continuous swallowing, maximize the rate of food intake. The extraordinary movements of the tongue are controlled by a sternoglossus muscle that attaches to the base of the sternum.

Tamanduas specialize in smaller-bodied termites and ants than do the giant anteater, and also avoid the soldier castes. They also refrain from eating ant and termite species that have chemical defenses, and will eat bees and honey. A tamandua will typically consume 9,000 ants in a day. The average length of arboreal ants and termites eaten by silky anteaters is 4mm (0.15in) as opposed to the 8mm (0.3in) or larger prey of giant anteaters.

Precocious Young
SOCIAL BEHAVIOR

All species of anteater are usually solitary. Home ranges in giant anteaters may be as small as 0.5sq km in areas of high food availability, such as the tropical forests of Barro Colorado Island, Panama, or the southeastern highlands of Brazil. In habitats that support fewer ant and termite colonies such as the mixed deciduous forests and semiarid

Above and below *Silky anteaters taking a break: above, curled in defensive posture with the claws in front of the face; below, suspended from a branch. An adaptation in the foot of silky anteaters allows the claws to be turned back under the foot to improve grip.*

llanos of Venezuela one individual giant anteater may require as much as 2,480ha (6,200 acres). The ranges of female giant anteaters may overlap by as much as 30 percent, while those of males typically overlap by less than 5 percent. Tamanduas are less than half the size of the giant anteater and in favorable habitats such as Barro Colorado, occupy home ranges of 50–140ha (124–346 acres). In the open llanos one animal may require as much as 340–400ha (840–988 acres). Silky anteater females on Barro Colorado have a home range that averages 2.8ha (7 acres) while that of a single male is approximately 11ha (27 acres). The home range of this male overlapped those of two females, but not the range of an adjacent male. Although the geographic distribution of the four anteater species differ, when they occur in the same habitat, home ranges of one do not appear to be affected by the presence of another.

Giant anteaters and tamanduas mate in the fall, and the single young is born in the spring. The giant anteater gives birth standing, using her tail as a third support. The young are precocious and have sharp claws that allow them to crawl to the mother's back shortly after being born. Twins occur rarely and the young are suckled for approximately six months but may remain with the mother up to the age of two years, by which time they will have reached sexual maturity. Young giant anteaters can gallop by about a month after birth, but generally either move slowly or are carried on the mother's back. Tamanduas may place the young one on a branch near a preferred feeding location, or leave them for a short period of time alone in a leaf nest, a practice that is shared with silky anteaters. The young of the silky anteater is fed semidigested ants that are regurgitated by both parents, and the infant may be carried by either parent. Giant anteater young are miniatures copies of their parents; however, tamandua infants do not resemble the parents and range in color from white to black.

Giant anteaters do not actually burrow, but instead scoop out shallow depressions in which they rest for up to 15 hours a day. They remain cryptic by covering their bodies with the great fanlike tail. Tamanduas generally rest in hollows in trees while silky anteaters sleep during the day curled up on a branch with the tail wrapped around the feet. They generally do not spend more than one day in a single tree.

Giant anteaters and tamanduas can produce strong-smelling secretions from their anal glands. Silky anteaters have a facial gland; however, its purpose is unknown. Giant anteaters can also distinguish the scent of their own saliva, although it is not known whether they use salivary secretions to communicate.

All anteaters have low metabolic rates: giant anteaters have the lowest recorded body temperature for a placental mammal, 32.7°C (90.9°F), and the tamanduas' and silky anteater's body

temperatures are not especially higher. Daily activity periods generally do not average more than eight hours for the giant anteater and tamandua and about four hours for the silky anteater.

Primarily resulting from slight color pattern differences, giant anteaters have been divided into three subspecies, and *T. mexicana* into five. Color variation in *T. mexicana* depends on the size and darkness of the black vest, although all individuals of this species show some degree of this marking. In contrast, *T. tetradactyla* shows great variation in this trait. In animals in the northern part of the range the coat is a uniform light color, while those in the southern part may have striking vest development. The species differences are most striking where the geographic ranges abut, and may be an excellent example of character displacement. This coat color variation probably explains why this species has been divided into thirteen subspecies. Differences in coat color probably also explain the naming of seven subspecies of silky anteater. In the northern regions the animal is a uniformly golden color, or has a darker dorsal stripe, but it becomes progressively grayer, and the mid-dorsal stripe darker, in the south.

○ **Above** *Inserting its long snout into a hollow log, a giant anteater feeds on the insects inside. Anteaters are choosy about the type of ants they consume, taking care to avoid the aggressive soldiers.*

▮ Prey for Trophy Hunters
CONSERVATION AND ENVIRONMENT

With the exception of small-scale use of tamandua skin in local leather industries, anteaters have little commercial value and are seldom hunted for food. However, the giant anteater has disappeared from most of its historic range in Central America as a result of habitat loss and human encroachment. In South America, it is frequently hunted as a trophy or captured by animal dealers. It has been extirpated in some parts of Peru and Brazil. Tamanduas also suffer when they occur near human habitations. They put on spectacular defenses and may be hunted with dogs for sport, or are often killed on the roads around areas of human settlement. In the Venezuelan llanos, young individuals may be tamed and prove to be popular as pets. However, the most serious threat to these creatures is the loss of habitat and the destruction of the limited number of prey species upon which they feed.   VN

Sloths

aLTHOUGH SLOTHS ARE RENOWNED FOR *their almost glacial slowness of movement, they are the most spectacularly successful large mammals in Central and tropical South America. On Barro Colorado Island, Panama, two species – the brown-throated three-toed sloth and Hoffmann's two-toed sloth – account for two-thirds of the biomass and half of the energy consumption of all terrestrial mammals, while in Surinam they comprise at least a quarter of the total mammalian biomass. Success has come from specializing in an arboreal, leaf-eating way of life to such a remarkable extent that the effects of competitors and predators are scarcely perceptible.*

Oviedo y Valdes, one of the first Spanish chroniclers of the Central American region in the 16th century, wrote that he had never seen an uglier or more useless creature than the sloth. Fortunately, little commercial value has since been attached to these animals, although large numbers, espe-

cially of two-toed sloths, are hunted locally for their meat in many parts of South America. Beauty, however, is in the eye of the beholder, and modern-day tourists will pay to have their photograph taken with sloths stolen from the forests and touted on the streets of South American cities. The maned three-toed sloth of southeastern Brazil is considered endangered due to the destruction of its coastal rain forest habitat, and the pygmy three-toed sloth, known only from the Isla Escudo de Veraguas, Panama, is vulnerable. The fortunes of all six species are inextricably bound up with the future of the tropical forests.

A Walking Ecosystem
FORM AND FUNCTION

Sloths have rounded heads and flattened faces, with small ears hidden in the fur; they are distinguished from other tree-dwelling mammals by their simple teeth (five upper molars, four lower), and their highly modified hands and feet, which terminate in curved claws 8–10cm (3–4in) long.

◗ **Below** *At home in the trees, a brown-throated three-toed sloth takes its ease in Bolivia's Gran Chaco National Park. The three-toed sloths spend almost all their lives in the branches, only descending to the ground once or twice a week to defecate.*

Their general appearance is extraordinary, but most remarkable of all is the fact that sloths are green; they possess a short, fine underfur and an overcoat of longer and coarser hairs which, in moist conditions, turn green, owing to the presence of two species of blue-green algae that grow in longitudinal grooves in the hairs. This helps to camouflage animals in the tree canopy. The ecology of sloth fur does not end there, for it also harbors animals, including moths (*Cryptoses* spp.), ticks (*Amblyomma varium*, *Boophilus* spp.), and beetles (*Trichilium* spp.). All species have extremely large, multicompartment stomachs, which contain cellulose-digesting bacteria. A full stomach may account for almost a third of the body weight of a sloth, and meals may be digested there for more than a month before passing completely into the relatively short intestine. Feces and urine are passed only once or twice a week, at habitual sites at the bases of trees.

The sloths are grouped into two distinct genera and families, which can be distinguished most easily by the numbers of fingers: those of genus *Choloepus* have two fingers and those of genus

○ **Left** *A southern two-toed sloth rests on the fork of a branch. Two-toed sloths spend much of their lives hanging upside down, supported by their hooked claws; they even sleep and give birth in that position.*

◑ **Below** *This brown-throated three-toed sloth clinging to a tree in Panama owes its green coloration to an algal growth. The algae provide camouflage and possibly also a source of nutrition, either absorbed through the skin or licked directly from the hair.*

Bradypus have three. Misleadingly, despite the fact that both genera have three toes, the two-fingered forms are known as two-toed and the three-fingered forms as three-toed sloths.

Both two- and three-toed sloths maintain low but variable body temperatures, from 30–34°C (86–93°F), which fall during the cooler hours of the night, during wet weather, and whenever the animals are inactive. Such labile body temperatures help to conserve energy: sloths have metabolic rates that are only 40–45 percent of those expected for their body weights as well as reduced muscles (about half the relative weight for most terrestrial mammals), and so cannot afford to keep warm by shivering. Both species frequent trees with exposed crowns and regulate their body temperatures by moving in and out of the sun.

■ **Sharing the Forest**
DISTRIBUTION PATTERNS

While representatives of both sloth families occur together in tropical forests through much of Central and South America, sloths within the same genus occupy more or less exclusive geographical ranges. These closely related species differ little in body weight (staying within a 10 percent range), and have such similar habits that they are apparently unable to coexist.

Where two- and three-toed sloths occur together, the two-toed form is 25 percent heavier than its relative and it uses the forest in different ways. In lowland tropical forest on Barro Colorado Island in Panama's Canal Zone, the brown-throated three-toed sloth achieves a density of 8.5 animals

per ha (3.5 per acre), over three times that of the larger Hoffmann's two-toed sloth. The smaller species is sporadically active for more than 10 hours out of 24, compared with just 7.6 hours for the two-toed sloth and, unlike its nocturnal relative, it is active both by day and by night. Three-toed sloths maintain overlapping home ranges averaging 6.6ha (16.3 acres), three times those of the larger species. Despite their apparent alacrity, however, only 11 percent of three-toed sloths travel further than 38m (125ft) in a day, and some 40 percent

FACTFILE

SLOTHS

Order: Pilosa

Families: Megalonychidae (two-toed sloths) and Bradypodidae (three-toed sloths)

6 species in 2 genera

DISTRIBUTION
C and S America

Equator

Habitat Lowland and upland tropical forest; montane forest to 2,100m/7,000ft (Hoffmann's two-toed sloth only).

Coat Stiff, coarse, grayish brown to beige, with a greenish cast provided by the growth of blue-green algae on the hairs; dark hair on face and neck, lighter fur on shoulders; hair grows to 6cm (2.4in) on three-toed sloths and to 15cm (6in) on two-toed sloths.

Breeding Gestation period 6 months (Southern two-toed sloth, three-toed sloths); 11.5 months (Hoffmann's two-toed sloth).

Longevity 12 years (up to at least 31 in captivity).

TWO-TOED SLOTHS Genus *Choloepus*
From Nicaragua S through C American isthmus to Colombia, Venezuela, Surinam, Guyana, French Guiana, NC Brazil, and N Peru. 2 species: **Hoffmann's two-toed sloth** (*C. hoffmanni*); **Southern** or **Linnaeus's two-toed sloth** (*C. didactylus*). HBL 58–70cm (23–28in), WT 4–8kg (8.8–17.6lb), tail absent.

THREE-TOED SLOTHS Genus *Bradypus*
From Honduras S through C American isthmus to Colombia, Venezuela, Surinam, Guyana, and French Guiana; coastal Ecuador, Bolivia, Paraguay, and N Argentina. 4 species: **Brown-throated three-toed sloth** (*B. variegatus*), **Pale-throated three-toed sloth** (*B. tridactylus*), **Maned three-toed sloth** (*B. torquatus*), and **Pygmy three-toed sloth** (*B. pygmaeus*). HBL 56–60cm (22–24in), TL 6–7cm (2.4–2.8in), WT 3.5–4.5kg (7.7–9.4lb). The Maned three-toed sloth is classed as Endangered and the Pygmy sloth as Vulnerable.

Abbreviations HBL = head–body length TL = tail length WT = weight

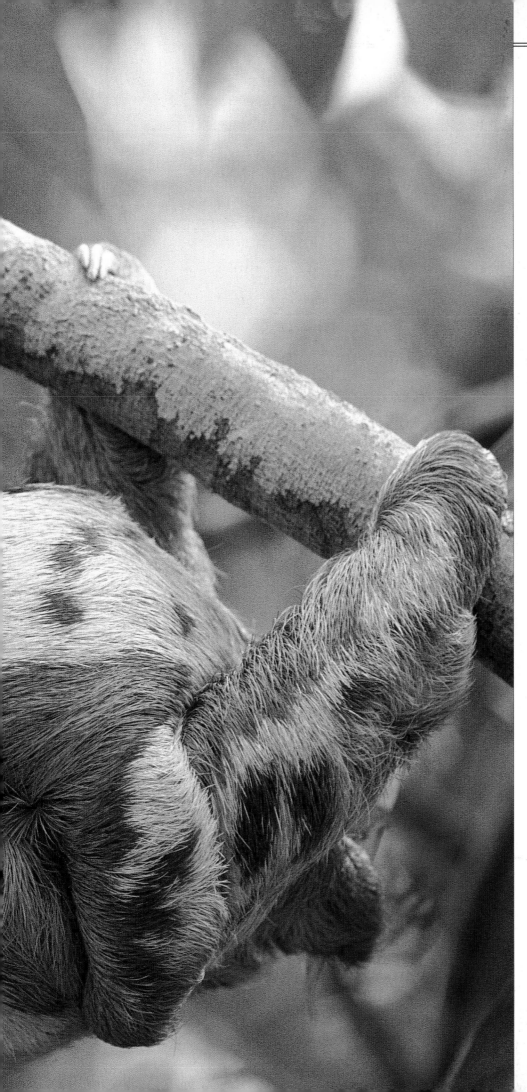

remain in the same tree on two consecutive nights; the three-toed sloths, by contrast, change trees four times as often.

Three maned three-toed sloths in an Atlantic forest reserve of south-eastern Brazil were observed to eat 99 percent leaves, with tree leaves (83 percent) preferred to liana leaves (16 percent). Moreover, young leaves (68 percent) were favored over mature ones (7 percent) throughout the year. Their diet included a total of 21 plant species (16 tree and 5 liana), but each individual made up its diet from an even smaller number of plant species (7–12). The sloths consumed only a tiny fraction of the species available to them, and those they ate were not particularly abundant. It seems likely that sloths have evolved resistance to the defensive poisons produced by certain plants and so eat predominantly those. Their metabolism is extremely slow, which may allow their gut to neutralize the plant toxins as they pass through, contributing to the sloth's success as the ultimate plant eater.

Inheriting the Mother's Domain
SOCIAL BEHAVIOR

Sloths are believed to breed throughout the year, but in Guyana births of the pale-throated three-toed sloth occur only after the rainy season, between July and September. Reproduction in the maned three-toed sloth is aseasonal. The single young, weighing 300–400g (10.5–14oz), is born above ground and is helped to a teat by the mother. The young of all species cease nursing at about 1 month, but may begin to take leaves even earlier. They are carried by the mother alone for 6–9 months and feed on leaves they can reach from this position; they utter bleats or pure-toned whistles if separated. After weaning, the young inherit a portion of the home range left vacant by the mother, as well as her taste for leaves. A consequence of inheriting preferences for different tree species is that several sloths can occupy a similar home range without competing for food or space; this will tend to maximize their numbers at the expense of howler monkeys and other leaf-eating rivals in the forest canopy. Two-toed sloths may not reach sexual maturity until the age of 3 years (females) or 4–5 years (males).

Adult sloths are usually solitary, and patterns of communication are poorly known. However, males are thought to advertise their presence by wiping secretions from an anal gland onto branches, and the pungent-smelling dung middens conceivably act as trysting places. Three-toed sloths produce shrill "ai-ai" whistles through the nostrils, while two-toed sloths hiss if disturbed.   CRD

◖ **Left** *A large adolescent pale-throated three-toed sloth clings protectively to its mother in the rain forest of Brazil's Manaus province. Even though they are weaned at 4 weeks, the young usually stay with their mothers for at least another 5 months, relying on them for transport through the trees.*

Armadillos

aRMADILLOS ARE ONE OF THE OLDEST, AND *oddest, groups of mammals. Because of the tough protective carapace they all possess, early zoologists often linked them with shelled verte-brates such as turtles. Modern taxonomists put them in the order Cingulata.*

The Xenarthra was the name given to one of the four basal groups of placental mammals, diverging from other mammals as long as 103 million years ago. Within the Xenarthra, armadillos split off into their own taxonomic branch about 55–75 million years ago. Recent molecular genetic studies suggest armadillos may be closely related to the fer-roungulates, which include the carnivores, cetaceans, and artiodactyls.

Although they are now classified in the order Cingulata, armadillos were previously included in the order Xenarthra along with anteaters and sloths. Prior to the Xenarthra they were included in the now obsolete order Edentata, which means "without teeth." This was always spurious, as they all possess rudimentary, peglike teeth that are undifferentiated (in other words, not divided into incisors, canines, or molars) and that serve to mash up their food. Most species have 14–18 teeth in each jaw, but the giant armadillo, with 80–100, has more than almost any other mammal. In the long-nosed species of the genus *Dasy-pus*, the jaws do not open very wide, so, as with the anteaters, they capture prey with their long, flexible tongues.

Though hardly lightweights, modern armadillos are puny compared with their ancestors. The largest extant species, the giant armadillo (*Pri-odontes maximus*), weighs 30–60kg (66–132lb), but the extinct glyptodonts were far more massive, with weights estimated at 100kg (220lb) or more. Some of these fossil forms were so large that their carapaces (up to 3m/10ft long) were used as roofs or tombs by early South American Indians.

Our knowledge of living armadillos is extremely sparse. Many species have not been studied extensively in the wild, and attempts to breed armadillos for study in captivity have been largely unsuccessful. The only well-known species currently is the nine-banded armadillo, which has been the subject of a few long-term field studies.

Insect-eaters in Armor
FORM AND FUNCTION

All armadillos possess a number of distinctive features, most notably a tough carapace that covers some portion of the upper surface of their bodies.

This shell probably provides some protection from predators and minimizes damage from the thorny vegetation that armadillos frequently pass through. The carapace develops from the skin, and is composed of strong bony plates, or scutes, overlaid by horny skin. There are usually broad and rigid shields over the shoulders and hips, and a variable number of bands (from 3–13) over the middle of the back that are connected to the flexible skin beneath. The tail, the top of the head, and the outer surfaces of the limbs are also usually armored (although the tail is not covered in the genus *Cabassous*), but the undersurface is just soft, hairy skin. To protect this vulnerable area, most species are able to withdraw the limbs under the hip and shoulder shields and sit tight on the ground, while some, such as the three-banded armadillos of the genus *Tolypeutes*, can roll up into a ball. While this strategy may prove effective against most predators, it has unfortunately made these species easy prey for human hunters.

While apparently well protected, armadillos are not invulnerable to predation. Juvenile mortality can be twice that of adults, possibly due to predation by bobcats, mountain lions, some raptors,

⬤ *Above A three-banded armadillo rolling itself up into a defensive ball. When fully curled, it has the appearance of a puzzle ball, leaving no chinks for natural predators to attempt to prize it open. Yet this defense has afforded little help against predation by humans, who have exploited armadillos as a source of food for centuries.*

ARMADILLOS AND LEPROSY

In the 1960s, Eleanor Storrs made the remarkable discovery that armadillos inoculated with the leprosy bacillus can develop the disfiguring human disease, and in the 1970s the condition was found in wild populations. In wild nine-banded armadillos, its occurrence varies regionally: Floridian armadillos lack leprosy, while as many as 20 percent of the animals from populations in Texas and Louisiana may be infected.

Unlike humans, armadillos exhibit no external symptoms until the disease has progressed sufficiently to fatally damage the internal organs. It is not yet known whether people can contract leprosy from armadillos, but the risk may depend on where they are from: unlike individuals from more tropical regions, people of northern European descent are relatively immune to the malady.

and even domestic dogs. Juveniles may be more vulnerable to predators because of their small size and softer carapace, but adult carcasses have also been found in the guts of large predators, such as jaguars, alligators, and black bears.

Most armadillos find prey by digging in the soil. In addition, many species excavate burrows that are used as refuges, resting places, and nest sites for rearing young. Consequently, most armadillos have muscular fore- and hindlimbs, ending in large, sharp claws that facilitate digging. While the hindlimbs always bear five-clawed digits, the fore-limbs may have from three to five digits with curved claws, depending on the species. In some species such as the naked-tailed armadillos and the giant armadillo the front claws are greatly enlarged, perhaps to facilitate opening ant and termite mounds for foraging. As a result, however, these species are unable to run quickly when danger appears.

Because they are usually active at night, most armadillos have poor eyesight. They seem, how-ever, to have well-developed senses of hearing and

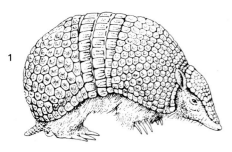

♠ **Above** The nine-banded armadillo, unlike the other species, is able to traverse water by inflating its stomach and intestine with air for buoyancy. Since it can hold its breath for several minutes, it can cross smaller streams underwater.

♥ **Below** The configuration of the armored shell varies markedly between species of armadillo: **1** the southern three-banded armadillo (Tolypeutes matacus); **2** the pichi (Zaedyus pichiy); **3** the lesser fairy armadillo (Chlamyphorus truncatus).

smell, which may be used in the detec-tion of both predators and prey. Olfaction may also be employed to determine the identity (and, during the breeding season, the reproductive con-dition) of other armadillos. The yellow armadillo and species in the genus *Chaetophractus* have 3–4 gland pits located on the back carapace. The long-nosed armadillos of the genus *Dasypus* have glands on the ears, eyelids, and soles of the feet, as well as a bean-shaped pair of anal glands that produce a yellowish secretion. These glands may be important in chemical communication, as armadillos are frequently observed sniffing this area when they encounter one another; they may also rub the glands on the ground in spots along the periphery of their home range. Although their hearing seems fairly acute, most armadillos are silent. What sounds they do produce are usually just low grunts or squeals, so most communica-tion is probably chemical.

While there are reports of modest differences in body size between the sexes, the males being larger than the females, most armadillos exhibit no obvi-ous sexual dimorphism. One interesting anatomi-cal feature is the male penis, one of the longest among mammals, extending two-thirds of the body length in some species. Armadillos were at one time thought to be the only mammals other than humans to copulate face to face, though this is now no longer believed to be the case; it seems instead that the males mount females from behind, as in most other mammals. If so, then the long penis may be necessary to permit intromis-sion, given the necessity to extend beyond the

FACTFILE

ARMADILLOS

Order: Cingulata

Family: Dasypodidae

21 species in 9 genera

DISTRIBUTION
Florida (except Ever-glades), Georgia, and South Carolina W to Kansas; E Mexico, C and S America to Straits of Magellan; Trinidad and Tobago, Grenada, Margarita.

Equator

HABITAT Savanna, pampas, arid desert, thorn scrub, and deciduous, cloud, and rain forest.

SIZE Head–body length ranges from 12.5–15cm (5–6in) in the Lesser fairy armadillo to 75–100cm (30–39in) in the Giant armadillo; **tail length** ranges from 2.5–3cm (1–1.2in) to 45–50cm (18–20in) and **weight** from 80–100g (2.8–3.5oz) to 30–60kg (66–132lb), both in the same two species.

COAT Broad shield of pale pink or yellowish dark brown armor (scute plates) over shoulders and pelvis, with varying numbers of flexible half-rings over middle of back; some species have white to dark brown hairs between the scute plates.

DIET Soil invertebrates, especially ants and termites. Will also feed on some plant matter, and are occasionally observed preying on small vertebrates (live or dead).

BREEDING Both sexes are sexually mature at about 1 year. Breeding can occur year-round, but is most frequent during summer. Gestation varies from 60–65 days (in the Yellow and hairy armadillos) to 120 days (prolonged by delayed implantation) in the Nine-banded armadillo. Litter size usually 1–4, but reaching 8–12 in some species.

LONGEVITY Unknown in the wild, but may be about 8–12 years (up to 20 in captivity).

CONSERVATION STATUS At present, 4 species are considered Vulnerable by the IUCN, and 6 more are list-ed as Lower Risk: Near Threatened. Two species are classed as Data Deficient.

See genera box ▷

1

2

3

armored carapace to reach the vaginal opening. The musculature of the penis consists of a series of longitudinal and circumferential supporting fibers, an arrangement that is thought to be common to all mammals.

New World Burrowers
DISTRIBUTION PATTERNS

Armadillos are strictly New World species; the majority of fossil forms come from South America, suggesting that this was where the group originally evolved. They subsequently colonized North America, where glyptodont fossils are found as far north as Nebraska, during periods when a land bridge connected the two continents. These fossil forms eventually went extinct, leaving no armadillos in North America until recent times, when, from the late 1800s onward, the nine-banded armadillo (*Dasypus novemcinctus*) rapidly expanded its range from northern Mexico to include much of the southern USA, with current sightings as far north as southern Illinois, Nebraska, Missouri, and southwestern Tennessee. In Florida, several armadillos escaped from zoos or private owners in the 1920s, and these also established wild populations, which have slowly spread northward and westward. Florida-derived and Texas-derived populations of armadillos have probably made contact by now, possibly in Alabama or Mississippi.

Although normally associated with moist, tropical habitats, armadillos can be found almost anywhere in the New World. For example, the pichi is found in the Patagonian region of Argentina all the way south to the Straits of Magellan; the hairy long-nosed armadillo is known only from high-altitude regions of Peru from 2,400–3,200m (7,900–10,500ft); while the greater long-nosed armadillo occurs only in the rain forests of the Orinoco and Amazon basins.

Species of armadillo vary dramatically in their abundance. The nine-banded armadillo, also aptly known as the common long-nosed armadillo, can reach population densities of 50 per sq km (130 per sq mi) in the coastal prairies of Texas and elsewhere. However, the maximum density estimated for the southern naked-tailed armadillo in the Venezuelan llanos is only 1.2 per sq km (3.1 per sq mi), and the giant armadillo, even in optimum lowland forest habitat in Surinam, was only found to reach half that figure. Yellow armadillos have been found in Brazilian savanna and forest at densities of up to 2.9 animals per sq km (7.5 per sq mi), while southern three-banded armadillos in southern Brazil may reach densities of 7 animals per sq km (18 per sq mi).

Even if no live animals are observed, a good sign of the presence of armadillos in a habitat is a burrow. Armadillos dig between 1 and 20 burrows, each 1.5–3m (5–10ft) long, in their home ranges, occupying a given burrow for anything from 1–29 consecutive days. Because armadillos use multiple burrows, counting burrows in a hab-

◐ **Above** The southern naked-tailed armadillo has five curved claws on each forefoot, the middle one of which is especially powerful. Its gait is unusual – it walks on the soles of its hindfeet (plantigrade), but on the tips of the claws on its forefeet (digitigrade).

itat may not provide a reliable estimate of actual population density. Burrows are generally not very long and tend to run horizontally under the surface rather than to extend vertically down into the ground. Most burrows usually have just one or two entrances.

Snuffling through the Leaf Litter
DIET

Perhaps because of their armor, armadillos are often fairly conspicuous, making a considerable racket as they snuffle along searching for food in dry vegetation. For armadillos, foraging consists of moving slowly along with the nose in the soil and leaf litter, then digging up material with the foreclaws. The animals may also use their claws to rip open rotting logs.

With their large front claws, giant and naked-tailed armadillos seem specialized for ripping open ant and termite mounds. Other species have a more catholic diet; analyses of gut contents have revealed a mix of invertebrates, mostly beetles and ants. The nine-banded armadillo is one of the few species to have been observed bravely feeding on fire ants (*Solenopsis invicta*), enduring their painful stings to dig open the nest and eat the larvae within. In addition to invertebrates, armadillos are also known to feed on some vegetable matter, including persimmons and other fruits, and, rarely, on certain vertebrates, such as snakes and small lizards; they may also scavenge carrion and the eggs of ground-nesting birds.

NATURE'S CLONES

Armadillos in the genus *Dasypus* are the only vertebrates known to exhibit obligate polyembryony, in which a female produces one fertilized egg that divides into multiple embryos. Because of this, all the offspring produced are genetically identical to one another. Genetic uniformity of siblings in the nine-banded armadillo (BELOW) has been confirmed using modern molecular techniques.

One proposed reason for such a strange system may be to encourage offspring to help each other out. Altruistic behavior reaps more evolutionary dividends when directed towards relatives, as they share a higher proportion of genes. Because of polyembryony, armadillo littermates are clones, and thus might be predicted to be particularly helpful to each other. As it turns out, however, armadillos get very little opportunity to mix with their siblings as adults, and it seems more likely that polyembryony represents an ingenious way of countering a physical restriction on reproduction, helping to overcome a constraint in the female's reproductive system that leaves space for only one egg prior to implantation.

Armadillo Genera

Long-nosed armadillos

Genus Dasypus

S USA, Mexico, C America, Colombia, Venezuela, Guiana, Surinam, Brazil, Paraguay, Argentina, Ecuador, Peru; also Grenada and Trinidad and Tobago. 7 species: the **Nine-banded** or **Common long-nosed** (*D. novemcinctus*), **Seven-banded** or **Brazilian lesser** (*D. septemcinctus*), **Greater** (*D. kappleri*), **Southern lesser** (*D. hybridus*), **Hairy** (*D. pilosus*), and **Northern** (*D. sabanicola*) **long-nosed armadillos**; and **Yepes's mulita**, *D. yepesi* (from northeastern Argentina). The Southern lesser long-nosed armadillo is classed as Near Threatened, the Hairy long-nosed armadillo is Vulnerable.

Naked-tailed armadillos

Genus Cabassous

C and S America E of the Andes from S Mexico and Colombia to Paraguay, Uruguay, and N Argentina. 4 species: the **Southern** (*C. unicinctus*), **Northern** (*C. centralis*), **Chacoan** (*C. chacoensis*), and **Greater** (*C. tatouay*) **naked-tailed armadillos**. The Chacoan naked-tailed armadillo is classed as Lower Risk, Near Threatened.

Yellow armadillo

Euphractus sexcinctus

Yellow or **Six-banded armadillo**. S Surinam and adjacent areas of Brazil; also E Brazil to Bolivia, Paraguay, N Argentina, Uruguay.

Giant armadillo   *Priodontes maximus*

S America E of the Andes, from N Venezuela and the Guianas to Paraguay and N Argentina. Vulnerable.

Hairy armadillos

Genus Chaetophractus

Bolivia, Paraguay, Argentina, Chile. 3 species: the **Andean** (*C. nationi*), **Screaming** (*C. vellerosus*), and **Larger** (*C. villosus*) **hairy armadillos**. The Andean hairy armadillo is classed as Vulnerable.

Three-banded armadillos

Genus Tolypeutes

Brazil and E Bolivia S through the Gran Chaco of Paraguay to Buenos Aires (Argentina). 2 species: the **Southern** (*T. matacus*) and **Brazilian** (*T. tricinctus*) **three-banded armadillos**. The Brazilian three-banded armadillo is classed as Vulnerable, while the Southern three-banded armadillo is Lower Risk, Near Threatened.

Fairy armadillos

Argentina, Paraguay, Bolivia. 2 species in 2 genera: the **Greater** or **Chacoan** (*Calyptophractus retusus*), and the **Lesser** or **Pink fairy armadillo** (*Chlamyphorus truncatus*). The Lesser fairy armadillo is classed as Endangered, while the Greater fairy armadillo is Vulnerable.

Pichi   *Zaedyus pichiy*

C and S Argentina, and E Chile S to the Straits of Magellan. LR, Near Threatened.

▌ Life beneath the Carapace

SOCIAL BEHAVIOR

Most armadillos are relatively solitary, and with a few exceptions most species are active at night, although this can vary with age – juveniles are often active in the late morning or early afternoon – and with the time of year: there is more diurnal activity when the weather is colder.

Among adults, most social interactions usually occur during breeding. For most species, breeding is seasonal, with matings occurring primarily during the summer months, although captive animals may breed year-round. Prior to mating, males and females may engage in extended bouts of courtship in which the males avidly follow the females. After mating, most species initiate embryonic development right away, but in northern populations of the nine-banded armadillo (*Dasypus novemcinctus*), possibly as an adaptation to the different timing of the seasons, implantation of the fertilized egg may be delayed by 3–4 months or more; one captive female of this species reportedly gave birth at least three years after the last date at which she could possibly have been inseminated. *D. novemcinctus* may be polygynous, with males mating with 2–3 females per breeding season, while females typically mate with just a single male. Yet not all individuals are reproductively successful: as many as one third of the females in a population may not reproduce in a given year, and, in a 4-year study, only about a third of all adults were identified as parents of at least one litter. Litter sizes are usually small, varying from 1–4 young per litter for most species, with a maximum of 8–12 reported for captive *D. hybridus*. The majority of species only reproduce once per year.

In *D. novemcinctus*, males occasionally chase, kick, and scratch each other with their claws either in defence of their home ranges or when competing for access to females. Although female home ranges may overlap quite extensively, pregnant or lactating adult females can also be quite aggressive, primarily targeting other females and younger individuals of both sexes.

D. novemcinctus home ranges vary from about 1.5ha (4 acres) for a population in Oklahoma to over 10ha (25 acres) for a population in Florida. Home range sizes for other species are largely unknown, but the low population densities of most species suggest they may range widely.

▌ Conserving the Hoover Hog

CONSERVATION AND ENVIRONMENT

For centuries, armadillos have been exploited by humans for their meat, and they continue to be a favored food item in many areas of Latin America. In North America people partake of armadillo meat less frequently; however, during the Great Depression of the 1930s, destitute southern sharecroppers came to rely on armadillos for food, and the animals were nicknamed "Hoover hogs," a wry allusion to US President Herbert Hoover.

Habitat loss from deforestation, agriculture, and other sources is another significant cause of declining populations, as is the eradication of digging armadillos from both agricultural areas and the well-manicured lawns of suburban communities. On the bright side, the Brazilian three-banded armadillo, which was formerly classed as extinct in the wild, has been rediscovered recently in several areas of Brazil.   CMM/WJL

◗ **Right** *The larger hairy armadillo has been known to burrow under animal carcasses in order to feed on the maggots and other insects that accumulate there. This species relies on insects, rodents, and lizards in summer, but half of its winter diet is vegetation.*

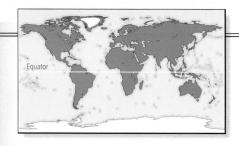

RODENTS

rODENTS HAVE INFLUENCED HISTORY AND human endeavor more than any other group of mammals. Over 42 percent of all mammal species belong to this one order, whose members live in almost every habitat, often in close association with humans. Frequently this association is to people's disadvantage, since rodents consume prodigious quantities of carefully stored food and spread fatal diseases. It is said that rat-borne typhus has had a greater influence upon human destiny than has any single person, and in the last millennium rat-borne diseases have taken more lives than all wars and revolutions put together.

It is nevertheless testimony to the entrepreneurial spirit of rodents that they have thrived in human-dominated environments from which so many other animal groups have been extinguished. Furthermore, many rodent species have an important function in ecosystems, and are therefore highly beneficial to man. Rodents play key roles in maintaining the relationship between plants and fungi. Many fungi form mycorrhizal (mutually beneficial) associations with the roots of plants that increase the ability of the plants to extract nutrients and water from the soil by many thousands of times. So important is this relationship that many plants simply cannot survive without the fungi, and vice versa. One of the most important groups of mycorrhizal fungi are the truffles, which are related to mushrooms but form their fruiting bodies underground. Truffles and trufflelike fungi rely on animals to dig up the fruiting bodies and to disperse the spores, either in the wind or in the animal's feces after eating the fungus. When gaps form in forests, for example, small mammals deposit fungal spores in their feces in the gaps, thereby bringing the fungi to the places where plant seeds are germinating. In the forests of North America and Australia, it is believed that this three-sided relationship between plants, fungi, and small mammals – including rodents – is vital for ecosystem

◗ **Right** A giant among rodents, the capybara can weigh up to 66kg (146lb) – fully 10,000 times the weight of the smallest mice. The animals share the close-knit social life and herbivorous diet of many other rodent species, but are unusual in their semi-aquatic lifestyle.

◖ **Left** On the alert for food, a Eurasian harvest mouse (Micromys minutus) *investigates a wheat crop in summer. Rodents are supreme opportunists; their rapid rate of reproduction and wide-ranging diets have made them among the most successful mammals.*

function. The role of rodents in other ecosystems, like grasslands, is not so well studied but is probably just as important.

In South America, Africa, and Asia, some larger species are also an important source of protein, being trapped or deliberately bred for food. Species in the latter category are the guinea pigs in South America, and the grasscutter rats and the edible dormouse (*Myoxus glis*) in Africa. Among other rodents, hamsters and gerbils are popular pets in the western world, with the prairie dog becoming increasingly common in the United States. Moreover, rats, mice, and guinea pigs today play an indispensable role in the testing of drugs and in biological research. Rodents are also keystone species in many ecosystems, providing an important food source for many species of medium-sized carnivores and birds of prey. For example, in agricultural ecosystems it is not unusual to have 50–100kg (110–220lb) of rodents per hectare distributed over tens of thousands of hectares. This provides a huge variety of food for predators living in agricultural systems or in neighboring forest habitats. The black-footed ferret (*Mustela nigripes*), which is the subject of much human nurturing through a reintroduction program after having become extinct in the wild, relies on a diet of prairie dogs for its survival.

Equipped for Gnawing
FORM AND FUNCTION

Rodents occur in virtually every habitat, from the high arctic tundra, where they live and breed under the snow (for example, lemmings), to the hottest and driest of deserts (gerbils). Others glide from tree to tree (flying squirrels), seldom coming down to the ground, or else spend their entire lives in underground networks of burrows (mole rats). Some have webbed feet and are semiaquatic (muskrats), often undertaking complex engineering programs to regulate water levels (beavers), while others never touch a drop of water throughout their entire lives (gundis). Such species can derive their water requirements from fat reserves.

Most rodents are small, weighing 100g (3.5oz) or less. There are only a few large species; the biggest of them, the capybara, may weigh up to 66kg (146lb).

The term *rodent* derives from the Latin verb *rodere*, which means "to gnaw." All rodents have characteristic teeth, including a single pair of razor-sharp incisors. With these teeth, the rodent can gnaw through the toughest of husks, pods, and shells to reach the nutritious food contained within. Gnawing is facilitated by a sizable gap, known as the diastema, immediately behind the incisors, into which the lips can be drawn, so sealing off the mouth from inedible fragments dislodged by the incisors. Rodents have no canine teeth, but they do possess a substantial battery of molar teeth by which all food is finely ground. Convoluted layers of enamel traverse these often

massive and intricately structured teeth. The pattern made by these layers is often of taxonomic significance. Most rodents have no more than 22 teeth, although one exception is the silvery mole rat from Central and East Africa, which has 28. The Australian water rat has just 12. Since rodents feed on hard materials, the incisors have open roots and grow continuously throughout life. They are constantly worn down by the action of their opposite number on the other jaw. If the teeth of rodents become misaligned so that they are not automatically worn down during feeding, they will continue to grow and may eventually end up piercing the skull.

Most rodents are squat, compact creatures with short limbs and a tail. In South America, where there are no antelopes, several species have evolved long legs for a life on the grassy plains (e.g., maras, pacas, and agoutis), and show some convergence with the antelope body form. A very variable anatomical feature is the tail (see panel overleaf and Squirrel-like Rodents).

Modern taxonomists divide rodents into two suborders. For convenience, we present these in three sections, the squirrel-like and the mouselike forms – both part of the suborder Sciurognathi – and the porcupine and cavy-like forms, the suborder Hystricognathi. Rodents were formerly split into three suborders on the basis of jaw musculature. The main jaw muscle is the masseter, which not only closes the lower jaw on the upper, but also pulls the lower jaw forward, so creating the unique gnawing action. In the extinct Paleocene

ORDER: RODENTIA
28 families: 435 genera: 1,999 species

SCIUROGNATHS Suborder Sciurognathi

SQUIRREL-LIKE RODENTS p140

284 species in 56 genera in 5 families
Includes **beavers** (Family Castoridae); **squirrels** (Family Sciuridae); **springhare** (Family Pedetidae).

MOUSELIKE RODENTS p168

1,480 species in 316 genera in 5 families
Includes **rats, mice, voles, gerbils, hamsters,** and **lemmings** (Family Muridae); **jumping mice, birch-mice,** and **jerboas** (Family Dipodidae).

HYSTRICOGNATHS Suborder Hystricognathi

CAVY-LIKE RODENTS
Suborder Hystricognathi p222

235 species in 63 genera in 18 families
Includes **New World porcupines** (Family Erethizontidae); **cavies** (Family Caviidae); **capybara** (Family Hydrochaeridae); **agoutis and acouchis** (Family Dasyproctidae); **chinchillas** and **viscachas** (Family Chinchillidae); **octodonts** (Family Octodontidae); **tuco-tucos** (Family Ctenomyidae); **cane rats** (Family Thryonomyidae); **Dassie rat** (Family Petromuridae); **coypu** (Family Myocastoridae); **Old World porcupines** (Family Hystricidae); **gundis** (Family Ctenodactylidae); **African mole rats** (Family Bathyergidae).

rodents, the masseter was small and did not spread far onto the front of the skull. In the squirrel-like rodents the lateral masseter extends in front of the eye onto the snout; the deep masseter is short and used only in closing the jaw. In the cavy-like rodents it is the deep masseter that extends forward onto the snout to give the gnawing action. Both the lateral and deep branches of the masseter are thrust forward in the mouselike rodents, providing the most effective gnawing action of all, with the result that they are the most successful in terms of distribution and number of species.

Most rodents eat a range of plant products, from leaves to fruits, along with small invertebrates, such as spiders and grasshoppers. Many northern rodents such as the field vole (*Microtus agrestis*) eat the bark of woody trees in times of food scarcity due to high populations. In field voles the toxic effects of bark seem to be neutralized by specially secreted enzymes in the stomach, which allow dietary flexibility in times of famine. A few species are specialized carnivores; for example, the Australian water rat (*Hydromys chrysogaster*) feeds on small fish, frogs, and mollusks.

To facilitate bacterial digestion of cellulose rodents have a relatively large cecum (appendix) that houses a dense bacterial flora. After the food they have eaten has been softened in the stomach, it passes down the large intestine and into the cecum. There the cellulose is split by bacteria into its digestible carbohydrate constituents, but absorption can only take place higher up the gut, in the stomach. Therefore rodents practice refection – reingesting the bacterially treated food taken directly from the anus. On its second visit to the stomach the carbohydrates are absorbed and the fecal pellet that eventually emerges is hard and dry. It is not known how rodents know which type of feces is being produced. The rodent's digestive system is very efficient, assimilating as much as 80 percent of the ingested energy.

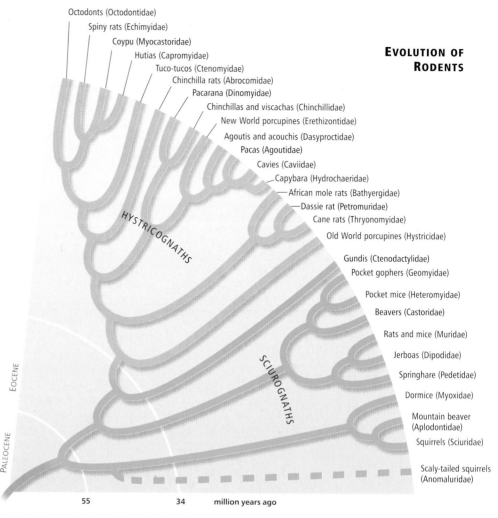

EVOLUTION OF RODENTS

Octodonts (Octodontidae)
Spiny rats (Echimyidae)
Coypu (Myocastoridae)
Hutias (Capromyidae)
Tuco-tucos (Ctenomyidae)
Chinchilla rats (Abrocomidae)
Pacarana (Dinomyidae)
Chinchillas and viscachas (Chinchillidae)
New World porcupines (Erethizontidae)
Agoutis and acouchis (Dasyproctidae)
Pacas (Agoutidae)
Cavies (Caviidae)
Capybara (Hydrochaeridae)
African mole rats (Bathyergidae)
Dassie rat (Petromuridae)
Cane rats (Thryonomyidae)
Old World porcupines (Hystricidae)
Gundis (Ctenodactylidae)
Pocket gophers (Geomyidae)
Pocket mice (Heteromyidae)
Beavers (Castoridae)
Rats and mice (Muridae)
Jerboas (Dipodidae)
Springhare (Pedetidae)
Dormice (Myoxidae)
Mountain beaver (Aplodontidae)
Squirrels (Sciuridae)
Scaly-tailed squirrels (Anomaluridae)

HYSTRICOGNATHS

SCIUROGNATHS

EOCENE

PALEOCENE

55   34   million years ago

All members of at least three families (hamsters, pocket gophers, pocket mice) have cheek pouches. Fur-lined folds of skin projecting inwards from the corner of the mouth, these may reach back to the shoulders, and can be everted for cleaning. They are used for carrying provisions, and rodents equipped with them often build up large stores – up to 90kg (198lb) in common hamsters.

Rodents are intelligent and can master simple tasks for obtaining food. They can be readily conditioned, and easily learn to avoid fast-acting poisoned baits – a factor that makes them difficult pests to eradicate. Their sense of smell and their hearing are keenly developed. Nocturnal species have large eyes; in addition, all rodents have long, touch-sensitive whiskers (vibrissae).

Above In evolutionary terms, rodents are quite young and so retain large, untapped stocks of genetic variability. This evolutionary tree, compiled by biologist Rodney Honeycutt, is based on relationships revealed by molecular techniques. Thus the lengths of the branches are proportional to genetic similarity, and not necessarily to time of separation, which is largely unknown thanks to limited fossil evidence.

Left A South African ground squirrel nibbles on a melon. Manual dexterity is particularly well developed in squirrels, although other rodents also make good use of their front paws for digging, grooming, grasping, and gathering food and nesting materials.

RODENT BODY PLAN

◑ **Below** *The skeleton of a roof rat (Rattus rattus) exhibits typical rodent features in its squat form, short limbs, plantigrade gait ((meaning that the animal walks on the soles of its feet), and long tail.*

◑ **Right** *Skull of the roof rat. Clearly shown are the continuously growing, gnawing incisors and the chewing molars, with the gap (diastema) left by the absence of the canine and premolar teeth. All mouselike rodents lack premolars, but the squirrel- and cavy-like rodents have one or two on each side of the jaw.*

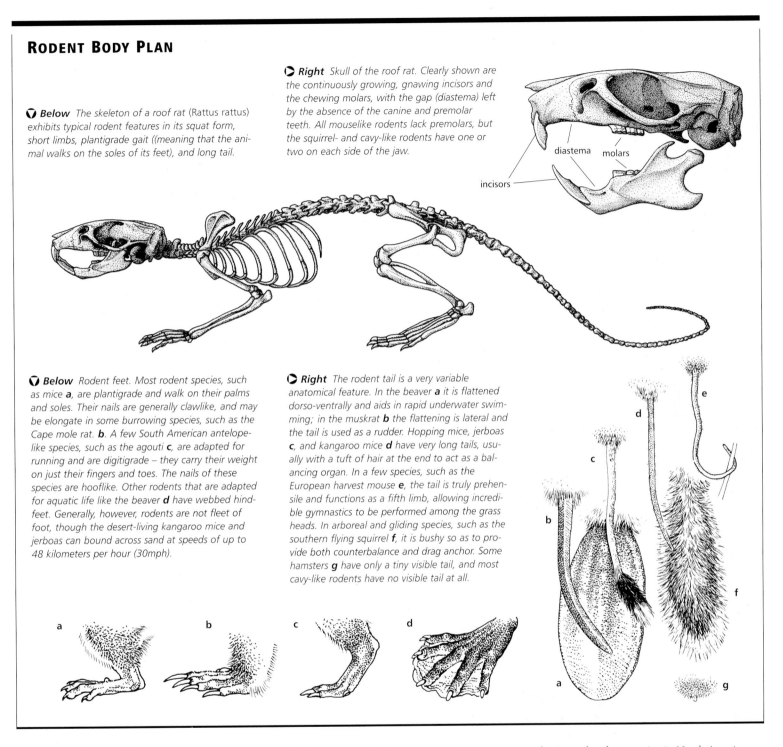

diastema   molars

incisors

◑ **Below** *Rodent feet. Most rodent species, such as mice **a**, are plantigrade and walk on their palms and soles. Their nails are generally clawlike, and may be elongate in some burrowing species, such as the Cape mole rat. **b**. A few South American antelope-like species, such as the agouti **c**, are adapted for running and are digitigrade – they carry their weight on just their fingers and toes. The nails of these species are hooflike. Other rodents that are adapted for aquatic life like the beaver **d** have webbed hind-feet. Generally, however, rodents are not fleet of foot, though the desert-living kangaroo mice and jerboas can bound across sand at speeds of up to 48 kilometers per hour (30mph).*

◑ **Right** *The rodent tail is a very variable anatomical feature. In the beaver **a** it is flattened dorso-ventrally and aids in rapid underwater swimming; in the muskrat **b** the flattening is lateral and the tail is used as a rudder. Hopping mice, jerboas **c**, and kangaroo mice **d** have very long tails, usually with a tuft of hair at the end to act as a balancing organ. In a few species, such as the European harvest mouse **e**, the tail is truly prehensile and functions as a fifth limb, allowing incredible gymnastics to be performed among the grass heads. In arboreal and gliding species, such as the southern flying squirrel **f**, it is bushy so as to provide both counterbalance and drag anchor. Some hamsters **g** have only a tiny visible tail, and most cavy-like rodents have no visible tail at all.*

The Prehistory of Rodents
EVOLUTION AND RADIATION

Almost two-thirds of all rodent species belong to just one family, the Muridae, with 1,303 species at present, although numbers change constantly as new species are identified. Its members are distributed worldwide, including Australia and New Guinea, where it is the only terrestrial placental mammal family found (excluding dingoes, introduced approximately 4,000 years ago, and modern introductions such as the rabbit). The second most numerous family is that of the squirrels (Sciuridae), with 273 species distributed throughout Eurasia, Africa, and North and South America.

The fossil record of the rodents is pitifully sparse, partly because finding small bones requires very careful looking. Rodent remains are known from as far back as the late Paleocene era (57 million years ago), by which time all the main characteristics of the order had already developed. The earliest rodents apparently belonged to an extinct sciuromorph family, the Paramyidae.

During the Eocene era (55–34 million years ago) there was a rapid diversification of the rodents, and by the end of that epoch it seems that leaping, burrowing, and running forms had evolved. By the Eocene/Oligocene boundary (34 million years ago) many families recognizable today were already occurring in North America, Europe, and Asia, and during the Miocene (about 20 million years ago) the majority of present-day families had arisen. Subsequently the most important evolutionary event was the appearance of the Muridae from Europe in the Pliocene epoch (5–1.8 million years ago). At the start of the Pleistocene, they entered Australia, probably via Timor, and then underwent a rapid evolution. At the same time murids invaded South America from the north once it was united to North America by a land bridge, with the result that there was an explosive radiation of New World rats and mice across South America.

How Rodents Interact
SOCIAL BEHAVIOR

Rodents are often highly social, frequently living in huge aggregations. Prairie dog townships may contain more than 5,000 individuals. The solitary way of life appears to be restricted to those species that can defend food resources against intruders. These include some that live in arid grasslands and deserts – hamsters and some desert mice – and also species such as the North American red squirrel (*Tamiasciurus hudsonicus*), which lives in northern coniferous forests and stores cones in large central caches called middens.

The Norway or brown rat (*Rattus norvegicus*) is a miscreant species that originated in Southeast Asia but has spread right around the globe in company with humans. Its social structure is central to the species' ecology and hence to the effectiveness of control measures. Socially dominant rats gain feeding priority and greater reproductive access and success. Social pressures force subordinate male rats to migrate into less favorable areas, resulting in a strongly unbalanced sex ratio (with more females than males) in breeding areas. Larger male rats tend to win dominance contests with smaller rats but, strangely, retain their higher social status long after subsequently losing body weight to levels at or below younger rats in the group. This means that dominance tends to be age related, with the dominant alpha male often being smaller than many of his subordinates. Rats, it seems, respect their elders. Larger rats tend to accept the status quo because the costs of aggression are too great relative to the value of the contested resource. Moreover, dominant males cannot strictly control access to receptive estrous females. Sometimes, lower-ranking males actually achieve more matings.

Indications are that male Norway rats undergo scramble competition for mates. In naturalistic enclosures, a string of up to seven males may pursue a receptive female whenever she leaves her burrow. To test if female rats actually selected mates in this mad scramble or whether they mated promiscuously by choice, female rats were placed in a central arena surrounded by cubicles in which males were housed (a "rodent inverta-brothel"). A circular passage gave the female access to the males but was too narrow for the males to pass. In such conditions, females formed enduring bonds with a single male, but also mated promiscuously. Even solitary rats seem to be profoundly affected by the knowledge that others of their species are in the vicinity. When female captive Heerman's kangaroo rats were entirely separated from males by wooden barriers rather than by clear plastic barriers, their estrous cycles were immediately doubled in length.

Rodent behavior is as adaptable as every other aspect of rodent biology. Having alert and active senses, rodents communicate by sight, sound, and smell. House mice have a sophisticated system of scent communication (see A Scent-based Information Superhighway). Kangaroo rats, however, tap dance to talk. Three species living in the same area in California were each found to have a different rhythm when drumming on the desert floor. The desert kangaroo rat thumped every 0.2–0.3 seconds, while the giant kangaroo rat drummed long footrolls that could last for 100 drums at 18 drums per second; the banner-tailed thumped footrolls at 3–38 drums per second. Even more intriguing is that individual banner-tails seemed to have their own signature rhythms. The sounds travel seismically through the ground to the ears of listening kangaroo rats hidden in burrows. Rats in burrows respond with carefully-timed drumming which does not overlap with those of the above-ground drummer. Drumming provides useful information about spacing and serves to reinforce territorial ownership. Female rats drumming at males tend to be saying "go away." Mother banner-tails drum vigorously at snakes. Banner-tails moving into a new neighborhood were found to alter their drums to be different from their neighbors.

While the social systems of some rodents have been well studied (see African Mole Rats), the habits of most of the 2,000 or so species are still a mystery awaiting investigation. Some insights have been achieved. Female Gunnison's prairie dogs mate with several males whereas they should be able to gain all the sperm necessary to fertilize their eggs from a single male. However, the probability of getting pregnant increases from 92 percent to 100 percent if they mate with three males instead of one, and females who mate with more males tend to have larger litters.

Some of the best-known visual displays are seen in the arboreal and the day-active terrestrial species. Courtship display in tree squirrels may be readily observed in city parks in early spring. The male pursues the female through the trees, flicking his bushy tail forward over his body and head when he is stationary. The female goads him by running slightly ahead, but he responds by uttering plaintive sounds similar to those that infants make to keep their mothers close. These sounds stop the female, allowing the male to catch up. Threat displays are dramatic in some species.

Rodents make considerable use of vocalizations in their communication. North American red squirrels and ground squirrels use a wide range of calls to advertise their presence to neighbors, to defend territories, and to sound the alarm when predators are detected. In other rodents, the sounds are far above the range of human hearing (at about 45kHz).

Rodents communicate extensively through odors produced by a variety of scent glands. Males tend to produce more and stronger odors than females, and young males are afforded a measure of protection from paternal attack by smelling like their mothers until they are sexually mature.

ODOR AND RODENT REPRODUCTION

Every phase of rodent reproduction, from initial sexual attraction to mating and the successful rearing of young, is influenced, if not actually controlled, by odor signals. Male rats are attracted to the urine of sexually receptive females, and sexually experienced males are more strongly attracted than naive males. Furthermore, if an experienced male is presented with the odor of a novel mature female alongside that of his mate, he prefers the novel odor. Females, on the other hand, prefer the odor of their mate to that of a stranger. The male's reproductive fitness is, it seems, best suited by seeking out and impregnating as many females as possible. The female, however, needs to produce many healthy young, so her fitness is maximized by mating with the best-quality male – one who has already proved himself. In gregarious species like the house mouse, a dominant male can mate with 20 females in 6 hours if their cycles are synchronized.

In young females, the odor of male urine accelerates not only the peak of sexual receptivity but also the onset of sexual maturity; it also brings sexually quiescent females into breeding condition. The effect is particularly strong from the urine of dominant males, while urine from castrated males has no such effect. It would appear, then, that the active ingredient – a pheromone – is made from, or is dependent upon the presence of, the male sex hormone testosterone. Male urine has such a powerful effect that if a newly-pregnant female is exposed to the urine odor of an unfamiliar male, she will resorb her litter and come rapidly into heat. In contrast, the odor of female urine has either no effect on the onset of sexual maturity or else slightly retards it.   DMS

○ **Above** *Disturbed by an intruder, a North American porcupine displays its quills. The species is found in forests across most of the USA, northern Mexico, and Canada. Porcupines have quite poor eyesight, move slowly, and cannot jump, but nonetheless frequently climb trees to enormous heights in search of food.*

◁ **Left** *Threat displays are very dramatic in some rodent species.* **1** *When slightly angry the Cape porcupine raises its quills and rattles the specialized hollow quills on its tail. If this fails to have the desired effect the hindfeet are thumped on the ground in a war dance accompaniment to the rattling. Only if the threat persists will the porcupine turn its back on its opponent and charge backward with its lethal spines at the ready.* **2** *Slightly less dramatic is the threat display of the Kenyan crested rat. This slow and solidly built rodent responds to danger by elevating a contrastingly colored crest of long hairs along its back, and in so doing exposes a glandular strip along the body. Special wicklike hairs lining the gland facilitate the rapid dissemination of a strong, unpleasant odor.* **3** *Finally, the little Norway lemming stands its ground in the face of danger and lifts its chin to expose the pale neck and cheek fur, which contrast strongly with the dark upper fur.*

Controlling Spiraling Populations
RODENTS AND HUMANKIND

With their high powers of reproduction and ability to invade all habitats, rodents are of great economic and ecological importance. Most rodent species are pregnant for just 19–21 days, mate again within 2 days of giving birth, and the young begin breeding at 6 weeks of age; theoretically, a single breeding pair of mice can generate 500 mice in 21 weeks. In good conditions, rodent numbers can soar, up to 1,000–2,000 per hectare (400–800 per acre). Aperiodic outbreaks occur repeatedly in the house mouse on farmland in Australia, in rat species in the uplands of Laos, and among grassland species such as the common vole.

Of approximately 2,000 rodent species, about 200–300 are economically important, and some of these occur worldwide. A telling example of their economic impact comes from Southeast Asia, where rodents are economically the most important preharvest pest. In Indonesia, rodents cause annual losses of around 17 percent of rice production; if these could be halved, there would be enough rice to provide 70 percent of the energy requirements of an extra 17.5 million people. In Vietnam, rodent damage to rice affected 63,000ha (155,000 acres) in 1995, rising to more than 700,000ha (1.7 million acres) in 1999. In 1998, an estimated 82 million rats were killed under bounty schemes. Over 5 million rat tails were returned from January to September in the province of Vinh Phuc alone, where the authorities estimate that there are more than 10 million rats and only 1.1 million people.

For farmers in mountainous regions of Laos, rodents are the pest problem they currently have least control over. It is not unusual for a family to lose more than 70 percent of its crop to rodents; if this occurs to one crop it is a major cause for concern, but if it happens to two crops in a row, the situation becomes catastrophic. And the impact of rodents does not stop once the crop is harvested; they also consume and contaminate significant amounts of stored grain. It is estimated that postharvest losses are of a similar magnitude to those that occur before harvest.

Other than rice, tropical crops damaged by rodents include coconuts, maize, coffee, field beans, oil palm, citrus, melons, cocoa, and dates. Every year rodents consume food equivalent to the world's entire cereal and potato harvest; it has been estimated that a train 5,000km (3,000mi) long – as long as the Great Wall of China – would be needed to haul the take.

zokor (*Myospalax fontanierii*), and ground squirrels of the Mongolian and Californian grasslands.

The characteristics that enable these animals to become such a problem are a simple body plan adapted to a variety of habitats and climates; opportunistic feeding behavior; gnawing and burrowing habits; and high reproductive potential. Many rodents of the arctic tundra and taiga undergo population explosions every 3-4 years (for instance, the Norway lemming in Europe and the brown and collared lemmings in North America). The population density builds up to a high level and then dramatically declines. Several theses have been advanced to explain the decline, none of them wholly satisfactory; for example, it was long held that disease (tularemia or lemming fever, found in many rodent populations) was the root cause of the decline, but it now seems more likely that it simply hastens it. Other suggestions are that the rodents become more aggressive at high density, leading to a failure of courtship and reproduction, or that the decline is due to the action of predators or the impoverishment of the forage. Objective observation of lemming behavior at high density shows it to be adaptive, providing the lemmings with the best chances for survival (see Voles and Lemmings).

In Britain, Norway rats may live in fields during the warm summer months when food is plentiful, and they seldom reach economically important numbers; but after harvest, with the onset of cold weather, they move into buildings. Also in Britain, and some other western European countries, the long-tailed field mouse (*Apodemus sylvaticus*), normally only a pest in the winter when it may for example nibble stored apples, has learned to locate, probably by smell, pelleted sugar-beet seed. The damage it causes, which possibly went unnoticed before the advent of precision drilling, can lead to large barren patches in fields of sugar beet and sometimes necessitates complete resowing.

Although rodents usually consume about 15 percent of their body weight in food per day, much of the damage they do is not due to direct consumption. Three hundred rats in a grain store can eat 3 tonnes of grain in a year; but every 24 hours they also contaminate the grain with 15,000 droppings, 3.5 liters (6 pints) of urine, and countless hairs and greasy skin secretions. In sugar cane, rats may chew at the cane directly, consuming only a part of it; the damage, however, may cause the cane to fall over, so the impact of the sun's rays is reduced and harvesting impeded. In addition, the gnawed stem allows microorganisms to enter, reducing the sugar content. Apart from the value of the lost crop itself, a 6 percent drop in sugar content represents an equivalent reduction in the return on investment on land preparation, fertilizers, pesticides, irrigation water, management, harvesting, and processing.

Structural damage attributable to rodents results, for example, from the animals burrowing

The challenge of managing the rodent impact in Southeast Asia is complicated because there are at least 15 major pest species, each with its own peculiarities. The variables include their level of tolerance to a commensal life with humans; their breeding ecology; use of habitat; social behavior; feeding behavior; climbing, swimming, or burrowing abilities; physiological tolerances to climatic conditions (including periods when water is scarce or only present at high levels of salinity); and responses to major disturbances such as fire, new cultivation practices, or floods. Although the use of rodenticides offers short-term respite from the depredations of most species, more environmentally benign and sustainable approaches to pest management demand good knowledge of the ecology of the particular species to be controlled.

The most universal pests are the Norway rat, the roof rat, and the house mouse. House mouse populations undergo spectacular eruptions in Australian cereal-growing areas, with devastating economic, environmental, and social consequences.

Squirrel-like pests include the European red and gray squirrels, but in terms of the damage they cause, these are relatively minor. Other problem species include the gerbils, the multimammate rats, and the Nile rat, all of which devastate agricultural crops in Africa. In North America as well as eastern and western Europe, voles are prominent pests: they strip bark from trees, often killing them, and consume seedlings in forest plantations or fields. When vole populations peak (once every 3–4 years) there may be 2,000 voles per hectare (almost 5,000 per acre). Other major pests include the cotton or cane rat and web-footed marsh rat (*Holochilus brasiliensis*) from, principally, Latin America; the Polynesian rat (*Rattus exulans*) of the Pacific Islands and Southeast Asia; the Bandicota rats of the Indian subcontinent and Malaysian Peninsula; the ricefield rat (*Rattus argentiventer*), lesser ricefield rat (*Rattus losea*), and Philippines ricefield rat (*Rattus tanezumi*) in Southeast Asia; and the prairie dogs, marmots, pikas, Brandt's vole (*Microtus brandti*), Chinese

◐ **Left** *A brown rat (*Rattus norvegicus*) cares for a helpless infant. Although the young are born naked and blind, they are quick developers; within 15 days they are fully furred, and after another week are weaned and ready to leave the nest. Newborns will themselves be ready to start breeding within 90 days.*

◐ ◑ **Above and below** *Competition for food is a major cause of conflict between rodents and humans. Species like the roof rat (*Rattus rattus*; below) are famed marauders of stored vegetables and grains; and rats will also attack fruit on the tree, as a damaged Egyptian orange (above) testifies. In Asia, rodents routinely consume 5–30 percent of the rice crop, sometimes devastating areas of 10,000 hectares (25,000 acres) or more; they have also been held responsible for destroying annually 5–10 percent of China's stored grain – enough to feed up to 100 million people.*

THE IMPACT OF RODENT-BORNE DISEASES

Rodent pests are involved in the transmission of more than 20 pathogens, including bubonic plague (transmitted to man by the bite of the rat flea), which was responsible for the death of 25 million Europeans from the 14th to the 17th century. Rats also transmit debilitating chronic diseases. In the late 1970s, 80 percent of the inhabitants of the capital of one developing Asian country were seropositive for murine typhus. Forty percent of those admitted to hospital were diagnosed as having fever of unknown origin; at least some of these, and maybe most, were probably suffering from murine typhus. The impact of the disease on the economy of the country is impossible to determine – and the same country also suffered frequent outbreaks of plague.

Apart from plague, which persists in many African and Asian countries as well as in the USA (where wild mammals transmit the disease, killing fewer than 10 people a year), murine typhus, salmonella food poisoning, leptospirosis, and the West African disease Lassa fever, to mention just a few, are all potentially fatal diseases transmitted by rats.

In the late 1990s, however, attention has tended to focus on rodent-borne hemorrhagic fever viruses. From 1995–2000, at least 25 "new" hantaviruses and arenaviruses were identified, all of them associated with rodents from the family Muridae. The hantaviruses cause pulmonary ailments in the New World (50 percent of infected humans die) and fever with renal ailments in the Old World (approximately 200,000 human cases each year in Asia, with 1–15 percent mortality). The arenaviruses cause South American hemorrhagic fever in the New World (mortality in humans is 10–33 percent) and Lassa fever in the Old World (100,000–300,000 human infections each year in West Africa, causing 5,000 deaths annually). Each virus is normally associated with a specific rodent host. Infection is passed on to humans via rodent urine, feces, or saliva.

After a period in which much work was done on describing and understanding the degree of rodent viral diversity that can generate human infections, the focus for the control or prevention of rodent-borne hemorrhagic disease is now switching to understanding the biology and ecology of the host–disease association.

◐ **Right** *A German engraving shows the bizarre protective clothing worn by a doctor to treat victims of bubonic plague in Nuremberg in 1656.*

into banks or sewers, or under roads. The effects include subsidence, flooding, and even soil erosion in many areas of the world. Gnawed electrical cables can cause fires, leading to enormous economic impact. Rodents also gnaw through electric wires in the insulated walls of modern poultry and pork units, causing malfunctions of air-conditioning units and subsequent severe economic losses.

Apart from the immediate economic costs that the hordes may bring to farmers, high densities can have a profound effect upon the ecological balance of an entire region. First, considerable damage is often inflicted on vegetation, from which it may take several years to recover. Second, predators increase in numbers in response to the abundance of rodents, and when the rodents have gone they turn their attention to other prey. Eruptions of long-haired rat (*Rattus villosissimus*) populations over hundreds of thousands of square kilometers in northwestern Queensland and the Northern Territory of Australia lead to a feeding bonanza for letter-winged kites, dingoes, foxes, and cats, and these predators in turn increase dramatically in numbers. In the mid-1990s there were so many cats living in the area that after the rat populations rapidly declined there was grave concern for other native fauna – in some areas many trees were literally a ball of cat fur. The situation was so desperate that the army was called in to help eradicate the feral cat population.

The simplest method of controlling the impact of rodents is to reduce harborage and available food and water. This, however, is often impossible. At best such "good housekeeping" can prevent rodent numbers building up, but it is seldom an effective method for reducing existing populations. One imperative is to develop management techniques based on an understanding of the ecology and behavior of the pest species concerned. The same principles of management apply in controlling the impact of rodents in fields, stores, or domestic premises.

To reduce existing populations of rodents, predators – wild (for example, birds of prey) or domestic (cats or dogs) – have relatively little effect. Their role may lie in limiting population growth. It is a widely accepted principle that predators do not control, in absolute terms, their prey, although the abundance of prey may affect the numbers of predators. Mongooses were introduced to the West Indies and Hawaiian Islands and cobras to Malaysian oil palm estates, both to control rats. The rats remain, however, and the mongooses and cobra are themselves now considered pests, the one a reservoir for rabies, the other a direct risk to people. Even the farm cat will not usually have a significant effect on rodent numbers: the reproductive rate of rodents keeps them ahead of the consumption rate of cats.

One of the simplest methods for combating small numbers of rodents is trapping. Few traps, however, are efficient: most simply maim their

○ Above *Indian villagers dig out rats' nests in their fields. For farmers, the battle against rodent damage is worldwide and never ending. Over the centuries poison has been a favorite weapon, but the use of powerful pesticides can come at a cost, as the toxins may also harm nontargeted species, and there is also a risk of contaminating human food supplies. In the fight against rodent-borne maladies, an alternative approach is to dust nests with insecticides to kill disease-bearing parasites, like the exterminator dusting a ground squirrel's den in California (inset).*

○ Left *A barn owl heads for the nest with a field mouse clasped firmly in its beak. Many terrestrial predators as well as birds of prey rely on a plentiful supply of fast-breeding rodents for a large part of their diet. Programs aimed at the local eradication of pest species can have unintended knock-on effects higher up the food chain by depriving these species of their prey.*

victims. One promising method of physical control is the use of multiple capture traps placed at the base of fences (25 x 25m) that enclose early-planted crops (lure crops). These "trap-barrier" systems, which remain in place for the duration of the crop, have significantly reduced the impact of the ricefield rat in lowland irrigated rice crops in Indonesia, Malaysia, and Vietnam. In Malaysia, 6,872 rats were caught in one night and over 44,000 rats in a 9-week period. In Indonesia and Vietnam, yield increases from surrounding crops have ranged from 0.3 to 1.0 tonne per ha (0.1–0.4 tonnes an acre), representing a 10–25 percent increase in production. The disadvantage of this approach is that it is labor intensive and requires a coordinated community approach.

The oldest kind of rodenticide – fast-acting, nonselective poison – appears in the earliest written record of chemical pest control; the Greek philosopher Aristotle described the use of strychnine as early as 350 BC. However, fast-acting poisons such as strychnine, thallium sulfate, sodium monofluoroacetate (Compound 1080), and zinc phosphide have various technical and ecological disadvantages, including causing long-lasting poison shyness in sublethally poisoned rodents. They also represent a hazard to other animals.

Since 1945, when warfarin was first synthesized, several anticoagulant rodenticides have been developed. These compounds decrease the blood's ability to clot, and consequently bring about death by internal or external bleeding. The first generation of anticoagulants required multiple feeds of the poison, and were initially effective at controlling susceptible species such as the Norway rat. However some Norway rats have since acquired genetic resistance to the substances, while other species, such as the roof rat, had a natural resistance from the start. These inadequacies have led to the development of more potent "second generation" anticoagulants, with active ingredients such as brodifacoum and bromadiolone, that only require single feeds and generally have a high kill rate for most rodent species. However, there are concerns about the risk to nontarget species from these more potent chemicals, which are more persistent in the environment and which accumulate in predators as they eat more and more poisoned rodents until the predators themselves succumb to the poison.

Apart from the choice of toxicant, the timing of rodent control and the coordinated execution of a planned campaign are important in serious control programs. The most effective time to control agricultural rodents, for example, is when little food is available to them and when populations are low (probably just before breeding). Avant-garde methods of rodent control involving such relatively novel means as chemosterilants, ultrasonic sound, or electromagnetism are sometimes suggested, but none can yet claim to be as effective as anticoagulant rodenticides.

Species at Risk
CONSERVATION AND ENVIRONMENT

Not all rodents have thrived with the spread of humans. At least 54 species have become extinct in the last two centuries, and another 380 currently face a similar fate. At greatest risk are 78 critically endangered species that have small, isolated populations (often less than 250 individuals) that are continuing to decline. For some of these, such as Margaret's kangaroo rat and the Brazilian arboreal mouse, habitat protection offers hope that extinction will be averted. For others, such as the Bramble Cay mosaic-tailed rat, the future is bleak. This stocky rodent occurs on only one sparsely vegetated coral cay, 340m (1,100ft) long and 150m (500ft) wide, at the northern tip of Australia's Great Barrier Reef. Although its population numbers several hundred individuals, the rat is declining inexorably as the tides erode the coral and threaten to inundate the land.

At slightly less risk are the 100 or so endangered species. These may have total populations of up to 2,500, often scattered among several locations that are at risk of disturbance. Two species of Central American agoutis fall within this category, as do six species of Mexican woodrats.

Active management is assisting the survival of some endangered species. For example, greater stick-nest rats numbered less than 1,500 individuals in 1990 and were restricted to Franklin Island off the southern coast of Australia. Successful translocations of captive-bred animals to three new islands and also to three large enclosed areas on the Australian mainland allowed the total population to double within nine years. Programs of captive breeding and habitat management currently benefit over 20 endangered species, including Vancouver marmots, Stephens' kangaroo rats, and Shark Bay mice.

While still threatened, almost 200 species classed as vulnerable face less risk of imminent extinction than their endangered relatives, and may achieve populations up to 10,000 individuals. Examples include the plains rat and dusky hopping mouse of central Australia, the Utah prairie dog, and Menzbier's marmot of Tien Shan.

Some rodents are elusive, making it difficult to confidently identify their status. Arboreal species such as the prehensile-tailed rat and the South American climbing rats do not readily enter traps, while others, such as the southern Australian heath rat, so resemble other common species that they are easily overlooked. In many instances a lack of recent survey work makes status assessment impossible. The New Britain water rat and the orange and Mansuela mosaic-tailed rats of Ceram are known only from one or two specimens collected in the early 20th century. Whether abundant or extinct, these rodents will remain known only from museum specimens until intrepid biologists foray back to the sites where they were originally collected.   GS/CRD/DMS

THE DADDY OF THEM ALL?

Sperm competition and ejaculation strategies in rodents

THE SEX LIVES OF RODENTS ARE MORE COMPLEX and interesting than one might imagine. Much of this complexity stems from female tendencies towards promiscuity. Whenever a female mates with more than one partner during a single estrous period, the sperm from different males must compete to fertilize her ova. Males are under intense evolutionary selection pressure to win these contests, and have developed diverse and sophisticated strategies for maximizing their fertilization success under sperm competition. Female promiscuity is common in a wide range of other mammals, but the diversity and accessibility of rodents make them particularly fruitful model species for studying male adaptations to sperm competition.

As in other mammals, sperm competition in rodents appears to be largely a numbers game, rather like a raffle or lottery: the male who enters the most "tickets" (sperm) into the competition typically has a strong advantage in contests for fertilizations. For example, when female Norway rats, *Rattus norvegicus*, receive varying numbers of ejaculates from different males, most of the resultant offspring are fathered by the male that ejaculated most frequently, and hence transferred the most sperm. So, successful strategies for winning fertilizations often involve a male transferring more sperm than his rivals. However, ejaculates are not necessarily cheap to produce, and males need to be prudent in their strategies of sperm allocation in order to maximize their overall reproductive success. Careful allocation of ejaculates is illustrated by the male mate choice behavior of thirteen-lined ground squirrels, *Spermophilus tridecemlineatus*.

In this species, ovulation is induced by the act of mating, and the probability of fertilization success declines for males mating with previously mated females, particularly when there is a long delay between copulations. Rather than "waste" their ejaculates for a relatively low pay-off in terms of likely reproductive success, male thirteen-lined ground squirrels often refuse copulations with previously mated females, instead preferring to search for, and mate promiscuously with, females that offer higher potential fertilization rewards.

Theory predicts that males should typically increase the total number of sperm transferred under conditions of high levels of sperm competition risk or intensity, within certain constraints. Hence the most obvious adaptation for sperm competition, from both a theoretical and anatomical point of view, is to have big testes that can produce large quantities of sperm. The benefits of having large testes when sperm competition is intense have been demonstrated in natural populations of yellow-pine chipmunks, *Tamias amoenus*. Genetic paternity analyses in this species reveal that males with large testes for their body size have higher annual reproductive success than those with relatively small testes. More generally, species with high levels of sperm competition typically have relatively large testes for their body size. As an extreme example, the spinifex hopping mouse (*Notomys alexis*) has a monogamous mating system (females rarely, if ever, produce litters sired by more than one male), and testes that make up only about 0.15 percent of male body mass. In contrast, the plains rat (*Pseudomys australis*) has a more promiscuous mating system

(litters may be sired by more than one male) and, at nearly 4 percent of male body mass, the testes of this species are approximately 25 times larger than those of the hopping mouse, relative to body size. Other rodent species in which litters often have two or more different fathers include deer mice (*Peromyscus maniculatus*), Belding's ground squirrels, (*Spermophilus beldingi*), and bank voles (*Clethrionomys glareolus*). In general, in species such as these where multiple paternity of litters is common, males tend to have relatively large testes for their body size, as expected if investment in sperm production is important for winning fertilizations under sperm competition.

While an important role for sperm numbers in mammalian sperm competition is well established, relatively little is known about other components of the ejaculate. Seminal fluid contains a diverse combination of secretions produced by the accessory reproductive glands, which include the seminal vesicles and the multi-lobed prostate gland. Comparative studies of rodents show that in addition to having large testes for their body size, species with high levels of sperm competition also have relatively large seminal vesicles and anterior prostate glands. The major product of these glands is the copulatory plug (a coagulated mass of protein deposited in the female reproductive tract at mating), and rodent species with high levels of sperm competition also produce relatively large plugs. As yet, the benefits of producing a large copulatory plug under sperm competition are unclear. One possibility is that the plug functions as a chastity enforcement device, delaying female remating behavior. This appears to be true for guinea pigs (*Cavia porcellus*), but in other species, such as deer mice (*P. maniculatus*), plugs appear to have no effect on female remating behavior. Moreover, female fox squirrels (*Sciurus niger*) and eastern grey squirrels (*S. carolinensis*) often simply remove the plugs within 30 seconds of mating and discard or consume them. An alternative function is suggested by studies of Norway rats (*Rattus norvegicus*) in which the copulatory plug seems to be important for assisting sperm transport in the female reproductive tract, and could therefore also promote male success in sperm competition.

◁ *Left A typical litter of deer mice (P. maniculatus) consists of full- and half-siblings that have been fathered by at least two males. This situation arises despite the formation of a copulatory plug after the female has been inseminated. Although these plugs may be a device to prevent the female mating again, they do not have this outcome in all rodent species.*

Right *Having large testes confers a male rodent with definite advantages in passing on his genes. Males that produce large quantities of sperm are likely to father more of the offspring in a multi-paternal litter.*

In addition to its role in the evolution of male reproductive anatomy, sperm competition may also explain much of the diversity observed in male copulatory behavior. Comparative studies of rodents show that species with large testes for their body size, and hence relatively high levels of sperm competition, are more likely to ejaculate repeatedly with each female mated than are species with relatively small testes. For example male golden hamsters (*Mesocricetus auratus*), whose testes weigh on average about 3 percent of their body mass, will typically ejaculate around 14 times before losing interest in a particular mating partner. In contrast, male house mice (*Mus musculus domesticus*), whose testes weigh less than 1 percent of their body mass, will usually only ejaculate only once with each female mated. Males adapted to high levels of sperm competition are also more likely to copulate at a faster pace, with shorter intervals between intromissions, and require shorter recovery periods after each ejaculation before they are able to resume copulating again. Similar variation can also be observed within the copulatory behavior of individual male house mice, exposed to differing perceived levels of sperm competition risk under experimental conditions. When mating in the presence of a rival male, male house mice are more likely to ejaculate twice, and copulate with fewer pre-ejaculatory intromissions per ejaculation.

Other male rodents respond to an elevated sperm competition risk by increasing the number of sperm per ejaculate. Experimental studies have shown that when male Norway rats, mate in the presence of a rival male they transfer on average 43 percent more sperm per ejaculate than when mating on their own with a female. Male meadow voles (*Microtus pennsylvanicus*) demonstrate a similar response to the odor of a rival male, transferring on average 72 percent more sperm when copulating in the presence of a rival male odor compared with when the odor is absent. These findings are consistent with expected optimal sperm allocation strategies under elevated sperm competition risk, as predicted by theoretical models called "sperm competition games." Interestingly, a very different result is found for male house mice mating under elevated sperm competition risk – in this case, the number of sperm transferred per ejaculate is significantly lower when subject

males mate with virgin females in the presence of a rival. The reasons for these different sperm allocation responses to elevated sperm competition risk in male rodents may relate to the average levels of sperm competition to which these different species are adapted. Their social lives are such that male house mice typically experience lower average levels of sperm competition compared with Norway rats and meadow voles, have smaller reserves of sperm, longer copulation durations, and are less likely to ejaculate repeatedly with the same female. Male house mice may thus trade-off sperm numbers per ejaculate to increase the

rate of sperm transfer under an elevated risk of sperm competition.

Detailed studies of rodent reproductive anatomy and behavior are now producing significant advances in understanding how the ejaculation strategies of male mammals are designed to maximize their reproductive success under sperm competition. The complex sex lives of these fascinating small mammals illustrate the amazing diversity of adaptations resulting from sexual competition, and the extent to which evolutionary selection pressure to succeed in reproduction can influence the minute detail of animals' lives. PS

Squirrel-like Rodents

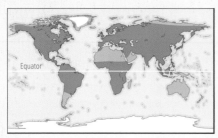
SQUIRRELS ARE PREDOMINANTLY SEEDEATERS and are the dominant arboreal rodents in many parts of the world. However, in the same family there are almost as many terrestrial species, including the ground squirrels of the open grasslands – also mostly seedeaters – as well as the more specialized and herbivorous marmots, and the semiaquatic beavers.

Although they may be highly specialized in other respects, members of the squirrel family have a relatively primitive, unspecialized arrangement of the jaw muscles and therefore of the associated parts of the skull, in contrast with the mouselike ("myomorph") and cavy-like ("hystricognath") rodents, which have these areas specialized in ways not encountered in any other mammals. In squirrels the deep masseter muscle is short and direct, extending up from the mandible to terminate on the zygomatic arch. Because this particular feature is shared by some smaller groups of rodents, notably the mountain beaver and the true beavers, these families have been grouped together with the squirrels in the suborder Sciuromorpha.

These families appear to have diverged from each other and from other rodents very early in the evolution of rodents and have very little in common other than the retention of the "sciuromorph" condition of the chewing apparatus.

A further primitive feature retained by these rodents is the presence of one or two premolar teeth in each row, giving four or five cheek teeth in each row instead of three as in the murids.

The superficially similar scaly-tailed squirrels of the African rain forests are only distantly related and are now placed within a separate suborder, Anomaluromorpha, which also includes the aberrant springhare of the African plains.   GBC

DIFFERENT STROKES...

There is a great deal of variation in the shape and function of the tail among the families of squirrel-like rodents. One highly specialized adaptation is found in the various species of flying squirrel (RIGHT), in which the tail is used in conjunction with the gliding membrane to control the precise angle of descent. In another group of "flying" squirrel-like rodents – the scaly tailed squirrels of the tropical African rain forests – the tail aids not only gliding but also climbing; overlapping scales on its underside give the squirrel purchase as it lands and grips onto the bark of trees. The semiaquatic beaver employs its broad, flat tail both as a means of propulsion and as a rudder. When slowly patrolling on the lake's surface, its tail moves from side to side. However, when swimming fast underwater (INSET) the beaver propels itself with powerful up-and-down thrusts of the tail. The long, bushy tail of the kangaroo-like springhare acts as a counterbalance, helping it maintain equilibrium while hopping along at speed. When the springhare is at rest, and standing on its hindfeet, it braces itself with its tail. The familiar, bushy tails of squirrels perform different roles depending on the habitat of the individual species – serving as warm cloaks for the denizens of northern forests, and as parasols to shade Cape ground squirrels from the fierce heat of the sun in the Kalahari desert.

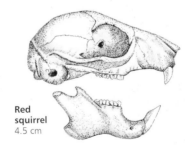

SHAPING THE ENVIRONMENT

Among squirrel-like rodents, the beaver is renowned for its skill in altering the landscape of its habitat. It cuts down trees with its strong incisors, uses the felled material to build dams and lodges, and excavates canals with its forepaws.

Somewhat less spectacular is the way that smaller sciuromorphs such as squirrels shape their environment, and yet this devastation is far more significant, thanks to the prolific and widespread nature of the squirrel family. Red squirrels, which live predominantly in conifer plantations, cause much damage by feeding on young shoots. Their cousins the gray squirrels specialize in peeling the bark from relatively

◁ **Left and above** A red squirrel, from Europe and Asia, and (above) a Douglas squirrel from western North America both display the classic squirrel profile – a long body and bushy tail.

young trees, up to 30–40 years old. The reasons for doing this are twofold: some bark is taken as a soft lining for nests; but the majority is stripped to gain access to the sweet, tasty sap beneath – a valuable dietary supplement when other food is in short supply (for example, in midsummer). This destructive activity is especially prevalent where squirrel populations are dense and low-status males are forced to search widely for food during lean times. Bark stripping presents the forestry industry with a serious problem; though trees are remarkably resilient, if their bark is stripped off entirely around the trunk and the soft tissue gnawed away, the vascular bundles that transport water, sugar, and nutrients through the tree are severed and it dies.

Crop raiding is also a cause of conflict between humans and squirrel-like rodents. Ground squirrel species feed principally on low-growing vegetation.

SKULLS AND DENTITION

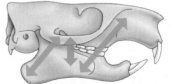

Beaver

Red squirrel

Red squirrel
4.5 cm

Skulls of squirrels show few extreme adaptations, although those of the larger ground squirrels, such as marmots, are more angular than those of the tree squirrels. Most members of the squirrel family have rather simple teeth, lacking either the strongly projecting cusps or the sharp enamel ridges found in many other rodents. In the beavers, however, there is a pattern of ridges, adapted to their diet of bark and other fibrous and abrasive vegetation and convergent with that

found in some unrelated but ecologically similar rodents like the coypu.

The primitive jaw musculature is characteristic of squirrel-like rodents. The lateral masseter muscle (blue) extends in front of the eye onto the snout, moving the lower jaw forward during gnawing. The deep masseter muscle (red) is short and used only in closing the jaw. Shown above is the skull of a marmot.

Beavers

EW WILD ANIMALS HAVE HAD AS GREAT AN *influence on the world's history and economics as the beaver. Exploration of the North American interior by Europeans was stimulated in large part by the demand for beaver pelts, used for hats and clothing. Records of the Hudson's Bay Company show an annual catch of 100,000 animals. So lucrative was this fur trade that conflicts erupted over access to trapping areas – notably the series of French and Indian Wars in the 18th century, which culminated in Britain gaining control over the whole of northern North America.*

The former importance of beavers may be judged from the fact that they are portrayed on the coats of arms of cities as distant as Härnösand in Sweden and Irkutsk in Siberia. In North America, many indigenous peoples valued the beaver both as a resource and as a spiritual totem. Central to the religion of the Montagnais of Quebec was a benevolent beaver guardian spirit, while the tribe west of Lake Athabasca in Alberta were named for the main river of their homeland: *Tsades*, or "River of Beavers" (now called the Peace River).

Heavyweights of the Rodent World
FORM AND FUNCTION

Biologically, the beaver's large incisor teeth, flat, scaly, almost hairless tail, and webbed hindfeet with a split grooming claw on the second digit are all distinctive, as is the internal anatomy of the throat and digestive tract. Beavers display a rich variety of construction, communication, and social behaviors that set them apart from other mammals. Like humans, beavers live in family groups, have complex communication systems, build homes (lodges and burrows), store food, and develop transportation networks (ponds linked by canals). Furthermore, they too change their environment to suit their needs; the dams they build promote ecological diversity, increase wetlands, affect water quality and yields, and help shape landscape evolution.

After the capybaras of South America, beavers are the heaviest rodents in the world; adults average 20–30kg (44–66lb), up to a maximum recorded weight of 45.5kg (100lb). Beavers always live near water. The animals scull slowly along the surface of lakes, using side-to-side movements of the tail for steering and propulsion. By contrast, when swimming fast or diving, the beaver moves its tail up and down in synchrony with powerful thrusts of the hindfeet.

Beavers may appear slow and awkward on land, waddling on large, pigeon-toed rear feet, short front legs, and trim forefeet. Yet they can put on a turn of speed if alarmed, outpacing both animal predators and humans as they race for the water.

A History of Comings and Goings
DISTRIBUTION PATTERNS

The North American beaver ranges over most of the continent from the Mackenzie River delta in Canada south to northern Mexico. By the late 1800s, beavers had effectively been extirpated locally over much of this range, especially in the eastern United States, but state and federal wildlife agencies have reestablished many populations through translocations and reintroductions. The animals have also been introduced into Finland, Russia (to the Karelian Isthmus, the Amur basin, and the Kamchatka peninsula), and in many central European countries, including Germany, Austria, and Poland. The largest population of North American beavers in Europe is today in southeastern Finland, numbering an estimated 10,500. North American beavers were also introduced in

FACTFILE

BEAVERS

Order: Rodentia

Family: Castoridae

2 species of the genus *Castor*

DISTRIBUTION N America, Scandinavia, W and E Europe, C Asia, NW China, Far E Russia, S America.

Equator

Habitat Riparian, semiaquatic wetlands associated with ponds, lakes, rivers, and streams.
Diet Wood (especially aspen), grasses, roots.

NORTH AMERICAN BEAVER *Castor canadensis*
North American or Canadian beaver
N America from Alaska E to Labrador, S to N Florida and Tamaulipas (Mexico); introduced to S America (Tierra del Fuego, Argentina), Europe, and Asia. HBL 80–120cm (32–47in); TL 25–50cm 10–20in); SH 30–60cm (12–23in); WT 11–30kg (24–66lb); no difference between sexes. Coat: yellowish brown to almost black; reddish brown is most common. Underfur is dense and dark gray. Breeding: gestation about 105–107 days. Longevity: 10–15 years. 24 subspecies are recognized. *C. c. phaeus* is Data Deficient; *C. c. frondator* and *C. c. mexicanus* are Not Evaluated; otherwise Lower Risk.

EURASIAN BEAVER *Castor fiber*
Eurasian or European beaver
NW and C Eurasia, in isolated, but increasing, populations from France E to Lake Baikal and Mongolia; also in far-eastern Russia (Khabarovsk). Other details as for *C. canadensis*. 8 subspecies are recognized. Critically Endangered as *C. f. tuvinicus*; Vulnerable as *C. f. birulai* and *C. f. pohlei*; otherwise Near Threatened.

Abbreviations HBL = head–body length TL = tail length SH = shoulder height WT = weight

◔ Above *Though somewhat ungainly when out of water, the semiaquatic beaver (Castor canadensis) is perfectly adapted to a wetland environment. Its dense, luxuriant pelage made the beaver vulnerable to hunting by fur trappers, and it was exterminated in many countries. However, aided by reintroduction programs, it is now making a comeback.*

◔ Left *Battling against the current, a beaver feeds on the bark of a silver birch branch. When a beaver dives, it shuts its nose and ears tight, while a translucent membrane covers its eyes and the back of the tongue prevents water from entering its throat. This effective, watertight adaptation allows beavers to gnaw and carry sticks underwater without choking; but the comic aspect of closing the lips behind the front teeth is much beloved of cartoonists when depicting the animals.*

South America (to Tierra del Fuego) in 1946. While 24 subspecies are recognized, local exterminations, translocations, and reintroductions have altered the genetic purity of many of these.

The Eurasian beaver was once found throughout Europe and Asia, but only isolated populations have survived the long association with humans. By the early 1900s, only eight relic populations totaling an estimated 1,200 individuals remained, in France, Germany, Norway, Belarus, Russia, Ukraine, Mongolia, and China respectively. Reintroduction and translocation programs began in most European countries in the early- to mid-1900s, and many continue at the present time. The Eurasian beaver population is growing (the current estimate is 500,000–600,000 animals) and its range is expanding throughout Europe and Asia. Eight subspecies are recognized, but translocations and reintroductions have altered their historic distributions.

The earliest direct ancestor of the Eurasian beaver was probably *Steneofiber* from the Oligocene, about 32 million years ago. The genus *Castor*, which originated in Europe during the Pliocene (5–1.8 m.y.a.), entered North America while the continents were still connected; thus the present-day North American beaver is thought to be evolutionarily younger than the Eurasian beaver. During the Pleistocene, 10,000 years ago, the two species coexisted with giant forms that weighed 270–320kg (600–700lb), for example *Castoroides* in North America and *Trogontherium* in Eurasia. The two present species are externally similar in size and coloration and are indistinguishable in appearance, but they differ in cranial morphology and chromosome number (*C. fiber* has 48 chromosomes, *C. canadensis* 40). The North American beaver is believed to be derived from the Eurasian beaver because it has fewer

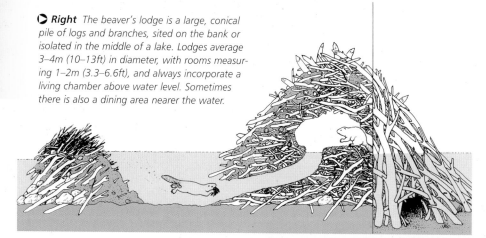

○ **Right** *The beaver's lodge is a large, conical pile of logs and branches, sited on the bank or isolated in the middle of a lake. Lodges average 3–4m (10–13ft) in diameter, with rooms measuring 1–2m (3.3–6.6ft), and always incorporate a living chamber above water level. Sometimes there is also a dining area nearer the water.*

chromosomes. It is thought that the reduced number of chromosomes in *C. canadensis* resulted from the fusion of 8 chromosome pairs in the ancestral *C. fiber*, and that this difference prevents the two species from interbreeding.

Choosy Generalists
DIET

Beavers are generalist herbivores whose diet varies seasonally. In spring and summer they feed on relatively nonwoody plants (leaves, roots, herbs, ferns, grasses, and algae), but they turn to trees and shrubs, especially in the fall. Aspen is the preferred tree species, but birch, maple, oak, dogwood, and fruit trees are also taken. In many regions, shrubs such as willow and alder form the bulk of the diet. Wood is not easy to digest; to cope with it, beavers have special microbial fermentation in the cecum, and digestion occurs twice to extract the maximum nutritive advantage.

Beavers are only able to survive the harsh winters of northern latitudes by caching food. Woody stems are stored underwater, where they are safe from other browsers. The beavers can then swim under the ice to fetch the food without having to leave the safety of the pond.

Many European beavers do not cache food (in some populations, only 50 percent of families do so). Instead, they venture onto land to find food in winter. Another strategy that beavers use to survive at this time is to live off the fat stored in the tail.

How Colonies Work
SOCIAL BEHAVIOR

Beavers live in small, closed family units, which are often referred to as "colonies." An established colony contains an adult pair, young of the current year (called kits), yearlings born the previous year, and possibly one or more subadults from previous breeding seasons. There are typically four to eight beavers in a family. The inclusion of offspring older than 24 months usually occurs in high-density populations, and these young adults generally do not breed. Under high-density conditions, the normal family structure has been reported to change, with more than one reproductively active adult female present.

The main beaver predator, beside humans, is the wolf, for which beavers are an important prey item. Other large carnivores, such as lynx, coyotes, wolverines, bears, and foxes, may also kill them.

Beavers are unusual among mammals in that they exhibit long-term monogamy. The mated pair occupies a discrete, individual territory, and the relationship usually lasts until one adult dies. The family unit is exceptionally stable, thanks to a low birth rate (one litter annually of 1–5 young in the Eurasian and up to 8 in the North American beaver), a high survival rate for all age–sex classes, and long-term parental care, with the young usually staying in the colony for 2 years. Both Eurasian and North American beavers have an average litter size of 2–3 kits, and the dominance hierarchy within the family is by age class, with adults dominant to yearlings and yearlings to kits. A sex-based hierarchy, with the adult female dominant to all other family members, has occasionally been reported. Physical aggression is rare, although beavers in dense populations are reported to have more tail scars – a sign of fighting, usually with outsiders over territorial boundaries.

Mating occurs in winter, usually in the water but also in the lodge or burrow. Kits are born in

○ **Above** *Beaver kits are extremely precious – females produce only one small litter each year. At birth, they have a full coat of fur and open eyes, and are able to move around inside the lodge. All family members share in bringing the kits solid food, with the adult male most actively supplying provisions.*

THE BEAVER'S 29-HOUR DAY

For most of the year, beavers are active at night, rising at sunset and retiring to their lodges at sunrise. This regular daily cycle is termed a circadian rhythm. During winter at northern latitudes, however, when ponds freeze over, beavers stay in their lodges or under the ice, because temperatures there remain near 0°C (32°F), while air temperatures are generally much lower. Activity above ice would require a very high use of energy.

In the dimly lit world of the lodge and the water surrounding it, light levels remain constant and low throughout the 24-hour day, so that sunrise and sunset are not apparent. In the absence of solar "cues," activity, recorded as noise and movement, is not synchronized with the solar day. The circadian rhythm breaks down, and "beaver days" become longer, varying in length from 26 to 29 hours. This type of cycle is described as a free-running circadian rhythm.

late spring, which may coincide with the dispersal of 2-year-olds away from the family territory. Though they can swim within a few hours, the kits' small size and dense fur make them too buoyant to submerge easily, so they are unable to dive down the passage out of the lodge. Kits nurse for between 6–8 weeks, although they may begin eating solid food before they are weaned.

While the kits are very young, the adult male may spend more time in territorial defense (patrolling and scent marking the family territory) while the female is more involved in care and nursing. The kits grow rapidly, but require many months of practice to perfect their ability to construct dams and lodges. As yearlings, they participate in all family activities, including construction. Dispersal of the young adults usually occurs in the spring of their second year, when they are approximately 24 months old; they head off to set up territories of their own, usually within 20km (12mi), although they may travel as far as 250km (155mi).

One of the ways in which beavers communicate is by depositing scent, usually at the borders of the family territory. Both species of beaver scent mark on small waterside mounds made of mud and vegetation dredged up from underwater. Eurasian beavers also mark tufts of grass, rocks, and logs, as well as directly onto the ground. The scent, produced by the substance known as castoreum (from the castor sacs) and secretions from the anal glands, is pungent and musty. All members of a beaver family participate, but the adult male marks most frequently. Scent marking is most intense in the spring, and probably serves to convey information about the resident family to passing strangers and to neighbors. Another mode of communication is to slap the tail against the water. Adults do this more often than younger animals, to let an approaching interloper know they have been spotted. The slap often elicits a response from the stranger, which enables the beaver to gauge what level of threat is posed. Beavers also communicate through vocalizations (hissing and grunting), tooth sharpening, and posture.

Of the various construction activities in which beavers engage, canal building is the least complex and was probably the first that the animals developed. They use their forepaws to loosen mud and sediment from the bottom of shallow streams and marshy trails, pushing it out of the way to the sides. The resulting channels enable the beavers to stay in the water while moving between ponds or to feeding areas. This behavior occurs most often in summer when water levels are low.

Beavers are efficient excavators and usually dig multiple burrows in the family area. A burrow may be a single tunnel or a whole maze, hollowed into the bank from a stream or pond and ending in one or more chambers. In many habitats, beaver families use burrows as the primary residence. Alternative riverside accommodation is provided by the beaver equivalent of a log cabin – the lodge.

○ **Above** *Of all rodents, the beaver is one of the best adapted for movement in water. Its torpedo-shaped body is hydrodynamically efficient and its fur is waterproof. It uses its broad tail for propulsion and steering, and also gains thrust from its webbed feet.*

Meat, Fur, and Medicines

CONSERVATION AND ENVIRONMENT

Historically, beavers have provided humans with meat, fur, and medicinal products, and they continue to supply the first two to this day. Between 200,000–600,000 pelts are collected in Canada each year, while the harvest in the United States is 100,000–200,000. Scandinavian countries take around 13,000 pelts, and Russia some 30,000. However, the global fur market is depressed, and there is little economic incentive for trappers.

Another beaver product of value to humans – especially in the past – was castoreum, a complex substance consisting of hundreds of compounds, including alcohols, phenols, salicylaldehyde, and castoramine. This substance is produced in the animal's castor sacs. As far back as 500–400 BC Hippocrates and Herodotus note its efficacy in treating diseases of the womb. Later writers, such as Pliny the Elder and Galen, mention it as a remedy for cramps and intestinal spasms. Down the ages, castoreum has also variously been suggested as a treatment for sores, ulcers, earache, constipation, and even as an antidote to snake venom. Modern studies have remarked on its similarity to the synthetic drug aspirin, which is derived from salicylic acid; castoreum also contains salicin, which the beavers obtain by eating the bark of willow and aspen. Although it no longer appears in the conventional pharmacopoeia, it is still used by homeopathic practitioners, and also serves as a base for perfume.

Beavers are today established once more in Belgium and the Netherlands, and a reintroduction program is planned in Britain. As with most such initiatives, there is controversy over the potential effect on land used by humans. North American beavers in Europe add to an already charged situation. Currently, large populations exist in Finland and northwestern Russia and there is no consensus on how the two species are competing for the limited wetland resource. New techniques make it possible to distinguish the two species in the field, either by using genetic analysis of hair-root cells or else by comparing anal-gland secretions.

Beavers and humans conflict when beavers make wetlands out of agricultural fields. In the midwestern and eastern United States, where beavers were once nearly extirpated, they have made a tremendous comeback, and beaver–human conflict is growing, a trend that is likely to continue. Beavers are keystone species in wetland habitats, and it remains for humans to acknowledge their environmental contributions and develop strategies that allow both humans and beavers to share the landscape.   PB/GH

THE CONSTRUCTION WORKER RODENT

3 *Although many beaver barrages are built across streams under 6m (20ft) wide and in water less than 1m (3.3ft) deep, the animals keep adding material until some dams end up over 100m (330ft) long and 3m (10ft) high. Dam-building is at its most intense in the spring and fall, although construction may go on throughout the year.*

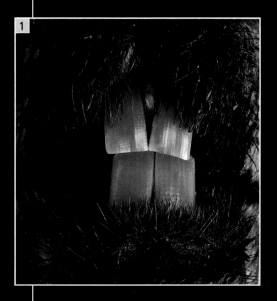

1 *Just as a lumberjack's ax is hardened with iron, so the front enamel of beaver teeth is reinforced. The softer inner surface wears down more rapidly, creating a sharp, chisel-like edge that makes cutting down trees for food and building easier. In common with all rodents, beavers have large incisors that grow as fast as they are worn down.*

2 *Trees felled by beavers; although the damage caused by gnawing may appear terminal, the trees that beavers favor (aspens, poplars, cottonwoods, and willows) are characterized by rapid growth, and beaver "pruning" often stimulates reinvigorated growth the next spring.*

4 In areas where beavers and humans coexist, beavers' dam-building activity (especially their propensity to block culverts and cause road flooding) is seen as a hazard. But the ecological advantages are often overlooked; by slowing the flow of rivers and streams, dams boost sediment deposition – a natural filtration system that removes potentially harmful impurities from the water. In addition, the large areas of wetland that dams create bring other benefits, such as reduced erosion damage and greater biodiversity.

5 The mud, stones, sticks, and branches that beavers use to construct their dams make for a very robust structure, behind which a substantial pond will form. By impounding a large body of water, they effectively surround their home with a wide moat, which increases their security from predators. Moreover, the bigger the lake, the more access the beavers have by water to distant food items. Several lakes and lodges may be the work of a single colony (so, simply counting these in any one area is not a reliable way of estimating the local beaver population). Colonies are forced to move on when the accumulation of sediment in a pond becomes too great. Abandoned, silted-up beaver ponds form the basis of rich new ecosystems; they develop into wetland meadows whose soil, rich in decaying plant matter, supports reeds and sedges, and eventually even large trees.

Mountain Beaver

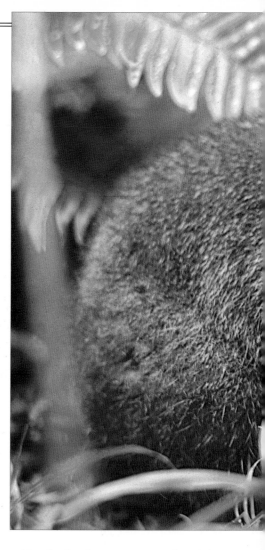

tHE MOST PRIMITIVE OF ALL PRESENT-DAY *rodents, mountain beavers live only in southwestern Canada and along the west coast of the USA, where they inhabit some of the most productive coniferous forest lands in North America.*

Not to be confused with the flat-tailed stream beaver (genus *Castor*), mountain beavers are strictly terrestrial animals. They are secretive and nocturnal, spending much of their time in burrows, where they sleep, eat, defecate, fight, and reproduce; they even do most of their traveling underground. Consequently, they are seldom seen in the wild.

MOUNTAIN BEAVER

Aplodontia rufa

Mountain beaver, Boomer, or Sewellel

Order: Rodentia

Sole member of family Aplodontidae

DISTRIBUTION USA and Canada along Pacific coast

Tropic of Cancer

HABITAT Coniferous forest

SIZE Head–body length 30–41cm (12-16in); tail length 2.5–3.8cm (1–1.5in); shoulder height 11.5–14cm (4.5–5.5in); weight 1–1.5kg (2.2–3.3lb). Sexes are similar in size and shape, but males weigh slightly more than females.

COAT Young in their year of birth have grayish fur, adults blackish to reddish brown, tawny underneath.

DIET Leafy materials, grasses, roots.

BREEDING Gestation 28–30 days

LONGEVITY 5–10 years

CONSERVATION STATUS Lower Risk: Near Threatened; two subspecies – the Point Arena and Point Reyes mountain beavers – are listed as Vulnerable.

Built for Burrowing

FORM AND FUNCTION

Mountain beavers are medium-sized, bull-necked rodents with a round, robust body and a moderately flat and broad head that is equipped with small, black, beady eyes and long, stiff, whitish whiskers (vibrissae). Their incisor teeth are rootless and continuously growing, as are their premolars and molars. Their ears are relatively small, and covered with short, soft, light-colored hair. Their short legs give them a squat appearance; the tail is short and vestigial. The fur on their back presents a sheen, whereas white-to-translucent-tipped long guard hairs impart their flanks with a grizzled effect. A distinctive feature is a soft, furry white spot under each ear.

Mountain beavers can be found at all elevations from sea level to the tree line, and in areas with rainfall of 50–350cm (20–138in) per year and where winters are wet, mild, and snow free, summers moist, mild, and cloudy. Their home burrows are generally in areas with deep, well-drained soils and abundant fleshy and woody plants. In drier areas mountain beavers are restricted to habitats on banks and to ditches that are seasonally wet or have some free-running water available for most of the year.

The distribution of mountain beavers is in part explained by the fact that they cannot adequately regulate the temperature of their bodies and must therefore live in stable, cool, moist environments. Nor can they effectively conserve body moisture or fat, which prevents them from either hibernating or spending the summer in torpor. Mountain beavers require considerable amounts of both food and water, and they must line their nests well for insulation. They satisfy most of their requirements with items obtained from within 30m (100ft) of their nest. Water is obtained mainly from succulent plants, dew, or rain.

Unlike any other rodent or rabbit, mountain beavers extract fecal pellets individually with their incisors when defecating and toss them on piles in underground toilet chambers. However, they also share with other rodents and rabbits the habit of reingesting some of the pellets.

Mountain beavers are strictly vegetarians. They harvest leafy materials such as fronds of sword fern, new branches of salal and huckleberry, stems of Douglas fir and vine maple, and clumps of grass or sedge, and also seek out succulent, fleshy foods, such as fiddleheads of bracken fern and roots of false dandelion and bleeding heart. If these foods are not eaten immediately they will be stored underground for subsequent consumption.

Most food and nest items are gathered above ground between dusk and dawn and consumed underground. Decaying, uneaten food is abandoned or buried in blind chambers; dry, uneaten food is added to the nest.

Life below the Forest Floor

SOCIAL BEHAVIOR

It used to be thought that all mountain beavers were solitary except during the breeding and rearing season, but recent studies using radio tracking have demonstrated that this view is inadequate. Some mountain beavers spend short periods together in all seasons. Neighbors, for example, will share nests and food caches, or a wandering beaver will stay a day or two in another beaver's burrow system. Sometimes a beaver's burrow will also be occupied, in part if not in its entirety, by any of a range of other animals, such as salamanders, frogs, or deer mice.

Unlike many rodents, mountain beavers have a low rate of reproduction. Most do not mate until they are at least 2 years old, and females conceive only once a year, even if they lose a litter. Breeding is to some extent synchronized. Males are sexually active from about late December to early March, with aggressive older males doing most of the breeding. Conception normally occurs in January or February. Litters of between 2–4 young are born in February, March, or early April. The young

◁ **Left** Mountain beavers seldom appear above ground during daylight hours. This rare image shows well the squat, thickset appearance of this most elusive of North American mammals.

land. Both sexes disperse in the same manner. Dispersing young travel mainly above ground: they become very vulnerable to predators, for example, owls, hawks, ravens, coyotes, bobcats, and man. Those living near roads are liable to be killed by vehicles.

The Forester's Foe
CONSERVATION AND ENVIRONMENT

Mountain beavers are classed as nongame mammals, and so are not managed in the same way as game animals like deer and elk or furbearing animals such as beavers and muskrats. They can pose a huge threat to young conifers planted for timber; the damage they cause affects about 111,000ha (275,000 acres). Almost all damage occurs while they are gathering food and nest materials.

Although some of the mountain beavers' forest habitat has given way to urban development and agriculture, they range over almost as extensive an area now as they did 200–300 years ago. They are probably more abundant now than they were in the early 20th century, thanks to forest logging practices. Mountain beavers do not appear to be in any immediate danger of extermination from man or natural causes.   JE

are born blind, hairless, and helpless in the nest. They are weaned when they reach about 6–8 weeks old and continue to occupy the nest and burrow system with their mother until late summer or early fall. Juveniles disperse and leave their natal site to find a territory and burrow system of their own.

Once on its own, a young beaver may establish a new burrow system or, more commonly, restore an abandoned one. New burrows may be within 100m (330ft) of the mother's burrow, or up to 2km (1.2mi) away, the distance depending on population densities and on the quality of the

◁ **Right** The burrow system of a mountain beaver. Each burrow system consists of a single nest chamber and underground food caches and fecal chambers which are generally close to the nest. Most nests are about 1m (3.3ft) below ground in a well-drained, dome-shaped chamber, although some may occur 2m (6.6ft) or more below ground. Tunnels are generally 15–20cm (6–8in) in diameter and occur at various levels; those closest to the surface are used for travel; deep ones lead to the nest and food caches. Burrow openings occur every 4–6m (13–20ft) or more, depending on vegetative cover and number of animals occupying a particular area. Densities vary from 1 or 2 mountain beavers per hectare (2.5 acres) in poor habitat to 20 or more per hectare in good habitat. Up to 75 per hectare have been kill-trapped in reforested clear-out areas, but such densities are rare. Individual burrow systems often interconnect.

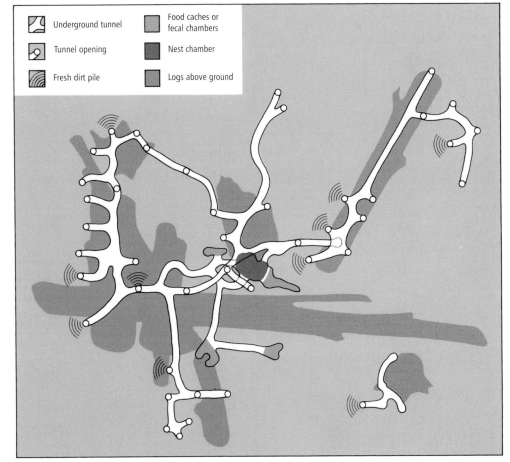

▨ Underground tunnel	▨ Food caches or fecal chambers
▨ Tunnel opening	▨ Nest chamber
▨ Fresh dirt pile	▨ Logs above ground

Squirrels

t EMPERATE-ZONE SQUIRRELS ARE A LITTLE *like daffodils: they appear suddenly in early spring, add life to the habitat for a few months, and then disappear again. For the ground dwellers, disappearance signals the start of hibernation, for many of these mammals spend at least half their lives in dormancy: they are active above ground for only 4–6 months and hibernate for the rest of the year in grass-lined nests deep underground.*

Squirrels are in general relatively unspecialized. They have evolved different body forms and habits that fit them for life in a broad range of habitats, from lush tropical rain forests to semiarid deserts, and from open prairies to town gardens. This successful family includes such diverse forms as the ground-dwelling and burrowing marmots, ground squirrels, prairie dogs, and chipmunks; the arboreal and day-active tree squirrels; and the nocturnal flying squirrels. The scaly-tailed squirrels (Anomaluridae) are also treated here, though they are taxonomically distinct from true squirrels.

Squirrel Groups and Genera

Pygmy squirrels: *Exilisciurus, Glyphotes, Myosciurus, Nannosciurus, Sciurillus*
Dwarf squirrels: *Microsciurus, Prosciurillus*
Giant squirrels: *Ratufa, Rubrisciurus*
Flying squirrels: *Aeretes, Aeromys, Belomys, Biswamoyopterus, Eupetaurus, Glaucomys, Hylopetes, Iomys, Petaurillus, Petinomys, Pteromys, Pteromyscus, Trogopterus*
Giant flying squirrels: *Petaurista*
Beautiful squirrels: *Callosciurus*
Sun squirrels: *Heliosciurus*
Groove-toothed squirrels: *Rheithrosciurus, Syntheosciurus,*
Palm squirrels: *Epixerus, Funambulus, Menetes, Protoxerus*

Long-nosed squirrels: *Hyosciurus, Rhinosciurus*
Rock squirrels: *Sciurotamias*
Red-cheeked squirrels: *Dremomys*
American red squirrels: *Tamiasciurus*
Tree squirrels: *Sciurus, Sundasciurus*
Striped squirrels: *Funisciurus, Lariscus, Tamiops*
African bush squirrels: *Paraxerus*
Chipmunks: *Tamias*
Ground squirrels: *Ammospermophilus, Atlantoxerus, Xerus (Geosciurus), Spermophilus, Spermophilopsis*
Prairie dogs: *Cynomys*
Marmots: *Marmota*

For full species list see Appendix ▷

Diggers, Climbers, and Gliders
FUNCTION AND FORM

Squirrels are instantly recognizable, with their cylindrical bodies, bushy tails, and prehensile limbs. They have short forelegs, with a small thumb and four toes on the front feet, and longer hindlegs with either four (woodchucks, *Marmota monax*) or five toes (ground squirrels and tree squirrels) on the hindfeet. Most are diurnal, conspicuous, active, and – often – amusingly clever. They exhibit a wide array of body sizes and behaviors, from ground-dwelling, fossorial species (marmots, ground squirrels, prairie dogs) to arboreal tree squirrels and nocturnal flying squirrels. Their abilities to live in contrasting habitats and to forage opportunistically are the bases for their widespread distribution and numerical abundance, both in species and populations.

Squirrels have large eyes, surrounded by light-colored rings, that are placed on the sides of their heads, affording them a broad field of vision. Keen eyesight enables them to recognize dangerous predators from nondangerous conspecifics at

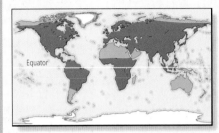

FACTFILE

SQUIRRELS

Order: Rodentia

Family: Sciuridae

273 species in 50 genera

DISTRIBUTION Among the most widespread of mammals, found worldwide except for in Australia, Polynesia, Madagascar, S South America, and the Sahara desert (Africa and Arabia).

Equator

HABITAT Various, from tropical rain forests to temperate and boreal coniferous forests, tundra and alpine meadows to semiarid deserts, and cultivated fields to city parks. Some species are arboreal and nest in tree branches or cavities; others are terrestrial and excavate subterranean burrows.

SIZE Head–body length ranges from 6.6–10cm (2.6–3.9in) in the diminutive African pygmy squirrel, *Myosciurus pumilio* to 53–73cm (20.8–28.7in) in the Alpine marmot, *Marmota marmota*; tail length from 5–8cm (2–3in) to 13–16cm (5.1–6.3in); weight from 10g (0.35oz) to 4–8kg (8.8–17.6lb), in the same two species.

COAT Squirrels come in many colors. Most squirrels molt twice per year. In northern areas a soft, fine summer coat alternates with a stiff, thick winter coat. There are no sexual dimorphisms or age variations in coat texture or colors.

DIET Tree and flying squirrels eat nuts, seeds, fruits, buds, flowers, sap, and occasionally fungi; ground-dwelling squirrels eat grasses, forbs, flowers, bulbs, and especially seeds (*Spermophilus* means "seed loving"). Most species will also eat insects, birds' eggs and nestlings, and small vertebrates if they are available.

BREEDING In most species, females mature sexually before males, usually reproducing by age 1 year. Males are polygynous and, in some species, females also mate with multiple partners, resulting in litters of mixed paternity. Most ground-dwelling squirrels, flying squirrels, and northern populations of tree squirrels bear one litter in late spring; temperate-zone tree squirrels and chipmunks often have another summer litter. Litters typically contain 1–6 (up to 11) pups; larger species have smaller litters.

LONGEVITY Ground and tree squirrels live 2–3 years on average and 6–7 years maximum; larger species, such as Yellow-bellied marmots (*Marmota flaviventris*), live 4–5 years on average and 13–14 years maximum. Females usually live longer than males.

CONSERVATION STATUS Many species are threatened or endangered due to loss of habitat, introduction of exotic species, and harassment. Red squirrels are listed as Near Threatened in the UK and N Italy due to exclusion by the introduced Gray squirrel.

○ *Above The Harris' antelope squirrel inhabits burrows that it has excavated. Within its range it may have several burrows, one of which will have a nest. The species is diurnal and quite conspicuous.*

◒ *Left The red squirrel, which lives in woodland across Europe and Central Asia, has distinctive tufting on its ears. It is hunted in Russia for its dark brown winter pelage.*

great distances. Tree and flying squirrels and chipmunks also have large ears; some, like red squirrels and tassel-eared squirrels (*Sciurus aberti*), have conspicuous ear tufts. All squirrels have touch-sensitive whiskers (vibrissae) on the head, feet, and the outsides of the legs.

Squirrels have an unusual arrangement of teeth for a rodent: a single pair of chisel-shaped incisors in each jaw, a large gap in front of the premolars, and no canine teeth. Their incisors grow continuously and are worn back by use; the cheek teeth are rooted and have abrasive chewing surfaces. The lower jaw is movable, and the lower incisors can operate independently. Some chip-

munks and ground squirrels have internal cheek pouches for carrying food.

Ground-dwelling squirrels are heavy-bodied, with powerful forelimbs and large scraping claws for digging, whereas arboreal squirrels have lighter, longer bodies, less muscular forelimbs, and sharp claws on all toes. Tree squirrels descend tree trunks head first, turning their hindfeet backward and sticking the claws into the bark to act as anchors. Their bushy tails are multifunctional: they serve as a balance when the squirrel runs and climbs, as a rudder when it jumps, as a flag to communicate social signals, and as a wrap-around blanket when the animal sleeps. All squirrels have soft pads on the soles of their feet, affording them a better grip of the substrate and food items. When feeding, squirrels squat on their haunches and hold the morsel in their forepaws. The foot pads of desert-living long-clawed ground squirrels (*Spermophilopsis leptodactylus*) are furry, which insulates them as they scurry over hot sand; in addition, fringes of stiff hairs on the outside of the hindfeet serve to push away sand during burrowing.

Flying squirrels, like other gliding mammals such as flying lemurs and flying phalangers, have a furred, muscular membrane (or "patagium") that extends along the sides of the body and acts as a parachute when the animal leaps. The patagium stretches from the hindlegs to the front limbs, and is bound in front by a thin rod of cartilage attached to the wrist. Once airborne, the squirrel steers by changing the position of its limbs and bushy tail and by varying the tension in the patagium. Flying squirrels descend in long, smooth curves to the base of tree trunks, where they brake by turning the tail and body upward. The larger flying squirrels can glide for 100m (330ft) or more; smaller species cover much shorter distances. Gliding is an economical way to travel and facilitates quick escape from flightless tree predators such as pine martens. When on trees, however, flying squirrels are hindered in their movements by the membrane, which may explain why they are all nocturnal – to evade keen-sighted birds of prey.

The Winter Larder
DIET

Squirrels are primarily vegetarians. Tree squirrels favor nuts and seeds, but will also eat leafy greenery. Gray squirrels in the United Kingdom and the Malabar giant squirrels (*Ratufa indica*) of Indian rain forests will also debark branches and feed on the underlying growing tissue; horsetail squirrels in Malayan rain forests specialize on bark and sap

from the boles of trees. In addition, insects are an important dietary component for some species. Gray and red squirrels in broadleaf woodlands feed on caterpillars in the spring and early summer when other nutritious foods are scarce. Several tropical squirrels only eat insects; indeed, the long-nosed squirrel (*Rhinosciurus laticaudatus*) has incisors modified into forcepslike vices perfect for grabbing such small prey. Most tree and flying squirrels will also eat birds' eggs and nestlings.

Ground-dwelling squirrels are similarly omnivorous. Although they feed primarily on plant parts, they will in addition eat insects, birds' eggs, carrion, and, occasionally, each other's young. Typically, no one plant makes up more than 10 percent of a species' diet. Early in the growing season, ground squirrels seek out new grass shoots, which they pull up and eat blade by blade, starting at the base. As the season progresses, flowers and unfurling leaves of forbs are their mainstays. In late summer, species that hibernate concentrate on energy-rich bulbs and seeds of grasses and

◁ **Left** *Representative species of squirrels:*
1 Southern flying squirrel (Glaucomys volans) gliding from a nest hole in a tree trunk; 2 Prevost's squirrel (Callosciurus prevostii); 3 African pygmy squirrel (Myosciurus pumilio) descending a tree head-first; 4 Abert or tassel-eared squirrel (Sciurus aberti); 5 American red squirrel (Tamiasciurus hudsonicus) hanging by its hindlegs; 6 Indian giant or Malabar squirrel (Ratufa indica); 7 Asiatic or Siberian chipmunk (Tamias sibiricus) with filled cheek pouches; 8 Alpine marmot (Marmota marmota) in vigilant upright posture giving alarm whistle; 9 Shrew-faced ground or long-nosed squirrel (Rhinosciurus laticaudatus) foraging for termites; 10 Geoffroy's or western ground squirrel (Xerus erythropus) with its tail arched and fluffed, an indication of anxiety.

legumes, and on nuts. Sometimes foraging activities affect the local vegetational structure: prairie dogs bite off and discard tall plants around their burrows to enhance their field of view, and this constant cropping discourages all but the fastest-growing plants. Most squirrels get all the water they require from ingested plant materials; however, tree squirrels regularly visit sources of drinking water, especially during hot, dry summers.

Because of the seasonal nature of flowering and fruiting in temperate forests, the squirrels that live there depend on different foods at different times of year. Another way of ensuring a constant food supply is to cache seeds and nuts, which can be unearthed and eaten during the winter. From July, when the first fruits mature, until the following April, gray and red squirrels in broadleaf woodlands depend on fresh and buried nuts. A poor mast crop can have disastrous consequences in terms of high overwinter mortality (particularly of subadults), and may even prevent breeding the following spring. Adult red squirrels that recover many cached pine cones and beechnuts are more likely to survive the next spring and summer than those that must rely only on buds, shoots, and flowers; and females are more likely to produce a spring litter if they feed heavily on cached seeds than if they feed mainly on other vegetation.

Tree squirrels within forests may incidentally act as reforesters; by burying seeds and nuts safely in the soil they promote regeneration of the trees. Squirrels of all ages hoard nuts and seeds; even juveniles exhibit characteristic burying behaviors. As poaching of squirrels' larders is not uncommon, some scatter their stores widely to avoid theft by neighbors. Individual red and gray squirrels may bury hundreds of nuts in a season, some close to the tree that bore them but others as much as 30–60m (100–200ft) away. And, although individuals can smell nuts buried as deep as 30cm (12in) below the surface, many are never retrieved. Burying behavior and failed retrieval result, inadvertently, in tree-seed dispersal. There has been a long coevolution of tree squirrels with many coniferous and mast-producing trees, such as pine, oak, and beech. This may seem odd, as squirrels' teeth can gnaw through hard shells and destroy the embryo of any nut they discover; but trees in fact benefit, by producing crops so abundant that many buried nuts are never recovered, enabling them to germinate.

Douglas squirrels (*Tamiasciurus douglasii*) and American red squirrels (*T. hudsonicus*) do not scatter hoard. Instead they cut unopened pine and spruce cones off trees and cache them in a single larder, often located in a hollow stump or under a log. Larders may contain up to 4,000 cones in jack pine forests, and as many as 18,000 in white spruce forests. The food contained in these so-called middens is essential for surviving the long winters in the boreal forest, so each squirrel defends a territory surrounding 1–3 middens.

Males and females defend similar-sized territories: 0.4–0.5ha (about 1 acre) in spruce forests, and 0.6–0.7ha (1.5 acres) in jack pine forests. Territories are defended year-round: females rarely leave home, and males depart only for a few days in the spring when neighboring females are sexually receptive. The squirrels warn away potential rivals by screeching and rattling calls; if an intruder persists, they will resort to chases and physical combat. Territorial defense is most intensive close to the midden, where the stakes are highest, and most evident in the autumn, when new cones are ready to harvest and dispersing juveniles are attempting to establish territories of their own.

The area defended around "primary" middens varies in size between years. When cone crops are good, juvenile recruitment is high, because territories of adults shrink and there is plenty to eat. Young, transient animals can temporarily reside between territories centered on primary middens. When cone crops fail, however, juvenile recruitment drops due to starvation and lack of living space. Interestingly, female American red squirrels may in very good years leave their territory and its middens to one or two sons or daughters. Being

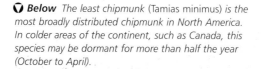

◐ **Below** *The least chipmunk* (Tamias minimus) *is the most broadly distributed chipmunk in North America. In colder areas of the continent, such as Canada, this species may be dormant for more than half the year (October to April).*

◐ **Above** *A white-tailed prairie dog eating a flower. Prairie dogs live in colonies or "towns." Populations of these animals fell during the 20th century, mostly as a result of poisoning programs; indeed, some prairie dog species have been reduced by several hundred million.*

larger, older, and more experienced, the mother is more likely to compete successfully for a new territory than her young would be, so leaving her territory to her offspring increases their likelihood of survival and reproduction.

North American flying squirrels also hoard food and guard their larders throughout the year. These larders are hidden in tree cavities or underground, and are marked by sweat and sebaceous gland secretions. Larders of southern flying squirrels (*Glaucomys volans*), primarily containing acorns, may be defended by a single individual or, in winter, by aggregations of up to 15 squirrels. Huddling together reduces daily energy expenditure by about 30 percent, and squirrels in a group are less likely to be taken by predators than an individual living on its own.

In coniferous forests, northern flying squirrels (*G. sabrinus*) do not have access to acorns, so lichens and hypogeal (subterranean) fungi are the predominant winter food. Nests are constructed in tree cavities or attached to branches, and are composed almost entirely of certain special arboreal lichens that lack acids and other secondary compounds. The lichen-covered walls then serve not only as insulation but also as winter food caches. By spring, the squirrels have almost literally eaten themselves out of house and home.

Photos and documentary film of tree squirrels curling up in their winter nests have led to the popular misconception that all squirrels hibernate. Tropical and desert-dwelling species may remain active all year round, and even Holarctic tree squirrels stay alert, putting on limited fat reserves in the autumn and relying on the constant availability of high-energy nuts and seeds to get them through the winter. Their winter activity pattern represents a balance between short, frenetic feeding bouts (of about 3–4 hours per day) to meet their energy demands – about 400–700 kJ/24–42kcal per day for a red squirrel weighing 300–350g (10–12oz) – and long resting periods in the nest (or "drey").

Slightly flattened and spherical in shape, the drey is made of small branches, twigs, and grasses (or a tree cavity may be used), and is thickly lined with dry grass, moss, and fur. It is so well insulated that, in freezing conditions when the owner is inside, the internal temperature is about 20°C higher than the air temperature outside. During a squirrel's extended resting periods, its body temperature decreases from about 41°C to 39°C, which further reduces energy expenditure. Nonetheless, the animal cannot afford to spend more than two days inside its cozy drey without foraging outside, even in bad weather.

Ground-dwelling squirrels living in temperate and northern climates spend the winter in subterranean burrows. They prepare for this period of forced inactivity either by storing food in their dens or by accumulating fat on their bodies; some will undertake both activities. Food-storing species typically undergo long bouts of torpor that are interspersed with brief periods of activity. Siberian chipmunks (*Tamias sibiricus*) store seeds, acorns, buds, and mushrooms, each in a different burrow compartment. They can carry up to 9g (0.3oz) of grain in their cheek pouches for distances in excess of 1km (0.6mi), and an individual animal may store as much as 2.6kg (5.7lb) of winter food.

Most fat-storing ground squirrels and marmots spend the winter months in hibernation, sometimes in groups of close relatives. The last animal into the den (among alpine marmots, *Marmota marmota*, this is usually an adult male) plugs the entrance hole with hay, earth, and rocks, for insulation and safety from predators.

Physiologically, hibernation is a state of suspended animation during which a squirrel's metabolism slows down to one-third of its normal

> **Right** A Eurasian red squirrel (Sciurus vulgaris) – a species that occurs throughout Europe and northern Asia – drinking from a pond. Most species of squirrel get most of the water they require from their food; however, tree squirrels will visit watering spots quite frequently, especially during hot periods.

rate, and its heartbeat, body temperature, and respiratory rate plummet. When the temperature outside is below freezing, a hibernating alpine marmot's body temperature will drop to 4.5–7.5°C (40–45.5°F), and the animal may breathe only once or twice per minute. Every 2–4 weeks, hibernators awaken to defecate and urinate; by the time they emerge properly from hibernation in the spring, they will have lost more than half their prehibernation body weight. At that point they may feed on the bulbs and seeds that they stored away the previous fall. Such stores are essential when late spring storms keep the animals below ground.

Some ground-dwelling hibernators also become torpid during the summer (estivation) if the vegetation withers away due to heat and drought. In such circumstances it is much better to be safely out of sight doing nothing rather than busily scurrying around on the hot surface, especially when there is no food to be found there. When entering estivation, the animals conceal and insulate the mouth of their den with plugs of grass and sand.

SCALY-TAILED SQUIRRELS

The tropical and subtropical forests of the Old World are inhabited by an interesting array of gliding mammals. In tropical Africa this niche is filled by the scaly-tailed squirrels, members of the Anomaluridae family (7 species in 3 genera – see Appendix for full list), which apparently share only a distant evolutionary relationship with true squirrels.

With the exception of the Cameroon scaly-tail, which does not fly, the anomalures' most distinctive feature is a capelike membrane, stretched between their four limbs, that lets them glide from branch to branch in the depths of the African rain forest. The membrane is supported at the front by a rod of cartilage extending from the elbow or the wrist; at the rear it attaches to the ankles. Spread out in flight, it forms a rough square that permits the squirrels to soar over distances that can exceed 100m (330ft). Although this adaptation resembles the patagia of the flying squirrels and the Australian flying possums, these species too

are evidently not closely related; instead, they have developed along convergent lines to fill similar ecological niches in different parts of the world.

The anomalures are squirrel-like in form, with a relatively thin, short-furred tail. They take their name from an area of rough, overlapping scales near its base. The scales help the squirrels get a purchase on trees when they land from a glide, and also provide grip for climbing trunks.

The ecology and behavior of scaly-tailed squirrels are poorly known, because they live in areas that are rarely visited by outsiders and are nocturnal in their habits. Even so, such species as the Lord Derby's squirrels are relatively common, and do sometimes come into contact with humans.

The scant information available about anomalure reproduction indicates that females may have two litters of 1–3 young per year. At birth babies are large, well furred, and active, and their eyes are open. Female pygmy scaly tail squirrels apparently leave the colonies to bear their single young alone.

Except for Lord Derby's scaly-tailed flying squirrel, these interesting but poorly known rodents depend entirely on primary tropical forest for their existence. To the extent that African primary forests are being destroyed, they are endangered, for they require for their survival a mature forest habitat with hollow trees in which they can nest. For want of more detailed information on their condition, the IUCN currently lists most species as near threatened.   THF

⊙ **Above** A white-tailed antelope squirrel on a Joshua tree. This species, which is found in Baja California and New Mexico, has stable dominance hierarchies. The breeding season for this species is from February to June.

⊙ **Below** Cape ground squirrels sunning themselves in the Kalahari Gemsbok Park. The species lives in social groups in burrows that may have anything up to 100 openings. Colonies average about 5–10 members, but can number as many as 25–30 individuals.

Living in Clusters

SOCIAL BEHAVIOR

All squirrels raise young. Ground-dwelling hibernators reproduce very early in the spring, presumably to maximize the time their young have to grow and fatten before winter returns. Males typically emerge first and wait for the females, who mate soon after emergence. The exact timing of emergence and mating depends on the severity of the preceding winter, and it differs greatly between species, among populations of the same species at different altitudes and latitudes, and within the same population under different weather conditions. For example, Belding's ground squirrels (*Spermophilus beldingi*) living at 2,200m (7,200ft) emerge and mate 5–8 weeks before conspecifics living just 800m (2,600ft) higher and 15km (9mi) away; however, the timing of emergence at 3,000m (9,800ft) may itself vary by 5–6 weeks, depending on snow depth and spring weather.

Squirrels' mating systems are diverse. In some species, such as Belding's ground squirrels, males defend small mating territories which females visit when they are receptive. The males of other species such as thirteen-lined ground squirrels (*S. tridecemlineatus*) search for widely scattered females, and wait in line to mate with them. At the opposite extreme, some marmots mate while still submerged in their winter burrows. Sometimes, as in the case of Idaho ground squirrels (*S. brunneus*), males guard females closely before and after mating. And, in most marmots, many ground squirrels, and black-tailed prairie dogs, males vigorously defend territories surrounding the burrows of several females, who mate exclusively with the territory holder.

In tree squirrels and chipmunks, receptive females attract males using chemical signals and vocalizations, then lead the males on long, spectacular mating chases that may last from 4 to 10 hours. Often numerous males simultaneously chase the same female (3–5 in red squirrels, up to 10 in gray squirrels, and 9–17 in beautiful squirrels). By running away but remaining conspicuous (rather than hiding), receptive females force males to compete, enabling the females to compare their suitors' stamina and fighting abilities. In general, the dominant male stays closest to the female and accounts for 80–90 percent of copulations. After mating, he guards the female for up to an hour. In some species males also hinder further mating with physical barriers of coagulated sperm and seminal fluids. However, females occasionally solicit matings with males other than the alpha (up to 4 or more in beautiful squirrels), and females often remove copulatory plugs to facilitate

remating, as in the case of gray and fox squirrels (*Sciurus niger*). Multiple mating may enable females to hedge their bets against the possibility of the dominant male being infertile. Ground squirrel females also mate with multiple males after removing copulatory plugs. Genetic analyses of arctic (*S. parryii*), Belding's, and thirteen-lined ground squirrel litters indicate that mixed paternity is frequent, though the first male to mate with a female (usually the dominant male) sires the majority of each litter.

The young are gestated for 3–6 weeks and then suckled for slightly longer again, especially in tree and flying squirrels. Litter sizes range from 1 in the giant squirrel (*Ratufa macroura*) and giant flying squirrel (*Petaurista elegans*) to 2 in beautiful squirrels, 2–5 in most tree squirrels and marmots, 4–6 in prairie dogs and chipmunks, and 5–11 in ground squirrels. In many species, middle-aged females in good condition produce larger litters and heavier pups than younger or older females and than females in poor condition. Across species, litter sizes vary inversely with female body size and degrees of sociality: bigger, more social species have smaller litters.

Young squirrels are born naked, toothless, and helpless, with skin over their eyes. They develop rapidly. Young red squirrels begin to sprout hair at 10–13 days, and are fully furred by 3 weeks; lower incisors appear at 22 days, upper ones at 35 days; eyes open at 30 days; self-cleaning begins around 35 days. Juveniles take their first solid food and begin venturing from the nest at about 40 days. At 8–10 weeks juveniles are independent, although they remain near their mother

⬤ Above *Idaho ground squirrels. The male is on guard against rivals and stays close to the female with whom he has just mated. Since females of this species are widely dispersed and locating them is a time-consuming activity, to ensure he fathers some young each season, the male adopts the strategy of keeping competitors away rather than looking for more females. The females are only sexually receptive for a few hours, just after they emerge from hibernation.*

⬤ Below *The average litter size of the eastern gray squirrel is three. The young are born naked and blind and will not open their eyes until about four weeks old. Fur begins to appear about a fortnight after birth and the young will remain in the nest for a further 3–4 weeks thereafter.*

and may still share her nest. The ontogeny of young flying squirrels is similar.

Interestingly, young ground-dwelling squirrels develop much more rapidly: chipmunk and ground squirrel pups are independent by 3–4 weeks, and marmot pups by 6 weeks. These differences probably relate to each species' ecology. So, for ground dwellers it is dangerous to remain in the maternal nest too long because pups can be trapped by digging predators, whereas for young tree and flying squirrels it is risky to leave the nest too soon because climbing about in trees requires considerable balance and coordination.

In most tree squirrels, ground squirrels, and chipmunks, parental care is provided solely by the mother, but marmots, prairie dogs, and certain other ground squirrels live in family groups. The basic social unit is a cluster of female kin, with daughters spending their lives in the group they were born into (natal philopatry). Females display nepotism (kin-assisting behavior) by sharing and jointly defending territories, and giving warning calls when predators approach (see the Role of Kinship special feature page).

In some species, one or more males append themselves to these female clusters; they sire the next generation and, sometimes, help care for the young. Alpine marmots live in just such mixed-sex colonies, ranging in size from 2 or 3 to over 50 animals. One large colony may occupy an immense burrow system. Colony members scent mark their territory with substances secreted from cheek glands, and chase unrelated intruders, accompanied by tooth gnashing and calling. While the young marmots play, other members of the family stand guard. Juveniles hibernate and live together in the parents' burrow for the summer or two after they are born. Black-tailed prairie dogs also live in mixed-sex family groups, and these too are aggregated into immense colonies. Each female has her own burrow, but families cooperate to defend their shared territory, to nurse hungry pups, and to warn each other of danger.

Among tree squirrels, social behavior often varies between populations of the same species according to seasonal and spatial variation in seed and nut crops. Among red squirrels, when food availability is stable in time and space, site fidelity is high and home-range size is small (about 2–4ha/5–10 acres in females and 6–8ha/15–20 acres in males). Females defend territories (especially the core area around the nest) against other females, and dominant individuals will not move unless a territory with greater food abundance becomes available nearby. Males do not defend territories, but neighboring males that share foraging areas differ in social status: heavy, old males dominate the rest. Both sexes exclude dispersing juveniles and subadults from territories, and these young become "floaters," searching over large areas for a vacant home range. In high-quality woodlands in central Europe, red squirrel

NICHE SEPARATION IN TROPICAL TREE SQUIRRELS

For two or more species to live in the same habitat, their use of resources must be sufficiently different to avoid the competitive exclusion of one species by another. Such lifestyle differences as ground living or tree dwelling, daytime or nocturnal activity, and insectivory or frugivory are obvious types of ecological separation. Sometimes, however, squirrel species occurring naturally in the same habitat appear to utilize the same food resources. Do they actually occupy different niches?

This situation is illustrated by squirrels found in the lowland forests of West Malaysia. Of the 25 species found there, 11 are nocturnal and 14 diurnal. The latter can be divided into terrestrial, arboreal, and climbing categories, with different species making different use of the various forest strata. For example, the three-striped ground squirrel and long-nosed squirrel feed on the ground or around fallen trees, whereas the slender squirrel is most active on tree trunks at lower forest levels. Plantain and horse-tailed squirrels travel and feed mainly in the lower and middle forest levels, but nest in the upper canopy. The three largest species live highest in the canopy.

Malaysian squirrels show considerable divergence in food choices when food is abundant, but considerable overlap when it is scarce; then, all species rely heavily on bark and sap. Unlike African or temperate forest species of comparable size, none of the smaller species, except *Sundasciurus hippurus*, are seed specialists. The three-striped ground squirrel feeds on plant and insect material, and the long-nosed squirrel is an insectivore; diets of these species overlap with those of tree shrews more than with other arboreal squirrels. Horse-tailed squirrels feed mainly on bark and sap, and most beautiful squirrels feed opportunistically on a variety of plant materials and insects. The larger flying squirrels eat a higher proportion of leaves than the smaller species, which eat mainly fruit.

The three largest species of diurnal squirrels diverge less than the smaller species in the lower forest levels. All three are fruit eaters, but the pale giant squirrel (*Ratufa affinis*) primarily uses the middle canopy levels and prefers leaves. The black giant squirrel (*Ratufa bicolor*) and Prevost's squirrel (*Callosciurus prevostii*) are often seen feeding together at the same fruit trees, but the latter eats a smaller range of fruit, and the two species also have different foraging patterns. The giant squirrel is larger, giving it a competitive advantage, but it cannot move as far or as fast as the smaller Prevost's squirrel; the latter can afford to spend less time feeding each day and is able to travel farther to scattered food sources, consuming them before the giant squirrels arrive.　　　　KMacK

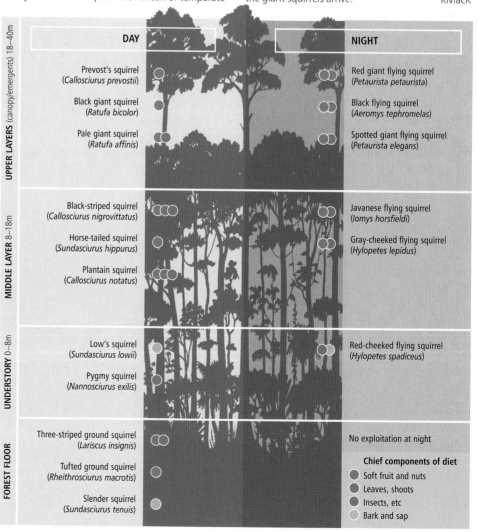

numbers vary little between years (numbering 0.7–2.2 squirrels per hectare, or 0.3–0.9 an acre). By contrast, in boreal coniferous forests in which pine and spruce seed abundance varies over time and between areas, both males and females frequently abandon territories when food becomes scarce. When the spruce-cone crop fails, adult males disperse after mating, and adult females after they wean their litter. Since reproductive rates and adult and juvenile survival are directly related to the food supply, red squirrel numbers within an area can vary between years by an order of magnitude of 0.03–0.3 squirrels per hectare (0.01–0.1 squirrels an acre).

Gray squirrel populations also fluctuate annually in size, and density varies with habitat (e.g., 2–10 squirrels a hectare, or 1–4 per acre). These differences can be traced to variations in acorn and hickory nut production, through their effects on the animals' reproductive rates, litter sizes, and, ultimately, survival. Population density is determined largely by the recruitment or otherwise of locally born young, but interactions between resident squirrels and juveniles drive dispersal behavior. Adult males aggressively chase juveniles of both sexes (but especially males), whereas females allow daughters to remain on their home range. For females, living together with relatives leads to communal nesting and other forms of amicable behavior.

Squirrels, Predators, and Man

CONSERVATION AND ENVIRONMENT

Squirrels are prey for many carnivores, including badgers, weasels, foxes, coyotes, bobcats, and (feral) cats on the ground, and hawks, eagles, falcons, and owls from the air. Sometimes squirrel populations are decimated by infectious diseases, particularly bubonic plague and tularemia.

Yet the greatest threat to squirrel populations worldwide is undoubtedly human population expansion, and the associated habitat fragmentation and loss due to the growth of cities, changes of land-use practices in rural areas (e.g., from rangeland to intensive agriculture), tree harvesting, fire suppression, and the introduction of non-native plants. Squirrels are hunted for pelts and meat and for sport, and both hunting and poisoning is still largely unregulated – if not actually encouraged – by governmental agencies that consider squirrels primarily as pests and carriers of disease. Little notice has been taken of the ecological and aesthetic losses associated with the dwindling size of many squirrel species, or of the benefits their activities bring. For example, the burrowing activities of ground-dwelling squirrels aerate the soil and bring nutrients to the surface, promoting plant growth, while the health of many forest ecosystems depends critically on tree squirrels' role as seed dispersers and controllers of insect outbreaks.   PWS/LW

⬆ Above *The northern striped palm squirrel is quite social and several may be observed in the same tree. Found in parts of Iran, India, Nepal, and Pakistan. Females can produce several litters per year.*

⬇ Below *In its woodland domain, the Malabar or Indian giant squirrel is very agile, rarely descending to the ground. However, along with all other species in the genus Ratufa, it is listed as vulnerable, largely as a result of extensive recent habitat loss.*

THE ROLE OF KINSHIP

The annual round in Belding's ground squirrels

BELDING'S GROUND SQUIRRELS ARE SOCIAL rodents inhabiting grasslands in the cold deserts of the far western United States (California, Nevada, Oregon, and Idaho). They are active above ground most of the day, going to subterranean burrows for refuge from predators and inclement weather and to spend the night. Primarily vegetarians, they forage on forbs and grasses, and are particularly fond of flower heads and seeds; but they will also eat birds' eggs, carrion, and, occasionally, each other's young.

A population of Belding's ground squirrels at Tioga Pass, high in the central Sierra Nevada of California (3,040m/9,945ft), has been studied for more than two decades. The animals are active only from May to October, hibernating for the rest of the year. Adult males emerge first each spring, often tunneling through several meters of accumulated snow to do so. Once the snow melts the females emerge, and the annual cycle of social and reproductive behavior starts – a complex and intriguing mix of competition and cooperation.

Females mate about a week after emergence. Although they are only receptive for a single afternoon, they take full advantage of this opportunity, typically mating with at least three (and sometimes up to eight) different males. Genetic analyses have revealed that about two-thirds of litters are fathered by more than one male, so that pups develop *in utero* among full- and half-brothers and sisters. Although a female's first mate is the predominant sire of her offspring, some litters are sired by as many as four different males.

In order to mate successfully, males defend small, exclusive territories. In the presence of receptive females, they threaten, chase, and fight with each other. Virtually every male sustains physical injuries during the mating period, some of them serious. The heaviest and most experienced males usually win such conflicts, and receptive females remain near those males. Dominant males copulate with multiple females (up to 13 in a season), but more than half of all males mate only once or not at all in any given year.

After mating, each female digs her own nest burrow in which she will rear her young. Females produce only one litter per season. Gestation lasts about 24 days, lactation 27 days, and the mean litter size is five pups. Females shoulder the entire parental role; indeed, some males do not even interact with the young, because by the time weaned juveniles begin to emerge above ground in July, they have already gone back into hibernation. Adult females hibernate early in the fall; and finally, when it starts snowing, the year's young begin their first long, risky winter underground.

The hibernation period, lasting 7–8 months, is a time of heavy mortality in which two-thirds of the juveniles and one-third of the adults perish. Most die because they deplete their stores of body fat and freeze to death; others are eaten by digging predators such as badgers and coyotes. Males live 2–3 years on average, whereas females typically live 3–4 years; the males apparently die younger due to infection from wounds incurred during fights over females or from the increased exposure to predators resulting from their higher levels of mobility, leading to more rapid aging (senescence). The sexes also differ markedly in their respective tendencies to leave the area where

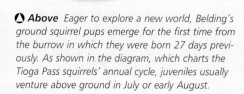

⬆ **Above** *Eager to explore a new world, Belding's ground squirrel pups emerge for the first time from the burrow in which they were born 27 days previously. As shown in the diagram, which charts the Tioga Pass squirrels' annual cycle, juveniles usually venture above ground in July or early August.*

◀ **Left** *A female ground squirrel gathers grass to line a nest. Typically, burrows are 5–8m (16–26ft) long, 30–60cm (12–24in) below ground, and have multiple surface openings. It can take more than 50 loads of dry grass to line a single nest.*

⚫ **Above** *Keeping watch for the benefit of the kin community in which she lives, a female squirrel notices the approach of a predator. She gives a repeated alarm cry, even at the risk of drawing the intruder's attention to herself.*

they were born. Juvenile males begin dispersing soon after they are weaned and never return home, whereas females seldom disperse, staying close to the natal burrow and interacting with maternal kin throughout their lives.

The ground squirrels' matrilocal population structure has set the stage for the evolution of nepotism (the giving of favors to family members) among females. This manifests itself in four main ways. First, close relatives (mothers and offspring and sisters) seldom attack or fight each other when establishing nests; females with living kin thus obtain residences with less expenditure of time and energy, and lower danger of injury, than those without kin. Second, close relatives share portions of their nesting territory and permit each other access to food and hiding places on these defended areas. Third, close kin help each other to evict distantly related and unrelated squirrels from each other's territories. Fourth, females give warning cries when predatory mammals approach.

At the sight of a badger, coyote, or weasel, some females stand erect and utter staccato alarm trills. A greater proportion of callers than non-callers are attacked and killed, so giving such calls

is dangerous. However, not all individuals take the same risks. The most frequent callers are old, lactating, resident females with living offspring or sisters nearby, whereas males and immigrant females with no relatives in the area call infrequently. Callers thus apparently behave altruistically – as if they were trading the risks of exposure to predators for the safety and survival of dependent kin.

The squirrels also vocalize when predatory hawks swoop at them, but these calls sound quite different: they are high-pitched whistles, each containing only a single note. Interestingly, these calls also apparently have a different function. Upon hearing a whistle, all the other squirrels scamper for cover, and their rapid flight inadvertently benefits the caller, both by creating pandemonium, which can confuse the predator's focus, and a scurrying group, in which there is numerical safety. So where the staccato alarm trill promotes the survival of offspring and other relatives, the single-note whistle call promotes self-preservation. The implication is that Belding's ground squirrels have different sounds for different degrees of danger.

Another important manifestation of nepotism is cooperative territory defense by related females.

During gestation and lactation, such females will exclude others from the area surrounding their nest burrow. Territoriality functions to protect the helpless pups from predation by other squirrels, for when territories are left unattended, even briefly, unrelated females or yearling males sometimes attempt to kill the young.

In the males' case, infanticide is motivated by hunger, since they typically eat their victims. Females seldom do so; in their case, the killing is triggered by the loss of their own litters to predators. After such a loss, they often leave the burrow that proved unsafe and move to a more secure site – and if there are young already present there, they will try to kill them, thereby reducing future competition for themselves and their daughters.

Females with close relatives as neighbors lose fewer offspring in this way than do females without neighboring kin, because groups detect marauders more quickly and expel them more rapidly; also, pups are defended by their mother's relatives even when she is temporarily away from home foraging. In sum, living in extended families is a strategy for survival and reproduction among female Belding's ground squirrels. **PWS**

THE ROOTS OF MARMOT SOCIALITY

The advantages of living in extended family groups

MARMOT SOCIALITY BEGINS WITH HIBERNATION. All 14 species of marmots live in the northern hemisphere, mainly in mountainous areas where food is unavailable during the winter. When the weather is fine, they lay down fat to keep them alive during a hibernation that may last 9 months. Some species, including the black-capped, long-tailed, and steppe marmots, live in environments so harsh that they mate, initiate gestation, and even give birth before emerging above ground.

When active, marmots use energy at a rate 8–15 times greater than during hibernation. To meet this heavy energy demand, they store copious amounts of body fat – comprising about 30 percent of body mass in the case of *Marmota bobak*, rising to 53 percent in *M. olympus*. Larger animals can store more fat and, relative to smaller animals, burn it more slowly. Marmots are the largest true hibernators, and the average adult body mass at the time of immergence ranges from 3.4kg (7.5lb) for *M. flaviventris*, the smallest species, to 7.1kg (15.7lb) for *M. olympus*, the largest. Even with the advantage of large body size, the demands on energy for reproduction, growth, activity, and hibernation are so great that individual females of at least 10 species, including *M. camtschatica*, *M. caudata*, and *M. menzbieri*, cannot accumulate sufficient resources for annual reproduction, which they skip, sometimes for two or more years.

To reach full size, marmots need to grow for a long time. Only one species, the woodchuck (*M. monax*), has an active season sufficiently long (at 5 months or more) to allow youngsters to mature and reproduce when 1 year old. Young woodchucks disperse and hibernate singly. The woodchuck is the only nonsocial species of marmot. Adult female woodchucks live alone, and males defend a home range that includes one or more females. Widespread forest–meadow-edge habitat enables the young to establish independence.

Marmots of most species live with their parents until they are 2 years old. The yellow-bellied marmot (*M. flaviventris*) requires one additional year. While male yellow-bellies disappear from the natal area to make their own way in the world, half of the females remain. Thus mother–daughter–sister assemblages of up to five are formed into matrilines. One male will enter an area containing more than one matriline and defend it.

Male Olympic (*M. olympus*) and hoary (*M. caligata*) marmots typically live with two females and their young. The females look after the young until they are 2 years old, and do not produce another litter during this time. Adolescent young disperse at age 2 and breed one year later. All members of the group hibernate together in a burrow.

The social lives of other marmot species involve living in extended family groups in which a dominant pair shares the home range with young of various ages that may stay at home beyond the age when they could be reproducing for themselves. This apparently paradoxical behavior would be explicable if the youngsters stood a chance of inheriting the parents' territory. In fact, however, if a member of the dominant pair were to die and a son or daughter inherited the territory, the new owner could end up mating with its own mother or father. To avoid this inbreeding, which could lead to physical inadequacies in the young, yearling yellow-bellied marmot males always disperse away from home, while half of the yearling females remain. The young females do not normally end up mating with their father, as he does not usually hold ownership of the territory long enough – for only 2.2 years on average. A female is in her third year of residency before she can breed, and her breeding career lasts an additional 2.95 years. Only about 17 percent of the males reach an age that makes reproduction likely. Male mortality is higher than that of females; at age 2, when many males are still in the dispersal stage, about 50 percent die, as opposed to only about 30 percent of the two-year-old females. Some level of inbreeding does occur in family groups, but there is no evidence of deleterious effects. In addition, relatedness, and hence inbreeding, is reduced when a male or female from some other family replaces the territorial dominant.

For yellow-bellied marmots, family living seems to bring all kinds of benefits. Animals in larger groups survive better and have more offspring. Group defense of resources ensures that they never go hungry, while the many extra pairs of eyes increase the chances of spotting a predator before it gets within striking distance. The rate of survival increases from about 0.6 for a single female to about 0.8 in groups of three or more. Net reproductive rate increases from 0.5 for a single female to 1.15 in groups of three.

Setting out to find a new home as a young marmot is a treacherous business, and waiting until 2 years or older increases the chances of success. Survival rates are significantly greater in *M. caudata* and *M. vancouverensis*, which disperse at age 3 or older, than in *M. flaviventris*, which disperses at 1 year old. However, staying at home with their parents results in reproductive suppression. In gray marmots (*M. baibacina*), most breeding is carried out by older females, and young females only get an opportunity when the population has been reduced. Reproductive suppression may be so pervasive that even when a dominant female alpine

⬥ Above A juvenile Olympic marmot approaches an adult marmot in grassland, Olympic National Park, Washington. Olympic marmots, the largest marmot species, are very tolerant and sociable and such face-to-face encounters are very common. The dispersal of young is a relatively slow process and appears to be determined by the young themselves rather than as a result of adult aggression driving them out.

marmot does not produce any young, as in the case of *M. marmota*, the subordinate females will still fail to reproduce.

Any animal that spends its entire life caring for others without having offspring of its own will die without passing its genes on to the next generation, and the genes responsible for causing such caring behavior will die with the childless carer. Thus such indiscriminate "caring genes" cannot evolve. Relatives, however, share genes, so those that cause individual animals to care for close kin and thus increase their likelihood of successfully rearing more young with more of those "relative-caring" genes can flourish. In biology, this principle is known as "kin selection." Individuals can afford to adopt an altruistic attitude toward family members because they share sufficient genes for their efforts not to be wasted. This is especially the case if having a family of one's own involves potentially dangerous activities, such as searching for a new home alone.

One reason why young marmots stay at home may be to help raise their siblings. Alpine marmots cuddle up to the young, preventing heat loss that would otherwise burn up fat reserves and hence cause weight loss, which in turn would reduce their chances of survival. When subordinate full siblings are present, juvenile mortality is about 5 percent, but this figure increases to about 22 percent when they are not present.

Even so, the benefits of kin selection hardly compensate fully for failing to produce young of one's own. A further reason why marmots stay at home when they could be establishing their own territories may be that there is simply nowhere for them to go. Habitats may become saturated, so that there are no territories available for a young family. In such circumstances they will stay at home, gaining experience by helping to raise their siblings and waiting for an opportunity to finally strike out on their own, richer in experience and still alive thanks to their parents' tolerance.   KBA

Springhare

S CATTERED THROUGH THE ARID LANDS OF East and South Africa are numerous flood plains and fossil lake beds. After the rainy season grass is superabundant here, but for much of the year it is too short and sparse for large grazers to forage efficiently. The result is an unused food supply or, to use the ecological term, an empty niche. To fill it requires an animal small enough to use the grass efficiently, yet large and mobile enough to travel to it from areas that can provide shelter from the weather and from predators. These are attributes of the springhare.

In spite of its adaptiveness, the springhare still faces formidable problems. In terms of its size (3–4kg/6–9lb) it is small enough to be killed by snakes, owls, and mongooses, and yet big enough to be attractive to large predators, including lions, leopards, wild dogs, and man. Many of the animal's specialized physical and behavioral features are adaptations, not just for an arid environment, but also for the efficient avoidance of predators.

Squirrel, Hare, or Kangaroo?
FORM AND FUNCTION

There is little evidence of the springhare's origins. Some people believe that its closest living relatives are the scaly-tailed flying squirrels of the genus *Anomalurus*. The springhare, except for the bushy tail, actually resembles a miniature kangaroo; its hindlegs are very long, and each foot has four toes, each equipped with a hooflike nail. Its most frequent and rapid type of movement is hopping on both feet. Its tail – slightly longer than its body – helps to maintain balance while hopping. The tail has a thick brush at the end that is of a darker coloration. The front legs, which are only about a quarter of the length of the hindlegs, have long, sharp claws that are curved for use in digging burrows and for grass corms. The head is rabbitlike, with large ears and eyes and a protruding nose; sight, hearing, and smell are well developed. When pursued by a predator, a springhare can leap 3–4m (10–13ft). If captured, it will try to bite the predator with its large incisors and to rake it with the sharp nails of its hindfeet.

Though springhares are herbivorous, they occasionally eat mineral-rich soils and accidentally ingest insects. They are very selective grazers, preferring green grass seeds and corms, which are high in protein and water. However, they also eat bulbs and roots. Springhares in the wild do not need to drink water, and have not been observed to drink water even during those brief periods when surface water is available.

Keeping Out of the Way of Predators
SOCIAL BEHAVIOR

Springhares are strictly nocturnal; shunning the midday sun means they avoid losing water in the arid regions they inhabit. While foraging, they are highly vulnerable to predators because they are completely exposed to detection. On nights with a full moon they appear to be particularly at risk, and venture only an average of 4m (13ft) to the feeding area; in contrast, on moonless nights they travel some 58m (190ft). When they are above ground springhares spend about 40 percent of their time in groups of 2–6 animals, presumably because a group is more efficient at detecting danger and avoiding predators.

Springhares spend the hours of daylight in burrows located in well-drained, sandy soils. Burrows lie about 80cm (31in) deep, have 2–11 entrances, and vary in length from 10–46m (33–151ft). Each burrow is occupied either by a single springhare or by a mother and an infant. Burrows provide considerable protection against the arid environment and also against predators. Some predators, such as snakes and mongooses, can enter burrows, however, so springhares often block entrances and passageways with soil after entering. When predators do enter, the tunnels and openings in the burrow system provide up to 10 escape routes. The absence of chambers and nests within the burrow suggests that springhares do not rest consistently in any one location – probably another precaution against predators.

In springhare populations the number of males equals the number of females. There is no breeding season, and about 76 percent of the adult females may be pregnant at any one time. Adult females undergo about three pregnancies per year, usually resulting in the birth of a single, large, well-developed infant; twins are born, but this is a rare occurrence.

Newborn springhares are well furred and are able to see and move almost immediately. However, they are confined to the burrow and are totally dependent on milk until they are half grown, at which time they can become completely active above ground and are quickly weaned. Immature springhares account for about 28 percent of all the individuals that are active above ground.

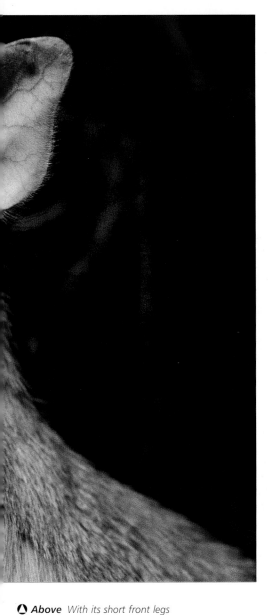

Although the reproductive rate of springhares is surprisingly low, there are two distinctive advantages to the animals' reproductive strategy. First, the time and energy available to the female for reproduction is funneled into a single infant, resulting apparently in low infant and juvenile mortality. When the juvenile springhare first emerges from its burrow, its feet are 97 percent, and its ears 93 percent, of their adult size: the young is almost as capable of coping with predators and other environmental hazards as an adult. Second, in having to provide care and nutrition for only one infant, the mother is subject to minimal stress.

A Tale of Declining Numbers
CONSERVATION AND ENVIRONMENT

Springhares are generally common where they occur, despite the fact that they are frequently hunted by man. In the best habitats there may be more than 10 springhares per hectare (4 per acre), and this can include areas where domestic stock have grazed the forage to a suitable height. However, when arid, ecologically sensitive areas are overgrazed by domestic stock, as occurs in the Kalahari Desert, springhare densities are lower.

Springhares are of considerable importance to man as a source of food and skins. In Botswana they are the most prominent wild animal in the human diet, and a single band of bushmen may kill more than 200 annually. They can be a significant pest to agriculture, feeding on a wide variety of crops including corn, sweet potatoes, and wheat. Partly as a result, there has been an upsurge in hunting activity that, together with habitat loss, is reckoned to have reduced springhare numbers by at least 20 percent in the 1990s alone. The animals are now classed as vulnerable by the IUCN.   TMB

FACTFILE

SPRINGHARE

Pedetes capensis, Pedetes surdaster

Springhare or springhass

Order: Rodentia

Family: Pedetidae (sole genus of family)

DISTRIBUTION Uganda, Kenya, Tanzania, Angola, Zimbabwe, Zambia, Botswana, Namibia, South Africa.

Equator

HABITAT Flood plains, fossil lake beds, savanna, other sparsely vegetated, short grass, arid and semiarid habitats on or near sandy soils.

SIZE Head-body length 36–43cm (14–17in); tail length 40–48cm (16–19in); ear length 7cm (3in); hind foot length 115cm (6in); weight 3–4kg (6–9lb). (Dimensions are similar for both female and male.)

COAT Upper parts, lower half of ears, basal half of tail yellow brown, cinnamon, or rufous brown; upper half of ears, distal half of tail, and whiskers black; underparts and insides of legs vary from white to light orange.

DIET Herbivorous, with a preference for protein-rich green grass, seeds, and rhizomes.

BREEDING Gestation about 77 days.

LONGEVITY Unknown in wild; more than 14 years in captivity.

CONSERVATION STATUS Vulnerable

⬤ **Above** *With its short front legs and hopping motion, the springhare resembles a miniature kangaroo. It is a vital resource for the Bushmen of southern Africa, who eat its meat, make its skin into garments, use its long tail sinew as thread, and even smoke its fecal pellets.*

◁ **Left** *Some typical postures of the springhare:* **1** *sitting down to groom;* **2** *hopping – when the springhare is in motion, it holds its tail (thought to be an aid to balance) either horizontally or curled up;* **3** *foraging on all fours;* **4** *standing on its hindlegs.*

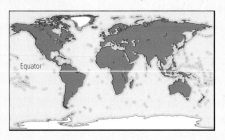

DISTRIBUTION Worldwide except for Antarctica.

Equator

SCIUROGNATHS (part only) Suborder Sciurognathi
1,480 species in 316 genera and 5 families

Mouselike Rodents

MORE THAN A QUARTER OF ALL SPECIES OF mammals can loosely be described as mouselike rodents. Although today they join the squirrels in the suborder Sciurognathi, they once occupied their own order, the Myomorpha. They are very diverse – so much so that they are difficult to describe in terms of a typical member. However, the brown rat and house mouse are fairly representative, both in size and overall appearance. The great majority are small, terrestrial, prolific, nocturnal seedeaters. The justification for believing them to comprise a natural group derived from a single ancestor is debatable but lies mainly in two features: the structure of the chewing muscles of the jaw and the structure of the molar teeth.

Most mouselike rodent species belong to the mouse family. The minority groups are the dormice, the jerboas and jumping mice, the pocket mice, and the pocket gophers. These represent early offshoots that have remained limited in species numbers and also somewhat specialized, the dormice being arboreal and (in temperate regions) hibernating, the jerboas adapted for the desert. The murids have undergone more recent and much more extensive changes (adaptive radiation) beginning in the Miocene epoch, i.e., within the last 24 million years. Some of the resultant groups are specialists, for example the voles and lemmings, which are adapted to feeding on grass and other tough but abundant vegetation. Yet many species have remained versatile generalists, feeding on seeds, buds, and sometimes insects, all more nutritious but less abundant than grass.

In ecological terms, most mouselike rodents may be classified as "r-strategists," that is, they are adapted for early and prolific reproduction rather than for long individual life spans ("k-strategists"). Although this applies in some degree to most rodents, the rats and mice show it more strongly and generally than, for example, their nearest relatives, the dormice and the jerboas.   GBC

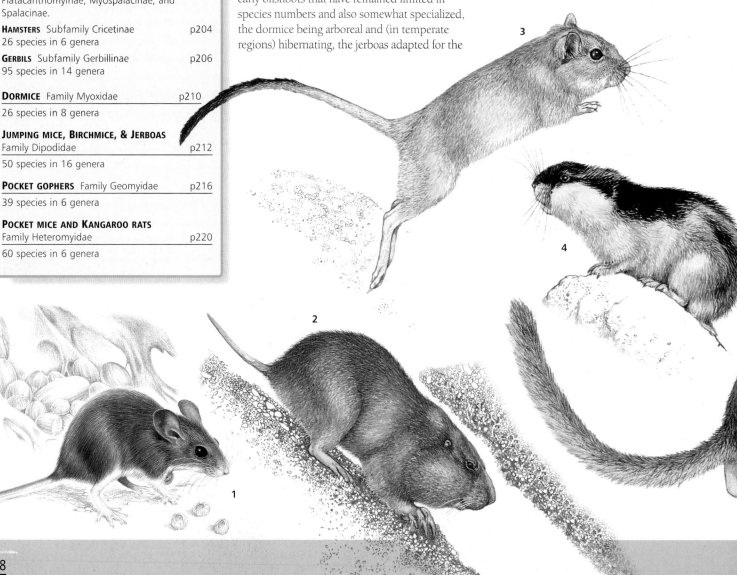

GREAT PROLIFERATORS

The greatest diversification of species in the entire evolution of mammals has occurred in the mouse family, which has over 1,000 living species. Its members are found around the world in almost every terrestrial habitat. Those that most closely resemble the common ancestor of the group are probably the common mice and rats found in forest habitats worldwide. These are versatile animals, predominantly seedeaters but capable of using their seedeating teeth to exploit many other foods, such as buds and insects.

From such an ancestor many more specialized groups have arisen, capable of exploiting more difficult habitats. Most gerbils (subfamily Gerbillinae) have remained seedeaters but have adapted to hot arid conditions in Africa and Central Asia. The hamsters (subfamily Cricetinae) have adapted to colder arid conditions by perfecting the arts of food storage and hibernation; the voles and lemmings (subfamily Arvicolinae) and the superficially similar African swamp rats (subfamily Murinae) have cracked the problem of feeding on tough and abrasive herbage, opening up fresh possibilities for expansion despite a restrictive diet.

✪ **Below** *Representative species of mouselike rodents (not to scale):*
1 *Wood mouse* (Apodemus sylvaticus) *with a store of nuts;* **2** *Plains pocket gopher* (Geomys bursarius) *descending its burrow;* **3** *Libyan jird* (Meriones libycus) *leaping;* **4** *Norway lemming* (Lemmus lemmus) *on the lookout;* **5** *Harvest mouse* (Micromys minutus) *entering its nest;* **6** *Woodrat* (genus Neotoma) *with a bone;* **7** *Merriam's kangaroo rat* (Dipodomys merriami);* **8** *Chocolate belted mouse – a domesticated variety of the house mouse* (Mus musculus) *– drinking.*

SKULLS AND DENTITION

Harvest mouse 1.6 cm

European hamster   Libyan jird

Harvest mouse   Norway lemming

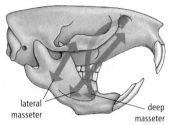
lateral masseter   deep masseter

Most mouselike rodents have only three cheek teeth in each row, but they vary greatly in both their capacity for growth and the complexity of the wearing surfaces. The most primitive condition is probably that found in the hamsters – low-crowned, with rounded cusps on the biting surface arranged in two longitudinal rows and no growth after their initial eruption. The rats and mice of the subfamily Murinae, typified by the harvest mouse, have developed a more complex arrangement of cusps, forming three rows, while retaining most of the other primitive characters. These two groups are often treated as separate families, the Cricetidae (so-called cricetine rodents) and Muridae (so-called murine rodents) respectively.

The gerbils have high-crowned but mostly rooted teeth, in which the original pattern of cusps is soon transformed by wear into a series of transverse ridges. The voles and lemmings take this adaptation to a tough, abrasive diet – in this case mainly grass – even further by having teeth with high crowns and complex shearing ridges of hard enamel that continue to grow and develop roots only late in life or, more commonly, not at all.

The other feature that principally distinguishes the mouselike rodents from other rodent groups is the structure of the jaw muscles. In the mouselike rodents, both the lateral (blue in the diagram LEFT) and deep (red) masseter muscles are thrust forward, providing a very effective gnawing action, with the deep masseter passing from the lower jaw through the orbit (eye socket) to the muzzle. Shown here is the skull of a muskrat.

RATS AND MICE AS PETS

Keeping mice as pets began in the Orient, probably first in China but also in Japan. Early records indicate that mouse breeding was flourishing in the 18th century; in 1787 a Japanese writer published a work on how to breed colored varieties, and domestication must have begun much earlier for such a pamphlet to have been produced. Sailors returning from the Far East probably took pet animals home with them, providing the stimulus for mouse breeding in the west.

Tame mice differ from wild ones in several respects. Apart from their docility, they are larger and have more prominent eyes, larger ears, and longer tails. All are bred to the same body conformation, implying that there are no breeds as such, only varieties.

Keeping rats as pets is a relatively recent activity. It probably began about 1850, possibly in England. The number of varieties is less than for mice, probably because of the shorter period of domesticity and smaller numbers.

5

7

6

8

New World Rats and Mice

THE INNOCENT PHRASE "NEW WORLD RATS
and mice" hides a plethora of 434 species in 86
genera, found in habitats ranging from the northern forests of Canada to the Americas' southernmost
tip. Their adaptations and habits are so diverse that
an entire volume could scarcely do them justice.

New World rats and mice are uniformly small: in
head–body length, even the largest living species
measure less than 30cm (12in). The length often
depends on how much tree-climbing their lifestyle
demands; the greater the need to balance in high
places, the longer the tail. Tails are usually almost
hairless but, as is to be expected in such a large
and diverse group, some species such as the aptly
named bushy-tailed wood rat buck the trend.
There are, however, very few exceptions to the
basic arrangement of teeth common to all highly-
evolved rodents, with three molars on each side
of the jaw separated by a distinct gap from a pair
of incisors, which grow continuously and have
enamel on their anterior surfaces, enabling a
sharp cutting edge to be maintained.

Natural selection has shaped the New World
rats and mice to a multitude of forms for different
habitats. Burrowing species have short necks,
short ears, short tails, and long claws, while those
living in water, such as the marsh rats, often have
webbed feet or, like the fish eaters, a fringe of hair
on the hindfeet that increases the surface area to
form a paddle. In forms even more developed for
aquatic life, the external ear is reduced in size or

even absent, as is the case with the Ecuadorian
fish-eating rat (*Anotomys leander*).

Above the generic level, the classification of
New World rats and mice is controversial. The
genera can be grouped into 15 tribes, and these in
turn can be thought of as belonging to six groups
(see table), though these groupings are of varying
validity; currently only one of the tribes has been
shown convincingly to be monophyletic.

FACTFILE

NEW WORLD RATS AND MICE

Order: Rodentia

Family: Muridae

Subfamily: Sigmodontinae (Hesperomyinae)

434 species in 86 genera and 15 tribes, combined
into 6 groups

HABITAT All terrestrial habitats (including northern forests,
tropical forest, and savanna) excluding permanently snow-
covered mountain peaks and extreme high Arctic.

SIZE Head–body length ranges from 5–8.1cm (2–3.2in)
in the Pygmy mouse to 16–28.7cm (6.3–11.3in) in the
South American giant water rat; tail length from 3.5–5.5cm
(1.4–2.2in) to 7.6–16cm (3–6.3in), and weight from 7g
(0.25oz) to 700g (1.5lb), both in the same two species.

COAT Most New World rat and mouse species have a
brown back and white belly, but some exhibit very attractive
coat colors; the Chinchilla mouse, for instance, has a strongly
contrasting combination of buff-to-gray back and white
belly. The color of the back often matches the surrounding
soil to provide camouflage against owls and other airborne
predators.

DISTRIBUTION N and S America and
adjacent offshore
islands

Equator

DIET Mostly plant material and invertebrates, though
some take small vertebrates including fish.

BREEDING Gestation 20–50 days

LONGEVITY Maximum 2 years in the wild; some species
live up to 6 years in captivity.

CONSERVATION STATUS 8 species are currently listed
as Critically Endangered, and a further 24 as Endangered,
including 6 species of wood rats (genus *Neotoma*) and 4
of the 5 species of fish-eating rats (*Neusticomys*).

See tribes table ▷

North American Rats and Mice

NEOTOMINE–PEROMYSCINE GROUP

The **white-footed mice and their allies** (tribe *Peromyscini*) are among the most extensively studied
murides. In particular, the white-footed mouse
itself (*Peromyscus leucopus*) has been used as a
model to investigate how males and females compete with members of their own sex to maximize
individual reproductive opportunities.

The mating systems of white-footed mice range
from polygyny to promiscuity. Males typically
occupy home ranges of approximately 500–
1,000sq m (600–1,200 sq yds), about twice the
size of those occupied by females. During the
breeding season, a male may spend most of his
time with one primary female, but his home range
often overlaps that of two or three others. Males
with larger home ranges have access to more
potential mates, thereby increasing mating opportunities. Males that mate with the most females
pass on the most genes, so males benefit by moving over large areas. At low densities, a male may
develop a wandering strategy; he may associate
with one primary female until she is pregnant,
then wander off to reside with neighboring, or
secondary, females while they are in estrus, before
returning eventually to his primary female.

Females usually mate with one male, but may
mate promiscuously with several, such that a
given litter may be sired by as many as three
males; however, the actual number of males a

⏺ **Below** *Restricted to salt marshes in
the San Francisco Bay area of California,
the salt-marsh harvest mouse is among
the rarer New World rodents; it was officially declared endangered by the US government in 1970. As an adaptation to its
salty habitat, it has become one of the
few mammals able to drink sea water.*

female mates with could be more. Mating with several males may increase the genetic diversity of the offspring or help ensure fertility, but it also functions to confuse the question of paternity. One reproductive strategy adopted by male white-footed mice is to kill offspring that they have not sired. Infanticide both removes the offspring of competitor males and provides a reproductive opportunity for the perpetrator. In white-footed mice, a female that loses her litter stops lactating and is ready to breed again within a few days, so by committing infanticide a male may be able to

mate sooner than if the young were permitted to suckle until weaning.

Males do not recognize their own offspring, but they do associate copulation with a given place and time, and will not kill pups within the area where they mated. Hence, a female who confuses paternity by mating with neighboring males also reduces the chances that these males will commit infanticide. Multimale mating appears to be a behavioral mechanism used by females as a counterstrategy to infanticide by males.

Female white-footed mice also commit infanticide, but as a mechanism to compete for breeding space. Dispersing females that do not have a territory of their own may attempt to kill the offspring of other females as a way of competing to take over their territories. At low densities when space is available for colonization, females space them-

selves out and are relatively nonaggressive, but when breeding space becomes limited, they aggressively defend their turf to ensure the survival of their offspring. At high densities, females defend breeding territories of approximately 300–500sq m (400–600sq yds).

Females provide most of the parental care in white-footed mice, but males do make some contributions. Males often nest with litters, retrieve wandering youngsters, provide warmth for the pups, and deter infanticide by intruding males. Pups are nursed for a period of 21–24 days and are then ready to leave the nest. Leaving involves risks, but if all the offspring were to remain at the natal site, unsustainable competition would ensue for resources and for mates.

An even greater cost to not dispersing is inbreeding, which is avoided in white-footed mice

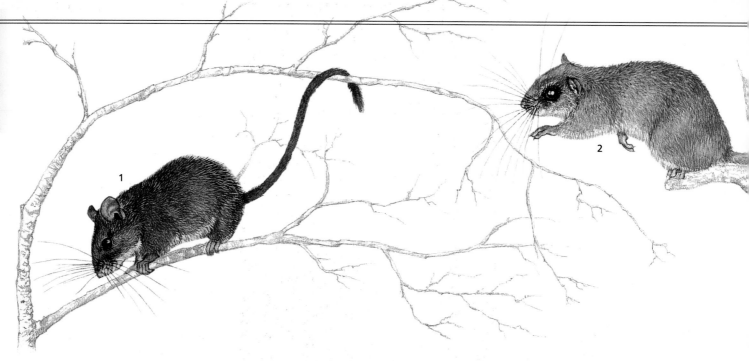

by sex-biased dispersal. At the time of weaning, young males will leave the natal site if their mothers are present in the territory, while young females depart if their fathers are present. In practice, mothers are almost always present, whereas fathers seldom are, so males disperse much more often than females. If for some reason offspring cannot disperse because all of the neighboring breeding sites are occupied, juveniles remain in their maternal site and form extended families for one to two generations. In these situations inbreeding is avoided by delaying the sexual maturation of older juveniles.

Sometimes mothers will share part of the natal site with their daughters. Mothers and daughters usually raise their young in separate nests, but at very high densities, when breeding space is limited, the two will occasionally raise them in the same nest, nursing each others' offspring indiscriminately. In such circumstances the same male may well be the father of both litters, although

other males may also have mated with either or both of the females.

During the winter nonbreeding season, white-footed mice often aggregate, with 5–8 individuals nesting communally and thereby sharing body heat. In some cases, these communal groups are relatives from the last litters of the breeding season, but occasionally they are unrelated. Food is typically stored during these inclement times. During food shortages, white-footed mice commonly enter daily torpor to conserve energy. Torpor periods vary in length, but typically last less than 12 hours.

White-footed mice are at risk from a variety of aerial and terrestrial predators. Their nocturnal lifestyle protects them from some of these, and they further increase their chances by being less active during full moons and by trying to avoid running on dry fall leaves that crunch underfoot, choosing instead to move over logs or else to forage among branches or shrubs. When active on a

◑ **Above** *Representative species from six tribes of New World rats and mice:* **1** *South American climbing rat (genus* Rhipidomys; *tribe Thomasomyini).* **2** *Central American vesper rat (genus* Nyctomys; *tribe Nyctomyini).* **3** *Central American climbing rat (genus* Tylomys; *tribe Tylomyini).* **4** *Pygmy mouse (genus* Baiomys; *tribe Baiomyini).* **5** *White-footed or deer mouse (genus* Peromyscus; *tribe Peromyscini).* **6** *Wood rat or pack rat, carrying a bone (genus* Neotoma; *tribe Neotomini).*

noisy substrate such as dry leaves, white-footed mice adjust their gait by placing their hindfeet in the path of their forefeet, thus halving the number of foot contacts with the ground. Unsurprisingly, they are most active on cloudy or rainy nights or when the ground is damp.

To have the option of selectively foraging or remaining inactive, the mice must have supplies of food readily on hand. Mice are seasonal hoarders and store nonperishable seeds for consumption in hot summer and cold winter periods. Acorns are a favorite crop that is harvested and stored in underground caches and hollow logs and trees. In fact, the abundance of the acorn crop determines to a large part survival rates and population size among white-footed mice. Following autumns of high mast production, which occur episodically once every 4–5 years, white-footed mice have high winter survival and may even breed all winter. Consequently, the following summers, mice are at their highest densities.

COLONIZING THE CONTINENTS

Rats and mice originated in North America from the same kind of primitive rodents as the hamsters of Europe and Asia and the pouched rats of Africa, their nearest Old World relatives today. These ancestors, the so-called cricetine rodents, first appeared in the Old World in the Oligocene era about 34 million years ago, and were found in North America by the mid-Oligocene some 5 million years later. They were adapted to living among the treetops in forest environments, but as land dried during the succeeding Miocene era (24–5 million years ago) some became more ground dwelling and developed into forms recognizable as those of modern New World rats and mice, the Sigmondontinae. In the course of their evolution they adapted to many habitats similar to those also occupied by Old World counterparts; for example, harvest mice of the genus *Reithrodontomys* reflect the Old World *Micromys*,

while *Peromyscus* wood mice have counterparts in the Murinae genus *Apodemus*.

The rats and mice of South America developed in a similar way. A land bridge formed between North and South America during the Pliocene era 5–1.8 million years ago, and several stocks of primitive North American rodents moved across it. Equipped for climbing and forest life, they underwent an extensive radiation in the new continent's spacious grasslands. Subsequently they adapted to many other habitats, some of which are not occupied by rodents in any other part of the world. The absence of insectivores and lagomorphs (rabbits and hares) from much of the continent allowed them room for maneuver, and some evolved to resemble shrews, moles, or even rabbits: today's South American species include mole mice, the shrew mouse, and the bunny rat.

When mice are abundant, they may selectively prey on larvae such as those of gypsy moths, reducing the numbers that defoliate oak and other deciduous trees in eastern North America. Less beneficially for humans, the mice can host a number of illnesses including Lyme disease and the deadly hantavirus that causes Hantaviral Pulmonary Syndrome.

Closely related to the white-footed mice is the volcano mouse of Mexico, a burrow user that is quite terrestrial in its habits. It occurs at elevations of 2,600–4,300m (8,530–14,100ft), and there is a birth peak in July and August.

The size of harvest mice varies considerably, from 6–14cm (2–5.7in) in head–body length and from 6.5–9.5cm (2.5–3.7in) in tail length. The North American species tend to be smaller than the Central American species, rarely weighing more than 15g (0.5oz). The western harvest mouse is typical of the species inhabiting the grassland areas of western North America, emerging at night to eat seeds or grain and living in a globular nest approximately 24cm (9in) off the ground in tall grass.

Grasshopper mice, which are about 10cm (4in) long with short tails, live in arid and semiarid areas, feeding on insects and small vertebrates. A pair will live together in a burrow during the breeding season, after which the weaned young disperse; it is not known whether the parents then stay together to raise further litters. These rodents are well-known for their high-pitched squeak (usually above 20kHz), which may be used to indicate tenancy of a patch as burrows are widely spaced.

The golden mouse (*Ochrotomys nuttalli*) is confined to the moderately wet, wooded habitats of the southeastern USA. The distinctive golden brown color of its back contrasts sharply with its white belly. This is an extremely arboreal form that builds a complex leafy nest in tangles of vines.

The **wood rats and their allies** (tribe Neotomini) are rat-sized rodents, varying in color from dark buff on the back to paler shades on the belly. In general they eat a wide range of foods, but some species are highly adapted for feeding on the green parts of plants; indeed, *Neotoma stephensi* feeds almost entirely on the foliage of juniper

◐ **Above** *Like a wolf howling, a northern grasshopper mouse (Onychomys leucogaster) raises its head to utter the shrill cry for which the species is famous. Humans can hear the calls, which can last for a second or more, from as much as 100m (330ft) away. The cries probably serve to warn approaching mice that a patch of land is already tenanted.*

173

trees. Some of the rats take refuge in crevices or cracks in rocky outcrops, while others construct burrows. All like to collect a mound of sticks and other detritus around the nest hole or crack.

The pads of spiny cacti may prove perfect tools for desert species; indeed, the name "pack rats" comes from this habit of transporting materials around their range. Each stick nest tends to be inhabited by a single adult individual, but they do make calls on neighboring nests; in particular, males visit receptive females.

The Magdalena rat occurs in an extremely restricted area of tropical deciduous forest in the states of Jalisco and Colima in western Mexico, where it may have an extended season of reproduction. This small, nocturnal wood rat is an excellent climber.

The diminutive wood rat (*Nelsonia neotomodon*) is found in the mountainous areas of central and western Mexico, where it is known to shelter in crevices of rock outcroppings at elevations exceeding 2,000m (6,500ft).

The home-range sizes of New World mice vary hugely. **pygmy mice** and **brown mice** (tribe Baiomyini) are the smallest New World rodents, and they possess correspondingly small home ranges that are often less than 900sq m (9,700sq ft) in extent; in comparison, a larger seedeating rodent such as *Peromyscus leucopus* has a home range of 1.2–2.8ha (2.9–6.9 acres). Pygmy mice are seed-eaters that inhabit a grass nest, usually under a stone or log. They may be monogamous while pairing and rearing their young. Brown mice are small, subtropical mice with a high-pitched call, probably used to demarcate territory. Males produce this call more frequently than females.

The **Central American climbing rats** (tribe Tylomyini) live in the forest canopy never far from water. They rarely descend from the trees or emerge before sundown, and eat mainly fruits, seeds, and nuts. The big-eared climbing rat, the smallest of these species, forages both in the trees and on the ground, and is unique among the New World rats in another crucial way: its young are born fully furred, are few in number, and are very well developed (precocial), opening their eyes after just 6 days. In contrast, most New World rats and mice produce hairless young whose eyes open only after 10–12 days. Furthermore, the big-eared climbing rat mother gestates her growing young for 6.5 weeks, while most New World rats and mice gestate for only 3 weeks.

Vesper Rats
NYCTOMYINE GROUP

The tribe Nyctomyini contains just two species of vesper rat. The Central American vesper rat is a specialized, nocturnal, arboreal fruit eater that builds nests in trees and has a long tail and large eyes. Its young are born furred with open eyes.

The Yucatan vesper rat, also highly arboreal, is a relict species in the Yucatan peninsula. It probably was once more broadly distributed under different climatic conditions, but became isolated during one of the drying cycles in the Pleistocene era 1.8 million–10,000 years ago.

Paramo and Rice Rats
THOMASOMYINE–ORYZOMYINE GROUP

The **Paramo rats** and their allies of the tribe Thomasomyini are distributed throughout South America. In the mountains of the Andes, many species are adapted for life at elevations exceeding 4,000m (13,000ft). Otherwise they are almost always confined to forests, or else live along rivers. All that is known about them is that they confine most of their activity to the hours of darkness, and that they eat fruit. Litters of two to four young have been recorded, but in general their reproductive potential is considered to be quite low.

The South American climbing mice are likewise adapted for life in trees. They are also nocturnal, and feed upon fruits, seeds, fungi, and insects. Their litter size is small: for the long-tailed climbing mouse (*Rhipidomys mastacalis*), two or three young per litter have been recorded.

▶ **Right** The vesper rat (Nyctomys sumichrasti) is a tree dweller in the rain forests of central America, where it builds nests rather like those of red squirrels. Individuals sometimes inadvertently find their way to the USA, concealed in bunches of imported bananas.

▼ **Below** The cotton mouse owes its name to its distribution in the cotton-growing states of the American south, where it can be found in woodland, swamps, and rocky areas. A nocturnal omnivore, it feeds on insects and other invertebrates as much as on plants.

ability of the genus; besides being active both by day and night, it is terrestrial and eats an array of different foods.

Members of the genus *Bolomys* are closely allied to *Akodon* but are more specialized for terrestrial existence. The tail, neck, and ears are shortened for burrowing, and the eyes are also reduced. Members of the genus *Microxus* are similar to *Bolomys* in appearance, but their eyes show yet further reduction in size.

Cane mice (tribe Zygodontomini) are widely distributed in South America, taking the place of *Akodon* at low elevations in grasslands and bushlands. The runways they construct can be visible to a human observer. Cane mice eat a considerable quantity of seeds and do not seem to be specialized for processing green plant food. In grassland habitats subject to seasonal fluctuations in rainfall, the cane mice may show vast oscillations in population density. In the llanos of Venezuela when the grass crop is exceptionally good, enabling them to harvest seeds and increase their production of young, they show population explosions. Densities can vary from a high of 15 per ha (6 per acre) to a low of less than 1 per ha (0.4 per acre), depending on the weather.

The **burrowing mice and their relatives** (tribe Oxymycterini) are closely allied to the South American field mice. These mice, like other rodents that feed on insects, have relatively small molar teeth and an elongated snout used for getting insects out of holes. Long claws help in digging for soil arthropods, larvae, and termites.

Feeding on insects and termites has its downside, however, which may be reflected in the limited number of offspring these groups are capable of producing. Termites are wrapped in protective armor in the form of an exoskeleton made of the protein chitin. The nutritional content of this substance is relatively low compared to other sources of protein or carbohydrate. Consequently, mammals relying on chitin for their daily supper tend to have low metabolic rates to compensate for the low energy return from their food. The relatively small litters of 2–3 young born to *Oxymycterus* species may be a constraint of their poor diet.

The shrew mouse, with its tiny eyes and ears hidden in its fur, represents an extreme adaptation for a tunneling way of life. It constructs a deep burrow under the litter of the forest floor. Its molar teeth are very reduced in size, a characteristic that indicates adaptation for a diet of insects.

Mole mice of the genera *Chelemys*, *Notiomys*, and *Geoxus* are widely distributed in Argentina and Chile and exhibit an extensive array of adaptations for exploiting both semiarid steppes and wet forests. Some species are adapted to higher-elevation forests, others to moderate elevations in central Argentina. They have extremely powerful claws, which may exceed 0.7cm (0.3in) in length. The name "mole mice" derives from their habit of spending most of their life underground.

Rice rats and their allies (tribe Oryzomini) are an assemblage with three tendencies: they may live in the trees, on the ground, or next to water. The species often replace each other up an altitudinal gradient. In northern Venezuela *Oryzomys albigularis* occurs above elevations of 1,000m (3,300ft), but at lower elevations it is replaced by *O. capito*. Alternatively, when two species occur in the same habitat, one may be more adapted to life in the trees than the other. *O. capito*, a terrestrial species, can happily share territory with *Oecomys bicolor*, a species adapted for climbing.

The South American water rat (one of the three species of *Nectomys*) is semiaquatic and the dominant aquatic rice rat over much of South America. *Oryzomys palustris*, found from northern Mexico up to southern Maryland, is also semiaquatic. This rat has catholic taste in food, though at certain times of year over 40 percent of its diet may consist of snails and crustaceans. It has an extended breeding season (from February to November) across much of its range, and so is able to produce four young every 30 days. As a consequence, it can become a serious agricultural pest.

The small bristly mice, which have a distinctive spiny coat, are nocturnal and eat seeds. *Neacomys tenuipes*, in northern South America, exhibits wide variations in population density.

Over evolutionary time rice rats have excelled at colonizing islands in the Caribbean and the Galápagos group, but many of the genus *Oryzomys* are currently threatened with extinction. The introduction of the domestic cat and murine rats and mice by humans has had a severe impact on the Galápagos population in particular.

South American Field and Burrowing Mice
AKODONTINE–OXYMYCTERINE GROUP

South American field mice (tribe Akodontini) are adapted for foraging on the ground, and many are also excellent burrowers.

The grass mice of the genus *Akodon* are another group that have excelled at occupying all the available vacancies in the ecosystems they inhabit. In general they are omnivorous, eating green vegetation, fruits, insects, and seeds, and most are adapted to moderate and high elevations. The northern grass mouse (*A. urichi*) typifies the adapt-

Fish-eating Rats and Mice

ICHTHYOMYINE GROUP

The **fish-eating** or **crab-eating rats and mice** (tribe Ichthyomyini) live the aquatic lives their name suggests, on or near higher-elevation freshwater streams, where they exploit small crustaceans, aquatic arthropods, and fish as their primary food sources. The rest of their biology remains a mystery.

Fish-eating rats of the genus *Ichthyomys* are among the most specialized of the genera. Their fur is short and thick, their eyes and ears are reduced in size, and their whiskers are stout. A fringe of hairs on the toes of the hindfeet aids in swimming, and the toes are partially webbed to propel a body about 33cm (9in) in length. They resemble large water shrews, or some of the fish-eating insectivores of West Africa and Madagascar.

Fish-eating rats of the genus *Neusticomys* are similar to *Ichthyomys*, and are distributed disjunctly in the mountain regions of Venezuela, Colombia, and Peru.

Water mice are smaller than the *Ichthyomys* species, rarely exceeding 19cm (7in) in head–body length. They occur in central American mountain streams, and are known to feed on snails, aquatic insects, and possibly fish.

Cotton and Marsh Rats and Allied Species

SIGMODONTINE–PHYLLOTINE–SCAPTEROMYINE GROUP

Cotton rats and marsh rats (tribe Sigmodontini) are united by a common feature, namely folded patterns of enamel on the molars that tend to approximate to an "S" shape when viewed from above. They exhibit a range of adaptations; the species referred to as marsh rats are adapted for a semiaquatic life, whereas the cotton rats are terrestrial. Both groups, however, feed predominantly on herbaceous vegetation.

The marsh rats, which are web footed, form the genus *Holochilus*. Two species are broadly distributed in South America, while another is limited to the chaco of Paraguay and northeastern Argentina. The underside of the tail has a fringe of hair that functions as a rudder when swimming. These rats build a grass nest that may exceed 40cm (15.7in) in diameter, locating it near water, sufficiently high up to avoid flooding. In the more southerly parts

of their range in temperate South America, breeding tends to be confined to the spring and summer (September–December).

Cotton rats are broadly distributed from the southern USA to northern South America. In line with their adaptations for terrestrial life, tail length is always considerably shorter than head–body length. Cotton rats are active both by day and night; they are omnivores, taking advantage of the fresh growth in herbs and grasses that follows after the onset of rains.

A striking feature of the hispid cotton rat is that its young are born fully furred; their eyes open within 36 hours of birth. This species has a very high reproductive capacity, and although it produces precocial young, the gestation period is only 27 days. Litter sizes are quite high, ranging from five to eight, with 7.6 as an average. The female is receptive after giving birth and only lactates for 10–15 days. Thus the turn-around time between litters is very brief; a female can produce a litter every month during the breeding season. In agricultural regions this prolific rat can quickly become a serious pest.

Leaf-eared mice and their allies (tribe Phyllotini) are typified by the genera *Phyllotis* and *Calomys*. *Calomys* (vesper mice) includes a variety of species distributed over most of South America. They feed primarily on plant material; arthropods form an insignificant portion of their diet. Most of the species making up the genus *Phyllotis* (the leaf-eared mice) occur at high altitudes. They are often active by day, and may bask in the sun. They feed primarily on seeds and herbaceous plant material.

◐ **Above** Large ears have given South America's leaf-eared mice their common name. This Darwin's leaf-eared mouse (Phyllotis darwini) is foraging 4,300m (14,000ft) up on the Andean altiplano.

◑ **Below** Representative New World rats and mice: **1** South American grass mouse (genus Akodon; tribe Akodontini) grooming its tail; **2** Cotton rat (genus Sigmodon; tribe Sigmodontini) attempting to move an egg; **3** Mole mouse (genus Chelemys; tribe Akodontini) in an underground burrow; **4** South American water rat (genus Nectomys; tribe Oryzomini) at the water's edge; **5** Fish-eating rat (genus Ichthyomys; tribe Ichthyomyini); **6** Swamp rat (Scapteromys tumidus; tribe Scapteromyini); **7** Leaf-eared mouse (genus Phyllotis; tribe Phyllotini).

The variations in form, and the way in which several species of different size occur in the same habitat, are reminiscent of the white-footed mice of the tribe Peromyscini.

The vegetarian, cathemeral bunny rat (*Reithrodon physodes*) is of moderate size and has thick fur adapted to the open-country plains of temperate Chile, Argentina, and Uruguay.

The highland gerbil mouse (*Eligmodontia puerulus*) is one of the few South American rodents specialized for semiarid habitats. Its hindfeet are long and slender, resulting in a peculiar, galloping gait in which the forelimbs simultaneously strike the ground, and then are driven upward by a powerful thrust from the hindlegs. The kidneys of this species are very efficient at recovering water; it can exist for considerable periods of time without drinking, being able to derive its water as a by-product of its own metabolism.

Patagonian chinchilla mice are distributed in wooded areas from central Argentina south to Cape Horn. The puna mouse is found only in the altiplano of Peru. This rodent is the most volelike in body form of any South American rodent. It is active both by day and night, and its diet is apparently confined to herbaceous vegetation. The Chilean rat is an inhabitant of humid temperate forests; this extremely arboreal species may be a link between the phyllotines and the oryzomyine rodents or rice rats. The Andean marsh rat occurs at high elevations near streams and appears to occupy a niche appropriate for a vole.

The **southern water rats and their allies** (tribe Scapteromyini) are adapted for burrowing in habitats by or near rivers. The swamp rat (*Scapteromys tumidus*), also known as the Argentinian water rat, is found near rivers, streams, and marshes. It has extremely long claws and can construct extensive burrow systems.

The giant South American water rats prefer moist habitats and have considerable burrowing ability. The woolly giant rat (*Kunsia tomentosus*) is one of the largest living New World rats, with a head–body length that may reach 28cm (11in) and a tail length of up to 16cm (6.3in).

Red-nosed rats are small burrowing forms allied to the larger genera. As with so many of the animals in this section, their biology and habits are poorly understood.   JFE/RB/JOW

New World Rat and Mouse Tribes

THE SHEER NUMBER OF NEW WORLD RAT and mouse species makes it convenient to have some grouping system through which to make sense of their diversity. Yet attempts to combine them at anything between subfamily and genus level (and, in some cases, even at that) have proved taxonomically controversial. The arrangement of groups and tribes suggested here is only provisional; readers should be aware that only one tribe has been convincingly shown to be monophyletic (arising from a single ancestor).

North American Neotomine–Peromyscine Group

White-footed Mice and their Allies
Tribe Peromyscini

10 genera: **White-footed** or **deer mice** (*Peromyscus*, 54 species), from N Canada (except high Arctic) S through Mexico to Panama. **Harvest mice** (*Reithrodontomys*, 19 species), from W Canada and USA S through Mexico to W Panama. **Crested-tailed deer mice** (*Habromys*, 4 species) from C Mexico S to El Salvador. **Florida mouse** (*Podomys floridanus*), Florida peninsula. **Volcano mouse** (*Neotomodon alstoni*), montane areas of C Mexico. **Grasshopper mice** (*Onychomys*, 3 species), SW Canada, NW USA S to north-central Mexico. **Michoacan deer mouse** (*Osgoodomys banderanus*), W C Mexico. **Isthmus rats** (*Isthmomys*, 2 species), Panama. **Thomas's giant deer mouse** (*Megadontomys thomasi*), C Mexico. **Golden mouse** (*Ochrotomys nuttalli*), SW USA.

Wood rats and their Allies
Tribe Neotomini

4 genera: **Wood rats** (*Neotoma*, 19 species), USA to C Mexico. **Allen's wood rat** (*Hodomys alleni*), W C Mexico. **Magdalena rat** (*Xenomys nelsoni*), W C Mexico. **Diminutive wood rat** (*Nelsonia neotomodon*), C Mexico.

Pygmy Mice and Brown Mice
Tribe Baiomyini

2 genera: **Pygmy mice** (*Baiomys*, 2 species), SW USA S to Nicaragua. **Brown mice** (*Scotinomys*, 2 species), Brazil, Bolivia, Argentina.

Central American Climbing Rats
Tribe Tylomyini

2 genera: **Central American climbing rats** (*Tylomys*, 7 species), S Mexico to W Columbia. **Big-eared climbing rat** (*Ototylomys phyllotis*), Yucatan peninsula of Mexico S to Costa Rica.

Nyctomyine Group

Vesper Rats   Tribe Nyctomyini

2 genera: **Central American vesper rat** (*Nyctomys sumichrasti*), S Mexico S to C Panama. **Yucatan vesper rat** (*Otonyctomys hatti*), Yucatan peninsula of Mexico and adjoining areas of Mexico and Guatemala.

Thomasomyine–Oryzomyine Group

Paramo Rats and their Relatives
Tribe Thomasomyini

8 genera: **Paramo rats** (*Thomasomys*, 25 species), Andean areas of high altitude from Colombia S to Bolivia. **Atlantic forest rats** (*Delomys*, 2 species), SE Brazil to adjacent areas of Argentina. **Wilfred's mice** (*Wilfredomys*, 2 species), SE Brazil to NW Argentina and Uruguay. **Ruschi's rat** (*Abrawayaomys ruschii*), SE Brazil. **South American climbing rats** (*Rhipidomys*, 14 species), low elevations from extreme E Panama S across northern S America to C Brazil. **Colombian forest mouse** (*Chilomys instans*), high elevations in Andes in W Venezuela S to Colombia and Ecuador. **Montane mice** (*Aepomys*, 2 species), high elevations in Andes in Venezuela, Colombia, Ecuador. **Rio de Janeiro rice rat** (*Phaenomys ferrugineus*), vicinity of Rio de Janeiro, Brazil.
Note: *Chilomys, Delomys, Wilfredomys, Phaenomys* have uncertain affinities.

Rice Rats and their Allies
Tribe Oryzomini

13 Genera: **Dusky rice rats** (*Melanomys*, 3 species), Central America S to Peru. **Montane dwarf rice rats** (*Microryzomys*, 2 species), mountains of Venezuela S to Bolivia. **Arboreal rice rats** (*Oecomys*, 12 species), lowland tropical forest of C. America to Brazil. **Pygmy rice rats** (*Oligoryzomys*, 15 species), S Mexico to S Brazil. **Rice water rats** (*Sigmodontomys*, 2 species), forests of Costa Rica to Ecuador. **Rice rats** (*Oryzomys*, 36 species), SE USA S through C America and N S America to Bolivia and C Brazil. **Galápagos rice rats** (*Nesoryzomys*, 5 species), Galápagos archipelago of Ecuador. **Spiny mouse** (*Scolomys*, 3 species), Ecuador, Peru. **False rice rats** (*Pseudoryzomys*, 2 species), Bolivia, E Brazil, N Argentina. **Bristly mice** (*Neacomys*, 3 species), E Panama across lowland S America to N Brazil. **South American water rats** (*Nectomys*, 3 species), lowland S America to NE Argentina. (*Amphinectomys savamis*), E Peru. **Brazilian arboreal mouse** (*Rhagomys rufescens*), SE Brazil.

▷ **Right** *Some desert-dwelling wood rats like this white-throated individual (Neotoma albigula) make elaborate dens that may be passed down through successive generations. The spiny materials used in their construction makes it difficult for enemies to enter them, though the rats themselves apparently come and go unscathed.*

Wied's Red-nosed Mouse
Tribe Wiedomyini

Wied's red-nosed mouse (*Wiedomys pyrrhorhinos*), E Brazil. Relationships uncertain.

Akodontine–Oxymycterine Group

South American Field Mice
Tribe Akodontini

11 genera: **South American field mice** (*Akodon*, 45 species), found in most of S America from W Colombia to Argentina. **Bolo mice** (*Bolomys*, 6 species), montane areas of SE Peru S to Paraguay and C Argentina. **Microxus** (3 species), montane areas of Colombia, Venezuela, Ecuador, Peru. **Altiplano mice** (*Chroeomys*, 2 species), Andes from Peru to N Argentina. **Mole mice** (*Chelemys*, 2 species), Andes on the Chile–Argentina boundary. **Long-clawed mole mouse** (*Geoxus valdivianus*), S Chile and adjacent Argentina. *Pearsonomys annectens*, montane-central Chile. **Cerrado mice** (*Thalpomys*, 2 species), cerrado of S Brazil. **Andean rat** (*Lenoxus apicalis*), SE Peru and W Bolivia. **Edwards's long-clawed mouse** (*Notiomys edwardsii*), Argentina and Chile. **Mount Roraima mouse** (*Podoxymys roraimae*), at junction of Brazil, Venezuela, Guyana.

Cane Mice
Tribe Zygodontomini

Cane mice (*Zygodontomys*, 3 species), Costa Rica and N S America. Relationships uncertain.

Burrowing Mice and their Relatives
Tribe Oxymycterini

4 genera: **Burrowing mice** (*Oxymycterus*, 12 species), SE Peru, W Bolivia E over much of Brazil and S to N Argentina. **Brazilian shrew mouse** (*Blarinomys breviceps*), E C Brazil. **Juscelin's mouse** (*Juscelinomys candango*), vicinity of Brasilia. *Brucepattersonius* (7 species), S C Brazil and adjacent northeastern Argentina and Uruguay.

Ichthyomyine Group

Fish-eating Rats and Mice
Tribe Ichthyomyini

5 genera: **Fish-eating** or **crab-eating rats** (*Ichthyomys*, 4 species), premontane habitats of Venezuela, Columbia, Ecuador, Peru. **Chibchan water mice** (*Chibchanomys*, 2 species), W Venezuela S in the Andes to Peru. **Ecuador fish-eating rat** (*Anotomys leander*), montane Ecuador. **Fish-eating rats** (*Neusticomys*, 4 species), Andes region of S Colombia and N Ecuador, N Venezuela, W Peru, and French Guyana. **Water mice** (*Rheomys*, 5 species), C Mexico S to Panama.

Sigmodontine–Phyllotine–Scapteromyine Group

Cotton Rats and Marsh Rats
Tribe Sigmodontini

3 genera: **Marsh rats** (*Holochilus*, 4 species), most of lowland S America. **Cotton rats** (*Sigmodon*, 10 species), S USA, Mexico, C America, NE S America as far S as NE Brazil. **Giant water rat** (*Lundomys molitor*), extreme S Brazil and adjacent areas of Uruguay.

Leaf-eared Mice and their Allies
Tribe Phyllotini

17 genera: **Leaf-eared mice** (*Graomys*, 3 species), Andes of Bolivia S to N Argentina and Paraguay. **Chaco mice** (*Andalgalomys*, 3 species), Paraguay and NE Argentina. **Garlepp's mouse** (*Galenomys garleppi*), high altitudes in S Peru, W Bolivia, N Chile. **Big-eared mice** (*Auliscomys*, 3 species), mountains of Bolivia, Peru, Chile, and Argentina. **Puna mouse** (*Punomys lemminus*), montane areas of S Peru. **Bunny rat** (*Reithrodon physodes*), steppe and grasslands of Chile, Argentina, Uruguay. **Vesper mice** (*Calomys*, 9 species), most of lowland S America.

Chinchilla mouse (*Chinchillula sahamae*), high elevations S Peru, W Bolivia, N Chile, Argentina. **Chilean rat** (*Irenomys tarsalis*), N Argentina, N Chile. **Andean mouse** (*Andinomys edax*), S Peru, N Chile. **Gerbil mice** (*Eligmodontia*, 4 species), S Peru, N Chile, Argentina. **Leaf-eared mice** (*Phyllotis*, 12 species), from NW Peru S to N Argentina and C Chile. **Patagonian chinchilla mice** (*Euneomys*, 4 species), temperate Chile and Argentina. **Andean swamp rat** (*Neotomys ebriosus*), Peru S to NW Argentina. **Bolivian big-eared mouse** (*Maresomys boliviensis*), N Argentina and adjacent Bolivia. **Southern big-eared mouse** (*Loxodontomys micropus*), W

Argentina. *Salinomys delicatus*, known from just 9 specimens found in NW Argentina.

Southern Water Rats and their Allies
Tribe Scapteromyini

3 genera: **Red-nosed rats** (*Bibimys*, 3 species), SE Brazil W to NW Argentina. **Argentinean water rat** (*Scapteromys tumidus*), SE Brazil, Paraguay, E Argentina. **Giant South American water rats** (*Kunsia*, 2 species), N Argentina, Bolivia, SE Brazil.

For full species list see Appendix ▷

DRIVEN TO THE EDGE

Endangered survivors of the Galápagos rat race

THE ISLANDS OF THE REMOTE GALÁPAGOS Archipelago once boasted a diverse assemblage of endemic rodent species – the Galápagos rice rats. This group consisted of 12 species of the Cricetine tribe Oryzomyini. The ancestral colonizers may hold the mammalian record for long-distance ocean crossing – a journey that would have involved at least two weeks of drifting on vegetation rafts over at least 960km (576mi) from the South American mainland. The ancestor (a Thomasomyine rodent) of the giant rice rat genus *Megaoryzomys* was the first to colonize, followed, about 3–3.5 million years ago, by the ancestor of *Nesoryzomys*. Finally, the yellowish rice rat *Oryzomys xanthaeolus* from coastal Peru is believed to have rafted over in recent historical times giving rise to the *Oryzomys* species of the Galápagos.

However, since the discovery of the archipelago in 1535, this enigmatic group has lost the most species of any vertebrate taxa in the Galápagos. Circumstantial evidence suggests that the introduction and spread of the black rat, *Rattus rattus*, played a leading role in the extinction of the Galápagos *Nesoryzomys* (five of eight) and *Oryzomys* (one of two) species. Both members of the giant rice rat genus *Megaoryzomys* are also extinct although the cause remains unclear. Today, just four species remain and three of these thrive on black-rat-free islands. The extermination of rice rats was rapid and nothing, except anatomical

information from fossil remains, is known of the biology and ecology of the extinct species or the process of their demise.

However, the rediscovery of the Santiago rice rat *Nesoryzomys swarthi* has since provided a unique opportunity to find out what may have happened to the extinct relatives of the surviving species. No trace of the Santiago rice rat had been found since its original collection in 1906 at Sullivan Bay on the northeast coast of Santiago and it was believed to be extinct. Then, in 1997, a population of this species was located on the north-central coast of Santiago, at a site known locally as La Bomba, where it appears to coexist with the exotic black rat. The two species intermix freely and there is no evidence of segregation in their activity patterns. This mix is particularly intriguing when the chronology and geography of the black rat invasion is considered. Genetic analyses suggest that black rats first landed ashore at James Bay, Santiago in the late 1600s. Subsequent, separate introductions to the archipelago, resulting in the current colonization of 33 islands coincided with the loss of *Nesoryzomys* and *Oryzomys* species wherever the black rat became established.

These historical patterns raise a question mark over the puzzling coexistence between the black

rat and the Santiago rice rat – can it continue? Are the two species at equilibrium or is the black rat slowly displacing the vulnerable rice rat? And, if black rats impact Santiago rice rats – how has endemic managed to live alongside invader for up to 400 years?

In fact, research has proved that the snapshot view of stable coexistence is a misleading one. An experiment that involved removing black rats revealed that they have a detrimental impact on the survival of rice rats. Intriguingly, this inter-specific competition appears to be sex mediated. Survival of rice rat females was enhanced where black rats had been removed, and in those places females, relative to males, showed some resistance to the usual seasonal decline in abundance. The plot thickened as behavioral investigations involving staged encounters, and field observations at artificial food patches, established that black rats are behaviorally dominant to rice rats and that the smaller the subordinate rice rat the greater the likelihood that a black rat will aggressively displace it. The rice rats are sexually dimorphic (the males are larger than the females) and so the smaller female rice rats are more vulnerable than are males to interference competition from black rats.

● **Above** *The area shaded in red denotes the part of Santiago island covered by vegetation. The remaining area is bare volcanic rock.*

◁ **Left** *The Opuntia cactus-scrub habitat at La Bomba is ideal for rice rats. However, increased rainfall would make the area more favorable to black rats and may deprive the Santiago rice rat of its last refuge on the island.*

rich resource, and the *Opuntia* may provide the rice rat with a vital resource refuge. Another factor that may facilitate coexistence at this site is the particularly arid local climate at La Bomba, caused by the rain-shadow effect of the island's topography. Interestingly, the rice rats are relatively drought resistant, while black rat numbers crash during dry years. It seems that three-and-a-half-million years of exposure to the harsh Galápagos environment has provided a competitive advantage as the rice rat has evolved a strategy of high survival and low reproduction that ensures population stability under conditions of ephemeral resource availability. Long lives may, in turn, have selected for the relatively large body size of *N. swarthi*. This species is the largest of the Galápagos *Nesoryzomys* and *Oryzomys* species, another definite advantage in the fight against the aggressive alien black rat.

The situation is, however, precarious. Perhaps the greatest threat to the future survival of the Santiago rice rat is climate change. It is predicted that the Galápagos islands will be subject to a greater frequency and intensity of El Niño events (prolonged warming of tropical currents in the east Pacific). This may have important negative implications for the rice rat. Stronger El Niño events are associated with heavier rainfall, which causes vegetation, and associated food supplies, to flourish. Conditions may then resemble those in the feeding experiment, enabling black rat populations to explode. Furthermore, *N. swarthi* could face a double onslaught as a strong El Niño can decimate *Opuntia* cactus populations. Climate change, therefore, could end the rat race for the Santiago rice rat.   DH/DWM

◐ **Above** *A rice rat chews on a cocoon. Competitive interference by black rats reduces the survival of smaller female rice rats, which may explain why the range of rice rats on the islands has contracted.*

◐ **Below** *The black rat has increased in abundance in all the islands where it has been introduced, displacing the native rice rats and resulting in the extinction of many rice rat species.*

The disadvantage of female rice rats was confirmed when food was provided for the rodents in two different patterns. In some plots the food was provided in discrete patches to simulate the clumped resource distribution typical of the Galápagos arid zone; elsewhere the same quantity of food was dispersed evenly. Black rats exhibited a rapid and dramatic response. Increased adult immigration and enhanced survival resulted in a seven-fold increase in black rat density on patchy plots. Black rats also increased where supplementary food was evenly dispersed, but only four-fold. Adult black rats monopolized the food patches. Benefits of priority access included weight gain, enhanced male survival, and an increase in the proportion of pregnant and lactating females on the patchy plots, indicating a reversal of the usual seasonal hiatus in breeding.

In contrast, rice rat abundance remained unaffected by the added food, but while their numbers were unchanged the rice rats did gain weight and juveniles grew faster on all the supplemented grids, showing that the black rats were unable to exclude them from the food. However, and especially where the food was provided in patches (where the densities of black rats grew highest), female rice rats suffered reduced survival relative to their male counterparts. Overall, it seems that the smaller female rice rats are losing the battle against the dominant black rat. This may explain the range contraction of the rice rats on Santiago as evidenced by their disappearance from Sullivan Bay. The question thus remains; how has the Santiago rice rat resisted extinction at just one tiny stretch of coast?

One striking feature of the habitat at La Bomba may provide a clue to coexistence – the high density of the cactus *Opuntia galapageia*. This endemic species is a potentially rich source of food, water, and nesting sites. Rice rats actively select habitat containing high shrub and cactus density; the density of rice rats is strongly correlated with cactus density and such habitat is unique to La Bomba – the last remaining stronghold of the Santiago rice rat. Coexistence is believed possible where the weaker competitor is the superior exploiter of a

Voles and Lemmings

POPULAR LEGEND TELLS OF LEGIONS OF lemmings periodically flinging themselves into rivers or the sea to drown en masse. However, there is no factual evidence of suicidal tendencies either in lemmings or in voles, their partners in the subfamily Microtinae, although it is true that lemmings embark from time to time on mass migrations, in the course of which thousands of individual animals may die.

Lemmings and voles have two features of particular interest. First, their populations expand and contract considerably, in line with cyclical patterns. This has made them the most studied subfamily of rodents (and the basis of much of our understanding about the population dynamics of small mammals). Second, though they neither hibernate like such larger mammals as ground squirrels nor can rely on a thick layer of fat like bears, many voles and lemmings live in habitats covered by snow for much of the year. They are able to survive thanks to their ability to tunnel beneath the snow, where they are insulated from extreme cold.

Thickset Bodies and Rounded Muzzles
FORM AND FUNCTION

Voles and lemmings are small, thickset rodents with a bluntly rounded muzzle, and a tail that is usually less than half the length of the body. Only small sections of their limbs are visible. Their eyes and ears tend to be small, and in lemmings the tail is usually very short. Coat colors vary not only between species but often within them. Lemmings' coats are especially adapted for cold temperatures: they are long, thick, and waterproof. The collared lemming is the only rodent that molts to a completely white coat in winter.

Some species display special anatomical features. The claw on the first digit of the Norway

○ **Above left** *A field vole eating. Although males are quite territorial, the females tend to be less so, with considerable overlapping of territories. Young males will be forced to disperse by older resident males.*

FACTFILE

VOLES AND LEMMINGS

Order: Rodentia

Family: Muridae

Subfamily: Arvicolinae (Microtinae)

143 species in 26 genera. Species include: Collared lemming (*Dicrostonyx torquatus*); Norway lemming (*Lemmus lemmus*); Northern mole-vole (*Ellobius talpinus*); Bank vole (*Clethrionomys glareolus*); and Muskrat (*Ondatra zibethicus*).

DISTRIBUTION N and C America, Eurasia from Arctic S to Himalayas; small relict population in N Africa.

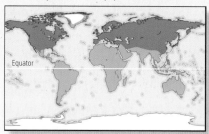

Equator

HABITAT Burrowing species are common in tundra, temperate grasslands, steppe, scrub, open forest, rocks; 5 species are aquatic or arboreal.

SIZE In most species, head–body length 10–11cm (4–4.5in), tail length 3–4cm (1.2–1.6in), weight 17–20g (0.6–0.7oz).

COAT Thickly furred in various shades of gray and brown.

DIET Herbivorous; mostly the green parts of plants, though some species eat bulbs, roots, and mosses. Muskrats occasionally eat mussels and snails.

BREEDING Gestation 16–28 days. Litter size varies between species from 1–12; at least 2 litters, and sometimes 4 or more, are produced each year.

LONGEVITY 0.5–2 years

CONSERVATION STATUS 3 species are listed as Critically Endangered and 3 more as Endangered. The Bavarian vole (*Microtus bavaricus*) is now considered Extinct.

See tribes table ▷

◁ **Left** *Muskrats are well adapted to life around water. They have partial webbing on their back feet and can use their tail, which is slightly flattened, as a rudder. Consequently, muskrats occur in a wide variety of aquatic environments.*

lemming is flattened and enlarged for digging in the snow, while each fall the collared lemming grows an extra big claw on the third and fourth digits of its forelegs, shedding the claws in spring. Muskrats have a long tail and small webbing between toes that assist in swimming. The mole lemmings, adapted for digging, have a more cylindrical shape than other species, and their incisors, used for excavating, protrude extremely.

Adult males and females are usually the same color and approximately the same size, though the shade of juveniles' coats may differ from the adults'. Although most adult voles weigh less than 100g (3.5oz), the muskrat grows to over 1,400g (50oz). The size of the brain, in relation to body size, is lower than average for mammals.

Smell and hearing are important, well-developed senses, able to respond, respectively, to the secretions that are used to mark territory boundaries, to indicate social status, and perhaps to aid species recognition, and to vocalizations (each species has a characteristic range of calls). Calls can be used to give the alarm, to threaten, or as part of courtship and mating. Brandt's voles, which live in large colonies, sit up on the surface and whistle like prairie dogs.

Tundra, Grassland, Forest
DISTRIBUTION PATTERNS

Microtines, especially lemmings, are widely distributed in the tundra regions of the northern hemisphere, where they are the dominant small mammal species. Their presence there is the result of recolonization since the retreat of the last glaciers. Voles are also found in temperate grasslands and in the forests of North America and Eurasia.

Because the Pleistocene era (1.8 million–10,000 years ago) has yielded a rich fossil record of microtine skulls, much of the taxonomy of this subfamily is based on the structure and kind of teeth, which are also used to distinguish the microtines from other rodents. All microtine teeth have flattened crowns, and prisms of dentine surrounded by enamel. There are twelve molars (three on each side of the upper and lower jaws) and four incisors. Species are differentiated by the particular pattern of the enamel of the molars. Dentition has not proved sufficient for solving all taxonomic questions, and some difficulties remain both in delimiting species and defining genera. It is often possible to distinguish the species of live animals from the general body size, coat color, and length of tail. The subdivision of species into many subspecies (not listed here) reflects geographic variation in coat color and size in widely distributed species. *Microtus*, the largest genus (accounting for nearly 50 percent of the subfamily), is a heterogeneous collection of species.

Many species have widely overlapping ranges. For example, there are six species – two lemmings and four voles – in the southern tundra and forest of the Yamal Peninsula in Russia. Each can be differentiated by its habitat preference or diet. The ranges of Siberian lemmings and collared lemmings overlap extensively, but collared lemmings prefer upland heaths and higher and drier tundra, whereas Siberian lemmings are found in the wetter grass-sedge lowlands. Competition between closely related microtines has been suggested but rarely demonstrated by field experiments.

Busy Grazers and Diggers
DIET

Voles and lemmings are herbivores that usually eat the green parts of plants, though some species prefer bulbs, roots, mosses, or even pine needles. The muskrat occasionally eats mussels and snails. Diet usually changes with the seasons and varies according to location, reflecting local abundances of plants. Species living in moist habitats, such as lemmings and the tundra vole, prefer grasses and sedges, while those inhabiting drier habitats, such as collared lemmings, prefer herbs. But animals select their food to some extent; diets do not just simply mimic vegetation composition.

Voles and lemmings can be found foraging both by day and night, although dawn and dusk might be preferred. They obtain food by grazing or digging for roots; grass is often clipped and placed in piles in their runways. Some cache food in summer and fall, but in winter, when the snow cover insulates the animals that nest underneath the surface, food is obtained by burrowing; animals also feed on plants at ground surface. The northern red-backed vole feeds on (among other items) berries, and in summer has to compete for them with birds; in winter, when the bushes are covered with snow, this vole can burrow to reach the berries, so only during the spring thaw is the animal critically short of food. In winter the sagebrush vole uses the height of snow packs to forage on shrubs it normally cannot reach.

Most microtines – for example the Florida water rat, the steppe lemming, and all species of *Microtus* – have continuously growing molars, and can chew more (and more abrasive) grasses than species with rooted molars. In tundra and grasslands, voles and lemmings help the recycling of nutrients by eliminating waste products and clipping and then storing food below ground.

A Short, Hectic Life

SOCIAL BEHAVIOR

The life span of microtines is short. They reach sexual maturity at an early age and are very fertile. Mortality rates, however, are high: during the breeding season, only 70 percent of the animals alive one month will still be alive the next. The age of sexual maturity can vary considerably. The females of some species may become mature only 2–3 weeks after birth. Males take longer, usually 6–8 weeks. The common vole has an extraordinarily fast development. Females have been observed coming into heat while still suckling, and may be only 5 weeks old at the birth of their first litter. In species that breed only during the summer, young born early will probably breed that summer, while later litters may not become sexually mature until the following spring.

The length of the breeding season is highly variable, but lemmings can breed in both summer and winter. Winter breeding is less common in voles, which tend to breed from late spring to fall. Voles in Mediterranean climates, on the other hand, breed in winter and spring, during the wet season, but not in summer. Within a species, the breeding season often varies widely in different years or in different parts of the range. The muskrat breeds all year in the southern part of its range but only in summer elsewhere. Some meadow vole species breed in winter during the phase of population increase, but not when numbers are falling.

In many species, such as the montane, field, and Mexican voles, the presence of a male will induce ovulation in a female. (Physical contact is unnecessary; ovulation is probably induced by social odors produced by the male.) The normal gestation time is 21 days, but it may be less if conditions are good, falling to just 17 days in a bank vole with optimal nutrition. The gestation period may also lengthen – up to 24 days in the bank vole's case – if a female has mated within a few hours of giving birth and is therefore pregnant while lactating.

The reproductive cycle is liable to be disrupted. A mated female can sometimes fail to become pregnant, or will abort spontaneously if exposed to a strange male (both have been observed in field, meadow, and prairie voles in the laboratory; however, attempts to show it in the field have so far failed). Males are under pressure to sire as many litters as possible in the short breeding season. Collared lemming females have been known to kill nestlings of other females.

WATER VOLES IN BRITAIN

The changing fortunes of British water vole populations through the 20th century have only recently come to light following the pioneering national surveys carried out by the Vincent Wildlife Trust in 1989–90 and 1996–98. These surveys confirmed that the species had been getting scarcer along waterways since the 1930s due to habitat loss and land-use change associated with the intensification of agriculture. In recent years this decline has accelerated due to predation by feral American mink (established as escapees from fur farms).

The decline has now developed into a serious population crash with a further loss of the remaining population by 88 percent in only seven years. The 1996–98 survey reports that the population loss has been most severe in the north and southwest of England, reaching 97 percent of the population in Yorkshire. This makes the water vole Britain's most rapidly declining mammal, and as such it has been given legal protection under the Wildlife and Countryside Act 1981.

The threats to water voles are complex but involve habitat loss and degradation (due to river engineering or agricultural practice), population isolation and fragmentation, fluctuations in water levels, pollution, predation (especially by mink), or indirect persecution through rat control operations.

Saving the water vole is going to take some complex habitat manipulation, and cooperation between many sectors of British society. Habitat restoration creates dispersal corridors for isolated populations to reach each other between restored backwaters, ponds, wet grassland, marshes, reedbeds, and a network of ditches. Riverbanks are central to water vole activity and the possibility of a coordinated scheme to connect whole lengths of river along their banks by the withdrawal of farming would be invaluable. When banks are left free from cultivation, wild plants perfect for water vole food and cover often soon colonize, their seeds carried along the river by water or wind. Where this doesn't happen, planting can speed things considerably. Highly layered bankside vegetation with tall grasses and stands of flowers such as willowherb, loosestrife, and meadowsweet, fringed with thick stands of rushes, sedges, or reed are the best habitat. In winter, the roots and bark of woody species such as willows and sallows are an important part of the water vole's diet, together with rhizomes, bulbs, and roots of herbaceous species. Already underway are projects on the River Cole at Coleshill, Wiltshire, in which 2km of degraded river has been restored to meanders, and on the River Skerne at Darlington, County Durham, where backwater pools are creating small-scale water vole havens.   RS

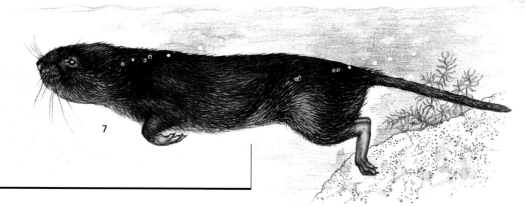

The young are born small, blind, and helpless; they usually weigh 1–10g (0.04–0.35oz), and the whole litter amounts to 22–28 percent of the adult female's weight. They are born in a nest, often below ground, which is made of dried grass, lichen, or other vegetation. Litter sizes and the number of litters per year vary enormously between species, in part reflecting the length of the breeding season and the availability of resources. The mean litter size is two for the red tree vole but over eight in the larger taiga vole, though any given litter may vary from one to over 12 in the more fecund species. At least two litters – but often four or more – are produced per year.

Parental care is the work of the females, who are strongly protective of their young. If any wander from the nest, they are located by their squeaks and will be retrieved by the female. Males do not appear to participate in parental care, except in the monogamous prairie vole and pine vole, whose males retrieve and groom the young, and help keep runways and burrows clean.

While the young are living in the nest, they learn to recognize the scent and behavioral cues of their species. So, if young brown lemmings are fostered (artificially) with collared lemmings, they will be more aggressive towards their own species as adults than to their fostered species. The length of lactation varies but usually lasts about 3 weeks, and in some species is terminated by the female abandoning the nest.

The two sexes and different species have different social behaviors, and these may change radically between seasons. The key to understanding both the social relationships and the spatial organization of voles and lemmings is the spacing behavior of males and females. In the breeding season males and females form territories delimited by scent marks. Males compete for access to receptive females, while females compete for

⬤ **Above** *Representative species of voles and lemmings:* **1** *Muskrat (Ondatra zibethicus) sitting on its house of branches and twigs;* **2** *Red tree vole (Arborimus longicaudus), a highly specialized, tree-living vole;* **3** *Norway lemming (Lemmus lemmus);* **4** *Southern (or Afghan) mole vole (Ellobius fuscocapillus);* **5** *Taiga vole (Microtus xanthognathus);* **6a** *Collared (or arctic) lemming (Dicrostonyx torquatus) in its winter coat, with double foreclaws;* **6b** *Collared lemming in its summer coat, with single foreclaws;* **7** *European water vole (Arvicola terrestris);* **8** *Meadow vole (Microtus pennsylvanicus), drumming an alarm signal with its hindfoot.*

space that contains high-quality food and serves to protect their litters from infanticide. Male and female territories may be separate (as in the montane vole and the collared lemming) or else overlap (as in the European water and meadow voles); alternatively, several females may live in overlapping ranges within a single male territory (for example, in taiga and field voles). Males form hierarchies of dominance – subordinates may be excluded from breeding – and may act to exclude strange males from an area. The common, sagebrush, and Brandt's voles live in colonies. The animals build complicated burrows.

Although in most species males are promiscuous, a few are monogamous. In the prairie vole the males and females form pair-bonds, while the montane vole appears to be monogamous at low density as a result of the spacing of males and females, but with no pair-bond. At high density this species is polygynous (males mate with several females). Monogamy is favored when both adults are needed to defend the breeding territory from intruders bent on infanticide.

The social system may vary seasonally. In the taiga vole, the young animals disperse and their territories break down late in summer. Groups of five to ten unrelated animals then build a communal nest, which is occupied throughout the winter by both sexes. Communal nesting or local aggregations of individuals are also observed in the meadow, gray, and northern red-backed voles. Huddling together reduces energy requirements.

Dispersal (the movement from place of birth to place of breeding) is an important aspect of microtine behavior, and has been the subject of considerable research. It plays an important role in regulating population size, and allows the animals to exploit efficiently the highly seasonal, patchy nature of their habitat: strategies change according

Vole and Lemming Tribes

Lemmings Tribe Lemmini

17 species in 4 genera. N America and Eurasia, inhabiting tundra, taiga, and spruce woods. Skull broad and massive, tail very short, hair long; 8 mammae.
Collared lemmings (*Dicrostonyx*, 11 species).
Brown lemmings (*Lemmus*, 3 species). Includes Norway lemming (*L. lemmus*).
Bog lemmings (*Synaptomys*, 2 species).
Wood lemming (1 species) *Myopus schisticolor*.

Mole voles Tribe Ellobiini

5 species in 1 genus. C Asia, inhabiting steppe. Form is modified for a subterranean life; coat color varies from ocher sand to browns and blacks; tail short; no ears; incisors protrude forward. Species include Northern mole vole (*Ellobius talpinus*), Southern mole vole (*E. fuscocapillus*).

Voles Tribe Microtini

121 species in 21 genera. N America, Europe, Asia, the Arctic.
Meadow voles (*Microtus*, 61 species). N America, Eurasia, N Africa. Coat and size highly variable, molars rootless, skull weak; 4–8 mammae; burrows on surface and underground. Includes Common vole (*M. arvalis*), Field vole (*M. agrestis*), American pine vole (*M. pinetorum*).
Mountain voles (*Alticola*, 12 species). C Asia. Includes Large-eared vole (*A. macrotis*).
South Asian voles (*Eothenomys*, 9 species) E Asia, includes Père David's vole (*E. melanogaster*).
Red-backed voles (*Clethrionomys*, 7 species). Japan, N Eurasia, N America, inhabiting forest, scrub, and tundra. Back usually red, cheek teeth rooted in adults, skull weak; 8 mammae. Includes Bank vole (*C. glareolus*).
Musser's voles (*Volemys*, 4 species). China.
Tree voles (*Arborimus*, 3 species). W USA.
Brandt's voles (*Lasiopodomys*, 3 species). C Asia.
Snow voles (*Chionmys*, 3 species). S Europe, SW Asia, Turkey.
Japanese voles (*Phaulomys*, 2 species). Japan.
Kashmir voles (*Hyperacrius*, 2 species) Kashmir and the Punjab. Includes True's vole (*H. fertilis*).
Water voles (*Arvicola*, 2 species). N America, N Eurasia. Includes European water vole (*A. terrestris*).
Heather voles (*Phenacomys*, 2 species) W USA and Canada. Includes Red-tree vole (*P. longicaudus*).
Afghan voles (*Blanfordimys*, 2 species). C Asia.
Martino's snow vole (1 species), *Dinaromys bogdanovi*. Yugoslavia.
Duke of Bedford's vole (1 species), *Proedromys bedfordi*. China.
Sagebrush vole (1 species), *Lemmiscus curtatus*. W USA.
Muskrat (1 species), *Ondatra zibethicus*. N America.
Round-tailed muskrat (1 species), *Neofiber alleni*. Florida.
Long-clawed mole vole (1 species), *Prometheomys schaposchnikowi*. Caucasus, Russia.
Steppe lemming (1 species), *Lagurus lagurus*. C Asia .
Yellow steppe lemmings (*Eolagurus*, 2 species). E C Asia.

For full species list see Appendix ▷

LEMMING MIGRATIONS

According to Scandinavian legend, every few years regimented masses of lemmings descend from birch woods and invade upland pastures, where they destroy crops, foul wells, and infect the air with their decomposing bodies. Driven by an irresistible compulsion they press on, not pausing at obstacles, until they end their suicidal march in the sea.

The truth is in fact very different. The life cycle of Norway lemmings is not exceptional. The animals are active throughout the year. During the winter, they tunnel and build nests under the snow, where they can breed in safety from predators except for an occasional attack by a weasel or ermine. With the coming of the spring thaw, the burrows risk collapse, so the animals are forced to move to higher ground, or lower to parts of the birch–willow forest, where they spend the summer months in the safety of cavities in the ground or in burrows dug through shallow layers of soil and vegetation. In the fall, with the freezing of the ground and withering of the sedges, there is a seasonal movement back to sheltered places in the alpine zone. Lemmings are particularly vulnerable at this time: should freezing rain and frost blanket the vegetation with ice before the establishment of snow cover, the difficulties in gathering food can prove fatal.

The mass migrations that have made the Norway lemming famous usually begin in the summer or fall following a period of rapid population growth. The migrations start as a gradual movement from densely populated areas in mountain heaths down into the willow, birch, and conifer forests. At first the lemmings seem to wander at random, but as a migration continues, groups of animals may be forced to coalesce by local topography, for instance if caught in a funnel between two rivers. In such

situations the continuous accumulation of animals becomes so great that a mass panic ensues and the animals take to reckless flight – upward, over rivers, lakes, and glaciers, and occasionally into the sea.

Although the causes of mass migrations are far from certain, it is widely thought that they are triggered by overcrowding. Females can breed in their third week and males as early as their first month; reproduction continues year-round. Litters consist of five to eight young, and may be produced every 3–4 weeks, so in a short period lemmings can produce several generations. Short winters without sudden thaws or freezes, followed by an early spring and late fall, provide favorable conditions for continuous breeding and a rapid increase in population density.

Lemmings are generally intolerant of one another and, apart from brief encounters for mating, lead solitary lives. It is possible that in peak years the number of aggressive interactions increases drastically, and that this triggers the migrations. Supporting evidence comes from reports that up to 80 percent of migrating lemmings are young animals (and thus are likely to have been defeated by larger individuals). Food shortages do not seem to be an important factor, since enough food seems to be available even in areas where there is a high density of animals.

The essential feature of long-distance migrations would therefore seem to be a desire for survival. Lemming species in Alaska and northern Canada also engage in similar, if less spectacular, expeditions. Although countless thousands of Norway lemmings may perish on their long journeys, the idea that such ventures always end in mass suicide is a myth. UWH

The numbers of juvenile males and females are equal, except in the wood lemming, which has an unusual feature for mammals: some females are genetically programmed to have only daughters, which is advantageous in an increasing population. In most species, however, there are usually more female adults than males, probably as a consequence of dispersal by males, which are then more susceptible to predators. In the European water vole it is the females who usually disperse, and there is a slight excess of males. In Townsend's vole, the survival and growth of juveniles are higher when the density of adult females is low and adjacent females are relatives.

Territory size varies, but males usually have larger territories than females. In the bank vole, home ranges were found in one study to be 0.7ha (1.7 acres) for females and 0.8ha (2 acres) for males. Territory size decreases as population density rises. In the prairie vole, home range length drops from 25m (82ft) at low density to 10m (33ft) at high density.

Potential for Harm
CONSERVATION AND ENVIRONMENT

Many microtines live in areas of little or no agricultural value, or in areas little changed by human habitation. These species are neither persecuted nor endangered. However, species living in temperate areas can be agricultural pests. The American pine vole burrows in winter around the base of apple trees and chews on the roots or girdles the stems, resulting in a loss in apple production. The extensive underground burrows of Brandt's vole can become a danger to grazing stock.

In addition to their status as pests, many species harbor vectors of diseases such as plague (mole voles) and sylvatic plague (sagebrush vole). In parts of eastern Europe and central Asia, *Microtus* species and water voles carry tularemia, an infectious disease that causes fever, chills, and inflammation of the lymph glands. The clearing of forest has increased both *Microtus* habitat and the incidence of tularemia. In the 1990s, hantavirus disease, which is carried by several species of voles and lemmings, emerged as an important viral ailment that can be fatal in more than 50 percent of cases. As a result, considerable research effort is now being directed to the epidemiology of the rodent-borne hemorrhagic fevers. CJK

○ **Left** In normal years, the distribution of the Norway lemming covers the tundra region of Scandinavia and northwestern Russia. However, during "lemming years," when there is a vast increase in the size of the population, the distribution expands considerably.

○ **Below** Norway lemmings are individualistic, intolerant creatures. When their numbers rise so does aggressive behavior, which is well developed. In the conflict shown here, two males box **1**; engage in wrestling **2**; and adopt a threatening posture toward one another **3**.

to population density. Norway lemmings move in summer onto wet, grassy meadows but in the fall move into deep mossy hillsides to overwinter.

Dispersers differ from nondispersing animals in several ways. There is some evidence that, in the meadow and prairie voles, animals that disperse are on average genetically different from permanent residents. Juvenile males disperse from their natal site to seek unrelated mating partners and to avoid inbreeding. Additionally, in field, prairie, meadow, tundra, and European water voles, many young pregnant females will disperse. This is quite unusual for mammals, but it does enable voles to rapidly colonize vacant habitats.

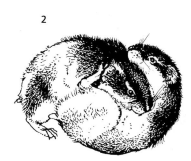

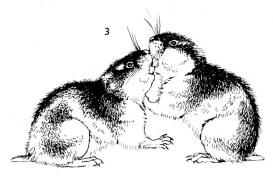

THE SCENT OF DEATH

The effect of weasel odor on vole reproduction

FOR MANY DESERT RODENTS, IT IS BETTER BY FAR to stay hungry but safe for a night or so than to risk death by seeking a meal outside of the burrow during the full moon. In open deserts and other arid areas, birds of prey are a serious threat. They have keen vision, which in many birds extends to seeing UV reflectance. Hunting raptors can even see the scent trails of voles reflecting UV light better than they can the average surroundings.

Things are different in Holarctic and boreal areas with a dense cover, whether in forest, meadow, or agricultural areas. Preferred rodent habitats in these areas are characterized by an undercover of grasses, herbs, scrubs, ferns, and bushes. Protection provided by this low canopy of vegetation considerably reduces the risk of airborne predation, and the same applies where there is permanent snow cover that forms a canopy during the winter. However, under the snow's protective canopy, the rodents face the threat of Europe's smallest carnivore, the least weasel (*Mustela nivalis*). Along with its slightly larger cousin, the stoat (*M. erminea*), it is the only predator of boreal areas that can follow prey into their own world: the burrows and crevices they occupy in old fields and forests, and the subnivean space under the snow.

Small mustelids are specialized vole hunters, and their population fluctuations closely follow those of the boreal voles on which they depend. The least weasel is committed to a lifestyle based on eating rodents; some specialists reckon that weasel predation is among the forces causing the three-yearly round known as the Northern European vole cycle. During vole population peaks, the least weasel and stoat can be responsible for 90 percent of total field and bank vole mortality.

Any strategy that helps the voles to avoid being killed will be favored in this harsh natural-selection regime. One way of assessing danger is to tap into the communicatory systems of the enemy themselves, and to use the information gained to predict areas of highest risk. Both weasels and stoats secrete a strong odor from their anal glands that is used in territory marking and sexual behavior. So alarming is the scent of weasels to voles that it has been used as a repellent to protect forestry and orchards from browsing. When the presence of scents indicates a lot of predator activity, voles stay in their burrows, becoming less active and avoiding going to distant foraging sites. If they do go out, they are more likely to forage in trees, keeping above the ground and out of the weasels' way.

These behaviors might well decrease the number and intensity of signs left to orient a weasel or stoat lurking somewhere inside the grass thicket or behind stones. Yet there is a price to pay for the enhanced security, in that the voles go hungry. This is especially a problem for females. Breeding is energetically costly, and, during pregnancy and lactation, reproductively active females need two or three times the amount of food required by nonbreeding females.

However, the most intricate tangle of adaptation and counteradaptation concerns the impact of weasel odors on the vole's sex life. Like weasels, voles also communicate by scent, so just as voles can spy on weasel activity by reading their scent messages, so too can weasels use vole scent marks to track them down. More chillingly still, weasels may even be able to distinguish the scents left by voles of different ages and reproductive condition to ensure that, when they do hunt, they are led to the best possible prizes. Female voles that have just given birth make for large, slow, and profitable prey, and the weasel may also benefit from an additional meal – the pups.

Thus if the risk of mortality from weasels is already high, and if it is particularly directed toward breeding females, what can the voles do? Laboratory experiments on the bank vole and the field vole have revealed that, in both species, the impact of mustelid odor on breeding was the same: in risky environments over 80 percent of females suppressed breeding, while in safe conditions the same percentage of control-group females bred successfully. Females exposed to mustelid treatment also lost weight, indicating decreased foraging success. Young females were more responsive to predator odor, while older females, closer to death anyway, were more likely to risk breeding.

Field experiments also showed that additional weasel smells suppressed field vole activity, while removing predators from some areas caused an upturn in reproduction. Yet some parts of this puzzle are still missing. Further experiments are needed in the field to compare rich habitats with dense and thriving rodent populations with the pattern among more marginal, less successful populations. Such studies would clarify the picture by showing what happens when rodents occupying marginal habitats face a strong risk of predation in addition to hunger and cold. Nonetheless, the exciting finding that vole breeding is influenced by the scent of the animals' predators is in itself a clear illustration of the pervasive importance of odor in most mammalian lives.　　HY

❍ **Right** A female bank vole with young that are just over a week old. Female voles, especially younger ones, will suppress breeding if they detect a powerful presence of weasel odor.

Old World Rats and Mice

tHE OLD WORLD RATS AND MICE, OR MURINAE, *include at least 542 species distributed over the major Old World land masses, from immediately south of the Arctic Circle to the tips of the southern continents. If exuberant radiation of species and the ability to survive, multiply, and adapt quickly are criteria for success, then the Old World rats and mice must be regarded as the most successful of all mammals.*

The Murinae probably originated in Southeast Asia in the late Oligocene or early Miocene about 25–20 million years ago from a primitive (cricetine) stock. The earliest fossils (*Progonomys*), in a generally poor fossil representation, are known from the late Miocene of Spain, about 8–6 million years ago. Slightly younger fossils (*Leggadina*, *Pseudomys*, and *Zyzomys*) have been discovered recently from the early Pliocene of Australia (5 m.y.a.). Old World rats and mice are primarily a tropical group that have sent a few hardy migrant species into temperate Eurasia.

An Evolutionary Success Story
FORM AND FUNCTION

The murines' success lies in a combination of features probably inherited and adapted from a primitive, mouselike archimurine. This is a hypothetical form, but many features of existing species point to such an ancestor, from which they are little modified. The archimurine would have been small, perhaps about 10cm (4in) long in head and body, with a scaly tail of similar length. The appendages would have been of moderate length, thereby facilitating the subsequent development of elongated hindlegs in jumping forms and short, robust forelimbs in burrowers. It would have had a full complement of five fingers and five toes. The sensory structures (ears, eyes, whiskers, and olfactory organs) would have been well developed. Its teeth would have consisted of continuously growing, self-sharpening incisors and three elaborately rasped molar teeth on each side of each upper and lower jaw, with powerful jaw muscles for chewing a wide range of foods and preparing material for nests. The archimurine would have had a short gestation period, would have produced several young per litter, and therefore would have

◗ Right *Although the tiny wood mouse* (Apodemus sylvaticus) *is often held responsible for the destruction of young plants, it also plays a role in the dispersal of seeds, which it buries underground. The wood mouse does not move far from its burrow and may never travel more than 200m (660ft) from its home.*

multiplied quickly. With its small size, it could have occupied many different microhabitats. Evolution has produced a wide range of adaptations, but only a few, if highly significant, lines of structural change.

Modifications to the tail have produced organs with a wide range of different capabilities. It has become a long balancing organ, sometimes with a pencil of hairs at its tip (as in the Australian hopping mice) and sometimes without (as in the wood mouse). In the harvest mouse it has developed into a grasping organ to help in climbing. In some species including the greater tree mouse it serves as a sensory organ, with numerous tactile hairs at the end furthest from the animal; in others like the bushy-tailed cloud rat, it is now thickly furred. In some genera, for example rock rats and spiny mice, as in some lizards, the tail is readily broken, either in its entirety or in part, though unlike lizards' tails it does not regenerate. In species where the proximal part of the tail is dark and the distal part white (for example the smooth-tailed giant rat), the tail may even serve as an organ of communication.

Hands and feet show a similar range of adaptation. In climbing forms, big toes are often opposable, though sometimes relatively small, as in the palm mouse. Both the hands and feet can be broadened to produce a firmer grip, for instance in the pencil-tailed tree mouse or Peter's arboreal forest rat. In jumping forms, the hindlegs and feet may be much elongated (as in Australian hopping mice), while in species living in wet, marshy conditions (for instance, African swamp rats), the hindfeet can be long and slightly splayed, somewhat reminiscent of the webbed feet of ducks. This type of adaptation is at its most pronounced in the Australian and New Guinea water rats and the shrew rats of the Philippines, which possess broadly webbed hindfeet.

The claws are also often modified. They may be short and recurved for attaching to bark and other rough surfaces, as in Peter's arboreal forest rat, or large and strong in burrowing forms like those of the lesser bandicoot rat. In some of the species with a small, opposable digit, the claw of this digit becomes small, flattened, and nail-like (for instance in the pencil-tailed tree mouse).

Fur is important for insulation. In some species such as spiny mice, some hairs of the back are modified into short, stiff spines, while in others the fur can be bristly (harsh-furred rats), shaggy (African marsh rat), or soft and woolly (African forest rat). The function of spines is not known, although it is speculated that they deter predators.

⟩ **Right** The Norway rat – also called the brown or common rat – is practically omnivorous (even eating soap) and found mainly in urban areas, where it causes a good deal of damage. The species' particular preference is for animal matter; it has been known to attack poultry and even young lambs.

OLD WORLD RATS AND MICE

Order: Rodentia

Family: Muridae

Subfamily: Murinae

542 species in 118 genera

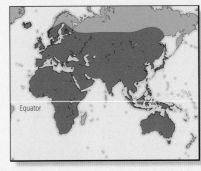

Equator

DISTRIBUTION Europe, Asia, Africa (excluding Madagascar), Australasia; also found on many offshore islands.

HABITAT Very varied; mostly terrestrial, but some are arboreal, fossorial, or semiaquatic.

SIZE Head–body length ranges from 4.5–8.2cm (1.7–3.2in) in the Pygmy mouse to 48cm (19in) in Cuming's slender-tailed cloud rat; **tail length** from 2.8–6.5cm (1.1–2.5in) to 20–32cm (8–13in); **weight** from about 6g (0.2oz) to 1.5–2kg (3.3–4.4lb), both in the same two species.

COAT Typically medium to dark brown on the back and flanks, sometimes with a lighter-colored belly. Some species are striped for camouflage.

DIET Mostly plant material and invertebrates, though some take small vertebrates.

BREEDING In most small species, gestation lasts 20–30 days, though longer in species that give birth to precocious young (e.g., 36–40 days in spiny mice), and also in "old endemic" Australian rodents (e.g., 32–50 days in Australian hopping mice). Duration not known for large species.

LONGEVITY Small species live little over 1 year; larger species like the Giant naked-tailed rats over 4 years.

CONSERVATION STATUS Although many Murinae species are flourishing, 15 are currently listed as Critically Endangered, including 2 species each of the genera *Zyzomys* (rock rats) and *Pseudomys* (Australian pseudomice); 36 are Endangered.

For full species list see Appendix ▷

Ears can range from the large, mobile, and prominent (as in the rabbit-eared tree rat) to the small and inconspicuous, well covered by surrounding hair (the African marsh rat). As its common name indicates, the earless water rat of Papua New Guinea lacks any external ears, an adaptation that helps streamline its body for a life spent in water. In addition, this highly specialized species has a longitudinal fringe of long white hairs on its tail, remarkably similar to that found in the completely unrelated elegant water shrew (*Nectogale elegans*) of the Himalayas. The tail fringe is thought to act as an effective rudder.

In teeth, there is considerable adaptation among murines in the row of molars. In what is presumed to be the primitive condition, there are three rows of three cusps on each upper molar tooth, but the number of cusps is often much smaller, particularly in the third molar, which is often small. The cusps may also coalesce to form transverse ridges. But the typical rounded cusps,

although they wear with age, make excellent structures for chewing a wide variety of foods.

The molars of Australian water rats and their allies, however, show great simplification, lacking as they do the strong cusps or ridges found in most of the murine rodents. In some species the molars are also reduced in number, the extreme being seen in the one-toothed shrew mouse which has only one small, simple molar in each row. This adaptation is most likely to be related to a diet of fruit or soft-bodied invertebrates.

The shrew rats of the Philippines have slender, protruding incisor teeth like delicate forceps, presumably adapted, as in the true shrews, for capturing insects and other invertebrates. However, the remaining teeth are small and flat-crowned, quite unlike the sharp-cusped batteries of the true shrews. The two species of the genus *Rhynchomys* offer pronounced examples of this adaptation.

These adaptations of teeth have, at the extremes, resulted in the development of robust

◁ **Left** *Old World rats and mice: 1 Smooth-tailed giant rat (Mallomys rothschildi); 2 Pencil-tailed tree mouse (Chiropodomys gliroides); 3 African marsh rat (Dasymys incomtus); 4 a spiny mouse (genus Acomys); 5 Natal multimammate rat (Mastomys natalensis); 6 Fawn-colored hopping mouse (Notomys cervinus); 7 Vlei rat (Otomys irroratus) sitting in a grass runway; 8 Brush-furred rat (Lophuromys sikapusi) eating an insect; 9 Four-striped grass mouse (Rhabdomys pumilio); 10 Australian water rat (Hydromys chrysogaster) diving; a tail of a field mouse (genus Apodemus); b tail of the harvest mouse (Micromys minutus); c tail of the greater tree mouse (Chiruromys forbesi); d tail of the bushy-tailed cloud rat (Crateromys schadenbergi); e hindfoot of the Asiatic long-tailed climbing mouse (Vandeleuria oleracea); first and fifth digits opposable to provide grip for living in trees; f hindfoot of the shining thicket rat (Grammomys rutilans); has broad, short digits for providing grip; g paw of the lesser bandicoot rat (Bandicota bengalensis) showing long, stout claws; h hindfoot of an African swamp rat (genus Malacomys) showing long, splayed foot with digits adapted for walking in swampy terrain.*

and relatively large teeth (in rufous-nosed and Nile rats) and in the reduction of the whole tooth row to a relatively small size, as in the lesser small-toothed rat of New Guinea. The food of this rat probably requires little chewing, possibly consisting of soft fruit or small insects.

Teeming and Ubiquitous
DISTRIBUTION PATTERNS

Murines are found throughout the Old World. There are considerable variations in the numbers of species in different parts of their range, though in examining their natural distribution the house mouse, roof rat, Norway rat, and Polynesian rat must be discounted, as they have been inadvertently introduced in many parts of the world.

The north temperate region is poor in species. In Europe, countries such as Norway, Great Britain, and Poland have respectively as few as 2, 3, and 4 species each. In Africa, the density of species is low from the north across the Sahara until the savanna is reached, where the richness of species is considerable. Highest densities occur in the tropical rain forest and adjacent regions of the Congo basin. This fact can be shown by reference to selected sites. The desert around Khartoum, the arid savanna at Bandia, Senegal, the moist savanna in Ruwenzori Park, Uganda, and the rain forests of Makokou, Gabon, support 0, 6, 9, and 13 species respectively. The Democratic Republic of Congo boasts 45 species, and Uganda 37.

Moving to the Orient, species are most numerous south of the Himalayas. India and Sri Lanka have about 35 species, Malaysia 22. In the East Indies some islands are remarkably rich: there are about 60 species in New Guinea, 38 in Sulawesi (Celebes), and 35 in the Philippines. Within the Philippines there has been a considerable development of native species, with 10 of the 12 genera and a total of 30 species found only there (in other words, they are endemic); only two species of *Rattus* are found elsewhere. A notable feature is the presence of 10 large species having head–body lengths of about 20cm (8in) or more.

The largest known murine, Cuming's slender-tailed cloud rat, is found in the Philippines; it grows to over 40cm (16in) in head–body length, and the pallid slender-tailed rat and the bushy-tailed cloud rat are only slightly shorter. This high degree of endemism and the tendency to evolve large species is also found in the other island groups. In New Guinea there are 8 species with head–body lengths of more than 30cm (12in), including the smooth-tailed giant rat, the rough-tailed eastern white-eared giant rat, the giant naked-tailed rats and the rock-dwelling giant rat. The most gigantic of all New Guinea's rodents, the subalpine woolly rat, which exceeds 40cm in length and weighs up to 2kg (4.4lb), was discovered only in 1989. There are only two small species, the New Guinea jumping mouse, about the size of the house mouse, and the diminutive delicate mouse, about half as small again. In Australia there are around 72 species, with the eastern half of the continent having a far greater diversity of species than elsewhere.

Niche Specialists
ECOLOGICAL ADAPTATION

It has proved difficult to give an adequate and comprehensive explanation of the evolution and species richness of the murines. There are some pointers to the course evolution may have followed, based on structural affinities and ecological considerations. The murines are a structurally similar group, and many of their minor modifications are clearly adaptive, so there are few characters that can be used to distinguish between, in terms of evolution, primitive and advanced conditions. In fact only the row of molar teeth has been used in this way: primitive dentition can be recognized in the presence of a large number of well-formed cusps. Divergences from this condition may represent specialization or advancement, while ecological considerations

account for a species' abundance and for the types of habitat preference it may show.

From this analysis, two groups of genera have been recognized. The first contains the dominant genera (African soft-furred rats, Oriental spiny rats, Old World rats, giant naked-tailed rats, the *Mus* species, African grass rats, and African marsh rats), which have been particularly successful, living in dense populations in the best habitats. These are believed to have evolved slowly, because they display relatively few changes from the primitive dental condition. The second group contains many of the remaining genera which are less successful, living in marginal habitats and often showing a combination of aberrant, primitive, and specialized dental features.

The dominant genera (with the exception of the African marsh rat) contain more species than the peripheral genera and are constantly attempting to extend their range. Considerable numbers of new species have apparently arisen within what is now the range center of a dominant genus (for example, soft-furred rats in central Africa and Old World rats in Southeast Asia). The reasons for this await explanation.

It is quite common for two or more species of murine to occur in the same habitat, particularly in the tropics. One of the more interesting and

important aspects of studies of the animals is to explain the ecological roles assumed by each species in a particular habitat, and then to deduce the patterns of niche occupation and the limits of ecological adaptations by animals with a remarkably uniform basic structure. A particularly favorable habitat, and one amenable to this type of study, is regenerating tropical forest.

In Mayanja Forest, Uganda, 13 species have been found in a small area of about 4sq km (1.5sq mi). Certain species – the rusty-bellied rat and the punctated grass mouse – are of savanna origin and are restricted to grassy rides. Of the remaining 11 species, all have forest and scrub as their typical habitat with the exception of the two smallest species, the pygmy mouse and the larger pygmy mouse, which are also found in grasslands and cultivated areas. Three species, the tree rat, the climbing wood mouse, and Peter's arboreal forest rat, seldom, if ever, come to the ground. The small climbing wood mouse – often found within the first 60cm (24in) off the ground – prefers a bushy type of habitat. The two other arboreal species are strong branch-runners and are able to exploit the upper and lower levels of trees and bushes. All three species are found alongside a variety of plant species (in the case of the wood mouse, 37 were captured beside 19 different plants, with *Solanum* among the most favored). All species are herbivorous and nocturnal, and the two larger species construct elaborately woven nests of vegetation.

Two species are found on both the ground and in the vegetation up to 2m (6.5ft) above ground level. Of these, the African forest rat is abundant and the rufous-nosed rat is much less common. The African forest rat lives and builds its nests in burrows whose entrances are often situated at the bases of trees; it is nocturnal, feeding on a wide range of both insect and plant foods. The rufous-nosed rat is both nocturnal and diurnal, and constructs nests with downwardly projecting entrances in the shrub layer, made out of grass, on which this species is known to feed.

Of the 11 forest species, Peter's striped mouse, the speckled harsh-furred rat, the long-footed rat, the pygmy mouse, the larger pygmy mouse, and Hind's bush rat are all ground dwellers. Of these, the striped mouse is a vegetarian, preferring the moister parts of the forest. The harsh-furred rat is an abundant species, predominantly predatory, favoring insects but also prepared to eat other types of flesh. The long-footed rat is found in the vicinity of streams and swamps; it is nocturnal, and includes in its diet insects, slugs, and even toads (a specimen in the laboratory constantly attempted to immerse itself in a bowl of water). The two small mice are omnivores, while Hind's bush rat is a vegetarian species that inhabits scrub.

A further important feature, which could well account for the dietary differences in these species, is their respective sizes. The three mice are in the 5–25g (0.2–0.9oz) range, with the

Above *The blind, hairless litter of the house mouse. This species is found almost worldwide, except in locations where it is excluded by either climate or competition from other small mammals.*

Right *A female Brants' whistling rat (*Parotomys brantsii*) with her young clinging to one of her nipples. Rodents of this species seldom venture far from their burrows, to which they return at the slightest provocation after emitting a loud alarm whistle.*

Below *A male harvest mouse with a nonreceptive female. Harvest mice construct nests for the young, usually about 1m (3.3ft) above ground. Litter size is about 4–7; sexual maturity is reached at five weeks.*

found in large cities and ports. The roof rat is more successful in the tropics, where towns and villages are often infested, though it cannot compete with the indigenous species in the field. In many Pacific, Atlantic, and Caribbean islands, roof rats are common in agricultural and natural habitats in the absence of competitors.

With even the solitary house mouse capable of causing considerable damage, the scale of mass outbreak damage is difficult to envisage. An Australian farmer recorded 28,000 dead mice on his veranda after one night's poisoning, and 70,000 were killed in a wheat yard in an afternoon.

There are many rodent-borne diseases, transmitted either directly or through an intermediate host. The roof rat, along with other species, hosts the plague bacterium, which is transmitted through the flea *Xenopsylla cheopis*. The lassa fever virus of West Africa is transmitted through urine and feces of the multimammate rat. Other diseases in which murines are involved include murine typhus, rat-bite fever, and leptospirosis.

In the past, some Old World rats and mice were persecuted for reasons other than pest control. Notably, the sheer size of the beaver rat of Australia – which weighs 650–1,250g (23–44oz) – once told against it, when it was hunted for its luxurious pelt from the 1930s onward. As a result of hunting restrictions, this species is now on the increase. Most murine species now regarded as threatened are in danger from habitat destruction.

The Old World rats and mice are a remarkably rich and adaptable group of mammals. In spite of their abundance and ubiquity in the Old World, particularly the tropics, the murines remain a poorly studied group. Exceptions include a few species of economic importance and the wood mouse. Many species are known only from small numbers in museums, supported by the briefest information on their biology. The Bisa rat, for example, is known only from a single skull retrieved from Bisa Island in 1990. There are undoubtedly endless opportunities for future research on this fascinating and accessible group of mammals.   GS/CRD/MJD

pygmy mouse rather smaller than the other two. The rufous-nosed rat is in the 70–90g (2.5–3.2oz) range, and the long-footed rat and Hind's bush rat above this. The remaining species – the tree rat, Peter's arboreal forest rat, the African forest rat, the speckled harsh-furred rat, and Peter's striped mouse – have weights between 35g and 60g (1.2–2.1oz).

Within the tropical forests there is a high precipitation, with rain falling in all months of the year. This results in continuous flowering, fruiting, and herbaceous growth, which is reflected in the breeding activity of the rats and mice found there. In Mayanja Forest, the African forest rat and the speckled harsh-furred rat were the only species obtained in sufficient numbers to permit the monthly examination of reproductive activity. The African forest rat bred throughout the year, while in the speckled harsh-furred rat the highest frequency of conception coincided with the wetter periods of the year, from March to May and October to December.

Of Mice and Men

CONSERVATION AND ENVIRONMENT

Some Old World rats and mice have a close, detrimental association with humans through consuming or spoiling their food and crops, damaging their property, and carrying disease.

The most important species commensal with humans are the Norway or brown or common rat, the roof rat, and the house mouse; now found worldwide, they originated from around the Caspian Sea, India, and Turkestan respectively. In addition to these cosmopolitan commensals, there are the more localized multimammate rat in Africa, the Polynesian rat in Asia, and the lesser bandicoot rat in India.

While the roof rat and the house mouse have been extending their ranges for centuries, the Norway rat's progress has been much slower. Unknown in the West before the 11th century, it is now established in urban and rural situations in temperate regions, and is the rodent most commonly found in sewers. In the tropics, it is mainly

Old World Rat and Mouse Species

Species include: African forest rat (*Praomys jacksoni*), African grass rats (genus *Arvicanthis*), African marsh rat (*Dasymys incomtus*), African soft-furred rats (genus *Praomys*), African swamp rats (genus *Malacomys*), Asiatic long-tailed climbing mouse (*Vandeleuria oleracea*), Australian hopping mice (genus *Notomys*), Australian pseudomice (genus *Pseudomys*), beaver rats (genus *Hydromys*), Bisa rat (as yet undescribed), Bushy-tailed cloud rat (*Crateromys*

schadenbergi), Cuming's slender-tailed cloud rat (*Phloeomys cumingi*), Delicate mouse (*Pseudomys delicatulus*), Giant naked-tailed rats (genus *Uromys*), Greater tree mouse (*Chiruromys forbesi*), Harvest mouse (*Micromys minutus*), Hind's bush rat (*Aethomys hindei*), House mouse (*Mus musculus*), Larger pygmy mouse (*Mus triton*), Lesser bandicoot rat (*Bandicota bengalensis*), Lesser ranee mouse (*Haeromys pusillus*), Lesser small-toothed rat (*Macruromys elegans*), Long-footed rat (*Malacomys longipes*), Multimammate mouse (*Mastomys natalensis*), New Guinea jumping mouse

(*Lorentzimys nouhuysi*), Nile rat (*Arvicanthis niloticus*), Norway, Brown, or Common rat (*Rattus norvegicus*), Old World rats (genus *Rattus*), Oriental spiny rats (genus *Maxomys*), Pallid slender-tailed rat (*Phloeomys pallidus*), Pencil-tailed tree mouse (*Chiropodomys gliroides*), Peter's striped mouse (*Hybomys univittatus*), Polynesian rat (*Rattus exulans*), Punctated grass mouse (*Lemniscomys striatus*), Pygmy mouse (*Mus minutoides*), Rabbit-eared tree rat (*Conilurus penicillatus*), Rock-dwelling giant rat (*Xenuromys barbatus*), Rock rats (genus *Zyzomys*), Roof rat (*Rattus rattus*), Rough-tailed eastern

white-eared giant rat (*Hyomys goliath*), Rufous-nosed rat (*Oenomys hypoxanthus*), Rusty-bellied brush-furred rat (*Lophuromys sikapusi*), Shrew rats (genus *Rhynchomys*), Smooth-tailed giant rat (*Mallomys rothschildi*), Yellow-spotted brush-furred rat (*Lophuromys flavopunctatus*), Spiny mice (genus *Acomys*), Subalpine woolly rat (*Mallomys istapantap*), thicket rats (genus *Thamnomys*), Vlei rats (genus *Otomys*), Whistling rats (genus *Parotomys*), Wood mouse (*Apodemus sylvaticus*).

For full species list see Appendix ▷

A SCENT-BASED INFORMATION SUPERHIGHWAY

Communication patterns among house mice

IN THE DARKNESS BEHIND OUR KITCHEN cupboards or in the house footings, mice live, feeding on the superabundant food that is a by-product of our wasteful lives. As many as 50 may live together in family groups, with several adult females, their offspring, subdominant males, and a dominant male defending the territory. They may be quiet, but be sure that they are communicating, relaying complex and subtle messages of life, death, property rights, sex, and family matters through the medium of their own urine.

Urine – a substance we think of as disposable if not disgusting – is the essence of the mouse information superhighway. In addition to urea and other waste products, their urine contains a complex mixture of chemicals: small-molecular-weight volatile odorants and much higher-weight non-volatile proteins. Together these are the mouse equivalent of visiting cards, providing information on identity, species, sex, social and reproductive status, and state of health. Many genetic differences between individual mice contribute to each individual's unique scent signature, including the highly variable (polymorphic) genes of the major histocompatibility complex (MHC). Because scents used for individual recognition are inherited, mice can recognize relatives they have not met before

from the similarity of their scents to that of known family members. The system is much more sophisticated than that used by humans to recognize their long-lost aunts or uncles.

Mice can produce their scent marks in slow-release capsules to ensure maximum effect. Mouse urine contains a high concentration of small (18–20kDa) lipocalin proteins, termed major urinary proteins (MUPs), that are manufactured in the liver and filtered through the kidneys into the urine. Adult males excrete around 30mg of protein per ml (.004oz per fluidram) of urine per day, while adult females excrete about 30 percent as much. These urinary proteins bind signaling chemicals inside a central cavity to cause their slow release from scent marks. In addition, each mouse produces a different combination of these proteins, allowing mice to recognize the individual producer of any scent mark.

All mice deposit urine in small streaks and spots as they move around their group home area, depositing their scents on any unmarked surfaces, so that all surfaces become covered with a pungent smear. Communication "posts" of dried urine mixed with dust build up like small stalagmites in frequently used locations, around feeding sites, at entrances to nest areas, or along trails.

Since mice are always surrounded by a familiar mixture of urine marks, they rapidly detect any new objects in their environment – or precipitous edges in the dark – by the absence of the strong, accustomed smell. Scent marks deposited around the territory also help to maintain familiarity and recognition between group members. Intruders can be recognized immediately because their scent contrasts with the background odors, stimulating investigation and attack by resident mice, and especially by the dominant male. In addition, adult males excrete signaling volatiles that are highly attractive to females and induce caution or stimulate aggression from other males.

Dominant males advertise their territory ownership and competitive ability by scent marking at a much higher rate than other mice. They deposit hundreds of urine marks per hour, compared with only tens of marks by females or subordinates, using hairs on the end of their prepuce as a wick. Since only a male successfully dominating an area can ensure that it is suffused with his own odor, this is a reliable signal that a territory is owned – by the male. Dominant territory owners seek out and attack any other males that deposit competing scent marks in their territory, and immediately countermark a competitor's scent by depositing

their own urine nearby, ensuring that their own scent is always the freshest. Other males will usually flee if they meet the owner of the scent marks within his scent-marked area, or will avoid entering it, considerably reducing the need for aggressive defence by the owner. However, if a male is not defending his territory very successfully and other males are able to deposit competing scents, the owner may be challenged.

Females take advantage of these scent competitions to select the best father for their young. While they will nest in one male's territory, they may well explore outside his territory and mate with other territory owners, particularly if their patch is exclusively and freshly scent marked. Given a choice between successful territory owners, they prefer mates whose scents are dissimilar to their parents', thus avoiding inbreeding problems. If there is no choice, however, they will mate anyway. Males do not distinguish their own young from those fathered by another male.

⊙ **Below** *At least since the start of cereal growing around 10,000 years ago, house mice have lived in wary coexistence with humans, using their sensitive noses to sniff out information about their environment and each other.*

◗ **Right** *As the table shows, the scent of urine has different priming effects on female house mice depending both on the reproductive state of the female and the identity of the donor. The strength of the inhibition caused by urine from nonbreeding females increases with the size of the group and length of exposure.*

	URINE DONOR		
	Unfamiliar adult male	**Non-breeding grouped female**	**Pregnant or lactating female**
Juvenile female	Accelerates puberty	Delays puberty	Accelerates puberty
Adult female	Induces estrus and shortens cycle	Prolongs anestrus or induces pseudopregnancy	Prolongs estrus
Pregnant female	Terminates early pregnancy and induces estrus		

If there is no territory available, some males will live within those of dominant males, spreading urine with low concentrations of signaling chemicals in fewer deposits. This allows the dominant male to recognize that they are not a threat, but it also means they are not attractive to females.

Mouse urine also plays an important role in the reproductive state of females according to their opportunities, as spelled out in the table above. A young female exposed to the scent of a new male will come into puberty, and therefore become ready to breed, up to 6 days earlier than normal (the familiar odor of a father has no such effects). A newly pregnant female will abort a pregnancy if the father disappears before the embryos have implanted in the wall of her uterus and she encounters the scent of a new male. She can then choose another mate that may have better genes to pass on to her offspring. Male urine also induces estrus and shortens the cycle of adult

females, thereby synchronizing their estruses. This may help them to share the chores of motherhood, as female mice prefer to nest communally with other familiar females (usually relatives). They will come into breeding condition earlier if they are receiving scent signals that other females in their group are already breeding. Overcrowding, however, is a problem, and may inhibit further reproduction. If three or more females live together and are waiting for an opportunity to breed, they produce a scent that can inhibit puberty in other young females by more than 20 days, and that inhibits estrous cycling among other adult females. This behavior delays reproduction in overcrowded conditions. These ingenious responses allow females to reproduce rapidly under favorable conditions, but to delay their reproduction at times of high population density when their offspring would stand little chance of survival. JH

Other Old World Rats and Mice

THROUGHOUT THE OLD WORLD THERE ARE *groups of rats and mice that cannot be included in the three major Muridae subfamilies. Here they are grouped in eight subfamilies, placed for convenience in a west–east geographical sequence. Some of these rodents are superficially similar to members of the major groups; for example, the zokors can be considered as specialized voles. Two groups, the blind mole rats and the bamboo rats, are more distinctive and are sometimes treated as separate families.*

Blind Mole Rats

SUBFAMILY SPALACINAE

Of all the subterranean rodents, the blind mole rats show the most extreme adaptations to life underground. Their eyes are completely and permanently hidden under their skin, and there are no detectable external ears or tail. The incisors protrude so far that they are permanently outside the mouth and can be used for digging without the mouth having to be opened. A unique feature is the horizontal line of short, stiff, presumably touch-sensitive hairs on each side of the head. Most blind mole rats are about 13–25cm (5–9in) long, but in one species, the giant mole rat of southern Russia, they can reach 35cm (14in).

Blind mole rats are found in dry but not desert habitats from the Balkans and southern Russia around the eastern Mediterranean to Libya. Apart from being entirely vegetarian they live very much like the true moles (which are predators belonging to the order Eulipotyphla). Each animal makes its own system of tunnels, which may reach as much as 350m (1,150ft) in length, throwing up heaps of soil. They feed especially on fleshy roots, bulbs, and tubers, but also on whole plants. Although originally animals of the steppes, they have adapted well to cultivation and are a considerable pest in crops of roots, grain, and fruit.

Blind mole rats breed in spring. There are usually two or three in a litter, and they disperse away from the mother's tunnel system as soon as they are weaned, at about 3 weeks. There is sometimes a second litter later in the year.

As in many other burrowing mammals, the blind mole rats' limited movement has led to the evolution of many local forms, making the individual species very difficult to define but providing a bonanza for the study of genetics and the processes of evolution and species formation. The number of species that should be recognized, and how they should best be classified, are still very uncertain. Eight species are recognized here, but these have been reduced to three elsewhere.

African Pouched Rats

SUBFAMILY CRICETOMYINAE

The five species of African pouched rats resemble hamsters in having a storage pouch opening from the inside of each cheek. The two short-tailed pouched rats are hamsterlike in general appearance also, but the other three species are ratlike, with a long tail and large ears.

The giant pouched rats are among the largest of the murid rodents, reaching 40cm (16in) in head–body length. They are common throughout Africa south of the Sahara, and in some areas are hunted for food. They feed on a wide variety of items, including insects and snails as well as seeds and fruit. In addition to serving to carry food to underground storage chambers, the cheek pouches can be inflated with air as a threat display. The gestation period is about 6 weeks, and the litter size is usually two or four.

The three large species are associated with peculiar, blind, wingless earwigs of the genus *Hemimerus*, which occur in their fur and in their nests, where they probably share the rats' food.

◖ **Left** *Species of Other Old World rats and mice:*
1 *Brant's climbing mouse* (Dendromus mesomelas);
2 *Savanna giant pouched rat* (Cricetomys gambianus) *with both pouches full of food;* **3** *East African root rat* (Tachyoryctes splendens) *burrowing with its incisors;* **4** *East Siberian zokor* (Myospalax aspalax), *kicking back excavated soil with its hindfeet;* **5** *Ehrenberg's mole rat* (Nannospalax ehrenbergi), *showing the broad nose used for ramming soil and tactile hairs on the face – note the absence of external eyes;* **6** *Crested rat* (Lophiomys imhausi) *with mane erect, showing a glandular patch;* **7** *Macrotarsomys ingens* (one of the Madagascan rats); **8** *Spiny dormouse* (Platacanthomys lasiurus).

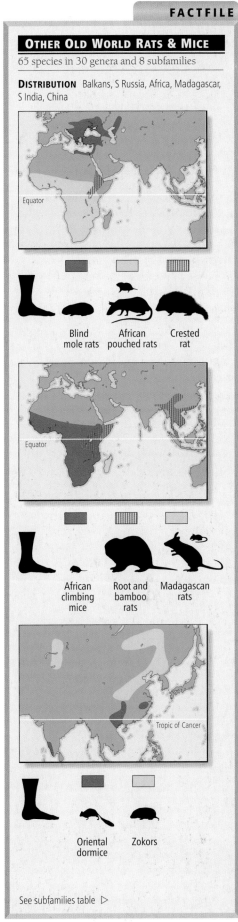

FACTFILE

OTHER OLD WORLD RATS & MICE

65 species in 30 genera and 8 subfamilies

DISTRIBUTION Balkans, S Russia, Africa, Madagascar, S India, China

Equator

Blind mole rats | African pouched rats | Crested rat

Equator

African climbing mice | Root and bamboo rats | Madagascan rats

Tropic of Cancer

Oriental dormice | Zokors

See subfamilies table ▷

Crested Rat
SUBFAMILY LOPHIOMYINAE

The crested rat has so many peculiarities that it is placed in a subfamily of its own, and it is not at all clear what its nearest relatives are. It is a large, dumpy, shaggy rodent with a bushy tail and tracts of long hair along each side of the back that can be erected. These are associated with specialized scent glands in the skin, and the individual hairs of the crests have a unique, latticelike structure that probably serves to hold and disseminate the scent. These hair tracts can be suddenly parted to expose the bold, striped pattern beneath, as well as the scent glands themselves.

The skull is also unique in possessing a peculiar granular texture and in having the cavities occupied by the principal, temporal chewing muscles roofed over by bone – a feature not found in any other rodent.

Crested rats are nocturnal and little is known of their way of life. They spend the day in burrows, rock crevices, or hollow trees. They are competent climbers and feed on a variety of vegetable materials. The stomach is unique among rodents in being divided into a number of complex chambers similar to those found in ruminant ungulates such as cattle and deer.

African Climbing Mice
SUBFAMILY DENDROMURINAE

The majority of African climbing mice are small, agile mice with long tails and slender feet, adapted to climbing among trees, shrubs, and long grass. Although they are confined to Africa south of the Sahara, some of them closely resemble mice in other regions that show similar adaptations, such as the Eurasian harvest mouse (subfamily Murinae) and the North American harvest mice (subfamily Sigmodontinae). They are separated from these mainly by a unique pattern of cusps on the molar teeth, and it is on the basis of this feature that some superficially very different rodents have been associated with them in the subfamily Dendromurinae.

Typical dendromurines, for instance those of the genus *Dendromus*, are nocturnal and feed on grass seeds, but are also considerable predators on small insects such as beetles and even on young birds and lizards. Some species in other genera are suspected of being more completely insectivorous. In the genus *Dendromus*, some species make compact, globular nests of grass above ground, for instance in bushes; others nest underground. Breeding is seasonal, with usually three to six naked, blind nestlings in a litter.

Of the other genera, the most unusual are the fat mice. They make extensive burrows and spend long periods underground in a state of torpor during the dry season, after developing thick deposits of fat. Even during their active season fat mice become torpid, with reduced body temperature during the day.

Many species of this subfamily are poorly known. Several distinctive new species have been discovered in the course of the past 40 years, and it is likely that others remain to be found, especially arboreal forest species.

The genera *Petromyscus* and *Delanymys* have sometimes been separated from the others in a subfamily of their own, Petromyscinae.

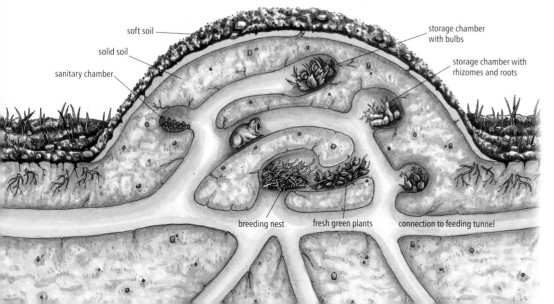

soft soil
solid soil
sanitary chamber
storage chamber with bulbs
storage chamber with rhizomes and roots
breeding nest   fresh green plants   connection to feeding tunnel

○ **Above** *Despite its common name, the island mouse (Nesomys rufus) is ratlike in appearance. It is one of a group of 14 rodents found only on the island of Madagascar, where it lives in complex burrows often located under fallen tree trunks.*

◁ **Left** *Breeding mound of a blind mole rat, Ehrenberg's mole rat (Nannospalax ehrenbergi). Each animal makes its own system of tunnels, which may be as long as 350m (1,150ft), throwing up heaps of soil. The rats feed especially on fleshy roots, bulbs, and tubers, but also on whole plants, which they pull down into their tunnels by the roots. Their food storage chambers have been known to hold as much as 14kg (31lb) of assorted vegetable matter.*

Root and Bamboo Rats

SUBFAMILY RHIZOMYINAE

Root rats are large rats adapted for burrowing, and they show many of the characteristics found in other burrowing rodents – short extremities, small eyes, large, protruding incisor teeth, and powerful neck muscles, reflected in a broad, angular skull. The bamboo rats, found in southeast Asian forests, show all these features in less extreme form than the East African root rats. They make extensive burrows in which they spend the day, emerging at night to do at least some feeding above ground. The principal diet consists of the roots of bamboos and other plants, but aboveground shoots are also eaten. In spite of their size, breeding is similar to the normal murid pattern.

The African root rats are more subterranean than the bamboo rats, but less so than African mole rats or the blind mole rats. They make prominent molehills in open country. Roots and tubers are stored underground. As in most molelike animals, each individual occupies its own tunnel system. The gestation period is unusually long – between 6 and 7 weeks.

Madagascan Rats

SUBFAMILY NESOMYINAE

It has long been debated whether the 14 indigenous rodents of the island of Madagascar form a single interrelated group (implying they have evolved from a single colonizing species), or whether there have been multiple colonizations, meaning that some of the present species may be more closely related to mainland African rodents than to their fellows on Madagascar. The balance of evidence seems to favor the first hypothesis – hence their inclusion here in a single subfamily.

The South African white-tailed rat has also been included – the implication being that it is the sole survivor on the African mainland of the stock that colonized Madagascar – although it actually might be best placed in a separate subfamily, Mystromyinae. The problem arises from the diversity of the Madagascan species, coupled with the fact that none of them match very closely any of the non-Madagascan groups of murid rodents.

The group includes small, agile mice with long tails, long, slender hindfeet, and large eyes and ears (e.g., *Macrotarsomys bastardi* and *Eliurus minor*). *Nesomys rufus* is typically ratlike in its proportions, while *Hypogeomys antimena* is rabbit-sized and makes deep burrows, although it forages for food on the surface. The two *Brachyuromys* species are remarkably volelike in form, dentition, and ecology. They live in wet grassland or marshes, and are apparently adapted to feeding on grass. Externally, they can only be distinguished with difficulty from Eurasian water voles.

Oriental Dormice

SUBFAMILY PLATACANTHOMYINAE

The three species of Oriental dormice have been considered to be closely related to the true dormice (family Gliridae), which they resemble externally and in the similar pattern of transverse ridges on the molar teeth, although there are only three molars on each row, not preceded by a premolar as in the true dormice. More recently, opinion has swung toward treating them as aberrant members of the family Muridae (in its widest sense, as used here). Whatever their affinities, they are distinctive arboreal mice with no close relatives, and little is known of their way of life. The spiny dormouse, a seedeater, is a pest of pepper crops in numerous parts of southern India.

Zokors

SUBFAMILY MYOSPALACINAE

Zokors are burrowing, volelike rodents found in steppes and open woodlands in much of China. Although they live almost entirely underground, they are less extremely adapted than the blind mole rats. Both eyes and external ears are clearly visible, although tiny, and the tail is also distinct. Digging is done mainly with the very large claws of the front feet rather than the teeth.

Like the blind mole rats, zokors feed on roots, rhizomes, and bulbs, but they also occasionally collect food such as seeds from the surface. Massive underground stores of food are accumulated, enabling the animals to remain active all winter.

Breeding takes place in spring, when one litter of up to six young is produced. Their social organization is little known, but the young appear to stay with the mother for a considerable time. GBC

Other Old World Rat and Mouse Subfamilies

Blind mole rats Subfamily Spalacinae

8 species in 2 genera: Greater blind mole rats (*Spalax*, 5 species); Lesser blind mole rats (*Nannospalax*, 3 species). Balkans, S Russia, E Mediterranean, N Africa. 5 species are Vulnerable.

African pouched rats Subfamily Cricetomyinae

5 species in 3 genera: Giant pouched rats (*Cricetomys*, 2 species); Lesser pouched rat (*Beamys hindei*); Short-tailed pouched rats (*Saccostomus*, 2 species). Africa S of the Sahara. 1 species is Vulnerable.

Crested rat Subfamily Lophiomyinae

1 species, *Lophiomys imhausi*. Kenya, Somalia, Ethiopia, E Sudan, in mountain forests from 1,200m (4,000ft).

African climbing mice Subfamily Dendromurinae

21 species in 10 genera: Climbing mice (*Dendromus*, 6 species); Nikolaus's mouse (*Megadendromus nikolausi*); Dollman's tree mouse (*Prionomys batesi*); Link rat (*Deomys ferrugineus*); Velvet climbing mouse (*Dendroprionomys rousseloti*); Groove-toothed forest mouse (*Leimacomys buettneri*); Gerbil mouse (*Malacothrix typica*); Fat mice (*Steatomys*, 6 species); Rock mice (*Petromyscus*, 2 species); Delany's swamp mouse (*Delanymys brooksi*). Subsaharan Africa. 2 species are Critically Endangered; 1 is Endangered, and 3, including Nikolaus's mouse, are Vulnerable.

Root and bamboo rats Subfamily Rhizomyinae

6 species in 3 genera: Bamboo rats (*Rhizomys*, 3 species); Lesser bamboo rat (*Cannomys badius*); Root rats (*Tachyoryctes*, 2 species). E Africa and SE Asia.

Madagascan rats Subfamily Nesomyinae

15 species in 8 genera: Big-footed mice (*Macrotarsomys*, 2 species); Island mouse (*Nesomys rufus*); White-tailed rat (*Brachytarsomys albicauda*); Tufted-tailed rats (*Eliurus*, 6 species); Voalavoanala (*Gymnuromys roberti*); Malagasy giant rat (*Hypogeomys antimena*); Short-tailed rats (*Brachyuromys*, 2 species); White-tailed mouse (*Mystromys albicaudatus*). Madagascar (1 species in S Africa). 2 species are Critically Endangered, 2 Endangered, and 2 Vulnerable.

Oriental dormice Subfamily Platacanthomyinae

3 species in 2 genera: Spiny dormouse (*Platacanthomys lasiurus*); Chinese pygmy dormice (*Typhlomys*, 2 species). S India (Spiny dormouse); S China and N Vietnam (Chinese dormice). 1 *Typhlomys* species is Critically Endangered.

Zokors Subfamily Myospalacinae

6 species in 1 genus (*Myospalax*). China and Altai Mountains. Underground. 1 species is Vulnerable.

For full species list see Appendix ▷

Hamsters

FAMILIAR IN THE WEST AS CHILDREN'S PETS, *hamsters in their natural setting are solitary animals that react with aggression when they encounter other members of their own species. One breed that currently flourishes in captivity virtually all around the world was on the brink of extinction less than a century ago.*

FACTFILE

HAMSTERS

Order: Rodentia

Family: Muridae

Subfamilies: Cricetinae and Calomyscinae

26 species in 6 genera: **Ratlike hamsters** (Genus *Cricetulus*, 11 species; SE Europe, Asia Minor, N Asia). **Common** or **Black-bellied hamster** (*Cricetus cricetus*; C Europe, Russia). **Golden hamsters** (Genus *Mesocricetus*, 4 species; E Europe, Middle East). **Dwarf hamsters** (Genus *Phodopus*, 3 species; Siberia, Mongolia, N China). **Gansu hamster** (*Cansumys canus*), China. **Mouselike hamsters** (Genus *Calomyscus*, 6 species; Iran, Pakistan Afghanistan, S Russia).

DISTRIBUTION Europe, Middle East, Russia, China.

Equator

HABITAT Arid or semiarid areas, varying from rocky mountain slopes and steppe to cultivated fields.

SIZE Ranges from **head–body length** 5.3–10.2cm (2–4in) to 20–28cm (7.9–11in), **tail length** 0.7–1.1cm (0.3–0.4in), **weight** 50g (1.8oz) to 900g (32oz)

COAT Soft, thickly furred in shades of gray and brown

DIET Mostly herbivorous – seeds, shoots, root vegetables – though occasionally hamsters will take insects, lizards, small mammals, and young birds.

BREEDING Gestation ranges from 15 days in the Golden hamster to 37 days in the White-tailed rat.

LONGEVITY 2–3 years

CONSERVATION STATUS *Calomyscus hotsoni* and *Mesocricetus auratus* are listed as Endangered; *Mesocricetus newtoni* is listed as Vulnerable; others not threatened.

For full species list see Appendix ▷

Until the 1930s the golden hamster was known only from a single specimen found in 1839. However, in 1930 a female with 12 young was collected in Syria and taken to Israel. There the littermates bred, and some descendants were taken to England in 1931 and to the USA in 1938, where they proliferated. Today the golden hamster is one of the most familiar pets and laboratory animals in the West. The other hamster species are less well known, though the common hamster has been familiar for many years.

Pouches for Foraging
FORM AND FUNCTION

Most hamsters have small, compact, rounded bodies with short legs, thick fur, large ears, prominent dark eyes, long whiskers, and sharp claws. Most have cheek pouches that consist of loose folds of skin, starting from between the prominent incisors and premolars and extending along the outside of the lower jaw. When hamsters forage they can push food into the pouches, which then expand, enabling them to carry large quantities of provisions to their underground storage chambers – a useful adaptation for animals that live in habitats where food may occur irregularly but in great abundance. The paws of the front legs are modified hands, giving the animals great dexterity when they manipulate food. Hamsters also use a characteristic forward squeezing movement of the paws as a means of emptying their cheek pouches of food. Common hamsters are reputed to inflate their cheek pouches with air when crossing streams, presumably to create extra buoyancy.

The group known as mouselike hamsters were previously considered hamsters based on their molars but they lack cheek pouches, sebaceous flank glands, and the short tail of the true hamsters. It is now thought that mouselike hamsters represent an early split from the rest of the mouse-like rodents and some authorities place them in their own family, the Calomyscidae.

Hamsters are mainly herbivorous. The common hamster may hunt insects, lizards, frogs, mice, young birds, and even snakes, but such prey contribute only a small amount to its diet. Normally hamsters eat seeds, shoots, and root vegetables, including wheat, barley, millet, soybeans, peas, potatoes, carrots, and beets, as well as leaves and flowers. Small items such as millet seeds are carried to the hamster's burrow in its pouches, larger items like potatoes in its incisors. Food is either stored for the winter, eaten on returning to underground quarters, or, in undisturbed conditions, eaten above ground. One Korean gray hamster

managed to carry 42 soybeans in its pouches. The record for storage in a burrow probably goes to the common hamster: chambers of this species have been found to contain as much as 90kg (198lb) of plant material collected by a single hamster. Hamsters spend the winter in hibernation in their burrows, only waking on warmer days to eat food from their stores.

Baby Machines
SOCIAL BEHAVIOR

Though considered docile pets, hamsters in the wild are solitary and exceptionally aggressive toward members of their own species. These characteristics may result from intense competition for patchy but locally abundant food resources, but may also serve to disperse population throughout a particular area. Large species, such as the Korean gray hamster, also behave aggressively toward other species, and have been known to attack dogs or even people when threatened. To defend itself from attack, the Korean gray may throw itself on its back and utter piercing screams.

Species studied in the laboratory have been shown to have acute hearing. They communicate with ultrasound as well as with squeaks audible to the human ear. Ultrasound appears to be most important between males and females during mat-

⬥ Above *The Chinese striped hamster (*Cricetulus barabensis*) has capacious cheek pouches, enabling it to transport large quantities of food quickly to its burrow. This species of ratlike hamster is reported to be very aggressive, especially toward conspecifics.*

ing. The sense of smell is also acute; the golden hamster can recognize individuals, probably from flank gland secretions, and males can detect stages of a female's estrous cycle and recognize a receptive female by odor.

Most hamsters become sexually mature soon after weaning (or even during it). Female common hamsters become receptive to males at 43 days and can give birth at 59 days. Golden hamsters have slightly slower development and become sexually mature between 56 and 70 days. In the wild they probably breed only once – occasionally twice – per year, during spring and summer, but in captivity they can breed year round.

Courtship is simple and brief, as befits animals that generally meet only to copulate. Odors and restrained movement indicate that the partners are ready and willing to mate. Immature animals or females not in heat will either attack or be attacked by other individuals. After copulation a pair separate and may never meet again. The female builds a nest for the young in her burrow from grass, wool, and feathers, and gives birth after 16–20 days (in the common hamster). The young – born hairless and blind – are cared for by

○ **Above** *The golden hamster* (Mesocricetus auratus) *has been familiar worldwide for several decades as a pet. However, in the wild it is found only in a small area of northwestern Syria and is classified as endangered by the IUCN.*

the female alone. During this time she may live off her food store in another section of the burrow. The young are weaned at about 3 weeks in the golden hamster. In the slowest-developing species, the mouselike hamster, adult coloration and size may not be reached until 6 months old.

One species, the Korean gray hamster (*Cricetulus triton*), has been extensively studied in the North China Plain. It begins to breed in March and ends by August. While older females can manage 3 litters in a year, hamsters born that year produce only 1–2 litters. Litter size may be between 2 and 22, but the average is 9–10, after a gestation of about 20 days. It takes 2 months for a newborn female hamster to produce a first litter. The interval between two litters for an adult female is also about 2 months. The population oscillates greatly from year to year. Weasels and hawks are the major predators.

Male Dzungarian hamsters are extraordinary fathers, and even act as midwife to their partner. They help pull the young from the birth canal, and then clean up the newborns, consuming the placenta and licking out the nostrils to allow the little ones to breath. The male then stays close to the mother and young to keep them warm. These behaviors may be mediated by hormonal changes, as just before a birth the male's levels of estrogen and cortisol – the female and stress hormones – rise, to be replaced by testosterone thereafter. The male also babysits while the female goes out to feed.

Pets or Pests?
CONSERVATION AND ENVIRONMENT

Hamsters are considered serious pests to agriculture in some areas – in some countries dogs are trained to kill them. Chinese peasants sometimes catch large hamsters to feed to cats or other pets, and may dig the burrows in autumn to recover stored grain; in addition, the common hamster is trapped for its skin. Despite these pressures, most hamster species are not endangered, perhaps because most live in inhospitable regions and have high reproduction rates.   JF/ZZ

Gerbils

tO MOST PEOPLE, GERBILS ARE ATTRACTIVE *pets with large, dark eyes, a white belly and feet, and a furry tail. The animal they have in mind, however, is the Mongolian jird, just one of the many species of gerbils, jirds, and sand rats that together make up the world's largest group of rodents adapted to arid environments.*

Gerbils are distinctive among rodents, mostly resembling the familiar Mongolian jird in overall appearance but varying in dimensions from the mouse-sized slender gerbils to robust-bodied jirds and sand rats. Within genera, however, the visible differences between species are subtle, often only expressed by small changes in fur and nail color, tail length, and the presence or absence of a tail tuft. Given such complexities, it is impossible to know for sure how many species exist; sometimes it is even hard to identify the genus to which a species belongs without using chromosomal, protein, and molecular comparisons.

Adaptations for Arid Climes
FORM AND FUNCTION
Most gerbils live in arid habitats and harsh climates, having adapted to both in interesting ways. To survive in such inhospitable conditions, an animal must not lose more water than it normally takes in. Water loss usually occurs by evaporation from the skin, in air exhaled from the lungs, and via urination and defecation. The gerbil's predicament is that it has a large body surface compared with its volume, and so has to find ways of minimizing water loss.

As a consequence, gerbils cannot afford to sweat, and indeed cannot survive temperatures of 45°C (113°F) or higher for more than about two hours. Most species are nocturnal; during the day they live underground, often with the burrow entrance blocked, at a depth of about 50cm (20in) where the temperature remains a constant 20–25°C (68–77°F). Only some northern species – for example, great gerbils and Mongolian jirds – live on the surface in daytime, though some jirds that live farther south also emerge during the day in winter.

In the arid world of the gerbil, the only foods that are often available are dry seeds or leaves. The animal's nocturnal activity enables it to make the most of this poor sustenance. By the time it comes out of its burrow, such foods are permeated with dew, and it can improve the burrow's humidity, already high in relative terms, by taking them back there to eat. The gerbil's digestive system extracts

water efficiently from the food, minimizing the water lost in feces, and the kidneys produce only a few drops of concentrated urine.

Other gerbil adaptations reduce the risk of capture by predators. Gerbils take on the color of the ground on which they live; this ability extends even to local populations of a single species living in different habitats, so animals found on dark lava soils are dark brown whereas conspecifics living on red sand are red. The effectiveness of the camouflage is only compromised by the tail, which ends in a tuft of a contrasting color. Even so, the tail is a vital survival aid; it helps with balance during movement; it can be used to twirl sand over a burrow entrance, effectively concealing it; and it may act as a decoy too, distracting predators from the animal's body and coming away either whole or in part if a predator happens to catch hold of it.

Another distinctive feature of gerbil anatomy is a particularly large middle ear, which is at its biggest in species living in open desert habitats; this enables the animals to hear low-frequency sounds such as the beating of an owl's wings. Gerbils also have large eyes, positioned high on the head so that they give the animals a wide field of vision.

The Three Gerbil Zones
DISTRIBUTION PATTERNS
The geographical range of gerbils can be divided into three major regions. The first includes not just the extensive savannas of Africa but also the Namib and Kalahari deserts, where the temperature rarely falls below freezing in winter. The second takes in the hot deserts and semidesert regions along the Tropic of Cancer in north Africa and southwest Asia, plus the arid Horn of Africa. The third covers the deserts, semideserts, and steppes of Central Asia, where winter temperatures fall well below freezing. The different gerbil genera fall broadly into groups linked to one or other of these regions. So, with the exception of the Indian gerbil, gerbils of the *Gerbillurus* and *Taterillus* groups occur in the first region, *Ammodillus*, *Gerbillus*, and *Pachyuromys* gerbils live in the second, while only species belonging to the *Rhombomys* group live in the third (though some of these also occur in the second region).

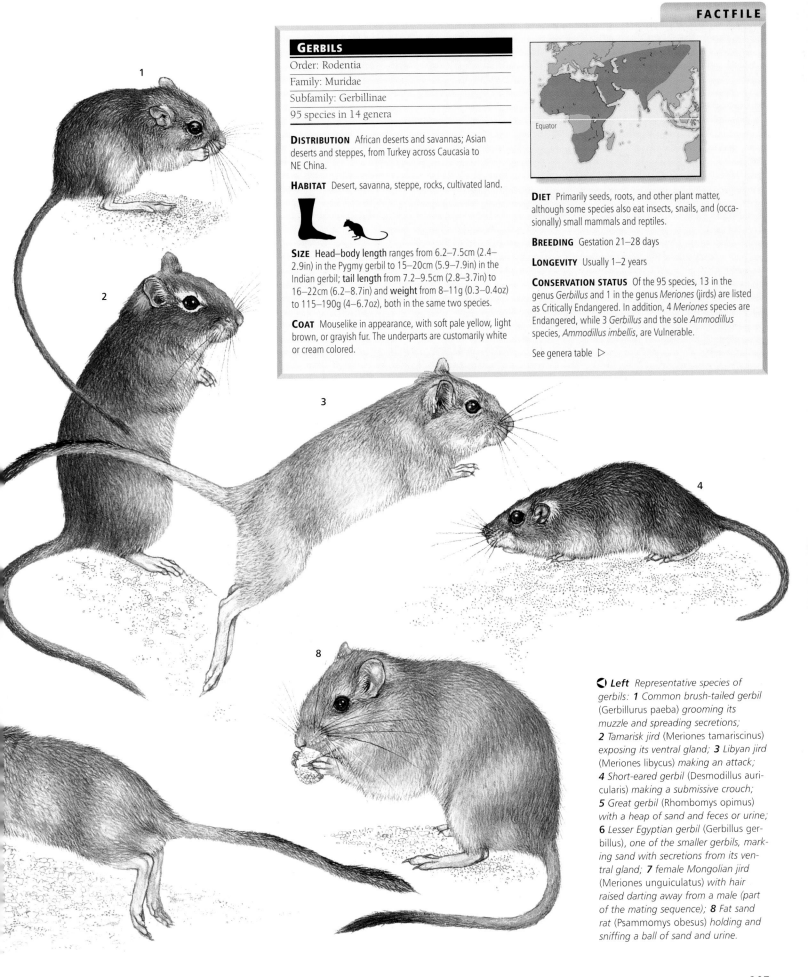

GERBILS

Order: Rodentia

Family: Muridae

Subfamily: Gerbillinae

95 species in 14 genera

DISTRIBUTION African deserts and savannas; Asian deserts and steppes, from Turkey across Caucasia to NE China.

HABITAT Desert, savanna, steppe, rocks, cultivated land.

SIZE Head–body length ranges from 6.2–7.5cm (2.4–2.9in) in the Pygmy gerbil to 15–20cm (5.9–7.9in) in the Indian gerbil; tail length from 7.2–9.5cm (2.8–3.7in) to 16–22cm (6.2–8.7in) and weight from 8–11g (0.3–0.4oz) to 115–190g (4–6.7oz), both in the same two species.

COAT Mouselike in appearance, with soft pale yellow, light brown, or grayish fur. The underparts are customarily white or cream colored.

DIET Primarily seeds, roots, and other plant matter, although some species also eat insects, snails, and (occasionally) small mammals and reptiles.

BREEDING Gestation 21–28 days

LONGEVITY Usually 1–2 years

CONSERVATION STATUS Of the 95 species, 13 in the genus *Gerbillus* and 1 in the genus *Meriones* (jirds) are listed as Critically Endangered. In addition, 4 *Meriones* species are Endangered, while 3 *Gerbillus* and the sole *Ammodillus* species, *Ammodillus imbellis*, are Vulnerable.

See genera table ▷

◁ **Left** *Representative species of gerbils:* **1** *Common brush-tailed gerbil* (Gerbillurus paeba) *grooming its muzzle and spreading secretions;* **2** *Tamarisk jird* (Meriones tamariscinus) *exposing its ventral gland;* **3** *Libyan jird* (Meriones libycus) *making an attack;* **4** *Short-eared gerbil* (Desmodillus auricularis) *making a submissive crouch;* **5** *Great gerbil* (Rhombomys opimus) *with a heap of sand and feces or urine;* **6** *Lesser Egyptian gerbil* (Gerbillus gerbillus), *one of the smaller gerbils, marking sand with secretions from its ventral gland;* **7** *female Mongolian jird* (Meriones unguiculatus) *with hair raised darting away from a male (part of the mating sequence);* **8** *Fat sand rat* (Psammomys obesus) *holding and sniffing a ball of sand and urine.*

Gerbil Groups

Ammodillus

1 genus: *Ammodillus*
Somali gerbil or **walo** (*Ammodillus imbellis*) Somalia, E Ethiopia, inhabiting savanna and desert.

Gerbillus

3 genera: *Desmodilliscus, Gerbillus, Microdillus*
Pouched pygmy gerbil (*Desmodilliscus braueri*) Senegal and Mauritania E to C Sudan, inhabiting savanna.
Northern pygmy gerbils (*Gerbillus*, 45 species) N Africa, Middle East, Iran, Afghanistan, to NW India, inhabiting desert, semidesert, and coastal plains. Species include Pygmy gerbil (*G. henleyi*),

Lesser Egyptian gerbil (*G. gerbillus*), Greater rock gerbil (*G. campestris*), Wagner's gerbil (*G. dasyurus*).
Somali pygmy gerbil (*Microdillus peeli*) Somalia, inhabiting dry savanna.

Gerbillurus

2 genera: *Desmodillus, Gerbillurus*
Short-eared gerbil (*Desmodillus auricularis*) S Africa, inhabiting desert, savanna.
Southern pygmy gerbils (*Gerbillurus* 4 species) S Africa, inhabiting savanna and desert. Species include Namib brush-tailed gerbil (*G. setzeri*).

Pachyuromys

1 genus: *Pachyuromys*
Fat-tailed jird (*Pachyuromys duprasi*) Morocco to Egypt inhabiting desert and semidesert.

Rhombomys

5 genera: *Brachiones, Meriones, Psammomys, Rhombomys, Sekeetamys*
Przewalski's gerbil (*Brachiones przewalskii*) N China, inhabiting desert.
Jirds (*Meriones*, 16 species) N Africa, Turkey, SW Asia, Kazakhstan, to Mongolia, N China and NW India inhabiting desert and semidesert. Species include Silky jird (*M. crassus*), Mongolian jird (*M. unguiculatus*).
Sand rats (*Psammomys*, 2 species) N African to Syria and Arabian peninsula inhabiting desert and semidesert. Species include Fat sand rat (*P. obesus*) and Lesser sand rat (*P. vexillaris*).
Great gerbil (*Rhombomys opimus*) Kazakhstan, Iran, Afghanistan, Pakistan to N China and Mongolia inhabiting steppe and desert.

Bushy-tailed jird (*Sekeetamys calurus*) E Egypt, S Israel, Jordan, to C Saudi Arabia inhabiting desert.

Taterillus

2 genera: *Tatera, Taterillus*
Large naked-soled gerbils (*Tatera*, 12 species) S, E, and W Africa, Syria to India, Nepal and Sri Lanka inhabiting savanna and steppe. Species include Indian gerbil (*T. indica*), Black-tailed gerbil (*T. nigricauda*).
Small naked-soled gerbils (*Taterillus*, 8 species) Senegal, Mauritania to S Sudan and S to N Tanzania inhabiting semidesert, savanna and wooded grassland. Species include: Emin's gerbil (*T. emini*), Harrington's gerbil (*T. harringtoni*).

For full species list see Appendix ▷

Omnivorous Vegetarians
DIET

Gerbils are basically vegetarians, eating various parts of plants – seeds, fruits, leaves, stems, roots, and bulbs; many species, however, will eat anything they encounter, including insects, snails, reptiles, and even other small rodents. The nocturnal *Gerbillus* species often search for wind-blown seeds in deserts. Gerbils living in the very dry desert regions of southern Africa are primarily insectivorous.

Some species are very specialized, living on a single type of food. The fat sand rat, great gerbil, and Indian gerbil, for example, are all basically herbivorous. Of these, the fat sand rat only occurs where it can find salty, succulent plants, while the Indian gerbil depends on fresh food all year round, so it tends to occur near irrigated crops. Wagner's gerbil has such a liking for snails that it threatens the existence of local snail populations; big piles of empty shells are found outside this gerbil's burrows.

Most gerbils take the precaution of carrying their food back to their burrows before they consume it. Species that live in areas with cold winters must hoard in order to survive. One Mongolian jird was found to have hidden away 20kg (44lb) of seeds in its burrow. Great gerbils not only hoard plants but also construct stacks outside the burrow that can be 1m (3.3ft) high and 3m (9.8ft) long.

A Link with Climate and Food
SOCIAL BEHAVIOR

The social organization of gerbils is only beginning to be studied. Species that live in authentic deserts, whatever genus or group they belong to, tend to lead solitary lives, sometimes in extensive burrow systems, though the burrows are often close enough not to preclude the existence of colonies. Perhaps because the supply of food

cannot be guaranteed in such an environment, each animal fends for itself. In contrast, species from savannas, where food is more abundant, are more social. There have been reports of stable pairs forming, and even of family structures emerging.

The most complex social arrangements of all have been observed in species in the Rhombomys group that live in regions with cold winters. Groups larger than families gather in single, extensive burrows, perhaps to huddle together for warmth but also maybe to guard food supplies. The best-known example is the great gerbil of the Central Asian steppes, which lives in large colonies composed of numerous subgroups that themselves have developed from male–female pairs. A similar social structure is found among Mongolian jirds, although other jird species in North Africa and Asia are reported to be solitary in hot climates but social in cooler regions.

◑ **Above** *The characteristically slender form of a northern pygmy gerbil, in this case a Cheesman's gerbil engaged in clearing sand from the entrance to its burrow in the Wahiba Sands, Oman. Many species of this genus are endangered.*

In savanna species, reproduction too seems to be linked to climate and food. These gerbils give birth after the rainy season. Species living in areas where fresh food is available may reproduce all the year round, with females giving birth to two or three litters a year. Some desert species, however, reproduce only in the cooler months, although those found in southern African deserts may give birth at any time.

Litter size can vary between 1 and 12, with a mean of 3–5, depending on species. The young are born helpless and hairless with their eyes closed, and are unable to regulate their body

◖ **Right** The bushveld gerbil has a ratlike appearance. These gerbils inhabit sandy plains, savannas, and woodlands. Despite their small stature they can leap vast heights and distances when frightened, fleeing from predators in a series of running bounds. Burrows for this genus may run up to 1m (3ft) underground.

THE COMMUNAL LIFE OF THE MONGOLIAN JIRD

Mongolian jirds live in sizable social groups that, at their largest in summer, consist of 1–3 adult males and 2–7 adult females, plus numerous subadults and juveniles, all dwelling in a single burrow system. Detailed studies have demonstrated that the animals engage in various group activities, for example collectively hoarding food for the winter and spending the cold months huddled together in the burrow. The integrity of the community seems, under normal circumstances, to be jealously guarded. Strange jirds and other animals are chased off.

Who, then, among the adults in the group are the parents of the subadults and juveniles? Parenthood is not evident from the behavior of the males and females within the community, even though they have been observed to form pairs.

The young might conceivably be the offspring of young adults that have migrated from another burrow, but for many reasons this has never seemed likely to be the case. If animals were to leave their own group late in the summer to establish another burrow community elsewhere, they would be vulnerable to predators and the effects of bad weather, and would also have to contend with other jirds into whose territories they might wander. (When population densities are high, there may be as many as 50 burrows per hectare, or 20 per acre). In addition, they would not have access to the food collected for the winter. The most serious objection, however, is

◖ **Right** This Mongolian jird is probably two to three weeks old. Litter size is usually 4–6; infants, which open their eyes at 2–3 weeks, are weaned after about 3–4 weeks.

that if the animals traveled in groups, such behavior would perpetuate inbreeding and so produce genetic problems.

The unexpected answer to this conundrum has come from observation of animals in captivity. Such studies have shown that communal groups do remain stable and territorial, but when females are in heat they leave their own territories and visit neighboring communities to mate. The females then return to their own burrows, where their offspring will eventually grow up under the protection and care not of their mother and father but rather of their mother and uncles.

temperature. For about two weeks they depend entirely on their mother's care, and are nursed constantly. Where there is a breeding season, only those born early within it become sexually mature in time to themselves breed in the same season (when aged about 2 months). Those born later become sexually mature after about 6 months, and breed during the following season.

Contradictory Relations with Humans
CONSERVATION AND ENVIRONMENT

Most gerbils live in largely uninhabited areas of the world. When they do come into contact with humans, especially in the African savannas, the Asian steppes, and India, their activities bring them into conflict with people. When collecting food, especially to hoard for winter, they pilfer from crops. When burrowing, they can cause great damage to pastures, irrigation channels, road and railway embankments, and even to the foundations of buildings. They also carry the fleas that transmit deadly disease, including plague, and are reservoirs of the skin disease leishmaniasis.

Though they serve humankind in medical research and as pets, they become pests when they interfere with peoples' lives. Many gerbils are destroyed by gassing; alternatively, burrow systems may be plowed up, even though they may have been used by generations of gerbils for hundreds of years. In some regions too, the sweet, lightly colored meat is considered a delicacy and is readily eaten.   DAS/GA

Dormice

○ **Right** *Worldwide, many dormouse species are at risk; the Japanese dormouse is classified by the IUCN as endangered.*

○ *Above Despite its name, the garden (or orchard) dormouse (Eliomys quercinus) is mostly found in forests across central Europe, though some inhabit shrubs and crevices in rocks.*

tHE DORMICE OR MYOXIDAE ORIGINATED AT *least as early as the Eocene era, 55–34 million years ago. In the Pleistocene (1.8 million–10,000 years ago), giant forms lived on some Mediterranean islands. Today dormice are the intermediates, in form and behavior, between mice and squirrels.*

Key features of dormice are their accumulations of fat and their long hibernation period (about seven months in most European species). The Romans fattened dormice for eating in a special enclosure, the *glirarium*, while the French have a phrase "To sleep like a dormouse," equivalent to the English "To sleep like a log."

Equipped for Scurrying
FORM AND FUNCTION
Dormice are extremely agile. Most species are adapted to climbing, but some – for example garden and forest dormice – also live on the ground; however, the masked mouse-tailed dormouse is the only species that does so exclusively. The four digits of the forefeet and the five digits of the hind-feet have short, curved claws. The underside of each foot is bare with a cushionlike covering. The tail is usually bushy and often long, and in some species such as the fat, hazel, garden, forest, and African dormice it can detach from the body when it is seized upon by predators – or even other dormice. The sense of hearing is particularly well-developed, as is the ability to vocalize. Fat, hazel, garden, and African dormice make use of clicks, whistles, and growling sounds across a broad range of behavior: antagonistic, sexual, explorative, playful.

The desert dormouse, which is placed in a genus of its own, occurs in deserts to the west and north of Lake Balkhash in eastern Kazakhstan, Central Asia. It has very dense, soft fur, a naked tail, small ears, and sheds the upper layers of skin when it molts. It eats invertebrates such as insects and spiders, and is mostly active at twilight and in the night. It probably hibernates in cold weather.

Feeding Up for Winter
DIET
Dormice are the only rodents that do not have a cecum, which indicates that their diet contains little cellulose. Analysis of the contents of their stomachs has shown that they are omnivores whose diet varies according to season and that there is dietary variation between species according to region. The fat and hazel dormice are the most vegetarian, eating quantities of fruits, nuts, seeds, and buds. Garden, forest, and African dormice are the most carnivorous – their diets include insects, spiders, earthworms, and small vertebrates, but also eggs and fruit.

In France, 40–80 percent of the diet of the garden dormouse is comprised of insects, according to region and season. However, there is also another factor to be considered. In summer the garden dormouse eats mainly insects and fruit while in the fall it eats little except fruit, even though the supply of insects is plentiful at this time of year. This change in the content of the diet is part of the preparation for entering hibernation; the intake of protein is reduced, and consequently sleep is induced.

A Long Time Sleeping
SOCIAL BEHAVIOR
In Europe, dormice hibernate from October to April with the precise length of time varying between species and according to region. During the second half of the hibernation period they sometimes wake intermittently – a sign of the onset of the hormone activity that stimulates sexual activity.

Dormice begin to mate as soon as they emerge from hibernation, females giving birth from May onward through to October according to age. (Not all dormice that have recently become sexually mature participate in mating.) The fat and garden dormice produce one litter each per year, but hazel and forest dormice can produce up to three. Vocalizations play an important part in mating. In the fat dormouse, the male emits calls as he follows the female; in the garden dormouse,

◁ **Left** *Curled up tightly, this hazel dormouse is in hibernation. For its long winter sleep this dormouse retires to a nest, either in a tree stump, amid debris on the ground, or in a burrow. The length of hibernation is related to climate and can last nine months.*

Dormouse Subfamilies

Subfamily Graphiurinae

African Dormice (*Graphiurus*, 14 species).
1 species Vulnerable.

Subfamily Leithiinae

Forest Dormice (*Dryomys*, 3 species). 1 species
Endangered.
Garden dormice (*Eliomys*, 2 species). 1 species
Vulnerable.
Mouse-tailed dormice (*Myomimus*, 3 species).
1 species Endangered, 2 species Vulnerable.
Desert dormouse (*Selvinia betpakdalaensis*).
Endangered.

Subfamily Myoxinae

Japanese dormouse (*Glirulus japonicus*). Endan-
gered.
Hazel dormouse (*Muscardinus avellanarius*).
Fat dormouse (*Myoxus glis*).

For full species list see Appendix ▷

the female uses whistles to attract the male. The female goes into hiding just before she is due to give birth, and builds a nest, usually globular in shape and located off the ground, for example in a hole in a tree or in the crook of a branch. Materials used include leaves, grass, and moss. The garden and fat dormice use hairs and feathers as lining materials. The female garden dormouse scent marks the area around the nest and defends it.

Female dormice give birth to between two and nine young, with four being the average litter size in almost all species. The young are born naked and blind. In the first week after birth they become able to discriminate between smells, although an exchange of saliva between mother and young appears to be the means whereby mother and offspring learn to recognize each other. This behavior may also aid the transition from a milk diet to a solid food one. At about 18 days the young become able to hear, and at about the same time their eyes open. They become independent after about 4–6 weeks. Young dormice then grow rapidly until the time for hibernation approaches, when their development slows. Sexual maturity is reached about one year after birth, towards the end of or after the first hibernation.

Dormice populations are usually less dense than those of most other rodents. There are normally between 0.1 and 10 dormice per ha (0.04–4 per acre). They live in small groups, half of which normally consist of juveniles, and each group occupies a home range, the main axis of which can vary from 100m (330ft) in the garden dormouse to 200m (660ft) in the fat dormouse. In urban areas the radio tracking of garden dormice has indicated that their home range describes an elliptical shape and is related to the availability of food. In the fall the home range is about 1,000sq m (10,800sq ft).

One study of the social organization of the garden dormouse revealed significant changes in behavior in the active period between hibernations. In the spring, when garden dormice are emerging from hibernation, males form themselves into groups in which there is a clearcut division between dominant and subordinate animals. As the groups form, some males are forced to disperse. Once this has happened, although groups remain cohesive, behavior within them becomes somewhat more relaxed, so that by the end of the

⬤ **Above** *Fat dormice have a predilection for fruit and are one of the most vegetarian species. This made them highly suitable for human consumption, hence their alternative name of edible dormice.*

summer the groups have a family character. In the fall social structure includes all categories of age and sex. Despite the high rate of renewal among its members, a colony can continue to exist for many years. CB

FACTFILE

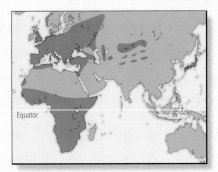

DORMICE

Order: Rodentia

Family: Myoxidae

26 species in 8 genera and 3 subfamilies

DISTRIBUTION Europe, Africa, Turkey, Asia, Japan.

HABITAT Wooded and rocky areas, steppe, gardens.

SIZE Head–body length 6.1–19cm (2.4–7.5in); tail length 4–16.5cm (1.6–6.5in); weight 15–200g (0.5–7oz).

COAT Soft furred and squirrel-like, with bushy tails (except in *Myomimus*).

DIET Omnivorous, including insects, worms, spiders, fruit, seeds, nuts, and eggs.

BREEDING Gestation 21–32 days

LONGEVITY 3–6 years in wild

CONSERVATION STATUS Half of all dormouse species are listed by the IUCN: 4 as Endangered, 4 as Vulnerable, and 5 as Lower Risk: Near Threatened.

See subfamilies table △

Jumping Mice, Birchmice, and Jerboas

T O A GREATER OR LESSER EXTENT, ALL THE members of the Dipodidae family have evolved to move in leaps and bounds. As their names suggest, jumping mice and birchmice are small and mouselike; the jerboas are mostly rather larger, and are remarkable for their kangaroo-like hindlegs.

These small and relatively defenseless rodents seem to have adapted to jumping as an antipredator strategy, but remain motionless once they have reached safety. Mostly nocturnal, they are shy and are seldom seen in the wild, not least because some species hibernate for up to 9 months of the year.

Jumping Mice
SUBFAMILY ZAPODINAE

The name "jumping mouse" is something of a misnomer. All jumping mice are equipped for jumping, with long back feet and long tails to help them maintain their balance in the air, but the most common species, those belonging to the genus *Zapus*, are more likely to crawl under vegetation or to run by making a series of short hops rather than long leaps. However, the woodland jumping mouse often moves by bounding 1.5–3m (5–10ft) at a time. In addition to the feet and tail, the outstanding characters of jumping mice are their colorful fur and grooved upper incisors. The function of the groove is unknown: it may improve the efficiency of the teeth as cutting tools, or it may just strengthen them.

◑ **Bottom** *A meadow jumping mouse. Its most important food is grass seeds, many of which are picked from the ground, but some are pulled from grass stalks. To eat timothy seeds, for example the mouse may climb up the stalk and cut off the seed heads. At other times the mouse will reach as high as it can, cut off the stalk, pull the top portion down, cut it off again , and so on, until the seed head is reached. The stem, leaf stalk, and uneaten seeds are usually left in a pile of match-length parts. Another favorite seed is that of the touch-me-not. These seeds taste of walnut, but the bright turquoise endosperm whirls turn the entire contents of the stomach brilliant blue.*

Jumping mice are not burrowers. They live on the surface, although their nests may be underground or in a hollow log or other protected place, and the hibernating nest is often at the end of a burrow in a bank or other raised area. For the most part, however, jumping mice hide by day in clumps of vegetation. They also usually travel about in thick herbaceous cover, although they will use runways or sometimes burrows of other species when present.

The habitat of jumping mice varies, but lush grassy or weedy meadows are the preferred habitat of meadow jumping mice, although they are often quite abundant in wooded areas, in patches of heavy vegetation (especially of touch-me-not, *Impatiens*), particularly in areas where there are no woodland jumping mice. Woodland jumping mice usually occur in woods, almost never in open areas, and are most abundant in wooded areas with heavy ground cover. Moisture is often mentioned as a factor favorable to jumping mice, but it seems more important as a factor favoring the development of lush vegetation rather than as a factor directly favoring the mice.

Jumping mice are profound hibernators, hibernating for 6-9 months of the year according to species, locality and elevation. The meadow jumping mouse in the eastern USA usually hibernates from about October to late April. Individuals that hibernate successfully put on about 6–10g (0.21–0.35 oz) of fat in the two weeks prior to entering hibernation. They enter hibernation by sleeping for increasingly longer periods until they attain deep hibernation, with their body temperature just a little above freezing. Their heart rate, breathing rate and all bodily functions drop to low levels. However, the animals wake about every two weeks, perhaps urinate, then go back to sleep. In the spring the males appear above ground about two weeks before the females. Of the animals active in the fall, only about a third – the larger ones -- are apparently able to put on the layer of fat, enter hibernation and awaken in the spring. The remainder -- young individuals or those unable to put on adequate fat – apparently perish during the winter retreat.

Jumping mice give birth to their young in a nest of grass or leaves either underground, in a clump of vegetation, in a log or in some other protected place. Gestation takes about 17 or 18 days, or up to 24 if the female is lactating. Each litter contains about 4–7 young. Litters may be produced at any time between May and September, but most young enter the world in June and August. Most females probably produce one litter per year.

FACTFILE

JUMPING MICE, BIRCHMICE, & JERBOAS

Order: Rodentia

Family: Dipodidae

50 species in 16 genera and 6 subfamilies

DISTRIBUTION N America, Eurasia, N Africa and Turkey.

Jumping mice and Birchmice	Jerboas

HABITAT Jumping mice: meadows, moors, steppe, thickets, woods. Birchmice: forests, meadows, steppe. Jerboas: desert, semidesert, steppe, including patches of bare ground.

SIZE Jumping mice: head–body length 7.6–11cm (3–4.3in), tail length 15–16.5cm (5.9–6.5in), weight up to 28g (1oz). Birchmice: head–body length 5–9cm (1.9–3.5in), tail length 6.5–10cm (2.6–3.9in), weight up to 28g (1oz). Jerboas: head–body length 4–23cm (1.6–9in), tail length 7–30cm (2.7–11in). hindfoot length 2–10cm (0.8–4in).

COAT Coarse in the jumping mice and birchmice, silky in the jerboas. Coloration usually matches the habitat in which the different species live.

DIET Jumping mice: moth larvae, beetles, fungi, and (in Meadow jumping mice) seeds. Birchmice: seeds, berries, insects. Jerboas: seeds, insects and insect larvae, fresh leaves and stems of succulent plants.

BREEDING Gestation times range from 17–21 days in jumping mice (*Zapus* and *Napaeozapus* species) to 18–24 days in birchmice (*Sicista betulina*) and 25–35 days in jerboas.

LONGEVITY Probably 1–2 years in jumping mice, at least 1.5 years in birchmice, and 2–3 years in jerboas.

CONSERVATION STATUS Among the 4 jumping mouse species, the Chinese jumping mouse (*Eozapus setchuanus*) is listed as Vulnerable. Of 16 birchmouse species, one (*Sicista armenica*) is Critically Endangered and another (*S. caudata*) Endangered. In the jerboas, one *Allactaga* species (*A. firouzi*) is Critically Endangered and another (*A. tetradactyla*) Endangered, as is the Long-eared jerboa (*Euchoreutes naso*). The Five-toed dwarf jerboa (*Cardiocranius paradoxus*) and one of the six Three-toed dwarf jerboa species (*Salpingotus crassicauda*) are Vulnerable.

Meadow jumping mice eat many things, but seeds, especially those from grasses, are the most important food. The seeds eaten change with availability. The major animal foods eaten by jumping mice are moth larvae (primarily cutworms) and ground and snout beetles. Also important in the diet are fungi related to the subterranean *Endogone*. This item forms about 12 percent of the diet (by volume) in the meadow jumping mice, and about 35 percent of the diet in the woodland jumping mouse.

Birchmice
SUBFAMILY SICISTINAE

Birchmice differ from jumping mice in having scarcely enlarged hindfeet and upper incisors without grooves. Moreover, their legs and tail are shorter than those of jumping mice, yet they travel by jumping, and climb into bushes using their outer toes to hold on to vegetation and their tails for partial support. Birchmice also, unlike jumping mice, dig shallow burrows and make nests of herbaceous vegetation underground.

Like jumping mice, birchmice are active primarily at night. They can eat extremely large amounts of food at one time and can also spend long periods without eating. Their main foods are seeds, berries, and insects. Birchmice hibernate in their underground nests for about half of the year. It has been suggested that *Sicista betulina* spends the summer in meadows but hibernates in forest. Gestation probably lasts about 18–24 days and

---

Subfamilies of Jumping Mice, Birchmice, and Jerboas

Jumping mice
Subfamily Zapodinae

5 species in 3 genera: **Meadow jumping mouse** (*Zapus hudsonius*), **Western jumping mouse** (*Z. princeps*), **Pacific jumping mouse** (*Z. trinotatus*), and **Woodland jumping mouse** (*Napaeozapus insignis*) N America, in meadows, moors, steppes, thickets, woods. **Chinese jumping mouse** (*Eozapus setchuanus*), China.
SIZE: HBL 7.6–11cm (3–4.3in); TL 15–16.5cm (5.9–6.9in); WT up to 28g (1oz).
BREEDING: about 17–21 days in *Zapus* and *Napaeozapus*.
LONGEVITY: probably 1–2 years.

Birchmice
Subfamily Sicistinae

13 species in 1 genus (*Sicista*). Mainly birch forests throughout Eurasia but also other habitats. Species include *S. betulina* (N Eurasia), *S. caucasica* (W Caucasus and Armenia), *S. concolor* (China), *S. subtilis* (Russia and E Europe).

SIZE: HBL 5–9cm (1.9–3.5in); TL 6.5–10cm (2.6–3.9in); WT up to 28g (1oz).
BREEDING: 18–24 days in *S.betulina*.
LONGEVITY: probably less than one year.

Jerboas

Habitat includes desert, semidesert steppe, including patches of bare ground.
SIZE: HBL 4–26cm (1.6–10in); TL 7–30cm (2.7–11in); hindfoot length 2–4cm (0.8–10in).
BREEDING: 25–42 days.
LONGEVITY: less than two years.

Subfamily Cardiocraniinae

7 species in 3 genera: **Five-toed dwarf jerboa** (*Cardiocranius paradoxus*), W China, Mongolia. **Three-toed dwarf jerboas** (*Salpingotus*, 5 species) Asian deserts. *Salpingotulus michaelis* Pakistan.

Subfamily Dipodinae

9 species in 5 genera: **Feather-footed jerboa** (*Dipus sagitta*) China and

Russia; **Lichtenstein's jerboa** (*Eremodipus lichtensteini*) Kazakhstan, Turkmenistan, Uzbekistan; **Desert jerboas** (*Jaculus*, 3 species, *J. blanfordi, J. jaculus, J. orientalis*) N Africa, Iran, Russia, Afghanistan, Pakistan, in various habitats; **Comb-toed jerboa** (*Paradipus ctenodactylus*) Russia in dry, sandy deserts; **Three-toed jerboas** (*Stylodipus*, 3 species, *S. andrewsi, S. sungorus, S. telum*) Russia, Mongolia, China, in clay and gravel deserts.

Subfamily Allactaginae

16 species in 3 genera: **Four- and five-toed jerboas** (*Allactaga*, 12 species) NE Africa (Libyan desert), Arabian Peninsula, C Asia. **Fat-tailed jerboas** (*Pygeretmus*, 3 species, *P. platyurus, P. pumilio, P. shitkovi*) Russia, in salt and clay deserts. **Bobrinski's jerboa** (*Allactodipus bobrinskii*).

Subfamily Euchoreutinae

1 genus: *Euchoreutes*
Long-eared jerboa (*Euchoreutes naso*) China and Mongolia, in gravel deserts.

⚅ **Bottom** *The Pacific jumping mouse is a very nervous creature and will turn aggressive and jump from side to side if trapped. It emits a high-pitched squeak and drums its long tail on the ground when fighting.*

parental care for another four weeks. Studies of *S. betulina* in Poland have shown that one litter a year is produced and that a female produces only two litters during her lifetime.

Jerboas
FORM AND FUNCTION

Jerboas are mouse- to rat-sized animals built for jumping. Their hindlimbs are elongated – at least four times the length of their front legs, and in most species the three main foot bones are fused into a single "cannon bone" for greater strength (in the subfamilies Dipodinae and Euchoreutinae, but not in the Cardiocraniinae). The outer toes on the hindfeet are small in size and do not touch the ground in species with five toes. In other species the outer toes are absent, so there are three toes on each hindfoot. One species, *Allactaga tetradactylus*, has four toes. Jerboas living in sandy areas have tufts of hair on the undersides of the feet that serve as "snowshoes" on soft sand and help them to maintain traction and kick sand backwards when burrowing. These jerboas also have tufts of hair to help keep sand out of the ears.

Some jerboas, those belonging to the genus *Jaculus* for example, have a fold of skin that can be pulled forward over the nostrils when burrowing. Jerboas use their long tail as a prop when standing upright and as a balancing organ when jumping. Jerboas are nocturnal and have large eyes.

The well-developed jumping ability of jerboas enables them to escape from predators as well as to move about, although they also move by slow hops. Only the hindlegs are used for movement; the front feet are used for gathering food. Jumps of 1.5–3m (5–10ft) are used when the animal moves rapidly. Desert jerboas, *Jaculus*, can jump vertically to nearly 1m (3ft).

Jerboas feed primarily on seeds, but sometimes also on succulent vegetation. In some areas they may be a pest to growers of melons. They also eat insects, and one species, *Allactaga sibirica*, feeds primarily on beetles and beetle larvae. One individual of *Salpingotus* in captivity ate only invertebrates. In *Dipus* all individuals in a population emerge for their nightly forays at about the same time, and move by long leaps to their feeding grounds, which may be some distance away. There they feed on plants, especially those with milky juices, but they can also smell underground nut sprouts and insect larvae in galls (gallnuts) below the surface. Like pocket mice, jerboas do not drink water; they manufacture metabolic water from food.

Some jerboas hibernate during the winter, surviving off their body fat. Also, some species enter torpor during hot or dry periods. They are generally quiet, but when handled will sometimes

shriek or make grunting noises. Some species have been known to tap with a hindfoot when inside their burrows. In northern species mating first occurs shortly after emergence from hibernation, but most female jerboas probably breed at least twice in a season, producing litters of 2–6 young.

There are four kinds of burrows used by various jerboas, depending on their habits and habitats: temporary summer day burrows for hiding during the day, temporary summer night burrows for hiding during nightly forays, permanent summer burrows used as living quarters and for producing young, and permanent winter burrows for hibernation. The two temporary burrows are simple tubes, which are in length respectively 20–50cm (8–20in) and 10–20cm (4–8in).

The permanent summer burrows have secondary chambers for food storage, and the permanent winter burrows are at least 22cm (9in) below the surface and also have secondary chambers.

◐ **Top** *The burrows used by desert jerboas can run as deep as 2m (about 6ft). At this depth the animals are insulated against fluctuations in outside temperature. Burrows can be complex, with passages off the main chambers from which the animals can burst through the soil to the surface when disturbed or threatened. There is usually one jerboa to a burrow, but the desert jerboas (as here) are fairly sociable and live in loose colonies with two or three animals often using the same nest. Desert jerboas are adept at burrowing, using their short front feet and incisor teeth for digging, and their hindfeet for kicking away the sand.*

Some species build a mound at the entrance, and some provide one or more accessory exits. The comb-toed jerboa lives in sand dunes where it burrows into the protected side of the dunes. Most of the burrows that have been dug up consisted of single passages. This is one species from which tapping sounds have been recorded from within the burrow.   GIS/JW

Pocket Gophers

POCKET GOPHERS ARE ONE OF SEVEN OR EIGHT *rodent groups around the world that spend most of their lives below ground in self-dug burrow systems. Native to North and Central America and to northwestern Colombia in South America, they present a paradox: they are extraordinarily diverse, even though all species share a common body plan and a similar life cycle, adapted for a life of digging.*

Pocket gophers take their name from the fur-lined cheek pouches that serve as built-in carrier bags both for food items and nesting materials. Unlike those of hamsters and squirrels, the gophers' pouches are external, located on either side of the mouth. They share this feature among mammals only with their close relatives in the family Heteromyidae – the pocket mice, kangaroo mice, and kangaroo rats.

Designed to Dig
FORM AND FUNCTION

Designed for digging, pocket gophers have thickset, tubular bodies, with no apparent neck. Fore- and hindlimbs are short, powerful, and of approximately equal size. The small, nearly naked tail is particularly sensitive to touch.

The front teeth project through furred lips, an adaptation that allows the gophers to use them for digging or cutting roots without getting dirt in their mouths. Even so, they generally excavate soil with the enlarged claws on their forefeet, and are thus categorized as "claw" or "scratch" diggers, though the incisors are used as helpful adjuncts in some genera. In *Thomomys* species, for example, populations living in harder soils tend to have more forward-pointing incisors that they use as chisels for digging. All pocket gophers push soil from their burrows with rapid movements of their forefeet, chest, and chin, and use an earthen plug to block the entrance. As a result, fresh gopher mounds can be distinguished by their characteristic triangular, or deltaic, shape, with an obvious round plug of soil located at the apex.

Gopher skin fits loosely. It is usually clothed in short, thick fur, interspersed with hairs sensitive to touch. The fur of more tropical species is coarser and less dense, perhaps as an adaptation for warmer climates. The loose skin enables individuals to make tight turns in their constricted burrows. Gophers are very agile and surprisingly fast, capable of rapid movement back or forward on their squat, muscular legs.

The gopher's skull is massive and strongly ridged, with heavy zygomatic arches and a broad temporal region holding powerful jaw muscles. The upper incisors may be either smooth or grooved on their anterior surface, depending on the genus. The four cheek teeth in each quarter of the jaw form a battery for grinding tough and abrasive foodstuffs. Strong and effective, these teeth grow continuously from birth to death, so that the grinding surface is present in all from the youngest to the oldest individuals. In Botta's pocket gopher, both teeth and foreclaws can grow at a rate of 0.5–1mm (0.02–0.04in) per day.

Male pocket gophers are larger than females, though the extent of this dimorphism varies greatly geographically. In Botta's pocket gopher, it seems to depend on habitat quality, and therefore on the density of animals in the population. In good habitat such as agricultural fields, males can have twice the body mass of females, and may be 25 percent larger in skull dimensions, but in poorer habitat such as deserts, the differences shrink to about 15 percent and 6 percent respectively. These variations are a result of both the nutritional quality of the food available to the animals – individuals of both sexes get larger if they eat well, particularly as juveniles – and the cessation of growth in females as they reach reproductive maturity and shift energy from growth to producing young.

Pocket gophers have the oldest fossil record of, and are taxonomically more diverse than, any other group of subterranean rodents. They originated in the late Eocene (36 million years ago) and underwent two pulses of diversification; the latest, beginning in the Pliocene (5 million years ago) led to the living genera. Fossils of both *Geomys* and *Thomomys* species date from Pliocene deposits; the other genera are known either from the early Pleistocene (*Pappogeomys*) or only from the modern record (*Orthogeomys* and *Zygogeomys*). Throughout the history of the family, there has been a relatively stable number of genera and constant extinction and origination rates.

The evolutionary history of the family is characterized by successive attempts to invade the fossorial (digging) niche. Each successive group exhibits better-developed adaptations for subterranean existence, with some modern pocket gophers exhibiting the best adaptations of all. The entire fossil history of the family is contained within North America.

In order to distinguish the genera, biologists examine overall size, details of the skull bones and the cheek teeth, and the presence and number of grooves found on the front surface of the upper incisors. The differences between populations of the same species that live apart can be more strik-

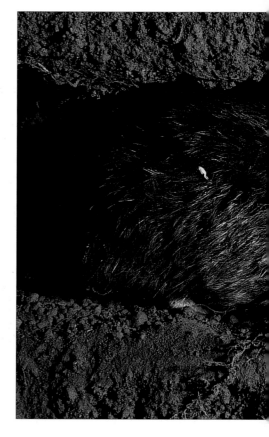

⬧ **Above** *In common with many other mammals that lead a subterranean existence, pocket gophers have certain adaptations, such as enlarged claws, sharp incisors, and furred lips, that make it easier to excavate burrows. The northern pocket gopher* (Thomomys talpoides) *inhabits a wider range of soil types than any other species in the family.*

⬧ **Below** *A northern pocket gopher feeding with filled pouches. When suitable vegetation is found, the gopher will cut this down into smaller pieces, which can be pushed into the cheek pouches using the forefeet, thus enabling the gopher to transport a relatively large quantity of food back to its burrow.*

FACTFILE

POCKET GOPHERS

Order: Rodentia

Family: Geomyidae

39 species in 6 genera, divided into 2 tribes

DISTRIBUTION N and C America, from C and SW Canada through the W and SE USA and Mexico to extreme NW Colombia.

Tropic of Cancer

HABITAT Friable soils in desert, scrub, grasslands, montane meadows, and arid tropical lowlands.

SIZE Head–body length ranges from 12–22.5cm (4.7–8.9in) in genus *Thomomys* to 18–30cm (7–11.8in) in genus *Orthogeomys*; **weight** from 45–400g (1.6–14oz) to 300–900g (11–32oz) in the same genera. Males are always larger than females, and up to twice the weight.

COAT Short and thick, in shades of brown and gray.

DIET Plant matter, particularly forbs, grasses, roots, and tubers.

BREEDING Gestation 17–21 days in *Thomomys* and *Geomys* genera.

LONGEVITY Maximum 5 years (6 years recorded in captivity).

CONSERVATION STATUS 2 species are listed as Critically Endangered, one as Endangered, and 2 as Vulnerable. 2 US subspecies are now classed as Extinct.

See tribes table ▷

ing than the differences that exist between separate species; so Botta's pocket gopher exhibits size, color, and habitat variations that span the entire range exhibited by all the other species in the genus *Thomomys*. As a consequence of this, species limits are, for the most part, poorly known, and a multitude of subspecies have been described – no fewer than 185 in the case of Botta's pocket gophers. Some species, including Wyoming, Idaho, and northern pocket gophers, are distinguished by hidden characteristics, such as chromosome number, rather than by any external features.

Species by Species
DISTRIBUTION PATTERNS

All genera and species are distributed contiguously; except in very narrow zones of overlap, only a single type of pocket gopher can be found in any particular area, as different species are apparently unable to share the space they occupy underground (the fossorial niche). In areas where several species or genera do meet, the pattern of species distribution is mosaic-like. In the mountains of the western USA and Mexico, for example, pocket gopher species replace each other in succession according to altitude.

Within the range of their distribution, pocket gophers are ubiquitous in virtually all habitats that have extensive patches of friable soil. The range of habitats in which they are found can be extreme: for instance, Botta's pocket gopher ranges from desert soils below sea level to alpine meadows that are – at 3,500m (11,500 ft) – well above the timberline. In tropical latitudes populations of the same species may be found in mountain forest meadows and in arid tropical scrub, although few species penetrate true tropical savannas.

Plants are the pocket gophers' dietary mainstay. Above ground, they take leafy vegetation from the vicinity of burrow openings; underground, they devour succulent roots and tubers. They often prefer forbs and grasses, but their diet shifts seasonally according to both availability and the gophers' requirements for nutrition and water. In deserts during the summer, water-laden cactus plants are consumed.

To transport food to caches in the burrow, gophers use their forepaws dextrously to fill their external cheek pouches. Food storage areas are usually sealed off from the main tunnel system.

A Lonely Life Underground
SOCIAL BEHAVIOR

Pocket gophers are solitary creatures. Individuals live in self-excavated burrows that abut those of other gophers. Male burrows tend to be longer and more dendritic than those of females, so that each male burrow might contact those of several females. In Botta's pocket gopher, the maximum territory size is about 250sq m (2,700sq ft), while in the yellow-faced pocket gopher individual burrow length may exceed 80m (260ft) of actual tunnel. Where habitat is good, the gophers become more crowded and space out evenly across the land; in low-quality habitat, groups of gophers concentrate in the best regions, while other areas remain gopher free. During breeding, this strict organization relaxes somewhat as males and

females briefly cohabit in the same burrow, and females share burrows with their young until they are weaned. Each individual gopher still maintains a tunnel system for its own exclusive use, but adjacent males and females may have both common burrows and deep, shared nesting chambers. Results from genetic studies would seem to suggest that females selected their mate from among the males whose territories are adjacent to their own.

Densities in small species such as Botta's pocket gopher rarely exceed 40 adults per ha (16 per acre), and they sink as low as 7 per ha (3 per acre) in the case of the large-bodied yellow-faced pocket gopher. In high-quality habitat, individual territories are stable in both size and position, with most individuals living their entire adult lives in very limited areas; in low-quality environments,

♦ **Above** *Members of the six pocket gopher genera:* **1** *male Botta's pocket gopher* (Thomomys bottae) *making a mound;* **2** *Botta's pocket gopher of a different color showing the pouch cheeks in detail;* **3** *Plains pocket gopher* (Geomys bursarius) *returning from foraging;* **4** *second color variant of Botta's pocket gopher, a female;* **5** *Giant pocket gopher* (Orthogeomys grandis) *in an underground food store making threats;* **6** *Michoacan pocket gopher* (Zygogeomys trichopus) *digging with its claws;* **7** *Buller's pocket gopher* (Pappogeomys bulleri) *using its incisors for digging.*

they shift throughout the year as animals search for food and mates.

Male and female young disperse from the mother's underground domicile at the same time, still wearing their juvenile coats. In Botta's pocket gopher, female young of the year initially move the farthest to establish territories, although most still seem to settle within 40–50m (130–165ft) of their natal area. If conditions are favorable, they may even breed in the same season as their birth, at just 70 days old. Male young tend to live in shallow systems in marginal and peripheral habitat, until they disperse to establish territories just prior to the next breeding season. As a consequence, their mortality is typically higher than that of females, which results in a prevalence of females in pocket gopher populations. Despite their adaptations for digging, pocket gophers can, and do, move considerable distances; most dis-

3

Soil Engineers
CONSERVATION AND ENVIRONMENT

Pocket gophers play a major role in soil dynamics, and in so doing become agriculturalists to suit their own needs. Cattle and other grazers compact soil, but underground, gophers counter this with their constant digging. They cycle soil vertically, which increases porosity, slows the rate of water runoff, and provides increased aeration. Gophers can thus have a profound effect on plant communities, often creating conditions that favor growth of the herbaceous plants that they prefer eating.

Voracious eaters, pocket gophers can become agricultural pests; in the western deserts of North America, the annual productivity of irrigated alfalfa fields can be reduced by as much as 50 percent in the year following an invasion by the animals. They also disturb irrigation channels. As a result, millions of dollars have been spent in the USA on programs to control gopher populations, but even so it has proved hard to curb their spread, so perfectly does agriculture suit their expansion.

Even so, some local US populations and subspecies are now considered threatened as a result of habitat loss, while in Mexico the Michoacan pocket gopher is at risk primarily because of its localized geographic distribution. Mostly, though, pocket gophers are among the few animals to have benefited from human development – particularly the replacement of native grass- and shrubland by agriculture.   JP

persal takes place above ground on dark nights, although movements over distances of just a few meters may take advantage of long tunnels just beneath the surface.

Individuals of both sexes are pugnacious and aggressive, and will fight for parcels of land. Males in particular exhibit heavy scarring around the mouth and on the rump, most of which will have been acquired during the breeding season.

As in most animals, reproduction is strongly affected by the changing seasons. In montane regions, breeding follows the melting snow in the late spring and early summer, but in coastal and desert valleys and in temperate grasslands, it coincides with winter rainfall.

Most Botta's gopher females have only one litter each season; however, some will have as many as three or four, depending on the quality of habitat – and therefore the nutrition – that is available to the mother. Animals that inhabit irrigated fields may breed nearly year-round while neighboring populations living amid natural vegetation have sharply delimited seasonal breeding. Females of yellow-faced and plains pocket gophers typically produce only one or two litters each year. Litter size varies between the species; *Pappogeomys* gophers usually give birth to twins, while *Thomomys* mothers typically produce five young, but may have to deal with as many as 10 per pregnancy. The onset of breeding, the length of the season, and the number of litters are largely controlled by local environmental conditions – primarily temperature, moisture, and the quality of the vegetation.

Pocket gophers are born with both their eyes and cheek pouches closed. The pouches open at 24 days and eyes and ears at 26 days. Additionally,

northern and Botta's pocket gophers have a juvenile coat that molts within 100 days of birth.

After a helpless early life spent in the shelter of the mother's burrow, infants are weaned at around 40 days. Within a couple of weeks of weaning the young head off alone, when still less than 2 months old. Unsurprisingly, most of the young that are produced each year do not survive long enough to be able to reproduce. In Botta's pocket gopher, only 6–12 percent of newborns are recruited into the breeding population the following year. The maximum longevity in nature can be as great as 4–5 years, but the average life span of an adult is usually only just over a year. No more than half of the population survive from one year to the next and some years only 15 percent will survive to the next year.

Females live nearly twice as long as males. Among yellow-faced pocket gophers, they survive on average for 56 weeks, as compared with the average 31-week lifespan of the male; in Botta's pocket gophers, females may live for as long as 4.5 years, compared with the maximum expectation of 2.5 years for the male. One possible explanation for this huge difference in longevity is the extreme intermale aggression that occurs during the breeding season. In addition, males appear to grow continuously throughout their life, while females cease growth when they reach reproductive maturity.

The sex ratio among adults varies geographically in all pocket gophers, a variation that in Botta's, northern, plains, and yellow-faced populations has been shown to be related to habitat quality. There are roughly equal numbers of both sexes in poor-quality habitats, such as desert areas, but in agricultural land there is a preponderance of females, with three to four for every adult male. As the population size increases males become less common, which is at least in part due to male mortality during or after fights over territories and access to mates. While almost all the adult females in a population breed each season, many males are not so lucky; some may never breed, while others will monopolize the females and father all the young.

Pocket Mice and Kangaroo Rats

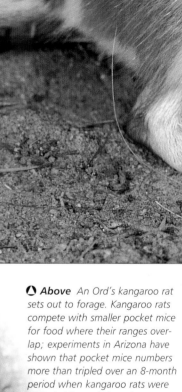

POCKET MICE AND KANGAROO RATS ARE *nocturnal burrow dwellers that inhabit many different American environments from arid deserts to humid forests. On returning from their nightly forays in search of food, they sometimes plug the burrow entrance with soil for added protection from predators and the weather.*

The Heteromyidae family brings together the pocket mice, which take their name from the deep, fur-lined cheek pouches in which they store food, and the kangaroo rats and mice, which as their name suggests are adapted to travel by hopping. They too have cheek pouches, the heteromyids' most distinctive feature; these can be turned inside out for cleaning, then pulled back into place with the help of a special muscle.

Built-in Carrying Pouches
FORM AND FUNCTION

Unusually for burrowers, the heteromyids are thin skulled, and do most of their digging with their front paws. The most distinctive feature of the head are the two cheek pouches, opening externally on either side of the mouth and extending back to the shoulders. The mice use their paws to fill the pouches with food and nest material for carrying back to the safety of the burrow.

While the pocket mice travel on all fours, the kangaroo rats and mice, in contrast, have long hindlimbs and shrunken forelimbs that are used mainly for feeding; these animals normally move in hops, only lowering themselves onto their front legs to scramble over short distances. The leg muscles are powerful enough to launch kangaroo rats 2m (6.6ft) or more with each leap when hurrying to escape from predators. All heteromyids have long tails; the jumping species rely on them to help keep their balance when traveling and as props to rest on when standing still.

In Search of Seeds
DISTRIBUTION PATTERNS

By day, summer conditions in the deserts of the southwestern USA are formidable. Surface temperatures soar to over 50°C (122°F), sparsely distributed plants are parched and dry, and signs of mammalian life are minimal. As the sun sets, however, the sandy or gravelly desert floor comes alive with rodents. The greatest diversity occurs among the pocket mice, of which five or six species can coexist in the same barren habitat.

Contrast these hot, dry (or in winter, cold and apparently lifeless) conditions with the tropical rain forests of central and northern South America. Rich in vegetation, the rain forest is nearly bare of heteromyid species: only one species, Desmarest's spiny pocket mouse, occurs at most sites.

The most likely explanation for this difference in species richness lies in the diversity and availability of seeds. In North American deserts, seeds of annual species can accumulate in the soil to a depth of 2cm (0.8in) in densities of up to 91,000 seeds per sq m (8,450 per sq ft). Patchily distributed by wind and water currents, small seeds weighing about 1mg tend to accumulate in great numbers under bushes and on the leeward sides of rocks, whereas larger seeds occur in clumps in open areas between vegetation, providing plentiful opportunities for the nocturnal seed-gathering activities of the heteromyid rodents.

Tropical forests are also rich in seeds, but many of those produced by tropical shrubs and trees are protected chemically against predation. This is especially true of large seeds weighing several grams, which considerably reduces the variety of seeds available to rodents. In effect, then, the tropical rain forest is a desert in the eyes of a seed-eating rodent, whereas the actual desert is a "jungle," as far as seed availability is concerned. Most of the 15–20 species of rodents inhabiting New World tropical forests are either omnivorous or exclusively fruit eating.

○ **Above** *An Ord's kangaroo rat sets out to forage. Kangaroo rats compete with smaller pocket mice for food where their ranges overlap; experiments in Arizona have shown that pocket mice numbers more than tripled over an 8-month period when kangaroo rats were excluded from their territory.*

◁ **Left** *The desert pocket mouse lives in arid areas of the American southwest and northwest Mexico. Like many heteromyids, it emerges from of its burrow at night to exploit the wealth of seeds blown across the desert floor.*

▷ **Right** *Long tails are a feature of Dipodomys species, like this Merriam's kangaroo rat; they serve as counterweights when the rats are traveling and as supports when they are resting.*

With large cheek pouches and a keen sense of smell, heteromyid rodents are admirably adapted for gathering seeds. Most of the time that they are active outside their burrow systems is spent collecting seeds within their home ranges. Members of the two tropical genera (*Liomys* and *Heteromys*) search through the soil litter for seeds, some of which will be buried in shallow pits scattered around the home range; others are stored underground in special burrow chambers.

Boom or Bust
SOCIAL BEHAVIOR

Breeding in desert heteromyids is strongly influenced by the flowering activities of winter plants, which germinate only after at least 2.5cm (1in) of rain has fallen between late September and mid-December. In dry years, seeds of these plants fail to germinate, and a new crop of seeds and leaves is not produced by the following April and May. In the face of a reduced food supply heteromyids do not breed, and their populations decline in size. In years following good winter rains most females produce two or more litters of up to five young, and populations increase rapidly.

This "boom or bust" pattern of resource availability also influences heteromyid social structure and levels of competition between species. When seed availability is low, seeds stored in burrow or surface caches become valuable, defended resources. Behavior becomes asocial in most arid-land species (including species of *Liomys*): adults occupy separate burrow systems (except for mothers and their young), and when two members of a species meet away from their burrows they engage in boxing and sand kicking. In the forest, in contrast, *Heteromys* species are socially more tolerant; individuals have widely overlapping home ranges, share burrow systems, and are less likely to fight.

The diversity and availability of edible seeds is the key to the evolutionary success of heteromyid rodents. Seed availability affects foraging patterns, population dynamics, and social behavior. In North American deserts, because seed production influences levels of competition not just between heteromyids themselves but also with ants and other seedeaters, there is a clear link between resources and the structure of an animal community. Thus the abundance and diversity of seed-eaters is directly related to plant productivity. THF

FACTFILE

POCKET MICE & KANGAROO RATS

Order: Rodentia

Family: Heteromyidae

60 species in 6 genera, 3 subfamilies

DISTRIBUTION
N, C, and northern S America

Equator

SUBFAMILY PEROGNATHINAE

SILKY POCKET MICE Genus *Perognathus*
SW Canada, W USA south to C Mexico. Quadrupedal. 9 species. HBL from 6–12.5cm (2.4–5in); TL from 4.5–14.5cm (1.8–5.7in); WT from 7–47g (0.25–1.7oz). Longevity: 2 years in the wild; up to 8 in captivity.

COARSE-HAIRED POCKET MICE Genus *Chaetodipus*
USA, Mexico. Quadrupedal. 17 species. HBL 6–12.5cm (2.4–5in); TL from 4.5–14.5cm (1.8–5.7in); WT from 7–47g (0.25–1.7oz).

SUBFAMILY HETEROMYINAE

SPINY POCKET MICE Genus *Liomys*
Mexico and C America S to C Panama. Mostly in semi-arid country. Quadrupedal. 5 species.

FOREST SPINY POCKET MICE Genus *Heteromys*
Mexico, C America, northern S America. Forests, up to 2,500m (8,200ft). Quadrupedal. 8 species including Desmarest's spiny pocket mouse (*H. desmarestianus*). Conservation status: *H. nelsoni* is Critically Endangered.

SUBFAMILY DIPODOMYINAE

KANGAROO RATS Genus *Dipodomys*
SW Canada and USA W of Missouri River to south C Mexico. Arid and semiarid country with some brush or grass. Bipedal (hindlegs long, front legs reduced). 19 species. HBL from 10–20cm (4–8in); TL from 10–21.5cm (4–8.5in); WT from 35–180g (1.2–6.3oz). Longevity: up to 9 years in captivity. Conservation status: 2 species – *D. ingens* and *D. margaritae* – are Critically Endangered; 1 more, the San Quintin kangaroo rat (*D. gravipes*) is Endangered, and the Texas kangaroo rat (*D. elator*) is Vulnerable.

KANGAROO MICE Genus *Microdipodops*
USA in S Oregon, Nevada, parts of California and Utah. Near shrubs in gravelly soil or sand dunes. Bipedal (hindlegs long, front legs reduced). 2 species.

Abbreviations HBL = head–body length TL = tail length WT = weight

For full species list see Appendix ▷

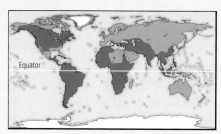
Cavy-like Rodents

THE FAMILIAR GUINEA PIG IS A REPRESENTATIVE of a large group of rodents classified as the suborder Hystricognathi (formerly Caviomorpha). Most are large rodents confined to South and Central America. Although they are extremely diverse in external appearance and are generally classified in separate families, the hystricognaths share sufficient characteristics to make it likely that they constitute a natural, interrelated group.

Externally, many of these rodents have large heads, plump bodies, slender legs, and short tails – as in the guinea pigs, the agoutis, and the giant capybara, the largest of all rodents at over one meter (39in) in length. Others, however – for example, some spiny rats of the family Echimyidae – come very close in general appearance to the common rats and mice.

Internally, the most distinctive character uniting these rodents is the form of the masseter jaw muscles, one branch of which extends forwards through a massive opening in the anterior root of the bony zygomatic arch to attach on the side of the rostrum. At its other end it is attached to a characteristic outward-projecting flange of the lower jaw. Hystricognaths are also characterized by producing small litters after a long gestation period, resulting in well-developed young. Guinea pigs, for instance, usually have two or three young after a gestation of 50–75 days, compared with seven or eight young after only 21–24 days in the brown (murid) rat.

The modern suborder name Hystricognathi serves to emphasize the close relationship of the Old World porcupines – family Hystricidae – with the South American "caviomorphs." However, despite the fact that both groups share the features described above, there has been considerable debate as to whether such features signify a common ancestry or are merely indicative of convergent evolution. This controversy over systematics is intrinsically linked to the question of whether the caviomorphs reached South America from North America or from Africa (rafting across in the late Eocene, when the continents were far closer together). The African cane rats (family Thryonomyidae) are closely related to the Hystricidae but some other families, namely the gundis (Ctenodactylidae) and the Dassie rat (Petromuridae) are much more doubtfully related, exhibiting only some of the "caviomorph" characters.

Most of the American caviomorphs are terrestrial and herbivorous but a minority, the porcupines (Erethizontidae) are arboreal, and one group, the tuco-tucos (Ctenomyidae) are burrowers. **GBC**

SKULLS AND DENTITION

Most cavy-like rodents have angular skulls and very strongly developed incisor teeth. The wearing surfaces of the four cheek teeth show enormous variation in pattern and complexity amongst the different species. Those of the coypu are typical of a large group of herbivorous species, including the agoutis and the American porcupines, and are closely paralleled in the Old World porcupines and cane rats. The teeth of the mara and of the capybara, although superficially very different in degree of complexity, resemble each other in being ever-growing as in the unrelated but also grass-eating voles and rabbits. At the other extreme, the tuco-tucos have surprisingly simple cheek teeth considering that they feed mainly on roots and tubers.

One distinguishing feature of cavy-like rodents is the deep masseter muscle in their jaws (see diagram BELOW). This extends forward through an opening in the zygomatic arch to attach to the muzzle and provides the powerful gnawing action characteristic of this suborder. The lateral masseter is only used in closing the jaw.

Coypu

Capybara

Mara

Tuco-tuco

Coypu 13cm

lateral masseter   deep masseter

⬥ *Above* *Representative species of cavy-like rodents (not shown to scale): **1** North African gundi (Ctenodactylus gundi); **2** a domesticated form of the cavy, or guinea pig (Cavia porcellus); **3** the distinctively deep, blunt muzzle of the capybara (Hydrochaeris hydrochaeris); **4** Paca (Agouti paca) – this sizable species is particularly prized as a game animal by indigenous peoples of Amazonia; **5** North American porcupine (Erethizon dorsatum); **6** Short-tailed chinchilla (Chinchilla brevicaudata) – hunted for its soft, valuable fur, this species is now listed by IUCN as critically endangered.*

⬥ *Below* *Perhaps the most bizarre of the cavy-like rodents are the naked mole rats of East Africa – virtually hairless creatures that spend almost all their time underground in extensive colonies. This is a breeding female.*

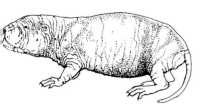

CAVIES AS A FOOD RESOURCE

The true cavy, or "guinea pig," has been highly regarded in South America since ancient times as an important source of meat for human consumption. There is clear evidence that many of the cultures that flourished along the Pacific coast of what is now Peru domesticated the cavy, adding variety to a diet based on fish and cultivated staple crops such as manioc and maize. Cavy bones dating from before 1800 BC were discovered in a midden at the coastal site of Culebras. Even the later cultures that arose on the High Andean altiplano and farmed llamas and alpacas continued to value the cavy; chroniclers of the 16th century reported that the animal was among sacrificial offerings made by the Inca. Cavies are still widely kept and traded in the region (RIGHT); they make ideal livestock for the smallholder, since they can be kept with little attention in compounds and thrive on green foods unpalatable to humans, such as brassicas.

New World Porcupines

NEW WORLD PORCUPINES BEAR A STRONG resemblance to Old World porcupines in both their adaptations and lifestyle. However, while the former are arboreal and have singly embedded quills, the latter are decidedly terrestrial and have quills that are grouped in clusters.

For heavy-bodied animals that can weigh as much as 18kg (40lb), the New World porcupines are excellent climbers, with well-developed claws and unfurred soles on their large feet. The soles consist of pads and creases that increase the gripping power of the feet.

Equipped for Climbing
FORM AND FUNCTION

Individual genera have further modifications to improve their climbing abilities. The prehensile-tailed porcupines and the hairy dwarf porcupines – the most arboreal genera – have smaller first digits on their hindfeet than those in the other genera, but they are incorporated in the foot pads, which increases the width and the gripping power of the pads.

The same genera also have long, spineless tails for grasping. Their tips form upward-directed curls and have a hard skin or callus on the upper surface. In the prehensile-tailed porcupines the tail contributes 9 percent of the total body weight; nearly half of the weight of the tail is composed of muscle fibers.

New World porcupines are very nearsighted, but have keen senses of touch, hearing, and smell. They produce a variety of sounds – moans, whines, grunts, coughs, sniffs, shrieks, barks, and wails. All porcupines have large brains and appear to have good memories.

In winter North American porcupines feed on conifer needles and on the bark of a variety of trees, excepting red maple, white cedar, and hemlock. During the summer these porcupines feed more frequently on the ground and select roots, stems, leaves, berries, seeds, nuts, and flowers. In the spring they frequently come out from forested areas into meadows to feed on grasses in the evening hours. They will eat bark at all times of the year, however, and can be destructive to forest plantations.

Prehensile-tailed and hairy dwarf porcupines feed more on leaves and both have many characteristics of arboreal leaf eaters. However, they are also reported to feed on tender stems, fruits, seeds, roots, tubers, and insects, and will even consume small reptiles.

FACTFILE

NEW WORLD PORCUPINES

Order: Rodentia

Family: Erethizontidae

12 species in 4 genera

DISTRIBUTION N America (except SE USA), S Mexico, C America, northern S America

Habitat Forest areas, open grasslands, desert, canyon.
Coat Sharp, barbed quills interspersed with long guard hairs cover the upper part of the body. Each quill protrudes individually from the skin, unlike in Old World porcupines in which they are clustered in groups of 4–6.
Diet Bark, leaves, and conifer needles; also roots, stems, berries, fruits, seeds, nuts, grasses, flowers, and, in some species, insects and small reptiles.

PREHENSILE-TAILED PORCUPINES Genus *Coendou*
S Panama, Andes from NW Colombia to N Argentina, NW Brazil. Forest areas. 4 species: Brazilian porcupine (*C. prehensilis*), Bicolor-spined porcupine (*C. bicolor*), Koopman's porcupine (*C. koopmani*), and Rothschild's porcupine (*C. rothschildi*). HBL 30cm (12in); WT 900g (32oz).

HAIRY DWARF PORCUPINES Genus *Sphiggurus*
S Mexico, C America, S America as far S as N Argentina. Forest areas. 6 species, including: Mexican tree porcupine

(*S. mexicanus*), South American tree porcupine (*S. spinosus*). Conservation status: one species, *S. vestitus* from Colombia and W Venezuela, is listed as Vulnerable.

NORTH AMERICAN PORCUPINE *Erethizon dorsatum*
Alaska, Canada, USA (except extreme SW, SE, and Gulf coast states), N Mexico. Forest areas. HBL 86cm (34in); WT 18kg (40lb). Breeding: gestation 210 days. Longevity: up to 17 years.

STUMP-TAILED PORCUPINE *Echinoprocta rufescens*
C Colombia. Forest areas.

Abbreviations HBL = head–body length WT = weight
For full species list see Appendix ▷

On the Move
SOCIAL BEHAVIOR

In habits porcupines range from the North American porcupine, which is semiarboreal, to prehensile-tailed and hairy dwarf porcupines, which are specialized arboreal feeders. All forms spend much of their time in trees, but even tree porcupines are known to come to the ground to feed and to move from one tree to another.

In the North American porcupine, the female reaches sexual maturity when about 18 months old. The estrous cycle is 29 days, and these animals may have more than one period of estrus in a year. They have a vaginal closure membrane, so females form a copulatory plug. The gestation period averages 210 days, and in both North American and prehensile-tailed porcupines usually one young is produced (rarely twins). The weight of the precocial newborn is about 400g (14oz) in

▶ **Right** The prehensile-tailed porcupines (Coendou spp.) live mainly in the middle and upper layers of forests in Central and South America, only descending to the ground to eat. The tail, which can be coiled around branches, has a callus pad which provides grip.

prehensile-tailed porcupines and 600g (21oz) in the North American porcupine. Lactation continues for 56 days, but the animals also feed on their own after the first few days. Porcupine young are born with their eyes open and are able to walk. They exhibit typical defensive reactions, and within a few days are able to climb trees. These characteristics probably explain why infant mortality is very low. Porcupines grow for 3–4 years before they reach adult body size.

The home range of the North American porcupine in summer averages 14.6ha (36 acres). In winter, however, they do not range great distances, instead staying close to their preferred trees and shelters. Prehensile-tailed porcupines can have larger ranges, though these vary from 8 to 38ha (20–94 acres). They are reported to move to a new tree each night, usually 200–400m (660–1,300ft) away, but occasionally up to 700m (2,300ft). Prehensile-tailed porcupines in South Guyana are known to reach densities of 50–100 individuals per sq km (130–260 per sq mi). They have daily rest sites in trees, usually on a horizontal branch 6–10m (20–33ft) above the ground. These porcupines are nocturnal, changing locations each night and occasionally moving on the ground during the day. Male prehensile-tailed porcupines are reported to have ranges up to four times as large as those of females.

Sharing their Fate with the Forests
CONSERVATION AND ENVIRONMENT

Porcupines, in general, are not endangered, and the North American porcupine can in fact be a pest. The fisher (a species of marten) has been reintroduced to some areas of North America to help control porcupines, one of its preferred prey. The fisher is adept at flipping the North American porcupine over so that its soft and generally unquilled chest and belly are exposed. The fisher attacks this area. A study found that porcupines declined by 76 percent in an area of northern Michigan following the introduction of the fisher.

Prehensile-tailed porcupines are often used for biomedical research, which contributes to the problem of conservation, but the main threat is habitat destruction. In Brazil prehensile-tailed porcupines have been affected by the loss of the Atlantic forest, and the Paraguayan hairy dwarf porcupine is on the endangered species list published by the Brazilian Academy of Sciences. One species of porcupine may have become extinct in historic times: *Sphiggurus pallidus*, reported in the mid-19th century in the West Indies, where no porcupines now occur.   CAW

Cavies

FACTFILE

CAVIES

Order: Rodentia

Suborder: Hystricognathi

Family: Caviidae

14 species in 5 genera

DISTRIBUTION

S America (mara in C and S Argentina only)

Equator

GUINEA PIGS AND CAVIES Genus *Cavia*

S America, in the full range of habitats. Coat: grayish or brownish agouti; domesticated forms vary. 5 species: *C. aperea, C. fulgida, C. magna, C. porcellus* (Domestic guinea pig), *C. tschudii*.

MARA Genus *Dolichotis*

Mara or Patagonian hare or cavy

S America (C and S Argentina), occurring in open scrub desert and grasslands. HBL 50–75cm (19.7–30in), TL 4.5cm (1.8in), WT 8–9kg (17.6–19.8lb). Coat: head and body brown, rump dark (almost black) with prominent white fringe round the base; belly white. Gestation: 90 days. Longevity: up to 15 years. 2 species: *D. patagonum* and *D. salinicola*. Conservation status: Lower Risk, Near Threatened.

YELLOW-TOOTHED CAVIES Genus *Galea*

Yellow-toothed cavies or cuis

S America, in the full range of habitats. Coat: medium to light brown agouti, with grayish white underparts. Gestation: 50 days. 3 species: *G. flavidens, G. musteloides, G. spixii*.

ROCK CAVY *Kerodon rupestris*

NE Brazil, occurring in rocky outcrops in thorn scrub. HBL 38cm (15in), WT 1kg (2.2lb). Coat: gray, grizzled with white and black; throat white, belly yellowish white, rump and backs of thighs reddish. Gestation: 75 days.

DESERT CAVIES Genus *Microcavia*

Argentina and Bolivia, in arid regions. HBL 22cm (8.7in), weight 300g (10.7oz). Coat: a coarse dark agouti, brown to grayish. Gestation: 50 days. Longevity: 3–4 years (up to 8 in captivity). 3 species: *M. australis, M. niata, M. shiptoni*.

Abbreviations HBL = head–body length TL = tail length WT = weight

mOST PEOPLE ARE FAMILIAR WITH CAVIES, but under a different and somewhat misleading name: guinea pigs. "Guinea" refers to Guyana, a country where cavies occur in the wild, while "pig" derives from the short, squat body of this rodent (the porklike quality of the flesh doubtless also played a part in its naming). The domestic guinea pig was being raised for food by the Incas when the conquistadors arrived in Peru in the 1530s, and is now found the world over, with one exception: it no longer occurs in the wild.

Cavies are among the most abundant and widespread of all South American rodents. They live in a variety of habitats ranging from tropical floodplains through open grasslands and forest edges to rocky meadows 4,000m (13,000ft) up. For a long time, they – or at least their domesticated cousins – were considered very stupid animals; psychologists found it difficult to set up tests in which guinea pigs showed any sign of learning or intelligence. However, it now appears that the tasks set for them may have been inappropriate.

To remedy this and to give cavies a fair chance to display their brainpower, experiments have recently been designed to play to their strengths. The basic prerequisites are a satisfactory laboratory and experiment habituation period; providing the animal with its daily requirements of vitamin C; a choice of task adapted to the animal's natural habits; and, finally, a controlled environment with as little extraneous noise as possible, to prevent the guinea pig from "freezing." In these conditions, guinea pigs have shown that they can learn at a similar rate to other mammalian species, particularly rats. Furthermore, when they were trained to forage under different experimental conditions (which included manipulations of travel time between food sources, food gain rates, and food availability), guinea pigs proved adept at optimizing their foraging efficiency.

☝ Above *The Brazilian guinea pig (Cavia aperea) is one of three wild species from which the familiar domestic guinea pig may have derived. The coats of the wild species are relatively long and coarse.*

☝ Below *Rock cavies' unusual mating behavior entails defending isolated rock piles to which females are drawn in search of shelter; in this way, the males accumulate harems. When approaching a female in estrus, the male circles around her to block her path* **1**, *then passes under her chin* **2** *before attempting to mount* **3**.

The 12 remaining species of the subfamily Cavi-inae, which comprises all the cavies except the *Dolichotis* species, are widely distributed throughout South America. All 12 are to a degree specialized for exploiting open habitats. Cavies are found in grasslands and scrub forests from Venezuela to the Straits of Magellan, but each genus has evolved to exist in a slightly different habitat.

Cavia is the genus most restricted to grasslands. In Argentina, *Cavia aperea* is limited to the humid pampas in the northeastern provinces. *Microcavia australis* is the desert specialist, and is found throughout the arid Monte and Patagonian deserts of Argentina. Other *Microcavia* species, *M. niata* and *M. shiptoni*, occur in the arid, high-altitude puna (subalpine zone) of Bolivia and Argentina. The specialized genus *Kerodon* is found only in rocky outcrops called *lajeiros* that dot the countryside in the thorn-scrub of northeastern Brazil. *Galea* seem to be the "jacks-of-all-trades" of the cavies, found in all the above habitats; it is also the only genus that coexists with other genera.

Regardless of habitat, all cavies are herbivorous. *Galea* and *Cavia* feed on herbs and grasses. *Microcavia* and *Kerodon* seem to prefer leaves; both genera are active climbers, which in the case of the *Kerodon* species is surprising because they lack claws and a tail, two adaptations usually associated with life in trees. The sight of an 800g (28oz) guinea pig hurrying along a pencil-thin branch high in a tree is quite striking.

All cavies become sexually mature early, at 1–3 months. The gestation period is fairly long for rodents, varying from 50–75 days. Litter sizes are small, averaging about 3 for *Galea* and *Microcavia*, 2 for *Cavia*, and 1.5 for *Kerodon*. The young are born highly precocial. Males contribute little obvious parental care, and generally ignore the female and her young once the litter is born.

Three species of cavies have been studied in northeastern Argentina: *Microcavia australis*, *Galea musteloides*, and *Cavia aperea*. *Cavia* and *Microcavia* never occur in the same area, *Cavia* preferring moist grasslands and *Microcavia* more arid habitats. *Galea* occurs with both genera. Competition between *Galea* and *Microcavia* seems to be minimized by the use of different foraging tactics: *Microcavia* is more of a browser, and arboreal. The degree to which *Cavia* and *Galea* interact within the same areas is unknown. Home-range sizes are, on average, 3,200sq m (34,500sq ft) for *Microcavia*, and 1,300sq m (14,000sq ft) for *Galea* and *Cavia*. They are diurnal, and are active mainly during early morning and evening hours.

The genus *Cavia* is the most widely distributed of all cavies, ranging over almost all South America from Colombia to Argentina. *Cavia* species breed year-round, but are less active in the winter. In the pampas region they can occur in high densities, especially in late autumn, typically inhabiting

Small, Alert, and Nervous
FORM AND FUNCTION

Cavies are among the most abundant and widespread of all South American rodents. All except the mara share a basic form and structure. The body is short and robust and the head large, contributing about one-third of the total head–body length. The eyes are fairly large and alert, the ears big but close to the head. The fur is coarse and easily shed when the animal is handled. There is

no tail. The forefeet are strong and flat, usually with four digits, each equipped with a sharp claw; the hindfeet, with three clawed digits, are elongated. Cavies walk on their soles, with the heels touching the ground. The incisors are short, and the cheek teeth, which are arranged in rows that converge towards the front of the mouth, have the shape of prisms and are constantly growing. Both sexes are alike, apart from each possessing certain specialized glands.

Cavies are very vocal, making a variety of chirps, squeaks, churrs, and squeals. One genus, *Kerodon*, emits a piercing whistle when frightened. *Galea* species rapidly drum their hindfeet on the ground when anxious.

Cavies first appeared in the mid-Miocene era in South America. Since their appearance some 20 million years ago, the family has undergone an extensive adaptive radiation, reaching peak diversity between 5 and 2 million years ago. From a peak of 11 genera during the Pliocene, they fell to their current 5 genera during the Pleistocene, about 1 million years ago.

3

linear habitats such as field margins and roadsides which have a zone of tall and dense vegetation. They feed in open areas of short vegetation, but return to the borders for protection.

The amount of time cavies spend watching for danger while feeding varies with the chances of being attacked by predators. In the open delta of the Paraná river, Argentina, those feeding in short grass away from cover were found by researchers to look up for danger three times more often than those close to shelter. Almost 50 percent of feeding occurred within 1m (3.3ft) of shelter, and the animals never strayed more than 4m (13ft) from cover. They recognized safety in numbers, staying in the open more than twice as long when in groups than when they were alone.

Cavies have several important predators. The grison – a South American weasel – has been known to almost wipe out a population of cavies over a period of five months. High-density populations also attract several species of raptor, which seem to kill more prey than they can consume, as evidenced by the presence of uneaten cavy carcasses where raptors have been.

Little is known of cavy reproductive behavior in the wild. Captive males are very aggressive, making it almost impossible to keep them together in the presence of females. As a result, only one male is present whenever a female comes into estrus. Females organize themselves in linear dominance hierarchies that are strictly age dependent.

Cavies are considered a major pest of tree crops in many regions of Argentina. For example, in the Paraná delta, cavies and red rats (*Holochilus brasiliensis*) destroyed more than 50 percent of the cultivated salicaceous trees by gnawing a fringe of bark 40cm (16in) up above ground level. Several methods of reducing their impact on forestry have been experimentally introduced, including chemical repellents and covering the stalks of seedlings with polyethylene tubes.

⚫ **Below** *Two rock cavies (*Kerodon rupestris*) huddle on a branch in northeast Brazil. The animals take their name from the rock piles in which they live and breed, leaving them each evening to forage. Agile climbers, they spend much of their feeding time in trees, where they go in search of their chief staple, tender leaves.*

Galea musteloides can live both at sea level and at altitudes up to 5,000m (16,400ft). Males living in large, mixed-sex groups form hierarchies in which higher-ranking animals sire more young than do subordinates – between 70 and 90 percent of all offspring, according to one observation of captive animals that employed DNA fingerprinting techniques. Aggression directed toward subordinates in the colony by higher-ranking individuals may have the effect of suppressing the losers' sex hormones. Equally intriguing is the fact that females appear to be tolerant of unfamiliar pups while they are breeding, probably as an adaptation to living in reproductive groups of related females with synchronized births and communal suckling.

In *Microcavia* species, aggression between males defines a linear dominance hierarchy within colonies. The stability of the social groups seems to vary between habitats: in deserts they keep strict fidelity to a burrow system to which their

⬥ **Above** *A southern mountain cavy (*Microcavia australis*) keeps watch over her growing brood on the Valdés Peninsula in Argentina. Three is a typical litter size for this short-lived species; mothers become receptive again immediately after giving birth, and can have up to five litters a year.*

group territoriality is restricted, but in less arid habitats they show a lax social organization without permanent groups. *Microcavia* sites its colonial burrows beneath bushes with broad canopies that are low to the ground, presumably as protection from predators. Grazing by *Microcavia* can damage an important number of plants; a study conducted in the Nacuñán Reserve, western Argentina, showed that herbivory by highland tuco-tucos (*Ctenomys opimus*) and *Microcavia* species affected 35 percent of the total plants of a creosote bush community dominated by *Larrea cuneifolia*.

Two species of cavies coexist in northeastern Brazil: *Kerodon rupestris* and *Galea spixii*. *Galea*

spixii is similar to the Argentine *Galea* in ecology, morphology, color, and behavior. The animals inhabit thorn forests, are grazers, and have a non-cohesive social organization.

The rock cavy (*Kerodon rupestris*) is markedly different from all the other small cavy species. It is larger and leaner, and has a face that is almost dog-like. All small cavies except *Kerodon* have sharply clawed digits; *Kerodon* has nails growing under the skin, with a single grooming claw on each inside hindtoe, and extensively padded feet. The modifications of the feet facilitate movement on slick rock surfaces. Rock cavies are strikingly agile as they leap from boulder to boulder, executing graceful mid-air twists and turns. They are also exceptional climbers, and forage almost exclusively on leaves in trees. There is little competition for resources with *Galea*.

Perhaps the most interesting difference between *Kerodon* and *Galea* is behavioral. *Galea* species, like the Argentine cavies, live in thorn-

scrub forest and have a promiscuous mating system. Rock cavies inhabit isolated patches of boulders, many of which can be defended by a single male, and single males seem to have exclusive access to two or more females. The boulder piles attract females, so by defending these sites males monopolize the female tenants. This system parallels that of the unrelated hyraxes of eastern Africa (see Hyraxes).

Natural Adaptors in Need of Help

CONSERVATION AND ENVIRONMENT

Most cavy species can adapt to altered and disturbed habitat, and some do well among human settlements. But one species, *Kerodon*, is in trouble. Hunted extensively, these rock cavies are declining in numbers and are in desperate need of protection. Because they are dispersed patchily throughout their range, large areas will have to be set aside; indeed, two such research reserves have already been established in Brazil.   TEL/MC

LIFELONG PARTNERS

Colonial breeding in the monogamous mara

AS DAWN BROKE ACROSS THE PATAGONIAN thorn scrub a large female rodent, with the long ears of a hare and the body and legs of a small antelope, cautiously approached a den, followed by her mate. They were the first pair to arrive, and so walked directly to the mouth of the den. At the burrow's entrance the female made a shrill, whistling call, and almost immediately eight pups burst out. The youngsters were hungry and all thronged around the female, trying to suckle. Under this onslaught she jumped and twirled to dislodge the melee of unwelcome mouths which sought her nipples. The female sniffed each carefully, chasing off all but her own. Finally, she managed to select her own two offspring from the hoard and led them 10m (33ft) to a site where they would be nursed.

In the meantime her mate sat alert nearby. If another adult pair had approached the den while his female was there, coming to tend their own pups, he would have made a vigorous display directly in front of his mate. If the newcomers had not moved away he would have dashed towards them, with his head held low and neck outstretched, and chased them off. The second pair would then have waited, alert or grazing, at a distance of 20–30m (65–100ft). When the original pair had left the area the new pair would then approach the den, to collect their own pups.

The animal being observed was the mara or Patagonian cavy, an 8kg (17.6lb) harelike diurnal cavy, *Dolichotis patagonum*. (The behavior of the only other member of the subfamily Dolichotinae, the salt-desert cavy, *Dolichotis salinicola*, is unknown in the wild.) A fundamental aspect of the mara's social system is the monogamous pair-bond, which in captivity, and probably in the wild,

lasts for life. The drive that impels males to bond with females is so strong that it can lead to "cradle snatching" – adult bachelor males attaching themselves to females while the latter are still infants. Contact between paired animals is maintained primarily by the male, who closely follows the female wherever she goes, discouraging approaches from other maras by policing a moving area around her about 30m (100ft) in diameter. In contrast, females appear less concerned about the whereabouts of their mates. While foraging, members of a pair maintain contact by means of a low grumbling sound.

Monogamy is not common in mammals and in the mara several factors probably combine to favor this system. It typically occurs in species where there are opportunities for both parents to care for the young, yet in maras virtually all direct care of the offspring is undertaken by the mother. However, the male does make a considerable indirect investment. Due to the high amount of energy a female uses in bearing and nursing her young, she has to spend a far greater part of the day feeding than the male: time during which her head is lowered and her vigilance for predators impaired. On the other hand, the male spends a larger proportion of each day scanning and is thus able to warn the female and offspring of danger. Also, by defending the female against the approaches of other maras, he ensures uninterrupted time for her to feed and care for his young. Furthermore, female maras are sexually receptive only for a few hours twice a year; in Patagonia females mate in June or July and then come into heat again in September or October, about 5 hours after giving birth, so a male must stay with his female to ensure he is with her when she is receptive.

Mara pairs generally avoid each other and outside the breeding season it is rare to see pairs within 30m (about 100ft) of each other. Then their home ranges are about 40ha (96 acres). Perhaps the avoidance between pairs is an adaptation to the species' eating habits. Maras feed primarily on short grasses and herbs, which are sparsely, but quite evenly, distributed in dry scrub desert. So far, detail of their spatial organization is unknown, but there is at least some overlap in the movements of neighboring pairs. Furthermore, there are some circumstances when, if there is an abundance of food, maras will aggregate. In the Patagonian desert there are shallow lakes, 100m to several kilometers in diameter, which contain water for only a few months of the year. When dry, they are sometimes carpeted with short grasses that maras relish. At these times, toward the end of the breeding season, up to about 100

◑ **Above** *A mother and pups. A female mara will normally give birth at one time to a maximum of three well-developed young. She will nurse them for an hour or more once or twice a day for up to four months.*

◑ **Left** *Foraging and feeding can be a dangerous time for maras, since it leaves them more vulnerable to attacks from predators. It is therefore essential that one of a pair remains alert.*

maras will congregate. However, individual pairs remain loyal to one another after the congregations have dispersed.

The strikingly cohesive monogamy of maras is noteworthy in its contrast with, and persistence throughout, the breeding season when up to 15 pairs become at least superficially colonial by depositing their young at a communal den. The dens are dug by the females and not subsequently entered by adults. The same den sites are often used for three or more years in a row. Each female gives birth to one to three young at the mouth of the den; the pups soon crawl inside to safety. Although newborn pups are moving about and grazing within 24 hours of birth, they remain in the vicinity of the den for up to four months, and are nursed by their mother once or twice a day during this period. Around the den an uneasy truce prevails amongst the pairs whose visits

⬙ **Above** *In the open grasslands of Patagonia, where cover is scarce, maras spend a large part of the day grazing or basking, but keep their keen sense of hearing attuned to any potential danger.*

coincide. The number of pairs of maras breeding at a den varies from 1 to at least 15 and may depend on habitat. Pairs come and go around the den all day and in general at the larger dens at least one pair is always in attendance there. Even when 20 or more young are kept in a crèche, cohabiting amicably, the monogamous bond remains the salient feature of the social system. Each female sniffs the infants seeking to suckle and they respond by proffering their anal region to the female's nose. Infants clambering to reach one female may differ by at least one month in age. A female's rejection of a usurper can involve a bite and violent shaking. However, interlopers

occasionally secure an illicit drink. Although females may thus be engaging in communal nursing they rarely seem to do so willingly.

The reasons why normally unsociable pairs of maras keep their young in a communal crèche are unknown, but it may be that it lowers the likelihood of them falling victim to a predator; indeed, the more individuals at a den (both adults and young) the more pairs of eyes there are to detect danger. Furthermore, some pairs travel as much as 2km (1.2mi) from their home range to the den, so the opportunities for shared surveillance of the young may diminish the demands on each pair for protracted attendance at the den. The unusual breeding system of the monogamous mara may thus be a compromise, conferring on the pups the benefits of coloniality, in an environment wherein association between pairs is otherwise apparently disadvantageous.   AT/DWM

Capybara

SAVANNA-DWELLING SOCIAL GRAZERS *averaging a hefty 50kg (110lb), capybaras are unusual animals. They are found only in South America, where they live in groups near water. Members of the suborder known as caviomorphs, which also includes cavies and chinchillas, they are in fact the largest of all the rodents.*

The first European naturalists to visit South America called capybaras "water pigs" or "Orinoco hogs," and the first of those names has carried over into their present scientific designation as hydrochoerids. Yet in truth, they are neither pigs nor totally aquatic; their nearest relatives are actually the cavies. The other hydrochoerids, now all extinct, were larger than present-day capybaras; the biggest were twice as long and probably weighed eight times as much, making them heavier than the largest North American grizzly bear.

The Biggest Rodents
FORM AND FUNCTION

Capybaras are ponderous, barrel-shaped animals. They have no tail, and their front legs are shorter than their back legs. Their slightly webbed toes, four on the front feet and three on the back, make them very strong swimmers, able to stay under water for up to 5 minutes. Their skin is extremely tough and covered by long, sparse, bristlelike hairs. The nostrils, eyes, and ears are situated near the top of the large, blunt head, and hence protrude out of the water when the animal swims. Two pairs of large, typically rodent incisors enable capybaras to eat very short grasses, which they grind up with their molar teeth. There are four molars on each side of each lower jaw. The fourth molar is characteristic of the subfamily in being as long as the other three.

Two kinds of scent glands are present in the capybara. One gland, highly developed in males but almost nonexistent in females, is located on top of the snout and is known as the *morrillo* (literally, "hillock" in Spanish). This is a dark, oval-shaped, naked protrusion that secretes a copious, white, sticky fluid. Both sexes also produce odors from two glandular pockets located on either side of the anus. Male anal glands are filled with easily detachable hairs abundantly coated with layers of hard, crystalline calcium salts. Female anal pockets also have hairs, but theirs are not detachable and are coated in a greasy secretion rather than with crystalline layers. The proportions of each chemical present in the secretions of individual capybaras are different, providing a potential for individual recognition via personal "olfactory fingerprints." The snout scent gland also plays a role in signaling dominance status, while the anal gland appears to be important in group membership recognition and perhaps in territoriality.

CAPYBARA

Hydrochaeris hydrochaeris

Order: Rodentia

Family: Hydrochaeridae

Sole member of genus and of family. 2 populations, one E of the Andes from Venezuela to N Argentina, the other from NW Venezuela through N Colombia up to the Panama Canal. Some authorities regard the two as separate species, named respectively *Hydrochaeris hydrochaeris* and *H. isthmius*.

DISTRIBUTION South America

Equator

HABITAT Flooded savanna or grassland next to water holes; also, along ponds and rivers in tropical forest.

SIZE Head–body length 106–134cm (42–53in); shoulder height 50–62cm (20–24in); weight male 35–64kg (77–141lb), female 37–66kg (81.6–146lb).

COAT Light brown, consisting of short, abundant hairs in young; adults have long, sparse, bristlelike hairs of variable color, usually brown to reddish.

DIET Mostly grasses, especially aquatic; occasionally water hyacinths and other dicotyledons.

BREEDING Females are sexually mature at 12 months, males at 18 months. Gestation 150 days. 1–8 (average 4) young, born mostly at the end of the wet season, after 150-day gestation. Very precocial: young graze within hours of birth.

LONGEVITY About 6 years (12 in captivity).

CONSERVATION STATUS Lower Risk, Conservation Dependent.

⬥ Above *Capybaras are born after a long gestation of five months. Even though they emerge in a well-developed condition and can eat soon after birth, it is over a year before they reach sexual maturity. Although the young are conceived in water, they are born on land.*

⬥ Left *Water is a place of refuge for capybaras. Capybaras live either in groups averaging 10 in number or in temporary larger aggregations, which may contain up to 100 individuals and will be composed of the smaller groups. The situation varies according to the season.*

Capybaras have several distinct vocalizations. Infants and the young constantly emit a guttural purr, probably to maintain contact with their mothers or other group members. This sound is also made by losers in altercations, perhaps to appease their adversary. Another vocalization, the alarm bark, is given when a predator is detected. This coughing sound is often repeated several times, and the reaction of nearby animals may be to stand alert or to rush into the water.

Recycling Cellulose
DIET

Capybaras are exclusively herbivorous, feeding mainly on grasses that grow in or near water. They are very efficient grazers, and can crop the short, dry grasses left at the end of the tropical dry season. Because a large proportion of the grasses they eat consists of cellulose, which is indigestible by any mammal's digestive enzymes, capybaras possess a huge fermentation chamber called the cecum, equivalent to the tiny human appendix. However, since the cecum is located between the small and large intestine, the animal cannot

absorb the products of the fermentation carried out by microbial symbionts. To solve this problem, capybaras resort to coprophagy – reingestion of feces – to take advantage of the work of their symbionts. Thus, for a few hours every morning during their resting period, capybaras recycle what they ate the previous evening and night. Usually they spend the morning resting, then bathe during the hot midday hours; in the late afternoon and early evening they graze. At night they alternate rest periods with feeding bouts. They never sleep for long, instead dozing in short bouts throughout the day.

Gregarious Grazers

SOCIAL BEHAVIOR

Capybaras live in groups of 10–30 animals, apparently depending on the habitat: greener and more homogeneous pastures promote larger groups. Pairs are rarely seen, but a proportion of adult males are solitary or loosely associated to one or more groups. In the dry season groups coalesce around the dwindling pools, forming temporary aggregations of 100 or more animals. When the wet season returns, these large aggregations split up into the original groups that formed them. Thus, capybara social units may last three years, and probably more.

Groups of capybaras are closed social units, in which little variation in core membership is observed. A typical group is composed of a dominant male (often distinguishable by his large morrillo), one or more females, several infants and young, and one or more subordinate males. Among the males there is a dominance hierarchy, maintained by aggressive interactions that usually take the form of simple chases. Dominant males repeatedly shepherd their subordinates to the periphery of the group, but fights are rarely seen. Females are much more tolerant of each other, although the precise details of their social relationships, hierarchical or otherwise, are unknown. Territories are defended by all adult members of the group against conspecific intruders. Any animal of either sex may chase an interloper away, irrespective of its sex, as long as the chaser is within its own territory.

Capybaras are found in a wide variety of habitats, ranging from open grasslands to tropical rain forest. Groups may occupy an area varying in size from 2–200ha (4–494 acres), with 10–20ha (24.7–49.4 acres) being most common. Each home range is used mainly, but not exclusively, by one group and can therefore be considered a territory. Territories are defended against conspecific intruders by all adult members of the group. Particularly in the dry season, but at other times as well, two or more groups may be seen grazing side by side. In some areas density may reach two individuals per hectare, but lower densities of fewer than one per hectare are more frequent.

Capybaras reach sexual maturity at 18 months. In Venezuela and Colombia they appear to breed year round, with a marked peak at the beginning of the wet season in May. In Brazil, in more temperate areas, they probably breed just once a year. When a female becomes sexually receptive, a male will start a pursuit that may last for an hour or more. The female will walk in and out of the water, repeatedly pausing while the male follows close behind. Mating takes place in the water; the female stops, and the male clambers on her back, sometimes pushing her underwater with his weight. As is usual in rodents, copulation lasts only a few seconds, but each sexual pursuit typically involves several mountings.

150 days later, up to seven babies are born; four is the average litter size. To give birth the female leaves her group and walks to nearby cover. Her young are born a few hours later, and are precocial, able to eat grass within their first week. A few hours after the birth the mother rejoins her group, the young following as soon as they become mobile, which should occur when the babies are still very young. Females seem to share the burden of nursing by allowing infants other than their own to suckle. The young in a group spend most of their time within a tight-knit crèche, moving between nursing females. When active, they constantly emit a churring purr.

Capybara infants tire quickly, and are therefore vulnerable to predators. They have most to fear from vultures and feral or semiferal dogs, which prey on them. Caymans and foxes may also take young capybaras. Jaguar and smaller cats were certainly important predators in the past, though today they themselves are nearly extinct in most of Venezuela and Colombia and are therefore less of a threat to capybara populations. In some areas of Brazil, however, jaguars seize capybaras in substantial numbers.

When a predator approaches a group the first animal to detect it will emit an alarm bark. The normal reaction of other group members is to stand alert, but if the danger is very close, or the caller keeps barking, they will all rush into the water, where they form a close aggregation with young in the center and adults facing outward.

Putting a Cap on Hunting
CONSERVATION AND ENVIRONMENT

Capybara populations have dropped so substantially in Colombia that, from 1980 onward, the government prohibited capybara hunting. In Venezuela they have been killed since colonial times in areas that are devoted to cattle ranching. In 1953 hunting became subject to legal regulation and controlled, but to little effect until 1968 when, after a 5-year moratorium, a management plan was devised, based on a study of the species' biology and ecology. Since then, 20–30 percent of the annually censused population in licensed ranches with populations of over 400 animals have been harvested every year. This has apparently resulted in local stabilization of capybara populations. Capybaras are now listed as conservation dependent by the IUCN, in recognition of the fact that control on hunting and harvesting must remain if population levels are to be maintained.

DWM/EH

◁ **Left** *A capybara marking its territory. It is instantly recognizable as a male from the prominent, bare lump on top of its snout – the morrillo sebaceous gland, which contains the animal's highly individual scent.*

◒ **Below** *A South American waterbird – the jacana – searches a capybara's coat for parasitic insects. The capybara spends much of its time in water and can travel long distances submerged; its small eyes and ears are thought to be an adaptation for living in water.*

FARMING CAPYBARA

In Venezuela there has been a demand for capybara meat at least since the early 16th century, when Roman Catholic missionary monks classified it, along with terrapin, as legitimate Lenten fare; the amphibious habits of the two species presumably misled the monks into thinking they had an affinity with fish. Today, because of their size and high reproductive rate as well as the tasty meat and valuable leather they can provide, capybaras are candidates for both ranching and intensive husbandry.

It has been calculated that, where the savannas are irrigated to mollify the effects of the dry season, the optimal capybara population for farming is 1.5–3 animals per hectare (or about 1 per acre), yielding 27kg of meat per ha (24lb per acre) per annum. Ranches licensed to harvest the population can sustain yields of about 1 animal per 2 ha in good habitat. An annual cull takes place in February, when reproduction is at a minimum and the animals congregate around waterholes. Horsemen herd them together, and they are then surrounded by a cordon of cowboys on foot. An experienced slaughterman selects adults weighing over 35kg (77lb), excluding pregnant females, and kills them with a blow from a heavy club. The average animal weighs 44.2kg (97.4lb), of which 39 percent (17.3kg; 38lb) is dressed meat. These otherwise unmanaged wild populations thus yield over 8kg of meat per hectare (7lb per acre) annually.

In spite of this yield, farmers have traditionally feared that large populations of capybaras would compete with domestic stock. In fact, however, capybaras selectively graze on short vegetation near water and so do not compete significantly with cattle, which take taller, drier forage, except in wet, low-lying habitats. In these regions, capybaras are actually much more efficient at digesting the plant material than are cattle and horses. So, ranching capybara in their natural habitat appears to be, both biologically and economically, a viable adjunct to cattle ranching.

Other Cavy-like Rodents

1

tHE FAMILIES ASSEMBLED HERE ARE PART OF *a disparate group of predominantly South American hystricognath rodents. The diversity they show is in marked contrast to the relative homogeneity of other rodent groups, such as the squirrels or the rats and mice.*

The group includes small, medium, and very large rodents; some are covered with barbed spines, others have soft, silky fur; nearly all are herbivorous, although a few are not averse to including insects or larger prey in their diet. Many are terrestrial but others live as burrowers or tree dwellers, or else spend much of their time swimming and feeding in water. They inhabit forests and grasslands, water and rocky deserts, coastal plains and high mountains; some are solitary, others colonial. Some species are common and widespread, others known only from a few specimens in museums; yet others have become extinct, some of them

within historical times, often as a result of human activities. Many species are eaten by humans, others are prized for their fur; some are pests, while others carry the diseases of humankind and domestic animals.

The larger species of South American rodents, such as agoutis, pacas, pacaranas, and viscachas, are prey for the large- and medium-sized carnivores (jaguars, ocelots, pampas cats, maned wolves, bush dogs, foxes, and others). They are herbivorous, and may be considered the South American equivalents of the vast array of ungulate herbivores that are so important in the African ecosystems. It is thought that these rodents radiated into this role as the primitive native herbivores became extinct, and before the arrival of the new fauna from the north.

Despite their obvious diversity, the cavy-like rodents have many anatomical and other features in common. Particularly striking are the similarities in reproduction, such as the long gestation period exhibited by many species, the small number of young in each litter, and the advanced state of development many show at birth. Especially in many of the medium-to-large species, the young are born fully furred and with their eyes open; some are able to run within a few hours of birth, and many become independent of their mothers relatively soon afterward.

Dassie Rat
FAMILY PETROMYIDAE

The dassie rat is superbly adapted to the dry, rocky hillside country of southern Africa in which it lives. The soft pelage is gray, buff, or tawny in color, making the animal difficult to spot when lying on rocks, and it has a flattened skull and very flexible ribs, enabling it to squeeze into narrow crevices. It forages on the ground or in bushes for leaves, berries, and seeds, and is particularly active at dawn and dusk, resting and sunning itself below projecting rocks so as to avoid predatory birds. Dassie rats are solitary or else found in pairs, yet utter a warning whistling call if alarmed. One or two well-developed young are born once per year, at the start of the rainy season, so the species has a relatively slow reproduction rate for a small tropical mammal.

Cane Rats
FAMILY THRYONOMYIDAE

Cane rats or grasscutters are robust African rodents with a coarse, bristly pelage, the bristles being flattened and grooved along their length. The pelage is brown speckled with yellow or gray above, buff white below, allowing them to blend well with the grasses and reeds in which they feed and live. The preferred semiaquatic habitat for *Thryonomys swinderianus* is reed beds, marshes,

2

3

4

5

6

and the margins of lakes and rivers, while *T. grego-rianus* occurs in dryer areas of moist savanna grasslands. Cane rats live in small groups, communicating by calls and stamping their hindfeet. They shelter among tall grasses or in rock crevices, or in the abandoned burrows of other animals; they also sometimes excavate their own shallow burrows. As their common name suggests, they feed mainly on grass and cane, but also a variety of other vegetation, including bark, nuts, and fruits, and they may be pests of plantations and cultivated land, especially where population densities are high. Cane rats are prey for leopards, mongooses, snakes, birds of prey, and humans. In some parts of their range, they breed all year round, but most have two litters each year with an average of four young per litter. The young are well-developed at birth.

Chinchillas and Viscachas
FAMILY CHINCHILLIDAE

Chinchillids live in relatively barren regions, and all have thick, soft fur, although chinchillas and mountain viscachas, occurring at higher elevations, have denser fur than that of the pampas-dwelling plains viscacha. They are slender-bodied animals with large ears and tails up to one-third the length of the body. Their long, strong hindlegs enable them to run and jump with ease.

All the family are colonial. Chinchillas live in holes and crevices among rocks, and emerge at dusk to forage during the night for any available vegetation. In contrast, mountain viscachas forage for grasses, mosses, and lichens, and sun themselves on rocks during the day; they generally live in family groups that coexist with others to form small to very large colonies. Colonies of plains viscachas live in extensive and complex burrows, consisting of a central chamber from which radiating tunnels lead to various entrances; they feed mainly on grass and seeds at dawn and dusk.

All species are subject to pressure from human hunting. Chinchillas have been pursued for their valuable fur to near extinction; mountain and plains viscachas are prized for both food and fur, and the plains viscacha competes for grazing with domestic animals. In addition, they destroy pasture with their acidic urine, and so undermine the pampas that men, horses, and cattle are often injured by falling into their concealed tunnels.

Pacarana
FAMILY DINOMYIDAE

The pacarana is solitary or lives in pairs. It has a broad head with short, rounded ears, a robust body, and broad, heavily clawed feet. The pelage is coarse, black or brown with two more or less continuous white stripes on each side. A forest-dwelling species, seldom encountered and little known, this slow-moving, inoffensive herbivore is prey for jaguars, ocelots, and other medium-sized carnivores, and is hunted for food by humans.

◑ **Left** *Representatives of 10 of the 12 families of other cavy-like rodents: 1 Chinchilla, with soft fur and bushy tail; 2 Cane rat from sub-Saharan Africa; 3 Chinchilla rat (Abrocoma bennettii); 4 American spiny rat climbing a mound. 5 Paca (Agouti paca) – the species has internal and external cheek pouches; 6 Dassie rat (Petromus typicus); 7 Pacarana (Dinomys branickii) feeding on vegetation; 8 Tuco-tuco (Ctenomys opimus) digging with its incisors; 9 Hutia sunning itself on a branch; 10 Degu (Octodon degus).*

FACTFILE

OTHER CAVY-LIKE RODENTS
180 species in 12 families and 40 genera

DISTRIBUTION S America; West Indies; Africa S of the Sahara.

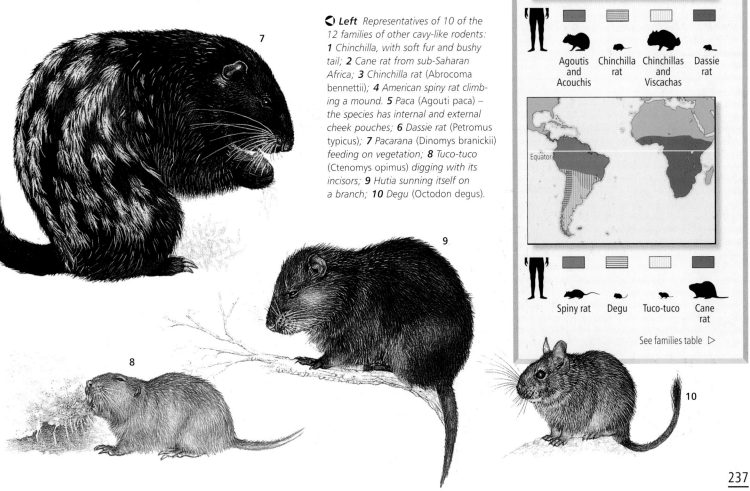

Coypu   Hutia   Pacarana   Paca

Agoutis and Acouchis   Chinchilla rat   Chinchillas and Viscachas   Dassie rat

Spiny rat   Degu   Tuco-tuco   Cane rat

See families table ▷

Agoutis and Acouchis
FAMILY DASYPROCTIDAE

Agoutis and acouchis are relatively large rodents with very short tails and a coarse, usually unpatterned pelage. The long limbs are modifications for running, as is the reduction in the number of toes on the hindfeet to three. The animals occur in a variety of habitats including forest, thick brush, and savanna; agoutis in particular are usually found close to water. All species are diurnal but secretive, and in areas of disturbance wait until dusk before emerging to forage for a wide variety of vegetation, especially fruit, nuts, and succulent parts of plants. When food is abundant, agoutis bury some for use in time of dearth, which is an important, if inadvertent, means of dispersing the seeds of many forest trees. In some areas, agoutis are known to breed throughout the year, litters normally consisting of one or two well-developed young that are able to run within an hour of birth. Agoutis and acouchis usually occur in small social groups of an adult male and female with several juveniles. They are preyed upon by a variety of carnivores including humans.

Pacas
FAMILY AGOUTIDAE

Pacas have often been included with the agoutis and acouchis as a separate subfamily of the Dasyproctidae; they are not dissimilar in appearance, but have relatively shorter legs, less reduced digits on the hindfeet, and a spotted pelage. To add to the confusion, the scientific name of the paca is *Agouti*, which in common parlance is

applied to the *Dasyprocta* species. Pacas usually occur in forested areas near water, often spending the day in burrows excavated by themselves or abandoned by other animals. They emerge at night to feed on leaves, stems, roots, nuts, seeds, and fruit, and may be a major pest of cultivated land. They are hunted by humans in addition to other large carnivores, and have become rare in some areas due to overhunting and habitat loss.

Tuco-tucos
FAMILY CTENOMYIDAE

The body form of tuco-tucos is robust and compact and shows many features associated with their burrowing lifestyle. The head is large, with small eyes and ears. The strong incisors, very prominent with their bright orange enamel, are used to cut through roots when tunneling. The limbs are short and muscular, and the claws on the forefeet in particular are long and strong, serving to dig the extensive burrow systems in which the animals live. The hindfeet bear strong bristle fringes, which are used for grooming; the animals' scientific name, meaning "comb toothed," is derived from the comblike nature of these bristles. The numerous species comprising this genus generally prefer the dry, sandy soils typical of coastal areas, grassy plains, and the altiplano, but also of forests. Some species are solitary, others colonial; most individuals occupy single burrows. Both sexes are territorial, with the more aggressive males holding larger territories than the females. Their shallow burrows may have several entrances. Although active mainly during the day, tuco-tucos

rarely emerge to forage until after dark. They feed mainly on roots, stems, and grasses. Tuco-tucos are considered pests of cultivated and grazing land in some areas, and their burrows occasionally collapse, injuring people and livestock. As a consequence, some species have been hunted intensively and their numbers greatly reduced.

Degus or Octodonts
FAMILY OCTODONTIDAE

Octodontids occur in southern South America from sea level to about 3,500m (11,500ft). The family name of Octodontidae refers to the worn enamel surface of their teeth, which forms a pattern in the shape of a figure eight. Most are adapted to digging, particularly rock rats and the coruro, and dig their own burrows, take over burrows abandoned by other animals, or live in rock piles and crevices. The pelage is usually long, thick, and silky. Degus and chozchoris are gray to brown above, creamy yellow or white below. Degus are active during the day; they are colonial and construct extensive burrow systems, with a central section connected to feeding sites by a complex maze of tunnels and surface paths. In contrast, the chozchoz is nocturnal and lives in burrows, rock crevices, and caves, feeding on acacia pods and cactus fruits. Coruros are brown or black, and rock rats dark brown all over; both are adapted to a burrowing lifestyle, with compact bodies, small eyes and ears, muscular forelimbs, and strong incisors, although these are less prominent in rock rats than in coruros. Little is known about the viscacha rats, which are buff above and whitish

---

Cavy-like Rodent Families

Dassie rat or African rock rat
Family: Petromuridae

1 species (*Petromus typicus*), S Angola, Namibia and NW South Africa

Cane rats or grasscutters
Family: Thryonomyidae

2 species in 1 genus (*Thryonomys*) Africa S of the Sahara

Chinchillas and viscachas
Family: Chinchillidae

6 species in 3 genera: Chinchillas (*Chinchilla*), 2 species; Mountain viscachas (*Lagidium*), 3 species; Plains viscacha (*Lagostomus maximus*). W and S South America. 1 species – the Short-tailed chinchilla – is listed by the IUCN as Critically Endangered, 1 other is Vulnerable.

Pacarana Family: Dinomyidae

1 species (*Dinomys branickii*) Venezuela, Colombia, Ecuador, Peru, Brazil, and Bolivia. Endangered.

Agoutis and Acouchis
Family: Dasyproctidae

13 species in 2 genera: Agoutis (*Dasyprocta*), 11 species; Acouchis (*Myoprocta*), 2 species. S Mexico to S Brazil and Lesser Antilles. 2 agouti species are Endangered, 1 Vulnerable.

Pacas Family: Agoutidae

2 species in 1 genus (*Agouti*) S Mexico to S Brazil

Tuco-tucos Family: Ctenomyidae

56 species in 1 genus (*Ctenomys*) Peru S to Tierra del Fuego. 1 species Vulnerable.

Octodonts Family: Octodontidae

10 species in 6 genera: rock rats (*Aconaemys*), 2 species; Degus (*Octodon*), 4 species; Mountain degu or chozchoz (*Octodontomys gliroides*); Viscacha rat (*Octomys mimax*); Coruro (*Spalacopus cyanus*); Plains viscacha rat (*Tympanoctomys barrerae*). Peru, Bolivia, Argentina, Chile. 2 species Vulnerable.

Chinchilla rats or chinchillones
Family: Abrocomidae

6 species in 2 genera: *Abrocoma*, 4 species; *Cuscomys*, 2 species. Peru, Bolivia, Chile, Argentina. 1 species Vulnerable.

Spiny rats Family: Echimyidae

70 species in 16 genera: Bristle-spined rat (*Chaetomys subspinosus*); Coro-coros (*Dactylomys*), 3 species; Atlantic bamboo rat (*Kannabateomys amblyonyx*); Olalla rats (*Olallamys*), 2 species; Arboreal soft-furred spiny rats (*Diplomys*), 3 species; Arboreal spiny rats (*Echimys*), 14 species; Toros (*Isothrix*), 2 species; Armored spiny rat (*Makalata armata*); Owl's spiny rat (*Carterodon sulcidens*); Lund's spiny rats (*Clyomys*), 2 species; Guiara (*Euryzygomatomys spinosus*); Armored rat (*Hoplomys gymnurus*); Tuft-tailed spiny tree rat (*Lonchothrix emiliae*); Spiny tree rats (*Mesomys*), 5 species; Terrestrial spiny rats (*Proechimys*), 32 species; Punare (*Thrichomys apereoides*) S and C America and West Indies.

5 species are currently listed as Vulnerable; in addition, 4 others have recently been declared Extinct.

Hutias Family: Capromyidae

15 species in 6 genera: Desmarest's hutia (*Capromys pilorides*); Bahaman and Jamaican hutias (*Geocapromys*), 2 species; small Cuban or sticknest hutias (*Mesocapromys*), 4 species; Long-tailed Cuban hutias (*Mysateles*), 5 species; Laminar-toothed hutias (*Isolobodon*), 2 species; Hispaniolan hutia (*Plagiodontia aedium*). W Indies. 6 species are Critically Endangered, and 4 more are Vulnerable; in addition, 6 species have recently been declared Extinct.

Coypu or Nutria
Family: Myocastoridae

1 species, *Myocastor coypus* S Brazil, Paraguay, Uruguay, Bolivia, Argentina, Chile; introduced into N America, N Asia, E Africa, Europe.

For full species list see Appendix ▷

from less than 200g (7oz) to 8.5kg (19lb), while the body mass of some extinct species is thought to have exceeded 20kg (44lb). The fur is harsh but with a soft underfur, and is generally brownish or grayish in coloration. Most of the living genera are partially, and the long-tailed Cuban hutias highly, arboreal. They live in forests, plantations, and rocky areas; in addition, small Cuban hutias occur in coastal swamps. Most are nocturnal, although Desmarest's hutia is diurnal in some areas. The diet includes a variety of vegetation but also small animals such as lizards. Hutias are and were preyed on by birds, snakes, introduced domestic dogs, cats, and mongooses, and they have been intensively hunted by humans for food; remains of several of the extinct species have been found in caves and kitchen middens.

below with a particularly bushy tail, except that they are nocturnal, burrowing herbivores inhabiting desert scrub. *Tympanoctomys* is similarly poorly known; it is apparently restricted to plains with salt-rich vegetation.

Chinchilla Rats
FAMILY ABROCOMIDAE

As their name suggests, chinchilla rats are soft-furred, ratlike rodents that live in burrows or rock crevices. They are mainly nocturnal and may be colonial. Little information is available about these animals. Their diet includes a wide variety of plant material, although in some places *Abrocoma cinerea* may be specialized to feed on creosote bush. The pelage is silver gray or brown above, white or brown below, and consists of soft, dense underfur overlain with long, fine guard hairs. The pelts are occasionally sold, but are of much poorer quality than those of true chinchillas.

Spiny Rats
FAMILY ECHIMYIDAE

Spiny rats comprise a diverse group of medium-sized, ratlike, herbivorous rodents, most of which have a spiny or bristly coat, although some are soft furred. Some are very common and widespread, while others are extremely rare; three genera

known only from skeletal remains are probably, and a fourth certainly, extinct. The taxonomy of some genera is poorly understood, and the number of species is only tentative. The body form in this family is correlated with lifestyle. Robust, short-tailed forms (*Clyomys*, *Carterodon*, and *Euryzygomatomys*) are burrowing savanna species; relatively slender, long-tailed forms (*Olallamys*, *Dactylomys*, *Kannabateomys*) are arboreal. Of the intermediate forms, *Proechimys*, *Isothrix*, and *Hoplomys* are more or less terrestrial, and *Mesomys*, *Lonchothrix*, *Echimys*, and *Diplomys* are mostly arboreal. Spiny rats are mainly herbivores: the diet of *Proechimys* and *Echimys* is mainly fruit, *Kannabateomys* and *Dactylomys* eat bamboo and vines, while *Mesomys* eats fruit and other plant material but also insects.

Hutias
FAMILY CAPROMYIDAE

Found only in the West Indies, hutias were once a very diverse group, with different genera grouped into several subfamilies. Approximately half of these genera are now extinct, most within historical times, and a further two include rare and endangered species. The living genera have a robust body, a broad head with relatively small eyes and ears, and short limbs. In size they range

Coypu
FAMILY MYOCASTORIDAE

The coypu is a large, robust rodent, well adapted to its semiaquatic life in marshes, lakes, and streams. The eyes and ears are small, the mouth closes behind the incisors while swimming, the whiskers are long, the limbs relatively short, and the hindfeet webbed. The pelage is yellowish or reddish brown; the outer hair is long and coarse and overlays the thick, soft underfur. Coypus live in burrows in riverbanks and are expert swimmers, able to remain underwater for up to five minutes. Their diet includes a wide range of vegetation, mussels, and snails. They are pests of cane fields and plantations. Coypus are nocturnal and live in pairs or small family groups. Females may have two or three litters a year, with an average of five young to a litter. The young are born fully furred and with their eyes open. Coypus are preyed on by alligators, fish, snakes, and birds of prey, and they are also hunted by humans for their meat. In addition, they are both hunted and farmed for their valuable pelt, known in the fur trade as nutria – a corruption of the Spanish for "otter." They have been introduced for fur farming to many parts of the world, where escaped individuals have formed feral populations (for example, in East Anglia, England), causing extensive damage to watercourses and cultivated land.   PJ

⬖ **Above** *In Brazil's Amazonas province a black agouti confronts the problem of opening a large brazil nut. Agoutis often squat on their haunches to consume smaller food items, holding them in their hands squirrel-style to eat.*

◗ **Right** *A swimming coypu reveals the bright orange incisors that are unexpected features of this semiaquatic species. Coypus spend most of their waking hours in water; they live in riverside burrows, and have webbed hindfeet.*

Old World Porcupines

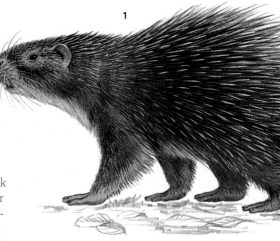

tO THE HUMAN EYE, PORCUPINES, WITH THEIR *array of quills, are among nature's strangest creations, though in terms of bodily protection for the porcupines themselves, the spikes make perfect sense. The two Old World subfamilies are mostly terrestrial, unlike the New World porcupines.*

Many people mistakenly believe that porcupines are related to hedgehogs or pigs, but in fact guinea pigs, chinchillas, capybaras, agoutis, viscachas, and cane rats are their closest relatives. Many of these animals have in common an extraordinary appearance, and are well known for their unusual ways of solving the problems of reproduction.

An Armor of Sharp Spines
FUNCTION AND FORM

Old World porcupines belong to two distinct subfamilies, Atherurinae and Hystricinae. The brush-tailed porcupines of the former branch have long, slender tails that end in tufts of stiff, white hairs containing hollow sections that rustle when the tail is shaken. The animals' elongated bodies and short legs are covered with short, dark brown bristles, with a few long quills on the back.

The crested porcupines of the Hystricinae subfamily have short tails surrounded by stout, sharp, cylindrical quills. The tip of the tail is armed with a cluster of hollow, open-ended quills. When the tail is shaken, these produce a rattle that acts as a warning signal that the animal is annoyed. The back of the upper parts and flanks is covered with black-and-white spines; as a modified form of hair, these are made of keratin.

When threatened, porcupines erect and rattle their quills, stamp their hindfeet, and make a grunting noise. If threatened further, they turn their rump to the intruder and run sideways or backward toward it. If the quills penetrate the skin, they become stuck and detach.

The rest of the body is covered with flat, black bristles. Most species have a crest of erectile hair extending from the top of the head to the shoulders. The head is blunt and exceptionally broad across the nostrils, with small, piglike eyes set far back on either side of the face. The two sexes look alike, though the females have mammary glands that are situated on the side of the body, enabling mothers to suckle lying on their stomachs.

The majority of Old World porcupines are vegetarians, feeding on the roots, bulbs, fruits, and berries of a wide variety of plants. Porcupines play a role in shaping local plant diversity and productivity; for example, the digging sites of Indian porcupines serve as important germination locations for seedlings. In cultivated areas, they will eat such crops as groundnuts, potatoes, and pumpkins. African porcupines are able to feed on plant species that are poisonous to domestic stock. Brush-tailed porcupines are tree climbers and feed on a variety of fruits.

Porcupines manipulate food with their front feet, pinning it to the ground and gnawing at it. Usually they feed alone, though they will eat in groups of two or three. Bones also appear occasionally in the porcupines' diets, littering their shelters. They are carried there for gnawing, either to sharpen teeth or as a source of phosphates.

◑ **Above** *The Indonesian porcupine **1** has a dense coat of flat, flexible spines. There are three species – in Borneo, Sumatra, and the Philippines. The African porcupine **2** is one of five crested species. It is very adaptable, inhabiting forest, grassland, and desert.*

Communities on the Cape
SOCIAL BEHAVIOR

Among Cape porcupines sexual behavior is normally initiated by the female. Approaching a male, she will take up the sexual posture – rump and tail raised and quills pointed away from her partner – who mounts her from behind with his forepaws resting on her back. Intromission only occurs when the female is in heat (every 28–36 days) and the vaginal closure membrane becomes perforated. Sexual behavior without intromission is exhibited during all stages of the sexual cycle.

The young are born in grass-lined chambers that form part of an underground burrow system. At birth they are unusually precocial: fully furred, they have their eyes open and are covered in

◑ **Left** *Although lions have been known to eat African porcupines, even they find it very difficult to penetrate the armory of quills. Contrary to folklore, the barbs cannot be projected; they can, however, become embedded and can cause septic, sometimes fatal, wounds.*

2

FACTFILE

OLD WORLD PORCUPINES

Order: Rodentia

Family: Hystricidae

11 species in 4 genera and 2 subfamilies

DISTRIBUTION Africa, Asia; some in S Europe.

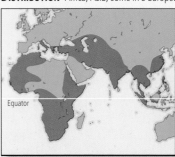

Equator

Habitat Varies from dense forest to semidesert.

Size Ranges from **head–body length** 37–47cm (14.6–18.5in) and **weight** 1.5–3.5kg (3.3–7.7lb) in the brush-tailed porcupines to **head–body length** 60–83cm (23.6–32.7in) and **weight** 13–27kg (28.6–59.4lb) in the crested porcupines.

Coat Head, body, and sometimes the tail, are covered in long, sharp quills – hardened hairs – that are brown or blackish in color, sometimes with white bands.

Diet Roots, tubers, bulbs, fruit, bark, carrion.

Breeding Gestation 90 days for the Indian porcupine, 93–94 days for the Cape porcupine, 100–110 days for the African brush-tailed porcupine, 105 days for the Himalayan porcupine, 112 days for the African porcupine.

Longevity Approximately 21 years recorded for crested porcupines in captivity.

BRUSH-TAILED PORCUPINES Genus *Atherurus* C Africa and Asia. Forests. Brown to dark brown bristles cover most of the body; some single-color quills on the back. 2 species: African brush-tailed porcupine (*A. africanus*), Asiatic brush-tailed porcupine (*A. macrourus*).

CRESTED PORCUPINES Genus *Hystrix* Africa, India, SE Asia, Sumatra, Java and neighboring islands, S Europe; recently introduced to Great Britain. Varied habitats. Hair on back consists of long, stout, cylindrical black-and-white erectile spines and quills; body covered with black bristles; grayish crest well developed. 5 species: African porcupine (*H. cristata*); Cape porcupine (*H. africaeaustralis*); Himalayan porcupine (*H. hodgsoni*); Indian porcupine (*H. indica*); Malayan porcupine (*H. brachyura*).

INDONESIAN PORCUPINES Genus *Thecurus* Indonesia, Philippines. Coat dark brown in front, black on posterior; body densely covered with flattened, flexible spines; quills have a white base and tip, with central parts black; rattling quills on tail are hollow. 3 species: Bornean porcupine (*T. crassispinis*); Philippine porcupine (*T. pumilis*); Sumatran porcupine (*T. sumatrae*).

LONG-TAILED PORCUPINE *Trichys fasciculata* Malay peninsula, Sumatra, Borneo. Forests. Body covered with brownish, flexible bristles; head and underparts hairy.

bristles that will become quills, although, fortunately for the mother, these only harden after birth. Newborn babies weigh 300–330g (10.6–11.6oz), and start to nibble on solids at 9–14 days. At 4–6 weeks they begin to feed, though they continue to be nursed for 13–19 weeks, by which time they weigh 3.5–4.7kg (7.7–10.4lb). Litter sizes are small; 60 percent of births produce one young and 30 percent produce twins. In the wild porcupines produce only one litter each summer.

Despite foraging alone, Cape porcupines are sociable, living in burrows with as many as 6–8 animals – usually an adult pair and their consecutive litters. Both sexes are aggressive toward strangers, and all colony members protect the young. Only one female in a group reproduces; should a litter be lost, she can conceive again within days. Sexual maturity is attained at 2 years.

Both parents may accompany the young when foraging for up to 6–7 months, although adult males are more frequently encountered with young than adult females. The occurrence of family groups is probably related to the opportunities available for mature offspring to disperse; when a population dips, young individuals are able to take advantage of newly available territories to reproduce. Thus disturbance can reduce the age of first reproduction from 24 to 12 months.

Porcupines live in groups in order to huddle together for warmth. Newborn offspring do not leave the burrow for the first 9 weeks of their lives, and, when warmed by the bodies of other group members, may be able to allocate more energy to growth. Sharing burrows also reduces porcupines' vulnerability to predation and encourages cooperative rearing.

Population density in the semiarid regions of South Africa varies from 1–29 individuals per sq km (up to 75 per sq mi). Forty percent of the population are less than one year old.

Territories are maintained by scent marking, using anal glands. Males mark more frequently in preferred feeding patches. Porcupines seem to forage up to 16km (10mi) from their burrows, moving along well-defined tracks, almost exclusively by night. They are catholic in their habitat requirements, provided they have shelter to lie in during the day.

On the Defensive

CONSERVATION AND ENVIRONMENT

Porcupines are often viewed as a threat to crops. In addition, African porcupines carry fleas, which are responsible for the spread of bubonic plague, and ticks, which spread babesiasis, rickettsiasis, and theilerioses. Brush-tailed porcupines are also known to be hosts of the disease organism of malaria, *Plasmodium atheruri*. As a result, they are often persecuted and killed as pests. Indigenous peoples eat their flesh and kill porcupines as a recreational pursuit.

Nevertheless, the animals occur in great numbers, thanks to the near absence of natural predators over much of their range, and also because of the increase in crop cultivation. At the time of writing, there is no reason to believe that porcupines as a whole are endangered, though certain species and subspecies are now considered at risk. For example, one subspecies of the Asiatic brush-tailed porcupine is currently listed as endangered by the IUCN, while the Malayan porcupine is classified as vulnerable.   RJvA

Gundis

◗ **Right** An extraordinary feature of the Mzab gundi is that its ears are flat and immovable.

GUNDIS ARE SMALL, HERBIVOROUS RODENTS *of North Africa's mountains and deserts. When the animals first came to the attention of Western naturalists, in Tripoli in 1774, they were given the name of "gundi mice" (gundi is the local word). The family name, Ctenodactylidae, means "comb toes."*

In the mid-19th century, the British explorer John Speke shot gundis in the coastal hills of Somalia, and later French naturalists found three more species; skins and skulls began to arrive in museums. But no attempt was made to study the ecology of the animal. Some authors said gundis were nocturnal, others diurnal; some claimed they dug burrows, others that they made nests; there were reports of the animals whistling, while other sources had them chirping like birds; and there were fantastic tales about them combing themselves with their hindfeet in the moonlight. In 1908 two French doctors isolated a protozoan parasite, now known to occur in almost every mammal, from the spleen of a North African gundi and called it *Toxoplasma gondii.*

Powder Puffs in the Desert Sun
FORM AND FUNCTION

Gundis have short legs, a short tail, flat ears, big eyes, and long whiskers. Crouched on a rock in the sun with the wind blowing through their soft fur, they look like powder puffs.

The North African and the desert gundi both have a tiny, wispy tail, but the other three have a fan that they use as a balancer. Speke's gundi has the largest and most elaborate fan, which it uses in social displays. Gundis also have rows of stiff bristles – their

"combs" – on the two inner toes of each hindfoot, and these stand out white against the dark claws. They use the combs for scratching. Sharp claws adapted to gripping rocks would destroy the soft fur coat that insulates them from extremes of heat and cold. The rapid circular scratch of the rump with the combed instep is characteristic of gundis.

The gundi's big eyes convinced some earlier authors that the animal was nocturnal. In fact the gundi is adapted to popping out of sunlight into dark rock shelters. Equally, the gundi can flatten its ribs to squeeze into a crack in the rocks.

◖ **Above** Gundi species, each of which has its own distinctive vocalizations: **1** Speke's gundi (Pectinator spekei), has a rich vocabulary of sounds; **2** Felou gundi (Felovia vae), makes a harsh "chee-chee" call when in danger; **3** Mzab gundi (Massoutiera mzabi), which is relatively succinct; **4** North African gundi (Ctenodactylus gundi), whose distinctive chirping helps members of this species recognize each other in the desert habitat that they share with the desert gundi (Ctenodactylus vali), a species that whistles.

FACTFILE

GUNDIS

Order: Rodentia

Family: Ctenodactylidae

5 species in 4 genera

DISTRIBUTION N Africa

SPEKE'S GUNDI *Pectinator spekei*
Speke's or East African gundi
Ethiopia, Somalia, N Kenya. Arid and semiarid rock outcrops. HBL 17.2–17.8cm (6.9–7.1in); TL 5.2–5.6cm (2–2.2in); WT 175–180g (6.2–6.3oz). Longevity: Unknown in wild; 10 years recorded in captivity.

FELOU GUNDI *Felovia vae*
SW Mali, Mauritania. Arid and semiarid rock outcrops. HBL 17–18cm (6.8–7.2in); TL 2.8–3.2cm (1.1–1.3in); WT 178–195g (6.3–6.9oz).

DESERT GUNDI *Ctenodactylus vali*
Desert or Sahara gundi
SE Morocco, NW Algeria, Libya. Desert rock outcrops. Breeding: gestation 56 days.

NORTH AFRICAN GUNDI *Ctenodactylus gundi*
SE Morocco, N Algeria, Tunisia, Libya. Arid rock outcrops. Longevity: 3–4 years.

MZAB GUNDI *Massoutiera mzabi*
Mzab or Lataste's gundi
Algeria, Niger, Chad. Desert and mountain rock outcrops.

Abbreviations HBL = head–body length TL = tail length WT = weight

Foraging in the Cool of the Day
DIET

Gundis are herbivores: they eat the leaves, stalks, flowers, and seeds of almost any desert plant. Their incisors lack the hard orange enamel that is typical of most rodents. Gundis are not, therefore, great gnawers. Food is scarce in the desert, and gundis must forage over long distances – sometimes as much as 1km (0.6mi) a morning. Regular foraging is essential as they do not store food. Home range size varies from a few square meters to 3sq km (1.9sq mi).

Foraging over long distances generates body heat, which can be dangerous on a hot desert day. It is unusual for small desert mammals to be active in daytime, but gundis behave rather like lizards. In the early morning they sunbathe until the temperature rises above 20°C (68°F), and then they forage for food. After a quick feed they flatten themselves again on the warm rocks. Thus they make use of the sun to keep their bodies warm and to speed digestion – an economical way of making the most of scarce food. By the time the temperature has reached 32°C (90°F), the gundis have taken shelter from the sun under the rocks, and they do not come out again until the temperature drops in the afternoon. When long foraging expeditions are necessary, gundis alternate feeding in the sun and cooling off in the shade.

In extreme drought, gundis eat at dawn when plants contain most moisture. They obtain all the water they need from plants; their kidneys have long tubules for absorbing water. Their urine can be concentrated if plants dry out completely, but this emergency response can only be sustained for a limited period.

Family Life in the Colonies
SOCIAL BEHAVIOR

Gundis are gregarious, living in colonies that vary in density from the Mzab gundi's 0.3 per ha (0.12 per acre) to over 100 per ha (40 per acre) for Speke's gundi. Density is related to the food supply and the terrain. Within colonies there are family territories occupied by a male, female, and juveniles or by several females and offspring. Gundis do not make nests, and the "home shelter" is often temporary. Usually a shelter retains the day's heat through a cold night and provides cool draughts on a hot day. In winter, gundis pile on top of one another for warmth, with juveniles shielded from the crush by their mother or draped in the soft fur at the back of her neck.

Each species of gundi has its own repertoire of sounds, varying from the infrequent chirp of the Mzab gundi to the complex chirps, chuckles, and whistles of Speke's gundi. In the dry desert air their low-pitched alert calls carry well. Short, sharp calls warn of predatory birds; gundis within range will hide under the rocks. Longer calls signify ground predators and inform the predator it has been spotted. The Felou gundi's harsh "chee-chee" will last as long as the predator is around.

Long complex chirps and whistles can be a form of greeting or recognition. The *Ctenodactylus* species – whose ranges overlap – produce the most different sounds: the North African gundi chirps, the desert gundi whistles. Thus members can recognize their own species.

All gundis thump with their hindfeet when alarmed. Their flat ears give good all-round hearing and a smooth outline for maneuvering among rocks. The bony ear capsules of the skull are huge, like those of many other desert rodents. The acute hearing is important for picking up the weak, low-frequency sounds of predators – sliding snake or flapping hawk – and for finding parked young. Right from the start, the young are left in rock shelters while the mother forages. They are born fully furred and open eyed. The noise they set up – a continuous chirruping – helps the mother to home in on the temporary shelter.

The young have few opportunities to suckle: from the mother's first foraging expedition onward they are weaned on chewed leaves. (They are fully weaned after a period of about 4 weeks.) The mother has four nipples – two on her flanks and two on her chest – and the average litter size is two. But a gundi has little milk to spare in the dry heat of the desert.   WG

African Mole Rats

WHILE AFRICAN MOLE RATS MAY NOT BE *the most aesthetically pleasing creatures in the animal kingdom, they nonetheless rank among the more interesting members. Discoveries made regarding the habits and behavior of the social species have rocked the scientific community.*

The African mole rat is a ratlike rodent that has assumed a molelike existence and become totally adapted to life underground. It excavates an extensive system of semipermanent burrows, complete with sleeping and food storage areas; and it pushes the soil it digs out to the surface as molehills. Whereas most rodents of comparable size grow rapidly and live for only a couple of years, mole rats take over a year to reach their full adult size and many can live for more than a decade. Indeed, the lifespan of captive naked mole rats may even exceed 25 years.

Teeth for Tunneling
FORM AND FUNCTION

Mole rats have cylindrical bodies with short limbs so as to fit as compactly as possible within the diameter of a burrow. Their loose skin helps them to turn within a confined space: a mole rat can almost somersault within its skin as it turns. Mole rats can also move rapidly backward with ease, and so they often shunt to and fro without turning round when moving along a burrow.

All genera except the dune mole rats use chisel-like incisors protruding out of the mouth cavity for digging. To prevent soil from entering the mouth, there are well-haired lip folds behind the incisors, effectively closing the mouth behind the gnawing teeth. Dune mole rats dig with the long claws on their forefeet and are less efficient at mining very hard soils; moreover, their body size is larger. These features restrict them to areas with easily dug sandy soil. This difference in digging method is reflected in the animals' teeth: the incisors of tooth-diggers protrude more than those of the dune mole rats, and the roots extend back behind the row of cheek teeth for strength.

When a mole rat is tunneling, it pushes the soil under its body with its forefeet. Then, with the body weight supported by the forefeet, both hindfeet are brought forward to collect the soil and kick it behind the animal. Once a pile has accumulated, the mole rat reverses along the burrow, pushing the soil behind it. Most mole rats force solid cores of soil out onto the surface, but naked mole rats kick a fine spray out of an open hole – an active hole looks like an erupting volcano. A number of naked mole rats cooperate in digging, one animal excavating, a number transporting soil, and another kicking it out of the hole – this unfortunate individual is particularly vulnerable to predation by snakes. All mole rats have hindfeet that are fringed by stiff hairs, as is the tail in all but naked mole rats; both adaptations help hold the soil during digging.

Because mole rats live in complete darkness for most of their lives, their eyes are small and can only detect light and dark. (Interestingly, the Cape mole rat, which occasionally travels on the surface, has eyes that are larger than those of other species.) It has been suggested that the surface of the eye may be used to detect air currents that would indicate damage to the burrow system; certainly, if damage occurs, the mole rats rapidly repair it. Touch is important in finding the way

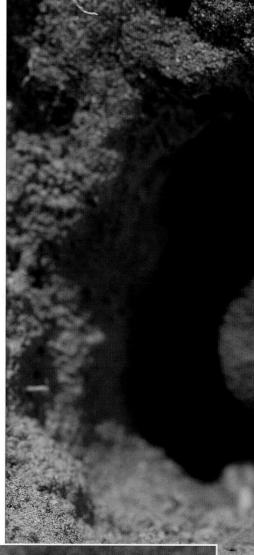

❯ Right *A Damara mole rat emerging from its tunnel. A tunnel system's depth usually depends on local soil conditions. In areas of loose soil, they lie deeper underground than in areas of hard soil.*

❯ Below *The powerful incisors of Mechow's mole rat are used for excavation. Clearly, keeping soil out of various orifices is important and its head is well adapted for this: the lips fold behind the incisors, the nostrils can be closed, and the ears and eyes are small.*

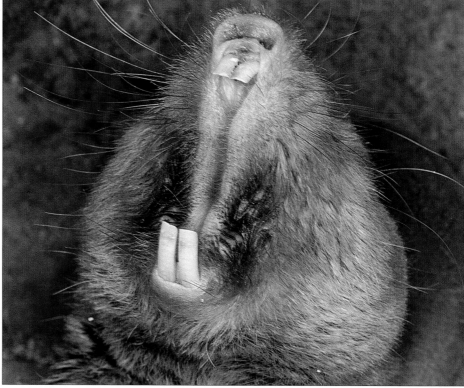

FACTFILE

AFRICAN MOLE RATS

Order: Rodentia

Family: Bathyergidae

At least 12 species in 5 genera: **Dune mole rats** (genus *Bathyergus*, 2 species), the largest mole rats, inhabiting sandy coastal soils of S Africa; **Common mole rats** (*Cryptomys*, at least 7 species), widespread in W, C, and S Africa; **Silvery mole rat** (*Heliophobius* argenteocureau), C and E Africa; **Cape mole rat** (*Georychus capensis*), Cape Province of the Republic of S Africa, along the coast from the SW to the E; and **Naked mole rat** (*Heterocephalus glaber*), in arid regions of Ethiopia, Somalia, and Kenya.

DISTRIBUTION Africa S of the Sahara

Equator

HABITAT Underground in different types of soil and sand.

SIZE Head–body length ranges from 9–12cm (3.5–4.7in) in the Naked mole rat to 30cm (11.8in) in the genus *Bathyergus*; **weight** from 30–60g (1–2.1oz) to 350–2,200g (26–63oz) in the same species.

COAT Thick, soft, and woolly or velvety in all but the Naked mole rat, which is almost hairless.

DIET Roots, tubers, geophytes, herbs, and grasses.

BREEDING Gestation 44–111 days (44–48 days in the Cape mole rat; 66–74 days in the Naked mole rat; 97–111 days in the Giant Zambian mole rat).

LONGEVITY Unknown (captive Naked mole rats have lived for more than 25 years and several species of *Cryptomys* for more than 10 years).

CONSERVATION STATUS Four species – *Bathyergus janetta, Cryptomys foxi, C. zechi,* and *Heliophobius argenteocinereus* – are currently listed as Lower Risk, Near Threatened. The other species are not considered threatened.

For full species list see Appendix ▷

around the burrow system; many genera have long, touch-sensitive hairs scattered over their bodies (in the naked mole rat, these are the only remaining hairs). The animals' sense of smell and their hearing of low-frequency sounds are good, and their noses and ears are modified on the outside so as to cope with the problems of living in a sandy environment: the nostrils can be closed during digging, while the protruding parts of the ears (pinnae) have been lost.

Subterranean Farmers
DIET

Mole rats are vegetarians, and obtain their food by digging foraging tunnels. These enable them to find and collect roots, storage organs (geophytes), and even the aboveground portions of plants without having to come to the surface. They appear to blunder into food rather than to detect it – tests failed to reveal any evidence that they could locate food items even half a meter (1.6ft)

from the foraging burrow. The large dune mole rats are not specialist feeders and live on grass, herbs, and geophytes, but common and naked mole rats live entirely on geophytes and roots.

Foraging burrows can be very extensive: one system containing 10 adults and 3 young common mole rats was 1km (0.6mi) long, and burrows of naked mole rats may exceed 3km (1.9mi) in length. Burrow length depends on the number and ages of mole rats in a system and on the abundance and distribution of food items.

Apart from providing nest, food storage, and toilet areas, the rest of the burrow system is dug in search of food. Excavating is easiest when the soil is soft and moist. After rain, there is a flurry of digging – indeed, in the first month after rain, colonies of naked and Damara mole rats can dig 1km (0.6mi) of burrows and throw up more than 2 tonnes of soil as molehills. In the arid regions where the two species live, many months may elapse before it next rains, so it is vitally important

to find enough food in these brief periods of optimal digging to see the colony through the drought. Small food items are eaten or stored (by Damara, common, and Cape mole rats, for example), while larger items are left growing in situ and are gradually hollowed out, thus ensuring a constantly fresh and growing food supply. At a later stage, the hollow is plugged with soil so the tuber will regenerate. This "farming" of geophytes enables colonies to remain resident in the same area for many years.

In some areas where naked mole rats occur, tubers may weigh as much as 50kg (110lb). When feeding, the mole rat holds small items with its forefeet, shakes them free of soil, cuts them into pieces with its incisors, and then chews these with its cheek teeth. In southwestern Cape Province, South Africa, differences in diet, burrow diameter and depth, and perhaps also of social organization enable three genera – *Bathyergus, Georychus,* and *Cryptomys* – to occupy different niches within the same area, and sometimes even the same field. This sympatry is unusual for burrowing mammals, where the normal pattern is for one species to occupy an area exclusively.

Life Below Ground
SOCIAL BEHAVIOR

The social behavior of three genera (*Bathyergus, Georychus,* and *Heliophobius*) follows the normal pattern for subterranean mammals: they are solitary, and aggressively defend their burrows against conspecifics. They signal to neighboring animals by drumming with their hindfeet; at the onset of breeding, *Georychus* males and females drum with a different tempo to attract a mate. Mating is brief, and the male then leaves the female to rear her pups. When about 2 months old, the pups begin to fight, and this is the prelude to dispersing; if forcibly kept together in captivity, siblings will eventually kill each other. In *Georychus,* the dispersing young often burrow away from the parent system and block up the linking burrows; this probably also occurs in the other solitary genera and would ensure that the young are protected from predators during this otherwise very vulnerable phase in their life history.

In the social mole rats (see box), only a single female breeds in each colony. In all the *Cryptomys* studied there is a strong inhibition against incest, and colonies are founded by a pair of animals originating from different colonies. The rest of the colony is composed of their offspring which, unlike the solitary mole rats, remain in the natal colony, helping to locate food and rear their siblings until conditions are favorable for dispersing. In fact, many never get the chance to breed.

Colony sizes of the common mole rat rarely exceed 14 animals, whereas 41 Damara mole rats may occur together (although 14–25 is more common). Naked mole rat colonies may contain over 300 individuals (the mean is about 80), but here there is no inhibition to incest and the breeders may come from within the colony. The breeding female is the dominant individual in the colony, which she controls through stress-related behaviors such as violent shoving. She has a distinctively elongated body (her vertebrae lengthen during her first few pregnancies), and this serves to better accommodate the large litters typical of this species. Up to three males may mate with her, and multiple paternity of litters can occur. Except for the dispersers, naked mole rats are very xenophobic and will kill foreign animals. They recognize colony members by scent, probably through a cocktail of odors that they spread on their bodies in the communal toilet area.

Because they live in a well protected, relatively safe environment, mole rats are less exposed to predators than are surface-dwelling rodents. This better life assurance may be why they produce smaller litters, usually of between two and five pups. There are exceptions: the Cape mole rat produces up to 10 pups, and the naked mole rat has as many as 28, although the average litter is 12. Naked mole rat pups weigh about 1g (0.04oz), while breeding females weigh 65–80g (2.3–2.8oz).

Snakes may occasionally pursue the solitary mole rats underground, but more often lie in wait for them. Field evidence suggests that the mole snake (*Pseudaspis cana*) is attracted to the smell of freshly turned soil and will penetrate the burrow system via a new molehill. It usually pushes its head into the burrow and waits for the mole rat as it reverses with its next load of soil. This may also be true of the eastern beaked snake (*Rhamphiophis oxythunchus rostrutus*), which has been seen preying on naked mole rats as they kick soil out of the burrow. Other predators also take mole rats: their skulls are not uncommon in the pellets of birds of prey and small carnivores such as jackals, caracals, and zorillas (African striped polecat).

In addition to protecting the mole rat against many predators, the underground environment provides a uniformly humid microclimate. This,

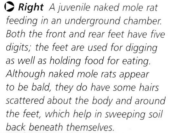

◐ **Right** *A juvenile naked mole rat feeding in an underground chamber. Both the front and rear feet have five digits; the feet are used for digging as well as holding food for eating. Although naked mole rats appear to be bald, they do have some hairs scattered about the body and around the feet, which help in sweeping soil back beneath themselves.*

◖ **Left** *A naked mole rat queen suckling several youngsters. The queen is effectively the leader of the colony and is a nonworker, and has a distinctively elongated body. Although only a small number of animals are actively involved in the breeding process, the others are not incapable of breeding, merely suppressed; research has shown that if nonbreeding females are removed from a colony and paired with a male, they become capable of breeding very quickly.*

THE INSECTLIKE RODENT

At least two species of mole rat, the naked and the Damara, have a colony structure similar to that of social insects. Within each colony, a single female and 1–3 males breed; the remaining males and females, while not infertile, remain nonreproductive while members of their natal colony. In naked mole rat colonies, the more numerous, small-sized, worker mole rats dig and maintain the foraging burrows and carry food and nesting material to the communal nest. Large-sized individuals spend much of the time in the nest with the breeding female. When the workers give an alarm call, however, they are mobilized to defend the colony.

The young born to the colony are cared for by all the mole rats but suckled only by the breeding female. Once weaned, they join the worker force, but whereas some individuals apparently remain workers throughout their lives, others eventually grow larger than the rest and become colony

When it does rain, a workforce must be mobilized rapidly to find sufficient food to see the colony through the dry months. By joining forces and channeling the energies of colony members along specific avenues (some finding food, some acting as soldiers, and a select few bearing young), these mole rats can survive in areas where single mole rats or pairs cannot.

Experiments have shown that nonbreeding mole rats are not sterile. Suppression is more severe in females than in males, which show some sperm production. Nonbreeders can rapidly become sexually active (within 7–10 days) and can found new colonies or, in the case of naked mole rats, can replace the breeding animals if they die. In this latter case, several of the older females initially show signs of sexual activity, and there is often a time of severe (sometimes fatal) fighting, before one female becomes sexually dominant, increases in

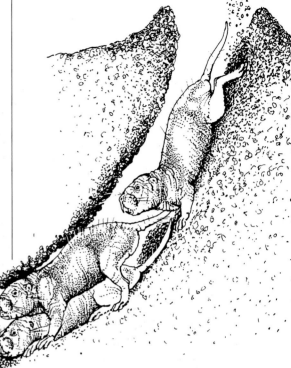

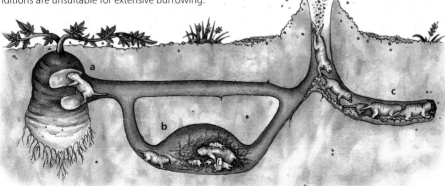

defenders. It is from these big, and usually older, individuals that new reproductive naked mole rats emerge when a breeder dies.

In naked as in all the social mole rats, therefore, a colony is composed of the progeny of a number of closely related litters. As with social insects, this relatedness is probably an important factor in the evolution and maintenance of a social structure in which some individuals in the colony never breed. By caring for closely related mole rats that share their genetic makeup, the nonbreeding individuals nonetheless ensure the passing on of their own genetic characteristics.

This system seems to prevail among social mole rats living in arid regions where for many months conditions are unsuitable for extensive burrowing.

body length, and becomes the new breeder. Occasionally succession occurs without fighting.

Unlike in social insects, pheromones do not seem to be the prime means of control. Yet in many captive colonies of naked mole rats, the whole colony is affected by the reproductive state of the breeding female. For example, just before a litter is born all colony members (male and female) develop teats, and some females come close to breeding condition. This strongly suggests that the colony is responding to chemical stimuli produced by the breeding female: these stimuli seem to prime the colony to receive and care for young that are not their own.

plus the high moisture content of the mole rat's food, precludes the necessity of having to drink free water. The burrow temperature remains relatively stable throughout the day, often in stark contrast to the surface temperature. In naked mole rat country, for example, surface temperatures of over 60°C (140°F) have been recorded while burrows 20cm (8in) below ground registered a steady 28–30°C (82–86°F). In response, naked mole rats have almost lost the ability to regulate body temperature, which consequently remains close to that of the burrow. If they need to alter it, they huddle together when cold or bask in surface burrows for warmth; they also take refuge in cooler areas within the system if they overheat, for example after digging near the surface

Helping and Harming

CONSERVATION AND ENVIRONMENT

Though inconspicuous, mole rats can cause considerable damage to property. Dune mole rats chew through underground cables, undermine roadways, and sometimes devour root and cereal crops. The molehills they create can damage the blades of harvesting machines, not to mention garden lawns and golf courses. The human response has been to attempt to exterminate all those causing the problems.

Yet mole rats also have beneficial effects on their environment. They are important agents in soil drainage and soil turnover (a Cape dune mole rat may throw up as much as 500kg/1,100lb of soil each month). They may play a role in dispersing geophytes (plants with underground storage organs) and they also eat geophytes that are poisonous to livestock.

JUMJ

⬥ **Above** *Cross-section of a burrow system. On the left **a** naked mole rats hollow out a growing tuber; in the center **b** is the main chamber, which is occupied by the breeding female, subsidiary adults and young; on the right **c** a digging chain is at work.*

⬥ **Top** *A mole rat digging chain. The lead animal digs with its teeth and pushes the soil backward. The one behind drags the load backward, keeping close to the tunnel floor, and passes it to the animal responsible for dispersal. It then returns to the front, straddling other mole rats pushing soil away.*

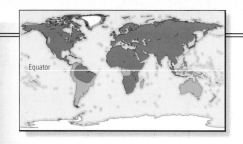

LAGOMORPHS

eITHER AS NATIVE SPECIES OR AS A RESULT OF *human introductions, lagomorphs – meaning literally "hare shaped" – are found all around the globe. The order contains two families: the small, rodentlike pikas, weighing under 0.5kg (1.1lb); and the rabbits and hares, weighing up to 5kg (11lb).*

The pikas are thought to have separated from the rabbits and hares in the late Eocene, around 38–35 million years ago. Recent DNA sequence analysis suggests that most rabbit and hare genera arose from a single rapid diversification event approximately 12–16 m.y.a. The first pikas appeared in Asia in the middle Oligocene and spread to North America and Europe in the Pliocene (5–1.8 m.y.a.). Pikas seem to have peaked in distribution and diversity during the Miocene (24–5 m.y.a.) and since declined, while the rabbits and hares have maintained a widespread distribution since the Pliocene.

Rabbits and hares have elongated hindlimbs adapted for running at speed over open ground. Their ears are long, the nasal region elongated, and their tail typically has conspicuous white underfur. By contrast, pikas are small with short legs, and are well adapted for living in open meadow and steppe habitats; the tail is virtually absent, and the ears short and rounded. They are far more vocal than rabbits and hares, but all three groups use scent products from special glands. Other features shared by all lagomorphs include coats of long, soft fur that fully covers the feet, ears that are large relative to body size, and eyes positioned for good broad-field vision.

What Makes a Lagomorph?
DIGESTION, DENTITION, AND DISTRIBUTION
Rabbits, hares, and pikas are all herbivores that feed predominantly on grasses but consume a range of other plant species in different habitats. Their digestive system is adapted for processing large volumes of vegetation, and they reingest some of their fecal matter, a behavior known as coprophagy. As herbivores with gnawing incisors, rabbits, hares, and pikas were initially classed by taxonomists within the order Rodentia, but in 1912 J. W. Cridley brought them together within

the new order Lagomorpha. Significant among the several distinctive features that set them apart from rodents is the possession of a second pair of small incisors, known as peg teeth, behind the long, constantlygrowing pair in the upper jaw. This gives rabbits and hares a total of 28 teeth and a dental formula of 2/1 incisors, 0/0 canines, 3/2 premolars, and 3/3 molars; while pikas have 26 teeth (one fewer upper molar on each side).

Only two pika species occur in North America; the rest are distributed across Asia. Rabbits and hares, on the other hand, have diversified to produce species occupying a wide range of habitats,

from tropical forest (the forest rabbit) through swamps, desert, and montane grassland (the North American marsh rabbit, black-tailed jackrabbits, and Mexico's volcano rabbit) to the snow-covered Arctic (snowshoe and arctic hares).

Phenomenal Numbers
BREEDING PATTERNS
Within their home ecosystems, lagomorphs are often key fodder for a range of mammalian and avian predators. To counter high mortality rates, they breed prodigiously. Most species reach sexual maturity relatively early (after just 3 months in

◗ **Right** *The European rabbit is a prodigious breeder, capable of producing between 10 and 30 young each year. And yet, in this species, over half of all pregnancies are aborted, with the embryos being resorbed into the female's body.*

female European rabbits). The gestation period is short – 40 days in *Lepus* species, and around 30 days in all other genera – and litter sizes are often large. Other features of lagomorph reproduction that minimize interbirth intervals for females include the phenomenon of induced ovulation, by which eggs are shed in response to copulation rather than on a cyclic basis; and postpartum estrus, permitting a female to conceive immediately after giving birth. Female lagomorphs are also capable of resorbing embryos under adverse conditions, for example in times of climatic or social stress. There is further evidence that species such as the European hare are capable of conceiving a second litter before the birth of the last young, an amazing feat called "superfetation."

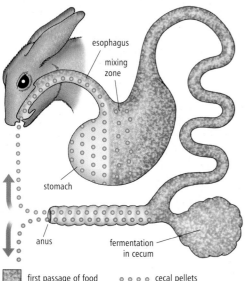

first passage of food ⚬⚬⚬⚬ cecal pellets

alimentary mass ⚬⚬⚬⚬ hard feces

Losses and Gains
CONSERVATION ISSUES

Over 20 percent of lagomorph species are currently listed as threatened. Some are island endemics, like the Mexican Tres Marías cottontail; others, such as Koslov's pika (China), the riverine rabbit (South Africa), and the volcano rabbit (Mexico), have a distribution that has been severely reduced by destruction of their highly specialized habitats.

More encouragingly, the Sumatran striped rabbit (*Nesolagus netscheri*) – representing a genus of striped rabbit until recently feared extinct – has been caught on autotrap camera in its tropical forest habitat. Furthermore, a second species of striped rabbit, the Annamite, has also come to light in remote montane forests between Laos and Vietnam. Three freshly killed specimens were found in a meat market in 1995–96, and live animals have subsequently been photographed. This new form of striped rabbit has been named the Annamite striped rabbit, *N. timminsi*.   ATS/DB

◁ **Left** The digestive system of lagomorphs is highly modified for coping with large quantities of vegetation. The gut has a large, blind-ending sac (the cecum) between the large and small intestines, which contains bacterial flora to aid the digestion of cellulose. Many products of the digestion in the cecum can pass directly into the blood stream, but others such as the important B vitamins would be lost if lagomorphs did not eat some of the feces (refection) and so pass them through their gut twice. As a result, lagomorphs have two kinds of feces. First, soft black viscous cecal pellets which are produced during the day in nocturnal species and during the night in species active in the daytime. These are usually eaten directly from the anus and stored in the stomach, to be mixed later with further food taken from the alimentary mass. Second, round hard feces which are passed normally.

◁ **Left** Alpine pikas have a fondness for sunning themselves and often bask on rocks, choosing for camouflage those with a similar color to their coat. Although many pikas live in regions with very severe winters, they do not appear to hibernate.

ORDER: LAGOMORPHA
92 species in 13 genera and 3 families. One family, the Prolagidae (Sardinian pika) is Extinct.

Distribution Worldwide, except for S South America, the West Indies, Madagascar, and some Southeast Asian islands.

RABBITS AND HARES Family Leporidae   p250

62 species in 11 genera
Includes **Riverine rabbit** (*Bunolagus monticularis*); **Hispid hare** (*Caprolagus hispidus*); **European rabbit** (*Oryctolagus cuniculus*); **Amami rabbit** (*Pentalagus furnessi*); **Volcano rabbit** (*Romerolagus diazi*); **Bunyoro rabbit** (*Poelagus marjorita*); **Pygmy rabbit** (*Brachylagus idahoensis*); **Sumatran rabbit** (*Nesolagus netscheri*); **Redrock hare** (*Pronolagus spp.*); **Tapeti** (*Sylvilagus brasiliensis*); **Eastern cottontail** (*S. floridanus*); **Antelope jackrabbit** (*Lepus alleni*); **Black-tailed jackrabbit** (*L. californicus*); **Snowshoe hare** (*L. americanus*); **European hare** (*L. europaeus*); **Arctic hare** (*L. arcticus*).

PIKAS Family Ochotonidae   p266

30 species in the genus *Ochotona*
Includes **Alpine pika** (*O. alpina*); **American pika** (*O. princeps*); **Northern pika** (*O. hyperborea*); **Royle's pika** (*O. roylei*); **Daurian pika** (*O. dauurica*); **Gansu pika** (*O. cansus*); **Moupin pika** (*O. thibetana*); **Koslov's pika** (*O. koslowi*); **Plateau pika** (*O. curzoniae*); **Steppe pika** (*O. pusilla*).

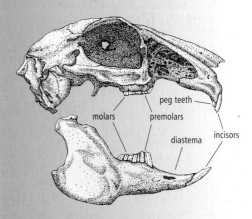

◁ **Above** The skull of a rabbit. Lagomorphs have long, constantly growing incisors, as do rodents, but lagomorphs differ in having two pairs of upper incisors, the back nonfunctional ones being known as peg teeth. There is a gap (diastema) between the incisors and premolars. The dental formula of rabbits and hares (family Leporidae) is I2/1, C0/0, P3/2, M3/3, with the pikas (family Ochotonidae) having one fewer upper molar in each jaw.

Rabbits and Hares

tHERE ARE FEW MAMMALS WHOSE FATE HAS *been so intimately intertwined over the centuries with humans' as the European rabbit. Its domestication probably began in North Africa or Italy in Roman times; today there are well over a hundred varieties of domestic rabbit, all selectively bred from a single species. In addition, wild or domesticated offspring of the original stock have, through invasion or deliberate introduction, spread worldwide, with many populations reaching pest proportions. Yet the European rabbit is just one of a family of more than 60 leporid species, some of which lead a far more precarious existence, numbering in the hundreds rather than the tens of millions.*

The family Leporidae splits broadly into two groups: the jackrabbits and hares of the genus *Lepus*, and the rabbits in the remaining 10 genera. Just to confuse matters, several species – for example, the African red rockhare and the endangered hispid hare – are commonly known as hares, even though behaviorally they are quite clearly rabbits.

Telling Rabbits from Hares
FORM AND FUNCTION

The major differences between the *Lepus* hares and the rabbits relate to differences in the strategies the two groups employ in evading predators and in reproduction. Basically, the longer-legged hares try to outrun their pursuers – some reputedly reaching speeds of 72 km/h (45 mph) in full flight – while the shorter-limbed rabbits run to seek refuge in dense cover or underground burrows. In addition, young hares (leverets) are better developed (precocial) at birth compared with altricial newborn rabbits (kittens). In the nonburrowing hares, the leverets are born after longer gestation periods (37–50 days) with a full covering of fur, their eyes open, and capable of coordinated movement. In contrast, rabbit kittens are born naked or with sparse fur covering after shorter gestation periods (27–30 days), their eyes opening after 4–10 days. Long ears are a conspicuous feature of all leporids, but typically these are at their most magnificent in the jackrabbits, where they can

RABBITS AND HARES

Order: Lagomorpha

Family: Leporidae

62 species in 11 genera, 7 of them monotypic (containing only a single species): the Riverine rabbit (*Bunolagus monticularis*), Hispid hare (*Caprolagus hispidus*), European rabbit (*Oryctolagus cuniculus*), Amami rabbit (*Pentalagus furnessi*),Volcano rabbit (*Romerolagus diazi*), Bunyoro rabbit (*Poelagus marjorita*), and Pygmy rabbit (*Brachylagus idahoensis*). In addition, there are 2 species of Striped rabbit (*Nesolagus*); 3 species of Red rockhare (*Pronolagus*); 17 species of Cottontail rabbit (*Sylvilagus*), including the Tapeti (*S. brasiliensis*) and Eastern cottontail (*S. floridanus*); and 32 species of hare (*Lepus*), including the Antelope jackrabbit (*Lepus alleni*), Black-tailed jackrabbit (*L. californicus*), Snowshoe hare (*L. americanus*), and European hare (*L. europaeus*).

DISTRIBUTION Americas, Europe, Asia, Africa; introduced (yellow) to Australia, New Zealand, and S America.

Equator

HABITAT Wide ranging; includes desert, montane forest, tropical rain forest, arctic tundra, swamp, tall grassland, agricultural landscapes.

SIZE Head–body length ranges from 25cm (10in) in the Pygmy rabbit to 75cm (30in) in the European hare; tail length from 1.5cm (0.6in) to 12cm (4.7in), and weight from around 400g (14oz) to 6kg (13.2lb), both in the same two species. Ear length reaches 17cm (7in) in the Antelope jackrabbit. Leporid hindlimbs are regularly longer than the forelimbs.

COAT Usually thick and soft, but coarse or woolly in some species (Hispid hare and Woolly hare); hair shorter/sparser on the ears; tail well furred or even bushy (Riverine rabbit and Red rockhares); feet hairy on both surfaces; coloration ranges through reddish brown, brown, buff, and gray, to white; the belly is often covered with lighter or pure white hair. Two species (*Nesolagus*) are striped, and arctic/northern species change to white for winter (Snowshoe, Arctic, Mountain, Japanese hares).

DIET Herbivorous

BREEDING Gestation typically longer in hares (up to 55 days in the Mountain hare) than in rabbits (30 days in the European rabbit). The young are precocial at birth in hares, but altricial in rabbits.

LONGEVITY Average less than 1 year in the wild; maximum of 12 years recorded in European hare and European rabbit.

CONSERVATION STATUS 12 species are listed as threatened (i.e. Critically Endangered, Endangered, or Vulnerable), and another 6 as Near Threatened.

See species table ▷

◐ *Above* Like several other northern species, snowshoe hares may molt twice a year, donning a white coat for camouflage each winter only to lose it again in the spring. Individuals of the species that live outside areas of continuous snow cover generally do not make the change.

◐ *Left* With its large ears pricked for unfamiliar sounds and its eyes wide open to catch sudden movements, a savanna hare in Tanzania's Serengeti National Park freezes briefly, alert for danger. In general, hares rely on their exceptional speed to outrun predators, while rabbits make rapidly for the nearest cover.

grow to over 17cm (7in). The eyes of both rabbits and hares are large and adapted to their crepuscular and nocturnal activity patterns. All leporids are herbivorous, but some, like the mountain and snowshoe hares, may be more selective in their choice of feeding material than others, including the European rabbit.

Open Terrain or Dense Cover
DISTRIBUTION PATTERNS

Apart from a few forest-dwelling species such as the snowshoe hare, most hares prefer open habitats with some cover offered by terrain or vegetation. They therefore have a widespread distribution, occurring in habitats ranging from desert to grasslands and tundra. Rabbits, on the other hand, are rarely found far from dense cover or underground tunnels. They occupy a variety of disturbed, successional, and climax habitats, often characterized by grass communities associated with dense cover; in the American cottontails this cover is often provided by plants such as sage brush and bramble. Other species are highly specialized in their habitat requirement, the two striped Sumatran and Annamite rabbits and the Japanese Amami rabbit living in tropical forest cover while the riverine rabbit and hispid hare (actually a rabbit) are restricted respectively to pockets of riverine scrub in the central karoo of South Africa and to tall grassland in the Indian subcontinent. In marked contrast to rabbits, hares tend to use cover for daytime shelter, but will run into the open when confronted with a predator.

Warrens and Absentee Parents
SOCIAL BEHAVIOR

The burrowing lifestyle familiar in the warren-digging European rabbit is actually rather unusual, even among leporid genera. Apart from the European rabbit, only the pygmy, Amami, and Bunyoro rabbits are reported to dig underground refuges themselves, while a few opportunists (for instance, the eastern, desert, and mountain cottontails) will use burrows dug by other species. A small number of hares are reported to dig burrows to avoid extreme temperatures: the black-tailed jackrabbit and Cape hare, for example, do so to escape high desert temperatures, while snowshoe and arctic hares may burrow into snow. Forms – surface depressions in the ground or vegetation – are more commonly used as resting-up sites by hares. These may be well-established sites used by successive generations or, alternatively, temporary refuges occupied for only a few hours.

The underground warrens dug by European rabbits form the focus of stable, territorial breeding groups – a social system unknown amongst other leporid species. Most hares and rabbits are nonterritorial, moving over individual home ranges of up to 300ha (740 acres) in some hares, with ranges overlapping in favored feeding areas. Temporary feeding aggregations have been seen in a number of leporids, including the Yarkand and mountain hares, the black-tailed jackrabbit, and the brush rabbit. In the European hare these aggregations may be structured, with dominant individuals maintaining priority of access to food patches. Large groups of snowshoe hares may be sighted in the winter months, when these animals are in their white camouflage coat. Individual animals are thought to gather together to reduce their chance of being preyed upon.

Apart from "policing," in which males intervene to protect young under attack from adult females, no form of male paternal care has been reported in the leporids, and even maternal care is pretty thin on the ground – a reproductive strategy known as "absentee parentism." In hares, the precocial, fur covered, fully mobile leverets are born into surface-depression forms, while the poorly developed rabbit kittens are delivered into carefully constructed fur-lined nests built in underground chambers or dense cover (thick clumps of montane bunch-grass in the case of the volcano rabbit). After birth, a consistent and unusual feature of leporid maternal care is the nursing or suckling of litters for just one brief episode, typically less than 5 minutes, once every 24 hours. In fact, the milk is highly nutritious, with a very high fat and protein content, and can be pumped into the youngsters at great speed during the short lactation period, which lasts for 17–23 days. In the European rabbit, for example, this will be the only contact between mother and young until the kittens are weaned at around 21 days, after which the mother will start preparing for the birth of the litter conceived as she emerged from giving birth to the last one.

As a strategy, this lack of social contact between the mother and her offspring may be designed to reduce the chances of drawing a predator's attention to the highly vulnerable nestlings. In the case of those rabbit species that breed in purpose-dug breeding tunnels, or stops, the soil entrance will be carefully resealed after each short suckling bout. In the surface-breeding hares, the leverets disperse to separate hiding locations about 3 days after birth, but regroup with littermates at a specific location at precisely defined intervals (often around sunset) for a frenzied, similarly brief, bout of suckling from mother.

Relationships between climate and reproduction are clearly demonstrated in both the hares and the New World cottontail rabbits. In the cottontails there is a direct correlation between latitude and litter size; species and subspecies in the north produce the largest litters during the shortest breeding season. The eastern cottontail appears to be the most fecund of the genus, producing up to 35 young a year, whilst the tapeti produces the least, at around 10 per annum. Amongst the *Lepus* hares and jackrabbits, productivity varies from a single litter of 6–8 in the far north to eight litters of 1–2 young at the equator, giving a fairly standard production statistic of about 10 young a year per female. Reproductive output is more variable in the snowshoe hare (5–18 young per female), a species well known for its population cycles, which are synchronous over a wide geographical range.

Compared with the more vocal pikas, communicating rabbits and hares appear to rely more heavily on scent than sound for communication. However, some species appear to be more vocal than others, and exceptions such as the volcano rabbit do exist. Most leporids make high-pitched distress squeals when captured by a predator, and five species of rabbit, all comparatively gregarious, give specific alarm calls. The European, brush, and desert rabbits are known to thump their hind-feet on the ground in response to danger, possibly as a warning to underground nestlings. In addition, many leporids possess a conspicuous white underside to their tail, which could serve as a visual warning signal during flight from a predator. Interestingly, those species with tail flags tend to be found in more open habitats than the forest and volcano rabbits and hispid hare, which have a dark underside to their tails.

All rabbits and hares have scent-secreting glands in the groin and under the chin. These appear to be important in sexual communication; in the gregarious European rabbit, where the activity of the glands is known to be related to testes size and levels of male hormones, they may also signal social status. Dominant male European rabbits are essentially the smelliest, scent marking at higher frequency with scent-gland secretions and carefully aimed squirts of pungent urine.

◁ **Left** *Representative species of rabbits and hares:* **1** *Antelope jackrabbit* (Lepus alleni)*;* **2** *Amami rabbit* (Pentalagus furnessi) *digging a burrow;* **3** *Riverine rabbit* (Bunolagus monticularis) *in an alert posture;* **4** *Bunyoro rabbit* (Poelagus marjorita), *hopping;* **5** *dominant male European rabbit* (Oryctolagus cuniculus) *scent marking with its chin;* **6** *Sumatran striped rabbit* (Nesolagus netscheri), *grooming its muzzle and spreading scent;* **7** *male eastern cottontail* (Sylvilagus floridanus) *in an alert posture;* **8** *European hare* (Lepus europaeus), *boxing;* **9** *Natal red rockhare* (Pronolagus crassicaudatus) *in an alert scanning posture;* **10** *Hispid hare* (Caprolagus hispidus), *sitting among cuttings and pellets;* **11** *Volcano rabbit* (Romerolagus diazi), *reingesting pellets amid a vegetation of zacatón grasses.*

⬤ Above Desert cottontail kittens crowd a shallow nest in California. The mother will not live in the nest with them, but will crouch over it to feed her young. This litter will be only one of several that she will raise in the course of the year, while the kittens themselves will be ready to start breeding within 3 months.

◁ Left Built to make quick getaways, a European hare shows a clean pair of heels to a pursuer. Hares are the champion sprinters among the smaller mammals; their long hindlegs can drive them forward at speeds of over 70 km/h (45mph).

UNWELCOME INTRODUCTIONS

Although many rabbit species are now at risk, the European rabbit (*Oryctolagus cuniculus*) is so successful that it has sometimes acquired the status of a major pest. Problems have arisen particularly following the introduction of the species to areas where it was previously unknown – for example Australia and New Zealand in the early 19th century. The result was a population explosion that proved highly costly for the nations' arable and livestock farmers. It was initially controlled by the deliberate introduction of the rabbit disease myxomatosis in the 1950s, although today the rabbit problem remains.

The reasons for the rabbit's dramatic capacity to increase its numbers are built into its biology. The European rabbit is not a fussy eater; it can feed off the same plants at many different stages in their growth. It is also almost unique in its habit of living communally in large burrows, a lifestyle that encourages high population densities. Above all, it is hugely prolific. Adult females can bear five litters a year, each containing an average of five or six young. Female offspring will themselves start breeding after just 5–6 months – an unfailing recipe for spiraling demographics.

Relict Species at Risk

CONSERVATION AND ENVIRONMENT

Sadly, the image of rabbits and hares has been somewhat tainted by a few species such as the European rabbit and hare, which are notorious for the damage they inflict on agricultural crops or forestry plantations. A preoccupation with rabbits' and hares' potential as pests has caused us to neglect the significant positive roles the leporid species play in ecosystems worldwide, both as prey items for small- to medium-sized vertebrate predators and through their grazing activities. Their pestilential reputation can also draw attention away from the larger number of rabbits and hares now listed as highly threatened in international registers.

Typically, those leporids threatened with extinction are primitive relict species, often the only members of their genus and usually the victims of habitat destruction by man. Most are highly specialized in their habitat requirements. The handsome riverine rabbit currently clings on in remnants of riverine scrub habitat associated with two seasonal rivers in the central karoo in South Africa: its habitat has been destroyed to promote the irrigation of encroaching agricultural crops. Similarly, the distribution of the primitive hispid hare is now restricted to isolated fragments of tall thatch grassland habitat located in a few protected areas across the northern Indian subcontinent, while the tiny Mexican volcano rabbit, or zacatuche, is isolated in pockets of endemic bunchgrass habitat on the slopes of just a few volcanoes around Mexico City, one of the world's largest conurbations. It is time that this group of attractive, long-eared mammals received more attention – and a far more positive press. DB/ATS

Rabbit and Hare Species

GENUS *BRACHYLAGUS*

Pygmy rabbit `LR`
Brachylagus idahoensis

SW Oregon to EC California, SW Utah, N to SW Montana; isolated populations in WC Washington State. Prefers habitat comprising clumps of dense sagebrush; extensive runways may cross the thickets. Lives in burrows of its own construction. HBL 21–27cm; TL 1.5–2cm; WT 50–470g. The smallest rabbit.
COAT: reddish, similar to red rockhares with bushy tail.
CONSERVATION STATUS: LR, Near Threatened. Widespread, but species has recently been in decline.

GENUS *BUNOLAGUS*

Riverine rabbit `Cr`
Bunolagus monticularis
Riverine rabbit or Bushman hare

Central Cape Province (South Africa). Dense riverine scrub (not the mountainous situations often attributed). Nocturnal, resting by day in hollows on the shady side of of bushes. Now extremely rare. HBL 34–48cm; TL 7–11cm; WT 1–1.5kg
FORM: coat reddish, similar to red rockhares with bushy tail.

GENUS *CAPROLAGUS*

Hispid hare `En`
Caprolagus hispidus
Hispid hare, Assam or Bristly rabbit

Uttar Pradesh to Assam; Tripura (India). Mymensingh and Dacca on the W bank of River Brahmaputra (Bangladesh). Sub-Himalayan *sal* forest where grasses grow up to 3.5m in height during the monsoon months; occasionally also in cultivated areas. Inhabits burrows that are not of its own making. Seldom leaves forest shelter. HBL 48cm; TL 5.3cm; EL 7cm; HFL 10cm; WT 2.5kg.
FORM: coat coarse and bristly; upperside appears brown from intermingling of black and brownish-white hair; underside brownish-white, with chest slightly darker; tail brown throughout, paler below. Claws straight and strong.

GENUS *LEPUS*

Most inhabit open grassy areas, but: Snowshoe hare occurs in boreal forests; European hare occasionally forests; Arctic hare prefers forested areas to open country; Cape hare prefers open areas, occasionally evergreen forests. Instead of seeking cover, hares rely on their well-developed running ability to escape from danger: also on camouflage, by flattening on vegetation. Vocalizations include a deep grumbling, and shrill calls are given when in pain. Usually solitary, but the European hare is more social. Habitat type has a marked effect on home-range size within each species, but differences also occur between species, e.g. from 4–20ha (10–50 acres) in Arctic hares to more than 300ha (745 acres) in European hares. Individuals may defend the area within 1–2m of forms, but home ranges generally overlap and feeding areas are often communal. Most live on the surface, but some species, e.g. Snowshoe and Arctic hares, dig burrows, while others may hide in holes or tunnels not of their making. HBL 40–76cm; TL 3.5–12cm; WT 1.2–5kg.
FORM: coat usually reddish brown, yellowish brown, or grayish brown above, lighter or pure white below; ear tips black-edged, with a significant black area on the exterior in most species; in some species the upperside of the tail is black. The Indian hare has a black nape. Species inhabiting snowy winter climes often molt into a white winter coat, while others change from a brownish summer coat into a grayish winter coat.
DIET: usually grasses and herbs, but cultivated plants, twigs, bark of woody plants are the staple food if other alternatives are not available.
BREEDING: breed throughout the year in southern species; northern species produce 2–4 litters during spring and summer. Gestation up to 50 days in Arctic hare, other species shorter. Litter size 1–9.
LONGEVITY: Only a minority of hares survive their first year in the wild, though survivors can reach 5 years; in captivity, hares can live to 6 or 7 years.

Antelope jackrabbit `LR`
Lepus alleni

S New Mexico, SC Arizona to N Nayarit (Mexico), Tiburon Island. Locally common. Avoids dehydration in hot desert by feeding on cactus and yucca.

Snowshoe hare
Lepus americanus

S and C Alaska, coast of Hudson Bay, Newfoundland, S Appalachians, S Michigan, N Dakota, N New Mexico, Utah, E California, introduced to Anacosti Isl (Canada). Locally common.

Arctic hare `LR`
Lepus arcticus

Greenland and Canadian Arctic Islands south to WC shore of Hudson Bay. Quebec and W maritime provinces of Canada.

Japanese hare `LR`
Lepus brachyurus

Honshu, Shikoku, Kyushu, Oki Isl, and Sado Isl (Japan). Locally common.

Black-tailed jackrabbit `LR`
Lepus californicus

N Mexico (Baja California), Oregon, Washington, S Idaho, E Colorado, S Dakota, W Missouri, NW Arkansas, Arizona, N Mexico. Locally common.

White-sided jackrabbit `LR`
Lepus callotis

SW New Mexico and southward discontinuously to Oaxaca (Mexico). Locally common, but declining.
CONSERVATION STATUS: Lower Risk, Near Threatened.

Cape hare
Lepus capensis

South Africa, Namibia, Botswana, Zimbabwe, S Angola, S Zambia, Mozambique; and to the north, Tanzania, Kenya, Somalia, Ethiopia, Sub-Saharan Africa. Locally common.

Broom hare `Vu`
Lepus castroviejoi

Cantabrian Mountains (N Spain).

Yunnan hare `LR`
Lepus comus

Yunnan and W Guizhou (China).

Ethiopian hare
Lepus fagani

N and W Ethiopia and neighboring SE Sudan south to NW Kenya.
CONSERVATION STATUS: Data Deficient

Korean hare `LR`
Lepus coreanus

Korean peninsula, S Kirin, S Liaoning, E Heilongjiang (China).

Corsican hare
Lepus corsicanus

Italy (including Sicily); introduced to Corsica (France).
CONSERVATION STATUS: Currently unknown, but likely to be listed as threatened due to overhunting and the introduction of the European hare.

European hare `LR`
Lepus europaeus
European or Brown hare

S Scandinavia, S Finland, Great Britain (introduced in Ireland), Europe south to N Iraq and Iran, W Siberia. Locally common but declining.

Tehuantepec jackrabbit `En`
Lepus flavigularis

Restricted to sand dune forest on shores of saltwater lagoons on N rim of Gulf of Tehuantepec (S Mexico). Nocturnal. Likely to be reclassified as Critically Endangered in near future.

Granada hare
Lepus granatensis
Granada or Iberian hare

Iberian peninsula except NE and NC parts (Spain, Portugal); Mallorca.

Abyssinian hare `LR`
Lepus habessinicus

Djibouti, E Ethiopia, Somalia, perhaps NE Kenya. Apparently replaces the Cape hare in open grassland, steppe, savanna, and desert habitats.

African savanna hare
Lepus victoriae

From Atlantic coast of NW Africa (Senegal, south to Guinea and Sierra Leone) eastward across Sahel to Sudan and extreme W Ethiopia; S through E Africa (E Republic of Congo, W Kenya) to NE Namibia, Botswana, and KwaZulu-Natal (S Africa). Small isolated population in W Algeria.

Hainan hare `Vu`
Lepus hainanus

Lowlands of Hainan Isl (China).

ABBREVIATIONS	HBL = head–body length TL = tail length EL = ear length		`Ex` Extinct	`En` Endangered
	HFL = hind-foot length WT = weight		`EW` Extinct in the Wild	`Vu` Vulnerable
	Approximate nonmetric equivalents: 10cm = 4in 30g = 1oz 1kg = 2.2lb		`Cr` Critically Endangered	`LR` Lower Risk

⚫ **Above** *The black-tailed jackrabbit lives in dry, sunny regions, where its huge ears help control heat intake. Even so, it is mostly active at night.*

Black jackrabbit `LR`
Lepus insularis

Espiritu Santo Island (Mexico).
CONSERVATION STATUS: Lower Risk,
Near Threatened.

Manchurian hare `LR`
Lepus mandshuricus

Jilin, Liaoning, Heilongjiang (NE China),
far NE Korea, Ussuri region (E Siberia,
Russia). Range decreasing.

Indian hare `LR`
Lepus nigricollis
Indian or Black-naped hare

Pakistan, India, Bangladesh (except Sun-
derbands), Sri Lanka (introduced into Java
and Mauritius, Gunnera Quoin, Anskya,
Réunion, and Cousin Isls in Indian
Ocean).

Woolly hare `LR`
Lepus oiostolus

Tibetan (Xizang) plateau and adjoining
areas.

Alaskan hare `LR`
Lepus othus

W and SW Alaska (USA), E Chukotsk
(Russia).

Burmese hare `LR`
Lepus peguensis

C and S Burma to Indochina and Hainan
(China).

Scrub hare `LR`
Lepus saxatilis

S Africa, Namibia.

Chinese hare `LR`
Lepus sinensis

SE China, Taiwan, S Korea.

Ethiopian highland hare `LR`
Lepus starcki

C Ethiopian mountains.

Mountain hare `LR`
Lepus timidus
Mountain or Blue hare

Alaska, Labrador, Greenland, Scandinavia,
N Russia to Siberia and Sakhalin, Hokkai-
do (Japan), Sikhoto Alin Mts, Altai, N Tien
Shan, N Ukraine, Baltic states. Locally
common. Isolated populations in the
Alps, Scotland, Wales, and Ireland.

Yarkand hare `LR`
Lepus yarkandensis

SW Xinjiang (China), margins of Takla
Makan desert.
CONSERVATION STATUS: Lower Risk,
Near Threatened

Tolai hare
Lepus tolai

N Caspian Sea S along E shore of Caspian
to N Iran, E through Afghanistan, Kazakhstan to Mongolia and W, C, and NE China.

White-tailed jackrabbit `LR`
Lepus townsendii

S British Columbia, S Alberta, SW

Ontario, SW Wisconsin, Kansas, N New
Mexico, Nevada, E California. Locally
common.

Desert hare
Lepus tibetanus

Afghanistan and Baluchistan eastward
through N Pakistan and Kashmir to the E
Pamir, NW Xinjiang and the Altai Mountains, eastward across S Mongolia to
Gansu and Ningxia (China).

GENUS *NESOLAGUS*

Sumatran striped rabbit `Cr`
Nesolagus netscheri
Sumatran rabbit or Sumatran short-eared hare

W Sumatra (1°–4°S) between
600–1,400m (2,000–4,600ft) in Barisan
range. Primary mountain forest. Strictly
nocturnal; spends the day in burrows or
in holes not of its own making.
HBL 37–39cm; TL 1.7cm; EL 4.3–4.5cm.
FORM: variable; body from buff to gray,
the rump bright rusty with broad dark
stripes from the muzzle to the tail, from
the ear to the chin, curving from the

shoulder to the rump, across the upper part of the hindlegs, and around the base of the hindfoot.
DIET: juicy stalks and leaves.

Annamite striped rabbit
Nesolagus timminsi

Annamite Mts. between Laos and Vietnam. Morphologically similar to *N. netscheri*. Little is known about this species but it is throught to be rare and potentially Endangered.

GENUS *ORYCTOLAGUS*

European rabbit   LR
Oryctolagus cuniculus
European or Old World Rabbit

Endemic on the Iberian peninsula and in NW Africa; introduced in rest of W Europe 2,000 years ago, and to Australia, New Zealand, S America, and some islands. Opportunistic, having colonized habitats from stony deserts to subalpine valleys; also found in fields, parks, and gardens, rarely reaching altitudes of over 600m (2,000ft). Very common. All strains of domesticated rabbit derived from this species. Colonial organization associated with warren systems. Utters shrill calls in pain or fear.
HBL 38–50cm; TL 4.5–7.5cm; EL 6.5–8.5cm; HFL 8.5–11cm; WT 1.5–3kg.
FORM: coat grayish with a fine mixture of black and light brown tips of the hair above; nape reddish to yellowish brown; tail white below; underside light gray; inner surface of the legs buff gray; total black is not rare.
DIET: grass and herbs; roots and the bark of trees and shrubs, cultivated plants.
BREEDING: breeds from February to August/September in N Europe; 3–5 litters with 5–6 young, occasionally up to 12; gestation period 28–33 days; young naked at birth; weight about 40–45g, eyes open when about 10 days old.
LONGEVITY: about 10 years in wild.

GENUS *PENTALAGUS*

Amami rabbit   En
Pentalagus furnessi
Amami or Ryukyu rabbit

Two of the Amami Islands (Japan). Dense forests. Nocturnal. Digs burrows.
HBL 43–51cm; EL 4.5cm.
FORM: coat thick and woolly, dark brown above, more reddish below. Claws are unusually long for rabbits at 1–2cm. Eyes small.
BREEDING: 1–3 young are born naked in a short tunnel; two breeding seasons.

GENUS *POELAGUS*

Bunyoro rabbit   LR
Poelagus marjorita
Bunyoro or Central African rabbit, or Uganda grass hare

S Sudan and Chad, NW Uganda, NE Zaire, Central African Republic, Angola. Savanna and forest. Locally common. Nocturnal. While resting, hides in vegetation. Reported to grind teeth when disturbed.
HBL 44–50cm; TL 4.5–5cm; EL 6–6.5cm; WT 2–3kg.
FORM: coat stiffer than that of any other African leporid; grizzled brown and yellowish above, becoming more yellow on the sides and white on the underparts; nape reddish yellow; tail brownish yellow above and white below. Ears small; hindlegs short.
BREEDING: Young reared in burrows; less precocious than those of true hares.

GENUS *PRONOLAGUS*

Nocturnal, feeding on grass and herbs. Inhabits rocky grassland, shelters in crevices. Utters shrill vocal calls even when not in pain.
HBL 35–50cm; TL 5–10cm; HFL 7.5–10cm; EL 6–10cm; WT 2–2.5kg.
FORM: coat thick and woolly, including that on the feet, reddish.

Natal red rockhare   LR
Pronolagus crassicaudatus
Greater red rockhare or Natal red rock rabbit

SE South Africa, extreme S Mozambique.

Jameson's red rockhare   LR
Pronolagus randensis

NE South Africa, E Botswana, Zimbabwe, W Mozambique, W Namibia, perhaps SW Angola.

Smith's red rockhare   LR
Pronolagus rupestris

South Africa to SW Kenya.

GENUS *ROMEROLAGUS*

Volcano rabbit   En
Romerolagus diazi
Volcano rabbit, Teporingo, or Zacatuche

Restricted to two volcanic sierras (Ajusco and Ixtaccihuatl–Popocatepetl ranges) close to Mexico City. Habitat unique "zacatón" (principally *Epicampes*, *Festuca*, and *Muhlenbergia*) grass layer of open pine forest at 2,800–4,000m. Lives in warren-based groups of 2–5 animals. Vocaliza-

tions resemble those of pikas.
HBL 27–36cm; EL 4–4.4cm; WT 400–500g.
FORM: coat dark brown above, dark brownish gray below. Smallest leporid; features include short ears, legs, and feet, articulation between collar and breast bones, and no visible tail.
BREEDING: breeding season December to July; gestation 39–40 days; average litter 2. Mainly active in daytime, sometimes at night.

GENUS *SYLVILAGUS*

Most species common. Range extends from S Canada to Argentina and Paraguay, and a great diversity of habitats is occupied. Distributions of some species overlap. Most preferred habitat open or brushy land or scrubby clearings in forest areas, but also cultivated areas or even parks. Various species frequent forests, marshes, swamps, sand beaches, or deserts. All species occupy burrows made by other animals or inhabit available shelter or hide in vegetation. Not colonial, but some species form social hierarchies in breeding groups. Active in daytime or at night. Not territorial; overlapping stable home ranges of a few hectares. Vocalizations rare. Most species are locally common.
HBL 25–45cm; TL 2.5–6cm; WT 0.4–2.3kg.
FORM: coat mostly speckled grayish brown to reddish brown above; undersides white or buff white; tail brown above and white below ("cottontail"); Forest rabbit and Marsh rabbit have dark tails. Molts once a year, except Tapeti and Marsh rabbits. Ears medium-sized (about 5.5cm) and same color as the upper side; nape often reddish, but may be black.
DIET: mainly herbaceous plants, but in winter also bark and twigs.
LONGEVITY: 10 years (in captivity).

Swamp rabbit   LR
Sylvilagus aquaticus

E Texas, E Oklahoma, Alabama, NW to S Carolina, S Illinois. A strong swimmer.
BREEDING: Gestation period 39–40 days; eyes open at 2–3 days.

Desert cottontail   LR
Sylvilagus audubonii
Desert or Audubon's cottontail

C Montana, SW to N Dakota, NC Utah, C Nevada, and N and C California (USA), and Baja California and C Sinaloa, NE Puebla, W Veracruz (Mexico).

Brush rabbit   LR
Sylvilagus bachmani

W Oregon to Baja California, Cascades to Sierra Nevada ranges.

BREEDING: Average 5 litters per year; gestation 24–30 days; young are covered in hair at birth.

Tapeti   LR
Sylvilagus brasiliensis
Forest rabbit or Tapeti

S Tamaulipas (Mexico) to Peru, Bolivia, N Argentina, S Brazil, Venezuela.
BREEDING: Average litter size 2; gestation about 42 days.

Manzano mountain cottontail
Sylvilagus cognatus

Restricted to Manzano Mountains, New Mexico, USA. Formerly included in *S. floridanus*.
CONSERVATION STATUS: Not evaluated, likely Endangered.

Mexican cottontail   LR
Sylvilagus cunicularius

Sinaloa to Oaxaca and Veracruz (Mexico).
CONSERVATION STATUS: Lower Risk, Near Threatened.

Dice's cottontail   En
Sylvilagus dicei

C American isthmus: SE Costa Rica to NW Panama.

Eastern cottontail   LR
Sylvilagus floridanus

N, C, and W Venezuela including all adjacent islands and adjacent Colombia, through disjunct parts of C America to NW Arizona, S Saskatchewan, SC Quebec, Michigan, Massachusetts, Florida. Very common.
BREEDING: Gestation period 26–28 days; young naked at birth.

Tres Marías cottontail   En
Sylvilagus graysoni

Maria Madre and Maria Magdalena Islands (Tres Marías Islands, Navarit, Mexico).

Omiltleme cottontail   Cr
Sylvilagus insonus

Sierra Madre del Sur, C Guerrero (Mexico).

Robust cottontail
Sylvilagus robustus

Chisos, Davis, and Guadalupe Mountains of Texas and New Mexico, and Sierra de la Madera of adjacent Coahuila (Mexico). Perhaps also in the Sierra del Carmen.
CONSERVATION STATUS: Not evaluated, likely Endangered.

ABBREVIATIONS		
HBL = head–body length TL = tail length EL = ear length	Ex Extinct	En Endangered
HFL = hind-foot length WT = weight	EW Extinct in the Wild	Vu Vulnerable
Approximate nonmetric equivalents: 10cm = 4in 30g = 1oz 1kg = 2.2lb	Cr Critically Endangered	LR Lower Risk

San José brush rabbit LR
Sylvilagus mansuetus

Known only from San José Island, Gulf of California. Often regarded as subspecies of *S. bachmani*.
CONSERVATION STATUS: Lower Risk, Near Threatened.

Marsh rabbit LR
Sylvilagus palustris

Marsh rabbit or Lower Keys marsh rabbit Florida Keys to SE Virginia on the coastal plain. Strong swimmer.

Mountain cottontail LR
Sylvilagus nuttallii
Mountain or Nuttall's cottontail

Intermountain area of N America from S British Columbia to S Saskatchewan, S to E California, NW Nevada, C Arizona, NW New Mexico.

Appalachian cottontail LR
Sylvilagus obscurus

New York State (W of Hudson River) to N Alabama along Appalachian Mountain chain.

Venezuelan lowland rabbit
Sylvilagus varyaensis

Presently known only from the states of Barinas, Guarico, and Portuguesa, Venezuela. Probably sympatric with *S. brasiliensis* and *S. floridanus*, but larger than both.
CONSERVATION STATUS: Not evaluated, likely Endangered.

New England cottontail Vu
Sylvilagus transitionalis

Boreal habitats from S Maine to N Ala-

⬓ *Above As its name suggests, the marsh rabbit is a habitat specialist, found only in swampy areas of the southern USA. A subspecies from the lower Florida Keys,* S. p. hefneri, *is considered endangered.*

bama. Distinguished from overlapping Eastern cottontail by presence of gray mottled cheeks, black spot between eyes and absence of black saddle and white forehead.   ES

THE SOCIAL LIFE OF RABBITS

How burrows shape interactions between group members

THE EUROPEAN RABBIT IS UNUSUAL AMONG rabbits and hares in constructing its own burrows. These can vary from single-entrance breeding "stops" through to extensive burrow systems, each containing a myriad of interconnected underground tunnels, accessed from as many as 60 entrances and containing a number of potential nest sites. Multiple-entrance burrow systems are generally referred to as warrens.

The burrowing habit has a number of implications for rabbit ecology and behavior. First, it allows rabbits to live in relatively open habitats, as the burrow affords shelter from predators. Rabbits can also raise large numbers of young by giving birth in the safe confines of the warren.

Female rabbits usually nurse their young in underground nesting chambers situated within preexisting burrow systems. Alternatively, young are raised in purpose-built stops with only one entrance. The mother animal visits the young only once a day for suckling, which may last as little as 5 minutes. When she leaves, she carefully covers the entrance. Despite these efforts, such stops are prone to being dug out by predators. Hence, nest sites deep in the main warrens are at a premium.

Where space underground is in short supply, natural selection should favor females that successfully defend nest sites. Good evidence of this was obtained from a long-term study of a population in southern England. There, the burrows were clustered together in tight groups in the form of warrens, which were themselves randomly distributed over the down.

Distinct social groups were established, the members of each having exclusive access to one or more burrow systems in their territory. Adult females, which do most of the burrow excavation, rarely attempted more than the expansion of an existing burrow system in the hard chalky soil. Completely new warrens hardly ever appeared, although breeding stops were constructed occasionally, and were at the core of the few new warrens that did appear during the study. Of the disputes between adult females, over 70 percent took place within 5m (16.5ft) of a burrow entrance. These were the most aggressive interactions seen during the course of the study, with the fur sometimes literally flying.

There was also a direct relationship between the size of a warren and the number of adult females taking refuge in it: the larger the warren, the more females that lived there. Thus a group of females sharing one or more warrens and feeding in extensively overlapping ranges around them are best regarded as reluctant partners in an uneasy alliance. This reluctance reflects the fact that only costs seem to accrue to group-living females, especially in terms of the survival of their offspring, which can be impaired by increases in both disease and predation. Solitary females, with exclusive access to a warren and attendant nest sites, do best in terms of reproductive success.

The pattern of dispersal also gave some insight into the importance of burrow availability. Overall, both adult males and females were rather sedentary, with only 20 percent and 5 percent respectively moving breeding groups between years. Dispersal was much more common among juvenile males, two-thirds of which bred in a different group from that into which they had been born, as compared with only one-third of juvenile

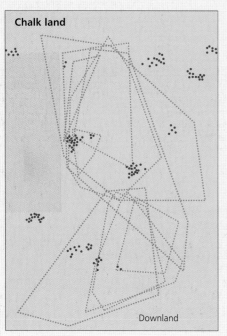

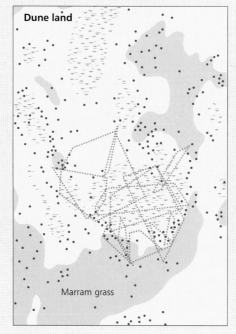

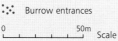

◐ **Above** *Maps comparing group-living and social behavior in European rabbits on chalk and dune land respectively. On chalk land rabbits have clustered burrows with females living as reluctant partners around each cluster. Fights often break out between females and their home ranges overlap considerably within each group but not with those of adjacent groups.*

On dune land rabbit burrows are not clustered and are randomly distributed, although they do not occur in the slacks, which are prone to flooding. Females move freely between burrows and there is little fighting between individuals. Home ranges overlap less than on chalk land. In both habitats males have larger territories that overlap those of several females.

relatedness of females in breeding groups is at least twice the average relatedness of males. This pattern is reinforced by very infrequent movement of individual rabbits between breeding groups once they reach adulthood.

Between 1987 and 1990, the number of adults in the population more than doubled, from 22 to 45. This resulted in an increase in the number of adults per social group rather than in the formation of new groups. Groups did seem to split when the number of female kin members expanded above six individuals; one or two females would restrict their activities to peripheral burrows within the group territory, and new males would start defending these does to form a new breeding group.

We can now recognize that the burrow shapes both the ecology and behavior of the wild rabbit. It is at the heart of its success as an invasive species throughout the world, so perhaps it is not surprising that it is also at the core of much conflict in rabbit societies.   DPC/DB

◑ **Above** *Post-coital grooming between a mating pair. Females enter estrus again shortly after giving birth. With a gestation period of only about 30 days, females can produce perhaps 4–5 litters per year.*

females. Interestingly, however, those juvenile females that did disperse entered breeding groups that were significantly less crowded in terms of burrow availability.

What of the males? Male rabbits do not contribute directly to parental care. Consequently, their reproductive success will reflect how many matings they have achieved. Females come into heat for 12–24 hours about every seventh day, or soon after giving birth. Males apparently monitor female condition closely: adult does were escorted by single males for about a quarter of their time above ground in the breeding season. Male home ranges were on average about twice the size of those of neighboring females, with which they had an extensive overlap. Consequently, these bucks could have been acquiring information, perhaps largely on the basis of scent rather than direct encounters, about the reproductive state of numerous females. The frequent aggressive interactions observed between males, whether or not they were escorting does, may be best interpreted

as attempts to curtail each other's use of space and access to females. The behavior of bucks following females around can be regarded as "mate-guarding." Each female is usually accompanied by only one male.

Despite bucks' efforts to monopolize matings with does, the females are promiscuous. An Australian study involved the genetic typing (using blood proteins) of all potential parents in a population, together with their weaned young. The resulting analysis showed that at least 16 percent of the young were not fathered by the male known to be the usual escort of their mother.

Long-term studies of a natural population of European wild rabbits living in eastern England have provided insights into relationships between social organization and the genetic structure of populations. Here, the rabbits live in highly territorial breeding groups that defend areas around the warrens. These breeding groups typically comprise 1–4 males and 1–9 females. Analyses of genetic relatedness between colony members confirmed predictions made from patterns of juvenile dispersal where sons disperse while daughters stay on to breed. As a consequence, females within breeding groups tend to be very closely related, with several generations living together. Indeed, the genetic

◑ **Above** *A European rabbit at a burrow entrance in southern England. Differences in soil type play a major role in social systems. Locations in which warrens can be dug quickly and easily cause rabbit populations to spread out, whereas in hard-soil areas populations center on long-established warren systems.*

THE TEN-YEAR CYCLE

Population fluctuations in the snowshoe hare

ANIMAL POPULATIONS RARELY, IF EVER, REMAIN constant from year to year. Populations of the great majority of species fluctuate irregularly or unpredictably. An exception is the snowshoe hare, whose populations in the boreal forest of North America undergo remarkably regular fluctuations that peak every 8–11 years.

These cycles were first analyzed quantitatively when wildlife biologists began to plot the fur-trading records of the Hudson's Bay Company during the early 1900s. Established in 1671, the company kept meticulous account of the numbers of furs traded from different posts across Canada. The most famous time series drawn from the records was that of the Canadian lynx published by Charles Elton and Mary Nicholson in 1942. The lynx is a specialist predator of snowshoe hares, and the 9–10 year rise and fall in lynx numbers turned out to mirror, with a slight time lag, the rise and fall of snowshoe hare populations (see graph).

The spectacular cycles of snowshoe hares and their predators seem to violate the implicit assumption of many ecologists that there is a balance in nature; anyone living in the boreal forest would be hard pressed to recognize any equilibrium in the boom-and-bust pattern of nature's economy. The challenge to biologists has been to understand the mechanisms behind these cycles. Over the last 40 years ecologists working in Alberta, the Yukon Territory, and Alaska have put together an array of studies that have resolved most, but not all, of the enigmas underlying them.

The demographic pattern of the hare cycle is remarkably clear and consistent. The key finding is that both reproduction and survival begin to decay in the increase phase of the cycle, two years before peak densities are reached. Maximal reproduction and highest survival rates occur early in this phase; as it progresses, reproduction slows and survival rates of both adults and juveniles fall. Both reproduction and survival rates continue to decline for 2–3 years after the cycle has peaked, then start to recover over the low phase. This time lag in changes in reproduction and mortality is the proximate cause of the variation in density that makes up the hare cycle, which can see populations rise or fall 30- or even 100-fold.

What causes the changes? The three main factors involved seem to be food, predation, and social interactions. There are two variants of the food hypothesis: first, that the hares may simply run out of food in winter and starve, or that the quality of the food available to them may decline. Yet feeding experiments have failed to change the pattern of the cycle or prevent the cyclic decline, so this hypothesis has now been rejected. Food by itself does not seem to be the primary limitation on hare numbers.

Predation is the next most obvious explanation. Studies with radio-collared hares have in fact shown that the immediate cause of death of 95 percent of adult hares is predation by a variety of animals, the main ones in Canada being lynx, coyotes, goshawks, and great horned owls. For leverets the figure is 81 percent, most of these being killed by various small raptors or else by red or arctic ground squirrels. Few animals die of malnutrition. Obviously such huge losses must play an important role in the cycle.

As for the predators themselves, the evidence indicates that all show strong numerical changes that lag behind the hare cycle by 1–2 years. In addition, both lynx and coyotes kill more hares per day in the peak and decline phases than during the increase. These kill rates have turned out to be well above previous estimates, and are also in excess of energetic demands. Surplus killing seems to be a characteristic of these predators.

By constructing electric fences around 1sq km (0.39sq mi) blocks of boreal forest, researchers have been able to test the impact of excluding

◁ **Left** *A snowshoe hare in its summer coat. Female hares show remarkable variations in litter size at different stages of the population cycle, bearing more than twice as many young when numbers are low.*

▷ **Right** *A lynx carries off its prey. When hare numbers decline, the shortage of alternative food sources leads to a rise in mortality among lynx kittens as well as to a drop in the number of young that are born.*

mammalian predators from hares. The main effects were to increase survival rates and to temporarily stop the cycle inside the fence, indicating that predation is indeed the immediate cause of the mortality changes over the cycle.

Yet if predation causes the changes in mortality, what about the varying rates of reproduction that accompany the cycle? Two possible explanations for these have been suggested. Lower-quality food in the time of high density may reduce reproductive output; alternatively, predators may cause the decline by stressing hares through repeated, unsuccessful attacks. Chronic stress has many direct detrimental effects on mammals, one of which is reduction in reproductive rate. Stress effects may also be indirect and long term, affecting offspring viability.

Ecologists are now close to understanding the snowshoe hare cycle. They believe that it results from the interaction between predation and food; but of these two factors, predation is clearly the main one. The impact of food shortages is felt largely in winter and is indirect; hares do not die directly of starvation or malnutrition. But food quality and quantity may nonetheless play a part by affecting the hares' body condition, and so predisposing them to increased parasite loads and higher levels of chronic stress, which in turn probably cause reduced reproductive output.

Hares in peak and declining populations must trade off safety for food. The result is a time lag in both the direct and indirect effects of predation that causes the cyclical pattern.   CJK

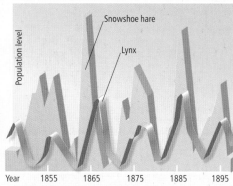

⬤ **Above** *The snowshoe hare makes up 80–90 percent of the Canadian lynx's diet. Populations of the two mammals closely mirror each other; when food shortages and predation bring about a decline in hare numbers, the lynx population drops sharply soon after; conversely, the recovery of hare populations presages an upturn in lynx numbers. This parallel fluctuation in the animals' fortunes is plotted on the graph, which derives from the records of the Hudson's Bay Company.*

MAD WORLD OF THE EUROPEAN HARE

① *With no underground sanctuary to provide refuge, the hare relies on its superb senses – and its long legs – for survival. Its sensory equipment includes eyes on the side of the head for all-round vision, huge ears, and a sensitive nose.*

②③ *"Mad as a March hare," people say, recalling the seemingly wild behavior of hares in the mating season (January–August). At this time does are receptive for just a few hours on one day in each of their six-weekly cycles, perhaps six well-spaced days in all. Local bucks then compete for their favors; the dominant male strives to keep all others at bay, while the doe herself will fight off any that approach before she is ready. "Mad" behavior becomes visible in March only because the nights, which hares prefer for their activities, become shorter, forcing them to enter the daylight arena.*

④ *Females do not pull their punches when beating off over-eager suitors, as the scarred ears of many bucks testify. When she is ready, the doe will start a wild chase over the countryside, shaking off the following bucks until only one, probably the fittest, remains. Then at last she will stop and allow him to mate.*

5 *A young hare shelters in its form, or daytime resting place; unlike their rabbit cousins, leverets enter the world fully coated, sighted, and mobile. Around sunset it will move cautiously to the spot where it was born a few days previously, where it will be joined by its littermates to await the mother. She will arrive about 45 minutes after sunset to suckle them for perhaps 5 minutes, and will then depart again, not to return for another 24 hours. By 4–5 weeks of age the leverets will be consuming vegetation and the doe's visits will cease.* TH

Pikas

PIKAS ARE SMALL, EGG-SHAPED LAGOMORPHS *with relatively large rounded ears, short limbs, and a barely visible tail. They are lively and agile, but often sit hunched up on a rock or in an alpine meadow, their long, silky fur making them resemble balls of fluff.*

Pikas' generic name, *Ochotona*, is derived from the Mongolian term for the animals (*ogdoi*), while the word "pika" itself evolved from a vernacular term used by the Tungus of Siberia in attempting to mimic the call ("peeka...") of the northern species. To this day, most pikas are denizens of high, remote mountains and wild country, serving as symbols of untamed nature.

Miniature Haymakers

FORM AND FUNCTION

Pikas are primarily active by day; only the steppe pika is predominantly nocturnal. They do not hibernate, and are well adapted to the cold alpine environments that they inhabit. They have a high body temperature, yet can perish in even moderately warm environmental conditions (American pikas have been known to die following a 30-minute exposure to 25°C/77°F). Thus they have little margin for error in their exposure to heat, and most species are active only during cool times of the day. High-altitude American pikas can be active all day, whereas populations at low altitudes (where it is hotter) emerge from their shelters only at dawn and dusk. Himalayan species demonstrate the same trend; Royle's pika is active in the morning and evening, while the large-eared pika, which lives at cooler elevations above 4,000m (13,000ft), basks in the midday sun.

Pikas either live among rocks or else dig burrows in open meadow–steppe environments. Afghan and Pallas's pikas are intermediate in their use of habitat (they sometimes live in rocks, but also burrow), but their life history closely parallels those of the burrowing pikas. Almost every facet of the biology of pikas is sharply divided between rock-dwelling and burrowing forms. Rock-dwelling pikas have very low reproductive rates due to the combination of small litter size and few litters per year; for example, most American pikas successfully wean only two young from one litter annually. In contrast, female burrowing pikas are baby machines; some species have as many as five litters containing up to 13 young.

Pikas eat whatever plants are available near their burrows or at the edge of their rocky scree territories, although they prefer those plants high-

est in protein or other important chemicals. They cannot grasp plants with their forepaws, so they eat grasses, leaves, and flowering stalks with a side-to-side motion of their jaws. During summer and fall, most species devote considerable time to harvesting mouthfuls of vegetation that they carry back to their dens to store for winter consumption in caches that resemble large piles of hay. American pikas may devote over 30 percent of their active time to haying, dashing back and forth with mouthfuls of vegetation. Haypiles rarely run out – pikas tend to overharvest, and there are often middenlike remains from the previous year.

In winter pikas also make tunnels in the snow to harvest nearby vegetation. Some species, such as Royle's, large-eared, and plateau pikas, live where winter snows are uncommon, and consequently do not construct haypiles – instead they continue to forage throughout the winter.

Pikas, like other lagomorphs, produce two different types of feces: small, spherical pellets resembling pepper seeds, and a soft, dark green, viscous excrement. The soft feces have high energy value (particularly in B vitamins) and are reingested either directly from the anus or after being dropped.

Gregarious or Reclusive?

SOCIAL BEHAVIOR

The dramatic differences between rock-dwelling and burrowing pikas are most apparent in their social behavior. Rock-dwelling pikas defend large territories, either as individuals (in North American species) or in pairs (Asian species). The resulting population density is low (about 2–10/ha, or 5–25/acre) and fairly stable over time. Rock-dwelling pikas rarely interact, and when they do it is usually to repel an intruding neighbor. Even the Asian forms that contribute to a shared haypile spend most of the day living solitary lives. The apparent lack of social activity can be somewhat misleading, however, as these animals are clearly aware of all the goings-on across the talus (see Securing a Vacancy).

In sharp contrast, burrowing pikas are among the most social of mammals. Family groups occupy communal dens, and local densities can exceed 300 animals per hectare (750 per acre) at the end of the breeding season, though the figures can fluctuate wildly, both seasonally and annually. During the breeding season family groups are composed of many siblings of different ages, and social interactions may occur as frequently as once

◗ **Left** The collared pika is found mainly on rocky outcrops in Alaska and northwestern Canada. Its name derives from the grayish patches below its cheek and around its neck. It spends roughly half its time above ground, sitting on prominent rocks.

FACTFILE

PIKAS

Order: Lagomorpha

Family: Ochotonidae

30 species of the genus *Ochotona*. Rock-dwelling species include: Alpine pika (*O. alpina*); American pika (*O. princeps*); Northern pika (*O. hyperborea*); Collared pika (*O. collaris*). Burrowing pikas comprise: Daurian pika (*O. dauurica*); Gansu pika (*O. cansus*); Koslov's pika (*O. koslowi*); Moupin pika (*O. thibetana*); Plateau pika (*O. curzoniae*); Steppe pika (*O. pusilla*).

DISTRIBUTION Mountains of W North America; across much of Asia N of the Himalayas, from the Middle East and the Ural Mountains E to the N Pacific Rim; from sea level to 6,130 m (20,100 ft).

HABITAT Rock dwellers: talus (rocky scree) on mountains or occasional piles of fallen logs. Burrowing forms: alpine meadow, steppe, or semidesert.

SIZE Head–body length 120–285mm (4.7–11.2in); **weight** 50–350g (1.8–12.3oz); **tail length** barely visible at about 5mm (0.2in); **ear length** 12–36mm (0.5–1.4in).

Equator

COAT Dense and soft; grayish brown in most species (though one is reddish), usually darker above than below.

DIET Generalized herbivorous

BREEDING Rock dwellers: litter size 1–5; 2 litters a year, but generally only 1 successfully weaned; gestation approximately 1 month. Burrowing forms: litter size 1–13; up to 5 litters a year; gestation approximately 3 weeks.

LONGEVITY Rock dwellers: up to 7 years. Burrowing forms: up to 3 years, but most live only 1 year.

CONSERVATION STATUS 5 species are listed as Vulnerable, 1 species as Endangered, and the Silver pika (*O. argentata*) is Critically Endangered. Several species are also listed as threatened in some measure.

For full species list see Appendix ▷

◗ **Above** A characteristic activity of pikas in late summer is the gathering of vegetation to store in haypiles, in part to serve as food during the winter. Most of these stores of food are kept under overhanging rocks.

a minute. Pikas sit in contact, rub noses, socially groom, and play-box together. Young line up behind an adult – generally their father – and follow him like a miniature train. Nearly all these friendly social interactions occur within family groups, while interactions involving animals from different groups are normally aggressive – most notably the long chases of adult males.

Communication styles also differ between rock-dwelling and burrowing pikas. Most rock dwellers have only two characteristic vocalizations: a short call used to announce their presence on the talus or to warn others of approaching predators, and a long call (or song) uttered by adult males during the breeding season. Some rock-dwelling species (large-eared and Royle's pikas, for instance) rarely utter even weak sounds. Burrowing pikas, on the other hand, have a vast repertoire: predator alarm calls (short, soft, and rapidly repeated); long calls (given by adult males); and also whines, trills, muffle calls, and transition calls, these last two usually uttered by young pikas and serving to promote cohesion among siblings.

Burrowing pikas also have an unusually flexible mating system. In adjoining plateau pika burrows,

◗ **Right** A pika at its burrow entrance in Ladakh, northeastern India. Only some pika species live in burrows and even these are not especially well adapted for digging. One of the main distinctions between burrowing and rock-dwelling pikas is that the former tend to be far more social than the latter.

one can observe monogamous, polygynous, polyandrous, and complex (multiple male and female) adult associations side by side. Polyandry is extremely rare in mammals, yet two males from the same burrow may be seen alternately mating with the resident female and then sitting alongside or grooming one another, even while the female is in estrus – apparently an adaptation to maximize reproductive rates in face of harsh environmental conditions.

Not Just a Pest
CONSERVATION AND ENVIRONMENT

Several species and subspecies of pika are globally listed as threatened. In general, these are forms confined to restricted rocky habitats or found in isolated locations of central Asia. In reality, the status of many pika species is difficult to determine because they inhabit such remote areas.

On the other hand, some of the burrowing pikas are treated as pests because they reach such high densities and are believed to cause rangeland degradation. For example, the plateau pika has been poisoned across 200,000sq km (77,000sq mi) in the Qinghai province of China alone – an area half the size of California.

However, others consider the plateau pika a keystone species for biodiversity on the Tibetan plateau because its burrows contribute to increased plant diversity and are the primary homes for a wide variety of birds and lizards. In addition, it serves as the principal prey for many predator species; and it contributes positively to ecosystem-level dynamics by recycling nutrients and minimizing erosion. ATS/TK

SECURING A VACANCY

The social organization of the American pika

TWO AMERICAN PIKAS DARTED INTO AND out of sight on a rock-strewn slope (known as a talus). The second, a resident male, was in aggressive pursuit of the first, an immigrant male. The chase continued onto an adjoining meadow, before turning into the dense cover of a nearby spruce forest. When next seen, dashing back toward the talus, the pair were being chased by a weasel. The pursuing pika was caught, and death followed swiftly less than 1m (3.3ft) from the safety of the talus. Immediately, all the pikas in the vicinity, with one exception, broke into a chorus of consecutive short calls, the sounds that pikas utter when they are alarmed by the presence of predators. The dead pika had initiated the chase, but the object of his aggression had managed to escape the weasel. Perched in silence on a prominent rock, he now surveyed his new domain.

Most accounts of the natural history of pikas have emphasized their individual territoriality;

◐ **Above** A pika sits amid its pile of winter provisions. Many pikas have a tendency to overprovision and collect far more leaves and grass than they will consume over the cold season.

◐ **Left** Pikas have two characteristic vocalizations: the short call and the long call (or song). Long calls (a series of squeaks lasting up to 30 seconds) are given by males primarily during the breeding season. Short calls normally contain one-to-two note squeaks and may be given from promontories either before or after movement, in response to calls from another pika, while chasing or being chased, or when predators are active.

vigorously attack unfamiliar (immigrant) males. The pika described in the account above had forayed from his home territory to chase an unfamiliar, immigrant adult male.

Affiliative behavior is seen in pairs of neighboring males and females, who are not only frequently tolerant of each other but also engage in duets of short calls. Such behavior is rarely seen between neighbors of the same sex or between nonneighbor heterosexual pairs.

Adults treat their offspring in the same way as neighbors of the opposite sex. Some aggression is directed toward juveniles, but there are also frequent expressions of social tolerance. Most juveniles will remain on the home ranges of their parents throughout their first summer before subsequently dispersing.

Ecological constraints have apparently led to a monogamous mating system in rock-dwelling pikas. Although males do not contribute directly to the raising of their offspring, they still primarily associate with a single neighboring female. Polygyny evolves when males can either monopolize sufficient resources to attract several females, or when they can directly defend several females. But in pikas the essentially linear reach of vegetation at the base of the talus precludes resource-defense polygyny, while males cannot defend groups of females because the females are dispersed and kept apart by their mutual antagonism, which thus precludes female-defense polygyny.

Juveniles of both sexes are likely to be repelled should they disperse and attempt to colonize an occupied talus. As a result, they normally settle close to their place of birth (philopatry). This pattern of settlement may lead to incestuous matings, which contributes to the low genetic variability that is found in pika populations.

The close association among male–female pairs and the near relatedness of neighbors may actually underlie the evolution of cooperative behavior patterns in pikas. First, attacks on intruders by residents may be an expression of indirect parental care: if the adults can successfully repel immigrants, they may increase the probability of their own offspring obtaining a territory should a local site subsequently become available for colonization. Second – to return to the opening account – the alarm calls given by both sexes when the weasel struck the resident pika served as a warning to the close kin – note that the unrelated immigrant was the only pika that did not call out. Uncontested, the newcomer immediately moved across the talus to claim the slain pika's territory, a half-completed haypile, and access to a neighboring female.   ATS

however, studies conducted in the Rocky Mountains of Colorado have helped add detail to this basic insight. For example, adjacent territories are normally occupied by pikas of opposite sexes. Male and female neighbors overlap each other's home ranges more, and have centers of activity that are closer to one another's than the ranges or activity centers of same-sex neighbors. The possession and juxtapositions of territories tend to be stable from year to year, consequently – as American pikas can live for up to 6 years – the appearance and whereabouts of vacant territories on the talus are unpredictable. For a pika, therefore, trying to secure a vacancy on the talus is like entering a lottery in which an animal's sex in part determines whether

or not it will have a winning ticket, for territories are almost always claimed by a member of the same sex as the previous occupant.

The behaviors that sustain this pattern of occupancy are apparently a compromise between the contrasting aggressive and affiliative tendencies of the pika. Although all pikas are pugnacious when they are involved in defending territories, females are less aggressive toward neighboring males, and conversely more aggressive to proximate females. Male residents rarely exhibit aggression toward each other because they do not come into contact with each other very frequently, apparently avoiding one another by the use of both scent marking and vocalizations. Resident males will, however,

Index

Page numbers in *italics* refer to captions; those in **bold** refer to extensive coverage or feature treatment of a subject.

Picture Credits

Front Cover: Digital Stock

viii BRG; ix Bruce Coleman Collection/Stephen Krasemann; x Denys Ovenden; xi Denys Ovenden; xii FLPA/Fritz Polking; xiii Graham Allen; xiv FLPA/Peter Davy; xv BRG; xvi BRG; xvii FLPA/Peter Davy; xix ICCE/Andy Purcell; xxi NHPA/Terry Andrewartha; xx BRG; xxii FLPA/Fritz Polking; xxv Olaf Bininda-Emonds/Technical University of Munich; xxvi Superstock/Mauritius; xxvii Superstock/Mark Newman; xxviii Reprinted with permission from Ricketts et al. 2005: data provided courtesy of the Alliance for Zero Extinction, www.zeroextinction.org; xxix Alamy/Robert Harding Picture Library; xxxi Reprinted with permission from Brooks et al., December 2004, Vol. 54, No. 12, page 1087, Fig. 3b global patterns of species richness for threatened mammals. Copyright, American Institute of Biological Sciences; xxxii Alamy/Darroch Donald; xxxiii Reprinted with permission from Rodrigues et al., December 2004, vol. 54, No. 12, page 1098, Fig. 5 global distribution a) irreplaceability, b) threat, and c) priority sites. Copyright, American Institute of Biological Sciences.

2b Auscape/Jean-Paul Ferrero; 2t M. McKelvey & P. Rismiller; 3 Dave Watts; 4 Dave Watts; 4–5 Dave Watts; 6–7 M. McKelvey & P. Rismiller; 6 BBC Natural History Unit/John Cancalosi; 7 Ardea/Jean-Paul Ferrero; 8 NHPA/Dave Watts; 8 Priscilla Barrett; 9 NHPA/A.N.T.; 10–11 BRG; 11 Bruce Coleman Collection/John Cancalosi; 12 Ardea/Jean-Paul Ferrero; 13 Ardea/M. W. Gillam; 14 NHPA/G. I. Bernard; 15 Corbis/D. Robert Franz; 16 Corbis/Lynda Richardson; 17 Priscilla Barret; 18 Oxford Scientific Films/J. Sauvanet/Okapia; 19l Oxford Scientific Films/Alan & Sandy Carey; 19r NHPA/T. Kitchen & V. Hurst; 20 BBC Natural History Unit/John Cancalosi; 20–21 C. Andrew Henley/LARUS; 22 NHPA Dave Watts; 22 Denys Ovenden; 23 Ardea/Jean-Paul Ferrero; 24r, 24l, 25r, 25l Bill Brown Dept. of Primary Industries, Water and Environment, Tasmania, Australia; 26 NHPA/A.N.T.; 26 Denys Ovenden; 27 Ardea/Jean-Paul Ferrero; 29 Ardea/Jean-Paul Ferrero; 29 Denys Ovenden; 30b C. Andrew Henley/LARUS; 30t Dave Watts; 31 C. Andrew Henley/LARUS; 32 BRG; 32–33 NHPA/A.N.T.; 34 BBC Natural History Unit/John Cancalosi; 35b NHPA/Dave Watts; 35t Ardea/Jean-Paul Ferrero; 36 Denys Ovenden; 38 Ardea/Hans & Judy Beste; 39 Ardea/Jean-Paul Ferrero; 40 Papilio Photographic; 40–41 NHPA/Daniel Heuclin; 43 Ardea /Jean-Paul Ferrero; 43 inset C. Andrew Henley/LARUS; 44–45 Denys Ovenden; 46–47 NHPA/Dave Watts; 48 NHPA/Martin Harvey; 48–49 C. Andrew Henley/LARUS; 49 BRG; 50 Denys Ovenden; 51 Oxford Scientific Films/Kathie Atkinson; 53 Dave Watts; 54 Dave Watts; 54 Denys Ovenden; 56 Corbis/Bruce Burkhardt; 57 BBC Natural History Unit/Pete Oxford; 58–59 Auscape/Jean-Paul Ferrero; 58b Auscape/D. Parer & E. Parer-Cook; 58tl Auscape/Jean-Paul Ferrero; 58tr Auscape/Jean-Paul Ferrero; 59b NHPA/Martin Harvey; 59t Still Pictures/Roland Seitre; 60c Andrew Henley/LARUS; 61 Oxford Scientific Films/Tom Ulrich; 62 NHPA/Martin Harvey; 64 BBC Natural History Unit/John Cancalosi; 64–0065 NHPA/Dave Watts; 66 Denys Ovenden; 66–67 A. Smith; 68–69 Calphotos/Dave Mangham; 70–71 Denys Ovenden; 72–73 BBC Natural History Unit/Pete Oxford; 75b Oxford Scientific Films/Michael Fogden; 75t Ardea/Peter Steyn; 76–77 Priscilla Barrett; 78 Ardea P. Morris; 78t BRG; 79 BBC Natural History Unit/Bruce Davidson; 80b–81b BRG; 80t–81t Ardea/P. Morris; 82 Denys Ovenden; 83 Rudi van Aarde; 84–85 Michael Long; 85 Bruce Coleman Collection/Steven Kaufman; 86 Ardea /John Cancalosi; 87 H.N. Hoeck; 88b–89b BRG; 88l BBC Natural History Unit/Peter Blackwell; 88t–89t Ardea/Kenneth W. Fink; 90 Malcolm McGregor; 91 Getty Images Stone Art Wolfe; 92 Oxford Scientific Films/G.I. Bernard; 92 BRG; 93b NHPA/Martin Harvey; 93t NHPA/Martin Harvey; 94 Oxford Scientific Films/ Martyn Colbeck; 94–95 Oxford Scientific Films/Martyn Colbeck; 96–97 Oxford Scientific Films/Martyn Colbeck; 96–97 BRG; 98b ICCE/Mark Boulton; 98t Oxford Scientific Films/Richard Packwood; 99b BBC Natural History Unit/David Shale; 99t Hoa-Qui/Jacana B. Francais; 100b Hoa-Qui/Jacana M. Denis-Huot; 100b–101b Oxford Scientific Films/Martyn Colbeck; 100t Oxford Scientific Films/Martyn Colbeck; 100t–101t Oxford Scientific Films/Martyn Colbeck; 101b Hoa-Qui/Jacana M. Denis-Huot; 101t BBC Natural History Unit/Anup Shah; 102 Priscilla Barrett; 102–103 Priscilla Barrett; 104–105 Bruce Coleman Collection/Bruce Coleman Inc.; 105b Planet Earth Pictures/Doug Perrine; 105t NHPA Haroldo Palo Jr.; 106 Planet Earth Pictures/Doug Perrine; 107l NHPA/Norbert Wu; 107r Pete Oxford; 108 Ardea Francois Gohier; 108–109 Planet Earth Pictures/Doug Perrine; 110 BRG; 110b CorbisHistorical Picture Archive; 111b BBC Natural History Unit Georgette Douwma; 111t NHPA/Trevor McDonald; 112 FLPA/Foto Natura Stock; 112–113 Corbis/Roger Garwood & Trish Ainslie; 114–115 Michael Long; 115 BRG; 116 Denys Ovenden; 116–117 NHPA/Kevin Schafer; 118b NHPA/Kevin Schafer; 118t BBC Natural History Unit/Pete Oxford; 119 Corbis/Tom Brakefield; 120b Bruce Coleman Collection/Luiz Claudio Marigo; 120t FLPA/Jurgen & Christine Sohns; 121 Michael & Patricia Fogden; 122–123 Bruce Coleman Collection/Staffan Widstrand; 124 BBC Natural History Unit/Mark Payne-Gill; 125 Denys Ovenden; 125 BRG; 126b BBC Natural History Unit/Jeff Foott; 126t FLPA/Foto Natura Stock; 127 BBC Natural History Unit/Pete Oxford; 128 BBC Natural History Unit/Mike Wilkes; 129 Ardea/François Gohier; 130 NHPA/Anthony Bannister; 130 BRG; 131 BRG; 132 BRG; 132–133 Oxford Scientific Films/Daniel J. Cox; 134 NHPA/Stephen Dalton; 135b ICCE/Andy/Purcell; 135tl ICI Plant Protection Division; 135tr Corbis/Bettmann; 136–137 Corbis/Michael Freeman; 136b FLPA/John Hawkins; 137t inset Corbis/Nicole Duplaix; 138 Alamy/Jeff Foott/Bruce Coleman Inc; 139 Alamy/Juniors Bildarchive; 140 NHPA/Manfred Danegger; 140 Denys Ovenden; 141 BRG; 141 inset Ardea/François Gohier; 141t Corbis/Joe McDonald; 142 Minden Pictures/Jim Brandenburg; 143 Oxford Scientific Films/Alan & Sandy Carey; 144 BRG; 144b Oxford Scientific Films/Mark Hamblin; 144t BBC Natural History Unit Jeff Foott; 145 Ardea/François Gohier; 146–147b BBC Natural History Unit/David Kjaer; 146–147t Bruce Coleman Collection/John Shaw; 146bl Bruce Coleman Collection/Janos Jurka; 146tl NHPA/Stephen J. Krasemann; 147 Oxford Scientific Films/Norbert Rosing; 148–149 Tom & Pat Leeson; 149 BRG; 150 Bruce Coleman Collection/Rob Jordan; 150–151 Oxford Scientific Films/John Brown; 152–153 Priscilla Barrett; 153 Ardea/John Cancalosi; 154b BBC Natural History Unit/Bernard Castelein; 154t Oxford Scientific Films/Wendy Shattil & Bob Rozinski; 156 BRG; 156–157 Bruce Coleman Collection/Paul van Gaalen; 158 Bruce Coleman Collection/Gunter Ziesler; 158–159 Ardea/Clem Haagner; 159 BBC Natural History Unit/Andrew Cooper; 159 Denys Ovenden; 160 BRG; 161b Oxford Scientific Films/Krupaker Senani; 161t BBC Natural History Unit/Pete Oxford; 162 Leppstock/George Lepp; 162 BRG; 162–163 Leppstock/George Lepp; 163 FLPA/T. & P. Gardner; 164–165 Corbis/George Lepp; 166–167 Oxford Scientific Films/Carol Farneti/Partridge Films Ltd; 167 BRG; 168–169 Denys Ovenden; 170 Ardea/B. "Moose" Peterson; 171 Corbis/Joe McDonald; 172–173 Priscilla Barrett; 173 Oxford Scientific Films/Claude Steelman/Survival Anglia; 174 Oxford Scientific Films/David M. Dennis; 174–175 Oxford Scientific Films/Michael Fogden; 176 Premaphotos Wildlife/Ken Preston-Mafham; 176–177 Priscilla Barrett; 178–179 Ardea /Wardene Weisser; 180b D. Harris Wildcru, Oxford; 180c BRG; 181t D. Harris WildCRU, Oxford; 181b Alamy/Che Garman; 182b Oxford Scientific Films/Tom Ulrich; 182t Bruce Coleman Collection/Colin Varndell; 183 NHPA/Stephen Dalton; 184–185 Priscilla Barrett; 186 NHPA/Paal Hermansen; 187 BRG; 188–189 Ecoscene/Robin Redfern; 190 Oxford Scientific Films/Press-Tige Pictures; 191 Denys Ovenden; 192–193 Priscilla Barrett; 194c Oxford Scientific Films/Kathie Atkinson; 194t Corbis/Yann Arthus-Bertrand; 195 Ardea/Jean-Paul Ferrero; 196b Oxford Scientific Films/G. I. Bernard; 196t Bruce Coleman Collection/Andrew Purcell; 197 Premaphotos Wildlife/Ken Preston-Mafham; 198–199 Ardea/Ian Beames; 199 BRG; 200–201 Priscilla Barrett; 202 BRG; 202–203 BBC Natural History Unit/Nick Garbutt; 204 Bruce Coleman Collection/Rod Williams; 205 Ardea/Dennis Avon; 206 Priscilla Barrett; 208 Oxford Scientific Films/Mike Brown; 208 BRG; 209b Oxford Scientific Films/Rodger Jackman; 209t Premaphotos Wildlife/Ken Preston-Mafham; 210 Priscilla Barrett; 210b Ardea/Ian Beames; 210t Bruce Coleman Collection/P. Kaya; 211 FLPA/Gerard Lacz; 212–212 FLPA/K. Maslowski; 214 Calphotos/Bill Leonard; 215 NHPA/Daniel Heuclin; 216 BBC Natural History Unit/Jeff Foott; 216–217 BBC Natural History Unit/Jeff Foott; 218–219 Priscilla Barrett; 220 Oxford Scientific Films/John Cancalosi/Okapia; 220–221 Oxford Scientific Films/Wendy Shattil & Bob Rozinski; 221Denys Ovenden; 222–223 Denys Ovenden; 223 Corbis/Ric Ergenbright; 223b Priscilla Barrett; 223t Priscilla Barrett; 224 Bruce Coleman Collection/Rod Williams; 225 NHPA/T. Kitchen & V. Hurst; 226 BRG; 226–227 FLPA/W. Meinderts/Foto Natura; 228 Ardea/Ian Beames; 228–229 Oxford Scientific Films/Jen & Des Bartlett/Survival Anglia; 230b BBC Natural History Unit/Pete Oxford; 230t FLPA/Terry Whittaker; 231 Oxford Scientific Films/Frank Schneidermeyer; 232–233 FLPA/Michael Gore; 233 Bruce Coleman Collection/Luiz Claudio Marigo; 234 NHPA/Eric Soder; 235b Ardea /François; 235t Still Pictures/Roland Seitre; 236–237 BRG; 239b Bruce Coleman Collection/Robert Maier; 239f Ardea/Nick Gordon; 240–241 Getty Images Stone/Barrie Wilkins; 240–241 Denys Ovenden; 242 Denys Ovenden; 243 W. George; 244 N. Eden (J.Jarvis); 244–245 J. Jarvis; 246b BBC Natural History Unit/Neil Bromhall; 246c Oxford Scientific Films/Neil Bromhall; 247b BRG; 247t BRG; 248 Oxford Scientific Films/Terry Andrewartha/Survival Anglia; 249FLPA/W. Wisniewski; 249l BRG; 0249r BRG; 250 BBC Natural History Unit/Mike Wilkes; 251 Ardea/Kenneth W. Fink; 252 Priscilla Barrett; 254–255 Bruce Coleman Collection/Jorg & Petra Wegner; 255 FLPA/K. Maslowski; 257 Agence Nature; 259 Bruce Coleman Collection/Steven Kaufman; 260 BRG; 260–261 Oxford Scientific Films/G.I. Bernard; 261BBC Natural History Unit/William Osborn; 262 FLPA/Leeson/Sunset; 262–263 BBC Natural History Unit/Lynn Stone; 263 BRG; 264–265 NHPA/Manfred Danegger; 264b NHPA/Manfred Danegger; 0264tl Bruce Coleman Collection/Jorg & Petra Wegner; 264tr NHPA/Manfred Danegger; 265 FLPA/D. A. Robinson; 266 Corbis/Geogre Lepp; 267b BBC Natural History/Unit/G. & H. Denzau; 267t Corbis/George Lepp; 268 Corbis/D. Robert Franz; 268–269/Bruce Coleman Collection.

Color and line artwork panels © Priscilla Barrett